Lecture Notes in Computer Science 3759

Commenced Publication in 1973
Founding and Former Series Editors:
Gerhard Goos, Juris Hartmanis, and Jan van Leeuwen

T0190019

Guihai Chen   Yi Pan   Minyi Guo
Jian Lu (Eds.)

Parallel and Distributed Processing and Applications – ISPA 2005 Workshops

ISPA 2005 International Workshops
AEPP, ASTD, BIOS, GCIC, IADS
MASN, SGCA, and WISA
Nanjing, China, November 2-5, 2005
Proceedings

 Springer

Volume Editors

Guihai Chen
Jian Lu
Nanjing University, Department of Computer Science
210093 Nanjing, China
E-mail: {gchen, lj}@nju.edu.cn

Yi Pan
Georgia State University, Department of Computer Science
34 Peachtree Street, Suite 1450
Atlanta, GA 30302-4110, USA
E-mail: pan@cs.gsu.edu

Minyi Guo
The University of Aizu, School of Computer Science and Engineering
Tsuruga, Ikki-machi, Aizu-Wakamatsu City, Fukushima 965-8580, Japan
E-mail: minyi@u-aizu.ac.jp

Library of Congress Control Number: 2005934459

CR Subject Classification (1998): F.1, F.2, D.1, D.2, D.4, C.2, C.4, H.4, J.3

ISSN   0302-9743
ISBN-10   3-540-29770-7 Springer Berlin Heidelberg New York
ISBN-13   978-3-540-29770-3 Springer Berlin Heidelberg New York

Springer is a part of Springer Science+Business Media

springeronline.com

© Springer-Verlag Berlin Heidelberg 2005
Printed in Germany

Typesetting: Camera-ready by author, data conversion by Scientific Publishing Services, Chennai, India
Printed on acid-free paper   SPIN: 11576259   06/3142   5 4 3 2 1 0

Preface

Welcome to the proceedings of the ISPA 2005 workshops, held in the city of Nanjing, China. For the first time eight workshops were held in conjunction with the 3rd International Symposium on Parallel and Distributed Processing and Applications (ISPA 2005), to encourage interaction between researchers and practitioners. Workshop topics are, of course, in line with the conference's scientific scope and the workshops provided a forum for groups of researchers and practitioners to meet together more closely, to exchange opinions and advanced ideas, and to share preliminary results on focused issues in an atmosphere that fostered interaction and problem solving.

The conference hosted eight half-day workshops: The International Workshop on Applications and Economics of Peer-to-Peer Systems organized by Qianni Deng and Zhichen Xu; the International Workshop on Advanced Storage Technology and Autonomic Distributed Data organized by Jiwu Shu and Weimin Zheng; the International Workshop on Bioinformatics organized by Mathew Palaka, Jake Chen and Zongben Xu; the International Workshop on Grid Computing in China organized by Hai Jin and Minglu Li; the International Workshop on Information Assurance in Distributed Systems organized by Peng Liu and Meng Yu; the International Workshop on Mobile Ad-hoc and Ubiquitous Sensor Networks organized by Anu Bourgeois and Wei Lou; the International Workshop on Service Grid Computing and Applications organized by Nong Xiao and Yunhao Liu; and the International Workshop on Web Information Systems and Applications organized by Baowen Xu. The eight workshops complemented the outstanding paper sessions. Indeed, ISPA deals with all the topics related to parallel and distributed processing and applications. The eight workshops are very specific and contributed to enlarging the spectrum of the more general topics treated in the main conference. Each workshop was organized by a group of international organizers, leading a program committee in the process of reviewing submission. Together the workshops selected 71 papers from a total of 323 papers, and gathered a good number of participants to the campus of Nanjing University on November 2, 2005.

Putting together eight workshops requires the time and effort of many people. First, we would like to thank Springer for publishing this year both the main conference and workshops proceedings in the Lecture Notes in Computer Science series. We would also like to thank all the authors for their hard work in preparing submissions. Finally we are very grateful for the support and collaboration of all the workshop organizers and program committee members.

November 2005   Guihai Chen, Yi Pan, Minyi Guo, Jian Lu

Preface

Organization

ISPA 2005 was organized mainly by the State Key Laboratory for Novel Software Technology, Nanjing University, China.

General Co-chairs
Jack Dongarra, University of Tennessee, USA
Jiannong Cao, Hong Kong Polytechnic University, China
Jian Lu, Nanjing University, China

Program Co-chairs
Yi Pan, Georgia State University, USA
Daoxu Chen, Nanjing University, China

Program Vice-Chairs
Ivan Stojmenovic, University of Ottawa, Canada
Mohamed Ould-Khaoua, University of Glasgow, UK
Mark Baker, University of Portsmouth, UK
Jingling Xue, University of New South Wales, Australia
Zhi-Hua Zhou, Nanjing University, China

Steering Committee Co-chairs
Sartaj Sahni, University of Florida, USA
Yaoxue Zhang, Ministry of Education, China
Minyi Guo, University of Aizu, Japan

Steering Committee
Jiannong Cao, Hong Kong Polytechnic University, China
Francis Lau, University of Hong Kong, China
Yi Pan, Georgia State University, USA
Li Xie, Nanjing University, China
Jie Wu, Florida Altantic University, USA
Laurence T. Yang, St. Francis Xavier University, Canada

Hans P. Zima, California Institute of Technology, USA
Weiming Zheng, Tsinghua University, China

Local Arrangements Chairs
Xianglin Fei, Nanjing University, China
Baowen Xu, Southeast University, China
Ling Chen, Yangzhou University, China

Workshops Chair
Guihai Chen, Nanjing University, China

Tutorials Chair
Yuzhong Sun, Institute of Computing Technology, CAS, China

Publicity Chair
Cho-Li Wang, University of Hong Kong, China

Publication Chair
Hui Wang, University of Aizu, Japan

Conference Secretary
Xuan Xu, Nanjing University, China

Program Committee

Selim G. Akl	Queen's University, Canada
Amy W. Apon	University of Arkansas, USA
Hamid R. Arabnia	University of Georgia, USA
Eduard Ayguade	UPC, Spain
David A. Bader	Georgia Institute of Technology, USA
Mark Baker	University of Portsmouth, UK
Anu Bourgeois	Georgia State University, USA
Wentong Cai	Nanyang Technological University, Singapore
Xing Cai	Univ. of Oslo/Simula Research Lab, Norway

Emmanuel Cecchet	INRIA, France
Weng-Long Chang	Southern Taiwan Univ. of Tech., Taiwan
Guihai Chen	Nanjing University, China
Su-Hui Chiang	Portland State University, USA
Yuanshun Dai	Purdue University, USA
Andrzej M. Goscinski	Deakin University, Australia
Dhrubajyoti Goswami	Concordia University, Canada
Ning Gu	Fudan University, China
Jieyue He	Southeast University, China
Yanxiang He	Wuhan University, China
Hung-Chang Hsiao	National Tsing-Hua University, Taiwan
Jenwei Hsieh	Dell Inc.
Ching-Hsien Hsu	Chung Hua University, Taiwan
Chun-Hsi Huang	University of Connecticut, USA
Tsung-Chuan Huang	National Sun Yat-sen University, Taiwan
Constantinos Ierotheou	University of Greenwich, UK
Stephen Jarvis	University of Warwick, UK
Chris Jeshsope	Universiteit van Amsterdam (UvA), Netherlands
Beihong Jin	Institute of Software, Chinese Academy of Sciences, China
Hai Jin	Huazhong University of Science and Technology, China
Weijia Jia	City University of Hong Kong, China
Ajay Katangur	Texas A&M University at Corpus Christi, USA
Hatsuhiko Kato	Shonan Institute of Technology, Japan
Daniel S. Katz	JPL, California Institute of Technology, USA
Jacques Chassin de Kergommeaux	INPG, LSR-IMAG, Grenoble, France
Raj Kettimuthu	Argonne National Laboratory, USA
Chung-Ta King	National Tsing-Hua University, Taiwan
Dieter Kranzlmueller	Linz University, Austria
Sy-Yen Kuo	National Taiwan University, Taiwan
Chokchai Leangsuksun	Louisiana Tech University, USA

Jie Li   University of Tsukuba, Japan
Minglu Li   Shanghai Jiao Tong University, China
Yamin Li   University of Hosei, Japan
Xiaola Lin   Sun Yat-sen University, China
Zhen Liu   Nagasaki Institute of Applied Science,
                               Japan
Peter Kok Keong Loh   Nanyang Technological University,
                               Singapore
Jianhua Ma   Hosei University, Japan
Praveen Madiraju   Georgia State University, USA
Geyong Min   University of Bradford, UK
Michael Ng   University of Hong Kong, China
Jun Ni   University of Iowa, USA
Manish Parashar   Rutgers University, USA
Andrea Passarella   University of Pisa, Italy
Rolf Rabenseifner   Rechenzentrum, Universität Stuttgart,
                               Germany
Alex Shafarenko   University of Hertfordshire, UK
Yuzhong Sun   Institute of Computing Technology,
                               CAS, China
Peiyi Tang   University of Arkansas at Little Rock,
                               USA
David Taniar   Monash University, Australia
Ruppa K. Thulasiram   University of Manitoba, Canada
Xinmin Tian   Intel, USA
Lorenzo Verdoscia   ICAR, Italian National Research
                               Council (CNR), Italy
Frederic Vivien   INRIA, France
Guojung Wang   Hong Kong Polytechnic University,
                               China
Xingwei Wang   Northeastern University, China
Allan Wong   Hong Kong Polytechnic University,China
Chengyong Wu   Chinese Academy of Sciences, China
Bin Xiao   Hong Kong Polytechnic University,
                               China

Nong Xiao   National University of Defense
                                 Technology, China
Cheng-Zhong Xu   Wayne State University, USA
Dongyan Xu   Purdue University, USA
Jianliang Xu   Hong Kong Baptist University, China
Xinfeng Ye   Auckland University, New Zealand
Kun-Ming Yu   Chung Hua University, Taiwan
Jun Zhang   University of Kentucky, USA
Yao Zheng   Zhejiang University, China
Bingbing Zhou   University of Sydney, Australia
Wanlei Zhou   Deakin University, Austraia
Xiaobo Zhou   University of Colorado at Colorado
                                 Springs, USA
Jianping Zhu   University of Akron, USA
A.Y. Zomaya   University of Sydney, Australia

Table of Contents

Workshop 2: International Workshop on Advanced Storage Technology and Autonomic Distributed Data (ASTD 2005)

Workshop 3: International Workshop on Bioinformatics (BIOS 2005)

Workshop 4: International Workshop on Grid Computing in China (GCIC 2005)

Workshop 5: International Workshop on Information Assurance in Distributed Systems (IADS 2005)

Workshop 6: International Workshop on Mobile Ad-Hoc and Ubiquitous Sensor Networks (MASN 2005)

Workshop 7: International Workshop on Service Grid Computing and Applications (SGCA 2005)

Workshop 8: International Workshop on Web Information Systems and Applications (WISA 2005)

Aurelia: Building Locality-Preserving Overlay Network over Heterogeneous P2P Environments

Di Wu, Ye Tian, and Kam-Wing Ng

Department of Computer Science & Engineering,
The Chinese University of Hong Kong,
Shatin, N.T., Hong Kong
{dwu, ytian, kwng}@cse.cuhk.edu.hk

Abstract. Traditional DHT-based overlays destroy data locality and make it hard to support complex queries (e.g., range query, similarity query, etc) in P2P systems. Additionally, the node heterogeneity is widely ignored in most existing overlay designs. In this paper, we propose a locality-preserving overlay design, called Aurelia, which can adapt to the heterogeneous P2P environment and exploit node heterogeneity to realize efficient routing and robust indexing. Aurelia preserves the data locality by abandoning the use of hashing for data placement and each peer is responsible for a continuous range of value. In Aurelia, the routing table size and index range are proportional to the node capacity, and multicasting is adopted for scalable routing table maintenance.

1 Introduction

In decentralized P2P systems, data locality is an important property to enable efficient complex queries, for the cost of performing a query is often proportional to the number of peers that need to process the query. Without data locality, a simple range query will require visiting a number of peers. To efficiently support complex queries (e.g., range query, similarity query, etc) in P2P systems, the overlay should preserve the data locality to guarantee data with similar values be stored in nearby nodes.

What is more, in real P2P file-sharing environments, previous measurements [1] have identified the tremendous heterogeneity among P2P nodes. The peers exhibit great diversity in their capacity (e.g., CPU processing, disk speed, bandwidth, etc) and behaviors (e.g., lifetime, altruism). However, most of current overlay protocols simply regard them as homogeneous during design. We believe it is an unreasonable assumption and also will cause the loss of efficiency. Obviously, it is a kind of waste for powerful nodes to maintain the same size of routing table as the weak nodes.

Based on the above design rationale, in this paper, we propose a locality-preserving overlay design, called Aurelia [1], which can exploit the node heterogeneity in bandwidth, storage and processing capability for more efficient routing

---

[1] Aurelia is a genus of jellyfishes, whose shape is similar to our proposed overlay structure. Therefore, we name it by Aurelia.

G. Chen et al. (Eds.): ISPA Workshops 2005, LNCS 3759, pp. 1–8, 2005.

and robust indexing. In Aurelia, peers maintain different sizes of routing table and index range according to their available capacity. Powerful nodes can achieve faster routing and quicker searching. The routing table maintenance is based on the multicast tree embedded in the overlay. Aurelia also preserves the data locality by abandoning the using of hash functions for data distribution and each node is responsible for a continuous range of values. This property makes it easy to support complex queries. The performance of Aurelia is evaluated through simulation. Experimental results validate the scalability and efficiency of Aurelia.

The reminder of the paper is organized as follows. We discuss the related work in Section 2 and then describe the detailed design of Aurelia in Section 3. In the following section 4, experimental results from the simulation are presented and analyzed. Finally, we conclude in Section 5.

2   Related Work

In the design of overlay protocols, there are only a few designs addressing both data locality and node heterogeneity. Existing DHT designs (Chord[2], Pastry[3], etc) use randomized hashing for data placement, but hashing will destroy the data locality. To preserve data locality in DHT, order-preserving hash function ([4], [5], etc) or another indexing layer(e.g., SFC[6], PHT [7]) was introduced. However, the design is likely to be complicated and to result in bad performance. SkipNet [8] is another kind of structured overlay, which provides data locality by organizing data by string names, but it suffers from the problem of load balancing. Additionally, they all ignore node heterogeneity in their design.

Previous proposals to utilize node heterogeneity are mainly based on the concept of "supernode". Nodes are simply classified into two categories: supernode or not. The system availability and performance greatly depend on the supernodes, and is contrary to the P2P design principle. In [9], Hu et al propose a new capacity-aware DHT design, in which the nodes can be further divided into different levels. However, due to node dynamism, it cannot perform well under non-uniform node distribution.

3   System Design

Like Chord, Aurelia organizes nodes into a circular ring that corresponds to the ID space $[0, 2^{128} - 1]$. Each node is assigned a unique identifier. However, we abandon the using of hashing to distribute the data objects across the nodes for it will destroy the data locality. Instead, each node of Aurelia is responsible for a contiguous range of data value, and Aurelia simply maps the data object to the node according to its value. In this way, the data locality can be preserved and range queries for a continuous data range become efficient.

To exploit the node heterogeneity, Aurelia differentiates the nodes according to their capacity. A node n's capacity C_n is determined by its bandwidth B, storage S, CPU processing capability P and the node lifetime L. We can represent it as $C_n = f(B, S, P) \times g(L)$, where f, g are monotonic increasing functions. For simplicity, we adopt a similar approach as [9]. Nodes are classified into levels (e.g., 0, 1, ... n, among them, 0 is the top level). The size of routing table and the index range of an Aurelia node are proportional to the node's capacity level. On the extreme, one very powerful node can have routes to all the nodes and host the full data index, just like Napster.

In the design of Aurelia, the main challenge is to maintain such a big routing table efficiently in a large system. There are two basic approaches: one is by periodical probing of all the nodes in the routing table entries, which will cause huge traffic when the table size is big; another is by event notification, when the node changes its status, its neighbors or itself can broadcast the event to all the related nodes. The latter is more scalable than the former. Aurelia adopts the latter approach. To avoid too many redundant messages, Aurelia uses multicast to notify all the relevant nodes when nodes join, leave, fail or change status. However, it is not necessary for Aurelia to explicitly maintain the multicast tree, because it is already embedded in the overlay. In the following sections, we will introduce the design of Aurelia in details.

3.1   Identification Scheme

Initially, the node ID can be assigned by uniform hashing, through which the nodes are distributed evenly across the ring. The node ID is divided into three parts: range ID, random bits and level ID. For example, for the node $\underline{001}010...10\underline{10}$, its range ID and level ID are $\underline{001}$ and $\underline{10}$ respectively, and the bits in between are random bits.

The range ID is the first r-bit prefix of the node ID, which defines the index range that the node will be responsible for. All the data keys whose first r-bit prefix is the same as the range ID will be placed in this node. The length of range ID determines the size of index range of that node if the objects are uniformly distributed. The nodes can choose a suitable length based on its capacity. When the node feels that the query workload is beyond its capacity, it can reduce the responsible index range by extending the length of range ID. Formally, supposing the range of the ring is mapped to $[0, 1]$, the node with range ID of $b_0 b_1 \ldots b_{r-1}$ will take charge of the range:

$$Range(b_0 b_1 \ldots b_{r-1}) = \left[\frac{\sum_{i=0}^{r-1} b_i \times 2^{r-i-1}}{2^r}, \frac{\sum_{i=0}^{r-1} b_i \times 2^{r-i-1} + 1}{2^r} \right)$$

The level ID is the l-bit suffix of the node ID, which represents the node capacity level. The level ID and routing range together determine the routing table size of the node. For a node n, only the nodes whose node ID is within the routing range and the last l bits are the same as its level ID will appear in its routing table. Supposing that nodes are uniformly distributed in the ID space, if there are N nodes in the system, the size of routing table is $N/2^l$. The shorter the level ID, the bigger the routing table. In the extreme case, if the length of level ID is zero, the routing table will include all the nodes in the system.

3.2   Routing Strategy

In case of uniform node distribution in the ring, the routing scheme of Aurelia will be similar to SmartBoa [9]. However, with node dynamism or load balancing reasons(e.g., under-loaded nodes quit their current position and rejoin the heavy-loaded region), the node distribution in the ring will become non-uniform. In such scenarios, SmartBoa's routing scheme will become inefficient. For the region with dense node distribution, more hops will be required than expected(as illustrated in Fig.1(a)). This drawback leads to the design of Aurelia.

The basic idea of Aurelia is to adjust the span of routing pointers adapting to the node distribution. In the sparse region, there are fewer routing pointers; while in the dense region, more routing pointers will be allocated for fast routing. The density of routing pointers is controlled by adjustment of level ID. The node seems like hosting multiple virtual nodes with different level ID and routing range. However, these virtual nodes share the same node ID. Fig.1(b) gives a simple example of Aurelia's routing pointers.

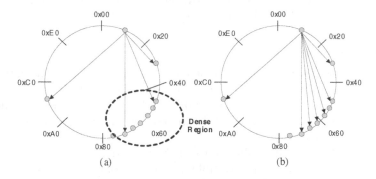

(a)   (b)

Fig. 1. Routing under non-uniform node distribution (a)SmartBoa's routing pointers (b)Aurelia's routing pointers

As to the routing strategy, Aurelia performs in a greedy-like style. Given a target key, the node always selects the nearest one in the routing table to forward it. For the powerful nodes, the big routing table enables them to complete the routing even in 1 hop.

To build such kind of routing table, a big challenge is to maintain the node-count distribution in a decentralized way. Aurelia adopts the technique of sampling to collect the statistical information and build the approximate node-count histogram locally. Each node in Aurelia maintains a leaf set with the size of k, which records the node's k nearest neighbors in the ID space. Normally, there will be $k/2$ nodes on each side of the node. Periodically, the node will probe the existence of the k neighbors and adjust the entries in case of node joining or leaving. If denoting the distance between the node's rightmost neighbor and the leftmost neighbor in the ring as d, then the node i can produce a local estimate D_i about node density in its nearby region, which is represented as $D_i = \frac{k+1}{d}$.

In addition to producing local estimate, the node also periodically makes sampling uniformly in the ring. According to the collected information, the node will choose the most recent statistical data to produce the node-count histogram. After the histogram is built and normalized, the node can adjust its routing pointers in the following way:

Each block in the histogram represents a continuous region with the size of $1/2^k$ of the whole ID space. Based on the ratio between the block's density level and the average density level, the length of virtual nodes' level ID will be increased or decreased accordingly. Such adjustment will impact the density of routing pointers in different routing ranges. For sparse routing range, fewer routing pointers are needed, so the level ID of virtual node in that region can be extended. On the contrary, for dense routing range, more routing pointers will be included by shortening the level ID. However, the extension and reduction of the level ID cannot deviate too much from its real level. Otherwise, it may cause problems in some situations. For example, if a weak node hosts a virtual node with high level and tiny routing range, it will join the high-level node group, which will result great update traffic beyond its capacity.

3.3   Routing Table Maintenance

The routing table of Aurelia includes four parts: routing pointers, top node pointers, leafset pointers and skip pointers.

The "routing pointers" part contains the nodes whose last l-bit suffix equals to the level ID and the node ID is within the routing range. The number of routing pointers scales nearly linearly with the increasing of node capacity. The "top node pointers" part is composed of the nodes whose level ID is the shortest suffix of current node's level ID. Top nodes are often powerful nodes that hold more routing pointers. The "leafset pointers" part includes the neighbors of current nodes in the ring. For the weak node's routing step span is still too large, there may be many nodes between two adjacent routing pointers. For fast routing, "skip pointers" are maintained in the region between the node's first right routing pointer and left routing pointer. Each of the skip pointers will skip $2^i (i = 0, 1, ...)$ nodes.

To maintain the routing pointers in a scalable fashion, Aurelia adopts multicast to distribute the events of node join, leave or status change. The multicast tree doesn't require explicit management. It is based on the level ID and routing range to disseminate the event from high-level nodes to low-level nodes.

The details of the multicast process are as follows: when a node joins or changes its status, it will first forward the event with the node ID to one of its top nodes randomly. Then this top node will multicast the event to all the nodes whose level ID is the suffix of the reported node ID. But for the virtual node, if an announced node ID is not within the routing range it wants to be notified, the event will be ignored. In every step of the multicast process, the node that receives the event will first send it to the next lower level, then notifies the other nodes with the same level ID. By this, we can guarantee the event to be exactly delivered from the high-level nodes to the low-level nodes. When a node leaves, its predecessor will detect this event and help to notify the top nodes and propagates the change information to all the related nodes.

A node can adaptively adjust its level and routing table according to the workload it experiences. In the high-level position, the node can establish a big routing table and do quick routing, but it is at the cost of more processing and bandwidth consumption.

3.4 Data Registration

To preserve the data locality, Aurelia avoids using hashing to distribute the data objects. Each node of Aurelia will be responsible for a contiguous range region, which is determined by its range ID. The data registration is simply based on the data value. If the value falls into the range of one node, then the node will hold the data object or the pointer to it. In this way, the objects with adjacent value will be assigned to the same node or the nearby nodes. This property makes range query to be efficiently supported in Aurelia. When publishing a new data object, its value is first normalized into the range [0,1]. Given that the normalized value is v, we can approximately represent v by a binary string $b_0 b_1 ... b_{n-1}$ (n is the maximum ID length). They satisfy the following relation: $v \approx \frac{b_0}{2} + \frac{b_1}{2^2} + ... + \frac{b_{n-1}}{2^{n-1}}$.

The binary string is the key of this data object, then this data will be registered into all the nodes whose range ID is a prefix of the key. In this way, one data object will have multiple index entries. It provides a kind of replication for index information and makes the indexing service more robust. Even when some nodes hosting the index information leave the system, the lookup may still be successful. For example, in Fig.2, two nodes are responsible for different range sizes in the ring. The index range of node $\underline{010}$xxxxx is covered by node $\underline{01}$xxxxxx.

The detailed registration process is as follows: Similar to the "top node pointers" in the routing table, every node also maintains "top index pointers", whose range ID is the prefix of the node's range ID and index range is not covered by any other nodes. This means that it keeps a bigger range that covers the range of this node. During data publishing, the registration message is firstly routed to the node whose ID is nearest to the data key; then the node will select a top

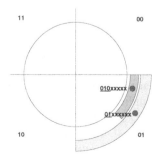

Fig. 2. Index Range Coverage

index node randomly and forward the message to it. This top index node will
be responsible for multicasting the message to all the nodes whose range is covered by it. The multicast algorithm is similar to the above-mentioned multicast
algorithm for routing table maintenance, except that it is based on the range ID
for multicasting. When a node feels overloaded by query traffic, it can adjust its
range ID to change index range.

4   Experiments

We evaluate the Aurelia protocol by simulation on a Sun Enterprise E4500
server(with 12 UltraSPARC-II 400MHz CPUs, 8GB RAM and 1Gbps network
bandwidth). To understand Aurelia's routing performance in practice, we simulate a network with N = 10,000 nodes and use the routing hops during a lookup
operation as the metric. We assume node distribution in the ring follows a Zipf-
like distribution. Each node in an experiment selects a random set of keys to
query from the system, and we measure the hops required to resolve each query.
To investigate the effects of node heterogeneity, the node capacity distribution
is based on the measurement results of Gnutella in [1].(as shown in Fig.3 (a))

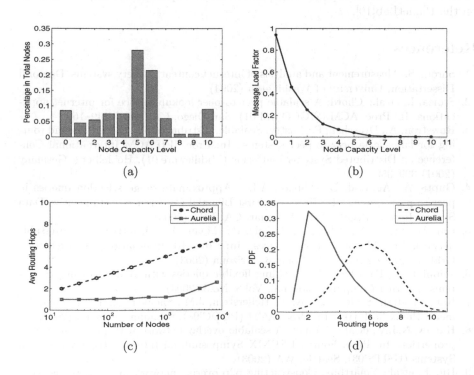

Fig. 3. (a)Node capacity distribution; (b)Message load factor of nodes with different capacity levels (c)Average routing hops as a function of network size (d) PDF(Probability
Distribution Function) of the routing hops for a network with 10000 nodes

Fig.3 (b) describes the message load factor of nodes with different capacity levels. High-level nodes are likely to have more message traffic. In our experiments, we take Chord[2] as a benchmark for routing performance comparison. Fig.3 (c) plots average routing hops as a function of network size. When the network size is small, even the weak nodes can maintain the routes to all nodes, and the average routing hops is near 1. With the increasing of node number, even the top nodes cannot maintain the full routing table, and the average routing hops will increase accordingly. However, the routing efficiency of Aurelia is still better than Chord. Fig.3 (d) plots the PDF(Probability Distribution Function) of the routing hops for a network with 10000 nodes. It is observed that most lookups can be completed within 5 hops.

5 Conclusion

We have presented a locality-preserving heterogeneous overlay design called Aurelia in this paper. It fully utilizes node heterogeneity to achieve fast routing and robust indexing. By guaranteeing data locality, complex queries like range query can be supported more efficiently. In the future, we will try to analyze its performance from theoretical perspective and conduct experimental implementation on the PlanetLab[10].

References

1. Saroiu, S.: Measurement and analysis of internet content delivery systems. Doctoral Dissertation, University of Washington (2004)
2. Stoica, I., et al.: Chord: A scalable peer-to-peer lookup service for internet applications. In: Proc. ACM (SIGCOMM'01), San Diego, CA (2001) 149–160
3. Rowstron, A., Druschel., P.: Pastry: Scalable, distributed object location and routing for large-scale peer-to-peer systems. In: Proc. IFIPACM International Conference on Distributed Systems Platforms (Middleware'01), Heidelberg, Germany (2001) 329–350
4. Gupta, A., Agrawal, D., Abbadi, A.E.: Approximate range selection queries in peer-to-peer systems. In: Proc. the First Biennial Conference on Innovative Data System Research (CIDR'03), Asilomar, CA, USA (2003)
5. Cai, M., Frank, M., Chen, J., Szekely, P.: Maan: A multi-attribute addressable network for grid information services. In: Proc. 4th International Workshop on Grid Computing (Grid'03), Phoenix, Arizona (2003)
6. Schmidt, C., Parashar, M.: Enabling flexible queries with guarantees in p2p systems. Internet Computing Journal, Vol.8, No.3 (2004)
7. Ramabhadran, S., Ratnasamy, S., Hellerstein, J.M., Shenker, S.: Brief announcement: Prefix hash tree. In: Proc. ACM (PODC'04), St. Johns, Canada (2004)
8. Harvey, N.J.A., et al.: Skipnet: A scalable overlay network with practical locality properties. In: Proc. Fourth USENIX Symposium on Internet Technologies and Systems (USITS'03), Seattle, WA (2003)
9. Hu, J., et al.: Smartboa: Constructing p2p overlay network in the heterogeneous internet using irregular routing tables. In: Proc. 3rd International Workshop on Peer-to-Peer Systems (IPTPS'04), San Diego, CA, USA (2004)
10. Planetlab: http://www.planet-lab.org/

On Building and Updating Distributed LSI for P2P Systems

Sanfeng Zhang, Guoxin Wu, Gang Chen, and Libo Xu

Department of Computer Science and Engineering, Southeast University,
210096 Nanjing China
sfzhangseu@hotmail.com

Abstract. Recently published studies have shown that Latent Semantic Indexing (LSI) plays an important role in content-based full text information retrieval
of P2P system. However, it is a challenging problem to generate global consistent LSI structures in P2P systems because their nodes are self-organizing and
their corpora are large, dynamic and distributed on different nodes. In this paper
we propose a method for building LSI structures from distributed corpora. Our
method is consisted with a network model for semantic information sampling
and exchanging and a Reduced-Dimension-Representation (RDR)s merging algorithm. By the signal and noise subspace model, we also provide a theoretical
justification that the RDR merging algorithm is sound. A simple numerical experiment shows that our RDR merging algorithm can keep query precision on
an acceptable level.

1 Backgrounds and Motivation

Due to the essential natures of P2P technologies such as scalability, fault tolerance,
and self-organizing, it is promising to build large-scale distributed Information Retrieval (IR) systems at low cost. Compared with conventional search engines, P2P
technologies can extend the searching scope to both servers and clients. However,
most current P2P search mechanisms [8][9][10] can only support exact match queries,
which limits their applications extremely. In IR area, Vector Space Model (VSM) [4]
and Latent Semantic Indexing (LSI) [5][6] are the most popular and well-studied IR
algorithms developed within last decades. To achieve effective semantic search, it's a
promising way to explore relationship between the k-dimensional semantic space
constructed by LSI and the Cartesian space formed by some P2P model (for example,
CAN [8]). In fact, recently published studies have attempted to do so.

In literature [1][2] C.Tang et al. proposed two content-based IR systems, pSearch
and eSearch, which both map high dimension semantic space formed by LSI to a low
dimension Cartesian space of CAN by rolling-index. When a peer need to share a
document, it first computes the document's coordinates in the semantic space according to LSI structures, then presents the document as a pair of (vector, URL) and sends
it to a special node to assure that indices of similar documents are stored on the adjacent nodes in the Cartesian space of CAN. When a query is initiated, it is first

G. Chen et al. (Eds.): ISPA Workshops 2005, LNCS 3759, pp. 9 – 16, 2005.

presented as a vector and then the vector is mapped to a node owning documents similar to the query, the whole process is just like that a document is shared. By this way, a query will not bother every node in the P2P system, so the communication overhead can be reduced that is main obstacle to carry out full text IR in P2P system, while keeping the recall-precision performance. The main shortcoming of the work in [1][2] is that they don't take the process of building and updating LSI from distributed corpus into account, they implicitly suppose that the semantic structure of corpora in P2P systems is known and the data structure of LSI is built previously, but this assumption doesn't suit to P2P system's environment.

In the dynamic and distributed environment, such as Web and P2P, documents are continuously added to or deleted from the whole corpus, and a same document may have many copies on different nodes. To compute data structures of LSI, one method is building a sample corpus previously, and then computing semantic vector of the document not in the sample set with Folding-in method. The computing cost of Folding-in is low, but sampling previously in P2P is difficult and destroys P2P system's self-organizing nature. Our motivation is to address this problem by proposing a method of building and updating LSI structures form distributed corpora in a self-organizing manner.

This paper is organized as follows. Section 2 introduces some related work. Section 3 proposes a network model for semantic information sampling and exchanging. Section 4 describes RDR-merging algorithm. Leveraging the signal and noise subspace model in array signal processing, section 5 provides a theoretical justification for the RDR-merging algorithm. Section 6 gives numerical experiments show that our RDR-merging algorithm can keep fair query precision. Section 7 concludes the paper.

2   Related Work

Deerwester, S. et al. first proposed LSI in [6]. It is an extension of VSM overcoming problems such as synonyms and polysemy. Its basic idea is described as follow. Let the term-by-document matrix derived by VSM be $A=[a_{ij}]\in R^{t\times d}$, where t denotes the number of terms in the corpus, d is the number of documents, the matrix's entry, a_{ij} is the weight of term i in document j. And a_{ij} can be compute with weighting schemes like TF-IDF. Let the Singular Value Decomposition (SVD) of A be:

$$A = U \sum V^T \tag{1.1}$$

Then we can get the reduced-dimension representation (RDR) of the matrix A, $A_k=U_k\Sigma_kV_k^T$□it is also a best rank-k approximation of A, where U_k and V_k are formed by the first k columns of U and V and constitute an orthogonal basis of the row and column space of A_k, respectively, and Σ_k is the k-th leading principal submatrix of A_k. Studies in [5] show that when k ranges from 50 to 350 LSI can make 30% progress in precision typically. One common metric of similarity between documents is the cosine of the angle document vectors.

$$\cos \theta_j = \frac{(A_k e_j)^T q}{\| A_k e_j \|_2 \| q \|_2} = \frac{(\Sigma_k V_k^T e_j)^T (U_k^T q)}{\| \Sigma_k V_k^T e_j \|_2 \| q \|_2} \quad (1.2)$$

In equation (1.2), e_j is defined as the j-th canonical vector of dimension d, $t_j = \Sigma_k V_k^T e_j$, $q' = U_k^T q$. q' denotes coordinate of the j-th document vector and q in the basis defined by U_k in the column space of A_k, The coordinate t_j and the norm c for each document usually are compute once and used for every query. Since computing and storing the complete U and V matrices is very costly, only U_k, V_k, and Σ_k are available in the memory or disk.

In literature [3], Heng Tao Shen et al. proposed a semantic-based content search schema in hierarchical p2p systems. On the peer and super peer level, they use the centroids as corpora's representation, which may drop important semantic information for building global semantic structures. Super peers will re-compute the SVD by new dictionary without leveraging current result, which wastes computing resource. Further more, how scalability can be achieved by hierarchical architecture is worth doubling.

Hongyuan Zha and H. Simon proposed an algorithm on updating LSI from the point of SVD in [7].

3   Network Model

In this section we describe a network model for semantic information sampling and exchanging to build LSI structures from distributed corpora. Fig.1 describes the basic model.

3.1   Two Assumptions

We separate nodes of P2P into clients and servers from the standpoint of indexing. Clients provide documents, parse documents to vectors of VSM, submit vectors to servers, but don't participate in the computation of LSI structures. Servers build and update LSI according to vector set. 10~100 client peers are connected to one server peer. Servers can be chosen from nodes of CAN P2P network considering computing and communication power. By the separating, the number of nodes computing SVD is reduced, and the document vectors are congregated.

We also assume the term set is fixed and adding documents only add a new vector to the matrix, and document vectors are generated using Term-Frequency (TF) weighting scheme.

3.2   Generate Document Vectors

Every node in the network runs a document parsing program and a global consistent term set. When a node shares a new document or submits a query, it parses the document or the query into a vector. Then the vectors are transported to the node's corresponding server in form of (URL, vector).

3.3 Derive Global RDR from Distributed Vector Sets

Each server N_i maintains three data structures. The first is the set of (URL, vector) pairs. (URL, vector) pairs are presentations of documents indexed by the server and D_i denotes the set. The second is a set of sample vectors gathered from the whole network, and S_i denotes this set. The last one is RDR which representing the semantic structure of the whole corpus in P2P network. In P2P systems, the corpora are so large and so dynamic that computing RDR from all the document vectors is not efficiency. An auto-sampling algorithm is designed for semantic information sampling. The algorithm is shown in Fig.2, where sim() is a function for computing similarity between two document vectors, for example $sim(x, y) = \dfrac{1}{\| x - y \|_2}$, λ is a threshold, its value decides the ratio of sampling. Experiments in [3] show that when the sampling ratio is greater than 15% the 85% of the query precision can be kept. By performing an union operation on vectors of S_i, N_i generate a vector V_{si} which denotes the centroid of S_i. N_i then broadcast V_{si} to other servers. When the scale of network is too large, TTL is used to limit hops of broadcast. N_i carries SVD computing and requests R_i of other servers. The next step is merging RDRs on server peers to a global one.

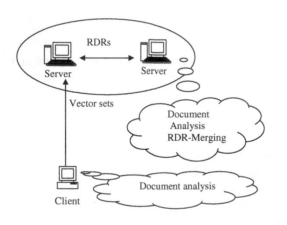

Algorithm 1:Document Sampling

1.   set D=document vector set
2.   set S=sample set=empty
3.   set i= size of D, j=1
4.   insert D_1 into S
5.   while i>0 {
6.   set k=1
7.   while k<=j {
8.   if sim(D_i,S_k)<λ {
9.   k++
10.   insert D_i into S
11.   j++
12.   }
13.   }
14.   i--
15. }

Fig. 1. Distributed building and updating of LSI   **Fig. 2.** Document sampling

RDR-merging process is shown in Fig.3, where sim() has the same meaning as Fig.2. Compared with [3], we generate new RDR with current RDR, and only use centroid vector as a criteria for choosing corpora dissimilar in semantic. Thus, communication overhead is reduced. In section 4 we will give details on computing new RDR matrix from two current RDR matrixes and proof that semantic structure is kept, while computing workload is reduced in section 5.

3.4 Add New Documents

When the initialization phase completes, each server owns an initial global consistent LSI data structure. Using the initial LSI, we can build a semantic overlay just like the process in [1]. Each server is mapped to a semantic range of documents. When new documents are shared, they are parsed into document vectors and submitted to servers. Eventually, they are transported to destination servers answering for indexing them. Then, each server N_i Samples from new document vectors according to algorithm-1. The centriod vector of the corpus of N_i $Vnew_{si}$ is computed. If $sim(V_{si}, Vnew_{si}) < \lambda_m$, N_i does SVD computation on new samples and gets a new RDR denoted by Rnew. N_i gets its new RDR of its corpus Leveraging RDR merging algorithm and broadcast $Vnew_{si}$ other server peers receive $Vnew_{si}$ decides whether it carry a RDR-Merging operation by semantic comparison.

Algorithm2 Merging RDRs

1. set S=set of vectors received
2. set V_i =local sample set vector
3. for each V_j in S{
4.   if $sim(V_i, V_j) < \lambda_m$ {
5. $V_i = V_i + V_j$
6.   request R_j
7.   merge R_j and R_i
8.   broadcast V_i }
9 }

Fig. 3. RDR- Merging

4 RDR-Merging Algorithm

In this section 4 we will give details on computing new RDR matrix from two current RDR matrixes.

Let $A_1 = [a_{ij}] \in R^{t \times d}$ be the term by document matrix on a server. $A_{k1} = U_{k1} \Sigma_{k1} V_{k1}^T$ is its RDR, $A_2 = [a_{ij}] \in R^{t \times p}$ and $A_{k2} = U_{k2} \Sigma_{k2} V_{k2}^T$ are matrix and RDR of another server. The goal is to find the RDR of matrix $C = [A_{k1}, A_{k2}]$, $C_k = U_k \Sigma_k V_k^T$.

$$C = \left(A_{k1}, A_{k2} \right)$$
$$= \left(U_{k1} \Sigma_{k1} V_{k1}^T, U_{k2} \Sigma_{k2} V_{k2}^T \right) = \left(U_{k1} \Sigma_{k1}, U_{k2} \Sigma_{k2} \right) \begin{pmatrix} V_{k1}^T & 0 \\ 0 & V_{k2}^T \end{pmatrix}$$
$$= \left(U_{k1}, X \right) \begin{pmatrix} \Sigma_{k1} & Y \\ 0 & Z \end{pmatrix} \begin{pmatrix} V_{k1} & 0 \\ 0 & V_{k2} \end{pmatrix}^T \tag{4.1}$$

In Equation (4.1), X should be an orthonormal matrix from orthogonal complement subspace of U_{k1}, Z should be an upper triangular matrix. Moreover, the QR decomposition of the projection of $U_{k2} \Sigma_{k2}$ in the orthogonal complement subspace of U_{k1} can be written as $(I - U_{k1} U_{k1}^T) U_{k2} \Sigma_{k2} = \widehat{U}_{k1} R$. We can write equations as follow.

$$X = \widehat{U}_{k1}, Y = U_{k1}^T U_{k2} \Sigma_{k2}, Z = R.$$

Then C is decomposed into product of two orthogonal matrixes and an upper triangular matrix.

$$C = \left(U_{k1}, \widehat{U}_{k1} \right) \begin{pmatrix} \Sigma_{k1} & U_{k1}^T U_{k2} \Sigma_{k2} \\ 0 & R \end{pmatrix} \begin{pmatrix} V_{k1} & 0 \\ 0 & V_{k2} \end{pmatrix}^T.$$

The mid of right part of the equation is a upper triangular of $(k_1+k_2)\times(k_1+k_2)$, its SVD can be computed at low computational workload.

$$\begin{pmatrix} \Sigma_{k1} & U_{k1}^T U_{k2} \Sigma_{k2} \\ 0 & R \end{pmatrix} = \left(P_k, \widehat{P_k}\right) \begin{pmatrix} \widehat{\Sigma_k} & 0 \\ 0 & \widehat{\Sigma_p} \end{pmatrix} \left(Q_k, \widehat{Q_k}\right)^T .$$

Eventually, we get the new RDR of C.

$$C = \left(\left(U_{k1}, \widehat{U_{k1}}\right)\left(P_k, \widehat{P_k}\right)\right) \begin{pmatrix} \widehat{\Sigma_k} & 0 \\ 0 & \widehat{\Sigma_p} \end{pmatrix} \left(\begin{pmatrix} V_{k1} & 0 \\ 0 & V_{k2} \end{pmatrix} \left(Q_k, \widehat{Q_k}\right)\right)^T \qquad (4.2)$$

$$C_k = \left(\left(U_{k1}, \widehat{U_{k1}}\right) P_k\right) \begin{pmatrix} \widehat{\Sigma_k} & 0 \\ 0 & 0 \end{pmatrix} \left(\begin{pmatrix} V_{k1} & 0 \\ 0 & V_{k2} \end{pmatrix} Q_k\right)^T \qquad (4.3)$$

From the analysis of the process, we can see that computing new RDR from current RDR reduces the dimensions of matrices participating SVD computation (approximately, from a 5000×1000 sparse matrix to a 200×200 upper triangular matrix).

5   Theoretical Interpretation of RDR-Merging

To compute the RDR of matrix C, we carry SVD computing according to RDRs of two sub matrixes of C instead of the original term by document matrix C, which reduces the computation workload efficiently. However, the cost of this benefit is dropping the semantic information contained by the triples corresponding to the smaller singular values. Will this semantic information dropping cause not acceptable error in SVD computation of C? In other words, does C_k depart from the true RDR of C too much to be acceptable? In this section we will give a theoretical interpretation for RDR-Merging algorithm described in last section.

In array signal processing, signal and noise subspace model divides the sample value into signal part and white noise part, $x(n) = A(\omega)s(n) + e(n)$. With several assumptions, the self-covariance matrix of sample value vectors can be written as $R_{xx} = APA^H + \Sigma^2 I$, where APA^H is signal self-covariance matrix; Σ^2 is white noise self-covariance matrix. Let $S^H R_{xx} S = diag(\sigma_1^2, ..., \sigma_m^2, \sigma^2, ..., \sigma^2)$, $\Sigma_1 \geq ... \geq \Sigma_m \geq \Sigma$, Σ_i^2 is signal eigenvalue, Σ^2 is noise eigenvalue. And each block-column of R_{xx} can be written in this form. In signal processing, Matrices like R_{xx} is called as low-rank-plus-shift structure.

We can proof THEOREM 5.1 on the assumption that matrix C has low-rank-plus-shift structure. Readers can repeat the deducing process with reference to literature [7]. We omitted the proof due to the space limit of paper.

THEOREM 5.1 Let $A_1=[a_{ij}] \in R^{t \times d}$ and $A_2=[a_{ij}] \in R^{t \times p}$ be two term-document matrices, A_{k1} and A_{k2} are their rank-k_1 and rank-k_2 RDR respectively, C=[A_1, A_2], furthermore assume that

$$\widetilde{C}^T \widetilde{C} = X + \sigma^2 I, (\sigma > 0), \tag{5.1}$$

X is symmetric positive semi-definite, rank(X)=k, Then $\widetilde{C}_k = C_k$.

THEOREM 5.1 tells us that the RDR from RDR-Merging algorithm is equal to the one from the SVD of complete corpus and what is dropped when replacing sub corpus with its RDR is just noise.

The precondition of THEOREM 5.1 is that matrix C has low-rank-plus-shift structure. To explore how matrix C has such a property, we plot a curve as Fig. 4 where values on the x-axis denotes sequence number of singular values and those on y-axis denotes corresponding singular values. The curve is get from a 5735×1033 term by document matrix of MED corpus. We can see that the curve has a flat tail and the assumption is approximately satisfied.

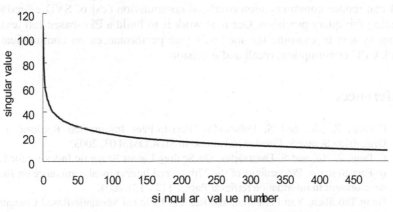

Fig. 4. Distribution of singular values

6 Numeral Experiment

Here we give a numeral experiment to proof that our RDR-Merging algorithm is sound. We use the MED corpus [12] provided by Cornell as test collection. MED corpus provides text collection, 30 queries and their related documents. Term by document matrix is generated by TMG [13]. The partial SVD computing is done with SVDPACKC [14]. The numeral experiment is carried on the MATLAB6.5.

Table 1. Precisions on MED corpus

d	933	833	733	633	533	433	333
p	100	200	300	400	500	600	700
RDR-Merging	70.56	70.72	71.24	73.37	74.68	73.21	72.13

Table.1 shows the experiment results on 5735×1033 term by document matrix, where d is the number of documents in A_1, p is that of A_2, k=100, values in row RDR-Merging are the precision. Compared with the precision 75.63% achieved with RDR derived from the complete matrix, RDR-Merging algorithm has acceptable precision.

7 Conclusion

In this paper, we propose a method for building LSI structures from distributed corpora. Our method is consisted with a network model for semantic information sampling and exchanging and a Reduced-Dimension-Representation (RDR)s merging algorithm. Using the signal and noise subspace model, we provide a theoretical justification for the algorithm and analysis its precondition. Theoretical analysis and numerical experiments show that our building and updating algorithm for distributed LSI can reduce communication overhead computation cost of SVD effectively while keeping fair query precision. Our next work is to build a P2P-based full text IR simulating system to examine the method's true performances on communication overhead, CPU consumption, recall and precision.

References

1. C.Tang, Z. Xu, and S. Dwarkadas. Peer-to-Peer Information Retrieval Using Self-Organizing Semantic Overlay Networks. In SIGCOMM'03, 2003.
2. C.Tang, Z. Xu, and S. Dwarkadas On Scaling Latent Semantic Indexing for Large Peer-to-Peer Systems. Proceedings of the 27th annual international conference on Research and development in information retrieval Pages: 112 - 121 2004.
3. Heng Tao Shen, Yan Feng Shu, and Bei Yu Efficient Semantic-Based Content Search in P2P Network IEEE Transactions on Knowledge and Data Engineering archive. Volume 16, Pages: 813 - 826 2004
4. M. Berry, Z. Drmac, and E. Jessup. Matrices, Vector Spaces, and Information Retrieval. SIAM Review, 41(2):335–362, 1999.
5. M. W. Berry, S. T. Dumais, and G. W. O'Brien. Using linear algebra for intelligent information retrieval. SIAM Review, 37(4):573-595,1995.
6. Deerwester, S., Dumais, S. T., Furnas. Indexing by latent semantic analysis. Journal of the American Society for Information Science, 41(6),391-407 1990
7. Hongyuan Zha and H. Simon. On Updating Problems in Latent Semantic Indexing, SIAM Journal of Scientific Computing. pp. 782-791, Vol. 21, 1999.
8. S. Ratnasamy, P. Francis, M. Handley, R. Karp, and S. Shenker, "A Scalable Content-Addressable Network," Proc. SIGCOMM, 2001.
9. I. Stoica, R. Morris, D. Karger, F. Kaashoek, and H. Balakrishnan,"Chord: A Scalable Peer-to-Peer Lookup Service for Internet Applications," Proc. SIGCOMM, 2001.
10. Rowstron, A. and P. Druschel. Pastry: Scalable, distributed object location and routing for large-scale peer-to-peer systems. IFIP/ACM Middleware 2001, Heidellberg, Germany, Nov
11. B. Yang and H. Garcia-Molina. Designing a super-peer network. In ICDE, 2003.
12. Cornell Smart System, ftp://ftp.cs.cornell.edu/pub/smart
13. TMG, http://scgroup.hpclab.ceid.upatras.gr/scgroup/Projects/TMG/
14. SVDPACKC, http://www.netlib.org/svdpack/

Performing Efficient Keyword Search by Keyword Grouping in DHT Peer-to-Peer Network[*]

Yin Li, Fanyuan Ma, and Liang Zhang

The Department of Computer Science and Engineering,
Shanghai Jiaotong University, Shanghai, China, 200030
{liyin, fy-ma, zhangliang}@cs.sjtu.edu.cn

Abstract. The primary challenge in developing a peer-to-peer file sharing system is implementing an efficient keyword search mechanism. Current keyword search system for structured P2P systems relies on the intersection of distributed inverted index. However, when executing multiple-attribute queries, the bandwidth overhead is unacceptable. In order to reduce query overhead, indexing can be done by a set of keywords which is adopted in KSS system. However, KSS index is considerably larger than standard inverted index and the insert and storage overhead are dramatically increased. In this paper, by adopting term ranking approach such as TFIDF and exploiting the relationship information between query keywords, the indexing is done by individual keyword while search can be done in a set of related keywords like KSS. Experiments results clearly demonstrated that the improved keyword search system can match standard inverted index in insert overhead and storage overhead, while can compete with KSS index in query overhead.

1 Introduction

Peer-to-peer (P2P) systems are distributed systems in which nodes of equal roles and capabilities exchange information and services directly with each other. In recent years, P2P has emerged as a popular way to share huge volumes of data. The key to the usability of a data-sharing P2P system, and one of the most challenging design aspects, is efficient techniques for search and retrieval of data.

Two classes of techniques have been proposed to perform keyword search in P2P networks: query flooding, and inverted list intersection. Unstructured P2P systems, such as Gnutella [1] and KaZaA [10], naturally support keyword search by flooding queries to some or all peers. Recently some efforts are made to improve scalability. For example, FastTrack[2] organizes subscribing nodes into loosely hierarchical structure where some nodes are selected as supernodes and cache the index. Multiple random walks [3] and associative overlays[4] reduce the number of forwarded queries by limiting searches to a fraction of the population. Though a lot of efforts have been

---

[*] Supported by The Science & Technology Committee of Shanghai Municipality Key Project Grant 03dz15027 and 03dz15028.

G. Chen et al. (Eds.): ISPA Workshops 2005, LNCS 3759, pp. 17–26, 2005.

made to the scalability of flooding-based search, flooding-based techniques are effective for locating highly replicated items, but they are poorly suited for locating rare items.

Another kind of P2P networks (structured P2P systems), such as CAN [7], Chord [6], Pastry [8], Tapestry [5], and SkipNet [18], don't support full text search directly. While, as they actually implement distributed hash tables (DHTs) over them, keyword search can easily be implemented by distributing inverted indices among hosts by keyword. Then a query with k keywords can be answered by at most k hosts through the intersection of inverted lists. This approach is adopted by some recent proposals [14][19] to add full text search functionality to structured P2P systems. However, Distributed inverted index by keywords may incur significant bandwidth for executing more complicated search queries such as multiple-attribute queries. This is unacceptably large bandwidth for query in a P2P system because bandwidth available to most nodes in the Internet is rather small.

In order to reduce query overhead, KSS (Keyword set Search)[10] partitions the index by a set of keywords. A KSS index is considerably larger than a standard inverted index, since there are more word sets than there are individual words. And insert overhead for KSS grows exponentially with the number of the keywords while query overhead is reduced because no intermediate lists are transferred across the network for the join operation. However, the insert overhead and storage overhead of KSS are obviously unacceptable for full-text search on a collection of documents.

Our work aims to design an efficient P2P keyword search system which has the same order of insert and storage overhead as standard distributed inverted index while has the same (or better) performance of keyword search as (or than) KSS. pKSS (P2P keyword search system), presented in this paper, adopts term ranking approach such as TFIDF and exploits the relationship information between query keywords to improve performance of P2P keyword search. In pKSS, instead of publishing keyword pairs as done in KSS, we only publish individual important keywords and associate each publishing keyword with a set of related keywords, and the insert and storage overhead can be greatly reduced when compared with KSS. When doing keyword search, related query keywords are grouped into sets, and search can be done in keyword set like KSS. Therefore the performance of keyword search can also be greatly improved when compared with standard distributed inverted index.

2 Background

pKSS is designed and implemented on top of Chord [6], of which we will first give a brief introduction. We will also briefly describe TFIDF(Term Frequency Inverse Document Frequency) and Bloom Filter techniques used in pKSS.

2.1 Chord

Chord organizes nodes into a circular distributed data structure. Any node in Chord has a unique identifier ranging from 0 to 2^{m-1}. These identifiers are arranged as a circle modulo 2^m, where each node maintains information about its successor and predecessor on the circle. Additionally, each node also maintains information about (at most) m other neighbors, called fingers, in a finger table. The ith finger node is the first node that succeeds the current node by at least 2^{i-1}, where $1 \le i \le m$. The finger table is used for efficient routing. An Example of Chord with m=3 is shown in Fig1.

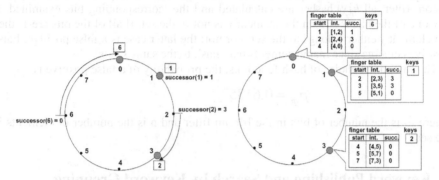

Fig. 1. The identity circle of Chord with three nodes whose identity is 0, 1, 3 separately

2.2 TFIDF

In classic information retrieval, documents are modeled as vectors in the dimensionality of the lexicon. Each entry in the term vector corresponds to the weight of the term in the document. A popular method for assigning term weights is called the TFIDF rule. The basic idea behind TFIDF is that by using some combination of term frequency (TF) in a document with the inverse of how often that term shows up in documents in the collection (IDF), we can balance: (a) the fact that terms frequently used in a document are likely important to describe its meaning, and (b) terms that appear in many documents in a collection are not useful for differentiating between these documents for a particular query.

Existing literature includes several ways of implementing the TFIDF rule [15]. In our work, we adopt the following system of equations as suggested by Witten et al. [16]:

$$IDF_t = \log(N / f_t) \tag{1}$$

$$w_{D,t} = (1 + \log(f_{D,t})) \times IDF_t \tag{2}$$

where N is the number of documents in the collection, f_t is the number of times that term t appears in the collection, and $f_{D,t}$ is the number of times term t appears in document D. In equation (1), IDF_t captures the "resolving power"[1] of term t, and $w_{D,t}$ in equation (2) describes the importance of term t in document D. It ensures that a term occurring very frequently in the document will not overpower a less frequent one with higher resolving power.

---

[1] The resolving power of a term is its usefulness in helping distinguish one document from another. It is also referred to as the term's discrimination value.

2.3 Bloom Filter

Bloom filters compactly represent set membership in an approach outlined by Reynolds and Vahdat [14]. A Bloom filter of a set $S = \{x_1, x_2, ..., x_n\}$ is implemented as a bit array of size m with all bits initially set to 0. Each element x_i is hashed by hash functions $h_1, h_2, ..., h_k$, each of which map into the range $\{0, ..., m-1\}$. Each bit corresponding to location $h_i(x_i)$ is set to 1. To test membership of an element y in a Bloom filter, all $h_i(y)$ hashes are calculated and the corresponding bits examined. If any one of the bits is 0, then the element y is not in the set. If all of the bits are 1, then the element y either belongs to the set S or not; the latter case is a false positive. False positives emerge since many elements may hash to the same k bits.

Given optimal choice of hash functions, the probability of a false positive is

$$p_{fp} = 0.6185^{m/n} \tag{3}$$

where m is the number of bits in the Bloom filter and n is the number of elements in the set.

3   Keyword Publishing and Search by Keyword Grouping

To support full text search functionality in structured P2P systems, the approach of distributing inverted indices among hosts by keyword is adopted in some recent proposals [14][19]. However, it has been demonstrated in [17] that inverted list intersection is not feasible to perform large scale keyword search because the bandwidth consumed by multiple-attribute queries exceed the internet's capacity.

In pKSS, we make two optimizations for keyword search in structured P2P network. Firstly, by adopting TFIDF technique, only important terms that best describe the document are selected as publishing keywords. This can reduce the costs for publishing inverted list of the documents at cost of ignoring some less important documents that may be queried by unimportant keywords which have low TFIDF weight. Secondly, by exploiting keyword relationship, the related keywords in query can be grouped together and thus the inverted list intersection cost for multiple-attribute queries can be greatly reduced.

3.1 Keyword Publishing

When a user shares a document, pKSS first builds the inverted list of the document with each term associated with a weight. The term weight is computed by TFIDF approach which is introduced in section 2.2. Then the most significant term list is selected as the publishing keywords. In pKSS, only the first L largest weighted terms are published, and if the number of terms in the inverted list is less than L, all the terms will be published. Therefore, if L is large enough, for example larger than the size of lexicon, all the keywords in inverted list will be published. In pKSS, we let $L=500$.

The index entry to publish in pKSS contains three parts: the keyword itself, the document ID, and a set of keywords that are in the document and related to the publishing keyword. The keyword set in the index entry can be expressed as follows:

$$KS_i = \{K_j \mid w_{i,j} \geq \theta, K_j \in D\} \qquad (4)$$

where K_i is the publishing keyword in index entry, D is the document, and K_j is the related keyword. To determine the keyword relationship, we take a query log which can be obtained from WWW or FTP search sites as input. According to the query log, we can obtain the keyword relationship matrix $M_{n \times n}$ where n is the size of lexicon. Element $w_{i,j}$ in M determine the relationship between keyword K_i and K_j. $w_{i,j}$ is computed as following:

$$w_{i,j} = \frac{freq(K_i \cap K_j)}{freq(K_i)} \qquad (5)$$

where $freq(X)$ represents the frequency that search term X occurs in users' query and $freq(X \cap Y)$ represents the frequency that search term X and Y both occur in users' query simultaneously. If $w_{i,j}$ is greater than *connectivity threshold* θ, we say that keyword K_i and K_j are related.

In pKSS, instead of storing related keyword set in the index entry, we use Bloom Filter to compress the keyword set and store the bloom filter in the index entry. $BF(KS_i)$ represents the bloom filter of the related keyword set KS_i. Thus the index entry of keyword K_i can be represented as follows:

$$IE_i = < K_i, DocID, BF(KS_i) > \qquad (6)$$

where IE_i is the index entry of keyword K_i, $DocID$ is the document ID.

To publish the index entry to the P2P network, pKSS first compute the hash of the keyword as key, then maps the key to the node in the network using Chord algorithm, and stores the index entry to that node at last. The algorithm of publishing keyword in pKSS works as shown in fig.2.

3.2 Keyword Search

Query in pKSS is consisted of a set of keywords. Thus, the query can be expressed as follows:

$$Q = \{k_1, k_2, ..., k_n\} \qquad (7)$$

where Q represents the query, $k_i(i=1,2,...n)$ is keyword in the query. To speed up the keyword search process, keywords in the query are grouped into sets of related keywords. Each group has a primary keyword which will be used to accomplish the keyword lookup process by Chord algorithm, while other keywords in the group set are the related keywords of the primary keyword that are used to filter the documents. The grouping method lies in two key points. The first is how to determine the primary keyword of the group set, and the second is how to select the related keywords of the primary keyword. In pKSS, the resolving power of the term is used to determine the primary keyword, and the keyword relationship matrix of the query log is used to select related keywords of the primary keyword. The grouping process can be divided by the following steps:

Input: the document D
Output: none
1   Build inverted list IL of document D with term in descended order of TFIDF weight
2   For each term K_i in IL where $1 \leq i \leq L$
3   create index entry $IE_i = <K_i, DocID, BF(KS_i)>$
4       $key = \text{hash}(K_i)$
5   Use Chord API insert to publish the index entry to the P2P network insert(key, $<K_i, DocID, BF(KS_i)>$)
6   End for

Fig. 2. The algorithm of publishing keyword in pKSS

Input: $Q = \{k_1, k_2, ..., k_n\}$
Output: *a list of documents that contain all the keywords in the query*

1.   While $Q \neq \varnothing$
2.   select the term k in Q with maximum IDF value
3. $Q = Q - \{k\}$
4. $G_k = \{k_i \mid (k, k_i) \in E \mid_\theta, k_i \in Q\}$
5. $Q = Q - G_k$
6.   Find node n storing index entries of keyword k
7.   Retrieve document list satisfying $G_k \subset KS_k$ by Bloom Filter
8.   End While
9.   intersect the result document list

Fig. 3. The algorithm of keyword search

Step1. In the query keyword set Q, select the term k that has maximum IDF value as the primary keyword, create a group set G_k, and remove this term from Q. The primary keyword k satisfies following equation.

$$IDF_k = \max(\{IDF_{k_1}, IDF_{k_2}, ... IDF_{k_n}\}) \qquad (8)$$

Step2. Find all the related keywords of primary keyword k, add them to the group set G_k, and remove these keywords from the query set Q. The related keywords can be selected by the following equation.

$$G_k = \{k_i \mid w_{m,i} \geq \theta, k_m = k, k_i \in Q\} \qquad (9)$$

Step3. If $Q \neq \Phi$, goto step1 to create another group set.

Unlike standard distributed inverted index approach, pKSS performs distributed search based on each group set, not the term only. This approach is somewhat like that of KSS, but differs in the keyword lookup and document filtering process. For each group set G_k, pKSS maps the primary keyword k onto the node in the network by Chord algorithm, then fetches all the document index entries and filters the satisfied documents according to the $BF(KS_k)$ field. The filtering condition is defined as following equation.

$$BF(G_k) \wedge BF(KS_k) = BF(G_k) \qquad (10)$$

where $BF(G_k)$ is the bloom filter of group set G_k. The filtering condition in equation (10) is in fact to test that every the keyword in set G_k appears in set KS_k. Finally, the intersection of documents fetched according to each group set is the final result that satisfy the query. Thus, compared to the standard inverted list intersection approach, the performance of keyword search in pKSS can be greatly improved by query keywords grouping. The algorithm of keyword search in pKSS is shown in fig.3.

4 Experiments

In this section, we evaluate pKSS by simulation. In order to analyze *pKSS* costs and efficiency for full-text search, we develop a web crawler that takes the web pages *www.edu.cn* and www.sohu.com as seeds and downloaded the text and HTML files recursively. Our crawler downloaded 42,238 HTML and text pages that occupied 492MB of disk space. In order to compare pKSS with existing KSS algorithms, we implemented KSS and standard inverted index. For the simulation we deployed 1800 nodes running on 12 personal computers in a 100M LAN, each of which has a 1.7 GHz processor with 512MB RAM running Linux AS 3.0.

In order to find the relationship between query keywords, we used the query logs of the FTP search website bingle.pku.edu.cn from Dec 1, 2002 to Dec 31, 2002.

We developed a scalable system iExtra, which is implemented purely in Java. In the preprocess phase, iExtra parses the HTML pages and removes the invalid characters. After parsing, Chinese paragraphs are extracted and segmented through Maximized-Matched Chinese word segmentation algorithm, and the resulted Chinese words were encoded with a unique ASCII string. We also selected a list of stopwords for filtering the English as well as Chinese stopwords.

We simulated inserting and querying of a document using pKSS. Next we ran the pKSS algorithm on each text file to create index entries and published them to corresponding virtual peers. We evaluated these algorithms by insert overhead and query overhead.

4.1 Insert Overhead

Insert Overhead is the number of bytes transmitted when a document is inserted in the system. When a user asks the pKSS system to share a file, the system generates index entries which are inserted in the distributed index. Unlike KSS, in which if we generate index entries for a document with n keywords for typical keyword-pair scheme the overhead required is bounded by $C(n,2)$, pKSS only generates small index entries which results in a small insert overhead.

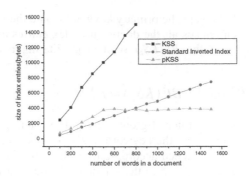

Fig. 4. Number of index entries generated vs. number of words in a document using the standard inverted indexing scheme, pKSS with θ=0.05, and KSS with window size of ten

Fig.4 gives the curves of size of index entries generated vs. number of words in a document using the standard inverted indexing scheme, pKSS with θ=0.05 and KSS with window size of ten. Fig.4 shows that the insert overhead for pKSS is much lower than that for KSS, is a little higher than that of the standard inverted index scheme when the document is small, and is lower than that of the standard inverted index scheme when the document is large.

4.2 Query Overhead

Query overhead is a measure of bytes transmitted when a user searches for a file in the system. As we know, the overhead to send the intermediate result list in the system from one host to another is the main part of the query overhead.

Fig.5 gives mean data transferred in KB when search using the standard inverted index with Bloom Filter, the standard inverted index without Bloom Filter, KSS with window size of 5, pKSS with θ=0.05, for a range of query words. Fig.5 shows that the query overhead for pKSS is much lower than that of the standard inverted index scheme, with or without bloom filter, and is a little lower than that for KSS when the number of keywords is greater than 3.

4.3 Connectivity Threshold

In section 3, we have mentioned that different connectivity threshold θ may impacts the relationship of query keywords. In this section, we evaluate the query overhead when connectivity threshold θ changes. Fig.6 shows the effect of connectivity threshold on query overhead. From Fig.6, we can see that the query overhead grows when connectivity threshold θ grows. This result is reasonable. With θ growing, the keywords pairs that were related before may not be related any more and inverted list intersection cost grows because more group sets of related keywords may be generated for a given query. From Fig.6, we can also see that when θ is lower than 0.05, the query overhead only drops a little. Therefore, in pKSS, we choose θ=0.05.

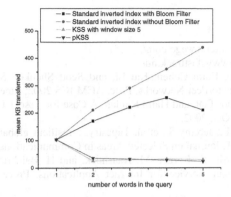

Fig. 5. Mean data transferred in KB when search using the standard inverted index with Bloom Filter, the standard inverted index without Bloom Filter, KSS with window size of 5, pKSS with θ=0.05, for a range of query words

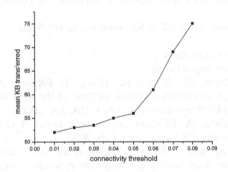

Fig. 6. Mean data transferred in KB when connectivity threshold θ changes

5 Conclusions

In this work, we adopt keyword ranking approach such as TFIDF and exploit the relationship between query keywords which can be extracted from users' queries logs, to improve the performance of P2P keyword search system. The main idea of this paper is as follows: At first, we find the relationship between query keywords from query logs obtained from WWW or FTP search sites such as bingle.pku.edu.cn, sheenk.com and so on. Next, by adopting TFIDF technique, the most significant *L* terms together with each related keywords are published to the network. When a user submit the query, the keywords in the query are grouped based on the keyword IDF value and their relationship, and thus the keyword search performance in pKSS can be greatly improved by approach of keyword grouping search. Experiments results clearly demonstrated that pKSS index is more efficient than KSS index in insert overhead and storage overhead, and more efficient than a standard inverted index in terms of communication costs for query.

References

1. Gnutella. http://gnutella.wego.com/.
2. FastTrack. http://www.fasttrack.nu/.
3. Qin Lv, Pei Cao, Edith Cohen, Kai Li, and Scott Shenker. Search and Replication in Unstructured Peer-to-Peer Networks. Proc. ACM ICS 2002, June 2002.
4. Edith Cohen, Amos Fiat, and Haim Kaplan. A Case for Associative Peer to Peer Overlays. Proc. HotNets-I, Oct. 2002.
5. Zhao B., Huang L., Jeremy S., et al. Tapestry: a resilient global scale overlay for service deployment. IEEE Journal on Selected Areas in Communications, 2004,22(1):41-53.
6. I. Stoica, R. Morris, D. Karger, M. Kaashoek, and H. Balakrishnan. Chord: A Scalable Peer-to-peer Lookup Service for Internet Applications. Proc. ACM SIGCOMM 2001, Aug. 2001.
7. S. Ratnasamy, P. Francis, M. Handley, R. Karp, and S. Shenker. A Scalable Content-Addressable Network. Proc. ACM SIGCOMM 2001, Aug. 2001.
8. A. Rowston and P. Druschel. Pastry: Scalable, distributed object location and routing for large-scale peer-to-peer systems. Proc. Middleware 2001, Nov. 2001.
9. Yang, B., Garcia-Molina, H., 2002. Improving Search in Peer-to-Peer Networks. In Proceedings of the 22nd International Conference on Distributed Computing Systems (ICDCS'02)
10. Omprakash, D. Gnawali, 2002. A Keyword-set Search System for Peer-to-Peer Networks. MIT's thesis Lib.
11. KaZaa. http://www.kazaa.com.
12. Napster. http://www.napster.com.
13. Clarke, I., Sandberg, O., Wiley, B., Hong, T. Freenet: A distributed anonymous information storage and retrieval system. In Proc. of the ICSI Workshop on Design Issues in Anonymity and Unobservability, Berkeley, CA, Jun. 2000.
14. Reynolds, P., Vahdat, A. Efficient peer-to-peer keyword searching. Technical Report 2002, Duke University, CS Department, Feb. 2002.
15. G. Salton, A.Wang, and C. Yang. A vector space model for information retrieval. In Journal of the American Society for Information Science, volume 18, pages 613"C620, 1975.
16. I. Witten, A. Moffat, and T. Bell. Managing Gigabytes: Compressing and Indexing Documents and Images. Morgan Kaufmann, San Francisco, second edition, 1999.
17. Jinyang Li, Boon Thau Loo, etc. On the Feasibility of Peer-to-Peer Web Indexing and Search. IPTPS 2003.
18. Nicholas J. A. Harvey, Michael B. Jones, Stefan Saroiu, Marvin Theimer and Alec Wolman. SkipNet: A Scalable Overlay Network with Practical Locality Properties. USITS'03, 2003.
19. Bobby Bhattacharjee, Sudarshan Chawathe, Vijay Gopalakrishnan, Pete Keleher and Bujor Silaghi. Efficient Peer-To-Peer Searches Using Result-Caching. IPTPS 2003.

Characterization of P2P File-Sharing System[*]

Hanyu Liu, Yu Peng, Mao Yang, and Yafei Dai

{lhy, py, ym, dyf}@net.pku.edu.cn

Abstract. Maze is a P2P file sharing system, which is developed, deployed and operated by our academic research team. With control over source code, we can leverage Maze as a large-scale measurement platform. By analyzing more than 600 million user shared files, as much as 100 million download session and users' online state for 4 months, this paper gives a complete study on file characteristics and user behavior in Maze system. Some valuable conclusions are derived from this measurement, which provide the first hand stuff to understand P2P system behavior.

1 Introduction

Maze[1] is a P2P file-sharing system that is developed and deployed by our academic research team. Maze is similar in structure to Napster, with a centralized, cluster-based search engine, but is additionally outfitted with a social network of peers. More details of the Maze architecture are available in [2][3].

Maze is currently deployed across a large number of hosts inside China's internal network and has become an excellent platform to observe many important activities inside the P2P network. In this paper we analyze 600 million shared files and 121-day log of user behavior which we collected at the central server of Maze. There are several lessons to be learned from our measurement results.

1. Few video files occupy a disproportionately high fraction of space and consume a disproportionately high fraction of bandwidth in the system. Furthermore, P2P software has become a platform for sharing all sorts of files, and it is not a system only for exchanging audio and video files.
2. A large percentage of shared files have never been downloaded by any user. It means these files are useless in the system. Furthermore, we find that a file's extension contains little information about whether it is useless. Whereas the replica number of a file is assumed to be a better candidate for predicting if a shared file is useless, more researches are needed to confirm this hypothesis.
3. Files' replica number and popularity do not follow Zipf distribution. In addition, we find mismatch in these statistics; the most popular file is not always the most replicated. We believe it is due to the large number of useless files in the system.

[*] Supported by National Grand Fundamental Reasearch 973 program of China under Grant No.2004CB318204, the National Natural Science foundation of China under Grant No.90412008

G. Chen et al. (Eds.): ISPA Workshops 2005, LNCS 3759, pp. 27 – 34, 2005.

4. Users in Maze share more files than users in other P2P file-sharing systems such as Napster and Gnutella. But it does not mean users are more willing to share. Contrarily, there exists a kind of free-rider who shares a lot of useless files.
5. In comparison with other P2P systems, users in Maze have two distinct characteristics: much better network bandwidth and much shorter online session.

The roadmap of the paper is as follows. Section 2 describes the data collection. Section 3 and Section 4 gives detailed analysis of files characteristics and user behavior in Maze. Section 5 contains related work and we conclude in Section 6.

2   Data Collection

In Maze, users are identified by immutable IDs, enabling us to track users by ID rather than by IP addressing, thus eliminating the problem of host aliasing due to wide use of DHCP and NAT. The Maze has a component to report their download behavior including the source or sink of the transfer, file type, file size, file signature (MD5) and the transfer bit rate. The central servers also log the following information per client: online time, IP address and network information (such as NAT or non-NAT). Also, the central servers log information about users' shared files. As long as its huge size, about totally 200GB, it is hard to log the update information for shared files. Therefore our analysis of files can not reflect the dynamic of users' sharing behavior.

Table 1 gives the summary of the logs. Unless otherwise stated, results are analyzed using logs from 2004/12/1 to 2005/3/31.

Table 1. Summary of log information (2004/12/1~2005/3/31)

Log duration	121 days
# of registered users	982,846
# of active users	498,903
# of transfer log	102,136,695
# of transfer unique files	12,991,876
Total transfer size	1,540.51 TB
# of shared files	616,964,867
Total shared file size	1,060.87 TB

3   File Characteristics

In this section, we will give a detailed analysis of the file that users share, upload and download in Maze. First, we analyze the features of files in the system, including their sizes, types, quantities, etc. Next, we will take a look at distributions of files' interesting attributes.

3.1   File Feature in Different Categories

There are totally 600 million shared files in the Maze System. According to their extensions, we classify these files into 9 categories which are shown in Figure 1.

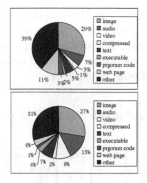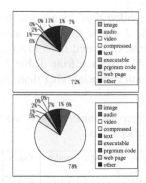

Fig. 1. Upper left: Number of files for different categories; Upper right: File sizes for different categories; Lower left: Number of downloaded files for different categories; Lower right: Download files size for different categories

The upper left of Figure 1 illustrates the breakdown of files with respect to their categories. As the graph shows, a high percentage of files, about 39% of total files, belong to other. There are 2 causes for this phenomenon. First, a part of preliminary users in the system shares many system files, such as *windows* directory. Second, we use file's extension as the criterion for classification, and therefore neglect some special-purpose file formats. On the upper right, Figure 1 shows the percentage of each category in size. Despite the fewer number of video files (3% of total files), they comprise as much as 72% of total file size. Obviously, few shared files take a large percentage of space in the system. During the experiment, there are almost 300 million of distinct files in the system, but only 1.7% of them have been downloaded at least once. In order to learn more about what types of files users care about in P2P system, we analyze the downloaded files. The lower 2 graphs of Figure 1 show the result. It can be seen that in today's P2P file sharing system the file types users tend to exchange are not only limited to music files which are the main type in Napster. People exchange a large variety of files of different categories. Also, few files consume a large percentage of bandwidth.

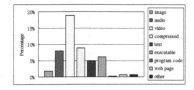

Fig. 2. The percentage of downloaded files for each category

Figure 2 depicts the percentage of downloading for each category. From the graph, we see that the percentage of downloading for shared video files is much higher than that of other categories. But the value is still small, only 18.9%. Therefore it is not appropriate to use file category to determine whether the file is useless. Furthermore, the shared files' average replica number is 2.1 and the average file size is 1.7MB while the downloaded files' average replica number is 31.8 and their average file size is 5.6MB. Table 2 shows that the downloaded files have larger replica number and file size than those of shared files. In some sense, the number of replica reflects if the file is useless. Also we see from Table 2 that the video files have an average replica number of 9 which is much higher than that of other categories.

Table 2. Average replica number (ARN) and the average file size (AFS) of each category, for shared and downloaded files

category / data		image	audio	video	zip file	text	exe.	program code	web page	other
Shared	ARN	1.81	4.389	8.92	3.86	2.1	7.00	1.80	1.91	2.05
	AFS	61K	1.9M	42.9M	10.2M	425K	2.4M	14K	10K	480K
Downloaded	ARN	23.87	31.33	39.05	22.40	16.29	65.13	86.33	28.17	58.22
	AFS	127K	2.3M	47.2M	14.5M	780K	3.5M	50K	36K	1.4M

3.2 File Distribution

The left of Figure 3 illustrates the shared files' replica distribution on a log-log scale. It is obviously that the distribution follows a heavy-tailed distribution. But the curve is not a straight line on the log-log scale, as the part with rank value less than 10000 is clearly deviated from the Zipf line. Therefore the distribution is not Zipf. On the right, Figure 3 shows the files' access popularity distribution on a log-log scale. Also this distribution follows heavy-tailed curve, but is not Zipf.

To our surprise, file's popularity does not match its replica number. We examine the top 100 downloaded files, and find that only 2 of them are in the first-100 files in term of replica number, 4 in first-1000, and 16 in first-10000. We think there are two reasons. First, many preliminary users share windows' *windows* directory and etc., however many files in these directories are the same for most users. This is also the main cause for the fact that the replica curve is noticeably flatter than the Zipf line Second, shared files' replica number is a static data in our experiment, which we need to improve in future analysis.

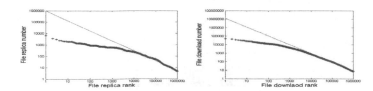

Fig. 3. Files' replica distribution (left) and Files' popularity (right) distribution on log-log scale

4 User Behavior

Another important issue in P2P system is the user. In this section we will analyze users' behavior in Maze system.

4.1 User Access Characteristics

The left of Figure 4 depicts that almost 35% of users share no file, while 12% of users shares more than 10GB files. In addition, the CDF curve of users' downloading is close to that of users' sharing, that is, 28% of the users have downloaded nothing, while 28% users have downloaded more than 3GB files. The CDF curve of users' uploading is much different from the former two. Up to 69% of users have never uploaded any file, and only 10% of users have uploaded more than 3GB files. On the right, Figure 4 illustrates that 97% of users upload and download less than 1000 files. Comparing the two graphs of Figure 4, we see that users in Maze system tend to transfer bigger files. But users' sharing behavior is different; 22% of users have more than 1000 shared files. It is distinct from that in Napster and Gnutella, in which only 7% of users share more than 1000 files[4][8].

To better understand users' behavior, we examine different types of special users. Figure 5 presents the CDF of file size and number of files, respectively, for users who only download but never share, users who only upload but never upload and users who share files but nobody download from them.

Sharing nothing means uploading nothing. 35% the users share nothing. Among them 48% download nothing. This means that 17% of users do nothing in the system. A majority of these users are preliminary users, they fear to share files in case that it may do harm to them; also they have short online time in the system.

During the experiment period, 28% of users have downloaded nothing, while 92% of them (26% of all users) have never uploaded any file. Excluding the 17% of users who share no files, 9% of users share files but download and upload nothing. After detailed case study, we find that there are 2 kinds of them. One is another kind of preliminary user, who randomly chooses a directory to share. That is why there are many shared *windows* directories in the system. In fact, they are a kind of free-riders.

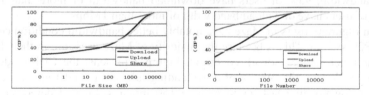

Fig. 4. CDF of size (left) and number (right) of files which users share, upload, and download

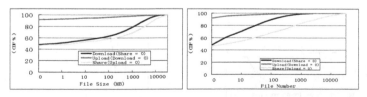

Fig. 5. CDF of file size and number of files for three kinds of users: those who share no files but only download, those who upload but never download, and those who share files which nobody has downloaded

The other one is collection users; they usually share their own collection of images, e-books, non-prevalent media files, etc. Although they are not active in the system, we think their existence is valuable to the system as a whole.

In addition, there are 2% of users in the system that only upload but never download. Their existence is the consequence of Maze's top user list which we publish daily in the forum. They are climbing the ladder and take part in the system only for the honor.

Table 3. Correlation between file size and file quantity

Variables	Correlation coefficient
Shared file size vs. Shared file quantity	0.27400
Downloaded file size vs. Downloaded file quantity	0.63746
Uploaded file size vs. Uploaded file quantity	0.58536

We have analyzed the users' file in term of size and quantity. Table 3 lists the correlation coefficient between files' quantity and their size, for which users share, upload and download, respectively. As the table shows, the correlation between size of files and file quantity of downloaded files and uploaded files is stronger than that of shared files. This reveals that there is a tendency that users transfer files of roughly the same size, while the shared files are dispersed in size. It is a distinct difference with other P2P systems in terms of shared file size.

4.2 User Bandwidth

Figure 6 shows that 94.4% of users have upload bandwidth of more than 100Kbps, and up to 66% of users have upload bandwidth of more than 1Mbps. The same as upload bandwidth, 93% of users have download bandwidth of more than 100Kbps and 69% of users have download bandwidth of more than 1Mbps.

Also in Figure 6, users in Maze have notably better bandwidth condition compared to other P2P system. This is because the majority of Maze users are in the CERNET, which has much better network condition. Figure 7 presents the CDF of download session time. We see that 95.8% of downloading last less than 10 minutes and only 0.044% of downloading last for more than 150 minutes. First, it demonstrates that users in Maze have better network condition. Second, some files are downloaded completely after several sessions because of the users' unstable online status.

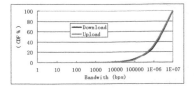
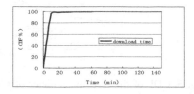

Fig. 6. CDFs of download and upload bandwidth   **Fig. 7.** CDF of download session time

4.3 User Online Time

The Maze software is divided into two parts: maze-client and maze-server, and each part can run independently. The online time of maze-client reflects the degree to which that a user searches and downloads in the system, while the online time of maze-server reflects the degree to which that a user provides service to other users. Besides, NAT plays a major role in influencing users' service.

Figure 8 presents the CDF of user's total online time, maze-client and maze-server's online time for NAT and non-NAT, respectively. It is noticeable that during the nearly 3000-hours experiment, as much as 94% of users have total online time less than 300 hours, reflecting that users' online time is much smaller than that in related works. In addition, 0.47% of users have a total online time of more than 1000 hours. This group is very small, but they tend to be the resource providers in the system.

As the figure shows, 90% of maze-clients' online time is less than 30 hours, which means maze-clients' online time is negligible. Therefore for a practical P2P system, it is essential to divide the program into two separate parts. Most popular P2P software, including Maze, has 2 separate parts, and makes it a little inconvenient to stop the server part. Although the maze-servers' online time is very close for NAT and non-NAT users, the non-NAT users are as twice as the NAT users in size.

Figure 9 depicts the number of online users as a function of time during March 25 and March 31. There exists a noticeable diurnal pattern for online users. The number of online user reaches the bottom on about 6AM, and reaches its peak on 11PM. It is interesting that the number of online users suffers a clear decrease between 1PM and 3PM every afternoon. That may be the case that students have the habit of noon break. There are 4 days in the graph which have sharp decrease. That is because during that time, the CERNET master node in Peking University had something wrong with its network equipment. The graph also shows that number of users recovered rapidly after the accident.

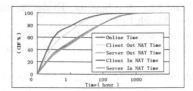

Fig. 8. CDF of user's online time

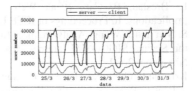

Fig. 9. Number of online users

5 Related Works

[4] and [8] demonstrated that only 7% of users share more than 1000 files. Breslau et al. [5] explored the impact of Zipf's law with respect to Web caching. In [7], they demonstrated that KaZaA traffic did not exhibit Zipf-like behavior.

Several measurement studies have characterized the basic properties of P2P file-sharing systems. Saroiu et al. [4] analyzed the behavior of peers inside the Gnutella and Napster file-sharing systems, showing that there is significant heterogeneity in peers' bandwidth, availability, and transfer rates. A study of AT&T's backbone traffic [6] confirmed these results.

[7] analyzed the patient behavior of users in KaZaA. In [4], they showed that 78% of the participating peers have downstream bottleneck bandwidths of at least 100Kbps.

6 Conclusion

Through the analysis of Maze's log data, we comprehend P2P system's development tendency that P2P system has become a platform for sharing all sorts of files. Also we analyze the user behavior in Maze and find that there is a kind of free-rider who share many useless files, which is much harmful to the system, especially for System that has a central index server such as Maze.

Acknowledgement

We are grateful to Wang Chong and Xiao Mingzhong for their suggestion and help.

Reference

1. http://maze.pku.edu.cn.
2. Mao Yang, Ben Y. Zhao, et al. Deployment of a large scale peer-to-peer social network, Proceedings of the 1st Workshop on Real, Large Distributed Systems.
3. Hua Chen, Mao Yang, et al. Maze: a Social Peer-to-peer Network. The International Conference on e-Commerce Technology for Dynamic e-Business (CEC-EAST'04). Beijing, China. September, 2004.
4. S. Saroiu, P. K. Gummadi, and S. D. Gribble. A measurement study of peer-to-peer file sharing systems. In Proceedings of Multimedia Computing and Networking (MMCN) 2002, January 2002.
5. L. Breslau, P. Cao, et al. Web caching and Zipf-like distributions: Evidence and implications. In Proceedings of IEEE INFOCOM 1999, March 1999.
6. S. Sen and J. Wang. Analyzing peer-to-peer traffic across large networks. In Proceedings of the Second SIGCOMM Internet Measurement Workshop (IMW 2002), Marseille, France, November 2002.
7. Krishna P. Gummadi, Richard J. Dunn and et al. "Measurement, Modeling, and Analysis of a Peer-to-Peer File-Sharing Workload". Proceedings of the 19th ACM Symposium on Operating Systems Principles (SOSP-19), Bolton Landing, NY.
8. P.Makosiej, G.Sakaryan, H.Unger, Measurement Study of Shared Content and User Request Structure in Peer-to-Peer Gnutella Network, http://wwwteo.informatik.uni-rostock.de.

Analysis of GHT in Mobile Ad Hoc Networks

Fang Liu and Ruonan Rao

Department of Computer Science and Engineering,
Shanghai JiaoTong University, Shanghai, China 200030

Abstract. Distributed Hash Table (DHT) is a technology widely used in today's network applications. With the rapid growth of mobile ad hoc network (MANET), a interface similar to DHT will be used in MANET. However the traditional approaches to construct DHT may not work in MANET due the routing problem in MANET. S. Ratnasamy etc. recently put forward the Geographic Hash Table (GHT) with the same interface as DHT in sensor networks. We wonder this approach can be used in MANET. In this paper, we provide some analyses and evaluations of GHT by means of simulation with *ns-2*. We present quantitative results with the cost of data dissemination and data query, the success rate, in various mobile scenarios and with different node density.

1   Introduction

A Mobile Ad hoc NETwork (MANET) [1] is a collection of wireless nodes communicating with each other in the absence of any infrastructure. With the rapid growth of wireless technology and the sharp decreasing of the prices of wireless devices, we believe that the applications of MANET will continue to grow. A characteristic of MANET similar to today's wired internet or intranet is the character of distributing. Distributed Hash Table (DHT) technologies, such as Chord [2], have been proved to be an effective way for building a variety of scalable and robust distributed applications in distributed systems. Inspired by the success of DHT , we believe a similar approach in MANET will bring similar benefits to the application developers and deployers for MANET [3] [4].

The traditional DHT technologies [1] concentrate on the efficient location of the node that stores a desired data item [2]. A significant difference between wired network and MANET is the cost of routing is much higher in MANET, and the routing problem is also a big problem faced by the researchers in this field [5] ([3] [4] gives tow ways to construct DHT in MANET above DSR). Therefore, the approaches taken in wired network, which associate data with node addresses, will not work effectively in MANET. Thanks to one of the characteristics of MANET, that the network topology is decided by the geographical position of the node, a natural way to construct DHT in MANET is using the geographical character of MANET. One may argue that knowing the locations of nodes is also a serious problem in MANET. But consider the availability of low price GPS devices for wireless devices, this problem is no longer a big one.

When we try to design a DHT working for MANET, GHT (Geographic Hash Table) designed to work in sensornets for data-centric strorage [6], comes

G. Chen et al. (Eds.): ISPA Workshops 2005, LNCS 3759, pp. 35–44, 2005.

to our horizon. GHT provides a similar interface of DHT. The main problem of applying GHT directly to MANET is that GHT is designed and evaluated in a more static, more dense environment—sensor networks [7]. To understand how to modify GHT to make it suitable for MANET, we must known which aspects or characteristics affect the performance of GHT, and how they make their effects. Thus, the major question this paper try to answer is whether or not GHT is suitable for MANET, an environment with higher mobility. We divide this question into several sub small questions listed bellow.

- What are the metrics to be used to evaluate the performance of GHT in MANET?
- Does the performance of GHT vary in different node mobility model? If the answer is Yes, then we should answer how node mobility affect GHT.
- Do other factors such as density of node, and the speed of nodes movement affect GHT and How?

In this paper, we try to answer these questions by simulation. In section 2 we review the literature and give the an introduction of GHT. Section 3 gives the methods and metrics we used to evaluate GHT, and in Section 4 we give the simulation results and a brief discussion of the way may improve the performance of GHT. Section 5 concludes this paper with a short discussion of future works.

2 Related Works and Background

2.1 Related Works

Although implement GHT in MANET using geographic information seems a new research issues, some similar works in scalable location services in MANET for geographical routing exits.

The Grid Location Servise (GLS) [8] is a scalable location service that performs the mapping of a node identifier to its location. GLS is designed to be combined with geographic forwarding to implement unicast. The implementation of GLS effectively provides a DHT interface; it routes a message with a nodeId Y to a node whose nodeId is closest to Y. [9] gives a geographic hashing based protocol (GHLS) to disseminate each nodes location to O(1) nodes. Similar works are also analyzed in [9], and a comparison is present. Nevertheless, more questions should be asked, such as these services can be directly used for various data hashing rather than only for location information.

2.2 GHT

The *Geographic Hash Table* (GHT), provides a similar interface as DHT:

- **Put(k; v)** stores v according to the key k, the name of the data.
- **Get(k)** retrieves the value stored associated with key k.

All data are assumed that can be mapped to a key, by using a hash function. GHT is based on GPSR [10] [11], a geographic routing protocol. There are 2 major aspects of GHT:

Data Dissemination and Storage. To disseminate data and store them in the network, GHT first map data to a geographic position according to the key of the data, and then, use GPSR to disseminate the data to the position. Note that the packet used to disseminate data does no target any node, but a geographic position, which means that no receiver ever sees the packet addressed to its own identifier. Thus, which nodes will consume this packet and how they consume it are two crucial problems in GHT. To answer these questions, two concepts are defined:

– Home node : The node geographically nearest the destination of the packet.
– Home perimeter : The entire perimeter that encloses the destination of the packet. Nodes on home perimeter will store the data.

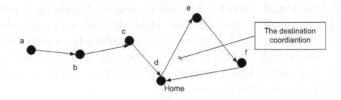

Fig. 1. GHT Example

Figure 1 gives an example. Node a call **put** to disseminate data to the network. GHT maps the data to a coordination in the network, which is marked in figure 1. Then, using GHT, the packet is forwarded to node d, where it enters the perimeter mode when no neighbor is more closer to the destination than node d, and then traverses the home perimeter that consists node d, node f, and node e. When the packet return to node d, node d knows that it is the closest one to the destination coordination, and becomes the home node and consumes this packet.

Data retrieval is also achieved by a similar approach: the request packet will target the same location, and will eventually arrive one of the nodes on the home perimeter. Then, this node will reply this request.

Data Refreshment and Release. To ensure the consistency of the data and handle the failure of nodes, three parameters are used:

– T_h: The interval between which the home node generates a refresh message to ensure that the nodes on the home perimeter have the data stored. This packet will be treat as a put packet.
– T_l: The interval between which the nodes storing data generate a refresh message to ensure a home node exists. This packet will be treat as a put packet.

– T_d: The live time of data. If data has not been refreshed in T_d seconds, the data will be released.

Obviously, $T_d > T_h$ and $T_l > T_h$. In [6] $T_d = 3T_h$ and $T_l = 2T_h$, we adopt the this equations in our evaluation.

2.3 Mobility Models

Towards a simulation that actually reflects the situations in the real word, the simulation model must be carefully selected [12]. As mentioned before, the goal of this paper is to answer whether GHT is suitable for a more mobile environment other than sensornets, and thus, the mobility model is the most important one that differs MANET from sensornets. We used RWP [12], an entity mobility model, and RPGM model, a group mobility model, to evaluate GHT:

- **Random WayPoint (RWP) model:** each node begins by staying in one location for a certain period of time then chooses a random destination in the simulation area and a speed that is uniformly distributed between [$minspeed, maxspeed$], and then travels toward the newly chosen destination at the selected speed. Upon arrival, the node pauses for a specified time period before starting the process again.
- **Reference Point Group Mobility (RPGM) model:** each group of nodes has a group leader that determines the groups motion. Within one group, each nodes velocity deviates slightly from that of the leader. The speed (V) and angle (Θ) are set as follows:
$$|\vec{V}_{node}(t)| = |\vec{V}_{leader}(t)| + random() \times SDR \times V_{max}$$
$$|\vec{\Theta}_{node}(t)| = |\vec{\Theta}_{leader}(t)| + random() \times ADR \times \Theta_{max}$$
(SDR is The Speed Deviation Rate and ADR is The Angle Deviation Rate)

3 Evaluation Method and Metrics

We ported the original GPSR package for ns-$2.1b6$ to current version ns-2.28 and extended the package to support our implementation of GHT. One feature of GHT that we do not realize in our current implementation is the structured replication [6], because we think that decide a suitable value of the depth of the hierarchy is another problem different from the one addressed by this paper, and the costs caused by structured replication may very high in mobile situations.

We analyze the performance of GHT under various node mobility conditions by changing node velocity, and mobility patterns using RWP and RPGM mobility models. We use the IMPORTANT [10] [11] framework to generate the mobile scenarios for evaluation. In mobile striations, we donate the first 50 seconds of total simulation time of 300 seconds to nodes movement, because the first a few seconds may be affected by the initial placement of nodes and lacks the generality.

Besides the mobility model, another important factor should be considered is the pattern of communication traffic, but traffic patterns may vary according to different applications. Thus, it is hard to define a general pattern when we only focus on the underlying GHT. We use a random traffic pattern. In a given time interval (20s), a node chooses to put data from a pre-defined data set, or perform a get or idle with equal probability. One more thing to say is that all data are loaded before the start of simulation, because the node may perform get in begin time.

The performance factors of GHT we mainly focus on are the cost of data dissemination, the cost of data maintain, and the success rate of query. Specially, the metrics we used to evaluate GHT are:

- The number of put message (No.of Put) and The number of get message (No. of Get). These two metrics reflect the traffic pattern.
- The number of refresh message generated in the a refresh interval (No. of Refreash). This metrics reflects the cost of data dissemination and consistence maintain.
- The success rate of data query (Success rate). This metrics is the most important one that reflects the overall performance of GHT in MANET.

4   Experimental Results and Analysis

In this section, we gives the experimental results based the methods defined in section 3, by varying the node density, changing the mobility model of nodes, and on different speed of node movement. We turn the parameters of ns-2 to model the Lucent Wavelan card at a 2 Mbps data rate, which means the effective transmission range is 250 meters, and the interfering range is about 550 meters. The values of parameters of GHT and GPSR we used in our experiments are given in Table 1.

Table 1. GHT and GPSR simulation parameters in *ns-2* simulation

GPSR Beacon Interval	1s
GPSR Beacon Expiration	4.5
Planarization	GG
Number of Nodes	100
Simulation Time	300s (The data used for statistic are obtained between[50, 290])
Refresh Interval	10s(static situations) 5s(mobile situations)
Number of items in data set	20 (The values of the data keys enables the data distributing uniformly)

4.1   Node Density on GHT

The first experiment is about the effect of node density on DHT. We vary the density of nodes to observe the performance of GHT based on the metrics defined in section 3. The nodes are placed uniformly in the whole simulation area. Table 2 gives the simulation results.

Table 2. GHT performance with different node densities

Density($m^2/node$)	Success rate (%)	No. of Put	No. of Get	No. of Refresh
5625	99.3%	390	371	0.6
10000	100%	367	391	0.8
22500	100%	398	394	1.4

As the results present in the original GHT paper [6], GHT works well in static networks. One observation we made is that the increase of refresh messages with the decrease of nodes density. In the situation of high node density, more contentions occur, and the rate of space reuse is down, and the latency of delivering a packet may increase. In GHT, this may cause the difference of time when nodes storing the same data begin to count T_l or T_h become larger, larger than the time interval needed for other node transferring a new refresh message and the possibility that a node expires its T_l are low. However, there is also another possibility, that it may let a refresh message take more time to arrival, and makes more refresh messages. Through the results, the first one seems win over the latter.

4.2   Mobility on GHT

In the following expirements, we evaluation the mobility effect on GHT. We fix the node density to 10000 $m^2/node$, 100 nodes in $1000m \times 1000m$ area.

RWP on GHT. The first experiment is about the speeds of RWP on GHT. We fix the *minspeed* to $0m/s$, and vary the *maxspee* among $0.5m/s, 1m/s, 5m/s$ (Choosing these values is because these values typical speeds for walking and jogging). The parse time is set to 60s. The results are shown in table 3. As

Table 3. GHT performance of RWP with different speed

Speed(m/s)	Success rate (%)	No. of Put	No. of Get	No. of Refresh
0.5	94.2%	391	372	0.9
1	92.1%	401	381	3.1
5	89.7%	395	371	11.2

we except, the performances of GHT in mobile situations are not very well. The success rate is decreasing with the speed increasing. The higher the speed of nodes is, the more frequently the topology changes, and the more often the fraction of the home perimeter. This is why the number of refresh messages raises. Concerning the success rate, the reason for its decreasing is due to tow factor. The first one is network partition. As mentioned in [12], nodes in RWP will gather to the center of the whole simulation area. We also get the same observation in our simulation. When most nodes gather to the center, the nodes in the edge may partitioned from the network. Another one is that the long home perimeter. When a message comes, either put, get, refresh, the message may expire its TTL. Thus, not all the nodes can get the new data or return the one they contains. In [6], the authors gives an augment on this problem.

RPGM on GHT. In this section, we deals the performance of GHT in RPGM. The node density is the same as we used in RWP. We fix the number of group to 1 (We believe that one group is the most frequently occurring situation). SDR and AGR are all set to 0.1. The movement of group leader is using one of the files shipped with IMPORTANT [13]. We vary the speeds as we do with RWP.

Table 4. GHT performance of RPGM with different number of GROUP

Speed(m/s)	Success rate (%)	No. of Put	No. of Get	No. of Refresh
0.5	97.2%	384	367	0.7
1	96.5%	391	398	1.6
5	93.7%	389	375	2.2

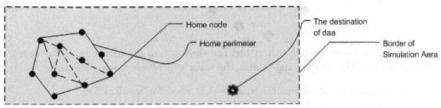

The home perimeter dose not encloses the destination. Before enter perimeter mode, and find the home node, GPSR may have to route through several routers (Indicating by dotted lines).

Fig. 2. An situation illustrating that perimeter may not enclose the destination in RPGM

The results are more promising than those in RWP, due to the correlation between nodes and higher link duration. However, another problem occurs. In RPGM, in a given time slice, the nodes may only cover a sect of the whole simulation area (If the nodes cover the whole area, then after some time, some nodes may cross the border of the simulation area), when the hash function maps the data uniformly to the whole area. As a result, there are situations, where the home perimeter is not the one encloses the coordination of data destination. One of such situations that we observed is shown in figure 2 In such situations, the long home perimeter problems may be encountered.

4.3   Discussion

To improve the performance of GHT, the most critical problem is the movement of nodes not the failure of nodes, unlike the cases in sensornets. Therefore, the method used by GHT to ensure the availability of data stored may not works well. The method, to generate refresh messages periodically, generates too many messages in our experiments, even no node failure occurs. To handle this problem, modify the parameters to make the refresh be generated when a node moves beyond some scope rather than expires some time may improve the performance of GHT. However, more evaluations should be done to check the results.

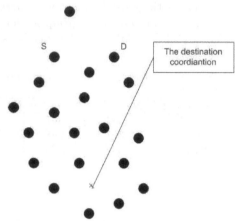

Node S and D are close to each other, but the destination coordination is far away. When using GHT to exchange data, the data will travel a long distance.

Fig. 3. An situation illustrating that need for localization

Another aspect to improve GHT in MANET is localization. In sensornets, GHT assumes an external data gatherer or a base station exits, and as a result, the cost for querying is approximately constant. However, in DHT for MANET, the data consumers are also in the same network boundary as the nodes that puts the data. When two nodes are close to each other, they also need to travel a long distance to exchange data. Such case may consume a lot of network bandwidths. Figure 3 gives an illustration to demonstrate the need of localization. Methods which can be used include hierarchy strategies or Iterative Bounded Flooding (IBF) [14] like methods. This aspect is the one worthy future evaluation.

5   Conclusion and Future Works

In this paper, we present a simulative study on the Geographic Hash Table in mobile ad hoc network. The results show that GHT works well in various node densities in static network. When concerned with mobile situations, the performances decrease when node speeds increase. With different mobility model, the one (RPGM) describing group mobility has a better performance than the one for entity mobility.

One of the problems this paper has not addressed is the data update and consistent. Unlike sensornets, where data are mainly gathered and delivered to base station, and the the data availability is more important than the consistent. This means, there are may obsoleted data in the networks. The success rate used in this paper and the original GHT paper [6] is based on this premise. But, in real applications that will run in MANET, obsoleted data should be removed, and therefore how accurately GHT can provides this capacity is worth for future evaluation.

The final goal of our research is to design a DHT like system in MANET. We believe geography based approach is advanced than other approaches based on network address, because it uses the distinguish feature of MANET, that the network topology is decided by its nodes' geographic positions. However, as we discussed, GHT works not well in mobile situations, thus how to improve the performance of GHT in MANET is the most significant one of our future works.

Acknowledgment

The authors would like to thank Mr. Zhang Xinyan for the helpful suggestions to our simulation, and others for the advices to our paper.

References

1. M. Frodigh et al. Wireless ad hoc networking: The art of networking without a network. *Ericsson Review*, 4, 2000.
2. I Stoica, R Morris, D Liben-Nowell, D R Karger, M F Kaashoek, F Dabek, and H Balakrishnan. Chord: A scalable peer-to-peer lookup protocol for internet applications. *IEEE/ACM Transactions on Networking*, 11(1):149–160, FEBRUARY 2002.
3. Himabindu Pucha, Saumitra M. Das, Y., and Charlie Hu. How to implement dhts in mobile ad hoc networks? In *the 10th MobiCom*, Philadelphia, PA, September 26-October 1 2004.
4. Himabindu Pucha, Saumitra M. Das, Y., and Charlie Hu. Ekta: An efficient dht substrate for distributed applications in mobile ad hoc networks. In *Sixth IEEE Workshop on Mobile Computing Systems and Applications (WMCSA 2004)*, 2004.
5. E.M. Royer and C.K. Toh. A review of current routing protocols for ad hoc mobile wireless networks. *IEEE Personal Communication*, pages 46–55, April 1999.
6. S. Ratnasamy, B. Karp, S. Shenker, D. Estrin, R. Govindan, L. Yin, , and F. Yu. Data-centric storage in sensornets with ght, a geographic hash table. *Mobile Networks and Applications (MONET)*, pages 427–442, 2003.
7. LF Akyildiz, Sankarasubramaniam Y Su WL, and Cayirci E. A survey on sensor networks. *IEEE Communications Magazine*, 40(8):102 114, 2000.
8. J. Liand J. Jannotti, D. DeCouto, D. Karger, and R. Morris. A scalable location service for geographic adhoc routing. In *Proceedings of Sixth Annual ACM/IEEE International Conference on Mobile Computing and Networking (MobiCom 2000)*, Boston, Massachusetts, August 2000.

9. Himabindu Pucha Saumitra M. Das and Y. Charlie Hu. Performance comparison of scalable location services for geographic ad hoc routing. In *24th Annual Joint Conference of the IEEE Computer and Communications Societies (INFOCOM 2005)*, 2005.

10. B. Karp and H.T. Kung. Greedy perimeter stateless routing for wireless networks. In *MobiCom 2000*, Boston, MA, August 200.

11. B. Karp. *Geographic Routing for Wireless Networks*. PhD thesis, Harvard University, 2000.

12. T. Camp, J. Boleng, and V. Davies. A survey of mobility models for ad hoc network research. *Wireless Communications & Mobile Computing(WCMC): Special issue on Mobile Ad Hoc Networking: Research, Trends and Applications*, 2(5):483–502, 2002.

13. F. Bai N. Sadagopan A. Helmy. The important framework for analyzing the impact of mobility on performance of routing for ad hoc networks. *Ad Hoc Networks Journal*, 1(4):383–403, November 2003.

14. F. Kuhn, R. Wattenhofer, , and A. Zollinger. Asymptotically optimal geometric mobile ad-hoc routing. In *Proc. of the 6th international workshop on Discrete algorithms and methods for mobile computing and communications (Dial-M)*, pages 24–33. ACM Press, 2002.

Attack Vulnerability of Peer-to-Peer Networks and Cost-Effective Immunization

Xinli Huang, Fanyuan Ma, and Yin Li

Department of Computer Science and Engineering,
Shanghai Jiao Tong University, 200030, Shanghai, P.R.China
{huang-xl, ma-fy, liyin}@cs.sjtu.edu.cn

Abstract. Currently, great efforts on network security are being made to concern software protection and prevention of loopholes, rather than the network topology. In this paper, we present a detailed and in-depth study on the response of peer-to-peer (P2P) networks subject to attacks, and investigate how to improve their attack survivability with a viewpoint of topological properties. We first, by extensive simulations, examine the attack vulnerability of P2P networks and find that these networks are extremely robust to random attacks whereas highly vulnerable under intentional targeted attacks. Based on these findings, we then develop a novel framework better characterizing the immunization of Gnutella-like P2P networks by taking into account the cost of curing infected peers. Finally, we propose a unique defense policy against intentional attacks and verify its performance merits via comprehensive experiments.

1 Introduction

Examples of complex networks are abundant in many disciplines of science and have recently received much attention. Many of such systems belong to a class of inhomogeneous networks, called *scale-free* networks [4, 5, 11, 12], for which the connectivity distribution $P(k)$ decays as a power-law following $P(k) \sim k^{-\lambda}$, free of a characteristic scale. So does the peer-to-peer networks, such as Gnutella [10]. This scale-free feature, which appears to be very efficient for a communications network, favors at the same time the spreading of computer viruses and attacks. The studies in [2, 6] reveal that scale-free networks display a surprisingly high degree of tolerance against random failures whereas at the expense of attack survivability. But the specialized BA-Network construction and the succeeding theoretic analysis in these papers do not characterize the Gnutella-like P2P networks well and can not be straightforward applied to them. The authors in [3], by extensive numeric simulations, study the response of complex networks subject to attacks on vertices and edges. But they tell neither how these attacks spread across the network, nor how to halt the spreading of these attacks. In [9], the authors propose a simple immunization algorithm for P2P networks. However, this algorithm itself does not take into account the cost of curing infected nodes and so is less cost-effective. In this paper, we aim at studying the impacts of topologies on the security and robustness of P2P networks. The main contributions of this paper are: first, we reveal the topological weaknesses of Gnutella-like

G. Chen et al. (Eds.): ISPA Workshops 2005, LNCS 3759, pp. 45–53, 2005.

P2P networks by identifying attack vulnerability via extensive simulations under realistic operating conditions; second, we work out a novel model that is better suitable for characterizing the immunization of Gnutella-like P2P networks by taking into account the cost of curing infected peers; and finally, we propose a unique cost-effective immunization policy to eradicate the viruses and intentional attacks.

The rest of this paper is organized as follows: In Section 2, we identify the vulnerability of P2P networks using various attack strategies over a Gnutella test-bed. And the new model special for cost-effective immunization of Gnutella's topologies is proposed in section 3. In section 4, we present the unique defense policy against intentional attacks, and we conclude the paper in the last section.

2   Identifying Attack Vulnerability of P2P Networks

Although it is generally thought that attacks on networks with distributed resource management are less successful, our results in this section indicate otherwise.

The *attack vulnerability* here denotes the decrease of network performance due to the removal of vertices or edges from a network [3]. In general, attack strategies can be boiled down to the following two kinds according to whether the attacked targets are deliberately selective or not: a) randomized (or uniform) attacks measuring the failure tolerance of a network, and b) intentional (or targeted) attacks measuring the attack tolerance of a network [2]. We start this section by introducing the attack strategies and the vulnerability metrics used in our simulations first and then give the experimental results and summaries.

2.1   Intentional Attack Strategies Used in Our Simulations

For the study of attack vulnerability of a network, the selection procedure of the order in which vertices are removed is an open choice. To better depict the impacts of topology changes before and after the intentional removal of vertices, we refine attacks into the following two ways and apply them in our simulations respectively.

- *ID Attack:* selects the vertices in the descending order of degrees in the initial network and then to remove vertices one by one starting from the vertex with the highest degree.
- *RD Attack:* uses the recalculated degree distribution at every removal step. As more vertices are removed, the network structure changes, leading to the different distributions of the degree than the initial ones. We design this attack strategy also as a measurement of the role of topological changes in attack tolerance.

It should be noted that both the ID attack and the RD attack are local attack strategies, which means that only local computing is needed during simulations.

2.2   Metrics of Attack Vulnerability

There are several ways of measuring the functionality of networks. To make a comprehensive description of failure and attack tolerance of Gnutella-like P2P networks, we use the following metrics to study the attack vulnerability according to [2]:

- *Diameter (d)*: defined as the average length of the shortest paths between any two nodes in the network. The diameter characterizes the ability of two nodes to communicate with each other: the smaller *d* is, the shorter is the expected path between them.
- *Fragmentation (S)* and *<s>*: Here, *S* is defined as the size of the largest cluster, shown as a fraction of the total system size; and *<s>* is defined as the average size of the isolated clusters (that is, all the clusters except the largest one). When nodes are removed from a network, clusters of nodes whose links to the system disappear may be cut off (fragmented) from the main cluster.

2.3 Simulation Results and Analysis

In the simulations, we consider a peer-to-peer network made of 20, 000 peers with a power-law exponent γ=2.4 (according to [10]), the smallest node degree *m*=3, which corresponds to an average-size Gnutella network [11]. We impose the aforementioned random removal strategy and the two intentional attack strategies respectively on the network, and compare the different response of the network subject to failures and attacks.

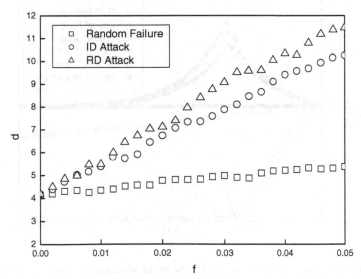

Fig. 1. Changes in the diameter *d* of the Gnutella network as a function of the fraction *f* of the removed nodes, using the attack strategies of random removal (□), ID attack (○), and RD attack (△) respectively

The simulation results are presented in Fig.1 and Fig.2, from which we observe a drastically different and surprising behavior for Gnutella network at different attacks:

When subject to random-removal attacks, the diameter (in Fig.1) almost remains unchanged under an increasing level of random failures. Thus even when as many as 5% of the nodes fail, the communication between the remaining nodes in the network is unaffected, which means that Gnutella networks display a surprisingly high degree of tolerance against random failures. It also explains why, despite frequent joining and leaving of nodes, the global functionality of P2P networks is almost unaffected. Similarly, such a conclusion can also be made from Fig.2, in which no threshold for fragmentation is observed; instead, the size of the largest cluster slowly decreases.

In contrast, as for the intentional attacks like *ID* removal and *RD* removal, when the most connected nodes are eliminated, the diameter of Gnutella in Fig.1 increases rapidly, more then twice of its original value if 5% of the nodes are removed, which is much different from the case of random failures. And such a difference is more obvious in Fig.2. We find that for Gnutella, as we increase f, S displays a threshold-like behavior such that for $f > f_c$ ($f_c^{ID} \approx 0.063$ with *ID* attack, $f_c^{RD} \approx 0.057$ with *RD* attack) we have $S=0$, which means that the network breaks into many isolated clusters and is almost completely fragmented. This behavior is also observed when we monitor the average size $<s>$ of the isolated clusters, finding that $<s>$ increasing rapidly until a peak value, after which it decrease to $<s>=1$. These behaviors show that the Gnutella network is extremely vulnerable to intentional attacks and breaks into many isolated fragments when the most connected nodes are targeted.

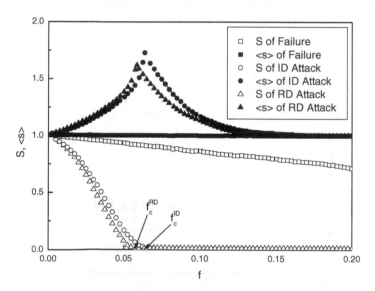

Fig. 2. Gnutella Network fragmentation under the attack strategies of random removal (□ for S, ■ for $<s>$), ID removal (○ for S, ● for $<s>$), and RD removal (△ for S, ▲ for $<s>$) respectively. The relative size of the largest cluster S and the average size of the isolated clusters $<s>$ as a function of the fraction of removed nodes f.

Besides, by comparing the simulations results between *ID* attack and *RD* attack, we find that the differences among the removal procedures are not significant in the early attack stage. However, as the removals proceed, the attack strategies harm the Gnutella network more in the order of *RD* > *ID*. As expected, strategies with recalculated degrees are more harmful. This is due to the large variation in the importance of the vertices, i.e., there exist very important vertices which play very important roles in the network functionality. In this sense, we identify the attack vulnerability of Gnutella-like P2P networks as the most connected nodes, especially the recalculated high-degree nodes during dynamic topology changes.

In summary, we find that Gnutella-like P2P networks display a surprisingly high degree of tolerance against random failures. However, such error tolerance comes at a high price in that these networks are extremely vulnerable to intentional attacks (that is, to the selection and removal of a few nodes that play a vital role in maintaining the network's connectivity). The topological weaknesses of these networks, rooted in the inhomogeneous connectivity distribution, seriously reduce their attack survivability.

The meaningful purpose for the attack vulnerability study in this paper is for the sake of protection: by identifying attack vulnerability of P2P networks, we can learn how to build attack-robust networks, or how to increase the robustness of networks.

3   Modeling Cost-Effective Immunization of P2P Networks

The analysis of computer viruses has been the subject of a continuous interest in the computer science community, mainly following approaches borrowed from biological epidemiology [1]. The standard model used in the study of computer virus spreading and cleanup is the *SIS* (Susceptible-Infective-Susceptible) epidemiological model. This model assumes that the nodes in a network can be in two states: susceptible (one node is healthy but could be infected by others) and infective (one node has the virus, and can spread it to others). Each susceptible node is infected with rate v if it is connected to one or more infected nodes. At the same time, an infected node is cured with rate δ, defining an effective spreading rate $\lambda = v/\delta$ for the virus model.

To address the effects of scale-free (SF) connectivity in epidemic spreading, Barabasi and Albert et al. study the SIS model in a BA scale-free network. They incorporate two key features of real-world networks (called *growth* and *referential attachment*) into topology generation and propose the *BA* model [1, 6], a currently widely used theoretical model for power-law networks. The construction of the BA graph starts from a small number m_0 of disconnected nodes; every time step a new vertex is added, with m links that are connected to an old node i with probability

$$\Pi(k_i) = \frac{k_i}{\sum_j k_j}. \tag{1}$$

where k_i is the connectivity of the i-th node. This algorithm implements the so-called "rich-get-richer" paradigm, which implies that highly connected nodes have always larger chances to become even more connected.

Based on further studies on the BA model, Satorras et al [1] find the absence of an epidemic threshold and its associated critical behavior, which implies that SF networks are prone to the spreading and the persistence of infections at whatever spreading rate the epidemic agents possess. In this sense, the key remedy is to introduce active and efficient immunization into these networks.

Computer viruses and attacks spread in environments characterized by scale-free connectivity. To stop epidemics on scale-free networks, possible solutions may be:

1. *Curing simultaneously all infected nodes:* This solution is obviously not realistic as for large-scale peer-to-peer networks, and another problem is that the number of available cures is often limited.
2. *Curing the hubs (all nodes with degree $k>k_0$):* It works: $(<k>/<k^2>) \neq 0$, but we can not effectively identify the hubs because this needs global knowledge. Here $<k>$ denotes the average degree of the nodes in a network.
3. *Probability of curing a node is proportional to k^α:* $\alpha=0$ for random immunization; $\alpha=\infty$ for treating all hubs with degree larger than k_0. The problem of this solution is that it is either inefficient ($\alpha=0$) or with too high curing cost ($\alpha=\infty$).

In this section, we extend the immunization model presented in [9] by taking into account the factor of cost-effectiveness, and then develop a new model that is more suitable for characterize the spreading and cleanup of viruses or intentional intrusions. We will also propose a novel cost-effective immunization policy for P2P networks in the next section based on this new model.

For convenience, we define α as the strength imposed upon the selecting probability of hubs, valuing between $[0, +\infty)$. As for the results in [9], $\alpha = +\infty$, corresponding to curing all hubs with degree larger than the pre-configured k_0. We denote the fraction of immunization nodes in the network as f_{cured}, according to the results in [9], we have the following equation:

$$\rho_{f_{cured}} = \frac{2e^{-1/m\lambda(1-f_{cured})}}{1-e^{-1/m\lambda(1-f_{cured})}}. \tag{2}$$

Here the prevalence ρ is defined as the average density of the infected nodes; λ defines the spreading rate of virus or attacks, and $m=<k>/2$.

We assume that the probability of curing a node is proportional to k^α, and thus make α be a factor of the epidemic threshold. Based on the results in [8], we obtain the epidemic threshold which depends on α as:

$$\lambda_c = \alpha m^{\alpha-1}. \tag{3}$$

Substituting (3) into Equation (2), we obtain:

$$\rho_{f_{cured}}^c = \frac{2e^{-1/\alpha m^\alpha(1-f_{cured})}}{1-e^{-1/\alpha m^\alpha(1-f_{cured})}}. \tag{4}$$

Equation (4) incorporates the factor of α into the immunization function, which helps us to develop efficient immunization policies with fewer cures required by populating the value of α.

4 Cost-Effective Immunization Policy for P2P Networks

The more successful is the policy in curing the hubs, the fewer cures are required. Based on such a principle, we then present a novel cost-effective immunization policy for P2P networks.

According to the analysis in Section 2, P2P networks are extremely vulnerable to deliberate attacks on the most connected nodes, so we prefer a small fraction of the most high-degree nodes as targets to inject immunization information in. And the immunization processes probe the network in a parallel fashion along links that pointing to a high-degree node with a probability proportional to k^{α}. It should be noted that, because this probability only depends on the variable k known locally as the degree of a node, our immunization policy does not need global knowledge and can be conducted in a completely decentralized manner, which also meets the intrinsic characteristics of peer-to-peer networks.

Furthermore, we also introduce a mechanism to isolate all hubs within two hops from an infected node when an intrusion or a virus is detected on it. Noteworthy, because the number of hubs that connect with a node within a very local range is usually very small in scale-free P2P networks [2, 10], the isolation mechanism in our immunization policy just increase the cost a bit, whereas result in a dramatic reduce of nodes required for curing. Due to the space limitation, we omitted the detailed design and implementation of the policy here and verify its merits via the simulations.

For comparing with the theoretical prediction, we formulate the highest degree k_{max} in the network as a function of the network size n. Given a specific degree distribution p_k, as stated in [12], we have $dp_k/dk \approx -np_k^2$. For Gnutella-like P2P networks, the probability distribution of degree is $p_k=ck^{-\gamma}$ (here c is a constant independent on k, γ is a power-law exponent valuing from 1.4 to 2.7 [10]). Substituting it into the above equation, we have $k_{max} = \sqrt[\gamma-1]{c \cdot n}$. For simplicity, suppose that the degrees of the nodes in the transferring sequence are all approximate to k_{max}, and then the number of steps needed to transfer the information in the network of size n is $s = \sqrt[1-\gamma]{n^{2-\gamma} \cdot c}$.

We perform extensive simulations to examine how our immunization policy works by making comparison with the aforementioned theoretical prediction and the results in [9]. In order to focus our experiments on examining the efficiency of various immunization policies during curing infected nodes, we make the assumption that the infections have been detected precisely beforehand. We focus on two main performance metrics: the number of steps needed to diffuse immunization information; and the critical point where the viruses or attacks are be eradicated. Fig. 3 shows that our immunization policy needs increasingly less steps to diffuse the immunization information with increasing of the network size, performing much better than the results in [9], as well as that of the borrowed theoretical prediction (denoted as Gnutella Max). Similarly, in Fig. 4, with increasing of f, ρ decays faster than that of [9], and the linear regression from the largest values of f yields the estimated thresholds $f_c^1=0.024$ using our policy, $f_c^2=0.03$ in [9] without any cost-effectiveness consideration, and $f_c^3=0.104$ obtained with the theoretical prediction. The value of f_c^1 indicates that, with our policy, the immunization of just a very small fraction (2.4%) will eradicate the spreading of viruses or attacks. Although this critical value is only a little better than that of [9], the number of steps needed is much smaller (shown in Fig. 3). In this sense, we can conclude that our immunization policy is more cost-effective.

Noteworthy, the results of the theoretical prediction are beyond our expectation. We conjecture that such a simple and arbitrary prediction model borrowed from other scale-free networks does not characterize the Gnutella-like P2P networks well. So, further studies are needed.

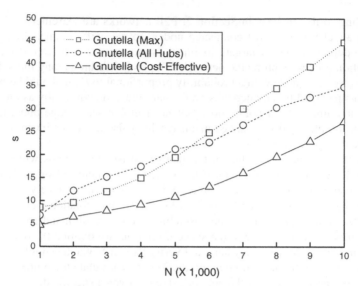

Fig. 3. The number of steps needed to diffuse immunization information through high-degree nodes as a function of the network size N, using immunization policies of theoretical prediction (□) denoted as Gnutella (Max), curing all hubs in [9] (○) and our cost-effective immunization policy (△) respectively. The simulation is performed with a power-law exponent γ=2.4, the number of the network size ranges from N=1,000 to N=10,000 with an increment of 1,000.

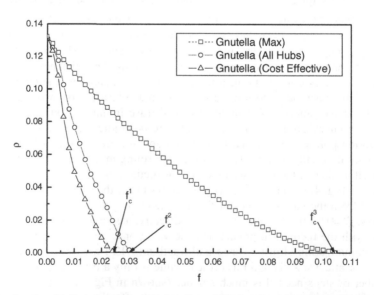

Fig. 4. The density of infected nodes ρ as a function of the fraction of immunized nodes f, using immunization policies of the theoretical prediction (□), curing all hubs in [9] (○) and our cost-efficient immunization policy (△) respectively. Here we take γ=2.4 and N = 4,096.

5 Conclusions and Future Work

Contrary to the traditional studies on network security, we take a viewpoint of the network topology, and investigate what its weaknesses are and how to remedy them. The main contributions of this paper are: first, we identify the attack vulnerability of Gnutella-like peer-to-peer networks by extensive simulations; second, by taking into account the cost of curing infected nodes, we propose a new cost-effective immunization model; and finally, we introduce an efficient but more economical immunization policy and justify its performance advantages by comparing with other studies through comprehensive experiments. Our further work will focus on identifying topological vulnerabilities using edge-removal-based intentional attack strategies, and try to find out those edges that play key roles in the attack-tolerance of P2P networks.

References

1. R. Paster-Satorras and A. Vespignani, Epidemics spreading in scale-free networks, Phys. Rev. Lett. 86(2001), 3200-3203.
2. R. Albert, H. Jeong, A.-L. Barabási, Error and attack tolerance of complex networks, Nature, 406(2000), 378-382.
3. P. Holme, B.J. Kim, C.N. Yoon and S.K. Han, Attack vulnerability of complex networks, Phys. Rev. E, 65(2002), 056109.
4. M. Faloutsos, P. Faloutsos, and C. Faloutsos, On power-law relationships of the Internet topology, Comput. Commun. Rev. 29(1999), 251.
5. L. A. Adamic and B. A. Huberman, Power-law distribution of the world wide web, Science 287(2000), 2115.
6. A.-L. Barabási and R. Albert, Emergence of scaling in random networks, Science, 286(1999), 509-512.
7. R. Albert, H. Jeong, and A.-L. Barabási, The Diameter of World Wide Web, Nature 401(1999), 130-131.
8. Z. Dezsö and A.-L. Barabási, Halting viruses in scale-free networks, Phys. Rev. E 65(2002), 055103(R).
9. Chen, H,. Jin, H., Sun J. H., and Han, Z.F., "Efficient immunization algorithm for peer-to-peer networks," Computational Science - Iccs 2004, Pt 1, Proceedings, vol.3036 pp623-626, 2004.
10. 10.Mihajlo A. Jovanovic, Fred S. Annexstein and Kenneth A. Berman, Modeling peer-to-peer network topologies through small-world models and power laws. IX Telecommunications Forum 2001.
11. 11.S. Saroiu, K.P. Gummadi, and S.D. Gribble, "A measurement study of peer-to-peer file sharing systems," in Multimedia Computing and Networking (MMCN), Jan. 2002.
12. 12.M. E. J. Newman, "The structure and function of complex networks", SIAM Review, Vol.45, pp.167-256, 2003.

A P2P Market Place Based on Aggregate Signatures

Dario Catalano[1], Giancarlo Ruffo[2], and Rossano Schifanella[2]

[1] École Normale Supérieure, Paris, France
[2] Dip. di Informatica - Università di Torino, Italy

Abstract. A peer-to-peer market place is likely to be based on some underlying micro-payment scheme where each user can act both as a customer and as a merchant. Such systems, even when designed for largely distributed domains, may be implemented according to hybrid topologies where trusted third intermediaries (e.g. the broker) are single points of failures. For this reason it is crucial that such central entities scale well w.r.t. the overall number of transactions. In this paper, we focus on PPay as a case study, to show how the broker would greatly benefit in terms of computational cost if aggregate signatures are adopted instead of RSA signatures.

1 Introduction

Incentives and micro-payments can be used to stimulate the users [1] and to avoid the free-riding phenomenon [2], and they are largely used in practice, e.g., BitTorrent [3], EMule [4] and Mojo-Nation[1]. In particular, a micro-payment scheme is an interesting alternative to a differential service incentives, especially when a market place is layered on top of a p2p system. Current peer-to-peer micro-payment schemes use an hybrid topology, because some central units (e.g., the broker, the certification authority) are needed. For example, PPay [5] is based on the idea of "transferable coins". Basically a tranferable coin allows a user to either cash it, by interacting with the broker, or to re-assign it to other peers. The second alternative has been introduced for fault tolerance reasons, because when millions of transactions occur during a short time period, the broker is likely to be responsible of many concurrent, computationally expensive, operations (such as digital signature verifications and generations). Moreover, the broker should be able to detect frauds (e.g. duplicate coins) and then it has to store all the information related to forged coins for future checkouts. For this reason coins should be kept on floating for a while, before the broker is asked to cash them. At the same time, digital coins should not (excessively) grow in size after each re-assignment.

The choice of a coin re-assignment strategy that is scalable in terms of the overall number of transactions is thus of crucial importance: as the broker is a single point of failure, the best (in terms of both space and time) assigment strategy should be used in a practical market place. For example, *FairPeers* [6], a p2p application that allows profit and file sharing, uses PPay coins extensively, and the entire system would break down if the broker is overwhelmed by an inefficient strategy.

---

[1] At the time of this writings the beta version of Mojo-Nation platform has been shut down by its creator Jim McCoy. He announced that another project will get the heritage.

G. Chen et al. (Eds.): ISPA Workshops 2005, LNCS 3759, pp. 54–63, 2005.

In this paper, we compare different coins management policies, introducing also a novel approach based on the idea of aggregate signatures [7]. PPay and aggregate signatures are briefly introduced respectively in Section 2 and 3. In Section 4 we outline the comparative model, and the results of our analysis are given in Section 5.

2   An Overview of PPay

PPay, proposed by Yang and Garcia-Molina [5], tries to minimize the interaction with the broker allowing direct transactions between peers. To this end, they suggested the idea of *floating and self-managed currency*. The coins can float from one peer to another, and the owner of a given coin manages the currency itself, except when it is created or cashed. In particular, the user manages all the security features of his/her coin(s). As other micro-payments systems, in PPay coin frauds are possible, but they are unprofitable. More precisely, frauds are detectable and malicious users can be punished as well. Moreover, each fraud concerns only small amounts of currency thus making the benefits not worth the risks. In what follows we provide a short overview of PPay, the interested reader is deferred to [5] for further details.

Table 1. Coins, assignments and re-assignments in PPay

$\gamma = \{X, sn\}_{SK_B}$	(raw coin)
$\lambda_X = \{X, lim_l, lim_u\}_{SK_B}$	(limit certificate)
$\gamma' = \{X, sn\}_{SK_X}$	(user signed raw coin)
$\alpha_{XY} = \{Y, seq_1, \gamma\}_{SK_X}$	(assigned coin)
$\varrho_{XYZ} = \{Z, \alpha_{XY}\}_{SK_Y}$	(re-assignment request)
$\alpha'_{XZ} = \{Z, seq_2, \gamma\}_{SK_X}$	(re-assigned coin)
$\alpha^B_{XZ} = \{Z, seq_2, \gamma\}_{SK_B}$	(broker's reassigned coin)
$\pi_{XYZ} = \{Z, Y, seq_3, \alpha_{XY}\}_{SK_Y}$	(layered coin)

Let X, Y and Z be three users of a p2p system, and let B be the broker. When setting up her own account, a user, say X, purchases digital coins from B. An user can buy a set of **raw coins** γ, signed by B, or a **limit certificate** λ_X that allows her to print her own raw coins γ'. Each raw coin has a serial number sn to detect double spending frauds. The serial number in a coin printed by a user, must belong to the interval defined in the corresponding limit certificate (i.e., $lim_l \leq sn \leq lim_u$).

When X wants to purchase an item or a service from Y, he will send to Y an **assigned coin** α_{XY}, that contains a sequence number of seq_1. The re-assignment of this coin will have a greater sequence number. Now Y is the owner of the coin, and he can decide to cash it or to re-assign it to another user (e.g., Z). In the latter case Y has to send a *reassignment request* ϱ_{XYZ} to X. After receiving ϱ_{XYZ}, X processes it and sends to Y and Z the new assignment α'_{XZ}, containing a sequence number $seq_2 > seq_1$. Of course, after α_{XZ} has been released, α_{XY} is no longer valid.

If X is down when Y wishes to reassign his own coin (or she simply denies to serve Y's request), the **downtime protocol** is used instead: the broker plays the role of the trusted intermediary, and she generates the newly assigned coin α_{XZ}^B in place of X. B sends the reassigned coin to X when this peer comes back on line. This is because X should be responsible for detecting frauds committed when it was off-line. Downtime protocol introduces a drawback due to high percentage of off-line periods in a lifetime of a peer: Broker's load significantly grows up to reassignment requests. Moreover, Broker must continuously check when peers came back on-line, because they must send back the newly assigned coin.

Another reassignment strategy is given by **layered coins**. In this case, Y can re-assign γ itself by sending to Z the assigned coin α_{XY} enveloped in a layer π_{XYZ}. If Z wishes to reassign the coin again, he has to add another layer to π_{XYZ}. Each layer represents a reassignment request and the broker and X can peel off all the layers to obtain all the necessary proofs. Although this protocol is still considered secure, it has the (relatively) negative drawbacks that fraud detection is delayed, and that floating coins grow in size.

3   Fraud Detection Using Aggregate Signatures

Basic re-assignments and layers have both some drawbacks: the former involves mainly the owner of the raw coin, but overloads the broker if she is off-line. The latter lets the coin grow in size, by adding a different signature to each re-assignment; moreover, when a layered coin is finally cashed, the broker has to verify many different signatures. As a consequence, even if this strategy results in better performances w.r.t the basic re-assignment strategy (see [8]), it remains of primary importance to investigate for solution that allows better performances in practice. Ideally, the best re-assignment strategy would be based on a layering scheme where: (a) the coin grows in size as little as possible after each transfer, and (b) the cost of signature verifications does not compromise the broker's efficiency, independently from the number of coins that reach the broker. In this paper we show how to meet both these requirements by using the recently introduced notion of aggregate signatures [7].

3.1   Aggregate Signatures

Aggregate signatures were introduced by Boneh *et al.* [7] to reduce the size of aggregate chains (by aggregating all signatures in the chain) and for reducing message size in secure routing protocols such as SBGP. An implementation of aggregate signatures using bilinear maps was given in [7] and uses the Boneh, Lynn and Shacham signature scheme [9] as underlying building block. Very informally a bilinear map is a function $e : G_1 \times G_2 \rightarrow G_T$ (where G_1, G_2 and G_T are groups) which is linear with respect to both G_1 and G_2. This means that for all integers a, b one has that $e(x^a, y) = e(x, y)^a$ and $e(x, y^b) = e(x, y)^b$. Of course, in order for a bilinear map to be useful in cryptography, some additional properties are required. For the purposes of this it is sufficient to say that "useful" bilinear maps can be constructed from the Weil pairing and the Tate pairing over groups of points of certain elliptic curves. For more details the interested reader is referred to [10].

The rest of this paragraph is devoted to briefly describe the aggregate signature scheme from [7]. For completeness, we give here a more formal definition of the bilinear maps used in cryptography.

BILINEAR MAPS. Let G_1 and G_2 be two cyclic (multiplicative) groups of prime order p. We denote with g_1 a generator of G_1 and with g_2 a generator of G_2. Moreover let ψ be a computable isomorphism from G_1 to G_2, such that $\psi(g_1) = g_2$. Now, let G_T be an additional group such that $|G_T| = |G_1| = |G_2|$. A bilinear map is a map $e : G_1 \times G_2 \to G_T$ with the following properties

1. Bilinear: for all $x \in G_1, y \in G_2$ and $a, b \in \mathbb{Z}$, $e(x^a, y^b) = e(x, y)^{ab}$.
2. Non-degenerate: $e(g_1, g_2) \neq 1$.

Notice that these properties imply that (1) for all $x \in G_1, y_1, y_2 \in G_2, e(x, y_1 y_2) = e(x, y_1)e(x, y_2)$ and (2) for any $x, y \in G_1$ $e(x, \psi(y)) = e(y, \psi(x))$.

THE SCHEME. An aggregate signature scheme allows to sign (distinct) messages $M_i \in \{0, 1\}^*$. A signature σ_i is an element in G_2. The groups G_1, G_2, their generators g_1, g_2, the computable isomorphism ψ from G_1 to G_2 and the bilinear map $e : G_1 \times G_2 \to G_T$ (where G_T is the target group), are all system parameters.

The key generation algorithm goes as follows. For each user it picks a random value $x \in \mathbb{Z}_p$, where p is an n-bit prime, and sets $v = g_1^x$ as the user public key. The user secret key is x. A user, holding secret key x, signs a message $M \in \{0, 1\}^*$ as follows. He computes $h = H(M)$ (where H is an hash function modeled as a random oracle mapping elements in $\{0, 1\}^*$ into elements in G_2). The signature is $\sigma = h^x$.

To verify the correctness of a signature σ on a message M, one computes $h = H(M)$ and checks whether $e(g_1, h) = e(v, h)$ holds.

To aggregate ℓ different signatures σ_i (on corresponding *different* messages M_i) one simply computes $\sigma = \prod_{i=1}^{\ell} \sigma_i$. The aggregate signature is $\sigma \in G_2$.

Finally to verify an aggregate signature σ, for the given (different) messages $M_1, \ldots, M_\ell$ and public keys $v_1, \ldots, v_\ell$ one proceeds as follows. First ensure that all the messages are different and reject otherwise. Next, compute $h_i = H(M_i)$ and accept if $e(g_1, \sigma) = \prod_{i=1}^{\ell} e(v_i, h_i)$ holds.

EFFICIENCY ANALYSIS. First notice that a signature is a single point in G_2. As pointed out in [7], on certain elliptic curves these signatures are very short: roughly the half the size of DSA signatures with comparable security. In particular one may set $n = 160$ as security parameter.

To sign one message costs one exponentiation in G_2, which costs $O(n^3)$ bit operations. Thus, signing is roughly 250 times faster than RSA-PSS.

Verification, on the other hand costs two pairing computations. Each pairing computation costs, roughly, 20 modular exponentiations. Thus the cost of verifying a signature is basically $40n^3$. Thus verifying a single signature is, roughly, 150 more expensive than RSA-PSS, with short public exponent.

Aggregation allows to verify ℓ signatures doing $\ell + 1$ pairing computations only. Still, verifying ℓ signatures remains 75 more expensive than RSA-PSS (again, with short public exponent).

4   Modeling Transferable Coins

The goal of modeling PPay is to numerically characterize the life-time of the coins, recalling that they can be printed, transferred and cashed. The computational cost is measured in terms of atomic operations, where an atomic operation is set, by construction, to a RSA digital signature verification.

We describes a framework where a set of peers interact reciprocally sharing items and (re-)assigning coins minted by the broker. We characterize the behavior of the peers in a time interval Δt. We do not make any assumptions about the duration of this time interval. Therefore, in order to simplify our analysis and without altering the results, we can reasonably suppose that all the coins printed during Δt are finally cashed.

Each coin γ is associated to a *re-assignment chain* rc_s^γ during its life-time. Such a chain is made of a sequence of peers, i.e., $rc_s^\gamma = \{p_0^\gamma, p_1^\gamma, \ldots p_s^\gamma\}$, where p_0^γ is the owner of γ, and $\forall i : 0 \leq i < s$, p_i transfers γ to p_{i+1}. Of course, p_s will give the coin back to the broker, to be properly cashed.

We define the *re-assignment limit* m as the maximum length of the re-assignment chain. Hence, $\forall rc_s : s \leq m$. Intuitively, higher m is, more the broker load is decreased, but the detection of double spending frauds is delayed. In the real world is reasonable to set such a boundary.

Let us define $a_0, a_1, \ldots, a_m$ where a_i represents the number of coins reassigned i times and that have been cashed by the broker during the time interval Δt. For example, let us suppose that during Δt, 10 coins are printed. Four of them are never reassigned [2] three are reassigned twice, and other three are reassigned once. If the limit m is set to 3, then we have that $a_0 = 4, a_1 = 3, a_2 = 3$, and $a_3 = 0$. Hence, we observe that C is equal to $\sum_{i=0}^{m} a_i$.

Therefore, we can derive the overall *number of transactions* performed in the market place, namely T, as the sum $\sum_{i=0}^{m}(i + 1)a_i$, observing that a coin reassigned i times corresponds to a re-assignment chain of length $i + 1$.

In such a scenario, a meaningful role is played by the distribution of the a_i coefficients. In fact, for a given number of transactions T that take place during Δt, the a_i distribution affects (1) the number of coins printed by the broker, (2) the amount of re-assignments, and, thus, (3) the load of the broker.

Unfortunately, we do not have any idea how users will behave in such a market place, because no one has experimented such technologies in the real world. This has the consequence that neither the analysis parameters can be set in an unique way, nor any empirical measure based on monitored peer-to-peer traffic can be used. Measures performed in the present p2p networks cannot be used in our study, because past analysis (e.g. [2] [11]) were conducted in domains where users download files for free without gaining any profit. Moreover, a fair micro-payment system, should seriously incentive users to reduce the free-riding phenomenon, e.g., as in *FairPeers* [6]. For such reason, we decided to evaluate the entire system making several hypotheses, and comparing reassignment strategies under these different settings.

We focus on two different distributions: *Pareto* and *FullChain*. When *Pareto* is used, the hypothesis is that an high number of coins will be cashed after few reas-

---

[2] i.e., These four coins corresponds to a re-assignment chain of length $s = 1$.

Table 2. Cost of atomic actions and modeling parameters

Name	Value	Description
$|check|$	1	Verification of one RSA digital signature
$|gen|$	$20 \cdot |check|$	Generation of one RSA signature
$\overline{check_1}$	$115 \cdot |check|$	Verification of one single aggr. sign.
$\overline{check_\ell}$	$57, 5 \cdot |check|$	Verification of ℓ aggr. signatures
$\overline{gen}$	$5.55 \cdot |check|$	Generation of one aggr. sign.
$aggr(\ell)$	$(\ell - 1)/6.4^2$	Aggregation of ℓ signatures ($\ell > 1$)
t	0.8	Off-line peer's rate
f	0.0, 0.05	Frauds rates
lim	10	numbers of coins in a limit certificate

signments, that is likely in the real world. The other distribution, namely $FullChain$, models an optimistic scenario, where each coin is *always* reassigned until it achieves the limit m, i.e., $a_0 = a_1 = a_{m-1} = 0$ and $a_m = C$. Other distributions can be used as well as in [8], but the significance of the results would not change and we did not include other diagrams for the sake of brevity.

Table 2 shows the set of system parameters and the cost of the operations considered in our analysis. The cost of each operation is normalized on the cost of an RSA signature verification ($|check|$). These values are based on the comparison times estimated in [12]. We can observe that the aggregate digital signature scheme looks much more expensive than RSA, except for generation ($\overline{gen} < |gen|$).

Moreover, broker's performances are sensibly affected when peers involved in transactions are off-line, and when frauds are detected. Let t be the off-line rate of a peer[3], f the fraud rate. Finally, let lim be the number of coins that a peer's user can print by herself when she owns a limit certificate.

5   Broker's Load Analysis

The broker is engaged when any coin is subjected to the following actions: **printing**, **reassignment**, and **cashing**. These actions affect the broker's performance dependently of the used coin management strategy. As a consequence, we use three functions, ω_P, ω_R, and ω_{Ca}, that respectively define the weights due to printing, reassigning or cashing a coin.

We define the broker's load L_B in terms of these three actions:

$$L_B = C * \omega_P + (T - C) * \omega_R + C * \omega_{Ca} \qquad (1)$$

If C and T are, respectively, the number of coins printed and the number of transactions occurred during the given time interval Δt, then $(T - C)$ is the number of reassignments performed during the time interval.

Definitions of ω functions change accordingly to three different coin management aspects: (1) the minting strategy, (2) the reassignment strategy, (3) the adopted digital signature scheme. As introduced in Section 2, there are two different coin *minting*

---

[3] As in [11], we suppose that a peer is off-line with a 0.8 probability.

strategies: the broker can mint a raw coin for a given peer X or can produce a limit certificate for X. We will refer to these approaches respectively with keywords **Raw** and **Limit**.

We classify *reassignment strategies* with labels **Basic** and **Layer**. In the Basic strategy, each reassignment involves the owner of the coin according to the scheme based on messages ρ and α' (Table 1). If the owner is down, the broker receives the reassignment request from the buyer and sends the reassigned coin α^B to the engaged peers. He has also the charge to contact the owner when he comes back on-line. If Layers are used instead, the coin floats from node to node until the limit m on the number of layers is reached or until a peer decides to cash it. After each hop, the coin grows in size and in number of attached signatures[4].

Finally, our evaluation considers two different *digital signature schemes*: **RSA** and **AS** (Aggregate Signature).

5.1 Computational Analysis

In the following, we compare the cost of all the strategies, identifying each combination with the triplet $[M, R, S]$, where M, R and S represents, respectively, the minting strategy, the reassignment policy, and the signature scheme.

For example, the triplet $[Limit, Basic, AS]$ identifies a system where the broker mints limit certificates, no layers are allowed during reassignment, and messages are signed under the aggregation scheme. Limit certificates represent an attempt to reduce the broker's load by way of allowing a peer to print a coin by himself. In fact, if C is the number of coins that circulates in the system during Δt, and lim is the number of coins that each peer can extract from a limit certificate, then each coin costs $\omega_P = |\overline{gen}| / lim$. Because layered coins are not allowed, the broker is involved during a reassignment with probability t (i.e., when a peer is likely to be off-line). Hence, ω_R is equal to the computational cost of checking a reassignment request ($|\overline{check_1}|$) and of generating a new assigned coin ($|\overline{gen}|$).

Finally, ω_{Ca} is the sum of the costs of (1) aggregating C signatures ($aggr(C)$), (2) verifying them ($|\overline{check_C}|$), and (3) detecting of the misbehaving peer(s) in presence of a fraud[5]. The last cost is particularly important, because we have two different scenarios: when we have no frauds ($f = 0$), all the C different signatures are proved valid. But if $f > 0$, the check will simply fail, without identifying the malicious signer(s). In this case, the broker should verify all the signatures one by one, in order to detect the misbehaving peer. For each assigned coin, ω_{Ca} is increased of a value equal to $f \cdot 2 \cdot |\overline{check_1}|$.

Table 3 shows all the computational costs of the ω functions, for different strategies.

As a final observation, observe that when layered coins are used, then $\omega_R = 0$, because the broker is never involved during reassignments. On the other hand, when a

---

[4] An hybrid strategy has been analyzed, too. In such a scenario, a peer tries to reassign the coin by way of the owner, but, if the latter is down, the coin is layered instead. We observed that this *Hybrid* strategy always outperforms the *Layer* one, even if they differ very slightly. Hence, for the sake of simplicity, we did not show results on this third reassignment strategy.

[5] Observe that the first two components of ω_{Ca} should be divided by the number of aggregated coins (see Table 3) in order to flatten their contribution in formula (1).

Table 3. Values of the weight functions in terms of cryptographic primitives

Strategy	ω_P	ω_R	ω_{Ca}
$[Raw, Basic, RSA]$	$|gen|$	$t(3\,|check| + |gen|)$	$2\,|check|$
$[Raw, Layer, RSA]$	$|gen|$	0	$(2+s)\,|check|$
$[Limit, Basic, RSA]$	$\frac{|gen|}{lim}$	$t(3\,|check| + |gen|)$	$2\,|check|$
$[Limit, Layer, RSA]$	$\frac{|gen|}{lim}$	0	$(2+s)\,|check|$
$[Raw, Basic, AS]$	$|\overline{gen}|$	$t(|\overline{check}_1| + |\overline{gen}|)$	$\frac{aggr(C)+|\overline{check}_C|}{C} + 2f\,|\overline{check}_1|$
$[Raw, Layer, AS]$	$|\overline{gen}|$	0	$\frac{aggr(C)+|\overline{check}_C|}{C} + (2+s)f\,|\overline{check}_1|$
$[Limit, Basic, AS]$	$\frac{|\overline{gen}|}{lim}$	$t(|\overline{check}_1| + |\overline{gen}|)$	$\frac{aggr(C)+|\overline{check}_C|}{C} + 2f\,|\overline{check}_1|$
$[Limit, Layer, AS]$	$\frac{|\overline{gen}|}{lim}$	0	$\frac{aggr(C)+|\overline{check}_C|}{C} + (2+s)f\,|\overline{check}_1|$

coin is cashed, it contains many signatures as the number of layers, and ω_{Ca} is higher than in the Basic reassignment strategy. In the estimation of ω_{Ca}, the number of layers in a coin is given by coefficient s, i.e., the length of the reassignment chain of the layered coin. In the next section, the size of layers (i.e., the value of s) is modeled using the *FullChain* and *Pareto* distributions, as previously introduced.

5.2 Results

The scalability of our market place is strictly bound to the load of the broker: less this central unit is overloaded, more the market place is resistant. As a consequence, we want to identify the combination of coin management policies that stresses the broker as less as possible. Hence, for comparing different strategies, we set T to a constant value. A spatial analysis (i.e., bandwidth and storage consumption) is trivial: an RSA signature is sized 128 bytes, against the 20 bytes needed under the AS scheme. As a generalization of [8], the best strategy is $[Limit, Layer, AS]$.

Computational analysis is not so straightforward, and we need an in depth analysis. In order to make our results independent from a given platform, we normalized all the costs at the value of an RSA verification cryptographic operation ($|check|$). Hence, the number of *check* operations is displayed in the y axes in diagrams showed below (Figures 1 and 2). The x axes are instead devoted to the maximum number of reassignment m. In Figure 1 we clearly see that a system adopting aggregate signatures outperforms, even from a computational point of view, an equivalent framework that uses RSA signatures. In fact, if we measure the system performance in terms of number of RSA signature verifications, we observe that when we have no fraudulent peers, and even when the rate of frauds is quite limited ($f < 5\%$), the usage of aggregate signatures appreciably improves the broker's load. This is observed in all the schemes, except for the $[\_, Basic, \_]$ strategies with *FullChain* distribution. However, the Basic reassignment strategy is failing w.r.t. Layer (confirming results in [8]). Observe that, whatever distribution is adopted in the model, the best strategy is definitely $[Limit, Layer, AS]$.

As expected, if the fraud rate grows (e.g., $f = 5\%$ in the diagrams of Figure 2), aggregate signatures deteriorates broker's performance. Anyhow, we can reasonably suppose that the rate of committed frauds will always be very limited, because of the low

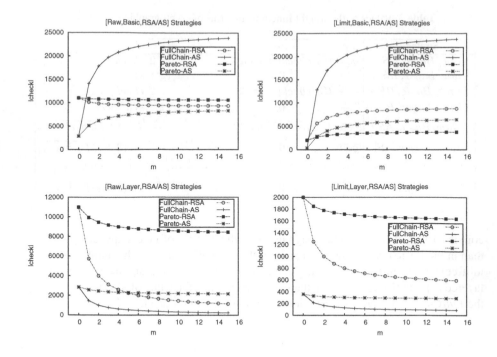

Fig. 1. Computational analysis of different strategies: fraud rate $f = 0\%$

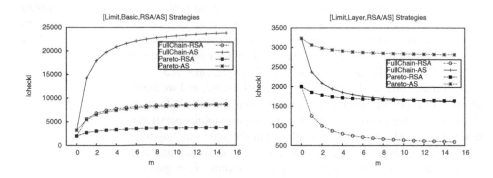

Fig. 2. Computational analysis of different strategies: fraud rate $f = 5\%$

value of the used currency: frauds are detactable and not profitable. In the real world, we can support the adoption of aggregate signatures to verify group of many signatures all at once after a periodical interval of time. Moreover, to enforce results of this study, the reader should observe that we adopted a heavy pessimistic estimation on the performance of cryptographic operations under an AS scheme. An efficient implementation of $\overline{check_\ell}$ would raise up the efficiency threshold based on f.

6 Conclusion

We evaluated the usage of an aggregate signature scheme in the PPay micro-payment system. We proved that aggregate signatures outperform RSA in terms of broker computational and spatial resources consumption. In particular, we showed that the broker's load scales well even if frauds are committed. Future work will focus on a deep analysis, taking advantage of simulators and a prototype implementation.

Acknowledgments

This work has been partially financially supported by the Italian FIRB 2001 project number RBNE01WEJT "Web MiNDS".

References

1. R. Dingledine, M.J.F., D.Molnar: Peer-To-Peer: Harnessing the Power of Disruptive Technologies, Chapter 16. O'Reilly (2001)
2. Adar, E., Huberman, B.A.: Free riding on gnutella. First Monday (2000)
3. Cohen., B.: Incentives build robustness in bittorrent. In: Proc. of the 1st Workshop on the Economics of Peer-to-Peer Systems. (2003)
4. eMule project: (http://www.emule-project.ne)
5. Yang, B., Garcia-Molina, H.: Ppay: micropayments for peer-to-peer systems. In: Proc. of the 10th ACM CCS, ACM Press (2003)
6. Catalano, D., Ruffo, G.: A fair micro-payment scheme for profit sharing in a p2p network. In: Proc. of HOT-P2P 04, IEEE Press (2004)
7. D. Boneh, C. Gentry, B.L., Shacham, H.: Aggregate and verifiably encrypted signatures from bilinear maps. In: Eurocrypt '03, LNCS 2656, Springer-Verlag. (2003) 416–432
8. Ruffo, G., Schifanella, R.: Scalability evaluation of a peer-to-peer market place based on micro payments. In: Proc. of HOT-P2P 05, IEEE Press (2005)
9. D. Boneh, B.L., Shacham, H.: Short signatures from the weil pairing. In: Asiacrypt '01, LNCS 2248, Springer-Verlag. (2001) 514–532
10. Boneh, D., Franklin, M.: Identity-based encryption from the weil pairing. In: Crypto '01, LNCS 2139, Springer-Verlag. (2001) 213–229
11. Gummadi, K.P., Dunn, R.J., Saroiu, S., Gribble, S.D., Levy, H.M., Zahorjan, J.: Measurement, modeling, and analysis of a peer-to-peer file-sharing workload. In: Proc. of SOSP '03, ACM Press (2003)
12. Barreto, P.S.L.M., Lynn, B., Scott, M.: Efficient implementation of pairing-based cryptosystems. J. Cryptology 17 (2004)

Proof of Service in a Hybrid P2P Environment

Jun Li and Xun Kang

Department of Computer and Information Science,
University of Oregon,
{lijun, kangxun}@cs.uoregon.edu

Abstract. In a hybrid peer-to-peer environment, clients can either directly download data from their server, or share data with each other. In order to create incentives for clients to share data and decrease server load, an effective economy model is for the server to credit those *provider* clients who provide data to others and offer discounts to those *recipient* clients who download data from provider clients instead of the server. To realize this model, the proof of service between provider and recipient clients must be provided.

We design and investigate three different schemes and compare them in terms of scalability, effectiveness, and cost. We emphasize the issues of lessening the number of proofs which must be provided, avoiding a heavy load on the server, and ensuring the proof for *every* piece of data served. Our study shows our enhanced public-key-based scheme to be the most effective.

1 Introduction

Sharing data over the network can either be based on a client-server model, or on a peer-to-peer mechanism. Interestingly, these seemingly contradictory paradigms can actually complement each other. While a server can independently serve data toward multiple individual clients, its clients can form a peer-to-peer relationship to share data from the server among themselves [1,2,3], reducing the amount of data clients must directly download from the server.

The combination of peer-to-peer and client-server paradigms creates a new, hybrid peer-to-peer data service environment. Both a server and its clients can potentially benefit from this environment: the server does not need to serve every client directly, and a client may also be able to obtain data from other peer clients that are closer than the server.

An obstacle to realizing such benefits is whether clients are willing to share data among each other. In another words, how can a client have incentives to provide services to its peer clients?

To answer this question, a simple but generic economy model can be introduced as follows: (1) Every client will only pay the server directly, and does not pay any other client; (2) A client who helps others (a *provider client* providing data, also called *provider*) will receive credits for assisting the server. (3) A client who is helped by other clients (a *recipient client* receiving data, also called

G. Chen et al. (Eds.): ISPA Workshops 2005, LNCS 3759, pp. 64–73, 2005.

recipient) will pay less for the data, since it does not directly utilize as much of the server's resources; (4) By offloading some tasks to provider clients, the server will serve more clients overall and thus make more profit, even though it charges each individual client less. Note that a provider may have stronger but indecent incentives if it violates this model and directly "sells" data illegally to other clients. Our focus in this paper is to provide positive incentives that will benefit everyone.

This economy model provides incentives to every entity involved, including the server, the provider clients, and the recipient clients. However, it also faces serious challenges with regards to the issue of trust. For instance, what if a client masquerades as a provider client and cheats the server by claiming that it has offered other clients a large amount of data, thus requesting credits? What if a recipient client lies to the server by reporting that it received much less data than it really received, or that it never received any data at all? Can a recipient client receive data from hundreds of providers but never acknowledge the service they provided?

In order to harden the economy model above, a trustworthy, effective proof-of-service mechanism must be designed. With proof of service, a client can present to its server a proof about its service to others, a server can verify whether or not a client has indeed served others, and a recipient cannot deny, cheat or be cheated about its reception of data from others.

In this paper, we first briefly describe related work, then illustrate the design of three proof-of-service schemes. We also report our experimental results to show that under this hybrid environment, effective proof of service can be implemented with a reasonable cost.

2   Related Work

The proof of service toward a recipient could be realized by obtaining a non-repudiable receipt about the service from the recipient. So proof of service in this paper can be regarded as one particular case of non-repudiation service. In fact, there have been quite a few non-repudiation schemes designed in different contexts, focusing on non-repudiation of origin, receipt, submission, and delivery [4]. Louridas also provided guidelines for designing non-repudiation protocols [5]. Verification of non-repudiation schemes have also been studied [6,7,8].

Proof of service is very similar to fair exchange of information, which can be either without or with a trusted third party (TTP) [4]. In the context of this paper, fairness would mean for a provider to receive a proof of its service and for a recipient to receive the desired data. (Note that unlike most fair exchange protocols, a recipient does not need to obtain the proof about the identity of the provider.) The most closely related to this paper is the fair exchange with an offline TTP. While leveraging current schemes, our solution in this hybrid environment has an important difference in that a server itself can act as a TTP for its provider and recipient clients. This is also an inherent advantage for enforcing fairness. Further note that the server is also the original source of the data that a provider offers to a recipient, bringing another advantage: If needed, a server can verify the data without requesting them from other nodes, thus avoiding a drawback in many TTP-based solutions, especially when the data is of large size.

Rather than alleviating the load on a TTP as in other fair exchange solutions, ours will focus on keeping the server lightly loaded. A big challenge in our context is that there can be thousands of clients of a server, and every recipient client may be related to a large number of providers. Our solution must scale as the number of clients grows. Furthermore, in this hybrid environment clients may collude to attempt to gain illegal proof of service.

3   Overview

Assuming every data object (such as a file) is divided into multiple blocks our general approach is to enforce an interlocking block-by-block verification mechanism between every pair of provider and recipient. ("Block" in this paper is an abstract concept which can just be an application-specific data transmission unit.) For every block that a provider has sent to a recipient, the recipient will verify the integrity of the block (which is through an orthogonal mechanism that we will not cover in this paper), and send back an acknowledgment to the provider. On the other hand, the provider will verify the acknowledgment *before* providing the next block. Those verified acknowledgments can then be used to form the proof of the service that the provider has offered to other clients, and they must be non-repudiable and can be verified by the server.

Three severe problems arise in this basic solution and must be handled:

- **Proof Explosion Problem.** If a provider has to present a separate proof for *every* block it served, it can be a very large number of proofs for its server to handle. Note that there can also be a large number of providers. So, an acknowledgment should be able to aggregate the receipts of recent blocks.
- **Server Overload Problem.** If a recipient has to resort to its server for composing every non-repudiable acknowledgment, or a provider has to fall back on the server for verifying every acknowledgment, or if they frequently seek other help from the server, this will not be a scalable solution. Especially since a large number of clients may be sharing a single server.
- **Last Block Problem.** After a recipient receives the last block it needs from a provider, the recipient could deliberately decide not to send an acknowledgment for this last block. *Note that this last block is not necessarily the last block of a data object.* Except for some simple cases (such as providing the last block of a data object), the provider has no way of knowing whether a particular block will be a recipient's last block to request.

In the following, we first introduce a simple solution based on shared secret key cryptography. It is not scalable as it heavily relies on the server as an inline TTP. Then we introduce the second solution based on public key cryptography, which scales in that the server will be used as an offline TTP. But, while this solution normally is effective, in some circumstances the last block problem is a concern, and we present a third solution.

We assume each client first contacts a server to establish a secure SSL channel between them. This is done by running the SSL protocol [9], which also helps the client obtain a certificate of the server's public key, and set up a secret key shared between the client and the server. The client then sends its request regarding particular data objects. While the server can directly serve the data, in this paper we assume that the server will issue a *ticket* to the client to authorize the client to retrieve data from other provider clients. The client then contacts one or more providers and presents its ticket to them. (A more detailed procedure on how clients find each other is out of the scope of this paper.) After verifying the ticket, a provider begins providing data to the client.

4   Shared-Secret-Key-Based Proof of Service

In this scheme, the server acts as an inline TTP. When a recipient sends back an acknowledgment for a block it received from a provider, the acknowledgment is protected using the secret key shared between the recipient and the server. The provider is not able to decrypt the acknowledgment, and it forwards the acknowledgment to the server. The server then verifies it and returns the verification result to the provider.

If the acknowledgment is verified as authentic, the server will also use it as a proof that the provider just sent a block to the recipient. Furthermore, only when the acknowledgment is verified as authentic will the provider go ahead and provide the next block to the recipient.

Figure 1 shows the procedure of this scheme. The recipient r has received block b_i. It verifies the integrity of the block, sends an acknowledgment $ack(b_i)$ to the provider p, and requests the next block b_{i+1}. The acknowledgment is in the following format:

$$k_r\{pid,\ rid,\ oid,\ i,\ timestamp\} \tag{1}$$

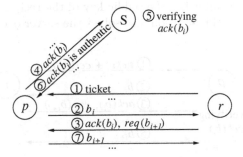

Fig. 1. Shared-secret-key-based proof of service

where k_r is the shared secret key between r and the server S for signing the acknowledgment; pid and rid are the ids of p and r, respectively; oid and i specifies which blocks of which data object are being acknowledged; $timestamp$ records when the request for b_i was issued.

This scheme is subject to the proof explosion problem, since a separate proof must be presented for every block that a provider served. It is also subject to the server overload problem in that the server has to verify the authenticity of *every* acknowledgment resulting from the interlocking verification process, and every block that a recipient receives will lead to a new acknowledgment. Lastly, it also does not address the last block problem.

5   Public-Key-Based Proof of Service

In this solution, when a recipient wants to receive data from a provider, it will not only present a ticket, which is prepared by the server to authorize the recipient to receive data from other providers, but it will also present the certificate of its own public key. When a recipient receives a data block, it will then apply the same procedure as in Section 4, except that it will (1) sign the acknowledgment using its private key, and (2) include a *sack* field instead of the index of the most recently received block. The following shows the format of the acknowledgment:

$$p_r\{pid,\ rid,\ oid,\ sack,\ timestamp\} \tag{2}$$

where p_r is the private key of the recipient client r.

The *sack* field solves the proof explosion problem. It is in a format similar to the SACK options for the TCP protocol [10]. It can express *all* the blocks that the recipient has received from the provider, instead of just the most recent one. For example, it can be $[0 - 56, 58 - 99]$ to confirm the reception of the first 100 blocks of a data object except for the block 57. This way, a provider only needs to keep the most recent—thus also the most complete—acknowledgment as the proof of its service to indicate all the blocks it provided.

Figure 2 shows an example when r acknowledges its receipt of blocks up to block b_i, and requests the next block b_{i+1}. Different from the shared-secret-key-based solution, here the provider verifies the acknowledgment by itself before sending block b_{i+1}. Recall it has the public key of the recipient and is thus able to verify it. Therefore, this solution also solves the server overload problem.

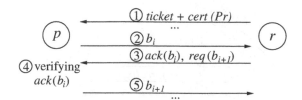

Fig. 2. Public-key-based proof of service

6   Enhanced Public-Key-Based Proof of Service

6.1   The Basic Idea and Its Issues

Neither of the above two solutions solves the problem of *last block cheating*. We now introduce a *block-key-based* mechanism. If a block is *not* the last block, we can just use the solution from Section 5. Otherwise, if the provider knows that the ith block b_i from a data object *oid* is the last block to send to a recipient *rid*, it will generate a secret *block key* k_i^r:

$$k_i^r = f(pid, rid, oid, i, k_p) \tag{3}$$

where f is a one-way hash function and k_p is the secret key shared between the provider and the server. Then, as shown in Figure 3, instead of delivering the original block b_i to the recipient, the provider will encrypt the block with this block key, and send the encrypted block to the recipient. Upon the receipt of the encrypted block, the recipient will acknowledge its receipt of this block, using the same format as in Equation (2). Here, the recipient *must* acknowledge the receipt of this block in order to receive the block key k_i^r to decrypt $k_i^r\{b_i\}$.

There are still a few issues to consider, however, given that both the provider and the recipient may be dishonest. First, this solution assumes that the provider knows block b_i is the last block that the recipient wants to receive. Second, this solution allows a provider to obtain an acknowledgment of the last block even if the provider did not provide the recipient with a correctly encrypted block or an authentic block key. Third, it is possible that the server may be overloaded with too many (honest or dishonest) requests related to the last block issues—for example, what if a recipient complains to the server frequently that it did not receive the block key even if it did? We address these issues in the following.

6.2   Determine the Last Block

The provider can treat every block as potentially the last block that a recipient would receive from it, and apply to every block the approach shown in Figure 3. Doing so, the provider will obtain the proof of its service of every block, including the last block. In case the provider is certain that the current data block is not the last block (such as via out-of-band knowledge), or if the provider does not mind missing the proof of just one last block, it can simply apply the original public-key-based proof-of-service scheme.

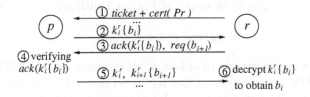

Fig. 3. Enhanced public-key-based proof of service

6.3   Ensure the Correctness of Encrypted Block

For acknowledging an encrypted block $k_i^r\{b_i\}$, we enhance Equation (2) to also include the digest (using a one-way hash function) of $k_i^r\{b_i\}$, denoted as $d(k_i^r\{b_i\})$, in the acknowledgment $ack(k_i^r\{b_i\})$:

$$p_r\{pid,\ rid,\ oid,\ sack,\ timestamp,\ d(k_i^r\{b_i\})\}. \qquad (4)$$

The provider p will verify $ack(k_i^r\{b_i\})$, including the digest, to decide whether or not to provide the block key k_i^r to the recipient r. This way, when p presents the server this acknowledgment as the proof of its service, the server can verify whether r received the correctly encrypted last block, i.e., correct block b_i encrypted using correct block key k_i^r. Note that the server can use Equation (3) to calculate the correct block key k_i^r.

Also, after r receives k_i^r, it can decrypt $k_i^r\{b_i\}$ to obtain b_i. Furthermore, it can verify the integrity of b_i. Only if b_i is integral will r continue with p for the next block. In case b_i appears to be corrupted, r knows that p cannot use $ack(k_i^r\{b_i\})$ as a proof of its service. r will not send $ack(k_{i+1}^r\{b_{i+1}\})$ to p; otherwise p can use it as the proof of its service, hiding the corrupted delivery of block b_i. The recipient r can either request b_i from p again, or decide not to continue with p.

Unfortunately, this stop-and-go process can have poor performance. To remedy this, we require every acknowledgment to include digests of last m encrypted blocks, and the server will verify whether the recipient received the correctly encrypted blocks for last m blocks (instead of just last one block). In step 5 of Figure 3, upon the receipt of k_i^r and the encrypted block b_{i+1} (i.e. $k_{i+1}^r\{b_{i+1}\}$), r will first immediately acknowledge the receipt of b_{i+1}, then invoke a separate process for decrypting block b_i and verifying its integrity. This process can be repeated for the next $m-1$ blocks, greatly improving the performance; in case that block b_i is discovered corrupted, p will still not be able to have a proof that it successfully delivered b_i—since the proof must show correct digests of all last m blocks. Here, we want to select m carefully such that it is small enough to be scalable, but large enough to keep a high level of parallelism.

6.4   Ensure the Correctness and Availability of Block Key

To ensure the correctness of a block key, the provider p can sign it with its private key p_p, replacing k_i^r in step 5 of Figure 3 with a *protected block key*:

$$p_p\{pid, rid, oid, i, k_i^r\}. \qquad (5)$$

The recipient r can decrypt it to obtain k_i^r. If r cannot decrypt $k_i^r\{b_i\}$ correctly, it can forward the protected block key to the server so that the server can verify if p sent a wrong block key. In case p did not provide a block key at all (i.e., no step 5 in Figure 3), r can retrieve it by asking the server to apply Equation (3) to calculate the block key.

6.5   Keep Server Lightly Loaded

Throughout the whole design, the server's load has been kept very light. A provider can wait until the end of serving a recipient to present a single proof of its service toward this client. Also, in addition to obtaining the ticket and certificate at the beginning, the only type of query that a recipient can issue is to verify or retrieve the block key of a block it receives from a provider (see Section 6.4). Because there can only be one last block between a recipient and a provider, this kind of query happens only once per recipient-provider pair.

7   Experimental Results

We have implemented a framework to support peer-to-peer data sharing among clients of a common server, and used this framework to evaluate the cost and performance when enforcing the public-key-based proof of service solution and its enhanced version, which we will denote as P and P_e, respectively. (Note that we do not evaluate the shared-secret-key-based solution since it is not feasible.) In addition, our framework can be configured to enforce a subset of three orthogonal security functions: client authentication, data integrity protection, and data confidentiality protection, denoted as A, I, C, respectively.

We measured several metrics with and without proof of service for comparisons. We compared the scenarios AI vs. AIP and AIP_e, and the scenarios AIC vs. $AICP$ and $AICP_e$. (Note that P or P_e always needs to be enforced together with A and I.) Cryptography parameters are: 112-bit 3DES for secret key, 1024-bit RSA for public key, and MD5 for message digest.

7.1   Server Capacity

Server capacity is defined as the number of client requests that a server can serve per time unit. Measuring the server capacity before and after applying a proof-of-service solution can test whether the solution would significantly impact the server. For both P and P_e, our design requires a server to perform the same operations; therefore, the server capacity will be exactly the same. We measured the server capacity of an iBook machine running MacOS X with a 700 MHz processor and 384 MB of memory. While the server capacity for the AI scenario is 360 requests per minute on average, it decreases by 93 (26%) to be 267 after adding P or P_e. At the same time, a 23% decrease (330 to 253 requests per minute) occurs when enforcing P or P_e on top of the AIC scenario.

7.2   File Downloading Time

File downloading time is the latency from the time that a client establishes a connection with a server for requesting a file to the time that it receives the whole file. It consists of a startup latency, which is the time that the client spends in handshaking with the server before sending out a request for the first block of a file, and data transferring time, which is the rest of file downloading time. Measuring file downloading time with and without P or P_e can indicate how a user may feel the impact of P or P_e when downloading a file.

In our experiment, we use the same server as in our server capacity measurement, and every client machine (either provider or recipient) is a Dell Latitude D810 machine running Linux 2.6.9-ck3 with a 1.73 GHz Pentium M processor and 512 MB of memory. We connect all of them on an isolated subnet to avoid background noise so that our comparison of file downloading times under different scenarios can be accurate and consistent.

Regarding the startup latency with and without proof of service, adding P or P_e on top of the AI scenario will increase the startup latency by approximately 0.2 and 0.3 seconds, respectively. The results for the AIC scenario is similar. Both are acceptable to users downloading files.

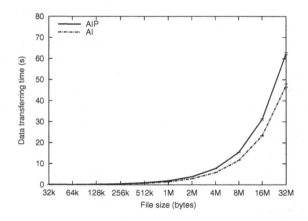

Fig. 4. Data transferring time (with 95% confidence interval)

We now analyze the data transferring time with and without proof of service. Since in our design whether or not the data is encrypted does not affect the data transferring time, we only look at scenarios without confidentiality. Furthermore, our design makes P and P_e have the same amount of data transferring time—in P_e, block encryption and decryption operations at a provider or a recipient are conducted out of band, and is not part of the data transferring time. As a result, we can just compare the data transferring times between the AI and AIP scenarios. Figure 4 shows the results. We can see that for each scenario, while the size of a file doubles, so does the data transferring time. Furthermore, for the same file size, adding P will increase the data transferring time, but within a reasonable range. For instance, adding proof of service can increase the data transferring time of a 4 MB file from 5.8 seconds to 7.7 seconds.

8 Conclusions

If clients of a server share data among themselves, great benefits can be obtained in that the server will have a reduced load and each client can choose close peer clients to obtain data. With such a hybrid peer-to-peer environment, an economy model can further be defined to create incentives for peer-level sharing: provider clients can gain credits, recipient clients can pay less, and the server can still make profit as it can afford to serve a larger population.

However, in order for the above to be true, a critical prerequisite is to enable providers to obtain non-repudiable, trustworthy proofs of the service they have given recipient clients. In this paper, we presented three different proof-of-service schemes—a shared-secret-key-based scheme, a public-key-based scheme, and an enhanced public-key-based scheme. While the shared-secret-key-based scheme is not scalable, we have shown that with the latter two schemes, a server will only be lightly loaded. The enhanced version can further ensure that a provider can obtain the proof for *all* the data it served. Experimental results have also shown that the final solution is effective and can be applicable for real usage with a reasonable cost. Future work of this research includes obtaining a formal verification of the protocol and conducting further studies on actual deployment.

Acknowledgements

We thank the anonymous reviewers for their comments. This research also benefited from discussions with Toby Ehrenkranz and Eric Anderson. Toby also helped prepare the camera-ready version of this paper.

References

1. BitTorrent, Inc.: BitTorrent. http://bittorrent.com (2005)
2. Stavrou, A., Rubenstein, D., Sahu, S.: A Lightweight, Robust P2P System to Handle Flash Crowds. In: ICNP. (2002) 226–235
3. Sherwood, R., Braud, R., Bhattacharjee, B.: Slurpie: A Cooperative Bulk Data Transfer Protocol. IEEE INFOCOM (2004)
4. Kremer, S., Markowitch, O., Zhou, J.: An Intensive Survey of Fair Non-Repudiation Protocols. Computer Communications **25** (2002)
5. Louridas, P.: Some Guidelines for Non-Repudiation Protocols. Computer Communication Review **30** (2000) 29–38
6. Zhou, J., Gollmann, D.: Towards Verification of Non-Repudiation Protocols. In: Proceedings of 1998 International Refinement Workshop and Formal Methods Pacific, Canberra, Australia (1998) 370–380
7. Schneider, S.: Formal Analysis of a Non-Repudiation Protocol. In: CSFW, Washington, DC, USA (1998) 54
8. Kremer, S., Raskin, J.F.: A Game-Based Verification of Non-Repudiation and Fair Exchange Protocols. Lecture Notes in Computer Science **2154** (2001) 551+
9. Freier, A.O., Karlton, P., Kocher, P.C.: SSL Protocol Version 3.0. http://wp.netscape.com/eng/ssl3/ssl-toc.html (1996)
10. Mathis, M., Mahdavi, J., Floyd, S., Romanow, A.: IETF RFC 2018: TCP Selective Acknowledgement Options (1996)

Construct Optimal Diameter Network and d-partition Routing Algorithm*

Qiang Ding, Ke Xu, and Hui-shan Liu

Department of Computer Science and Technology, Tsinghua University,
Beijing, 100084, P.R.China
{dingq, xuke, liuhs}@csnet1.cs.tsinghua.edu.cn

Abstract. This paper studies the topological structure of network using graph-theoretical properties and proposes a topology construction method of regular directed graphs (or digraphs). The diameter of the topological digraph is $\lceil \log_d n \rceil$. In this paper, we also propose a routing algorithm based this topological structure and find its complexity is $O(\lceil \log_d n \rceil)$. This algorithm has a smaller diameter and easier to construct than the existing algorithms, which can be used of downloading files and defending worms in structured peer-to-peer systems.

1 Introduction

In recent years, the application based on P2P network developed rapidly [1][2][3][4]. It is present not only in sending early-warning signals, but also in transferring file, etc. We consider the problem that each host has initially one early-warning signal and all these early-warning signals have to be distributed to all hosts in P2P network. We wish the speed of sending early-warning signals is faster than the speed of worms spreading so far. So we need to structure a P2P network with maximum delay as small as possible based the existing Internet topological structure.

The topology of network is made up with some vertices and some edges. We regard hosts as vertices and links as directed edges. In graphs theory, the maximum delay can be denoted the diameter. The diameter of graph [11] is an important parameter to measure the efficiency of a network. Some researchers have put forward some excellent algorithms, for example, Chord [3], Tapestry [4], etc.

In this paper, we explore the relationship between diameter of network and route policy. We present a topological structure of the optimal diameter network and give the proof of it. Additionally, we design d-partition routing algorithm of lower computation complexity.

The remainder of this paper is organized as follows. Section 2 introduces the background and related problems. Section 3 presents the basic definitions, and section 4 gives an important proposition and the proof of it. In section 5 we design the d-

---

* The research of this paper is supported by National Natural Science Fund Project of China (No. 60473082).

G. Chen et al. (Eds.): ISPA Workshops 2005, LNCS 3759, pp. 74–81, 2005.

partition routing algorithm. Section 6 provides the computation complexity of this route algorithm. Section 7 is conclusion and further research work.

2 Background

2.1 Remove and Add Edges Policy

Below graphs we will mention are all digraph (directed-graph). In order to reduce the problem, we only pay attention to the links and how to connect each other.

Small diameter represents small communication delay, then, the following problems arise. Which factor will influence the diameter of a network? How to decrease the diameter? We can transform this problem through the policy of removing or adding edges. Like this, for a digraph G, Let $f_d(G)$ be minimum (maximum) number of adding (removing) edges in order to make its diameter be d. We need to add edges to decrease its diameter. By a similar consideration, we need to remove edges to increase its diameter. It is clear that any digraph of n-vertices can be obtained by removing some edges from an n-vertices complete digraph. In general, it is NP-complete to determine the minimum (maximum) number of edges to be added (removed) to a digraph to make its diameter be d [5]. For an n-vertices digraph G of degree k, some literatures [6][7] have proved the following conclusions.

(1) $f_2(G)=n-k-1$

(2) $f_3(G)\geq n-O(k^3)$

(3) If $d\geq 4$: f_d (G) depends on the structure of digraph greatly besides d.

That is to say, $f_d(G)$ has a minimum when diameter is 2, $f_d(G)$ only has a low bound, and the situation will be complicated when the diameter exceeds 3. The conclusions of above-mentioned NP-complete problem can be showed as follows.

$G_0(n, k, h)$ ——remove $f_d(G_0)$ edges ——>$G_1(n, b, d)$ (b<k, d>h) (2.1)

If the n-vertices regular digraph G of degree k has minimum possible diameter x, the above question is equivalent to the problem that we remove $f_x(G)$ edges from the complete digraph G(n, k, 1) in order to obtain G(n, k, d). Then we have

$G_0(n, n-1, 1)$ —— remove $f_x(G_0)$ edges ——>$G_1(n, k, x)$ (k<n-1, x>1) (2.2)

It is easy to know (2.2) is a special case of (2.1) through comparing (2.1) and (2.2). Consequently, this proves (2.2) is a NP-complete problem.

2.2 Related Problems

We study the relationships between the number of vertices, degree and diameter of regular digraphs. These three problems are denoted by N(d, k), K(n, d) and D(n, k).

(1) N(d, k) Problem: Find the maximum possible number of vertices given degree d and diameter k.

(2) K(n, d) Problem: Find the minimum possible diameter given the number of vertices n and degree d.

(3) D(n, k) Problem: Find the minimum possible degree given the number of vertices n and diameter k.

In recent years the three problems have received much attention from researchers due to their possible applications in network design. N(d, k) problem shows how to make the size of network be maximum. K(n, d) problem shows how to make the delay be minimum. D(n, k) problem shows how to make the load of vertex be minimum. These three problems are related but not equivalent. The authors of [8] give the conclusions of N(d, k) and K(n, d) when n≤100. Obviously, if N(2,k)=n then K(n,2)=k while d=2, and

(1) if $n \leq 2^s$, then $K(n,2) \leq s$

(2) if $n=2^s+1$ and s is odd number, then $K(n,2) \leq s$

Let A be adjacency matrix of G=G(n, d, k), then we have

$$I+A+A^2+A^3+\ldots+A^k \geq E .\tag{1}$$

where I is the n × n identity matrix and E is the n × n the unit matrix. It follows that

$$1+d+d^2+d^3+\ldots+d^k \geq n .\tag{2}$$

must hold whenever G(n, d, k) exists, and

$$N(d, k) \leq 1+d+d^2+d^3+\ldots+d^k .\tag{3}$$

Toueg and Bridges have proved that the regular digraph $G(1+d+d^2+d^3+\ldots+d^k, d, k)$ can not exist (d>1,k>1)[9]. So, we have

$$N(d, k) \leq d+d^2+d^3+\ldots+d^k \quad (d>1,k>1) .\tag{4}$$

If we look the three problems as three functions, we shall draw the following conclusions easy.

(a) N increase monotonic in d if k given.

(b) N increase monotonic in k if d given.

(c) K decrease monotonic in d if n given.

3   Definition

In this section, we will define some graph-theoretical terms and notations used in this paper [10][11].

Definition 1 : Graph
A graph G=(V, E, φ_G) always means a simple graph with vertex-set V=V(G) and edge-set E=E(G). φ_G is the associate function.

Definition 2 : Digraph
A graph called digraph (directed graph) if all edges are directed edges.

Definition 3 : Order
The cardinality |V(G)| is called the order of G.

Definition 4 : Degree
Degree of a vertex v∈G is the number of edges (u, v) or (v, u) in G. Use the symbol $d_G(v)$ to denote the degree of a vertex v∈G.

The degree of G is the maximum degree of all vertices in G, denoted by △(G). We call digraph G is a d-regular digraph if the degree of all vertices are d. Below regular digraphs we will mention are all d-regular digraph.

Definition 5: Distance
The distance from vertex u to vertex v in G is defined as the length of the shortest directed of path from vertex u to vertex v, denoted by $d_G(u, v)$.

Definition 6: Diameter
The diameter k of a digraph G is the maximum distance between two vertices in G.

The maximum delay and average delay are two important parameters to measure the performance and efficiency of a network. The two parameters are defined as the diameter and the average distance of a digraph. The diameter of the digraph G is defined as

$$k=\max\{d_G(u, v)\}\ (u, v\in V).\tag{5}$$

4 Construct Optimal Diameter Network

In this section, we'll give and prove the following proposition, then construct an optimal diameter network.

Propositions. Let $\omega(n, d, k)$ be a set of regular digraph of order n, degree d and diameter k, where $n>0, d>1, k=\lceil \log_d n\rceil$, then $\omega(n, d, k)$ is nonempty.

Proof: Obviously, every digraph in $\omega(n, d, k)$ have d × n edges. This proposition is proved using construction method. We construct a topology graph using residue formula and prove the diameter of topology graph is $\lceil \log_d n\rceil$.

Assume the digraph $G(n, d, k) \in \omega(n, d, k)$ is a regular digraph of order n, degree d and diameter k($n>0, d>1$), denoted by G=(V,E) also. We construct the directed edges of G through constructing neighbor vertices. Let vertex set of digraph G be V={0,1,2,...,n-1}, for every i∈V, its neighbor vertices are

$$di + s + t\ (\text{mod } n)\ (1\le s\le d, t\in[0,n-1]).\tag{6}$$

The whole route table has a characteristic of periodic return (mod n). Consequently, it called periodic return method. We now prove the diameter of topology graph which constructed with this method is $\lceil \log_d n\rceil$.

We find neighbor vertices which are constructed with di + s +t (mod n) have following continuity.

(1) ID of neighbor vertices of a vertex is continuous.
The neighbor vertices of vertex i are di+1+t, di+2+t, di+3+t, ..., di + d+ t (mod n)
 (2) ID of neighbor vertices of adjoined two vertices is continuous.
We know neighbor vertices of vertex i are di+1+t,di+2+t,..., di + d +t (mod n)
The neighbor vertices of vertex i+1 are
d(i+1)+1+t,d(i+1)+2+t,d(i+1)+3+t,...,d(i+1)+d +t (mod n)
As, (d(i+1)+1+t)-(di+d+t) = (di+d+1+t)-(di+d+t) = 1
Consequently, the head neighbor vertex of vertex i+1 is bigger than the trail neighbor vertex of vertex i.

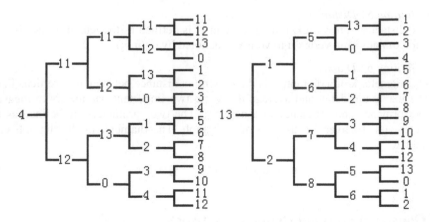

Fig. 1. Route trees of vertex 4 and vertex 13

The ID of neighbor vertex complete continuous in whole route table based the above attributes, and owing to repeat d times justly (mod n). For instance, we construct the whole route table using equation 6, where d=2, n=14, t=2 and diameter is 4.We present the route trees of vertices 4 and 13 that including all possible paths in the following figure.

Let the diameter of digraph G be k, then every vertex $i \in V(G)$ can reach every other vertex $j \in V(G)$ in at most k hops. As every layer in route tree of vertex i is continuous. Hence all n vertices will appear in k layer for the first time. i.e.

$$d^{k-1} < n \leq d^k . \tag{7}$$

From the left side of equation (7)

$$k < (\log_d n) + 1 . \tag{8}$$

From the right side of equation (7)

$$\log_d n \leq k . \tag{9}$$

Combining equation (8) with equation (9), we have that

$$\log_d n \leq k < (\log_d n) + 1 . \tag{10}$$

So, $k = \lceil \log_d n \rceil$

We have proved the maximum distance from one vertex to reach every other vertex is $\lceil \log_d n \rceil$, that is to say, the diameter of the topology graph is $\lceil \log_d n \rceil$. This proves the topology graph that meets n>0, d>1 and $k = \lceil \log_d n \rceil$ existing. Consequently, the set $\omega(n, d, k)$ is nonempty.   ■

Some classical algorithms present the degree $O(\log n)$ and the diameter $O(\log n)$ [5][6], but we have proved the diameter of diagraph which constructed using above method presents $O(\lceil \log_d n \rceil)$. And this method is very simply and feasible.

5 d-partition Routing Algorithm

Based on the above topology construction method, we design the following heuristic route algorithm which is called d-partition routing algorithm. Through dividing and classifying the target vertex continued, the vertices transmit the package to the target vertex along with the right path gradually. Then, how to a source vertex w_0 route a package to target vertex j? This algorithm processes as following.

(1) Let $x=\lceil \log_d n \rceil$. The neighbor vertices of the vertex w_k are

$$w_{k+1}=d*w_k+ s + t \ (\text{mod } n) \ (1 \le s \le d, t \in [0,n-1]) . \tag{11}$$

The source vertex computes the equation (11) x times iterative ($s=1$, w_0 is source vertex). We can obtain w_x and write out a sequence with w_x be the head number. The length of the sequence is d^x and difference is 1. Every number of the sequence is modeled by n. In this way we can obtain the sequence denoted by 'a'.

(2) The vertex w_0 divides the sequence 'a' into d parts same. We can obtain sub-sequences a_1, a_2, ..., a_d; We denote the neighbor vertices of w_0 by v_1, v_2,..., v_d according to their size. Then we confirm the position of vertex j based on the vertex attach algorithm. The vertex w_0 transmits the package P to the neighbor vertex v_i if the target vertex j belongs to a_i ($1 \le i \le d$). If the target vertex j belongs to many sub-sequences simultaneity, the vertex w_0 selects a sub-sequence a_k ($1 \le k \le d$) random and transmits the package P to the neighbor vertices v_k whose suffix is corresponding.

(3) Using the same way, the vertex which receive P operates the sub-sequence according to step (2). The vertex operates iterative until the neighbor vertex of one vertex is vertex j and transmits P to target vertex j.

We present target vertex attach algorithm following.

Let the head number of a_i be p, and the trial number of a_i is q. Let h be the length of sequence 'a'. Number h equals d^{x-k} after k times operations. thus, $q=p+(h/d-1)$

(1) while $p > q$: if $j \ge p$ or $j \le q$, then $j \in a_i$

(2) while $p < q$: if $p \le j \le q$, then $j \in a_i$

That is to say, the target vertex j belongs to sub-sequence a_i at the above two situations ($1 \le i \le d$).

Let us illustrate the route algorithm. We construct the topology graph using the periodic return method with $d=2$, $n=14$, $t=2$. The diameter of graph is 4. Every vertex need to compute its neighbor vertices. Assume vertex 4 wants to send a package P to vertex 5. It routes the package P as follows.

At first the vertex 4 computes the equation (11) (where $d=2$, $s=1$, $t=2$, $n=14$, $w_0=4$) 4 times iterative, and it gains the w_4 is 11. Then we write out the arithmetic progression whose length is 16 and 11 is the head number. We model every number by 14. Finally, we can obtain the sequence 'a'.

11 12 13 0 1 2 3 4 5 6 7 8 9 10 11 12

(1) The vertex 4 divides up the sequence 'a' symmetry.

11 12 13 0 1 2 3 4 ⦙ 5 6 7 8 9 10 11 12

The vertex 4 finds the target vertex 5 belonging to the back half of 'a'. So, the vertex 4 sends the package P to its neighbor vertex 12.

(2) The vertex 12 divides up the back half of sequence 'a' symmetry.

11 12 13 0 1 2 3 4 ┊ 5 6 7 8 ┊ 9 10 11 12

Then the vertex 12 finds the target vertex 5 belonging to the front half of sequence 'a'. Hence the vertex 12 sends the package P to its neighbor vertex 13.

(3) The vertex 13 divides up the front half of received sequence symmetry.

11 12 13 0 1 2 3 4 ┊ 5 6 ┊ 7 8 ┊ 9 10 11 12

Then the vertex 13 finds the target vertex 5 belonging to the front half of received sequence. Hence the vertex 13 sends the package P to its neighbor vertex 1.

The vertex 1 finds its neighbor vertex just is 5 when it receives the package P, thus, the whole transmitting process ends until it sends package P to vertex 5. The whole transmitting path is $4 \rightarrow 12 \rightarrow 13 \rightarrow 1 \rightarrow 5$.

6 Complexity

Let us appraise the complexity of this route algorithm.

(1) The source vertex computes the equation (11) x times ($s=1$, w_0).

Let $x= \lceil \log_d n \rceil$, we find w_x, the computation cost is $\lceil \log_d n \rceil$. We focus on the computation cost of multiplication and division and ignore addition. The model operation is division and finding remainder in fact. Consequently, once operation of the similar residue formula needs once multiplication and once division, and we need $\lceil \log_d n \rceil$ times multiplication and $\lceil \log_d n \rceil$ times division in this step in all.

(2) We write out sequence 'a' with w_x be head number, whose length is d^x and difference is 1. We only need to write out each number differ with 1 and judge whether or not it equals n-1 until all d^x numbers appear. The next number will change be 0 when it equals n-1. We need $\lceil \log_d n \rceil$ times multiplication of finding d^x.

(3) The vertex w_0 divides sequence 'a' into d parts equally and finds a sub-sequence which j belongs to, then the vertex w_0 transmits the package P to the neighbor vertex corresponding. So, we need once division and d times add operations.

(4) The latter vertices who receive the package P repeat the above d-partition operation, and transmit the package P to that neighbor vertex corresponding.

(5) This d-partition operation need to be done $\lceil \log_d n \rceil$ times in all.

The whole computation cost is $\lceil \log_d n \rceil$ times similar residue formula operations and $\lceil \log_d n \rceil$ times d-partition operations. We need $2 \times \lceil \log_d n \rceil$ times multiplication and $2 \times \lceil \log_d n \rceil$ times division altogether, for instance, if n=1000000, d=10, we need 24 times multiplication only. So, the complexity of this algorithm is $O(\lceil \log_d n \rceil)$.

We compare the d-partition routing algorithm with other algorithms. Chord maps keys onto vertices. In an N-vertices network, each vertex maintains routing information for about $O(\log_2 N)$ other vertices, and resolves all lookups via $O(\log_2 N)$ messages to other vertices. CAN uses a d-dimensional Cartesian coordinate space to implement a distributed hash table that maps keys onto values. Each vertex maintains $O(d)$ state, and the lookup cost is $O(dN^{1/d})$. Thus, in contrast to Chord and CAN, the computation cost of d-partition routing algorithm is $O(\lceil \log_d n \rceil)$ only. It is clear that the d-partition routing algorithm have not only smaller diameter but also lower complexity than others.

Table 1. Comparison of algorithms

Algorithm	Degree	Diameter	Complexity
d-partition	d	$\lceil \log_d n \rceil$	$O(\log_d n)$
Chord	$\lceil \log_2 n \rceil$	$\lceil \log_2 n \rceil$	$O(\log_2 N)$
Pastry	$(b-1)\log_b n$	$\log_b n$	$O(\log_b n)$
CAN	2d	$1/2dN^{1/d}$	$O(\log_e n)$

7 Conclusions and Future Work

In the present paper, we study the problem of the diameter of network with degree given based on graph-theoretical properties. Then, we construct an optimal diameter network. Additionally, we provide the d-partition routing algorithm whose complexity is $O(\lceil \log_d n \rceil)$.Compared to other algorithms, our algorithm not only greatly improves the speed of transmitting package, but also significantly reduces complexity. At the present time, we have finished the P2P worm defense system based on this algorithm.

Based on our experience with the algorithm mentioned above, we would like to improve upon the design in the following areas. The key point of our research will be failure recovery. That is to say, how to maintain the stabilization of P2P network after a vertex failure? Furthermore, the average delay is another mainly parameter to study. The meaning of studying the average delay is very important.

References

1. Rebecca Braynard, Dejan Kostic, Adolfo Rodriguez: Opus: an Overlay Peer Utility Service. 5th International Conference on Open Architectures and Network Programming (2002)
2. Andersen, D. G.: Resilient Overlay Networks. Master's thesis, Massachusetts Institute of Technology, (2001)
3. I. Stoica, R. Morris, D. Karger, M. F. Kaashoek: Chord: A scalable peer-to-peer lookup service for internet applications. SIGCOMM, San Diego, CA, (2001) 149-160
4. B. Y. Zhao, J. D. Kubiatowicz: Tapestry: An infrastructure for fault-tolerant wide area location and routing. Univ. California,Berkeley, CA, Tech. Rep. CSD-01-1141, (2001)
5. A.A. Schoone, H.L. Bodlaender, J. van Leeuwen: Diameter Increase Caused by Edge Deletion. Journal of Graph Theory 11, (1987) 409-427
6. A. Rucinski and N. C. Wormald: Random graph processes with degree restrictions. Combin. Probab Comput. 1, (1992) 169–180
7. P. Erdos, A. Gyarfas, M. Ruszinko: How to decrease the diameter of triangle-free graphs. Combinatorial, 18, (1998) 493-501
8. Mirka Miller, Ivan Fris: Minimum Diameter of Diregular Digraphs of Degree 2. Computer Journal, Volume 31, Issue 1, (1988) 71-75
9. W.G.Bridges and S.Toueg: On the impossibility of directed Moore graphs. J.Combinatorial Theory, Series B 29, no.3, (1980) 339-341
10. P. Erdos and A. Renyi: On random graphs I. Math. Debrecen 6, (1959) 290–297
11. Bondy, J.A and Murty,U.S.R.: Graphs Theory with Applications. Macmillan, (1976)

Decoupling Service and Feedback Trust in a Peer-to-Peer Reputation System

Gayatri Swamynathan, Ben Y. Zhao, and Kevin C. Almeroth

Department of Computer Science, UC Santa Barbara
{gayatri, ravenben, almeroth}@cs.ucsb.edu

Abstract. Reputation systems help peers decide whom to trust before undertaking a transaction. Conventional approaches to reputation-based trust modeling assume that peers reputed to provide trustworthy *service* are also likely to provide trustworthy *feedback*. By basing the credibility of a peer's feedback on its reputation as a transactor, these models become vulnerable to malicious nodes that provide good service to badmouth targeted nodes. We propose to decouple a peer's reputation as a *service provider* from its reputation as a *service recommender*, making the reputation more robust to malicious peers. We show via simulations that a decoupled approach greatly enhances the accuracy of reputations generated, resulting in fewer malicious transactions, false positives, and false negatives.

1 Introduction

The explosive growth in the Internet in the last decade has resulted in an increase in the use and popularity of online peer-to-peer (P2P) communities. P2P file sharing communities like Gnutella [9] involve millions of users who interact daily to transfer files among each other free of cost. The success of this type of a P2P community relies on cooperation amongst all the peers in the community. However, peers are anonymous and can act in their self-interests. This open and anonymous nature makes the network difficult to police and vulnerable to a variety of attacks.

A number of attacks can interfere with the operation of a P2P system. One common attack is the "whitewashing attack" where a free-riding node repeatedly joins the network under a new identity in order to avoid the penalties imposed on free-riders [8]. A more serious type of attack is when malicious peers exploit file sharing networks to distribute viruses and Trojan horses. The *VBS.Gnutella* worm, for example, stores trojan executables in network nodes. *Mandragore*, a Gnutella worm, registers itself as an active peer in the network, and in response to intercepted queries, provides a renamed copy of itself for download [5]. Peers also need to detect inauthentic file attacks, in which corrupted or blank files are passed off as legitimate files. Hence, it is necessary for P2P communities to combat these threats by motivating cooperation and honest participation within their network. Reputation systems help address this need by establishing a trust mechanism that helps peers decide whom to trust before undertaking a transaction.

A number of reputation systems have been proposed or deployed in practice. While systems like eBay use a centralized approach [7], a number of decentralized reputation systems encourage cooperation and punish malicious behavior. These systems, within

G. Chen et al. (Eds.): ISPA Workshops 2005, LNCS 3759, pp. 82–90, 2005.

the bounds of their assumptions, demonstrate the ability to significantly reduce the number of malicious transactions in a P2P system [1,3,5,6,10,12].

A central challenge in building a reputation system is to make it robust to misleading or unfair feedback. Malicious peers can subvert the reputation system by assigning poor reputation ratings to honest peers and good ratings to other malicious peers. To cope with malicious feedback, most existing reputation systems incorporate into their trust model the notion of *correlated trust*: peers reputed to provide trustworthy service, in general, will likely provide trustworthy feedback. Consequently, in these models the credibility of a peer's *feedback* is weighed by its reputation as a *service provider*.

While useful as a simple defense against malicious ratings, the correlated trust assumption can easily fail or be manipulated. A peer providing honest service can be incentivized to give false feedback about other peers' service. Similarly, colluding malicious nodes can offer honest service for the express purpose of boosting their reputations so they can badmouth the peers they are attacking.

This paper offers three key contributions. First, we propose a peer-to-peer reputation system that increases robustness against fake and misleading feedback by decoupling service and feedback reputations. Second, we show via simulation how our reputation system drastically reduces the rate of malicious transactions in a P2P system. Finally, we compare our scheme against correlated trust models in existing reputation systems. Our simulations show that strategic peers can exploit correlated trust models to increase malicious transactions, false positives and false negatives in the system. Our decoupled reputation system significantly reduces all of these behaviors.

The remainder of the paper is organized as follows. Related work is discussed in Section 2. In Section 3, we discuss our decoupled trust model and present our reputation system. In Section 4, we present our simulation settings and performance evaluation. Finally, Section 5 concludes the paper with suggested future work.

2   Related Work

Reputation management involves several components, including trust modeling, data storage, communication and reputation safeguards. Most research efforts have focused on solving only specific reputation management issues such as reputation storage, communication or attack safeguards [5,6,12].

eBay, the largest person-to-person auction site, uses a reputation-based trust scheme where, after each transaction, buyers and sellers rate each other using the *Feedback Forum* [7]. Reputation profiles are designed to predict future performance and help users decide whom to transact with [13]. eBay, however, uses a central authority to manage all communication and coordination between peers, essentially eliminating much of the complexity present in decentralized systems.

Aberer and Despotovic propose a decentralized reputation system for P2P networks where data is stored on a P-Grid [1]. Their system assumes most network peers are honest, and reputations in the system are expressed as complaints. Though the method works well, it is not at all robust to dynamic peer personalities.

EigenTrust [10] is a reputation system for P2P networks that attempts to combat the spread of inauthentic files. Each peer is associated with a global trust value that reflects the experiences of all other peers in the network with the target peer. Peers use these trust values to choose who they download from, as a consequence, the community identifies and isolates malicious peers from the network. The limitation of EigenTrust is that it assumes the existence of pre-trusted peers in the network.

While the systems mentioned so far assume a correlation between service and feedback reputations, a few have actually developed separate metrics for evaluating *service* trust and *feedback* trust [2,14]. PeerTrust [14] is a reputation framework that includes an adaptive trust model. To decouple feedback trust from service trust, peers use a *personalized similarity measure* to more heavily weigh opinions of peers who have provided similar ratings for a common set of past partners. In a large P2P system, however, finding a statistically significant set of such past partners is likely to be difficult. As a consequence, peers will often have to make choices among a set of candidates for which there is no information.

CONFIDANT [2] attacks the problem of false ratings using a Bayesian approach in a mobile ad-hoc network. They distinguish between reputation, how well a node behaves in routing and trust, and how well it behaves in the reputation system. A node distributes only first-hand information to other nodes, and only accepts other first-hand information if those opinions are similar (within a threshold) to its own opinion. Compared to this system where a node's referral is interpreted subjectively per node, our proposal produces a system-wide referrer rating per node. Our proposal is also generalizable to any environment using a reputation system.

Previous trust models do not provide a general model for decoupling service trust and feedback trust. In this paper, we propose a reputation system in which each peer is associated with two trust values: one for its role as a service provider in the P2P network, and the other for its role as a service recommender in the reputation system.

3   The Trust Model

Our reputation system associates with each peer two sets of reputation ratings: an aggregated service rating (*s-rating*) and an aggregated feedback rating (*f-rating*). Additionally, the system maintains for each peer a list of peers that has rated it and its rating. Service ratings are normalized values ranging from -1.0 to 1.0 with 0 indicating a neutral rating. Feedback ratings are normalized values that range from 0 to 1.0 with 1.0 indicating a good rater. Initially, the s-rating is set to 0, and the f-rating is set to 1.0 for all peers.

Consider a peer, A, that queries for a file. In order to make a decision on which responding peer to transact with, A chooses the peer with the highest aggregated service rating. While this can result in an unbalanced load distribution in the network, a probabilistic approach can be employed to distribute load [10]. After finishing a transaction with a service provider, B, A provides to B either a rating of -1 (unsatisfactory) or 1 (satisfactory) depending on the outcome. This rating is weighed by *f-rating(A)*, *i.e.* the feedback rating of A. This implies that A needs to be well-reputed as a feedback provider in order for its opinions to have an effect on B's service reputation. That is, the feedback from those peers with higher feedback trust ratings will be weighed more than those with lower feedback ratings.

At the end of the transaction, A also needs to send feedback rating updates to all peers that had rated B earlier. If A received good (or bad) service from B, it provides a rating of 1 to all the peers that rated B as good (or bad) prior to the transaction. This rating is in turn weighed by A's feedback rating. In the case that the outcome of A's transaction with B did not match with a prior service rating, A assigns a feedback rating of 0 to the originator of the rating. This process is shown in Figure 1, where peer A interacts with B, updates B's service reputation, and updates the feedback ratings of C and D, who contributed to B's service reputation.

Consequently, the service trust value and feedback trust value of a peer, u, denoted by *s-rating(u)* and *f-rating(u)*, are defined as:

$$s\text{-}rating(u) = \alpha * s\text{-}rating(u) + \beta * (r_u * f\text{-}rating(i))$$

$$f\text{-}rating(u) = \tfrac{1}{n_u} * \sum_{i=1}^{n_u} f_u * f\text{-}rating(i)$$

where r_u indicates a service rating of -1 or 1; f_u is the feedback rating which can be 0 or 1 depending on malicious feedback or helpful feedback; n_u represents the total number of transactions that have made use of u's feedback; and α and β are normalized weight factors, between 0 and 1, used to exponentially decay reputation ratings.

Peers can exhibit dynamic personalities, *i.e.* they are honest at times and dishonest at others. For example, once a peer has established a good reputation in the network, it can abuse it. Also, honest peers can be subverted at any time and begin behaving badly. Hence, peer reputations must be representative of more recent behavior rather than old ratings. Our model follows previous models in exponentially decaying reputation to weigh recent feedback more heavily than older feedback. This allows reputations to become negative if a node becomes malicious, or recover if a formerly malicious node becomes honest. Furthermore, a dynamic system also allows honest nodes to recover from poor ratings given by malicious nodes.

In our model, we do not explicitly define how reputations and records of ratings are stored. The issue of reputation storage is orthogonal to our problem of decoupling reputation. Different storage models would not impact our reputation accuracy. In a self-storing model, peers can compute and maintain their own reputations, storing them along with ratings signed by raters. Another option is to store each peer's reputations away from the peer. For example, Eigentrust [10] and P-Grid [1] use distributed hash tables to determine where individual reputations are stored in the P2P system.

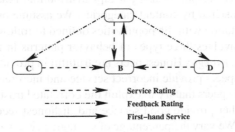

Fig. 1. Decoupling service and feedback reputation: after interacting with B, peer A modifies B's service reputation, but also modifies the feedback reputations of B's previous raters C and D

4   Performance Evaluation

We first evaluate the effectiveness of our method for limiting malicious behavior, then compare our approach to conventional correlated trust approach. Our results show not only a decrease in the number of malicious transactions, but also a significant reduction in the number of false positives and negatives reported.

To limit storage and communication overhead, we use a time window so that only records of a peer's transactions within the window are stored. Only the most recent service ratings are stored and feedback rating updates are only applied to those peers who rated a node recently. This reduces the communication costs associated with updating feedback ratings. The storage and communication costs of our reputation system are reasonable and justified given its significant benefits.

4.1   Simulation Environment

We implement our simulations in C using tools built on the Stanford Graph Base (SGB) [11]. The SGB platform represents a peer community and takes a peer model and topology graphs generated from the GT-ITM Topology Generator [4]. Table 1 summarizes the main parameters used and their default values.

Table 1. Simulation Parameters

	Parameter	Value Range	Nominal Value
Peer Model	Number of peers in the network	50-1000	500
	Percentage of honest peers	0-100	60
	Percentage of malicious peers	0-100	40
	Number of strategic peers	0-100	0
	Percentage of peers responding to a query request	0-20	10
Simulation	Number of query cycles in one experiment	50-1000	500
	Number of experiments over which results are averaged	5	5

Our network simulation proceeds in cycles. For simplicity, we assume that every peer in the network makes one transaction in each query cycle. We model the distribution of files and query responses using a Zipf distribution. Finally, P2P file sharing networks are often clustered by content categories. We assume only one content category in our implementation with file popularities defined to follow a Zipf distribution.

Our peer model involves three types of behavior patterns in the network, namely, *honest*, *dishonest* and *strategic*. Honest peers are truthful in providing service and feedback while dishonest peers provide incorrect service and incorrect feedback. Strategic peers are opportunistic peers that try to exploit the correlated trust model to spread bad information. They either provide good service and dishonest feedback or bad service and honest feedback. We vary the percentage of strategic peers in our experiments to illustrate the benefits of using our approach in scenarios where honest peers could report dishonest feedback about others, and vice versa.

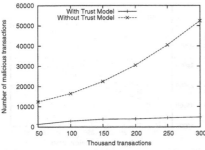

Fig. 2. Measuring malicious transactions in a network with and without our reputation model (40% nodes are malicious)

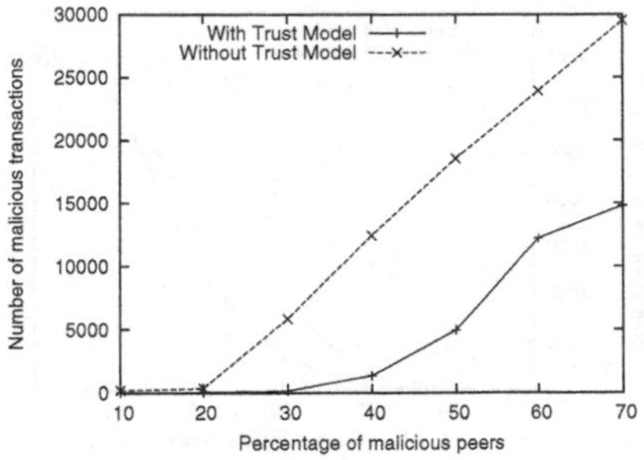

Fig. 3. Measuring malicious transactions in a network with and without our reputation model (Number of transactions is 50,000)

Our first set of experiments evaluates the effectiveness of our reputation system at detecting malicious behavior compared to conventional correlated trust. Each result presented is an average of five randomized runs, and the standard deviation is less than 2%.

4.2 Effectiveness Against Malicious Behavior

We set the number of malicious peers to 40% in a network of 500 peers. On the x-axis, the number of transactions ranges from 50,000 to 300,000. As seen in Figure 2, without a reputation system, an increase in the number of transactions results in a corresponding increase in the number of malicious transactions. However, our trust model results in a significant reduction in the number of bad transactions in the system. After about 100,000 transactions, the number of malicious transactions is close to constant.

Figure 3 shows results for a similar experiment, but instead of varying the total number of transactions, varies the number of malicious peers in the network. We perform the test for 50,000 transactions over 500 peers, and vary the percentage of malicious peers from 10% to 70%. As seen in the figure, the number of malicious transactions is substantially lower when a trust model is employed. When a small percentage of network peers are malicious, they are easily detected and avoided, resulting in a very low number of malicious transactions. However, as malicious nodes become the majority ($> 50\%$) they begin to overwhelm honest nodes, resulting in a significant increase in malicious transactions. This result demonstrates the natural collusion between dishonest nodes that form a network majority.

4.3 Benefits of Decoupling Service and Feedback Trust

In our second set of experiments, we evaluate the benefits of our approach compared to the conventional approach of correlating service trust and feedback trust. In the correlated approach, ratings assigned to the service provider at the end of a transaction are weighed only by the service rating of the rater. That is, the feedback from those peers with higher service ratings will be weighed more than those with lower service ratings.

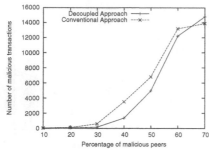

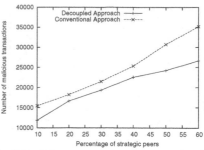

Fig. 4. Malicious transactions in networks with a conventional trust model and our decoupled model (50,000 transactions)

Fig. 5. Malicious transactions in networks with a conventional trust model and our decoupled model (40% malicious nodes, the percentage of strategic nodes varies)

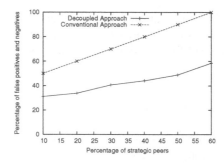

Fig. 6. False positives and negatives in a network with a conventional trust model and our decoupled model (40% malicious nodes, the percentage of strategic nodes varies)

We set the number of transactions to 50,000 for 500 peers. We first evaluate the number of malicious transactions using both approaches in a network with only static peer personalities. Honest peers always provide honest service and feedback, and dishonest peers always provide malicious service and feedback. We vary the percentage of malicious peers in the network from 10% to 70%. As seen in Figure 4, both approaches perform well in reducing the total number of malicious transactions, with our model generally being more accurate. When peers exhibit static personalities, the assumption that a honest peer will provide honest feedback holds true. Hence, correlated trust-based reputation models work as well as our decoupled model.

We introduce strategic behavior in our second experiment. Malicious peers may try to "rig the system" by providing honest service and feedback in some cases but dishonest feedback in others. Similarly, honest peers may, at times, give malicious feedback or service to some peers due to jealousy or competition. We use a network with 40% malicious peers who will provide both bad service and bad feedback. We vary the percentage of strategic peers from 10% to 60%, with the remaining nodes being totally honest. Half of the strategic peers provide good service as a service provider and malicious feedback as a service recommender. The other half provide bad service but honest feedback. Figure 5 demonstrates that our decoupled approach significantly outperforms the conventional approach in reducing the number of malicious transactions. While strategic peers take advantage of the correlated trust assumption in conventional systems to spread incorrect ratings, our decoupled model correctly identifies nodes as malicious service providers or sources of malicious feedback.

In our last experiment, we demonstrate how our decoupled trust model reduces the number of false positives and negatives reported in the P2P network. False positives and negatives represent the amount of false information fed into the reputation system. Such disinformation are the source of malicious transactions and are difficult to remove, once inserted. Again, we use a network with 40% malicious nodes, and vary the percentage of strategic peers in the network from 10% to 60%. As seen in Figure 6, our decoupled approach results in significantly fewer false positives and negatives than the conventional model. We note that the relatively high numbers of false reports are due to the high number (40%) of initial malicious nodes in these network setups.

5   Conclusions and Future Work

We have proposed a reputation-based trust model that improves accuracy by removing the assumption of correlation between service quality and feedback quality. The model decouples trust associated with each peer based on the role it plays, both as a service provider and as a service recommender. This decoupled approach incorporates reputations of both the service provider and the requester in the computation of trust values and, in this way, makes our model more robust to peer maliciousness. Our results report fewer false positives and negatives in the system as compared to the conventional approach of correlating the trust values. As ongoing work, we are building a more sophisticated trust model and working towards safeguarding our system from collusion.

References

1. ABERER, K., AND DESPOTOVIC, Z. Managing trust in a Peer-2-Peer information system. In *Proc. of CIKM* (Atlanta, GA, USA, Nov. 2001).
2. BUCHEGGER, S., AND BOUDEC, J. L. A robust reputation system for P2P and mobile ad-hoc networks. In *Proc. of the 2nd P2PEcon Workshop* (June 2004).
3. BURTON, K. Design of the openprivacy distributed reputation system, May 2002. http://www.peerfear.org/papers/openprivacy-reputation.pdf.
4. CALVERT, K. L., DOAR, M. B., AND ZEGURA, E. W. Modeling internet topology. *IEEE Communications Magazine 35*, 6 (June 1997), 160–163.
5. DAMIANI, E., DI VIMERCATI, D. C., PARABOSCHI, S., SAMARATI, P., AND VIOLANTE, F. A reputation-based approach for choosing reliable resources in peer-to-peer networks. In *Proc. of CCS* (Nov. 2002).
6. DEWAN, P., AND DASGUPTA, P. Pride: Peer-to-Peer reputation infrastructure for decentralized environments. In *Proc. of WWW* (May 2004).
7. EBAY. ebay home page, http://www.ebay.com, 2005.
8. FELDMAN, M., PAPADIMITRIOU, C., CHUANG, J., AND STOICA, I. Free-riding and whitewashing in peer-to-peer systems. In *Proc. of WEIS* (May 2004).
9. GNUTELLA. The gnutella protocol specification v0.4, 2001.
10. KAMVAR, S. D., SCHLOSSER, M. T., AND GARCIA-MOLINA, H. The eigentrust algorithm for reputation management in P2P networks. In *Proc. of WWW* (May 2003).

11. KNUTH, D. E. *The Stanford GraphBase: A Platform for Combinatorial Computing.* 1993.
12. OOI, B. C., LIAU, C. Y., AND TAN, K.-L. Managing trust in peer-to-peer systems using reputation-based techniques. In *Proc. of WAIM* (August 2003).
13. RESNICK, P., AND ZECKHAUSER, R. Trust among strangers in internet transactions: Empirical analysis of ebay's reputation system. *Advances in Applied Microeconomics 11* (Jan. 2001).
14. XIONG, L., AND LIU, L. Peertrust: Supporting reputation-based trust for peer-to-peer electronic communities. *IEEE Trans. on Knowledge and Data Engineering 16*, 7 (2004).

VTarget: An Improved Software Target Emulator for SANs

Hongcan Zhang, Jiwu Shu, Wei Xue, and Dingxing Wang

Tsinghua University, Beijing,China
zhanghc02@mails.tsinghua.edu.cn

Abstract. With the increasing of storage scale and complexity, the storage management for heterogeneous environments is becoming more and more important. This paper introduces an improved software target emulator integrated with storage virtualization management called VTarget, and some key technologies are explained in detail. The VTarget system can manage various heterogeneous storage resources and provides one virtualization interface for storage management. It is implemented in the storage network layer in the SAN and can support heterogeneous operation systems. The VTarget system also provides an access control mechanism to enhance device security and adapts multi metadata copy technology to improve reliability. We have implemented a prototype of VTarget system and the testing results showed that the storage virtualization management influences the I/O bandwidth less than 3.6% and less than 8% in latency, which only has a very slight effect on storage performance for the mass heterogeneous storage system management.

1 Introduction

The prevalence of e-business and multimedia applications has caused the capacity of data storage to increase rapidly, and accordingly the storage systems are rapidly expanding. As a new technology with features of high scalability, high performance and long distance connectivity, Storage Area Networks (SANs) currently play an important role in building large storage systems. In the construction of SAN systems, the technology of the software target emulator has a higher performance-cost ratio than that of all of the hardware. The software target emulator can be accessed as storage devices by the application servers in the SAN, which is relatively quite cheaper and more flexible. Recently some fibre target emulators and iSCSI target emulators have appeared, among which the SCSI Target Emulator developed by the University of New Hampshire [1] is widely used. Adapted with a different Front-End Target Driver (FETD), the SCSI Target Emulator can represent the storages it attaches to the application servers as different kinds of storage devices such as fibre devices, iSCSI devices, etc. But it can only represent the devices it has attached directly to the application servers, and lacks effective management of storage resources.

Increasing requirements of storage capacity also result in another problem that has become increasing more urgent: how to effectively manage storage resources. Storage virtualization management technology is applied to solve just

G. Chen et al. (Eds.): ISPA Workshops 2005, LNCS 3759, pp. 91–100, 2005.

this problem. It can manage various storage systems and provides a uniform storage resource view for users. It also provides functions of dynamic storage resource configuration, online backup, remote mirroring and so on. By striping one logical device across multiple physical disks, it achieves a higher I/O performance. Sistina's Logical Volume Manager (LVM[2]) is the most widely used storage virtualization technology, and it has become a part of the Linux OS kernel. The Enterprise Volume Management System (EVMS[3]]) provides virtualized storage management for enterprises, but can only be adapted to a certain kind of Operating System (OS) and it only runs in a single host environment. The SANtopia Volume Manager[4] is a storage virtualization system for the SAN environment, but it is dedicated to a certain file system, and is not compatible with multiple operating systems.

This paper introduces the VTarget system, which is a software target emulator integrated with storage virtualization management. It can provide a uniform storage view to heterogeneous platforms, and provides efficient management of storage resources, thus optimizing the storage resource utilization. The VTarget system can also control the access to virtual devices, and thus provides a certain degree of storage security.

2   Architectures

2.1   Hardware Architecture for Building an FC-SAN

As a software target emulator, VTarget can be connected directly into fibre networks or ethernet as a network storage device, which is shown by Figure 1. In the storage network, the Fibre HBAs on front servers work in an initiator mode, while those on VTargets work in a target mode. One or more FC-switches connect them. According to the requests from the front application servers, the VTarget system can create Virtual Devices (VD), which can be found and accessed by front servers, no matter which kind of OS is adopted (Linux, Solaris, Windows, etc.). Providing a uniform storage resource interface for heterogeneous platforms is an outstanding virtue of VTarget.

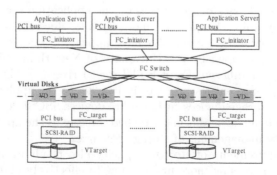

Fig. 1. Hardware architecture of FC-SAN Using VTarget

2.2 Software Architecture

As shown in Figure 2, the VTarget system is made up of two main modules: the SCSI Command Execute (SCE) Module and the Virtualization Module.

The SCSI Command Execute Module (SCE Module) is responsible for handling the IO requests from the FETD. In fact, the IO requests are called virtual IO requests, as they are aimed at virtual devices. They can not be implemented directly unless storage address remapping has been completed. The Address Mapping Sub-Module is responding for transforming one virtual IO request into one or more physical IO requests, which are the IO requests that can be implemented on physical devices.

The Virtualization Module is responsible for storage virtualization and access control. Storage virtualization includes physical storage device management, virtual storage device management and metadata management. The Physical Device Manager, Virtual Device Manager and Metadata Manager are designed for these functions respectively. The Storage Command Execute Module and Virtualization Module are connected by the Virtual Device's information structure, which will be introduced in section 3.1.

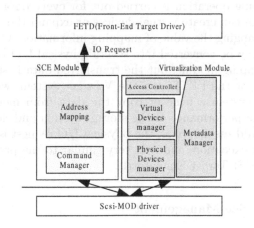

Fig. 2. Software architecture of VTarget

3   Key Technology

3.1   Address Mapping

When the SCE receives one IO request (or SCSI command) from the FETD, the type of this request is first tested. If it is one inquiry request, such as INQUIRY or READ CAPACITY, the SCE would return the virtualization information for this virtual device. If the request is a read/write command, the SCE should get the relevant physical addresses through the address mapping module first. One request from FETD may need read/write multiple physical data blocks, and

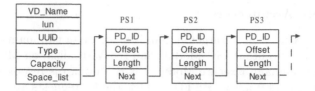

Fig. 3. Data structure of virtual device

VTarget system would transform the request into several physical I/O requests. Figure 3 shows the data structure of the virtual device.

As shown in Figure 3, the Physical Segment (PS) is one continuous storage space on a specified physical device. The address mapping module changes the logical address <lun,offset,length>to a physical operation address <PD_ID, offset,length>through the data structure of the virtual device. It finds the corresponding VD by seeking the lun-VD table and then determines the first PS according to the logical offset, and the length is used to determine the number of physical operations and the data size.

The I/O mapping operation is carried out for every data I/O request, and the VTarget system can create virtual devices or expand the virtual device size dynamically by changing the value of mapping information. One virtual request from the FETD may be converted into several physical I/O requests according to the address mapping module, but the transferred data is stored in one common storage pool for the FETD and the VTarget system, which ensures that the virtualization system can never copy the data from memory to memory, which improves the performance of the storage system and decreases the CPU utilization. After address mapping, the physical I/O request is sent to the command manager for execution, and it is very similar to the process of command execution in the SCSI Target Emulator[1].

3.2   Storage Device Management

Facilitating storage management is the main goal of storage virtualization. The VTarget system eliminates the need for the front server to know about the end devices' details, focusing instead on just one uniform storage pool. Further, the VTarget system has a set of storage device management tools, which provides the users great convenience for users. In detail, the physical device manager and virtual device manager are responsible for the management of physical devices and virtual devices respectively.

The physical device manager scans all of the physical devices, and records them into a storage pool. When a storage device is found, it sets up a physical device structure and identifies the device with a 64-bit Universal Unique Identifier (UUID), through which the system can find the device after being rebooted or physical moved. The physical device manager divides the capacity of the storage device into fixed-size blocks (64K for default) and adds the blocks into the storage pool, which is the platform for the management of all of the virtual devices. By this means, the details of physical devices such as capacity, rotation speed and so on are not taken into account; thus the virtualization function is free from having to monitor each device.

The virtual devices manager is one of the key parts of the VTarget system. It implements some key functions such as creating/deleting/expanding virtual devices and data snapshot/mirroring. It controls the algorithm for converting from logical addresses to physical addresses, so it can create different types of virtual devices through different address mapping algorithms. These virtual device types include linear, striped, mirror and snapshot. From figure 3,we know that the storage space of VD is a table of PS. As one PS in the table represents one continuous storage space whose capacity is determined by the user freely,the virtual device manager can manage huge storage spaces. And when a new PS is added into this table, the virtual device's size is expanded. Also the virtual device manager can decrease the virtual device capacity easily. With this technology, the VTarget system can dynamically manage the storage resources very well.

3.3   Access Control

Large data centers often need tens of thousands of virtual devices. If there is no efficient access control management of the devices, the application servers will have to receive too much unnecessary information about the network storage, and the security of data access can not be guaranteed. For example, without access control, one virtual device can be seen by two or more application servers. Therefore, these application servers may read from or write to the virtual device simultaneously. This probably would cause a conflict of data access and result in data loss. The access control function we implemented was to make one application server able to only read or write on the virtual devices with authority, and at the same time, each virtual device can only be seen by the servers that have authority to operate it. Details of the implementation of this system can be described as follows:

The system holds an access authority table. Every entry of this table contains a virtual device, an access bitmap and a privilege bitmap. The access bitmap and privilege bitmap have the same length and every bit represents the authority of an application server. Together they hold the access control information of the corresponding devices. A possible access authority table is shown in Table 1.

Table 1. Access authority information of virtual device

VD NUMBER	ACCESS BITMAP	PRIVILEGE BITMAP
VD 0	0001	0001
VD 1	0010	0010
VD 2	0110	0100
....		
VD n	0000	0000

Table 2. Access mode

Access bit	Privilege bit	Access Mode
0	0	ACCESS DENY
1	0	READ ONLY
1	1	READ/WRITE

Every bit in the Access Bitmap represents whether a certain application server can access that virtual device or not. The No. 0 bit represents whether the No. 1 server can access it or not, the No.1 bit represents where the No. 2 server can access it or not, and so on. Every bit in the Privilege Bitmap represents the operating authority of that particular application server. The combination of this pair of bitmaps can guarantee each server's access control information. The details of the access authority can be explained in Table 2.

Consequently, the access information of the virtual device in Table 1 is explained as follows: server 1 is permitted to read from and write to VD 0; server 2 is permitted to read from and write to VD 1; server 3 is permitted to read from and write to VD 2; server 2 is only permitted to read from VD 2; etc.

Every time when an application server loads the initiator-mode fibre driver, it must check the VTarget's Access Authority table to find which virtual devices are "visible" (whose corresponding access bit is 1), and then add the "visible" virtual devices to the server's SCSI device list. The application server then has the permission to perform IO operations on these virtual devices, but it has to consult the Access Authority table again to check if the device has permission for read or write requests. We can improve the security of the device access through this control mechanism, and thereby guarantee the data security of application servers.

3.4   Metadata Management

Metadata management is another important component of the virtualization module. The metadata of the VTarget system is the information of physical devices, virtual devices, access control and other related items. A rational metadata management method must ensure recovery of the previous system configuration when the system is reloaded. For this reason, the VTarget system provides a reentrant feature; the system's reliability is improved by providing multiple metadata copies, and therefore the system could be recovered even if some of the metadata copies are invalid. In addition, the metadata of this system is capable of checking the configuration and choosing the appropriate part of the metadata to recover, so the system has very high availability.

At present, the VTarget system saves the metadata to two SCSI disks, and both disks are called metadata disks. We named one of the double disks the primary metadata disk, and the other the secondary metadata disk. Each metadata disk uses its first 20M of space to save metadata. The two copies serve as backup copies of each other. Once the metadata is changed, the system must update both metadata disks. There is a special tag in the metadata information, which indicates whether the metadata has been written to the disk completely or not. Every time metadata is updated, this special tag of the primary metadata disk will be reset to zero first, and then the metadata update begins. After accomplishing the update, the tag will be set to WRITE_COMPLETE. Updating of the secondary metadata disk is implemented in the same way.

4   Performance Testing of VTarget

4.1   IO Performance

Compared with the SCSI Target Emulator, the VTarget system has more advantages in the management of storage resources and data security because of the virtualization function. But this is not implemented at the cost of losing the target's performance. We used Iometer at the application servers for testing, and measured the total bandwidth and average response time of multiple network disks in two cases: using VTarget as the target and using SCSI Target Emulator as the target.

The IO requests are totally sequential, and their sizes are all 128K. The proportion of the read and write operation is 80% and 20% respectively. (This proportion matches the common data stream's read-write feature.) We used the VTarget's virtualization function to create a virtual device on each physical device, and measured the different quantities of virtual devices' total bandwidth and average response time. We then compared VTarget system with the SCSI Target Emulator under the same test environment. The comparison of the total bandwidth and average response time are shown respectively in Figure 4-a and Figure 4-b.

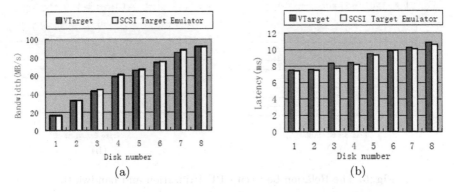

Fig. 4. IO Performance of VTarget and SCSI Target Emulator

The comparison of the performance testing results show that the total bandwidth of VTarget is less than that of the SCSI Target Emulator, but this proportion does not exceed 3.6%; the average response time is more but does not exceed 8%. This means the complex virtualization functions of VTarget did not cause too much extra cost. This is because the main latency of IO operations, which is at the millisecond level, happens on the read-write operation to the disks. The latency of address mapping on the data path is microsecond level. This can be ignored relative to the read-write latency, so the introduction of virtualization functions does not affect the IO performance very much.

4.2   CPU Utilizations

The performance test in section 4.1 considered the whole VTarget system as multiple virtual devices. It measured the access bandwidth and average latency that the system applies. This is VTarget's external appearance. Because an address mapping process was added in the IO accessing path, there would be some influences on the system itself. The most representational influence must be on CPU utilization. In this section,we tested the relationship between the read-write bandwidth and CPU utilization of the VTarget system and the SCSI Target Emulator system.

These relationships are shown in Figure 5-a and Figure 5-b. The corresponding parameters of Iometer were both 100% sequential requests, and blocks' size was 128K. What was different was the read-bandwidth test using 100% read requests and the write-bandwidth test using 100% write requests. The reason we used complete read or complete write requests to test the relationship between total bandwidth and CPU utilization is because write requests are more complicated than read requests in the VTarget system. For write requests, the VTarget system must be interrupted twice to accept commands and data separately. But for read requests, only one interruption for commands is necessary.

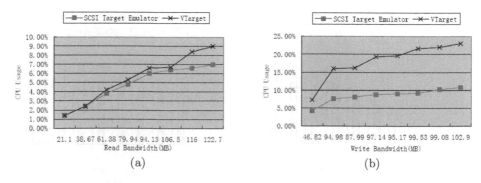

Fig. 5. The Relation between CPU Utilization and bandwidth

From the figures we can see that in both the VTarget system and SCSI Target Emulator, the increase of read/write bandwidth will certainly cause the increase of CPU utilization. But within the same changing range, the increase of CPU utilization of the VTarget system is more than that of SCSI Target

Emulator. This means the VTarget system definitely extends the process path of IO requests, and the load of the system grows. The VTarget prototype system reached about 120MB read bandwidth or 100MB write bandwidth in this study. This was limited by the 160MB SCSI bus bandwidth of the Ultra 160. Even when we reached these bandwidths, the CPU utilization was only less than 25%, leaving a good amount of computation resources free to be uses. Even if the computation resources happen to not be enough, this can be managed by increasing the computation resources or updating the hardware system.

5   Summary and Future Work

The VTarget prototype system we implemented is based on the UNH's SCSI Target Emulator. We added several modules like address mapping, storage device management, access control, and metadata management, so that the VTarget system is provided with virtualization storage management functions. When performing IO requests, the information of virtual devices and storage organization is queried first through the address mapping process. This causes the application servers to be aware of the changing of virtual devices. On the other hand, virtual devices are organized by the table mode, so the virtual storage spaces can be managed conveniently. The combination of these two gives the VTarget system the ability to dynamically create virtual devices and dynamically extend capacity, so application servers can use the storage more conveniently. The VTarget System thus satisfies the demand for dynamic configuration in e-business applications. The VTarget system applies device-level access control. Therefore, application servers only have the authority to perform IO operations on the virtual devices which are permitted. The security of application data is increased. In addition, the VTarget system is capable of checking the configurations of metadata, so it can be recovered selectively. Better availability is guaranteed in this way. The performance testing of the VTarget system showed that the additional virtual functions in VTarget do not impact the target's IO performance much. It only consumes a small amount of the CPU resources of the target itself.

The virtualization function in our VTarget prototype system only addresses the problem of the capacity of the server. Other dimensions are not considered (such as bandwidth, latency), and the system cannot adapt to sudden changes of the application servers' storage requirement. To achieve this goal we must do some job scheduling on the IO requests which the VTarget system is dealing with. We will monitor the features of all IO requests and schedule the IO requests rationally, according to the demand of storage requirements. In short, our next goal is to provide storage services with performance guarantees.

Acknowledgement

The work described in this paper was supported by the National High-Tech Program Plan of China under Grant No. 2004AA111120. We greatly appreciate our teachers' meaningful advice. We also are grateful to our colleagues including Bigang Li, Di Wang, Fei Mu and Junfei Wang for their kind help.

References

1. Ashish Palekar. Design and Implementation of A Linux SCSI Target for Storage Area Networks. Proceedings of the 5th Annual Linux Showcase & Conference, 2001
2. David C. Teigland, Heinz Mauelshagen. Volume Managers in Linux. Sistina Software,Inc. http://www.sistina.com, 2001
3. Steven Pratt. EVMS:A Common Framework for Volume Management. Linux Technology Center, IBM Corp., http://evms.sf.net
4. Chang-Soo Kim, Gyoung-Bae Kim,Bum-Joo Shin. Volume Management in SAN Environment. ICPADS 2001, pages 500-508. 1997
5. SCSI Primary Commands - 3 (SPC-3), SCSI Block Commands - 2 (SBC-2), Working Drafts. http://www.t10.org, 2004
6. C.R.Lumb, A. Merchant, and G. A. Alvarez. Fa?ade: Virtual storage devices with performance guarantees. In Proceedings of the 2nd USENIX conference on File and Storage technologies, pages 131-144, San Francisco, CA, April 2003.
7. StoreAge Networking Technologies Ltd. High-Performance Storage Virtualization Architecture. http://www.store-age.com, 2001
8. Intel Corp. "Intel iSCSI project". http://sourceforge.net/projects/intel-iscsi,2001
9. Li Bigang, Shu Jiwu, Zheng Weimin. Design and Optimization of an iSCSI system, .Jin, Y Pan, N. Xiao and J. Sun (Eds.), GCC'2004 Workshop on Storage Grid and Technologies, LNCS 3252, pages 262-269, 2004.
10. Shu Jiwu, Yao Jun, Fu Changdong, Zheng Weimin. A Highly Efficient FC-SAN Based on Load Stream. The Fifth International Workshop on Advanced Parallel Processing Technologies(APPT2003), Xiamen, China, September2003, LNCS 2834, pages 31-40,2003
11. John Wilkes. Traveling to Rome: QoS specifications for automated storage system management. In Proceedings of the International Workshop on Quality of Service (IWQoS), pages 75-91, June 2001
12. Lan Huang, Gang Peng, and Tzi-cker Chiueh. Multi-Dimensional Storage Virtualization. In Proceedings of the joint international conference on Measurement and modeling of computer systems, Pages 14 -24, New York, NY, USA, 2004. ACM Press.

Design and Implementation of an Efficient Multipath for a SAN Environment

Jun Luo, Ji-wu Shu, and Wei Xue

Tsinghua University, Beijing, China
luojun03@mails.tsinghua.edu.cn

Abstract. Multipath provides multiple paths between application Servers and storage devices. Multipath can overcome single point of failure, and improve a system's reliability and availability. This paper presents a multi-layer Multipath, and describes the design and implementation of a Multipath system in a storage area network (SAN). For an application server, we implemented Multipath in the volume management layer. For a storage server, we implemented Multipath in the SCSI Middle Level layer. This system can make the most use of the storage server's characteristics to decrease the time of failure discovery and location, and it is independent of lower SCSI cards and storage devices, so it has good compatibility. This paper also proposes methods for choosing paths, automatically recovering paths and balancing the load. We tested the read performance and the average response time, and the results showed that with the load balanced, the read performance improves 17.9% on average, and the average response time decreases 15.2% on average.

1   Introduction

In the SAN environment, data in a storage device can be protected by RAID technology, but RAID cannot increase the reliability of data transfers between the application server and the storage device. If one SCSI card or something in the data transfer path fails, the application server cannot access the storage device. Multipath technology can provide multi-paths between application servers and storage devices. Multipath can ensure a storage device's availability if one path has failed. Multipath is an important part of SAN disaster recoverability. And load balance technology in Multipath can improve system performance.

At present Multipath is commonly implemented on the application server, such as EMC's Powerpath [1] and HP's Securepath [2]. And Multipath is also implemented in the storage device itself. This is often based on a special storage device, and is integrated into the storage device controller. When one port or controller fails, the I/O can access the device through another port or controller. According to the device's different response time to the I/O through different ports, storage devices can be grouped into three behavior models [3]. Holding the device, the server should set a path-choosing policy according to the device's behavior model to achieve the best performance.

G. Chen et al. (Eds.): ISPA Workshops 2005, LNCS 3759, pp. 101–110, 2005.

For the application server Multipath, the path-choosing policy is set on the application server. But in SAN environments, different application servers can connect to different behavior model devices, and application servers with the same devices may even have different device orders. So the administrator should set the server's path-choosing policy independently. Management is very complicated and it may unnecessarily reduce the performance. Load balance in the application server Multipath is only based on the local load, and does not take into account the status of other servers. So it is hard for the storage device to achieve real load balance.

Multipath can be implemented at different levels in an operating system's I/O path. Usually Multipath can be implemented on three levels: volume management, SCSI level and SCSI card driver level. Volume management includes LVM [4] [5], EVMS [6] and MD. It can configure multiple devices exposed by operating system, which point to the same storage device, to form multiple paths for failover. Multipath at this level is very mature and easy to run, but it cannot shield the bottom devices and applications can directly access the bottom devices.

Multipath can also be implemented at the SCSI level. This level is closer to the bottom devices and can shield them from applications. For example, IBM's Michael Anderson and others have implemented a Mid Level Multipath in Linux-2.5+ kernel [3]. This was limited to a special operating system edition. Its compatibility was bad.

The implementation at the SCSI card driver level binds the same two or more cards to form a Multipath. This can also shield devices from the upper level. Once a path fails, the card driver will directly send commands through other paths. Adaptec's Qlogic 5.x edition [7] and Emulex's MultiPulse [8] both implement Multipath at the card driver level. And many companies' Multipath software is based on the card driver's Multipath function as designed by Adaptec or Emulex, for example EMC's Powerpath software is based on Emulex's MultiPulse. This method is based on a special SCSI card, and can only be used for the same edition card of the same company. It does not have good compatibility.

In this paper, we describe the design and implementation of a multiple layers Multipath for the Tsinghua Mass Storage Network System (TH-MSNS) [9]. The TH-MSNS has an additional storage server between Fabric and the storage device. In the storage server, the TH-MSNS has software to simulate a SCSI TARGET Driver. We added a Multipath layer on the storage server to implement Multipath for the storage device. According to the storage server's special software architecture, we implemented the Multipath layer between the SCSI Target Middle Level and the operating system's SCSI Mid Level. It is compatible with different Linux kernels, and is independent of the lower SCSI cards and storage devices. Storage devices are directly connected to the storage server, so the storage server can set the most suitable path-choosing policy for storage devices with different behavior models. And this method can also shield storage devices' characteristics from the application server, so the application server can set path-choosing policy according to the Fabric status. As for the application server we implemented Multipath at the volume management layer. This paper also proposes methods for choosing paths, automatically recovering paths and balancing loads.

In this paper, we first introduce the TH-MSNS and its Multipath architecture. Secondly, we describe the details of the design and implementation of the storage server Multipath. Finally, we discuss the testing results, which show that our storage server Multipath does significantly improve read performance and reduce the average response time in the conditions of varied block sizes.

2   The Architecture of Multipath for the TH-MSNS

2.1   The Brief Introduction of the TH-MSNS

The TH-MSNS is an implementation of a FC-SAN [10]. It adds a general-purpose server as a storage server between Fabric and the storage device to provide storage services. The storage server is connected to Fabric through the FC-HBA card. Ordinary storage devices such as SCSI Disk Array, SATA Disk Array, and FC storage devices can be directly connected to the storage server. In the storage server, the TH-MSNS has Front End Target Driver (FETD) and SCSI Target Middle Layer (STML) software modules to simulate the SCSI TARGET [11] [12]. So the application server can use any kind of storage device connected to the storage server as a FC storage device. The TH-MSNS is low cost, highly scalable and can achieve considerably high performance [9]. Figure 1 shows the I/O path of the TH-MSNS:

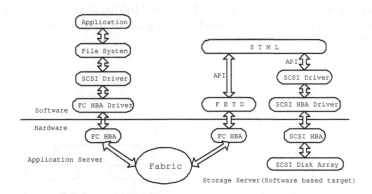

Fig. 1. The I/O path of the TH-MSNS

Applications send out I/O requests, and corresponding SCSI commands are formed through the local SCSI protocol stack. The FC-HBA card then encapsulates the SCSI commands and sends them to Fabric. On the storage server, the FC-HBA card receives FC Frames from Fabric, and then the FETD separates the SCSI command and data from the FC Frame and sends them to the STML.

When the STML receives the SCSI command and data from the FETD, it rebuilds the SCSI I/O request, and sends it to the local SCSI system. After the STML gets the command results from the local SCSI system, it will send them back to the FETD, and then to the application server through Fabric.

The FETD cooperates with the STML to directly map the storage device of the storage server to the application server. So the storage server and its storage device look just like the FC storage device in SAN.

2.2   The Architecture of Multipath

On the application server, we configured the devices from two or more FC-HBA cards to Multipath in the volume management layer. This can provide multiple paths from the application server to the storage device. But if Multipath is only implemented on the application server, the management will be complicated. And though an application server Multipath can discover and locate failures, there are many layers between the application server and the storage device, which may prolong the time it takes to discover and locate failure. Load balancing only on the application server does not take into account the load of other servers, and is not well suited to storage devices with different behavior models.

In order to reduce the time of failure discovery and location and provide whole load balance for all application servers, we implemented Multipath on the storage server. It provides multiple paths between the storage server and the storage device, and can shield these paths from the application server. And then the application server Multipath only takes into account the I/O path from the application server to the storage server. This reduces the complexity of the application server Multipath. The two Multipath layers are independent and complementary. Figure 2 shows the I/O path of Multipath designed for the TH-MSNS:

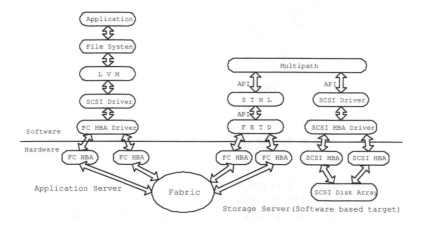

Fig. 2. The I/O path of Multipath for the TH-MSNS

As volume management Multipath has been thoroughly developed, this paper will mainly discuss the design and implementation of Multipath on the storage server.

3   Design and Implementation of Multipath

3.1   Design of Multipath

The FETD and STML are the main software modules that simulate the SCSI TARGET on the storage server. The FETD separates the SCSI command and data from the FC Frame, sends them to the STML, and sends back the command results returned by the STML to the application server through the FC-HBA card. The STML communicates with the local SCSI system to get device information, command results etc. The STML directly communicates with the local SCSI system, so it can fully control how to execute commands and return the results. We added a Multipath layer between the STML and the local SCSI system. Multipath gets device information from the local SCSI system, configures the same devices from different paths to form new virtual devices and returns virtual devices to the STML. The STML sends commands to Multipath instead of the local SCSI system, and then Multipath chooses the real device by a path-choosing policy, and sends the commands to it.

The STML reads SCSI devices from the local SCSI system's host list to form its device list, which is recorded in struct stml_device. Multipath adds multiple path struct to shield the same devices from different paths. Figure 3 shows the data structure of Multipath.

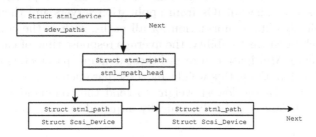

Fig. 3. The data structure of Multipath

Multipath defines struct stml_mpath to record all of the paths' information, such as the path-choosing policy. Each stml_path struct records path information. The scsi_device struct in the stml_path struct points to the real SCSI device. The same devices from different paths are linked one by one. The STML only maps stml_device instead of every SCSI device to the application server, so the application server does not see the multiple paths from the storage server to the storage device. When a command arrives, Multipath reads the path-choosing policy in the stml_mpath struct, selects one stml_path and sends the command to the real SCSI device recorded in stml_path.

Multipath information is written to a file. When Multipath module is loaded, it reads the file and fills the stml_device struct. And we can also dynamically set it by proc interface. Each stml_device records corresponding information such as the sequence, UUID, path-choosing policy etc. This can ensure that the information corresponding to the stml_device will not change after a system reboot and that the application server will see the same thing.

We implemented a Round Robin (RR) and Last Recent Used (LRU) path-choosing policy in Multipath. The RR policy means that paths will be rotated across all available paths on every request sent to the real SCSI device. The LRU policy means that every request will be sent through the last path used and other paths will be used only when the last path fails. The path-choosing policy can be dynamically changed through proc interface.

In the storage server, we can set suitable path-choosing policies for storage devices according to their different behavior models. So it is unnecessary to consider the storage device behavior model in the application server. In the application server, we can set an appropriate path-choosing policy according to the different services the applications provide and the status of Fabric.

In the shared storage environment, single application server Multipath cannot perform load balancing for all servers. The storage server Multipath can accomplish load balancing for all application servers. But the Round Robin policy cannot dynamically adjust command executive sequences. When we need different qualities of service for different application servers or when the lower SCSI card capability is different, the RR policy is not suitable. When the remote storage device is connected to the storage server through a network, the RR policy doses not reflect different network delays through different paths. The storage server Multipath handles all IOs from application servers and their results, so it can dynamically obtain information for all paths, such as the current load of each path, each SCSI card's ability, the average response time of each path, etc. The storage server Multipath can record these dynamic parameters in stml_path struct, and calculate the path's weight by these parameters. It can dynamically choose the path with the lowest weight to send the command through. This means the load balance can be dynamically adjusted for all application servers.

3.2   The Command Processing of Multipath

When it receives a SCSI command, the STML will judge its type. If it is a write command, the STML will allocate a data buffer and put the command into a waiting queue. When the data arrives, the STML fills in the command's data buffer, takes it out of the waiting queue and puts it into a dispatching queue. If it is a read command, the STML will directly put it into the dispatching queue. The dispatching thread takes the command out of the dispatching queue and sends it to Multipath. Multipath will select one path by the path-choosing policy and send the command to the real SCSI device.

The monitoring thread in Multipath will handle the command result. If the command fails, the monitoring thread first checks whether the status of that path is DEAD. If not, the monitoring thread will increase the error count of that path. The monitoring thread will rebuild the error command, set the command status as CMD_RETRY and put the command into a retry queue. The command in the retry queue has higher priority than that in the dispatching queue. The dispatching thread will take the command out of the retry queue and send to the SCSI device by another available path. If the command succeeds, the monitoring thread will return the processed information to the STML.

When the error count of the path reaches a predefined threshold, the monitoring thread will set the path status as DEAD and begin to check the path. If other devices of this path can be accessed successfully, it is not a path error but a disk error. Then the monitoring thread will mark the stml_device status as BAD and reset the path status as OPERATIONAL. And the monitoring thread will report the error information to the administrator. The whole error handling process is transparent to the application server.

In order to recover from errors automatically, the monitoring thread will periodically supervise the path. When a failure has been eliminated, the monitoring thread will find it in time and automatically set the stml_device status as NORMAL or the path status as OPERATIONAL. The dispatching thread will send SCSI commands by the path-choosing policy formerly defined. The error recovery process is also transparent to the application server.

3.3   About the UUID

Storage devices can show up multiple times through multiple paths. This may cause potential problems for applications. The UUID can hide the duplicate paths from applications and ensure that applications will access the same storage device through multiple paths. The UUID for each device must be unique. Some use one algorithm to produce unique serial number for each device. For example, LVM uses one function to assign a random number for each device as the UUID and needs to save this information in the device. But this information may not be accessed by another operating system.

SCSI devices commonly have the Vital Product Data (VPD) page information. The SCSI driver can get this information by the SCSI INQUIRY VPD page command. But some SCSI devices return no UUID, some return a UUID that is the same as the UUID on another SCSI device. Paper [3] adopts this method to get a device's UUID. When a UUID is not unique, it uses special prefix + vender + model + revision information as the device's UUID.

In this paper, we introduce a full user level scanning method. Through the proc interface by storage server Multipath, the administrator can scan all SCSI devices' VPD page information as a UUID. When a UUID is not unique, the administrator can set the SCSI device's UUID manually. And the administrator can save all the information for every SCSI device such as UUID, vender, model, host, and id in a file. After the storage server reboots, storage server Multipath will compare the newly acquired information with the saved information. If any difference exists, the administrator can handle it manually. So the device's UUID can remain unchanged. All application servers can get the device's UUID by the SCSI INQUIRY VPD page command. Storage server Multipath will capture this command and return the device's UUID. If there is some mistake such as a device failure, the administrator can retain the device's UUID and change other related information to match the new device. This handling is transparent to the application server.

4   Performance Evaluation

A test was designed and performed to evaluate and analyze the performance of storage server Multipath. The test used a 2-Gbps Fabric, two application servers, and one storage server. The application server uses two 2.4 GHz Xeon processor, with 1 GB memory and one Emulex LP982 HBA (2Gb/s), and run the Linux kernel version 2.4.26. The storage server uses one 2.4 GHz Xeon processor, with 1GB memory and one Qlogic ISP 2300 (Target mode, 2Gb/s), and runs the Linux kernel version 2.4.26. Five Seagate ST336607LW 10,000 RPM SCSI disks are connected to the storage server via two Emulex LP982 HBAs (2Gb/s).

The standard disk I/O testing kit IOmeter by the Intel Corporation [13] was used. The open mode of the physical disks was O_DIRECT. In this test, five disks were mapped to two application servers, and two application servers issued sequential read commands with different data block sizes to these five disks. The goal was to compare the performance and the average response time of the commands with no Multipath, Multipath LRU and Multipath RR. Figure 4 and figure 5 show the test results.

The results show that the storage server Multipath had little impact on system performance and average response time. And when Multipath used the Round Robin method to balance the load of the two Emulex FC-HBA cards, commands could be sent to the disk through two paths and the results could

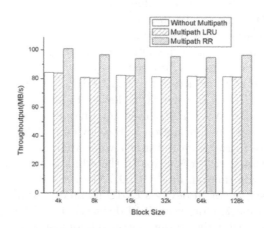

Fig. 4. The Performance of Storage Server Multipath

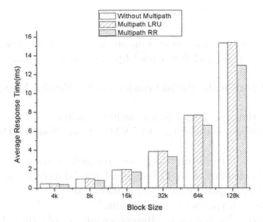

Fig. 5. The Average Response Time of Storage Server Multipath

be received through two paths. So the load of one path was reduced, and the command handling was sped up. The sequential read performance improved 17.9% on average. When the I/O request size was 4k, performance improvement reached 20%. The average response time decreased 15.2% on average.

With the increase of disks connected to the storage server, one path will quickly reach its top performance and become a bottleneck in data transfer. The storage server Multipath can balance the load and improve the data transfer rate, improving the performance of the TH-MSNS.

5 Conclusion

This paper describes the design and implementation of a multi-layer Multipath system. On the application server, we implemented Multipath in the volume management layer. And we added a Multipath layer on the storage server to provide multiple paths for the storage device and shield these paths from the application server. It is independent of lower SCSI cards and storage devices, so it has good compatibility. We can easily set a disk's UUID, choose paths, automatically recover paths and balance the loads of all application servers in the storage server Multipath.

With the introduction of a storage server in the TH-MSNS, the storage server may become a new single point of failure. We will investigate how to implement the technology such as high availability, load balance for two storage servers. And furthermore we will investigate how to configure many storage servers to form a storage cluster and provide transparent service for the application server.

Acknowledgement

The work described in this paper was supported by the National Key Basic Research and Development (973) Program of China (Grant No. 2004CB318205).

References

1. EMC PowerPath. http://www.emc.com/products/software/powerpath.jsp
2. HP Securepath. http://h18006.www1.hp.com/products/sanworks/secure-path/index.html
3. SCSI Mid-Level Multipath. Michael Anderson and Patrick Mansfield. Linux Symposium 2003.
4. Logical Volume Manager. http://www.sistina.com/lvm
5. Adding Multi Pathing Capabilities to LVM. Stefan Bader. LINUX-KONGRESS 2002.
6. The EVMS project. http://sourceforge.net/projects/evms
7. QLogic Fibre Channel Software: Enhancing Disk Adapter Performance, Function, and Control. White Paper, Qlogic Corporation, 2000.
8. Emulex MultiPulse. http://www.emulex.com/
9. Technical Report: Design and Implementation of the TH-MSNS. Computer Science Department, Tsinghua University, P.R. China, 2003, http://storage.cs.tsinghua.edu.cn/
10. A highly efficient FC-SAN based on load stream. Jiwu Shu and Jun Yao. The Fifth International Workshop on Advanced Parallel Processing Technologies, LNCS 2834, pp.31-40,2003.
11. Design and Implementation of A LINUX SCSI Target for Storage Area Networks. Ashish Palekar and Narendran Ganapathy. Proceedings of the 5th Annual Linux Showcase & Conference, 2001.
12. Design and Implementation of a Fibre Channel Network Driver for SAN-Attached RAID Controllers. Jae-Chang Namgoong and Chan-Ik Park. IEEE Parallel and Distributed Systems, 2001.
13. Iometer: The I/O Performance Analysis Tool for Servers. Jerry Sievert. http://www.intel.com/design/servers/devtools/iometer/index.htm

Research of Hot-Spot Selection Algorithm
in Virtual Address Switch

Tao Cai, ShiGuang Ju, JuenJie Zhao, and DeJiao Niu

Department of Computer Science, JiangSu University,
JiangSu, China 213013
caitao@ujs.edu.cn

Abstract. SAN-level buffer cache is an important factor in improving the efficiency of the storage area network (SAN). In this paper, we analyzed the SAN-level access pattern characterization, and designed a new hot spot selection algorithm called maximal access times and oldest access first select (MOFS) and minimal access times and oldest access first eliminate (MOFE) for SAN-level buffer cache. The line size for the hot spot is larger than the line size implemented in disk array caches. The algorithm calls in the block with the highest number of access times and oldest access to SAN-level buffer cache, and eliminates the block with the minimal access times and oldest access from the accessed block list. The algorithm uses the self-adapt mechanism to change the parameter's algorithm value dynamically. We implemented a virtual address switch in the SAN virtualization system to collect the access request information. Base on this we implemented the hot spot selection algorithm to select a block and send it to the SAN-level buffer cache. Lastly we evaluated the MOFS and MOFE algorithm and proved that this algorithm realizes a low call in ratio and high hit ratios in the SAN-level buffer cache and the self-adapt mechanism makes the MOFS and MOFE work efficiently with different types of workloads.

1 Introduction

In modern computer systems there are many multilevel and multi-purpose buffer caches. Systems access data in accordance with these levels. In the ideal conditions, a lower level cache will retain data missed from the upper level cache, and this data should be accessed in the future. Access types and management mechanisms between each level cache are different and must have different selection and replacement strategies. In SAN systems, the storage hierarchy and cache level are more complicated, where a device cache services the disk or disk array directly and the SAN-level cache serves the entire SAN system. The key problem of enhancing the SAN cache efficiency is to analyze the characteristics of SAN-level cache access, and to design the proper management strategy to complement other various caches.

The data are shared in a SAN; therefore data will not be monopolized by any single machine. And data sharing is an aspect of access pattern characterization. SAN virtualization improves management of the storage system, and at the same time, it also changes the data access pattern. The current selection algorithms can not adapt to new

G. Chen et al. (Eds.): ISPA Workshops 2005, LNCS 3759, pp. 111–119, 2005.

requirements, so how to deal with the change of access type in the SAN-level cache is very important.

This paper first introduces some past studies about cache management, and then analyzes the access pattern characterization of SAN-level buffer cache in SAN virtualization system. We then present new hot spot selection algorithm called the MOFS and MOFE. We also implement a virtual address switch and realize SAN-level cache call in. We use a feedback mechanism in the hot spot selection algorithm to adapt to different workloads. At the conclusion of paper, we discuss the evaluation and analysis of the algorithm.

2 Related Work

Munts and Honeyman have researched multilevel caches in distributed file system, and suggested that different level caches must use different management algorithms, but they did not give concrete access pattern characterizations and management algorithms [1]. Willick has proven the FBR replacement algorithm is more effective than the LRU replacement algorithm in low-level caches, but did not present a call in algorithm for use when accessing disks. Yuanyuan Zhou presented a second-level buffer cache management strategy [2], analyzed the access characteristics of buffer caches on both clients and servers under the workload of network database and file servers, and came to the conclusion that the data will be called in second level buffer cache is neither the hottest data nor the coldest data. He presented an MQ replacement algorithm, but it could not eliminate the effect on the cache by large sequence access, and only analyzed the access pattern characterization of the C/S mode. His algorithm still used the strategy of calling in the buffer cache when processing a request, without considering the changes of the SAN. The algorithm was difficult to implement because it was complicated and required modification of the first-level cache management algorithm. Elizabeth J. O'Neil proposed LRU-K hot spot discovery and cache replacement algorithm of database systems in SAN[3], which eliminated the effect on the cache caused by sequence access. The algorithm required on I/O command to be forged and the k times of accessed time to be saved for every accessed block. Many other studies were conducted concerning cache replacement algorithms. These algorithms include: FBR[4], LFRU[5], 2Q[6], LIRS[7] and ARC[8]. But call in algorithm was rarely studied.

Control theory has been used in more and more computer management systems. Feedback technology has been used in Web and e-mail service[9][10][11]. Y. Lu proposed a method which used feedback technology to allow Web systems to adapt to different types of workloads [12]. But no papers have been published about how to employ feedback technology in SAN-level buffer cache management.

This paper discuss the access pattern characterization of SAN-level buffer caches, and presents a new hot spot selection algorithm called the MOFS and MOFE, then also provides an analysis of its characterization.

3 Analysis of SAN-Level Buffer Cache Access Pattern Characterization

In SAN virtualization systems, clients access the logical disk organized by the disk arrays, and the logical disk is shared by many computers instead of being monopolized by a single computer. The client has its own cache, and the SAN-level buffer cache can demonstrably enhance SAN global performance. The level of the SAN-level buffer cache is under the client's cache. It retains data missing from the client's cache and shares it among different computers. Yuanyuan Zhou compared the different access pattern characterizations between the first-level (L1) cache and second-level（L2）cache. From the aspect of data reuse distance, for the L1 cache, more than 75 percent of the cache has a reuse distance less than or equal to 16, but for the L2 cache 99 percent has a reuse distance of 512 or greater[2]. Testing four kinds of workloads, the results showed that the L2 cache must maintain a reuse distance of at least 64k. Using the access probability and number of access times to describe the access frequency of blocks, the results indicated that 70 percent of the blocks had been accessed at least twice and contributed to 95 percent of the number of access times. However, only 40 percent of the blocks had been accessed at least four times, but contributed to 90 percent of the access times. Therefore, it is a useful to retain blocks accessed between two and four times and having a reuse distance of 64k or greater in the SAN-level buffer cache.

Different kinds of services have their own access pattern characterization. An effective SAN-level cache management strategy must be able to deal with complex and volatile workload environments. It is difficult for a single algorithm with fixed parameters i to meet the requirements of all kinds of applications. Yuanyuan Zhou evaluated four kinds of workloads: Oracle miss trace-16M, Oracle miss trace-128M, HP Disk trace and Auspex Server trace, and analyzed the data locality and access frequency [2]. They discovered that the changes in the characteristics of all applications seemed consistent, but the peak value was different and occurred on the same scope. The fact that the tendency to change remained consistent indicates that different kinds of workloads can use the same hot spot selection algorithm. And a dynamic tunable parameter can adjust a hot spot selection algorithm to adapt to different workloads. We used the Na as a tunable parameter.

In summary, the access pattern characterization of a SAN-level buffer cache is different from a single machine cache and similar to a level 2 cache. And the algorithm should deal with the effect of data sharing and adapt to different kinds of workloads. *Distance* presents the reuse distance of blocks, *atimes* presents the access times, *Nun* presents the sharing times of blocks, and Na is the tunable parameter. Then we can use a tetrad (*distance*, *atimes*, *Num*, *Na*) to present the access pattern characterization of a SAN-level cache. Next we will discuss how the parameters of the hot spot selection algorithm were quantified and simplified.

4 Hot Spot Selection Strategy for SAN-Level Buffer Cache

The reuse distance can be represented by a block's size. If every access is one byte, then a 64k block represents a reuse distance of 64k. In SAN-level buffer caches 64k is a fundamental block unit.

Blocks that have been accessed between two and four times contributs to 95 percent of the access times, which indicates that the blocks accessed between two and four times must be called in the SAN-level buffer cache instead of other hotter blocks (being accessed more than five times) and colder blocks (being accessed only once). Using *access_list* to record the number of times a block is accessed, once one block is accessed between two and four times, it can be called in the SAN-level buffer cache.

If the number of times a block is shared by different clients is the condition to decide whether it should be called in, a parameter must be added to the algorithm, which hinders the system's efficiency, flexibility and controllability. We converted share times to access times. One share time can be converted into K (tunable parameter) access times. When K equals zero, it indicates that the share factor is not in consideration in the hot spot selection algorithm.

4.1 Hot Spot Selection Algorithm

The selection of a hot spot block is performed by choosing suitable blocks from *access_list*. The MOFS algorithm selects the block with the most access times and oldest access, and then called it in the SAN-level buffer cache and MOFE algorithm eliminates the block with the fewest access times and oldest access from the access list.

To describe the new algorithm, first we must define some variables, Amax is the maximal length of *access_list*; K is the conversion ratio from shared times to accessed times, and *ttime* is the lowest number of access times to decide if a block should be called in the cache. *Amax, K* and ttimes are three tunable parameters. Access_list is a chained list saving the blocks that have been accessed; each node includes five data items: *devname, offset, atimes, hostid* and *next*. *Devname* is the name of the storage device; *offset* is the offset address of the blocks; *atimes* is the number of times a block is accessed; *hostid* is the identifier of a host that has accessed a block recently; *next* is the pointer of next node.

The MOFS and MOFE algorithm is presented as follows: (*access_list_n* is a node in *access_list*)

```
    If ( the request block  IN  access_list list)
    {
    access_list_n.atimes = access_list_n.atimes + 1;
     If ( access_list_n. hostid != accessed host's id)
              access_list_n.atimes = access_list_n.atimes + K;
    }
    Else
    {
       Insert new node into the tail of the access_list;
       access_list_n.atimes = 1;
    }
    If ( the number of access_list > amax)
    {
             While ( access_list_n.atimes != 1)
                    access_list = access_list.next;
             delete this node
    }
```

Search access_list, find the maximal of *atimes* → *maxtimes*;
If (*maxtimes* > *ttimes*)
{
    While (*access_list_n.atimes* != *maxtimes*)
            access_list = *access_list.next*;
    discover hot spot and call in the SAN-level buffer cache
    delete this node
}

Ttimes ensure the blocks in the SAN-level cache are hot (access times must be *ttimes or greater*). The strategy of choosing the block with the maximal access times and oldest access ensures the hot blocks will be discovered and called in the SAN-level buffer cache efficiently, quickly and fairly. The strategy of eliminating the blocks with minimal access times and oldest access from the accessed block list requires that the blocks accessed only once preferentially are eliminated to prevent the blocks accessed sequentially from being called into the SAN-level buffer cache. *Amax* controls the number of accessed nodes stored in the accessed queue and ensure there are not too many blocks in order to facilitate search efficiency, and save space and computer time.

4.2 Self-adapt Mechanism

It is difficult for unchangeable hot spot selection algorithms to work efficiently under different workloads. We used a feedback mechanism to make out algorithm self-adaptive. *Amax, K* and *ttimes* are three tunable parameters. We used a self-adapting mechanism to calculate new values for these three parameters according to the actual running condition of the SAN-level buffer cache when the system is running. By changing the three parameters, the algorithm can adjust different kinds of tracers.

The parameter represents *Amax* the size of access list. The system checks the ratio between the nodes having been accessed more than *ttimes* and all nodes in *access_list* periodically. If the ratio is high, the system increases *amax* to expand the *access_list* size and prevent the blocks from being eliminated too quickly. The system also decreases *amax* to shorten the *access_list* size and eliminate the blocks that are rarely accessed.

The parameter *Ttimes* decides the number of times that the blocks are called in the SAN-level buffer cache. The system checks the ratio between the hit blocks and all blocks in the SAN-level buffer cache. A high ratio means the system should increase *Ttimes* to prevent the blocks that are accessed rarely from being chosen. A low ratio means the system should decrease *Ttimes* to permit more blocks to be called into the SAN-level cache.

The value of *K* decides ratio for converting share times to access times. The system monitors the replacement frequency of *hostid* in *access_list*. If the frequency is high, it means there is a high number of block shared between the different hosts. Increasing the value of *K* could cause the shared blocks to be called into the SAN-level buffer cache more quickly. However, the system should decrease the value of *K* when the frequency is low.

4.3 Implementation

To implement the hot spot selection algorithm, all hosts' access requests are collected and traced. Therefore, a new application called the "virtual address switch" should be introduced as shown in Figure 1. It runs on a special server and simulates a virtual address switch using software. First of all, the address translation module in the host access request is modified. Secondly, the address transformation request is sent to the virtual address switch. Thirdly, the virtual address switch checks the SAN-level cache and sends a new address back to the host. Finally, the hosts sents an I/O command with the new address to the SAN switch and retrieves the wanted data. The virtual address switch collects all of the SAN's I/O commands, and use the MOFS algorithm to discover the hot spot blocks. The cache entity is composed of virtual discs implemented by the memory.

Figure 2 shows the process of SAN-level buffer cache hot spot selection, and adjustment in the virtual address switch. The address receiver thread accepts the I/O commands from the client and then inserts them into the request queue. The hot spot selection thread detects the request queue to get the I/O commands. We used the hot spot selection algorithm presented above to select the hot blocks and called them into the SAN-level buffer cache. The system checks whether the SAN-level buffer cache has a request block. If the SAN-level buffer cache has a request block, the new address should be inserted into the send back queue; otherwise, the original address should be inserted into *access_list*. The address sends back thread checks the send back queue, and sends the address back to the corresponding computer if the return queue has the address to be returned. The monitor thread collects statistics about the access queue and the SAN-level buffer cache periodically. The adjustment thread receives feedback information from the monitor thread periodically, and selects suitable valued for the three tunable parameters according to the hot spot selection self-adapt mechanism. In the virtual address switch, we adopted multi-threading to realize all functions such as receiving addresses, hot spot selection, monitoring and adjustment. In order to ensure requests from every host are handled promptly, we used threads to simulate the ports of the switch, which eliminated the performance cost brought by address translation centralization.

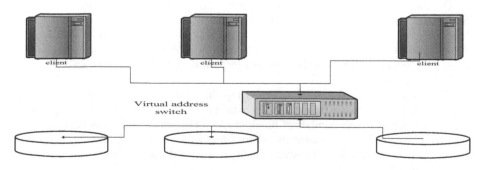

Fig. 1. The structure of the virtual switch address

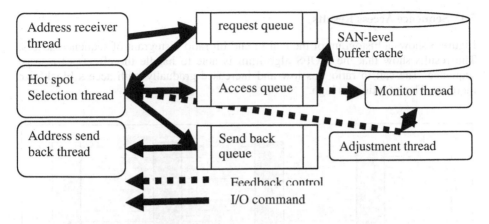

Fig. 2. Flow diagram of the selection, called in and adjustment process

5 Evaluation and Analysis

The experimental test beds contained two client computers running a Linux operating system, a virtual address switch running the Linux operating system and one optical fiber disk array. All computers and the disk arrays were connected together using an optical fiber switch. Table 1 shows the configuration of the client computers. Table 2 shows the configuration of the virtual address switch and optical fiber disk array.

Table 1. Configuration of client computers running the linux operating system

CPU	Intel Xeon 2.4GHz × 2
Memory	1GB
OS	Linux (kernel: 2.4.26)
FC HBA	Emulex LP982（2Gb/s）

Table 2. Configuration of the virtual address switch and optical fiber disk array

CPU	Intel Xeon 2.4GHz × 2
Memory	1GB
OS	Linux (kernel: 2.4.26)
FC HBA	Emulex LP9802
FC Disks	Seagate ST3146807FC × 5

Iometer was the software used for evaluation to test the SAN-level buffer caches with the four different size access blocks the statistics for the (8k, 16k, 32k and 64k) and two types of sequences and two types of random access lists. The statistics for the call in and hit ratio of the SAN-level buffer cache per second were also evaluated.

5.1 Sequence Access Results

Figure 3 shows a histogram of the call in and hit ratio histogram of sequence access. The results show that the MOFS algorithm is able to handle the effects of a large sequence. The call in ratio was low and increased gradually with access block size increase. The hit ratio was high.

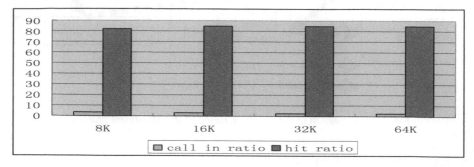

Fig. 3. Sequence access results

5.2 Random Access Results

Figure 4 shows the call in ratio percentage and hit ratio percentage according to the random access list. It shows the call in ratio was also low and decreased gradually with the increase of access block size.

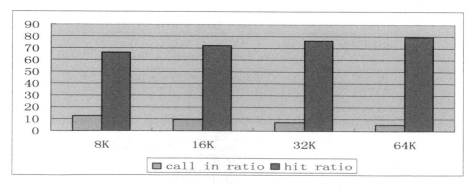

Fig. 4. Random access results

6 Conclusion

This paper describes the access pattern characterization of a SAN-level buffer cache. More specifically, it presents a new hot spot selection algorithm called MOFS, MOFE algorithm and a self-adapting mechanism to call the suitable block into the SAN-level buffer cache. We implemented the virtual address switch to collect the accessed information, and implemented the MOFS and MOFE in it to select the hot spot call in SAN-level buffer cache.

We evaluated MOFS and MOFE algorithm by testing it under four different kinds of workloads and monitoring the sequence and random access list. The implementation results show the MOFS and MOFE algorithm has a low call in ratio and high hit ratio in the SAN-level buffer cache, and can handle the negative effect of large sequence access. The self-adapting mechanism adjust the MOFS and MOFE algorithm dynamically and allow it to work efficiently with different types of workloads.

References

1. D. Muntz and P. Honeyman, Multi-Level Caching in Distributed File Systems-or-Your Cache Ain't Nuthiní but Trash, Proc. Usenix Winter 1992 Technical Conf., pp. 305-314, Jan. 1991.
2. Yuanyuan Zhou Zhifeng Chen and Kai Li, Second-Level Buffer Cache Management IEEE transactions on parallel and distributed systems, VOL. 15, NO. 7, JULY 2004.
3. Elizabeth J. O'Neil, Patrick E. O'Neill, Gerhard Weikum, The LRU-K Page Replacement Algorithm For Database Disk Buffering SIGMOD 93 Washington, DC, USA ACM.
4. J. Robinson and M. Devarakonda, Data Cache Management Using Frequency-Based Replacement,î Proc. ACM SIGMETRICS Conf. Measurement and Modeling of Computer Systems, 1990.
5. D. Lee, J. Choi, J.-H. Kim, S.L. Min, Y. Cho, C.S. Kim, and S.H. Noh, On the Existence of a Spectrum of Policies That Subsumes the Least Recently Used (LRU) and Least Frequently Used (LFU) Policies, Proc. ACM SIGMETRICS Int'l Conf. Measurement and Modeling of Computing Systems, SIGMETRICS Performance Evaluation Rev., vol. 27, no. 1, pp. 134-143, May 1999.
6. T. Johnson and D. Shasha, 2Q: A Low Overhead High Performance Buffer Management Replacement Algorithm, Proc. Very Large Databases Conf., pp. 439-450, 1995.
7. S. Jiang and X. Zhang, ìLIRS: An Efficient Low Inter-Reference Recency Set Replacement Policy to Improve Buffer Cache Performance, Proc. SIGMETRICS, pp. 31-42, 2002.
8. N. Megiddo and D.S. Modha, Arc: A Self-Tuning, Low Overhead Replacement Cache, Proc. Second USENIX Conf. File and Storage Technologies, 2003.
9. T. F. Abdelzaher and N. Bhatti, "Web Server QoS Management by Adaptive Content Delivery," International Workshop on Quality of Service, pp. 216-225, 1999.
10. R. Golding, P. Bosch, C. Staelin, T. Sullivan, and John Wilkes. "Idleness is not Sloth," Winter'95 USENIX Conference, pp 201-212, Jan. 1995.
11. S. Parekh, N. Gandhi, J. L. Hellerstein, D. Tilbury, T. S. Jayram, J. Bigus, "Using Control Theory to Achieve Service Level Objectives in Performance Management," IFIP/IEEE International Symposium on Integrated Network Management, 2001.
12. Y. Lu, A. Saxena, and T. F. Abdelzaher, "Differentiated Caching Services; A Control-Theoretical Approach," International Conference on Distributed Computing Systems, pp. 615-622, April 2001.

An Efficient Cache Replacement Policy with Distinguishing Write Blocks from Read Blocks in Disk Arrays[*]

Yulin Wang[1], Guangjun Li[1], Xiaojun Wu[2], and Shuisheng Lin[1]

[1] Inst. of Commun./Info. Engineering, Univ. of Electronic Science and Technology of China,
Chengdu, Sichuan, China
{wyl, gjli, sslin}@uestc.edu.cn
[2] Integrative Research Dept., Huawei Tech. Lmt. Corp. Shengzhen, Guangdong, China
xjwu@huawei.com

Abstract. The cache in disk array controller is critical to disk array performance. Many researches have been done to improve the hit-ratio in the cache, including the prefetch algorithms and the replacement algorithms, such as the LRU-K algorithm, the 2-Q algorithm and so on. All these algorithms assume that it takes the same cost to replace all the data blocks. But the cost of replacing write blocks is much higher than the cost of replacing read blocks. Based on the facts a new replacement algorithm named the write-prior least recently used (WP-LRU) algorithm is presented in this paper. The data blocks in the cache are divided into read blocks and write blocks according to the host access mode. The two types of data blocks are managed with different methods. The LRU algorithm is only used to read blocks and all victim blocks are read blocks. Some especial operations are performed for all write blocks in the cache. A simulation model is developed and the simulation results show that the WP-LRU algorithm can improve the performance of disk arrays by reducing the average service time remarkably while it keeps the same hit-ratio as the standard LRU.

1 Introduction

The Internet has been a phenomenon that has cultivated a worldwide revolution. At unprecedented paces and in unparalleled scales, the information digitalization processes have presented numerous new challenges to IT scientists and engineers. One of the major challenges is to design and advanced storage systems to meet the demanding requirements for high performance, high capacity, and strong reliability. RAID (Redundant Array of Independent Disks) architectures have become the architecture of choice for large storage systems since they employ striping (i.e., parallelism) and redundancy across multiple disks to increase capacity, speed, and availability of storage systems. Modern RAID disk arrays contain multiple disks, large caches, and sophisticated array controllers. The large caches are transparent to the host access and are managed by the array controllers. Good cache architectures and good

---

[*] Supported by the Huawei Science Research Foundation under Grant No. M16010101HW 04005.

G. Chen et al. (Eds.): ISPA Workshops 2005, LNCS 3759, pp. 120–129, 2005.

cache management policy can improve the performance of disk arrays remarkably. Takahashi, Naoya et al. [1] propose a hybrid cache architecture including control memory and data memory and the architecture has been proved to be more efficient. The data from the host is stored in the data memory temporarily. The control tables for cache memory and other types of control information are stored in the control memory. A two-level cache displays superior performance in comparison to a single level cache and is effective in temporal and spatial locality [2] [4].

The cache replacement policy is the same critical to the disk array performance as the cache structure. A good cache replacement policy should keep short access time in addition to high hit-ratio. We investigate the characters of data accessed by hosts and propose the WP-LRU algorithm. The data blocks in the cache are distinguished according to the host access mode as read blocks and write blocks in the proposed algorithm. Different management methods are used to the read blocks and the write blocks. The simulation results show that the WP-LRU algorithm can reduce the average service time remarkably while it keeps the same hit-ratio as the standard LRU.

The rest of the paper is organized as follows: Section 2 presents related work in the area of the disk array cache replacement algorithms. Section 3 explains the idea of the WP-LRU algorithm and its implementation in details. In section 4, the simulation result and performance analysis is presented. Section 5 discusses the algorithm extension in other cache architectures. Section 6 presents the conclusion.

2 Related Work

The LRU algorithm is one of the most popular cache replacement algorithms. It can get high hit-ratio with low implementation cost. Bently and McGeoch [17] proved that conventional LRU is superior to other replacement algorithms, such as *frequency count, FIFO,* or *transpose* by using real data to compare and rank. But the LRU algorithm doesn't perform best. Many advanced algorithms (like LRU-K [3], [13] and 2-Q [14], [16]) were developed with the intent to improve the performance (lower miss rate) for some specific applications. Thiebaut and Stone [5] propose a modified LRU, which considers the case that several processes compete the cache. Their work is the precursor of this work. Cache replacement policies have been studied by many people, with notable work by Smith and Goodman [6], by So and Recheschaffen [7] among others.

The disk array performance can be measured by the throughput and the access time. High hit-ratio can reduce the average access time and improve the throughput. The previous cache replacement algorithms assume that the replacement cost of every block is identical and evaluate the performance mainly by hit-ratio. The disk array performance can also be improved by reducing the access time. In this paper we investigate the facts that it takes much longer time to replace one write block than to replace one read block and it takes much longer time to write back one stripe unit to disks each time than to write back all stripe units as a whole. Based on the facts, the WP-LRU algorithm is proposed to reduce the average access time and to improve the disk array performance.

3 The WP-LRU Algorithm

High performance storage systems require high reliability and high availability in addition to high throughput, high scalability and high compatibility. A large capacity cache based on DRAM in disk array controllers is used to realize high throughput. According to the host access mode, the data in the disk array cache has the read data and the write data. The read data can be regained from disks at the cost of lower performance if the cache failures. But the write data can't be regained and will cause the data loss if the cache failures. So there are the read cache and the write cache in some disk array cache designs. The read cache is based on DRAM and the write cache is based on nonvolatile RAM (NVRAM) with low read/write speed. The advantage of this scheme is to be able to improve the reliability. But this scheme has more disadvantages than advantages. Firstly, the scheme has low adaptability. Both the read cache and the write cache have fixed sizes, which limits the host access modes, such as most-write access mode and most-read access mode. Secondly, the scheme has low write speed because Flash NVRAM has low read/write speed. Thirdly, the whole cache hit-ratio is not high because the read cache and the write cache are managed independently. Modern disk arrays adopt a unified cache instead of a read cache and a write cache, and the high reliability and the high availability are realized with the NVRAM based on battery backed RAM and the redundancy. So the cache replacement in this paper is referred to the unified cache.

There are two types of host requests in a storage system: read some data from disks and write some data to disks. The cache can improve the disk array performance with host asynchronous write and temporal store of the data accessed by host in future. The cache is managed in data blocks and accordingly there are two types of data blocks: the host read blocks and host write blocks. When host read or write requests arrive the whole cache will be searched. If one write block is requested by host write requests, the block content will be updated. If one read block is requested by host write requests, the block content will firstly be updated and the block becomes a write block. If one host read request arrives and the cache is hit, the data blocks are read from the cache directly. Because all write blocks in the cache are written to disks finally, we can't discard any write blocks in the cache replacement algorithm until the blocks are written to disks.

The cache also has two types of operations on disks: read some blocks and write back some blocks. But most RAID systems incorporate both redundancy and some form of data interleaving, which distributes the data over all the data disks in the array. Redundancy is usually in the form of an error correcting code, with simple parity schemes predominating. Data interleaving is usually in the form of data "striping" in which the data to be stored is broken down into blocks called "stripe units", which are then distributed across the data disks. A typical size of a stripe unit is 8K to 64K bytes. A "stripe" is a group of corresponding stripe units, one stripe unit from each disk in the array. Thus, the "stripe size" is equal to the size of a stripe unit times the number of data disks in the array. So the cost of writing one block to the disks is higher than the cost of reading one block from the disk in normal mode because it requires four disk accesses in RAID 5, which is widely used. Specifically, a data write to a single stripe unit requires that the old data and corresponding parity information be read from the appropriate data disk. Next, new parity information is computed with the old data, the new data and the old parity information. Finally, the new data and the new parity are written to the disks, respectively. The WPP-LRU algorithm tries to reduce the times of writing to disks to improve the performance.

Let's see an example. We use the RAID 5 and refer the jth stripe unit in the ith stripe as S_{ij}. The original write queue is given as Fig. 1.

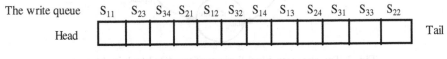

Fig. 1. The original write queue

We can know that the times of the disk access is 48 if we write the blocks to the disks in order, because it take four times of disk access to write one stripe unit to the disks in RAID 5. We prefer to store the write blocks in the cache temporarily and change the order of the write queue to realize writing all stripe units of one stripe to the disks in one time. So we give special attention to write blocks in the cache replacement algorithm. The changed write queue is given as Fig. 2.

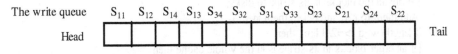

Fig. 2. The changed write queue

The parity information of the whole stripe is calculated one time when all the stripe units of one stripe are written to the disks at one time. The times of disk access is reduced to 15 in the changed write queue. The disks and the disk channels can service the prefetching and the host requests better in terms of the decrease of the disk access. So we try to write all stripe units of one stripe in one time when writing disks.

As a result the idea of the WP-LRU algorithm is:

- There are three types of queues in the data cache: the read queue, the write queue and the idle queue. All read blocks are in the read queue and all write blocks are in the write queue. The idle blocks are in the idle queue.
- The LRU algorithm is only applied to the read queue. The blocks in the read queues join in the write queue when host write requests update their contents. The victim blocks join in the idle queue.
- The coalescing write algorithm is applied to the write queue. Each disk writing operation tries to write more write blocks. The blocks in the write queue join in the read queue when they are written back to the disks. The LRU algorithm decides whether the block should be discarded together with all other blocks in the read queue.

Each data block in the cache has three types of states based on the idea of the WPP-LRU: idle, full of the data to read and full of data to write. The state transition diagram is given in Fig. 3.

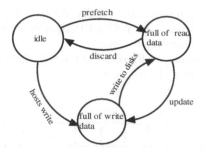

Fig. 3. The state transition diagram of the data block in the cache

The best case is to write the whole stripe to disks each time when writing disks. The read hit ratio will reduce if there are too many write blocks in the cache. To get better performance, we must tradeoff between the high read hit ratio and the low disk writing. One feasible scheme is given in Fig. 4.

Case host writes one block to the cache:
{The block joins in w_q;
if all other blocks in its stripe is in w_q then
    {Write all the blocks in its stripe to disks;
    Add them to r_q and delete them in w_q;}
else if length(w_q)>=2/3 limit then
    {if all other blocks in its stripe is in the whole cache then
        {Write the blocks to disks;
        Add them to r_q and delete them in w_q;}
    else if the whole stripe of a random block in w_q is in the whole cache then
        {Write the blocks to disks;
        Add them to r_q and delete them in w_q;}
else if length(w_q)>= limit then
    {Write the head block and the blocks which belong to the same stripe in w_q to disks;
    Add them to r_q and delete them in w_q;}}

Fig. 4. The special operations on the write queue

We can adjust the length limit of the write queue according to practical applications. The length limit can be large if the applications have much writing operation on disks. On the contrary, the length limit can be small if the applications have much reading operation on disks. The length limit is suggested to be one third of the total capacity of the cache if the users have no interest in the applications.

4 Simulation Results

In this section, we present results obtained through simulations to show the advantages of the proposed algorithm.

In order to check the validity of the algorithm presented, a model was worked out to simulate the behavior of the cache replacement. We constructed a disk array simulator through adding a new cache simulation module to the simulator RAIDSim. The simulator includes two kinds of cache replacement algorithms in addition to the WP-LRU algorithm, which are the absolute fair LRU (AF-LRU) and the direct write LRU (DW-LRU). AF-LRU means that all blocks including the read request blocks and the write request blocks are indiscriminatingly scheduled by the standard LRU and the write request block is written to the disks if it is the victim. DW-LRU means that the head block in the write queue is written to the disks and joins in the idle queue so long as the disks are idle. Only the read request blocks are scheduled by the standard LRU in the DW-LRU algorithm.

Various simulations were performed with different workloads and different cache replacement algorithms. There are two kinds of workload models, which are the OLTP load and the scientific load. The workload models have three parameters. W is the maximum number of blocks requested, p is the parameter for the geometric distribution and σ is the probability that a request accesses one block of data or accesses the maximum blocks of data [11] [12].

The system disks, which for the sake of simplicity are identical, are IBM 0661 3.5" 320 MB SCSI Hard disks [15]. The disk characteristics and the simulation parameters are given in Table 1.

Table 1. Simulation parameters

Parameter	Value	Disk parameters	Value
Capacity (C)	32G	Bytes per sector	512
Cache port number (P)	32	Sector per track	48
Host interface processors	16	Tracks per cylinder	14
Disk interface processors	16	Cylinders per disk	949
Block size (B)	4K	Revolution time	13.9ms
The maximum of W	10	Average seek time	12.6ms
The geometric distribution P	0.8	Max stroke seek time	25.0ms
The probability σ	0.7	Sustained transfer rate	1.8MB/s

Various simulations were performed with different methods. The simulation results of the overall hit ratio appear in Table 2. The table shows the overall hit ratio for the AF-LRU, the DW-LRU and the WPP-LRU, after 512M blocks and 1024M blocks have been processed by the hosts. It is known from the table that the DW-LRU has the lowest hit ratio and the WP-LRU has the same high hit ratio as the AF-LRU. So the WP-LRU doesn't reduce the hit ratio compared with the AF-LRU. So some good algorithms can also be used in the read blocks to improve the hit ratio, such as the LRU-K algorithm [13], the 2-Q algorithm [14] and so on.

Table 2. The overall hit ratio

	512M blocks			1024M blocks		
	AF-LRU	DW-LRU	WPP-LRU	AF-LRU	DW-LRU	WPP-LRU
OLTP workloads	65.79%	62.23%	65.71%	65.13%	62.33%	65.11%
Scientific workloads	72.15%	69.54%	72.18%	72.55%	69.64%	72.54%

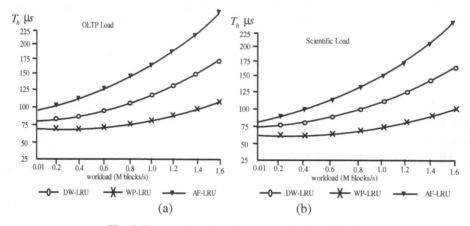

Fig. 5. The worst service time versus total workloads

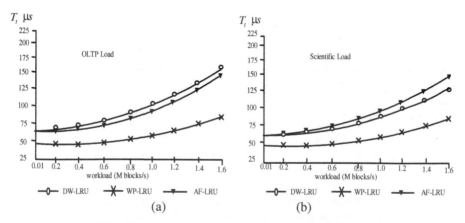

Fig. 6. The average service time versus total workloads

Fig. 5 shows the variation of the worst service time with total workloads. The worst service time is linear with total workloads whichever algorithm is adopted, because the wait time increases linearly when the workloads exceed one limit. The worst service time of the AF-LRU is the longest in the workload models because the operation must wait if the victim block needs to be written back to disks. The worst service time of the DW-LRU is the middle and the hit service time of the WP-LRU is the shortest.

Fig. 6 shows the variation of the average service time with total workloads. The average service time of the DW-LRU is as much as the time of the AF-LRU, because the hit ratio of the AF-LRU is higher than the hit ration of the DW-LRU although the hit service time of the DW-LRU is higher than the hit service time of the AF-LRU. The average service time of the WP-LRU is the shortest in three algorithms, because it has the shortest hit service time and has the same high hit ratio as the AF-LRU. The average service time of the WPP-LRU is reduced about 10% in normal workloads and more than 20% in heavy workloads compared to the DW-LRU and the AF-LRU.

5   Extension of the Algorithm

The WP-LRU algorithm is proven to have good performance through simulation. The algorithm has as high hit ratio as the AF_LRU and has less average access time than the DW_LRU and the AF_LRU. But the hit ratio of AF_LRU is not the highest and there are many methods to improve the hit ratio. One efficient method is two-level cache. Two-level cache makes better use of the spatial locality and temporal locality, and it has higher hit-ratio. The first level cache makes use of the temporal locality mainly and the second level cache makes use of the spatial locality mainly. The small accessed data block in the large block will be moved into the first level cache when the large data block will be replaced in the second level cache. All the replacement will proceed in the second level cache when prefetching data or the host writing data back. The WP-LRU algorithm can be used in the second level cache in case of two-level cache. This will not affect the cache hit-ratio and can farther improve the whole performance by reducing the average access time.

Two-level cache will increase the hardware cost although it can improve the hit-ratio. There are some algorithms which can also improve the hit-ratio, such as the 2-Q algorithm [16] and the LRU-K algorithm [3]. These algorithms have a presupposition that all replacement blocks have the same cost. In our WP-LRU algorithm, all replacement blocks are the read data blocks and have the same replacement cost. So we can use the 2-Q algorithm and the LRU-K algorithm instead of the LRU algorithm in the read queue to improve the hit-ratio. And this will not change the idea of the WP-LRU algorithm.

6   Conclusions

An algorithm named WP-LRU is presented in this paper based on the fact that it takes more cost to replace one write block than to replace one read block in the unified cache of disk arrays. The unified cache can gain more advantages by contrast with the read/write cache and the unified cache is popular in the practical applications. The write blocks are distinguished from the read blocks in the WP-LRU algorithm. And the LRU algorithm is only used to the read blocks and some special operations are performed for all write blocks in the cache. The effect of the WP-LRU on the performance of disk arrays is also explored. The simulation results show that the WP-LRU algorithm can reduce the average service time remarkably while it keeps the same hit ratio as the AF-LRU algorithm. The extension of the WP-LRU algorithm is also discussed in this paper. The WP-LRU can be used in the second level cache in two-level cache, which is popular in high-end disk array. At the same time, some good algorithms can also be used in the read blocks to improve the hit ratio, such as the LRU-K algorithm, the 2-Q algorithm and so on. This will not change the idea of the WP-LRU algorithm.

Reference

[1] Takahashi, Naoya (Disk Array Systems Division, Hitachi, Ltd.); Kurosu, Yasuo, Performance improvement of disk array subsystems having shared cache and control memories. *Electronics and Communications in Japan, Part III: Fundamental Electronic Science (English translation of Denshi Tsushin Gakkai Ronbunshi)*, v 87, n 10, October, 2004, pp. 1-14.

[2] Huh Jung-Ho, Chang Tae-Mu, Two-level disk cache of RAID 5 based on both temporal and spatial locality, *Proceedings of the International Conference on Parallel and Distributed Processing Techniques and Applications*, v2, 2003, p928-934.

[3] R. Pendse; U. Walterscheidt, A Low Overhead, Least Recently Used Block Replace Scheme with Flooding Protection. *International Journal of Computers and Their Applications*, pp 71-76. June 1998.

[4] Chen Yun, Yang Genke; Wu Zhiming, The application of two-level cache in RAID system, *Proceedings of the World Congress on Intelligent Control and Automation (WCICA)*, v2, 2002, p1328-1332.

[5] Dominique Thiebaut; Harold S. Stone; Joel L. Wolf, Improving Disk Cache Hit-Ratios Through Cache Partitioning. *IEEE Transactions on Computers*. Vol 41, No. 6, pp. 665-676. June 1992.

[6] J. E. Smith and J. R. Goodman. Instruction cache replacement policies and organizations. *IEEE Trans. Comput.* Vol C-34, no. 3, pp. 234-241, Mar. 1985.

[7] K So and R. N. Rechtschaffen, Cache operations by MRU change, *IEEE Trans. Comput.*, vol.37, no. 6 pp. 700-709, June 1988.

[8] Shih, F. Warren (IBM T J Watson Res Center, Yorktown Heights, NY, USA); Lee, Tze-Chiang; Ong, Shauchi, A file-based adaptive prefetch caching design, *Proceedings - IEEE International Conference on Computer Design: VLSI in Computers and Processors*, Sep, 1990, pp. 463-466.

[9] Grimsrud, Knut Stener (Brigham Young Univ); Archibald, James K.; Nelson, Brent E., Multiple prefetch adaptive disk caching, *IEEE Transactions on Knowledge and Data Engineering*, v 5, n 1, Feb, 1993, p 88-103 ISSN: 1041-4347 CODEN: ITKEEH.

[10] G.J. Mcknight; L.A. Riedle; C.T. Stephan, Method and System for Improving RAID Controller Performance through Adaptive Write Back/Write through Caching, technical report, *United States Patent and Trademark Office*, US Patent 6629211, Apr. 2001.

[11] S. Ng, Improving disk performance via latency reduction, *IEEE Trans. Comput.* 40 (1) (1991) pp. 22-30.

[12] S. Chen and D. Towsley, The design and evaluation of RAID5 and parity striping disk array architectures, *J. Parallel Distr. Comput.* 17 (Jan, 1993) pp. 58-74.

[13] E.J. O'Neil, P.E. O'Neil, G. WeiKum, The LRU-K Page Replacement algorithm for Database Disk Buffering, *Proc. of the ACM 1993 SIGMOD Conference*, pp 297-306, June 1993.

[14] T. Johnson, D. Sasha, 2Q: A Low Overhead High Performance Buffer Management Replacement Algorithm, *Proc. 20th International Conference on Very Large Data Bases*, pp 439-450, 1994.

[15] E.K. Lee, R. Katz, An analytic performance model of disk arrays, *Proc. ACM Sigmetrics Conf. On Measur. & Model. Of Comp. Sys.* (May 1993) 98-109.

[16] J-L. Baer; W-H. Wang, Multi-level cache hierarchies: Organizations, protocols and performance, *J.Parallel and Disistrivuted Computing,* vol.6, no.3, pp. 451-476, 1989.

[17] J. L. Bentley; C. McGeoch, Worst-case analysis of self-organizing sequential search heuristics. *Proc. of 20th Allerton Conf. Commun.*, Contr., Comput., Oct. 6-8, 1982, pp. 452-461.

An NFSv4-Based Security Scheme for NAS

Xiangguo Li, JianHua Yang, and Zhaohui Wu

Computer Science and Engineering College of Zhejiang University,
HangZhou, China, 310027
{lixg, jhyang, wzh}@cs.zju.edu.cn

Abstract. This paper presents a security scheme for network-attached storage based on NFSv4 frame. One novel aspect of our system is that it enhances NFSv4 to guarantee the security of storage. Another novel feature is that we develop new user authentication mechanism which outperforms Kerberos. It uses HMAC and the symmetric cryptography to provide the integrity and privacy of transmitted data. The system includes three essential procedures: authenticating user, establishing security context and exchanging data. Our scheme can protect data from tampering, eavesdropping and replaying attacks, and it ensures that the data stored on the device is copy-resistant and encrypted. In spite of this level of security, the scheme does not impose much performance overhead. Our experiments show that large sequential reads or writes with security impose performance expense by 10-20%, which is much less than some other security systems.

1 Introduction

Over the last decade, exponential growth in processor performance, storage capacity, and network bandwidth is changing our view of storage.Much effort has been made to improve distributed storage and to provide better performance and scalability [20, 6].

Traditionally, DAS (Direct-attached storage) is defined as one or more spinning or streaming devices that are connected to a single server via a physical cable. Unfortunately, this centralized file system design fundamentally limit storage performance and availability since all access go through the central server [7,24].The single server will be the bottleneck of the system. Thus, the demand for great scalability within heterogeneous systems has forced storage to adopt a decentralized architecture. Under the environment, NAS (Network-attached storage) comes into being. The NAS device is directly attached to network with scalability and it removes I/O bottleneck of single server, providing file sharing among different platforms.

By attaching storage directly to the network, the NAS now exposes disk drivers to outside direct attack, moreover, NAS stores much important information, so the security of NAS is significant.

Research on security of NAS includes user identification, data integration, data privacy and data recoverability. Few security solutions are considered in usual NAS architectures or only one aspect of the problem is solved in many systems ahead with strong security so as to lower storage efficiency [6].

Thus, we design integrated security architecture for network-attached storage based on NFSv4 [22,23] frame. The scheme employs Kerberos-like architecture to provide

G. Chen et al. (Eds.): ISPA Workshops 2005, LNCS 3759, pp. 130–139, 2005.
© Springer-Verlag Berlin Heidelberg 2005

user authentication. HMAC (Hash-based Message Authentication Code) and the symmetric cryptography provide the integrity and privacy of transmitted data [25,2].

Our scheme can protect data from tampering, eavesdropping [14] and replaying attacks, and it ensures that the data stored on the device is copy-resistant and encrypted. In spite of this level of security, our system does not impose much performance expense.

The rest of the paper is organized as follows. Section 2 discusses related work. Section 3 describes the system specification. Section 4 evaluates the performance of our security system. Finally, we conclude in Section 5.

2 Related Works

Much of recent storage security work has focused on authentication, data integrity, and data privacy [7]. Most of NAS systems allege that they have resolved the security issues. In fact, they somewhat have defects. Some systems still suffer from the security attack, the other impose much performance.

Some NAS systems use NFS developed by Sun Microsystems to deploy file system. However, the NFS involves few security mechanisms.

AFS [13,19] and NASD [8,10] employ Kerberos [15, 12] to provide user authentication by requiring users to obtain tickets used as proof of identity and access rights from KDC [15,12]. SFS [5] provides the mutual authentication of servers and users using self-certifying pathnames. However, these systems store data in clear on disks without privacy.

SCARED [1] provides a mechanism for authentication and protection of data integrity. However, it does not employ point-to-point data encryption. CFS[18] performs client-side encryption. The file system encrypts data before it is stored in a shadow file system and decrypts the data as it is read. The short of the CFS is that it has a key distribution problem, since users must remember and distribute the encryption keys.

SUNDR [4] and SNAD [6] use the encrypt-on-disk strategy, where data is concealed by keeping it encrypted on the disk. Revoking access in such systems is expensive because the involved data must be re-encrypted using a new key.

TCFS [9] uses a lockbox to store a single key and encrypts only file data and file names [7]. Some important directory structures left unencrypted. Furthermore, the security of TCFS is at the expense of performance. When write operation, the system performance decreases by more than 50%.

Some access control strategy [3] enlightens us to research further ACL methods.

The recent NFSv4 specifications [22, 23] propose several security mechanisms based on GSS-API [16]. All these mechanisms essentially need establish a secure context and enable mutual authentication. The shortcoming of the NFSv4 architecture is that it storages file in clear and lacks of protection for privacy.

Our system instead aims to provide strong security while preserving good performance. Our scheme uses HMAC [11, 17] and the symmetric cryptography to protect data and employs our authentication architecture to provide user identification.

3 System Specification

3.1 System Design

Client is a multi-user workstation. Client program communicates with user, authentication server and NAS server. Client program performs encryption/decryption for data. Authentication server is a simple module of Kerberos KDC [15, 12]. It administrates the user policy and grants right ticket. NAS Server stores and retrieves encrypted files data for client.

(1),(2) employ the processes like Kerberos authentication .The authentication processes obtain the Ticket and the secret Key K_f, which is used to encrypt the files;

(3),(4) present the tickets to NAS server and establish the security context;

(5),(6) The two processes use K_f to encrypt/decrypt the transmitted data and use HMAC to protect the data integrity.

The scheme provides four important features.

User authentication is the first important feature. User first has to be authenticated by the authentication server. After obtaining a ticket from the authentication server, the user sends it along with the request to the NAS server, allowing the server to authenticate it.

The second mechanism is encryption of all file system data, including data stored on disk and data transmitted. This method only allows the authenticated user to access to the right data while still allowing administrators to do their jobs. All file data are encrypted before transmitting to the NAS server. The NAS server stores the encrypted data.

Guaranteeing data integrity is the third feature. NAS system must guarantee that the transmitted data is intact. The system must detect the tamper and any modified data.

High performance is the fourth goal desirable for a secure file system. Normally, the operations of encryption and decryption consume much overhead. Our system performs the two operations at the client, shifting the bottleneck from the NAS server to the client.

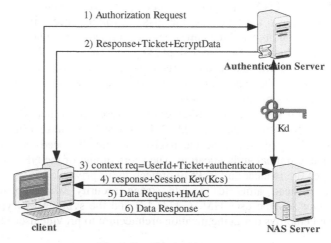

Fig. 1. System Architecture

3.2 System Security Protocol

In this system, NAS server shares the disk key K_d with the authentication server and uses it to produce authenticate key K_{ca} for user. Every NAS users and the authentication server share the K_{ca} that identifies them. In order to protect the privacy of data stored and transmitted, the file blocks are encrypted with the K_f. The authentication server generates the K_f according to K_{ca} and distributes it to NAS clients. NAS server only manages the disk key K_d, which reduces the difficulties of the key management.

Some notation is used in this section. In expression of Kx(M), Subscript x is the encryption Key. Kx(M) represents using x to encrypt the message M. HMACx(M) is a keyed message authentication code, generated by hashing the message M with the disk key x.

3.2.1 User Authentication

When a user firstly access to NAS file system, he has to be authenticated by the authentication server. User obtains the ticket to indicate his identity. In the later access operations, user need not access to the authentication server if the ticket is not expire.

The user presents the following request to authentication server:

$$\text{AuthReq} = \{\text{"UserAuthReq"}, \text{UserID}, \text{SeqNo}, \text{TimeStamp}, \text{RandNum}\} \tag{1}$$

The authentication request includes UserID, sequence number SeqNo, TimeStamp which to prevent the reply-attacks and the random number RandNum which is different from formers.

Upon receiving the request, the authentication server first verifies the request, checks the UserID in the database and obtains the corresponding user key K_{ca}. If the operation is successful, the request is valid. Server generates the AuthReply and sends it to client.

$$\text{AuthReply} = \{\text{"AuthReply"}, \text{SeqNo}, \text{EncryptData}, \text{Ticket}\} \tag{2}$$
$$\text{EncryptData} = \text{Kca} (\text{Kcs}, K_f, \text{ExpTime}, \text{RandNum}).$$

$$K_f = \text{HMAC}_{\text{Kca}} (\text{UserID}) \tag{3}$$

Fig. 2 illustrates the process of the user authentication.

The replied EncryptData includes the file key K_f and the session key K_{cs}. The K_{cs}, which is generated randomly by authentication server, is shared between client and NAS server.

$$\text{Ticket} = K_d (K_{cs}, \text{UserID}, \text{ExpTime}) \tag{4}$$

Ticket is encrypted by K_d, which contains K_{cs}, UserID and ExpTime. Other program and user cannot decrypt the Ticket except the authentication server and NAS server. After receiving the Ticket, the client saves it in local cache file for later use. ExpTime represents the expire-time of Ticket.

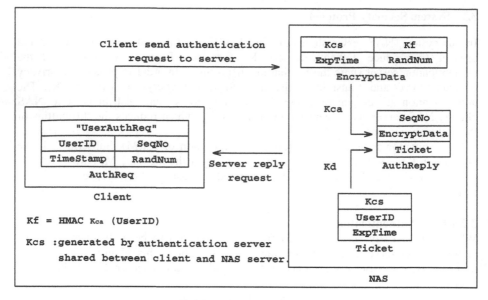

Fig. 2. User Authentication

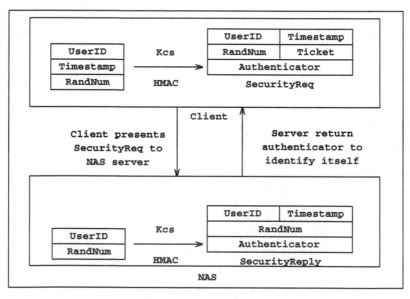

Fig. 3. Security Context Establishment

3.2.2 Security Context Establishment

The process of establishing security context is the mutual authentication of client and NAS server. Client presents SecurityReq to NAS server:

SecurityReq = {UserID, Timestamp, RandNum, Ticket, Authenticator}   (5)
Authenticator = $HMAC_{Kcs}$ (UserID,Timestamp,RandNum)

Upon receiving the request, the NAS server first decrypts the Ticket using Kd and performs the HMAC operation for UserID, Timestamp, and RandNum. Then comparing the HMAC with Authenticator, the client identity and data integrity are verified if equal.In order to mutual authentication, the server must return authenticator to identify itself.

SecurityReply = {UserID, Timestamp, RandNum, Authenticator}   (6)
Authenticator = $HMAC_{Kcs}$ (UserID, RandNum)

After receiving the response from NAS server, the client performs the same operation like server. The server identifies it and the data integrity can be verified.

If everything succeeds, the client and NAS server negotiate the mutual authentication and establish the security context.

Fig. 3. illustrates the process of establishing security context.

3.2.3 Data Exchange

After establishment of security context, the client can access the NAS server.

The client presents the following request to NAS server:

$$M = \{\text{"Request"}, UserID, ReqArgs, ReqData, SeqNum, Timestamp\}, \quad (7)$$
$$HMAC_{Kcs}(M)$$

ReqArgs includes some access parameters such as access type and access object. When write operations, the ReqData presents the write data that is encrypted with file key K_f in client. SeqNum used here is not for security purpose. It allows the client to correlate the UserID with the right user, because the client is a multi-user machine.

After receiving the request, NAS server performs the HMAC operation for M using K_{cs} and compares the result with $HMAC_{Kcs}(M)$.If they are equal, the integrity of message M can be verified and the file system can access disk according to the access permission table. The file system may write the encrypted ReqData to disk. Other program or user cannot read the file data directly without the correct K_{cs}.

NAS server returns the following response to client:

$$M=\{\text{"Response"}, ResponseArgs, data, SeqNum, Timestamp\}, HMAC_{Kcs}(M) \quad (8)$$

ResponseArgs includes many parameters from NAS such as access status. If read operation, data must be decrypted with K_f before understanding it. SeqNum allows the client to correlate the right user•

After receiving the response, client performs the HMAC operation for M using K_{cs} and compares with $HMAC_{Kcs}(M)$.If they are equal, the integrity of message M achieves to verify. When write operations, the client affirms the completion of write.

Fig. 4. explains the process of data Exchange.

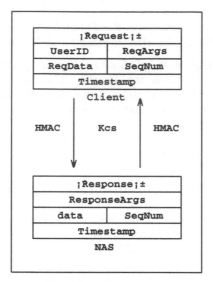

Fig. 4. Data Exchange

4 Performance Analysis

4.1 Simulation Experimental Environment

We have built a simulation prototype implementation of the cryptographic protocols. In addition, we have constructed simulation environment and ran our experiments to see how much performance penalty the cryptographic overhead will impose on the storage. In our simulation experiments, the authentication server is currently not involved. To ensure an impartial comparison, we tested the system using the same hardware configuration. We measured the system throughput using Iometer [21].

Table 1. The simulation environment use the computers listed in this table

Tested bed	configuration
NAS server	CPU P4 2.4G ;Memory 1G; Seagate 7200RPM, 3COM 3C905B
Client	CPU P4 1.8G ;Memory 256M; Seagate 7200RPM,3COM 3C905B

The NAS server and the client are connected each other by 100 MBits/s Ethernet using a switch. Our test items consist of reads and writes to logical blocks on the disk with random and sequential access patterns.

4.2 Prototype Performance

To make clear the impact of security on performance, we first tested the system without any security. This is our base system. Then we tested the system with security involved. Results show the network-attached storage simulation prototype's performance of reads and writes with/without security [7].

Comparing the performance of sequential accesses and that of random accessed by Fig. 5, we can conclude that the performance of sequential accesses is much better. In addition, with the block's size increasing from 1 KB to 32 KB, both random reads and random writes losing little performance for security. Results demonstrate, with block sizes increasing up to 32 KB, the system loses less performance for security. When the storage performs sequential writes or reads, the overhead of cryptographic work increases along with the amount of the data block transmitted growing up.

From the Fig.5, the results show that large sequential reads or write with security impose performance penalty by 10-20%, which is much less than some other security systems.

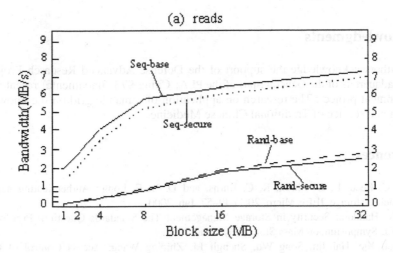

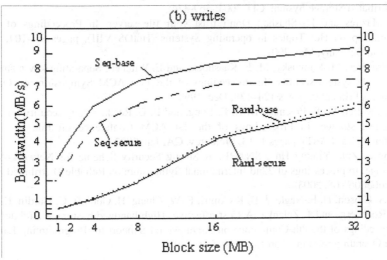

Fig. 5. Prototype Performance (read operations)

5 Conclusion

In this paper, we propose a security scheme for network-attached storage (NAS) that is based on NFSv4 security architecture and uses authentication infrastructure like Kerberos to provide user authentication. Our system uses HMAC and the symmetric cryptography to protect data from tampering, eavesdropping and replaying attacks; it also ensures that the data stored on the storage is copy-resistant and private.

It is important that our strong security does not impose much performance penalty. The simulation experiments show that large sequential reads or writes with security impose performance expense by 10-20%, which is much less than some other security systems.

The system is feasible to current computing power and becomes more attractive as processors become faster.

Acknowledgments

The authors acknowledge the support of the Defense Advanced Research Project of the Headquarters of the General Staff of the PLA; China 973 fundamental research and development project: The research on application of semantic grid on the knowledge sharing and service of Traditional Chinese Medicine.

References

1. B. C. Reed, E. G. Chron, R. C. Burns, and D. D. E. Long.: Authenticating network-attached storage. IEEE Micro, 20(1):49–57, Jan. 2000.
2. B.K. Haddon.: Security in Storage Management The Standards Question. Proc of 18th IEEE Symposium on Mass Storage Systems, 2001.
3. Chao Xie, Hai Jin, Song Wu, Shengli Li, Zhiping Wang: Access Control of Global Distributed Storage System. CIT 2004: 369-374
4. D. Mazires and D. Shasha.: Don't trust your file server. In Proceedings of the 8th Workshop on Hot Topics in operating Systems (HotOS VIII), pages 99–104, Schloss Elmau, Germany, May 2001.
5. D. Mazires, M. Kaminsky, M. F. Kaashoek, and E. Witchel.: Separating key management from file system security. In Proceedings of the 17th ACM Symposium on Operating Systems Principles, pages 124–139, Dec. 1999.
6. E. L. Miller, W. E. Freeman, D. D. E. Long, and B. C. Reed.: Strong secutity for network attached storage. In Proceedings of the 1st ACM Conference on File and Storage technologies (FAST), pages 1–13, Monterey, CA, Jan. 2002.
7. Yingwu Zhu, Yiming Hu : SNARE: A Strong Security Scheme for Network-Attached Storage, In processings of 22nd International Symposium on Reliable Distributed Systems October 06 ~08, 2003.
8. G. A. Gibson, D. F. Nagle, J. B. K. Amiri, F. W. Chang, H. Gobioff, C. Hardin, E. Riedel, D. Rochberg, and J. Zelenka: A Cost-effective, High-bandwidth Storage Architecture. In Proceedings of the 8th Conference on Architectural Support for Programming Languages and Operating Systems, San Jose, CA, Oct. 1998.

9. G. Cattaneo, L. Catuogno, A. D. Sorbo, and P. Persiano : The Design and Implementation of a Transparent Cryptographic File System for Unix. In Proceedings of the Freenix Track: 2001 USENIX Annual Technical Conference, Boston, MA, June 2001, pages 199–212.

10. H Gobioff : Security for a High Performance Commodity Storage Subsystem. PhD thesis, Carnegie Mellon University, 1999.

11. H Krawczyk, M Bellare, R Canetti : HMAC:Keyed-hashing for Message Authentication. Request for Comment (RFC) 2104, Internet Engineering Task Force (IETF), Feb. 1997.

12. J. G. Steiner, B. C. Neuman, and J. Schiller : Kerberos: An Authentication Service for Open Network Systems. In Proceedings of the Winter 1988 USENIX Technical Conference, Dallas, TX, Feb 1988.

13. J. H. Howard, M. L. Kazar, S. G. Menees, D. A. Nichols,M. Satyanarayanan, R. N. Sidebotham, and M. J. West : Scale and Performance in a Distributed File System. ACM Transactions on Computer Systems,Feb.1988.

14. J. Hughes.: Security in storage. Proc of 19th IEEE Symposium on Mass Storage Systems, 2002.

15. J.Kohl,C.Neuman : The Kerberos Network Authentication Service(V5). Request for Comment (RFC) 1510. September 1993.

16. J.Linn : Generic Security Service Application Program Interface Version 2, Update 1, Request for Comment (RFC) 2743, January 2000.

17. M Bellare , R Canetti , H Krawczyk: Message Authentication Using Hash Functions -The HMAC Construction . RSA Laboratories' CryptoBytes, Spring 1996, Vol.2,No.1

18. M.Blaze.: A cryptographic file system for unix. In Proceedings of the first ACM Conference on Computer and Communication Security, pages 9–15, Fairfax, VA, Nov. 1993.

19. M. Spasojevic and M. Satyanarayanan : An Empirical Study of a Wide-area Distributed File System. ACM Transactions on Computer Systems,May 1996,14(2), pages 200–222.

20. Weitao Sun, Jiwu Shu, Weimin Zheng: Storage Virtualization System with Load Balancing for SAN. GCC Workshops 2004: 254

21. Li Bigang, Shu Jiwu, Zheng Weimin, Design and Optimization of an iSCSI system, GCC'2004 Workshop on Storage Grid and Technologies, LNCS 3252, pages 262–269,WuHan,Nov. 2004.

22. S. Shepler, B. Callaghan, D. Robinson, R. Thurlow,C. Beame, M. Eisler, and D. Noveck: NFS Version 4 Protocol. Request for Comment (RFC) 3010, Internet Engineering Task Force (IETF), Dec. 2001.

23. S.Shepler B.Callaghan D.Robinson R.Thurlow C.Beame M.Eisler D.Noveck : Network File System (NFS) version 4 Protocol. Request for Comment (RFC) 3530, Internet Engineering Task Force (IETF), April 2003.

24. Thomas E. Anderson, Michael D. Dahlin, Jeanna M. Neefe, David A. Patterson, Drew S. Roselli, and Randolph Y. Wang. Serverless Network File Systems, ACM Transactions on Computer Systems, Feb. 1996.

25. W. Freeman and E. Miller.: Design for a Decentralized Security System for Network Attached Storage. Proc of 17th IEEE Symposium on Mass Storage Systems, 2000.

Using Blocks Correlations to Improve the I/O Performance of Large Network Storage System

ChangSheng Xie, Zhen Zhao, Jian Liu, and Wei Wu

National Storage System Laboratory, College of Computer Science & Technology,
Huazhong University of Science & Technology, HuBei, WuHan, 430074
zhaozhen1212@126.com, cs_xie@hust.edu.cn

Abstract. In the large network storage system, the operation of continuously reading discrete small blocks severely impacts the I/O performance. To solve this problem, this paper designs and implements a system prototype, which implements precise prefetch and regulates the data distribution according the small blocks correlations, mined by a novel heuristic algorithm between the file system and block device. The system performance can be improved evenly and continuously without interruption and sudden state transitions. Furthermore, compared with other algorithms, this heuristic algorithm thinks about both the locality and the globality of the correlations. Through the experiments, it has been proved that the prototype and the algorithm are effective and the system I/O performance can be enhanced distinctly. Furthermore, the prototype can be used universally by not modifying the file system and the storage devices

1 Introduction

For most large storage systems, the data layout is static, and can't adapt to the change of I/O characteristics. The unadaption of storage system data layout may also lead to the descending of the system performance with the increasing of system usage time. As it is known to all, disk fragment is a common problem which leads to the gradual descending of the disk performance. And it is also a hard problem to be solved, because it will take much time to complete the defragment process in a single disk. In the RAID system, this problem becomes even harder to solve.

In current large storage systems, RAID1 and RAID5 are used widely. Some of them will change data distribution according to the load characteristics, such as Auto Raid system. But it is a state transition, i.e. transiting from one state to another. This need transfer much data, and cause the performance dropping down, even system stopping. However, in many current systems, such as ECommerce system, the service of 24/7 is needed. So the adjustment of the system had better be performed evenly and continuously.

Prefetch is an important way to improve the performance. Many policies of prefetching have been brought forward but most of them are fit for certain access patterns. Someone supposed to select different policy according to different access pattern, but this also will lead to a sudden transition [1]. The historical information is useless, especially when scattered small blocks are continuously read. This phenomenon will happen frequently.

G. Chen et al. (Eds.): ISPA Workshops 2005, LNCS 3759, pp. 140–148, 2005.
© Springer-Verlag Berlin Heidelberg 2005

In most cases, those block continuously read are interdependent. For example, the operation of 'ls /usr/home' will get the inode block of '/usr/home', then the directory entry block. The two blocks are semantically associated. Some files are put discretely, or read jumpily. There are correlations among those small blocks.

Block correlations are useful for improving the system performance. It can be used for prefetch and data layout adjustment. There have been many discussions on mining data correlations, for example, GSP, SPAD and SPAM [2]. But these methods do not take locality and globality of those correlations into account. In the storage system, the correlations are not stable, and some of them will degenerate.

Getting the correlations can be implemented on three levels, application, file system, and block device driver level. Application level is suitable for special program, for example, in database system, where the speed of querying operation can be enhanced. We can also get abundant information, such as semantic information. Predicting the access pattern is another advantage. But this is only for special application, and is not universal.

File system is also a good level. Some techniques have been implemented to alleviate this problem. For example, the files in the same directory or the whole file try its best to be put together, thus make these blocks continual. Because the blocks in file system have their own logic meanings, it can have more hints to deal with those correlations. But implementation on this level must modify the file system.

While on Block level, it will be transparent to the top user. It need not modify anything, and can be widely used.

This paper provides a system prototype. In this prototype, a heuristic algorithm is used to get the correlations of small discrete blocks. According to the information, those correlative blocks scattered are put into continuous blocks and prefetched. The prototype has been test with both simulated and real-world data. Its performance is found to be better, and the system can reduce the response time. The prototype does not modify the system kernel, and do nothing with the file system.

This paper is organized in 5 sections. Section 2 presents the structure of the prototype. Section 3 explains the heuristic algorithm. Section 4 evaluates the proposed prototype and the algorithm. Finically, section 5 summarizes the main contributions of this work.

2 System Prototype

In the network storage system, when client continually read multiple discrete small blocks from a storage node, it will send many requests, and the disk head of the storage node will also make move several unordered movement, which will be the primary reason increasing the response time. If we put those discrete and interdependent blocks into continues blocks, prefetch some of them accessed frequently into a small RAM in storage nodes, and send them to the client in a single response, the mean response time of the system will be reduced.

During using the storage system, many such discrete and interdependent data will appear, but some of them will degenerate. After a long time, there will be a relative stable aggregate, and the system will gradually adjust the date layout, so the performance of the system will always be kept at a good state or even be enhanced.

2.1 The Structure of This Prototype

This system is consisted of three parts: blocks correlations discover (BCRD), correlations keep module (CRKM) in each storage node, and prefetched correlative data cache (PCRC) in client. The structure is showed in Figure 1. When all requests are sent to target nodes, the information of small read will be sent to read info collector (RIC), which can discard some info if the load is too heavy. When this information is collected for some time, it is sent to BCRD, in which correlations are mined. And when reliable correlations are gained, they are sent to the CRKM in proper storage node.

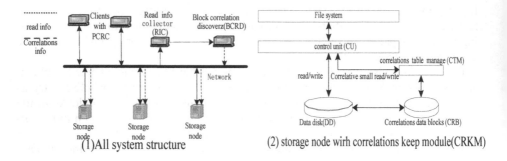

Fig. 1. Prototype Structure

As a block device driver, CRKM module locates between file system and block device in the storage node. Figure 1 (2) shows its structure. For file system, it is transparent just like a block device. The main function of this module is to implement in the control unit (CU). The correlations are kept in correlations table manager (CTM), and correlative blocks are put into Correlations data blocks (CDB). CDB can just be a small partition of disk or memory. If combining CRKM with disk catch disk (DCD) [3], the performance of small write can be improved also.

2.2 Read Path

How to select the read path mainly depends on the size of the read request. For large read, the CU passes the request to the data disk (DD) directly. At the same time, it also judges whether some of those blocks are in CRKM and have been updated. If that is true, the requests are sent to CDB, and all of those blocks are reorganized in CU at last.

For small read, the client first examines whether the data is in PCRC. If the result is positive, they will be got from PCRC directly, or the request will be sent to storage nodes. Those nodes should be checked whether the data is in CTBD. If the answer is false, data should be read from DD. Otherwise, data will be read form CTBD, and other correlative data in CTBD will be read together. After this, they will be sent back in a package, and those prefetched data are put into PCRC. The correlative blocks which are read from DD are sent to CDB. Then they will be transferred into CDB gradually.

2.3   Write Path and Consistency

Large write requests are sent to DD by CU. If blocks in those requests are kept in CRKM, they are just given an invalid mark. Small requests are sent to DD or CRKM according to the structure of RBK in CRKM. The data will be inconsistent between the DD and CRKM on condition that the data blocks in CRBK are modified, and the system crashes at the same time. If the RBK is a nonvolatile device, such as NVRM or disk, the requests are sent to CRKM directly. Otherwise DD is the best place to keep the latest data. In other words, the DD and RDK must be updated synchronously. In this way, the consistency of the system can be kept.

When the data in CRKM which are prefetched by some client are updated, it will be inconsistent between the storage node and the client. There are two schemes, push and pull, to solve this problem. In the scheme of push, while updating some correlative data, the storage node informs clients who prefetched these data, and send the new data to them at the same time. But there is a limitation that the storage node should remember who have prefetched those data.

In pull scheme, the client should send requests, regardless whether the data are in BCRD. If the data are in BCRD, the request is marked a special token. If the data have been updated, the token will not have any effect, and they will be read just as mentioned above. Otherwise, the storage node just gives that client an ACK package.

2.4   Adjusting the Data Layout

When the amount of data in CDB is more than the threshold and the correlations in storage node is stable, these data must be reconstructed as follows: allocate continuous free spaces in DD for locate those data, and keep the index table of them in CTM, which maps old position to new one. When the visited frequency of some blocks is more than a certain value, these blocks will be kept in CDB. Otherwise, they will be gradually swapped by new blocks.

When the replaced data in DD are too much, we can presume that the system's status is too bad. In this condition, any process will be worthless, and then a complete revival is needed, such as using defragmenter to the storage node.

2.5   Analyze the Mean Response Time

For each read request, the response time is made up by the following elements:

1. t_1 :request transfer time
2. t_2 :the time of storage node getting data
3. t_3 :response transfer time

In this prototype, the correlative blocks may be in continuous area for the sake of the adjustment on data layout, and t_2 of the following reads can be reduced. If clients prefetch these blocks, t_2 will be eliminated. The t_1 and t_3 will also be affected, but they are not similar in different updated scheme.

In push scheme, except the first block in a correlative blocks set, all blocks need not be read from storage node. But the update operation on those blocks will need some extra network packages. While, in pull scheme, the package size of some response is shortened, so t_3 is reduced, and t_2 is eliminated.

Push scheme can reduce the mean response time markedly, but pull scheme could be more robust in not reliable or low speed network environment.

3 The Heuristic Algorithms

3.1 Definition of the Block Correlation

If a block b_1 appears, block b_2 will be likely to appear. We call this a correlation, which is marked as $b_1 \rightarrow b_2$. The rest may be deduced by analogy that it may be $b_1 b_2 \rightarrow b_3$, $b_1 \rightarrow b_2 b_3$. The left is called the correlation's prefix, and the right is postfix.

On the level of block device driver, the block number is the single standard to judge the correlation. If and only if some sequence of block number appears many times, we could claim it a correlation. That is to say, if some blocks are considered correlative, firstly, all of them must have a high appearing frequency. Secondly, they must often appear in a fixed pattern. This algorithm is consisted of two steps: getting local correlative blocks and getting global correlative blocks. Every relation is marked with some info.

1. *prefix_count*: the appearance times of the prefix.
2. *postfix_count*: the appearance times of the postfix along with the prefix.
3. *cr_scale*: *prefix_count* / *postfix_count*.

Also some variants are defined.

1. *t*: the time of recording small read info.
2. *M:* the minimal appearing times of a correlation in our candidates set.
3. *Ms*: the minimal *cr_scale* of a correlation in our candidates set.

3.2 Get Local Correlative Blocks

After recording the small read info for some time *t*, all information form a block number aggregate L. After a long period of time, the series $L_0...L_n$ will be got. To each L, we sort it by block number. Then we could easily get the record set, m_1, whose visiting frequent is more than $\lfloor M/2 \rfloor$. Secondly, we make $C_2 = M_1 \times M_1$, C_2 is the Descartes set of M1. Then we remove the overlap items, such as 'aa', 'bb', getting the C2.the member of the candidate set is composed of two elements, $a_1 a_2$, we check whether a_2 appear in s steps after a_1. If it appears, the postfix count increases one. Then, if *cr_scale* <*Ms*/2, it will be removed. Finally, we get $M_2 = C_2$.

And so on, the $C_k = M_{k-1} \times M_1$, remove the improper elements. We got M_k. At last we get M_{n+1}, which is empty. Then we stop the cycle.

$$T_m = M_2 \bigcup ... \bigcup M_{k-1} \bigcup M_k, \tag{1}$$

Because we want to get more through less info, for example, if 'abc$\rightarrow$d' exists, 'ab$\rightarrow$cd' may be a candidate, even 'a->bcd'. But according to (2) and (3), we can get (4). So only if some correlation's *cr_scale* is bigger than *Ms* by a specifically value, and its length exceeds 4, we try the correlation's whole content with shorter prefix for some steps, until *cr_scale*<*Ms*.

$$P\ (nm|m) = F(nm)/F(m) \tag{2}$$

$$F(k_1) > F(k_2)\ (\ k_1 \text{ is the prefix of } k_2) \tag{3}$$

$$P\ (n|k_1) < P\ (n|k_2) \tag{4}$$

3.3 Get Global Correlative Blocks

After prior step, we get correlative blocks for each t. Some of them will degenerate. But the goal is to get the long-term relations. So something must be done to pre- result in next time. Those relations degenerating should gradually leave from the set. And the new seed should be added. Our method is this.

$$T_{k1} = T_{k-1} \cap T_k, \tag{5}$$

$$T_{k2} = \overline{T}_{k-1} \cap T_k, \tag{6}$$

$$T_{k3} = T_{k-1} \cap \overline{T}_k \tag{7}$$

$$T_k = T_{k1} \cup T_{k2} \cup T_{k3} \tag{8}$$

To T_{k1}, its element's *prefix_count* and *postfix_count* are the sum of the element in two set, T_{k-1} and T_k. For those in T_{k3}, they are not appearing in L_k, so they must be given penalty. If their prefix in T_k, they have been punished. Or its *postfix_count* subtracted some value. If their appearance count less than $\lfloor M/2 \rfloor$, or *cr_scale* less than $Ms/2$, it will be removed form T_{k3}. At last, the new T_k is got.

After a long time, we will get a steady correlations set. Before using that set, some redundant relations can be removed. For example, (a->b, ab->c, a->bc) could be replaced with (a->bc). Finally, we get a minimal effective aggregate.

3.4 Proper Parameters

In this algorithm, some parameters will affect the performance. Major of them are t, M and Ms. The value of t will affect the globality and validity. While, the *M* and *Ms* will affect how many relations will be kept. Improper values will lose too much info or aggravate the burden of the system.

The degree of punishment to these elements in T_{k3} mentioned above should be taken into account carefully also. This affects the degenerated rate of that aggregate. When it is too small, the aggregate will not be able to become steady soon, but too large value will make some elements lost irrelevantly.

Most of those parameters are interdependent, for example, *t* and *Ms*, *M* and *Ms*. Usually, just changing one value cannot get good performance.

4 Experimental Results

For the purpose of performance evaluation, we have implemented the system proto-type in Linux system. There are two machines both with a 1.7GHz Pretium-4 processor and 512 Mbytes of memory. One runs as the storage node, and another as the relation discover. An emulator is constructed contemporarily, in which every thread represents a client. A thread has its own cache space and PCRC, and it issues I/O request to the storage node.

4.1 Response Time of the Raw System and This Prototype

To compare the performance of the raw system and this prototype, we contrast their mean response time in 10M and 1000M-Ethernet. At the same time, there is a compare between the two update schemes (push and pull). The trace used in this experiment is the HP traces, which was collected from HP-UX systems during a 4-month period and it's typical for transaction. The result got by our simulator is shown in Figure 2.

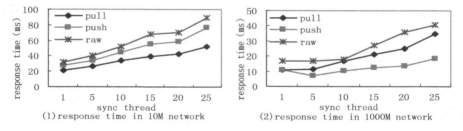

Fig. 2. The performance of this prototype in different network environment

From the result, we can see that the mean response time of the prototype is reduced distinctly compared to the raw system for the speedup on small read. It also can be found that in the 10M-Ethernet network, the pull scheme is better than another. The reason is that the update request should send updated notification to some clients in push scheme, and this operation will consume much time with low bandwidth. But in 1000M-Ethernet network, it can be ignored. It can be concluded that the push scheme would be preferred in high speed environment.

4.2 Selecting Appropriate t and Ms

The t and Ms in the mining algorithms play a larger role for system performance, and this experiment is to examine how it will impact the performance with varying values. We test the mean response time with the changing of t and Ms. The response time is presented in Figure 3.

Figure 3 (1) shows the mean response time of the prototype with the change of t. As we see, at the beginning, the response time reduces with t increasing, but increases with t after a certain point. The reason is that in a longer period of t, more info can be got. But too long a time of t will result in the not-timely info. In other words, the correlation may have degenerated already before the time point of t. So we must select the value of t carefully. It had better to use the t with a dynamic value, fluctuating near a assured value of 5 minutes.

Figure 3 (2) shows the response time with different Ms. Small Ms will make the block device use too much memory, and also cost more time to find appropriate pattern, while large Ms will lose too much relations info. Through the test we select 60% as the appropriate value.

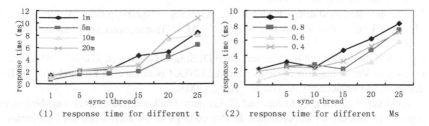

(1) response time for different t   (2) response time for different   Ms

Fig. 3. Mean response time with different t or Ms

5   Conclusions

Based on these experiments, the algorithm is proved to be efficient to mine the correlations in the network storage system, and the system prototype is a effective method to improve the I/O performance of the storage system. Furthermore, realizing this prototype needs no special hardware support, and does not change the existing software. At the same time, it will not change the disks data layout, which makes it able to be used universally.

Without any logistic and semantic information of these blocks, we cannot optimize single directory and file. And in the worst situation, lacking the criterion to abandon useless info will lead to some information interrupting us, such as, those data modified frequently. These are our future work.

This algorithm proposed in the paper is a general one, and can be used in many fields such as web prefetching. Furthermore we will use it in OBS (object based storage).

Acknowledgements

This paper is supported by national science foundation (60273073)

References

[1] KE ZHOU and JIANG-LING ZHANG: "Cache pfefetching adaptive policy based on access pattern", Proceedings of the first International Conference on machine leaning and cybernetics, Beijing, 4-5 November 2002

[2] J. Ayres, J. E. Gehrke, T. Yiu, and J. Flan nick. Sequential pattern mining using bitmaps. In Proc. 2002 ACM SIGKDD Int. Conf. Knowledge Discovery in Databases (KDD'02), pages 429–435, Edmonton, Canada, July 2002

[3] Yiming Hu and Qing Yang, "DCD—Disk Caching Disk: A New Approach for Boosting I/O Performance", in Proceedings of the 23td international Symposium on computer Architecture, pp.169-178,May 1996

[4] A. D. Brown, T. C. Mowry, and O. Krieger. Compiler-based I/O prefetching for out-of-core applications. ACM Transactions on Computer Systems,19(2):111–170, 2001.

[5] R. Agrawal and R. Srikant. Mining sequential patterns. In Eleventh International Conference on Data Engineering, 1995.

[6] GREGORY R. GANGER, CRAIG A. N. SOULES   " Soft Updates: A Solution to the Metadata Update Problem in File Systems" ACM Transactions on Computer Systems, May 2000

[7] Craig A.N. Soules, Garth R. Goodson, John D. Strunk, Gregory R. Ganger "Metadata Efficiency in Versioning File Systems" 2nd USENIX Conference on File and Storage Technologies, San Francisco, CA, Mar 31 - Apr 2, 2003.

[8] J. Schindler, J. Griffin, C. Lumb, and G. Ganger. Track-aligned extents: matching access patterns to disk drive characteristics. In Proceedings of the First USENIX Conference on File and Storage Technologies, 2002.

[9] A. Seifert and M. H. Scholl. A multi-version cache replacement and prefetching policy for hybrid data delivery environments. In 28th International Conference on Very Large Data Bases (VLDB), 2002

A Cluster LVM for SAN Environments

Bigang Li, Jiwu Shu, Fei Mu, and Weimin Zheng

Tsinghua University, Beijing, China
lbg01@mails.tsinghua.edu.cn

Abstract. Logical Volume Managers (LVM) have been a key component of storage systems. They can support volume online resizing and reconfiguration, snapshots, and various software RAID levels. But most logical volume managers are only suitable for single system environments. They are not adequate for Storage Area Network (SAN) environment where cluster hosts share same storage resources. In this paper, we present a cluster LVM (cLVM) for SAN environments, and explain the design and architecture of the cLVM in detail. The cLVM's key techniques include its management mechanism, device mapping method, metadata synchronization between cluster hosts and fault tolerance. The management mechanism controls all the cLVM operations and all of the storage resources. It provides a uniform view of the cLVM to users and includes a user-friendly interface. The fault tolerance is designed to deal with disk failures and to manage mode or cluster node shutdowns. One agent is set as the management node for synchronizing the metadata in the kernel space between the different nodes in the cLVM. Through the metadata synchronization and the device mapping method, the cLVM provides the file systems with a uniform virtualized view of the storage devices and supports cluster host environments. It achieves online resizing, movement of data between partitions and snapshots. We implemted and tested the cLVM. The result shows that it is also compatible with ordinary common single file systems or GFS. It has comparatively better fault tolerance than the LVM currently in use. The new cLVM system supports the computing needs of large enterprises and provides high scalability and high availability in the SAN environment.

1   Introduction

The increasing growth of the network data has stimulated the advancement of storage systems. Because of growing data storage needs, it has become urgent to develop an efficient, manageable, and expanded storage system with huge capacity[1]. To meet the practical demand, the Storage Area Network (SAN) has developed relatively quickly. In SAN systems, various servers can effectively share and expand storage resources by directly accessing the disks on the SAN (e.g., the Fibre-Channel network[2][3]). Thus, the SAN system has become the best solution for the storage problem large enterprises are currently facing.

The Sistina Company used the GFS (Global File System) as a parallel file system in a SAN environment, and issued the LVM (Logical Volume Manager) as

G. Chen et al. (Eds.): ISPA Workshops 2005, LNCS 3759, pp. 149–158, 2005.

one part of a Linux kernel. They provided a solution plan for the virtualization of storage in single systems[4][5]. IBM also used EVMS (Enterprise Volume Management System) to solve the problem of virtualized storage at the enterprise level[6]. However the solution plans mentioned above were quite complicated, making them inappropriate for practical operation. They have strict requirements for the software environment and are unsuitable for virtualized storage in a SAN environment. For other compares, Chang-Soo Kim used a SANtopia storage system, consisting of the SANtopia file system and volume management. Only by combining these two parts could this system support virtualized storage in SAN environment[7][8]. It was also incompatible with the current storage system for Linux/UNIX. Pool Driver[9] is another virtual storage system with functions similar to those of LVM. With the assistance of GFS, it can accomplish virtual storage in a SAN system. However, it is not capable of have online expansion or configuration. The Petal[16] is another distributed virtual disk, but it does not have fault tolerance. Another drawback to Petal is that there are few storage systems using Petal, while the LVM is very popular.

In this paper, we propose a plan for the implementation of the cLVM in a SAN environment, which is based on the current Linux LVM for single systems. We distribute the administrative responsibility of different volume groups to different hosts, and the agent in the host supervises its own volume group and synchronizes the metadata within hosts through configuration tools running in the user's space. Compared with other virtualization systems, our cLVM has some advantages, as described below:

- Our cLVM is a global aware system for SAN systems. If one node changes the configuration of the system, the other nodes are aware of it. In other virtualization systems, such as the LVM, nodes are not aware of the configuration of other nodes and two or more nodes, could use the same disk leading to the system failure,
- The cLVM has a global lock mechanism to ensure the logical correction of the virtualization system,
- The cLVM has a fault tolerance. If one or more nodes shut down unexpectedly, our virtualization system can provide uninterrupted service. The metadata of the virtualization system is kept on an extra node, so the system is able to provide high reliability for users.

This cLVM is suitable for the implementation of virtualized storage in a SAN environment and has such functions such as online alteration of disk capacity, snapshot and online backup, redundancy storage, and management of storage resources.

2   Basic Knowledge

The Linux LVM for single systems has many tasks to perform[10]. At present, the capacity of several disk drivers is often desirable for a large file system. Because most file systems can only be established on a single physical disk,

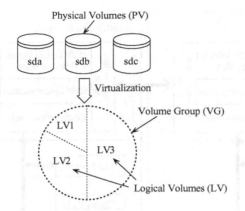

Fig. 1. Relationships of the PV, LV and VG

individual disks are combined into one logical device for the file system. LVM can easily achieve this, and furthermore, it can resize the disks online without being restricted by different disk sizes.

In the Linux system, the LVM accomplishes virtualized storage by mapping and changing the address of IO requests sent by file systems. It maps the logical device to the proper physical device, and changes the logic request offsets before transferring them to the bottom block device driver[10].

As a single device or domain, Physical Volume (PV) is the lowest unit in the Linux LVM storage hierarchy. Each PV includes a Volume Group Descriptor Area (VGDA) that consists of some special information about the LVM configuration. A PV can join the existing Volume Group (VG) at any time, and a VG can be seen as a big storage pool, consisting of one or several Logical Volumes (LVs) while each LV serves the file system as a practical logical device. Their relationship is shown in figure 1. The PV and LV are both made up of physical extent (PE). The LVM uses PEs to map the logical address to the physical address. One PE is typically a few megabytes, and PEs within one volume group are identical. Users can configure the size of the PEs using the configuration module.

For each volume group, a volume group descriptor area is allocated to contain the specific configuration information. In one host, after the LVM changed the VGDA in one Physical Volume, it must inform other hosts of the change in the LV and synchronize the data in the memory.

3   Overview of the Cluster LVM

Figure 2 represents the architecture of our storage system. It consists of file systems, the cLVM in the kernel space, configuration tools, a cLVM synchronization module and a cLVM control module. The cLVM kernel module and the configuration tools are much more like those found in single systems. In our system,

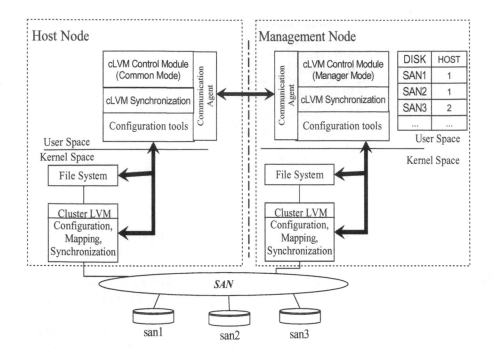

Fig. 2. The architecture of the cluster LVM

they were only slightly changed. The cLVM synchronization module in the user space was developed for the metadata synchronization between hosts. The communication agent is the cLVM control data channel, and it is based on the TCP and UDP networks. The cLVM control module can work in two modes: common mode and manager mode. In cLVM systems, only one host runs the control module in the manager mode. The file system will be GFS or SFS, even for common file systems, such as AFS[13], xFS[14], Zebra[15]and Petal[16].The ReiserFS and SGI XFS with the cLVM can be online resized without umounting the device. The cLVM collects various storage devices connected with SAN systems, and creates logical volumes for multiple hosts. Most of this paper will concentrate on the cLVM control module and the synchronization module, which are described in detail in the next part.

4   Implementation and Management

The cluster logical volume manager runs in all cluster hosts and makes it possible to provide file systems with a virtualized view of shared physical storage devices in a SAN environment. It provides logical volumes for file system and all of file system's I/O operations are performed in the logical address space. The cluster logical volume manager will map logic address to the proper physical disk and the proper offset in the same mode with the LVM for a single system.

4.1   Metadata Synchronization Between Hosts

One cLVM synchronization module operates on each host node, and is responsible for communication with the local cLVM kernel and for sending the cLVM
metadata synchronization information to other agents and the management host
node. When the host is in the process of creating a logical volume or expanding
its capacity, the cLVM synchronization module carries out the synchronization
of the cLVM between clustered nodes.

The cLVM metadata synchronization between host nodes includes VG and
LV synchronization. The synchronization operations can also be divided into two
parts: (1) the revision of user space data including the metadata of the storage
disk, that is the metadata backup file. (2) updating kernel space information
in detail, and updating cLVM information in the kernel space. The node being
synchronized simply updates the cLVM information in the cLVM kernel. The
most important synchronization operations are getting and inputting the correct cLVM metadata, which is implemented by IOCTL functions, and most of
these IOCTL functions are supplied by the LVM for single systems,such as the
LV_CREAT,LV_EXTEND,LV_RESIZE and so on.

4.2   Management Node

To ensure the synchronization of all of the virtualized operations in clustered
hosts and the unified management of all the storage resources, one node within
the cluster is chosen to be the management node. The management node employs
a lock mechanism to ensure that only one cLVM operation is executed at a
time. This can simplify the distributed virtual storage system and improve its
reliability.

The management node supervises all network storage resources and synchronizes the virtualized layer information between nodes to offer the file manager
a unified storage view.It assigns unified serial numbers(for example san1,san2
and host1,host2) to the network disks and host nodes in the SAN environment.
These disks and nodes are the basic units that the management software must
supervise. One or several of these network disks constitute the VG. The establishment and management competence of a single VG is simply assigned to a
single host node; thus a storage resources table is protected on the management
host node. Meanwhile, the cLVM control module for every host node also records
its own disk tabulation, and then the structure of the mapping table relates the
mapping information to a specific disk to be scattered over several hosts. The
cLVM on a specific host can freely control and manage the disks (or VG) of its
own. In the SAN environment, we assumed that the hosts trust each other. With
the management node, all logical volume operations can be synchronized. When
one host performs some operations such as creating or resizing logical volumes,
these steps must be followed:

  – the host notifies the management node of the operation,
  – the management node sets the operation lock,

– the management node informs other hosts related to that VG,
– the host preforms the operation through its cluster logical volume interface,
– the management node synchronizes the cluster logical volume information for related hosts,
– the management node releases the operation lock. The management node notifies the user of the result of this operation.

There are only a few of these operations, so only one can be operation constrained at a time. This is accomplished by the management node's locking mechanism. The management node controls lock's flag and decides which operation should be set. With this design, the cluster logical volume manager offers a uniform view of the logical devices for different SAN hosts.

The management node sets the physical disks as the basic administrative unit, and many key functions are implemented by the cluster hosts. So the single system Linux LVM provides many benefits. To synchronize the data of clustered hosts, the management node controls three mapping tables: the PV_VG table, which indicates the volume groups that every physical disk belongs to or just free space; the VG_Node table, which indicates the relationship between the volume groups and the hosts; and the LV_Node table, which consists of the logical volume information and permission for functions such as reading or writing. These managing data are scattered over all the SAN's hosts to prevent system failure. The management node is the key role for the uniform view of the clustered LVM. Additionally, the logical volume operations are not very frequently used and the metadata is also small, so the management node does not affect the performance of the whole storage system. The uniform management provides high scalability, high availability and high flexibility.

4.3   Device Mapping

The management node protects disk device tabulation not only by controlling the information about network disks, but also by distributing information to the proper hosts. It protects the information of this distribution table and synchronizes the tables included in the configuration module of other nodes at the same time. Each time the content gets updated, the data from this table is stored into a file for backup. Table 1 indicates one possible table message. According to table 1, disk1 and disk2 belong to VG1 used by host2, while disk3 serves as free space. When the space in disk3 needs to be distributed to host2, the cLVM module on the host node can ensure the management competence of disk3 merely by directly changing the value in the table. Each network disk corresponds to one row in the table, making it convenient to add or delete disks.

4.4   Fault Tolerance

We designed and implemented a fault tolerant mechanism for the cluster LVM. When one cluster node shuts down suddenly, the management module in the management node will first note its disconnection from the TCP network, and the management node will handle the problem using the following steps:

Table 1. The distribution of network disks

DISK	MAJOR& MINOR	VG	HOST
SAN1	[8,2] ...	VG1	Host 2
SAN2	[8,3] ...	VG1	Host 2
SAN3	[8,4] ...	VG2	Host 4

- clear up the cLVM operation of this host node which may be in the process of being executed,
- release the operation lock,
- set the HOST table state as DIS_ACTIVE to show that this host node cannot work normally,
- consult the MAPPING DEVICE table and recycle the disks (or VG) which have been distributed to this host node,
- broadcast the HOST table to other host nodes on the network,
- synchronize the data on other host nodes.

When the host node has recovered, it should first be reconnected to the management host and then get registered in the simultaneous operation with kernel figures. Since adequate independence is ensured between host nodes, when one host node shuts down, the whole virtual storage system can still work effectively.

When the management node fails, it produces a little more trouble. When the management node suddenly shuts down, no cLVM operation on the system can be carried out. However, the remaining host nodes can still work normally, ensuring regular performance. When the management node recovers, following steps are carried out:

- the management module reads the configuration file, establish HOST tabulation and the search network disk to create a uniform view for the disks,
- the management module reads the backup file and creates a MAPPING DEVICE table, a VG table and a DISK table,
- the management node issues a broadcast, asking each host node to send the table data from their internal memories,
- the management node chooses and updates the table data according to the timestamp,
- the management module resynchronizes the table data in the internal memories of each host node and resumes normal management function.

In the view of the three possible cases mentioned above, the distributed virtualized storage system can manage them well, ensure normal service, and safeguard the security and agreement of the overall figures.

5   Performance of the cLVM

Figure 3 illustrates our cLVM prototype, it is implemented on the TH-MSNS system[17]. Eight server nodes share the seven SCSI disks (73GB) via 2Gbps FC

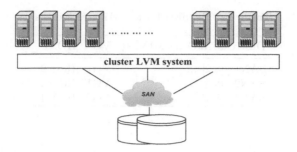

Fig. 3. One cLVM prototype

switch. Each node has two Intel Xeon 2.4G CPUs and 1GB of RAM. The OS
for these server nodes is RedHat 8.0.

These eight nodes are pre-installed in the cLVM to manage the storage pool.
The whole cLVM interface has more than 30 calls and many of these calls are
devoted to information inquiry and management functions, such as obtaining
the LV, PV and VG information and creating and deleting a logical volume,
and creating and deleting a snapshot volume or configuring the server nodes'
information. Mostly these calls are infrequently executed and take less than a
half-second to complete. Our primary performance goals were to provide latency
roughly comparable to a locally attached disk, and throughput that matched
the scale of the number of the servers.

Table 2. Latency comparison

(ms)	LOCAL DISK	CLVM
512byte/read	8	9
64KB/read	12	13
512byte/write	8	9
64KB/write	12	12

We used the iometeor to test the latency of the disks. Table 2 shows a comparison of the read and write latency in two conditions: with the cLVM and without
it. For read/write requests from 512 bytes to 128 KB, the cLVM latency only
slightly increases the latency of I/O operations. Most of the increased latency
is due to the mapping of the logical address to the physical address. Because
this mapping operation is implemented in the RAM or even the CPU cache, it's
not necessary to match the I/O latency to the physical disk's latency. Additionally, with the cLVM, multiple physical disks can be combined to improve the
performance of the storage system.

Figure 4 shows the time taken by the cLVM's function calls. The operation of
extending the logical volume size from 20GB to 200GB was set as representative
to test the functional call's latency. At the same time, we tested the latency for

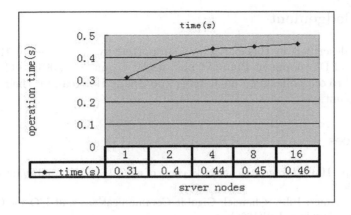

Fig. 4. The cLVM's operating time

cluster nodes with different sizes. The functional call latency is mainly due to
the additional difficulty in transmitting the data over the IP network. As the
server nodes increase, the operation's latency increases slightly. This results in
a time expenditure of less than half a second, while in the Petal system, it adds
around one second.

6   Conclusion

This paper has given one specific implementation plan for cLVM suitable for
a SAN environment, and we proved its performance by implementing it in our
SAN environment. This cLVM was implemented on the basis of a single system
LVM with an open source code, and it synchronized data on different host nodes
through broadcasting. In the cLVM, a specific management host is in charge of
all of the storage resources and is responsible for the synchronization of the data
on each host node. It also provides an error handling mechanism to ensure the
security of virtual storage system configuration data and the continuity of service. The cLVM offers simple and convenient implementation and fully preserves
the functions of the LVM for single system. Additionally, on the basis of unified
management over storage resources, it fully retains the independence of single
host node. Host nodes can be added or removed at any time, and other host
nodes can still work normally when one or more hosts shut down.

The distributed storage management system introduced in this paper greatly
improves the utilization ratio of storage resources, effectively and flexibly distributes storage resources and provides functions like online expansion and configuration of logical disk capacity, the configuration of software RAID and snapshot. With great expansibility, reliability and parallelism, it is a good candidate
for the implementation of virtualized storage pools in SAN environments. The
system's ability to manage uniform storage resources not only meets the users'
needs, but also ensures the integrity of shared data between different host nodes.

158   B. Li et al.

Acknowledgement

The work described in this paper was supported by the National High-Tech Research and Development Plan of China under Grant No. 2001AA111110. We are grateful to our colleague Pan Jiaming and Zhang Hongcan for their help and encouragement.

References

1. B.Phillips: Have storage area networks come of age?, IEEE Computer(1998), vol.31, no.7, 10-12
2. Alan F.Benner: Fibre Channel: Gigabit Communications and I/O for Computer Networks, McGraw-Hill(1996)
3. IBM Corp: Introduction to Storage Area Networks, http://www.redbooks. ibm.com/pubs/pdfs/redbooks/sg245470.pdf,2005
4. RedHat: Logical Volume Manager, http://sources.redhat.com/lvm/,2005
5. RedHat: Global File Systems, http://www.redhat.com/software/rha/gfs/, 2005
6. Steven Pratt : EVMS: A Common Framework for Volume Management,Linux Technology Center, http://evms.sf.net, 2005
7. Chang-Soo Kim, Gyoung-Bae Kim, Bum-Joo Shin: Volume Management in SAN Environment, ICPADS (1997)500-508
8. Yong Kyu Lee, Shin Woo Kim, Gyoung Bae Kim:Metadata Management of the SANtopia File System, ICPADS (1997)492-499
9. David Teigland: The Pool Driver: A Volume Driver for SANs, http://www.sistina.com, 2000
10. David Teigland, Heinz Mauelshagen: Volume Managers in Linux, Sistina Software Inc, http://www.sistina.com, 2000
11. Infiniband Trade Association: Infiniband Architecture Specification(2001) , Volume 1, Release 1.0a
12. Steve Soltis: The design and performance of a shared disk file system for IRIX, in the 6th Goddard Conference on Mass Storage Systems and Technologies in cooperation with the Fifteen IEEE Symposium on Mass Storage Systems(1998)
13. M. Stayanarayanan: Scalable, Secure, and highly available distributed file access. IEEE Computer(1990), 23(5):9-21
14. Thomas Anderson, Michael Dahlin, Jeanna Neefe: Serverless network file systems, ACM Transactions on Computer Systems(1996) 14(1):41-79
15. John Hartman and John Ousterhout: The Zebra striped network file system, ACM Transactions on Computer Systems(1995) 13(3):274-310
16. Edward Lee and Chandramohan Thekkath: Petal:Distributed Virtual Disks, The proceedings of the 7th International Conference on Architectural Support for Programming Languages and Operating Systems(1996)
17. Jiwu Shu,Bigang Li,Weimin Zheng:Design and Implementation of a SAN System Based on the Fiber Channel Protocol, IEEE Transactions on Computers, April 2005

COMPACT: A Comparative Package for Clustering Assessment

Roy Varshavsky[1,*], Michal Linial[2], and David Horn[3]

[1] School of Computer Science and Engineering,
The Hebrew University of Jerusalem 91904, Israel
royke@cs.huji.ac.il
[2] Dept of Biological Chemistry, Institute of Life Sciences,
The Hebrew University of Jerusalem 91904, Israel
michall@cc.huji.ac.il
[3] School of Physics and Astronomy, Tel Aviv University, Israel
horn@post.tau.ac.il

Abstract. There exist numerous algorithms that cluster data-points from large-scale genomic experiments such as sequencing, gene-expression and proteomics. Such algorithms may employ distinct principles, and lead to different performance and results. The appropriate choice of a clustering method is a significant and often overlooked aspect in extracting information from large-scale datasets. Evidently, such choice may significantly influence the biological interpretation of the data. We present an easy-to-use and intuitive tool that compares some clustering methods within the same framework. The interface is named COMPACT for **Comparative-Package-for-Clustering-Assessment**. COMPACT first reduces the dataset's dimensionality using the Singular Value Decomposition (SVD) method, and only then employs various clustering techniques. Besides its simplicity, and its ability to perform well on high-dimensional data, it provides visualization tools for evaluating the results. COMPACT was tested on a variety of datasets, from classical benchmarks to large-scale gene-expression experiments. COMPACT is configurable and expendable to newly added algorithms.[*]

1 Introduction

In the field of genomics and proteomics, as well as in many other disciplines, classification is a fundamental challenge. Classification is defined as systematically arranging entities (data-points) into specific groups. Clustering, being an unsupervised learning problem, may be regarded as a special case of classification with unknown labels (for more details see [1], [2]). In gene expression microarray technology, a hierarchical clustering algorithm was first applied to gene-expression data at different stages of cell cycle in yeast [3]. During recent years several algorithms, originating from various theoretical disciplines (e.g., physics, mathematics, statistics and computational neuroscience), were adopted and adjusted to gene expression analysis. They

---

[*] Corresponding author.

G. Chen et al. (Eds.): ISPA Workshops 2005, LNCS 3759, pp. 159–167, 2005.

are useful for diagnosis of different conditions for example differentiating between sick and healthy tissues, and classification to subtypes of a disease. An additional outcome of applying such algorithms to gene-expression data was the revealing of functional classes of genes among the thousands used in experimental settings [4]. Furthermore, it became possible, and useful, to isolate groups of relevant genes that mostly contribute to a particular condition, in the correlative or derivative perspective, a procedure called bi clustering [5].

By their nature, data points that are collected from large-scale experimental settings suffer from being represented in a high dimensional space. This fact presents a computational and an applicative challenge. Compression methods that maintain the fundamental properties of the data are called for.

As clustering algorithms are rooted in different scientific backgrounds and follow different basic principles, it is expected that different algorithms perform differently on varied inputs. Therefore, it is required to identify the algorithm that suits best a given problem. One of the targets of COMPACT is to address this requirement, and to supply an intuitive, user-friendly interface that compares clustering results of different algorithms.

In this paper we outline the key steps in using COMPACT and illustrate it on two well-known microarray examples of Leukemia [4], and yeast datasets [6]. For a comparative analysis we included routinely used clustering algorithms and commonly applied statistical tests, such as K-Means, Fuzzy C-Means and a competitive neural network. One novel method, Quantum Clustering (QC) [7], was added to evaluate its relative performance. The benefit of applying COMPACT to already processed data is demonstrated. All four algorithms that were applied in analyzing these datasets were compared with a biologically based validated classification. We conclude that the compression of data that comprises the first step in COMPACT, not only reduces computational complexity but also improves clustering quality. Interestingly, in the presented tested datasets the QC algorithm outperforms the others.

2 Implementation

After downloading and configuring COMPACT, four steps should be followed: defining input parameters, preprocessing, selecting the clustering method and presenting the results.

2.1 Input Parameters

COMPACT receives two input parameters that are Matlab variables: data (a two-dimensional matrix) – represents the elements to be clustered, and 'real classification' (an optional, one-dimensional vector) – representing the elements according to an expert view and is based on bulk biological and medical knowledge.

2.2 Preprocessing

  a) Determining the matrix shape and which vectors are to be clustered (rows or columns).
  b) Preprocessing Procedures: SVD, normalization and dimension selection.

2.3 Selecting the Clustering Method

a) Points' distribution preview and clustering method selection: The elements of the data matrix are plotted. If a 'real classification' exists, each of its classes is displayed in a different color. One of the clustering methods, K-means, FCM (fuzzy C-means), Competitive NN (Neural Network) or QC (Quantum Clustering) is to be chosen from the menu.
b) Parameters for clustering algorithms: depending on the chosen method, a specific set of parameters should be defined (e.g., in the K-Means method – number of clusters).

2.4 COMPACT Results

Once COMPACT completes its run, the results are displayed in both graphical and textual formats (results can be displayed also in a log window). In the graphical display, points are tagged by the algorithm. The textual display represents Purity and Efficiency (also known as precision and recall or specificity and sensitivity, respectively) as well as the joint Jaccard Score[1]. These criteria for clustering assessment are defined as follow:

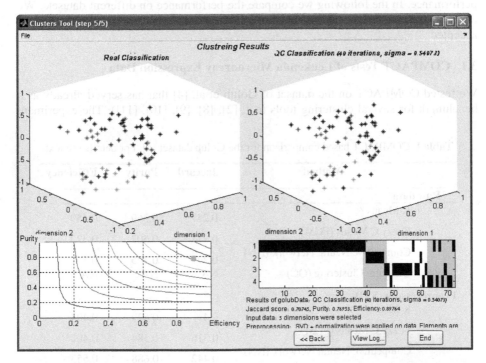

Fig. 1. A screenshot of the graphical view on the results produced by COMPACT

---

[1] The Jaccard score reflects the 'intersection over union' between the algorithm and 'real' clustering, and its values range from 0 (void match) to 1 (perfect match).

$$Purity = \frac{n_{11}}{n_{11}+n_{01}}, \quad \Box Efficiency = \frac{n_{11}}{n_{11}+n_{10}}, \quad Jaccard = \frac{n_{11}}{n_{11}+n_{01}+n_{10}} \qquad (1)$$

Where:

- n_{11} is the number of pairs that are classified together, both in the 'real' classification and in the classification obtained by the algorithm.
- n_{10} is the number of pairs that are classified together in the correct classification, but not in the algorithm's classification.
- n_{01} is the number of pairs that are classified together in the algorithm's classification, but not in the correct classification.

Ending the application will add a new variable to the Matlab workspace: calcMapping - a one-dimensional vector that represents the calculated classification of the elements.

3   Results

We applied several of the most commonly used clustering algorithms for gene expression data. By analyzing the results of COMPACT we observe significant variations in performance. In the following we compare the performance on different datasets. We choose to use datasets that were heavily studied and for which an expert view is accepted.

3.1   COMPACT Tests of Leukemia Microarray Expression Data

We tested COMPACT on the dataset of Golub et al. [4] that has served already as a benchmark for several clustering tools (e.g. [2], [8], [9], [10], [11]). The experiment

Table 1. COMPACT based comparison for the Golub dataset [4]. For details see text.

Method	Jaccard	Purity	Efficiency
Raw data			
K Means	0.257	0.369	0.459
Fuzzy C Means (FCM)	0.272	0.502	0.372
Competitive Neural Network (NN)	0.297	0.395	0.547
Quantum Clustering (QC)	NA	NA	NA
Preprocessing (SVD)			
K Means	0.4	0.679	0.494
Fuzzy C Means (FCM)	0.316	0.584	0.408
Competitive Neural Network (NN)	0.442	0.688	0.553
Quantum Clustering ($\sigma = 0.54$)	0.707	0.77	0.898

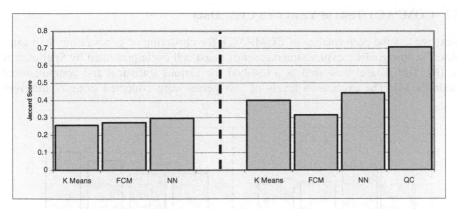

Fig. 2. Jaccard scores of the four algorithms tested by COMPACT on the Golub dataset. Left: before compression, Right: following application of the SVD compression step. Note that an improvement is detected for all methods by a preprocessing step.

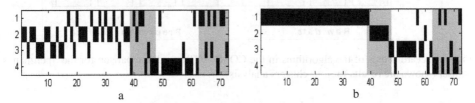

Fig. 3. A graphical comparison of COMPACT results on Leukemia dataset. The samples (patients) are ordered by their groups: samples 1-37: group #1, samples 38-47: group #2, samples 48-62: group #3 and samples 63-72: group #4. The four 'real' classes are distinguished by the background color (white, gray, white and gray), whereas black bars demonstrate the algorithm's classification. For example, in (a) the first sample belongs to the 'correct' first group (white background); while the algorithm placed it in the second group (the black bar is at group #2). Shown are the results of (a) K-means (K=4) and (b) QC (Quantum clustering, $\sigma = 0.54$) for clustering the AML/ALL cancer cells after SVD truncation to 5 dimensions.

sampled 72 leukemia patients with two types of leukemia, ALL and AML. The ALL set is further divided into T-cell leukemia and B-cell leukemia and the AML set is divided into patients who have undergone treatment and those who did not. For each patient an Affymetrix chip measured the expression of 7129 genes.

The clustering results for four selected clustering algorithms are shown in Table 1. A comparison of the Jaccard scores for all algorithms is displayed in Figure 2 and two clustering assignments are compared in Figure 3. Applying the selected algorithms to the raw data (i.e., without an SVD preprocessing) yields poor outcomes.

Next we applied the SVD preprocessing step selecting and normalizing the 5 leading SVD components ('eigengenes' according to Alter, [12]) thus reducing the matrix from 7129X72 to 5X72. Clustering has improved after dimensional truncation, yet not all algorithms correctly cluster the samples. Note that only QC shows a substantial degree of consistency with the 'real' classification (Jaccard. = 0.707, Purity = 0.77 and Efficiency = 0.898, for discussion see Horn & Axel [13]).

3.2   COMPACT Tests of Yeast Cell Cycle Data

Next we test the performance of COMPACT for clustering of genes rather than samples. For this goal we explore the dataset of yeast cell cycle presented by Spellman et al. [6]. This dataset was used as a test-bed for various statistical and computational methods 14]. The expression levels of 798 genes were collected from 72 different

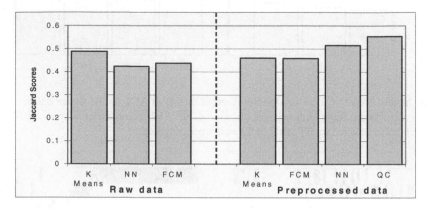

Fig. 4. Jaccard scores of the algorithms in the COMPACT based comparison for the Spellman dataset (shown are results for four clusters analysis)

Table 2. COMPACT based comparison to the Spellman dataset of Cell cycle in Yeast [6]

Method	Jaccard	Purity	Efficiency
Raw data			
K Means (5 clusters)	0.435	0.617	0.596
K Means (4 clusters)	0.488	0.64	0.673
Fuzzy C Means (5 clusters)	0.425	0.663	0.542
Fuzzy C Means (4 clusters)	0.438	0.458	0.912
Competitive Neural Network (4 clusters)	0.424	0.53	0.68
Quantum Clustering	NA	NA	NA
Preprocessing			
K means (5 clusters)	0.406	0.636	0.528
K means (4 clusters)	0.46	0.626	0.634
Fuzzy C means (5 clusters)	0.4	0.63	0.522
Fuzzy C means (4 clusters)	0.459	0.624	0.634
Competitive Neural Network (5 clusters)	0.33	0.55	0.458
Competitive Neural Network (4 clusters)	0.516	0.658	0.706
QC after SVD (σ =0.595)	0.554	0.664	0.77

conditions that reflect different time points in the yeast cell cycle. The task in this case is to cluster these 798 genes into five classes identified by Spellman et al. through functional annotations of individual genes.

We applied COMPACT both to 'raw' data and to SVD compressed data. In the latter case we selected two leading normalized SVD components ('eigensamples' according to Alter, [12]), thus reducing the matrix size from 798X72 to 798X2. All four clustering methods were tested as before. Once again the results obtained by the QC are moderately superior.

We have tested all methods for both 4 and 5 clusters (Table 2 and Figure 4). Interestingly enough, 4 clusters seem to be a better choice in all cases, although the 'real' classification defines 5 classes.

4 Discussion

In this paper we demonstrate how different clustering algorithms may lead to different results. The advantage of COMPACT is in allowing many algorithms to be viewed and evaluated in parallel on a common test set. Through COMPACT one can evaluate the impact of changing the algorithm or its parameters (e.g., sigma value in QC, number of iterations for the Competitive Neural Network, starting points of K-Means, Fuzzy C-Means and more). Being able to run a number of clustering algorithms, observe their results (quantitatively and graphically) and compare between them is beneficial for researchers using gene expression, proteomics, and other technologies that produce large datasets. We find it advisable to start with a problem that has a known classification (referred to as 'real classification') and use the statistical criteria (i.e., efficiency, purity and Jaccard score) to decide on the favorable clustering algorithm. For general research problems, where no known classification exists, the same statistical tools may be used to compare results of different clustering methods with one another. We presented here a comparative analysis of some well-known clustering methods with one relatively new method, QC. For the two datasets that we have explored, QC outperformed the other methods.

We have shown that dimensionality reduction improves the clustering quality. This observation is highly relevant when handling genomic data. Recall that for Affymetrix microarrays the number of genes tested reaches all known transcripts from the selected organism, producing 20,000-30,000 data points for a mammalian genome. Similarly, the application of the new SNP discovery chip produces a huge number of noisy data points in a single experiment. Besides its computational complexity, one of the major challenges when using massive data is to identify features and to filter out noise. Often handling such high dimensional noisy inputs can be a barrier. Hence it is important to develop more efficient and accurate tools to tackle these problems (see examples in [3], [4], [15], [16]). Thus, constructing a method that can significantly reduce data volume, and at the same time keep the important properties of that data, is obviously required.

COMPACT offers easy-to-use graphical controls for users to select and determine their own preferences, and graphical displays where the results can be presented or saved for later usage. It offers several clustering algorithms and allows the user to compare them to one another.

Although similar tools have already been proposed (e.g., [17], or [18]), the novelties of COMPACT are: (i) presenting an integrative, light package for clustering and visualization, (ii) integrating an efficient compression method and (iii) introducing the QC algorithm as part of the available clustering options.

The beginners will find this user-friendly tool with its graphical and textual displays useful in their data analysis. The experts will benefit from its flexibility and customizability that enables expanding the tool and modifying it for advanced, specialized applications.

Acknowledgment

We thank Inon Axel for helping in the initial stages of the development. We thank Noam Kaplan for critical reading the manuscript. We thank the ProtoNet team in the Hebrew University of Jerusalem for suggestions and helpful discussions. This work is partially supported by the BioSapiens NoE of the EU framework VI. R.V. awarded a fellowship by the SCCB, The Sudarsky Center for Computational Biology. His research is partially supported by the Israel Science Foundation.

Availability: COMPACT is available at http://www.protonet.cs.huji.ac.il/compact and at http://adios.tau.ac.il/compact . A detailed description of the application can be found on these websites.

References

1. Jain, A. K., Dubes R. C.: Algorithms for Clustering Data. Englewood Cliffs, NJ, Prentice Hall, Englewood Cliffs, NJ; 1988
2. Sharan, R., Maron-Katz A., Shamir, R.: CLICK and EXPANDER: a system for clustering and visualizing gene expression data. Bioinformatics. 2003, 19(14): 1787-99.
3. Eisen, M. B., Spellman, P. T., Brown P. O., Botstein D.: Cluster analysis and display of genome-wide expression patterns. Proc Natl Acad Sci U S A. 1998, 95(25): 14863-14868.
4. Golub T.R., Slonim D.K., Tamayo P., Huard C., Gaasenbeek M., Mesirov J.P., Coller H., Loh M.L., Downing J.R., Caligiuri M.A., Bloomfield C.D., Lander E.S.: Molecular classification of cancer: class discovery and class prediction by gene expression monitoring. Science. 1999, 286: 531-537.
5. Cheng Y., Church G. M.: Biclustering of Expression Data. Proceedings of the Eighth International Conference on Intelligent Systems for Molecular Biology; AAAI; 2000:93-103.
6. Spellman P.T., Sherlock G., Zhang M.Q., Iyer V.R., Anders K., Eisen M.B., Brown P.O., Botstein D., Futcher B. P. T.: Comprehensive identification of cell cycle-regulated genes of the yeast Saccharomyces cerevisiae by microarray hybridization. Mol Biol Cell. 1998, 9(12): 3273-97.
7. Horn, D., Gottlieb A.: Algorithm for data clustering in pattern recognition problems based on quantum mechanics. Phys Rev Lett. 2002, 88(1): 018702.
8. Yeang C.H., Ramaswamy S., Tamayo P., Mukherjee S., Rifkin R.M., Angelo M., Reich M., Lander E., Mesirov J., Golub T. C. H., Ramaswamy S.: Molecular classification of multiple tumor types. Bioinformatics. 2001, 17 Suppl 1: S316-22.

9. Pan, W.: A comparative review of statistical methods for discovering differentially expressed genes in replicated microarray experiments. Bioinformatics. 2002, 18(4): 546-54.
10. Mukherjee S., Tamayo P., Rogers S., Rifkin R., Engle A., Campbell C., Golub T.R., Mesirov J.P. S.: Estimating dataset size requirements for classifying DNA microarray data. J Comput Biol. 2003, 10(2): 119-42.
11. Pan, W.: A comparative review of statistical methods for discovering differentially expressed genes in replicated microarray experiments. Bioinformatics. 2002, 18(4): 546-54.
12. Alter, O., Brown P. O, Botstein D.: Singular value decomposition for genome-wide expression data processing and modeling. Proc Natl Acad Sci U S A. 2000, 97: 10101-10106.
13. Horn, D., Axel I.: Novel clustering algorithm for microarray expression data in a truncated SVD space. Bioinformatics. 2003, 19(9): 1110-5.
14. Friedman, N., Linial M., Nachman I., Pe'er D.: Using Bayesian networks to analyze expression data. J Comput Biol. 2000, 7: 601-20.
15. Sasson, O., Linial N., Linial M.: The metric space of proteins-comparative study of clustering algorithms. Bioinformatics. 2002, 18 Suppl 1: S14-21.
16. Sasson O., Vaaknin A., Fleischer H., Portugaly E., Bilu Y., Linial N., Linial M.: ProtoNet: hierarchical classification of the protein space. Nucleic Acids Res. 2003, 31(1): 348-52.
17. The Eisen Lab software page [http://rana.lbl.gov/EisenSoftware.htm]
18. The R project for statistical computing [http://www.r-project.org/]

Fast Sequence Similarity Computing with LCS on LARPBS[*]

Xiaohua Xu[1], Ling Chen[2,3], and Ping He[2]

[1] Department of Computer Science and Engineering,
Nanjing University of Aeronautics and Astronautics, Nanjing 210016, China
x.xu@citiz.net
[2] Department of Computer Science, Yangzhou University,
Yangzhou 225009, China
lchen@yzcn.net, angeletx@citiz.net
[3] National Key Lab of Novel Software Tech, Nanjing University,
Nanjing 210093, China

Abstract. The problem of the longest common subsequence (LCS) is a fundamental problem in sequence alignment. In this paper, we first present fast parallel algorithms for sequence similarity with LCS. For two sequences of lengths m and n ($m \leq n$), the algorithm uses n processors and costs $O(m)$ computation time. Time-area cost of the algorithm is $O(mn)$ which reaches optimality. Based on this algorithm, we also give a fast parallel algorithm which can compute the length of LCS in $O(\log m)$ time. To our best knowledge, this is the fastest one among the parallel LCS algorithms on array architectures.

1 Introduction

The longest common subsequence (LCS) problem is a fundamental problem in bioinformatics. Aho et al. [1] obtained a lower bound of $\Omega(mn)$ on time for the LCS problem using a decision tree model. By using dynamic programming technique, the LCS problem can be solved in $O(mn)$ time and $O(mn)$ space [2]. To further reduce the computation time, a lot of parallel algorithms have been proposed for the LCS problem on different models. On CREW-PRAM model, Aggarwal [3] and Apostolico et al [4] independently proposed an $O(\log m \log n)$ time algorithm using $mn/\log m$ processors. On the CRCW-PRAM model, Apostolico et al [4] gave a $O(\log n (\log \log m)^2)$ time algorithm using $mn/\log \log m$ processors. Unfortunately, these algorithms are designed on the theoretical models and need large number of processors (not less than $mn/\log m$) which are hardly applied in realistic bioinformatics problems. Several other algorithms have been proposed on systolic arrays. Chang et al [5] proposed a parallel algorithm with $n+5m$ steps using $m(m+1)$ processing elements. Luce et al [6] designed a systolic array with $m(m+1)/2$ processing elements and $n+3m+q$ steps where q is the

---

[*] This paper is supported in part by the Chinese National Natural Science Foundation under grant No. 60473012, Chinese National Foundation for Science and Technology Development under contract 2003BA614A-14, and Natural Science Foundation of Jiangsu Province under contract BK2005047.

G. Chen et al. (Eds.): ISPA Workshops 2005, LNCS 3759, pp. 168–175, 2005.
© Springer-Verlag Berlin Heidelberg 2005

length of the common subsequence. Freschi and Bogliolo [7] addressed the problem of computing the LCS between run-length-encoded (RLE) strings. Their algorithm executes in $O(m+n)$ steps on a systolic array of $M+N$ units, where M and N are the lengths of the original strings and m and n are the number of runs in their RLE representation.

Since these algorithms are designed on either theoretical models such as PRAM, or specialized hardware such as systolic arrays, they are not practical. Therefore, it is necessary to develop parallel algorithms for the LCS problem on a realistic computational model. Due to advances in optical technology, optical communication has been implemented in parallel computing systems. LARPBS presented by Pan and Li in [8] is a computational model based on optical bus technology. It has been shown that LARPBS is a realistic model and has been used as a standard computational architecture for parallel algorithm designing by many researchers [9][10].

In this paper, we first present a fast parallel algorithm for sequence similarity with LCS on LARPBS model. Our algorithm uses n processors to compute the length of LCS in $O(m)$ time. Time cost of the algorithm is $O(mn)$ which reaches optimality. Based on this algorithm, we also propose a faster parallel LCS algorithm on the LARPBS model. Our algorithm requires $O(\log m)$ time on an LARPBS with $mn^3/\log m$ processors. To the best of our knowledge, this is the fastest algorithm on a practical computational model.

2 Preliminaries

Let X and Y be two sequences with lengths of m and n respectively ($m \leq n$). The length of X is denoted as $|X|$, and $X[i]$ is the ith character of X. Let $A = (a[i, j])$ be an $m \times n$ matrix, and $a[i, j]$ be the length of the longest common subsequence of $X[1: i]$ and $Y[1: j]$. Matrix A can be computed with the following well-known recursive formula.

$$a[i, j] = \begin{cases} 0, & \text{if either } i = 0 \text{ or } j = 0 \\ a[i-1, j-1]+1, & \text{if } X[i] = Y[j] \\ \max\{a[i-1, j], a[i, j-1]\}, & \text{if } X[i] \neq Y[j] \end{cases} \quad (1)$$

We assume that all the indexes of the characters in Y matched with $X[i]$ are $0 < j_1 < j_2 < \ldots < j_r < n+1$. Let $j_0 = 0$ and $j_{r+1} = n+1$, we can get the following formula.

$$a[i, j] = \begin{cases} 0, & \text{if either } i=0 \text{ or } j = 0 \\ a[i-1, j], & j \in [0, j_1) \\ a[i-1, j-1]+1, & j \in \{j_1, j_2, \cdots, j_r\} \text{ where } Y[j_k] = X[i](k = 1, 2, \cdots, r) \\ \max\{a[i-1, j], a[i-1, j_k-1]+1\}, & j \in (j_k, j_{k+1}) \end{cases} \quad (2)$$

We define the block $B[i_1:i_2, j_1:j_2]$ as (3), where δ is the Kroneck delta function.

$$B[i_1 : i_2, j_1 : j_2] = \begin{pmatrix} \delta(X[i_1], Y[j_1]) & \cdots & \delta(X[i_1], Y[j_2]) \\ \vdots & \vdots & \vdots \\ \delta(X[i_2], Y[j_1]) & \cdots & \delta(X[i_2], Y[j_2]) \end{pmatrix} \qquad (3)$$

We use $c[i_1,j_1,i_2,j_2]$ to denote the length of the longest common subsequences $X[i_1:i_2-1]$ and $Y[j_1:j_2-1]$ represented by block $B[i_1:i_2-1, j_1:j_2-1]$. Namely, $c[i_1,j_1,i_2,j_2] = |LCS(X[i_1:i_2-1], Y[j_1:j_2-1])|$. Since $a[i, j] = c[1,1,i+1,j+1]$, it is obvious that $a[m, n] = c[1,1,m+1,n+1]$. Therefore the problem of computing $a[m, n]$ is actually the problem of computing $c[1,1,m+1,n+1]$ which can be computed by the method of divide and conquer using (4). For block $B[i_1:i_2-1, j_1:j_2-1]$, the corresponding LCS length $c[i_1,j_1,i_2,j_2]$ satisfies:

$$c[i_1, j_1, i_2, j_2] = \max_{j_1 \leq j \leq j_2} \left\{ c[i_1, j_1, i_m, j] + c[i_m, j, i_2, j_2] \right\} \qquad (4)$$

where i_m is a fixed number satisfying: $i_1 < i_m < i_2$.

3   Primitive Operations of LARPBS

Recently, arrays with reconfigurable optical bus systems [8] have been proposed and have drawn much attention from the researchers. In these systems, messages can be transmitted concurrently on a bus in a pipelined fashion and the bus can be reconfigured dynamically under program control to support different algorithmic requirements. LARPBS is one of such model where any processor involvement is not allowed during a bus cycle, except setting switches up at the beginning of a bus cycle. Hence, it can exploit the high bandwidth of optical buses used to connect processors there. Many algorithms have been designed for basic data movement operations, sorting and selection, computational geometry, and PRAM simulation on the LARPBS model.

Based on the coincident pulse addressing technique, the pipelined optical bus systems can support a massive volume of communications simultaneously and are particularly appropriate for applications that involve intensive communication operations such as broadcasting, one-to-one communication, multicasting, compression, split, and many irregular communication patterns. Here we describe implementation details of several primitive operations.

(1) **One-to-one communication.** Assume that processors $P(i_k)$ $(k=1,2,\ldots,M)$ are senders and processors $P(j_k)$ $(k=1,2,\ldots,M)$ are receivers. The operation is presented as:
  for $k \leftarrow 1$ *to* M *pardo* $R(j_k) \leftarrow R(i_k)$
(2) **Broadcasting.** In this operation, the source processor $P(i)$ wants to broadcast a message to all the other processors $P(i_k)$ $(k=1,2,\ldots,M)$ in the array:
  $R(i_1), R(i_2),\ldots, R(i_M) \leftarrow R(i)$
(3) **Multicasting.** The implementation of this operation is similar to that of broadcasting. Processor $P(i_k)$ $(k=1,2,\ldots,M)$ wants to broadcast a message to $P(j_{k,1})$, $P(j_{k,2})$, $P(j_{k,3}),\ldots$. Namely:
  for $k \leftarrow 1$ *to* M *pardo* $R(j_{k,1}),R(j_{k,2}),R(j_{k,3}),\ldots \leftarrow R(i_k)$

(4) Element pair-wise operations. Assume $\square$ is a binary operator. Element pair-wise operations are presented as:

for $k \leftarrow 0$ *to* N-1 *pardo* $R(i+k) \leftarrow R(i+k) \square R(j+k)$

(5) Binary prefix sum. Assume every processor $P(i)$ (i=0,1,...,N-1) has a register $R(i)$ which holds a binary value. The binary prefix sum operation is presented as:

for $i \leftarrow 0$ *to* N-1 *pardo* $R(i) \leftarrow R(0)+R(1)+...+R(i)$

(6) Extraction and compression. In this operation every processor $P(i)$ (i=0,1,...,N-1) has a value $x(i)$, and we wish to extract those $x(i)$ that have certain property and compact them to the beginning of the linear array. Suppose there are M $x(i_k)$ (k=1,2,...,M) that have such property and they stored in $R(i_1)$, $R(i_2)$,..., $R(i_M)$ ($i_1<i_2<,...,<i_M$), the operation can be presented as:

for $k \leftarrow 1$ *to* M *pardo* $R(N$-1-M+$k) \leftarrow R(i_k)$

The reader is referred to [8] for implementation details of other primitive operations on the LARPBS model. It has been shown that by using the coincident pulse addressing technique, all the above primitive operations take $O(1)$ bus cycles, where the bus cycle length is the end-to-end message transmission time over a bus. It was also shown in [8] that the minimum or maximum of n bounded numbers can be found in $O(1)$ time on a LARPBS of size n.

In addition to the tremendous communication capabilities, a LARPBS can also be partitioned into several independent subarrays. The subarrays can operate as regular linear arrays with pipelined optical bus systems, and all subarrays can be used independently for different computations without interference. Hence, this architecture is very suitable for many divide-and-conquer problems. The basic communication, data movement, and aggregation operations provide an algorithmic view on parallel computing using optical buses, and also allow us to develop, specify, and analyze parallel algorithms by ignoring optical and engineering details. These powerful primitives that support massive parallel communications plus the reconfigurability of optical buses make the LARPBS computing model very attractive in solving problems that are both computation and communication intensive. Although LARPBS has great potential of computational ability, it is still a theoretical computational model at present. But unlike many other theoretical models, such like PRAM, the LARPBS model is implementable and practical using current optical technologies.

4 Parallel Algorithm to Compute Longest Common Subsequence

Based on (2), we can compute the elements of $a[i, j]$ row by row sequentially and the entries of each row can be computed in parallel using the entries of the previous row.

4.1 Framework of the Parallel LCS Algorithm

In the process of the ith row, the elements of previous row $a[i$-1, $j]$ (j=1,2,...,n) are stored in the registers $d[j]$ and $q[j]$ of $P(j)$ (j=1,2,...,n), the value of $a[i$-1, j_k-1]+1 are stored in the registers $q[j_k]$ of $P(j_k)$ (k=1,2,...,r), and elements of $b[i, j]$ (j=1,2,...,n) are stored in the registers $e[j]$ of $P(j)$. The value of $a[i, j]$, i.e. the new value of $d[j]$ can be obtained by parallel computation of $d[j]$=max{ $d[j]$, $q[j]$ }(j=1,2,...,n). The value of $q[j]$ in $P(j)$ can be set by broadcasting $a[i$-1, j_k-1]+1 to all the $P(j)$ where j satisfies $j_k \leq$

$j < j_{k+1}$. Suppose $m \leq n$, in the LARPBS there are n processors which are denoted as $P(1)$, ..., $P(n)$. Elements of sequence $X=X[1 : m]$ and $Y=Y[1 : n]$ are stored in the processors: $X[i]$ is in $P(i)$ ($i=1,2,...,m$) and $Y[j]$ in $P(j)$ ($j=1,2,...,n$). Suppose in the ith row, $b[i, j_k]=1$ ($k=1,...,r$), $P(j_k)$ is called critical processor. The framework of the algorithm is as follows.

Algorithm *PLCS*   *//Parallel Algorithm for LCS Problem*
Input :   sequence $X=X[1 : m]$ and $Y=Y[1 : n]$ are stored in the processors:
        $X[i]$ is in $P(i)$ ($i=1,2,...m$) and $Y[j]$ in $P(j)$ ($j=1,2,...,n$).
Output :   The length of LCS of X and Y is in $d[n]$ of $P(n)$.
01   **for** $j \leftarrow 1$ **to** n **pardo**   // *Initialize the length array* $d[]$
02        $d[j] \leftarrow 0$ // $P(j)$ does
03   **end for**
04   **for** $i \leftarrow 1$ **to** m **do**
05        $P(i)$ broadcast $X[i]$ to all processors in the array.
06   **for** $j \leftarrow 1$ **to** n **pardo**   //*Compute* $e[j]$
07            $e[j] \leftarrow (X[i]=Y[j])$ //$P(j)$ computes $e[j]$ using $X[i]$ and $Y[j]$ stored in $P(j)$
08   **end for**
09   **for** $j \leftarrow 1$ **to** n **pardo**   // *Initialize* $q[]$
10            $q[j] \leftarrow 0$ // $P(j)$ initializes the register $q[j]$ 0
11   **end for**
12   **for** $j \leftarrow 1$ **to** n-1 **pardo**   //*One–to-One*
13            $q[j+1] \leftarrow d[j]$ //$P(j)$ sends $d[j]$ to $P(j+1)$, and $P(j+1)$ stores $d[j]$ as $q[j+1]$
14   **end for**
15   **for** $j \leftarrow 1$ **to** n **pardo**   //*Compute* $d[j]$ *where* $e[j] = 1$
16   **if** $e[j] = 1$ **then** $d[j] \leftarrow q[j] + 1$ // $P(j)$ does
17   **end for**
18   **for** $j \leftarrow 1$ **to** n **pardo**   //*Re-initialize* $q[]$
19            $q[j] \leftarrow d[j]$ // $P(j)$ does
20   **end for**
21   **for** $j \leftarrow 1$ **to** n **pardo**   //*Compress*
22   **if** $e[j] = 1$ **then**
23                $P(j)$ is a critical processor, denote the kth critical processor as $P(j_k)$.
                $P(j_k)$ ($k=1,2,...,r$) compress the index j_k and store j_k in $P(N-1-r+k)$.
24   **end if**
25   **end for**
26   **for** $k \leftarrow 2$ **to** r **pardo**   //*One–to-One*
27            $P(N-1-r+k)$ sends j_k to $P(N-1-r+k-1)$, hence $P(N-1-r+k-1)$ holds j_{k-1} and j_k
28   **end for**
29   **for** $k \leftarrow 1$ **to** r **pardo**   //*One–to-One*
30            $P(N-1-r+k)$ sends the index j_{k+1} to $P(j_k)$, where we let j_{r+1} be $n + 1$.
31   **end for**
32   **for** $k \leftarrow 1$ **to** r **pardo**   // *Multicasting*
33   //Critical processor $P(j_k)$ broadcasts the value of $q[j_k]$ to $q[j]$
            //for all j's satisfying $j_k \leq j < j_{k+1}$.
                $q[j_k], q[j_k+1], ..., q[j_{k+1}-1] \leftarrow q[j_k]$
34   **end for**

35   *for* $j \leftarrow 1$ *to* n *pardo*   //Compute $d[]$
36          $d[j] \leftarrow max\{d[j], q[j]\}$ // $P(j)$ does
37   *end for*
38   *end for*
39   *return* $d[n]$

4.2 Complexity Analysis of the PLCS Algorithm

For the two sequences $X = X[1 : m]$ and $Y = Y[1 : n]$ ($m \leq n$), it is obvious that the algorithm above uses n processors in the array. In each processor, only constant numbers of registers are required.

Next we will show the time complexity of the algorithm is $O(m)$ with n processors. In the algorithm, lines 1-3 are simply operations of assignment which takes $O(1)$ time. In each iteration of the i-loop, line 5 is a primitive operation of broadcast which takes $O(1)$ time. In lines 6-8 every processor computes the $e[j]$ in parallel, obviously this also requires $O(1)$ time. Lines 12-14, lines 26- 28 and lines 29-31 consist of primitive operations of one-to-one communication, they also take $O(1)$ time. Lines 21-24 use a compress operation which requires $O(1)$ time. Lines 32-34 use a multicasting operation which also requires $O(1)$ time. The other lines are simply operations of assignment which require $O(1)$ time. Therefore, the time complexity of each i-loop is $O(1)$. Since the algorithm can be completed after m iterations of i-loops, time complexity of algorithm is $O(m)$. Therefore, time cost of the algorithm is $O(mn)$ which is optimal for a parallel algorithm to compute the LCS of the two sequences with lengths of m and n .

4.3 Faster Parallel Algorithm for LCS

A faster parallel algorithm which can be implemented in $O(\log m)$ time using $mn^3/\log m$ processors is presented in this section. The algorithm consists of three steps as follows:

Step 1: The rows of $B[1:m,1:n]$ are partitioned into $m/\log m$ row-blocks each of which has $\log m$ rows. The kth row-block is $B[k \cdot \log m+1 : (k+1) \cdot \log m, 1 : n]$ ($k = 0,1,...,$ $m/\log m$ -1). The processors are also divided into $m/\log m$ groups each of which processes one row-block. For each row-block, all the sub-blocks $B[k \cdot \log m+1 : (k+1) \cdot \log m, j_1 : j_2](1 \leq j_1 \leq j_2 \leq n)$ are processed to compute $c[k \cdot \log m+1, j_1, (k+1) \cdot \log m+1, j_2+1]$ ($1 \leq j_1 \leq j_2 \leq n$) using algorithm PLCS.

Step 2: Combine the neighbor row-blocks $B[k \cdot \log m+1 : (k+1) \cdot \log m, 1 : n]$ and $B[(k+1) \cdot \log m+1 : (k+2) \cdot \log m, 1 : n]$ into larger row-block $B[k \cdot \log m+1 : (k+2) \cdot \log m, 1 : n]$ ($k = 0,2,..., m/\log m$ -2) using formula (4). At this moment, we have $m/(2\log m)$ row-blocks. In the meantime the corresponding sub-blocks $B[k \cdot \log m+1 : (k+1) \cdot \log m, j_1 : j_2]$ and $B[(k+1) \cdot \log m+1 : (k+2) \cdot \log m, j_1 : j_2]$ are also combined into larger sub-block $B[k \cdot \log m+1 : (k+2) \cdot \log m, j_1 : j_2]$ ($k = 0,2,..., m/\log m$ -2) ($1 \leq j_1 \leq j_2 \leq n$) using formula (4).

Step 3: Combine the pairs of neighbor row-blocks obtained in step 2 into $m/(4\log m)$ larger row-blocks. And the pairs of neighbor sub-blocks are also combined into larger sub-blocks recursively. It is easy to see that after $\log(m/\log m)$ tines of such recursions, the whole block $B[1:m,1:n]$ can be obtained and hence $c[1,m+1,1, n+1]$ can be computed.

4.4 Complexity Analysis of the Faster Parallel Algorithm

In step 1, the processors are divided into $m/\log m$ groups each of which processes one row-block. In each row–block, there are $(n+1)n/2$ sub-blocks to be processed in parallel. For sub-block $B[k\cdot\log m+1 : (k+1)\cdot\log m, j_1 : j_2]$ $(1 \leq j_1 \leq j_2 \leq n)$, computing $c[k\cdot\log m+1, j_1, (k+1)\cdot\log m+1, j_2+1]$ is actually to compute the length of the LCS of $X[k\cdot\log m+1 : (k+1)\cdot\log m]$ and $Y[j_1: j_2]$ which requires j_1-j_2+1 processors and $O(\log m)$ time using algorithm PLCS. Therefore the computation time required for step 1 is $O(\log m)$ and the number of processors used in this step is

$$\frac{m}{\log m} \sum_{\substack{1 \leq j_1 \leq n \\ j_1 \leq j_2 \leq n}} (j_2 - j_1 + 1) = \frac{m}{\log m} \sum_{j=1}^{n} \binom{j+1}{2} = \frac{m}{\log m} \binom{n+2}{3} \tag{5}$$

But in the computation of sub-block $B[k\cdot\log m+1 : (k+1)\cdot\log m, j_1 : j_2]$ to obtain $c[k\cdot\log m+1, j_1, (k+1)\cdot\log m+1, j_2+1]$ the value of $c[k\cdot\log m+1, j_1, (k+1)\cdot\log m+1, j_2'+1]$ $(1 \leq j_1 \leq j' \leq j_2 \leq n)$ has also been obtained, i.e. sub-block $B[k\cdot\log m+1 : (k+1)\cdot\log m, j_1 : j'_2]$ has also been processed. Therefore, the number of processor can be reduced to

$$\frac{m}{\log m} \sum_{1 \leq j_1 \leq n} (n - j_1 + 1) = \frac{m}{\log m} \binom{n+1}{2} \tag{6}$$

In step 2, two neighbor sub-blocks $B[k\cdot\log m+1 : (k+1)\cdot\log m, j_1 : j_2]$ and $B[k\cdot\log m+1 : (k+1)\cdot\log m, j_1 : j_2]$ are combined using (4) by obtaining the maximum of $j_2- j_1+1$ values . This can be completed in $O(1)$ time using $j_2- j_1+1$ processors. Therefore, the computation time of step 2 is $O(1)$, and the number of processors required is

$$\frac{m}{2\log m} \sum_{j=1}^{n} \left(\binom{j+1}{2} + \binom{j}{1} \right) = \frac{m}{2\log m} \left(\binom{n+2}{3} + \binom{n+1}{2} \right) \tag{7}$$

In step 3, after $\log(m/\log m)$ times of recursions, $c[1,m+1,1, n+1]$ can be computed. The computation time used is $O(\log(m/\log m))O(1) = O(\log m)$. After each recursion, the processors used are reduced by half. At the last recursion, $2(n+2)(n+1)n/3$ processors are used.

To sum up, the time complexity of the algorithm is $O(\log m) + O(\log m) = O(\log m)$, and the number of processors required by the algorithm is

$$\max\left\{ \frac{m}{\log m}\binom{n+2}{3}, \frac{m}{2\log m}\left(\binom{n+2}{3} + \binom{n+1}{2} \right) \right\} = \frac{m}{\log m}\binom{n+2}{3} \leq \frac{mn^3}{\log m} \tag{8}$$

Due to the symmetry of the sequences X and Y, the algorithm can also be completed in $O(\log n)$ time using $m^3 n/\log n$ processors.

5 Conclusions

In this paper, we present a parallel algorithm on LARPBS for computing the length of the longest common subsequence of two given sequences. For two sequences of lengths m and n, the first algorithm uses n processors and costs $O(m)$ computation time by using the method of row iteration instead of traditional diagonal iteration. Time-area cost of our algorithm is $O(mn)$ which reaches optimality, and its space cost is $O(1)$ which also reaches optimality. Therefore it is superior to the other parallel algorithms in systolic array in the aspect of efficiency. Based on this algorithm, we also give a faster parallel algorithm with time complexity of $O(\log m)$ using $mn^3/\log m$ processors, or time complexity of $O(\log n)$ using $m^3 n/\log n$ processors. To the best of our knowledge, this is the fastest one among the parallel LCS algorithms on array architectures. These algorithms can be used to compute the edit distance so as to speed up the process of sequences alignment which is important in bioinformatics.

References

1. A. Aho, D. Hirschberg, and J. Ullman, Bounds on the Complexity of the Longest Common Subsequence Problem, J. Assoc. Comput. Mach., vol. 23, no. 1, pp. 1-12, Jan. 1976.
2. Gotoh, O.: An improved algorithm for matching biological sequences, J. Molec. Biol. 162 (1982) 705–708
3. Aggarwal, A., Park, J.: Notes on Searching in Multidimensional Monotone Arrays, Proc. 29th Ann. IEEE Symp. Foundations of Comput. Sci. 1988, pp. 497–512
4. Apostolico, A., Atallah, M., Larmore, L., Mcfaddin, S.: Efficient Parallel Algorithms for String Editing and Related Problems, SIAM J. Computing, vol. 19, pp. 968-988, Oct. 1990
5. Chang, J.H., Ibarra, O.H., Pallis, M.A.: Parallel Parsing on a one-way array of finite-state machines, IEEE Trans. Computers C-36 (1987) 64–75
6. Luce, G., Myoupo, J.F.: Systolic-based parallel architecture for the longest common subsequences problem. Integration 25(1): 53-70 (1998)
7. Freschi, V., Bogliolo, A.,: Longest common subsequence between run-length-encoded strings: a new algorithm with improved parallelism, Information Processing Letters, Volume 90, Issue 4 (May 2004), pp. 167-173
8. Pan, Y., Li, K.: Linear Array with a Reconfigurable Pipelined Bus System – Concepts and Applications, Journal of Information Science 106 (1998) 237-258
9. Li, K., Pan, Y., Zheng, S.-Q eds.: Parallel Computing Using Optical Interconnections, Kluwer Academic Publishers, Boston, USA, Hardbound, ISBN 0-7923-8296-X, October 1998
10. Chen, L., Pan, Y., Xu, X.: Scalable and Efficient Parallel Algorithms for Euclidean Distance Transform on the LARPBS Model. IEEE Trans. Parallel Distrib. Syst. 15(11): 975-982 (2004).

Fast Scalable Algorithm on LARPBS for Sequence Alignment[*]

Ling Chen[1,2], Chen Juan[1], and Yi Pan[3]

[1] Department of Computer Science, Yangzhou University,
Yangzhou 225009, P.R. China
lchen@yzcn.net, angeletx@citiz.net
[2] National Key Lab of Novel Software Tech, Nanjing University,
Nanjing 210093, P.R. China
[3] Department of Computer Science, Georgia State University,
Atlanta, GA 30303, U.S.A.
pan@cs.gsu.edu

Abstract. Linear array with reconfigurable pipelined bus system (LARPBS) is a parallel computational model based on the optical bus system. In this paper, an $O(1)$ time algorithm on LARPBS for prefix computation based on the maximum operation is presented. We also present a fast and efficient sequence alignment algorithm on LARPBS. For two sequences with length of m, n respectively, the algorithm can be implemented in $O(mn/p)$ time with p processors($1 \leq p \leq \max\{m,n\}$).Since the time complexity of the algorithm can be adjusted by choosing different number of processors p , the algorithm is highly scalable.

1 Introduction

Sequence alignment is an important problem in bioinformatics and can be applied to DNA classification, structure prediction of protein, etc. The goal of sequence alignment is to estimate the difference between a pair of sequences, and to provide a basic tool for DNA classification and the secondary structure prediction of protein sequences. It was shown in [2] that the time and space complexity of sequence alignment is $O(mn)$ using the dynamic programming algorithm. Mayers and Miller [3] reduced the space complexity to $O(m+n)$ using the technique presented by Hirschberg [4]. Since the parallel processing can speedup the computation greatly, it has drawn much attention of the researchers to develop parallel algorithms for sequences alignment [5-7]. Many parallel algorithms have also been proposed on systolic arrays [8-11].

With the development of technique of optical technology, optical communication has been implemented in parallel computing systems. Some parallel computing models of reconfigurable pipelined bus system have been presented in the resent years.

---

[*] This paper is supported in part by the Chinese National Natural Science Foundation under grant No. 60473012, Chinese National Foundation for Science and Technology Development under contract 2003BA614A-14, and Natural Science Foundation of Jiangsu Province under contract BK2005047.

G. Chen et al. (Eds.): ISPA Workshops 2005, LNCS 3759, pp. 176–185, 2005.
© Springer-Verlag Berlin Heidelberg 2005

Among these models, the linear array with a reconfigurable pipelined bus system (LARPBS) presented by Y. Pan [12] is the most typical one. Chen Guo-Liang *et al* [1] presented an algorithm of $O(1)$ time for string matching allowing *k*-errors on LARPBS. But, the parallel algorithm of sequence alignment on LARPBS has not been reported so far. In this paper, we first present a constant time LARPBS algorithm for prefix computation based on the maximum operation. Based on this parallel prefix maximum algorithm, a fast sequence alignment algorithm on LARPBS is presented.

2 Prefix Computation Based on Maximum Operation on LARPBS

2.1 Prefix Computation Based on Maximum Operation

Definition 1.Given N elements R(0),R(1), ...,R(N-1), the prefix computation based on maximum operation is to compute: $M(j)=\max\{R(0),R(1), ...,R(j)\}$, $j=0,1,...,N$-1.

Here $M(j)$, $j=0,1,...,N$-1, is called the prefix maximum.

For an element R(*j*), if it satisfies: $R(j)>R(i)$ for $i=1,2,...,j$-1, R(*j*) is called a leader element. If $R(j_1)$ and $R(j_2)$ ($j_1< j_2$) are two adjacent leader elements, we call all the elements between $R(j_1)$ and $R(j_2)$ are followers of $R(j_1)$. Obviously, the prefix maximum $M(j)=R(j)$ for each leader R(*j*), and $M(i)=R(j)$ for each R(*j*)'s follower R(*i*), $i=j_1+1, j_1+2,..., j_2$-1.

2.2 The LARPBS Algorithm for Prefix Maximum Computation

Let $a_1, a_2, ...,a_n$ be *n* binary integers of *d* binary bits and $a(i,j)$ be the *i*th bit of a_j. All the elements of $a(i,j)$ form a $d \times n$ matrix A where the *j*th column consists of the binary bits of a_j and the the *i*th row consists of the *i*th bits of all the elements. A binary bit *flag*[*j*] is set for each element R(*j*): if R(*j*) is a leader, *flag*[*j*]=1, otherwise, *flag*[*j*]=0. All the *flag*[*j*] are initialized as 1 at the beginning of the algorithm.

Assuming that *n* processors are available in LARPBS, each of the *n* binary integers is stored in one processor. In the algorithm we process the matrix A from the top row to the bottom, i.e., we process the bit of the elements from the bit with greatest magnitude to the smallest one. For each row, we call the elements "0" between two adjacent "1" elements the follower of the left "1" element. In the process of the first row, if the first bit of an element is "1", its processor broadcasts the "1" to its followers and at the same time set the *flag* bit of the followers to "0". We call this the operation scatter. Then the array is reconfigured into two independent subarrays in the way that the processors whose first bits are "0" form one subarray, and the rest processors form the other. Now we process the second row in each array. For each processor, if its *flag* bit is "0", its second bit should be set as 0. Then perform the same process as for the first bit. After the process, each subarray is further divided into two smaller subarrays according to the second bits of the processors. Repeat this process until all the *d* bits are processed. At the end of the algorithm, the integer represented by the *j*th column of matrix A is just the *j*th prefix maximum *M*[*j*].

The framework of the algorithm is described as follows:

Algorithm-1.Prefix computation based on the maximum operation on LARPBS with n PEs
   Input: n binary integer $a_1, a_2, ..., a_n$ which are stored in n
processors, where a_j and flag[j] are stored in PE_j,
$a(i,j)$ indicates the i-th bit of a_j, $0 \leq i \leq d-1$, $1 \leq j \leq n$.
   Output: the result M[j]is stored in the jth processor
$1 \leq j \leq n$.
   Begin
      1   for j=1 to n par-do
             flag[j]=1
          Endfor-j
      2   Scatter operation on the a(1,1) …a(1,n), i.e. if
          a(1,j)=1 then its processor scatters "1" to all
          its followers and set their flag as "0".
      3   Reconfigure the array into two subarrays: the
          processors whose first bits are "0" form one su-
          barray, and the rest processors form the other.
      4   for i= 2 to d do
             for each subarray par-do
                for j=leftmost location to rightmost location
                   of the subarray par-do
                   4.1   if flag[j]=0 then a(i,j)=0
                   4.2   scatter for the ith row of A: if
                         a(i,j)=1 then its processor scatters
                         "1" to all its followers and set their
                         flag as "0".
                   4.3   Reconfigure the array into two subar-
                         rays: the processors whose ith bits are
                         "0" form one subarray, and the rest
                         processors form the other.
                Endfor-j
             Endfor-each sub pipelined bus
          Endfor-i
   End.

2.3 Time Complexity of Algorithm-1

In lines 2, and 4.2 the scatter operation is used. The operation of data scatter is to
broadcast "1" to their followers. Namely, the operation can be presented as: *for* $k \leftarrow$
1 *to* M *par-do* $R(i_k) \rightarrow R(i_k+1)$, $R(i_k+2)$, ..., $R(i_{k+1}-1)$. The data scatter operation
can also be completed in constant time on LARPBS. In algorithm 1, the first step is an
arithmetical operation, the third step is a reconfigure operation, they can both be finished in $O(1)$ time. The second step is a scatter and flag setting operation, it can be
finished in $O(1)$ time. In the loop body of the fourth step, step 4.1 is an arithmetical
operation, step 4.3 is a reconfigure operation, they can both be finished in $O(1)$ time.
4.2 step is a scatter and flag setting operation, it can be finished in $O(1)$ time. Therefore each execution of the loop body can be finished in $O(1)$ time. Obviously, the
forth step can be finished in $O(d)$ time. As a result, Algorithm 1 requires $O(d)$ time.
Because d is a constant, Algorithm 1 can be finished in $O(1)$ time.

2.4 Scalability of Algorithm-1

To implement the algorithm in $p(1\le p\le n)$ processors, we first partition the n data into $\left\lceil \dfrac{n}{p} \right\rceil$ segments labeled 0, 1, ..., $\left\lfloor \dfrac{n}{p} \right\rfloor$. There are p data in each segment except the last segment which has $n\ mod\ p$ data. First, we compute the prefix-maximum value in first segment using Algorithm 1 and save the maximum value as max. Then after replacing the first element value by the maximum of max and its original value, we compute the prefix-maximum value in second segment using Algorithm-1 and save the maximum value as max. All the other segments are similarly processed.

Since execution of each segment requires $O(1)$ time, time complexity of Algorithm-1 is $O(n/p)$ and its time-area cost is $O(n)$. This shows that for $1\le p\le$ n, Algorithm 1 is scalable.

3   The Basic Algorithm of Sequence Alignment

Let $A=$ "$a_1,a_2, . . . ,a_m$",$B=$"$b_1,b_2. . . . ,b_n$" be two sequences be compared, m, n be the length of A, B respectively. Σ denotes the alphabet□ '$-$' denotes the gap between two symbols. Penalty function f: $\sum\cup\{\text{'-'}\}\times\sum\cup\{\text{'-'}\}\to \mathbb{R}$ indicate the evaluation of the similarity of two symbols. The similarity of an alignment of two sequences can be measured by sim which is defined as follows:

Definition 2□Suppose the penalty function score depends only on the symbols compared regardless of their locations, assuming that the penalty function score of two symbols in ith location is f_i, then $sim= \sum\limits_{i=1}^{L} f_i$, here L is the length of the longer sequence after alignment.

Definition 3□The optimal alignment of two sequences is the alignment which gets the greatest sim score.

An $(m+1)\times(n+1)$ matrix T where $T[i, j]$ $(0\le i\le m,0\le j\le n)$ denotes the optimal alignment score of "$a_1,a_2,\square\square\square,a_i$" and "$b_1,b_2,\square\square\square b_j$". Initially, $T[0,0]$ is set as 0 and $T[0,j]$, $T[i,0]$ and $T[i,j]$ can be obtained as follows:

$$T[0, j] = \sum_{k=1}^{j} f('-',b_k) \tag{1}$$

$$T[i,0] = \sum_{k=1}^{i} f(a_k,'-') \tag{2}$$

$$T[i, j] = \max \begin{cases} T[i-1, j]+ f(a_i,'-') \\ T[i, j-1]+ f('-',b_j) \\ T[i-1, j-1]+ f(a_i,b_j) \end{cases} \tag{3}$$

The elements in array T can be computed in a row-wise fashion from top to bottom and from left to right in each row. Finally, $T[m,n]$ is just the optimal alignment score. It is obvious that the computation of matrix T can be finished in $O(mn)$ time. Thus, the optimal alignment can be found by tracing back in the digraph from $T[m,n]$ to $T[0,0]$ to search the shortest path between $T[m,n]$ and $T[0,0]$.

4 Parallel Sequence Alignment Algorithm on LARPBS

4.1 Transforming the Iteration Formula

Most of the parallel algorithms are based on dynamical programming method and process the matrix T in the wave front fashion. This is inefficient because the number of processors used is not constant. By transforming the iteration formula (3), the dependencies between entries on different rows can be partitioned, and we can compute the elements of $T[i, j]$ row by row sequentially and the entries of each row can be computed in parallel using the entries of the previous row[13].

Assuming that the $(i-1)$-th row has been computed, the value of $T[i-1,j]$ and $T[i-1,j-1]$ in (3) are already known since they belong to the $(i-1)$th row. But the value of $T[i, j-1]$ in (3) has not been computed. This data dependency can be partitioned by means of prefix maximum computation. Let:

$$w[j] = \max \begin{cases} T[i-1, j] + f(a_i, '-') \\ T[i-1, j-1] + f(a_i, b_j) \end{cases} \tag{4}$$

Then,

$$T[i, j] = \max \begin{cases} w[j] \\ T[i, j-1] + f('-', b_j) \end{cases} \tag{5}$$

Therefore, $T[i,j]$ is divided into two parts: one part depends only on the data which have been already computed (i.e. $w[j]$), the other part consists of data have not been computed. We define $x[j]$ as:

$$x[j] = T[i, j] - \sum_{k=1}^{j} f('-', b_k) = \max \begin{cases} w[j] - \sum_{k=1}^{j} f('-', b_k) \\ T[i, j-1] - \sum_{k=1}^{j-1} f('-', b_k) \end{cases}$$

$$= \max \begin{cases} w[j] - \sum_{k=1}^{j} f('-', b_k) \\ x[j-1] \end{cases}$$

Let:

$$y[j] = \sum_{k=1}^{j} f('-',b_k) \qquad (6)$$

$$z[j] = w[j] - y[j] \qquad (7)$$

Then:

$$x[j] = \max \begin{cases} z[j] \\ x[j-1] \end{cases} = \max\{z[0], z[1], ..., z[j]\} \qquad (8)$$

$$T[i,j] = x[j] + \sum_{k=1}^{j} f('-',b_k) = x[j] + y[j] \qquad (9)$$

Since the data in the $(i\text{-}1)$-th row have already been computed, obviously $w[j]$ can be computed by formula (4) directly. Using formula (6), $y[j]$ can be computed by parallel prefix-sum computation operation. Using the values of $w[j]$ and $y[j]$, $z[j]$ can be computed using formula (7). Consequently, $x[j]$ can be computed using parallel prefix maximum computation by (8). Finally, $T[i,j]$ can be computed using formula (9). The values of the elements $T[i,j]$ ($j=1,2,...,n$) in the ith row can be computed in parallel. All the rows are processed in a row wise fashion.

4.2   The Algorithm

Let $m \leq n$, there are n processors on LARPBS. Each processor PE_j has 8 registers named $a[j]$, $b[j]$, $top[j]$, $t[j]$, $y[j]$, $x[j]$, $w[j]$, $z[j]$, where a_i, b_j, $T[j,0]$, $T[i,j]$, $y[j]$, $x[j]$, $w[j]$, $z[j]$ are stored respectively. Additionally, a temporary variable $a1$ is used to store the value of a broadcasted and $t1[j]$ is used to store the value of $T[i,j-1]$ received from the point-to-point communication, here $1 \leq i \leq m$, $1 \leq j \leq n$.

```
Algorithm-2. Parallel sequence alignment algorithm on
LARPBS with n PEs
   Input : aᵢ in the sequence A ("a₁,a₂,. . . .,aₘ") is stored
in the register a[i] in PEᵢ, bⱼ in the sequence B ("b₁,b₂,
. . . bₙ") is stored in the register b[j] in PEⱼ, the pen-
alty function  f is stored in each processor.
   Output : the similarity score of A and B •sim.
   Begin
      1.  for i=1 to m par-do
              1.1 top[i]=f(a[i] ,'-')
              1.2 compute prefix-sum of array top[i], results
                  are stored in top[i]. //Initialize T[i,0]
          Endfor-i
      2.  for j=1 to n par-do
              2.1 t[j] =f('-',b[j])
              2.2 compute prefix-sum of array t[j], results
```

```
                are stored in t[j]. //Initialize T[0,j]
         2.3  y[j] =t[j]      //formula (1), (6)
      Endfor-j
   3.  for i=1 to m do
         3.1  a[i]• a1[1],a1[2],...,a1[m]  //broadcast aᵢ
         3.2  top[i]• t[0] //point-to-point communication
         3.3  for j=1 to n par-do
            3.3.1          t[j-1]•t1[j]    // point-to-point
               communication
            3.3.2          w[j] =max{t[j]+f(a1[j], '-'),
               t1[j]+f(a1[j],b[j])}  //formula (4)
            3.3.3  z[j]=w[j]-y[j]     //formula (7)
            3.3.4          compute prefix-maximum value of
               array z[j], results are stored in x[j]
               // formula (8)
            3.3.5  t[j] =x[j]+y[j]  // formula (9)
            Endfor-j
      Endfor-i
   4.  sim=t[n]
End.
```

4.3 Analysis of Algorithm-2

In *Algorithm*-2, steps 1.2 and 2.2 are the operation of prefix-sum, step 3.1 is the broadcasting operation, steps 3.2 and 3.3.1 are point-to-point communications, step 3.3.4 is the prefix-maximum operation, and other steps are all arithmetic operations. Since each of these operations can be finished in constant time on LARPBS, the first, second, and forth steps can be done in $O(1)$ time and the third step requires $O(m)$ time if the number of processors is n. Therefore, the whole algorithm can be finished in $O(m)$ time.

4.4 The Case of $p \leq n$

In case the number of processors is p satisfying $1 \leq p \leq n$, the prefix-sum operation can be implemented in $O(n/p)$ time. To implement *Algorithm*-2 in $p(1 \leq p \leq n)$ processors, we partition the m elements in A into $\lfloor \dfrac{m}{p} \rfloor$ groups and each group has p elements which are scattered to the p processors. Elements of sequence B are partitioned and scattered in a similar way. Let $M = \lfloor \dfrac{m}{p} \rfloor$, $N = \lfloor \dfrac{n}{p} \rfloor$ be the number of symbols of sequence A, B stored in each processor. There are some registers in PE_j named $a[j,k]$, $b[j,l]$, $top[j,k]$, $t[j,l]$, $y[j,l]$, $x[j,l]$, $w[j,l]$, $z[j,l]$ where a_{kp+j}, b_{lp+j}, $T[kp+j,0]$, $T[i,lp+j]$, $y[lp+j]$, $x[lp+j]$, $w[lp+j]$, $z[lp+j]$ are stored respectively. Additionally, a temporary variable $a1$ is used to store the value of a broadcasted and $t1[j,l]$ is used to store the value of $T[kp+i,lp+j-1]$ received from the point-to-point communication, here $1 \leq i \leq p$, $1 \leq j \leq p$, $1 \leq k \leq M$, $0 \leq l \leq N$.

Algorithm-3. Parallel sequence alignment algorithm on LARPBS with p(1≤p≤n) PEs

Input : a_i, a_{p+i},. . . ,a_{Mp+i} are stored in registers a[i,0] . . . ,a[i,M] in PE$_i$, a_{kp+i} is stored in a[i,k], b_j,b_{p+j},. . . ,b_{Np+j} are stored in registers b[j,0] . . . ,b[j,N] in PE$_j$, b_{lp+j} is stored in b[j,l], the penalty function is stored in each processor.

Output : the similarity score of A and B ∙sim.

Begin
```
1. sum=0
2. for k=0 to M do
      if (k+1)p≤m then p'=p else p'=m mod p;
      for i=1 to p par-do
      2.1 top[i,k]=f(a[i,k] ,'-')
      2.2  top[1,k]=sum+ top[1,k]
      2.3 compute the prefix-sum of array
         top[1,k]…,top[p',k]    //Initialize T[i,0]
      2.4 save the final prefix-sum as sum
      Endfor-i
Endfor-k
3. sum=0;
4. for l=0 to N-1 do
      if (l+1)p≤m then p'=p else p'=m mod p;
      for j=1 to p par-do
      4.1 t[j,l]=f('-',b[j,l])
      4.2  t[1,l]=sum+ t[1,l]
      4.3 compute the prefix-sum of array
         t[1,l]…,t[p',l] //Initialize T[0,j]
      4.4 save the final prefix-sum as sum
      4.5 y[j,l]=t[j,l]       //formula (1), (6)
      Endfor-j
   Endfor-l
5. for k=0 to M do
      for i=1 to p do
      5.1 if (k+1)p≤m then p'=p else p'=m mod p;
      5.2 a[i,k]∙ a1[1,k],a1[2,k],…,a1[p',k]
      // broadcast a_{kp+i}
      5.3 for l=0 to N do
         5.3.1 top[i,k] ∙ t[0,l]
         //point-to-point communication
         5.3.2 if (l+1)p≤m then p'=p else p'=m mod p;
         5.3.3 for j=1 to p' par-do
            5.3.3.1 t[j-1,l] ∙ t1[j,l]
            //point-to-point communication
            5.3.3.2 w[j,l] =max{t[j,l]+f(a1[j,k], '-'),
            t1[j,l]+f(a1[j,k],b[j,l])}  //formula (4)
            5.3.3.3 z[j,l]=w[j,l]-y[j,l];//formula (7)
            5.3.3.4 computer prefix-maximum value for
            z[j,l],result are stored in x[j,l]
            //formula (8)
            5.3.3.5 t[j,l] =x[j,l]+y[j,l]//formula (9)
               Endfor-j
```

```
        Endfor-l
      Endfor-i
      Endfor-k
  6. sim=t[n mod p,N]
End.
```

4.5 Analysis of Algorithm-3

In the algorithm, steps 2.3 and 4.3 are the operation of prefix-sum, step 5.2 is broadcasting operation, step 5.3.1 and 5.3.3.1 are point-to-point communication, step 5.3.3.4 is a prefix-maximum operation, and other steps are simple arithmetic operations. Since each of these operations can be finished in constant time on LARPBS, the second and the forth steps can be finished in $O(m/p)$, $O(n/p)$ time respectively, the fifth step can be finished in $O(mn/p)$ time and the first, the third and the sixth step can be finished in $O(1)$ time. Therefore, the time complexity of the whole algorithm is $O(mn/p)$,here $p(1 \leq p \leq n)$.

If $m>n$, algorithm 2 can be modified so that array T can be processed in a column-wise fashion. The time complexity of the algorithm is also $O(mn/p)$ for p satisfying $1 \leq p \leq m$. Therefore, the time complexity of the algorithm is $O(mn/p)$, if the number of processors p satisfies $(1 \leq p \leq \max\{m,n\})$. This means our parallel algorithm is not only optimal in time-area complexity but also scalable.

5 Conclusions

In this paper, an algorithm of prefix computation based on the maximum operation is presented. Using the algorithm, the prefix-maximum of n elements can be obtained in $O(1)$ time on LARPBS with n processors. Based on the parallel prefix-maximum algorithm, a fast sequence alignment algorithm on LARPBS is presented. For two sequences with length of m, n respectively, the algorithm can be implemented in $O(mn/p)$ time with p processors$(1 \leq p \leq \max\{m,n\})$. In this algorithm, by choosing different p values, the time complexity can be adjusted flexibly. This means our parallel algorithm is scalable. Furthermore, the time-area cost of the algorithm is optimal, and the algorithm is highly efficient. To the best of our knowledge, this is the first parallel algorithm for sequence alignment on LARPBS, it is also better than other parallel algorithms in the aspects of speed and efficiency.

References

1. Zhong Chen, Chen Guo-Liang, Parallel algorithms for approximate string matching on PRAM and LARPBS, 2004 Journal of Software, vol.15, No.2.
2. O. Gotoh, An improved algorithm for matching biological sequences, J. Molec. Biol. 162 (1982) 705-708
3. E. W. Mayers, W. Miller, Optimal Alignment in Linear Space, Comput. Appl. Biosci. 4(1) (1998) 11-17
4. D. S. Hirschberg, A Linear Space Algorithm for Computing Maximal Common Subsequences, Commun. ACM 18 (6) (1975) 341-343.

5. A. Aggarwal and J. Park, Notes on Searching in Multidimensional Monotone Arrays, Proc. 29th Ann. IEEE Symp. Foundations of Comput. Sci. 1988, pp. 497-512
6. A. Apostolico, M. Atallah, L. Larmore , and S. Mcfaddin, Efficient Parallel Algorithms for String Editing and Related Problems, SIAM J. Computing, vol. 19, pp. 968-988, Oct. 1990.
7. M. Lu, H. Lin, Parallel Algorithms for the Longest Common Subsequence Problem, IEEE Transaction on Parallel and Distributed System, vol 5. No. 8, August 1994.
8. Y. Robert, M. Tchuente, A Sytolic Array for the Longest Common Subsequence Problem, Inform. Process. Lett.21 (1985) 191 – 198
9. J. H. Chang, O.H. Ibarra, M.A. Pallis, Parallel Parsing on a one-way array of finite-state machines, IEEE Trans. Computers C-36 (1987) 64-75
10. G. Luce, J.F. Myoupo, Systolic-based Parallel Architecture for the Longest Common Subsequences Problem, Integration 25(1): 53-70 (1998).
11. V. Freschi, A. Bogliolo, Longest Common Subsequence between Run-length-encoded Strings : a New Algorithm with Improved Parallelism, Information Processing Letters, v.90 n.4, p.167-173, 31 May 2004.
12. Y. Pan, K. Li, Linear Array with a Reconfigurable Pipelined Bus System – Concepts and Applications, Journal of Information Science 106 (1998) 237-258.
13. S. Aluru, N. Futamura, K. Mehrotra☐Parallel Biological Sequence Comparison Using Prefix Computations, Journal of Parallel and Distributed Computing, Vol. 63, No. 3, pp. 264-272, 2003.

Identification, Expansion, and Disambiguation of Acronyms in Biomedical Texts

David B. Bracewell, Scott Russell, and Annie S. Wu

School of Electrical Engineering and Computer Science,
University of Central Florida,
Orlando, FLA 32816
davidb@cs.ucf.edu, srussell@cs.ucf.edu, aswu@cs.ucf.edu

Abstract. With the ever growing amount of biomedical literature there is an increasing desire to use sophisticated language processing algorithms to mine these texts. In order to use these algorithms we must first deal with acronyms, abbreviations, and misspellings.In this paper we look at identifying, expanding, and disambiguating acronyms in biomedical texts. We break the task up into three modular steps: Identification, Expansion, and Disambiguation. For Identification we use a hybrid approach that is composed of a naive Bayesian classifier and a couple of handcrafted rules. We are able to achieve results of 99.96% accuracy with a small training set. We break the expansion up into two categories, local and global expansion. For local expansion we use windowing and longest common subsequence to generate the possible expansions. Global expansion requires an acronym database. To disambiguate the different candidate expansions we use WordNet and semantic similarity. Overall we obtain a recall and precision of over 91%.

Keywords: Acronyms, Text Cleansing, Information Retrieval, Natural Language Processing

1 Introduction

Out of the ever growing amount of data made available to biomedical researchers and the resulting new literature, an equally ever growing amount of ambiguous and incomprehensible acronyms and abbreviations have arisen. These acronyms and abbreviations as well as misspellings represent a serious problem for language processing algorithms. Acronyms and abbreviations that have not become common in a language's lexicon will typically be treated as misspellings in most systems. [2] look at the affect misspellings play in part-of-speech taggers and [3] find that acronyms and abbreviations create trouble for automatically generating lexicons. Only with the addition of a system that can expand acronyms and abbreviations and correct misspellings will information retrieval using language processing algorithms be possible.

In this paper we will look at identification, expansion, and disambiguation of acronyms in biomedical texts. There are many approaches for dealing with misspellings such as [12]. However, for biomedical texts, which are mostly made up

G. Chen et al. (Eds.): ISPA Workshops 2005, LNCS 3759, pp. 186–195, 2005.

of journal articles and conference papers, misspellings are not much of a problem. Abbreviations and acronyms have been lumped together in many other approaches such as [1] and [14]. In fact the line between abbreviations and acronyms is quite fuzzy. For example state abbreviations look and act more like acronyms than abbreviations. In this paper we will focus on acronyms and those abbreviations that act or function like acronyms.

The difficulty with acronyms is the ambiguity caused by the large number of possible expansions. We can think of this as meaning acronyms are highly polysemous. In general, however, this may not be a problem as the expansions can be partitioned into much smaller domain sets, where all the members of the set belong to some common domain. For example according to Acronym Finder (http://www.acronymfinder.com/) the acronym TWA has 20 possible expansions, but depending on the choice of domains these 20 expansions could be partitioned into 9 domains with the largest domain containing 5 expansions.

In the general case of acronym expansion this ability to break down expansions into smaller domains is easily seen. Many approaches for the general case such as [15], [9], [11] have achieved good precision. However, the acronyms that are inside of the biomedical domain are still highly polysemous as [6] shows and general acronym expansion techniques perform poorly on medical texts as [10] shows. As such, approaches for their expansion, as of yet, have not caught up with the results for the general case. Therefore, we look at a new method for the identification, expansion, and disambiguation of acronyms in biomedical texts.

The problem of identifying correct acronym/expansion pairs in text can be broken down as follows:

1. Identify acronyms in the document
2. Find candidate expansions for the acronyms
3. Disambiguate to find the correct expansion.

The identification of acronyms in biomedical texts cannot be done using a simple heuristic such as acronyms are words in all capital letters. In the biomedical field there are many acronyms that would break such a heuristic. As such we have developed a naive Bayesian classifier and augmented its output with a couple of handcrafted rules. The classifier requires only a small training set and is able to achieve a good balance of recall and precision.

Expansion can be broken down into two categories: global and local. Local expansion means that the expansion is given in the text. Most documents should have local expansions for the majority of their acronyms as it is good writing habit to define acronyms once before they are used. Global expansion means that the expansion is not in the text. Instead the author assumes it is so common in the domain that it is a priori knowledge for the reader. Examples of these in the biomedical field are DNA, RNA, mRNA, HIV, etc. For local expansion we employ a commonly used windowing technique. In addition we use the longest common subsequence algorithm to eliminate erroneous expansions. Global expansion requires an acronym database. In such we chose to use the acronym database that is part of UMLS [17].

Disambiguation for acronym expansion entails finding which expansion out of a list of candidates is the correct one. Support Vector Machines, Maximum Entropy Models, and rule based systems are just some of the methods used for this task. In our approach we try to learn the possible senses for an abstract using WordNet [7]. We then find the possible senses for the candidate expansions and pick the candidate that most closely matches the abstract.

The paper will proceed as follows. First, We will look at the identification method that used. Next, we will look at the expansion process. We will categorize the two different types of expansions and propose ways of dealing with them and then look at the expansion method we employ. Then we will take a look at disambiguation and how to find semantic similarly between expansions and abstracts. Next, We will look at the training and testing data we used. Then we will look at the results of our system. Finally we look at future work and then make our conclusions.

2   Identification

Identifying acronyms is the first the step in normalizing them. Other approaches to acronym expansion include Park and Byrd's approach that uses a set of conditions and rules for identification [9]. Taghva and Gilbreth used the simple assumption that acronyms are words that have a length between 3 and 10 characters and are all capital letters [11].

We chose to use a hybrid approach composed of a naive Bayesian classifier, using a maximum a posterior approach, and two handcrafted rules. We looked a set of 5 attributes for the identification process.

1. In Parentheses: Boolean indicating if the word appears in a parenthesis.
2. In Dictionary: Boolean indicating if the word is in the dictionary.
3. Capital Letter Percentage: Percentage of letters that are uppercase (rounded to the nearest percent).
4. Consonant Letter Percentage: Percentage of letters that are consonants (rounded to the nearest percent).
5. Length: Length of the word.

For the Bayesian classifier we used the first 4 attributes. During testing we found that thresholding the Capital Letter Percentage and Consonant Letter Percentage to binary values increased the performance. We chose 66% to be the threshold value for both. These values were chosen, because we believed they would maximize performance for acronyms with length greater than 3. If we had chosen 50% then we would have problems with 2 letter words being misidentified. 66% also came out to be the best value for both when we tested. The increase in performance due to thresholding is seen because we have made the hypothesis space smaller. Instead of looking at two values that are binary and two other values that range from 0 to 100 we only have to look at 4 binary values, which greatly simplifies the problem. This allows for much easier learning.

In addition to increasing the performance, thresholding also allows us to use a smaller training set.

We used two commonsense handcrafted rules. The first rule was added to fix overfitting caused by the training process. During classification, words in parenthesis were found to have a high probability of being acronyms and this caused some all lowercase words to be mis-identified as acronyms. To fix this we added a rule stating that if a word is all lowercase and in parenthesis it is not an acronym. The second handcrafted rule takes care of the general acronym case. That is the rule states that if a word is in all capitals and has a length greater than 1 then it is an acronym. This rule is similar to the one Taghva and Gilberth used only less restrictive.

3   Expansion

In dealing with expansion we have to handle global and local expansions. In addition we have to be able to handle things like plural and variant forms of acronyms. A variant form of an acronym is typically made up of a base and number. For example, the acronym TT could be defined in a paper as time trial and then later on TT1 and TT2 could be seen. It is obvious to the reader that TT1 and TT2's expansions are time trial 1 and time trial 2. These variant forms can be thought of as local expansion, but in order to get their expansion we have to look at the expansion for the base. First we will look at the assumption we make about acronyms and their expansions. Next, we will look at how to handle the plural and variant forms of acronyms. Then we will look at how to handle global and local expansions. Finally, we present the expansion we use in a step by step fashion.

Our expansion method makes use of the one sense per discourse rule introduced by [4] and used by [14] in the domain of acronyms. One sense per discourse in terms of acronyms means that all occurrences of an acronym, in an abstract, have the same expansion. Unlike, Yu, Tsuruoka, and Tsujii though we do not find expansions for each acronym occurrence and then use some means of choosing the best one. Instead we combine information from all of the occurrences together to find the expansion.

To group plural and variant forms of acronyms with their base forms we use two rules. The first rule checks if there is a lowercase 's' at the end of the acronym. If there is, we see if there is another acronym that is exactly the same except for the lowercase 's.' The second rule is similar to the first one except we check for digits instead of a lower case 's.'

Global expansion means that the author has not given an expansion for the acronym in the text. For the most part these acronyms are common and domain specific. The only way to retrieve candidate expansions is with the use of an external acronym database. We have chosen to use the acronym database from UMLS [17].

Local expansion means that somewhere in the text, typically to the left or right of the first occurrence, an expansion is given for the acronym. Using this knowledge we can construct windows around the different occurrences. These windows then become the candidate expansion. Doing this creates $2 \times N$ different candidates, where N is the number of occurrences of the acronym and its plural and variant forms. The window size is determined by the length of the acronym. Stop words (and, the, of, etc.) and numbers are ignored when creating the window. Since $2 \times N$ will result in a large number of windows, we also use techniques to eliminate erroneous windows.

Our expansion method tries to exploit local expansion as much as possible. The overall expansion process is done in the following four steps:

1. Group acronyms
2. Local expansion with restrictive longest common subsequence
3. Global expansion
4. Local expansion with non-restrictive longest common subsequence

The first step groups the acronyms together. This step combines the variant and plural forms with their base form. The second step attempts to find local expansions using the windows and the longest common subsequence (LCS) algorithm. This technique is based on the approach by [11]. The first letter from all the words in the window are extracted and used in the LCS with the letters from the acronym. In our approach we assign each window a score. The score is the percentage of the acronym that the LCS covers. We compute the LCS and the resulting scores for each window. After all windows have been seen we return the windows with the maximum score.

Next, if we are unable to find an expansion we then do global expansion (step 3) by consulting the acronym database and retrieving expansions. However, the acronym database does not always contain expansions for an acronym. Therefore, if we still have not found an expansion then in the final step we try once again to do local expansion. This time instead of using the LCS with only the first letters of the words in the window we do the LCS with all the letters in the window. Every window that has a LCS length equal to the length of the acronym becomes a candidate expansion, effectively making the acronym a regular expression.

4   Disambiguation

Disambiguation, in terms of acronyms, means finding the correct expansion among multiple candidate expansions. Support Vector Machines [14] and Maximum Entropy [8] are some of the methods used in disambiguation of acronyms in medical texts. We use, what could be thought of as, conceptual clustering based on semantic similarity. Each cluster describes a set of semantically similar senses. The senses and the semantic similarity are computed using WordNet [7].

The disambiguation process starts by building a set of sense clusters that describe the abstract. The top 15% most occurring words in the abstract except numbers, stop words, and acronyms are looked up in WordNet for noun senses. The noun senses are then clustered based on semantic similarity. The clustering process simply loops through the senses and the available clusters adding the new sense to a cluster if it is within a threshold. To compute the similarity between a sense (S) and a cluster (C) we simply find the maximum similarity measure between S and each sense (cs) in C, see equation 1. Any similarity measure that computes the similarity between two WordNet senses can be used for $Similarity(S, cs_i)$. If the new sense was not semantically similar, as defined by the threshold, to any of the clusters then a new cluster is created.

$$Similarity(S, C) = \arg\max_{cs_i \in C}(Similarity(S, cs_i)) \qquad (1)$$

No attempt is made to disambiguate word senses in the abstract, instead we use all word senses. The resulting cluster sizes should give a good approximation on what the correct senses are in the abstract. The reason we use such a shallow approach, instead of parsing the abstract, is because, as we stated in the beginning, the presence of acronyms and abbreviations are a detriment to language processing algorithms. It seems to make more sense to deal with too many senses than it does to deal with a smaller possibly incomplete set of senses.

After we have created the set of sense clusters for the abstracts we are ready to disambiguate expansions. To do so we look at each candidate expansion individually. We assign a score to each candidate expansion (E) based on similarity with the abstract (A), see equation 2. The similarity measure for an expansion and a cluster is simply the sum of the similarity measures for each sense of each word in the expansion and the cluster, see equation 3. The candidate expansion with the highest score is then chosen as the correct expansion.

$$Score(E, A) = \sum_{C_i \in A} Similarity(E, C_i) \qquad (2)$$

$$Similarity(E, C) = \mid C \mid \times \sum_{S_i \in E} Similarity(S_i, C) \qquad (3)$$

5   Training and Testing Data

For training and test data we used abstracts extracted from PubMed [16]. PubMed currently contains over 15 million citations from various journals. We randomly extracted 300 abstracts for our test set. This set was split up into 20 abstracts for training and the rest for testing. The 300 abstracts had over 56,000 words and resulted in around 562 unique acronyms for a total of 1,728 occurrences. We also found that that 61.25% of the acronyms had local expansions.

The abstracts have in them section headings. These section headings are in all capital letters and could cause problems for identification purposes. As such we created an ignore list which is made up of these section headings. Other data files that we used were a dictionary [18] and a list of stop words. The dictionary is used during identification and the list of stop words is used during expansion.

6   Results

6.1   Identification

In looking at the results of identification we compare our naive Bayesian classifier to the approaches by [9] and [11]. We use recall, precision, F-Measure, and accuracy to compare the results. Recall is a measure of how well the method was able find all the "real" acronyms. Precision is a measure of how accurate the method is in identifying only "real" acronyms as acronyms. F-Measure is a way to combine recall and precision into one measure [13]. Accuracy is a measure of how well the method is at identifying words (acronyms and non-acronyms). Typically there is a trade off between recall and precision, meaning we can increase recall at the expense of precision or increase precision at the expense of recall.

We used a three-way-cross-validated experiment. We randomly chose 20 abstracts for training and tested on the remaining 280. We then repeated this two more times, each time picking a new random set of 20 training abstracts. In tables 1, we show the average results of the methods over the three different testing sets. Bayesian is the naive Bayesian classifier without the handcrafted rules and Hybrid is the naive Bayesian classifier with the handcrafted rules. Park and Taghva refer to the approaches by [9] and [11] respectively.

The trade off between recall and precision can be seen in the approaches by Park and Byrd and Taghva and Gilbreth. Taghva and Gilbreth's approach is very restrictive, but because of this it is able to achieve a good precision. Park and Byrd's approach was less restrictive, which allowed it find most of the "real" acronyms, but the lax restrictions also caused it to misidentify many non-acronyms as acronyms. Using just the Bayesian classifier resulted in a recall and precision of greater than 91%. The simple handcrafted rules were able to help boost the precision, recall, and accuracy.

Table 1. Identification Results

Method	Recall	Precision	F-Measure	Accuracy
Bayesian	92.35% (±.75%)	97.23% (±.73%)	94.73% (±.66%)	99.73% (±.03%)
Hybrid	99.22% (±.03%)	99.45% (±.03%)	99.34% (±.02%)	99.96% (±.00%)
Park	95.93% (±.19%)	39.71% (±.20%)	56.17% (±.18%)	96.04% (±.05%)
Taghva	66.75% (±.32%)	99.56% (±.05%)	79.92% (±.21%)	99.11% (±.01%)

The Bayesian hybrid approach clearly outperforms the others. The Bayesian classifier was able to learn which attributes were most closely related to acronyms and non-acronyms. The handcrafted rules helped by alleviating overfitting and helping to model certain attributes not possible with the classifier alone, when using a small training set. The only cost of using this method is training and we were able to achieve these results with only a 20 abstract training set.

6.2   Expansion

For testing the expansion method we looked at the recall rate. In this case the recall rate is simply the number of acronyms that we found expansions for divided by the total number of acronyms. We calculated the recall rates of those acronyms that we manually marked as local expansion and those we marked as global expansion separately.

Table 2. Expansion & Disambiguation Results

Expansion Type	Recall	Precision
Local	97.25%	95.14%
Global	81.70%	80.98%
Local & Global	93.21%	91.93%

In table 2 we show the results for the entire set of 300 abstracts. We found that the expansion method worked well for those acronyms we had identified as having local expansions. However, we were not as fortunate when it came to those acronyms we marked as having global expansions. The reason for this low recall rate is that the acronym database was inadequate. To overcome this in the future we will look at mining abstracts for acronyms and expansions, using only the restrictive local expansion, to build up the acronym database. The larger database should help in the recall rate for those acronyms that use global expansion. However, the draw back to this is that we will introduce many new possible expansions, which may cause an overall decline in precision. The overall recall was just under 94%. In contrast Acrophile had a recall of 60% and Acromed had a recall of 72% on similar texts [10].

6.3   Disambiguation

For disambiguation we again looked at the entire 300 abstract test set. We used the similarity measure by [5] for computing similarity measures between two WordNet senses. This technique uses information content and the edge distance between the sense nodes in WordNet. We used the implementation that is available in the WordNet::Similarity Perl module (http://wn-similarity.sourceforge.net/). The threshold that we chose for clustering was 0.8, which was chosen through experimentation.

In table 2 we also see the results for the acronyms from the 300 abstracts. We can see from the results that disambiguating acronyms with local expansions did considerably well. This is partly do to the fact that there were much fewer candidate expansions. Disambiguating acronyms with global expansions was just under 81%. The reason for the low precision is due to an inadequate acronym database and due to the error in the disambiguation process. Most of the error in the disambiguation process can be attributed to the coverage of WordNet. WordNet does not contain many of the more complicated biomedical terms. If these terms are frequent, as one would expect, in the abstract then we will be unable to find senses for them. As such, the completeness of the sense clusters we create for the abstract will be diminished. To alleviate this we need to look at incorporating a biomedical ontology into the WordNet ontology.

6.4   Overall System Results

In table 3 we show the overall results of the system. Like we did with identification we used a three-way-cross-validated experiment. The results show that the system achieves better than 91% for recall, precision, and F-Measure.

Table 3. Overall System Results

Measure	Result
Recall	91.90% ($\pm$.44%)
precision	91.29% ($\pm$.42%)
F-Measure	91.60% ($\pm$.42%)

7   Conclusions

We have presented a modular approach for identifying, expanding, and disambiguating acronyms in biomedical texts. While there exist very accurate methods for doing this in the general case, their accuracy does not carry over to biomedical texts. In addition most other methods dealing directly with biomedical texts have focused either on building acronym databases or just the disambiguation of acronyms.

For identification we used a naive Bayesian classifier with two handcrafted rules. The classifier was able to achieve a recall and precision of greater than 99% with a small training set. For finding expansions we tried to exploit the idea of local expansion as much as possible and achieved a recall of over 97% for them. Finally, for disambiguation we presented a method that clusters words from an abstract based on similarity. We then used these clusters to help find the correct expansion for an acronym. In the future we hope to achieve better results by improving the acronym database and coalescing a biomedical ontology into WordNet.

References

1. H. Ao and T. Takagi, "An Algorithm to Identify Abbreviations from MEDLINE", *Genome Informatics*, Vol. 14, 2003, pp. 697-698.
2. J. Bigert, O. Knutsson and J. Sjobergh, "Automatic Evaluation of Robustness and Degradation in Tagging and Parsing", *In Proceedings of the 2003 International Conference on Recent Advances in Natural Language Processing*, 2003, pp. 51-62.

3. C. Friedman, H. Liu, L. Shagina, S. Johnson and G. Hripcsack, "Evaluating the UMLS as a Source of Lexical Knowledge for Medical Language Processing", In *Proceedings of American Medical Informatics Association Symposium*, 2001, pp. 189-193.

4. W. Gale, K. Church and D. Yarowsky, "One Sense Per Discourse", In *Proceedings of the DARPA Workshop on Speech and Natural Language Processing*, 1992, pp. 233-237.

5. J.J. Jiang and D.W. Conrath, "Semantic Similarity Based on Corpus Statistics and Lexical Taxonomy", In *Proceedings of the Int'l Conf. on Research on Computational Linguistics*, 1997.

6. H. Liu, AR. Aronson and C. Friedman, "A study of abbreviations in MEDLINE abstracts", In *Proceedings of American Medical Informatics Association Symposium*, 2002, pp. 464-469.

7. G. Miller, "WordNet: a lexical database for English", *Communications of the ACM*, Vol. 38, 1995, pp. 39-41.

8. S. Pakhomov, "Semi-supervised maximum entropy based approach to acronym and abbreviation normalization in medical texts", In *Proceediags of the 40th Annual Meeting of the Association for Computational Linguistics (ACL)*, 2002, pp. 160-167.

9. Y. Park and R. Bryd, "Hybrid Text Mining for Finding Abbreviations and their Definitions", In *Proceedings of the 2001 Conference on Empirical Methods in Natural Language Processing*, 2001, pp. 126-133.

10. J. Pustejovsky, J. Castano, B. Cochran, M. Kotecki, M. Morrell and A. Rumshisky, "Linguistic Knowledge Extraction from Medline: Automatic Construction of an Acronym Database", In *Proceedings of Medinfo*, 2001.

11. K. Taghva and J. Gilbreth, "Recognizing Acronyms and their Definitions", Technical Report 95-03, ISRI (Information Science Research Institute) UNLV, 1995.

12. S. Van Delden, D.B. Bracewell and F. Gomez, "Supervised and Unsupervised Automatic Spelling Correction", In *Proceedings of the 2004 IEEE International Conference on Information Reuse and Integration*, 2004.

13. Y. Yang and X. Liu, "A Re-Examination of Text Categorization Methods", In *Proceedings of the 22nd annual international ACM SIGIR conference on Research and development in information retrieval*, 1999, pp. 42-49.

14. Z. Yu, Y. Tsuruoka and J. Tsujii, "Automatic Resolution of Ambiguous Abbreviations in Biomedical Texts using Support Vector Machines and One Sense Per Discourse Hypothesis", In *Proceedings of the SIGIR'03 Workshop on Text Analysis and Search for Bioinformatics*, 2003, pp. 57-62.

15. M. Zahariev, "Efficient Acronym-Expansion Matching for Automatic Acronym Acquisition", In *Proceedings of the International Conference on Information and Knowledge Engineering*, 2003, pp. 32-37.

16. National Library of Medicine, PubMed, Internet. http://www.ncbi.nlm.nih.gov/PubMed.

17. National Library of Medicine, Unified Medical Language System (UMLS), Internet. http://www.nlm.nih.gov/research/umls/.

18. G. Ward, A Set of Lexical Resources, Internet. http://www.dcs.shef.ac.uk/research/ilash/Moby/ .

A Knowledge-Driven Method to Evaluate Multi-source Clustering

Chengyong Yang, Erliang Zeng, Tao Li, and Giri Narasimhan

Bioinformatics Research Group (BioRG), School of Computer Science,
Florida International University, Miami, FL 33199, USA
{cyang01, ezeng001, taoli, giri}@cs.fiu.edu

Abstract. Recent research demonstrated that biological literature can complement the information extracted from gene expression data to obtain better gene clusters. The Multi-Source Clustering (MSC) algorithm, which was recently proposed by the authors, performs semantic integration of information obtained from gene expression data and biomedical text literature. To address the challenge of evaluating clustering results, a new knowledge-driven approach is proposed based on information extracted from a database of published binding sites of known transcription factors (TF). We propose the use of a measure called C-index for an objective, quantitative evaluation. We compare the results of algorithm MSC for the integrated data sources with the results obtained (a) & (b) by clustering applied to the two sources of data separately, and (c) by clustering after using a feature-level integration. We show that the C-index measurements of the clustering results from MSC are better than that from the other three approaches.

1 Introduction

Clustering genes based on gene expression data is now a routine method to partition genes into groups (or clusters) sharing similar expression patterns [1], [2], [3], [4]. Two critical questions have been pursued by researchers: (a) How to improve the clustering by combining information from different biological data sources? (b) How to validate or evaluate the resulting clusters?

The large (and growing) biological literature database has been considered as an important source of additional information for any exploratory analysis of biological data. It was shown to be useful for identifying functional commonalities of genes and to help drive the interpretation and organization of the expression data [5]. Several algorithms have been proposed to combine gene expression data and text literature data sources to perform clustering [6], [7], [8], [9], [10], [11]. Many other sources of data have also been successfully used to perform exploratory analysis. These sources include annotations form biological databases, protein interactions, transcription factor binding, etc [12], [13], [14].

In general, there are two existing clustering approaches for combining multiple sources of data: semantic integration and feature-level integration. Methods that use feature-level integration combine the features and then perform the analysis in the joint feature space [10]. On the other hand, the semantic level integration methods first build individual models based on separate information sources and then combine these

G. Chen et al. (Eds.): ISPA Workshops 2005, LNCS 3759, pp. 196–202, 2005.
© Springer-Verlag Berlin Heidelberg 2005

models via techniques such as mutual information maximization [15]. In a recent paper, a generative probabilistic model for combining promoter sequence data and gene expression data was developed to extract biologically meaningful clusters (transcriptional modules) on a genome-wide scale in S. cerevisiae [16]. The MSC algorithm, which was recently devised by the authors, is an example of the semantic integration method [11]. It implicitly learns the correlation structure among heterogeneous data sources and provides a semantic scheme to analyze data from them. Using a measure called z-score [17], it was shown that the MSC clustering outperformed those using single data source only or multiple sources combined at the feature level [11].

To address the question of validating or evaluating clustering outcomes, researchers have used annotations from the Gene Ontology (GO) database. The Gene Ontology (GO) represents an important knowledge resource to describe the function of genes, and the GO database contains annotations for a large number of genes from a variety of organisms [18]. The z-score evaluation measure is based on mutual information between cluster membership and GO annotations, and was used to judge the quality of clustering methods [17], [11]. A different approach based on similarity information extracted from GO annotations has also been proposed [19]. An important point to note is that if GO annotations are to be used for evaluation purposes, then it should not be used as a data source in the clustering algorithm, since this would bias the evaluation. By the same token, it would be inappropriate to use GO terms and attributes to perform text mining of biological literature databases. This raises some general questions: what other sources of data can be used for the purpose of evaluating clustering outcomes? And what evaluation measures are appropriate for these data sources? In this paper, we explore new data sources and measures for evaluating clusters. The idea is to use databases containing information about transcription factors (TF), which are involved in gene regulation, and their binding sites (i.e., the regulatory elements, or TFBS).

The remainder of the paper is organized as follows. In Section 2, we briefly review the previously described MSC algorithm, describe our new gene cluster assessment using information about TF binding sites in the promoter regions of the genes, and then introduce the evaluation measures used in our experiments. In Section 3, we show the performance of different clustering approaches through a typical example and present TF enrichment results. We conclude with a discussion in Section 4.

2   Methods

2.1   The MSC Algorithm

Intuitively, clustering is the problem of partitioning a set of points in a multi-dimensional space into clusters such that the points belonging to the same cluster are similar while the points belonging to different clusters are dissimilar [20]. For our purposes, the goal is to identify clusters of related genes using the available datasets. The MSC algorithm, a variant of the EM method [21], stochastically builds the models for each data source by boosting the models using the cluster assignments from the other models. In each iteration, we first randomly select a data source based on the weight vector. We then perform the following steps: (i) find the model parameters that maximize the likelihood of the data given the current cluster assignment; (ii) assign the data points to the cluster that maximizes the posterior probability. Our previously reported experimental results show that the MSC algorithm implicitly learns the correlation structure among the multiple data sources [11].

In order to obtain the final clustering, the cluster assignment for each point, for each data source, can be thought of as a k-dimensional vector in which only one entry (corresponding to the assigned cluster) is equal to 1 and all the others are zero. By combining the results obtained from the m data sources, the cluster assignment for each data point now constitutes a km-dimensional vector and the whole data set corresponds to an n × km matrix, which is used to cluster using one of standard clustering algorithms, such as K-means. Detailed descriptions of the MSC algorithm can be found in [11].

2.2 Cluster Validity Assessment

Here we propose a method to use a new source of knowledge — gene regulatory information — to evaluate the validity of clusters. A key source of information used is TRANSFAC, which is a database containing information on eukaryotic transcription factors and profiles of their genomic binding sites [22].

Similar to the approach used for other data sources, we propose a binary matrix M, such that its ij-th entry, $m_{ij} = 1$ if there is at least one TFBS for TF_j in the promoter region of gene G_i, and 0 otherwise. The matrix provides a basis for defining a distance function between the genes. Using the cosine distance measure (other distance measures could also have been used), we define the distance between gene i and gene j as:

$$d_{ij} = 1 - \frac{\sum_k m_{ik} m_{jk}}{\sqrt{\sum_k m_{ik} \cdot \sum_k m_{jk}}} \tag{1}$$

The above distance measure can be used to compute the C-index, a cluster validity estimator [23], which was recently used in a different context [19]. It is defined as follows:

$$C = \frac{S - S_{min}}{S_{max} - S_{min}} \tag{2}$$

Here S is the sum of distances over all pairs of genes from the same cluster (over all clusters). Let l be the number of those pairs, then Smin is the sum of the l smallest distances between all pairs of genes and Smax is the sum of the l largest distances. It is easy to see that the numerator in the above formula will be small for pairs of genes with a small distance. Hence, a small value of C-index indicates a good clustering.

2.3 Data Sources and Representation

Briefly, the goal is to build numeric vectors from each data source for each gene for further analysis. In our analysis, all genes of interest have two representations: Term

Vector based on information from the literature repository, and Expression Vector from the gene expression data (obtained from microarray data).

To represent information from text data, the Document-Term matrix was constructed from a biomedical literature repository (MEDLINE abstracts) using tf-idf indexing [24]. Then a Gene-Term matrix was obtained by combining the Document-Term matrix with the Gene-Document matrix from the SGD database [ftp://genomeftp.stanford.edu/pub/yeast/data_ download/literature_curation/].

Data sources and representations are similar to that in our previous study [11]. One difference from the previous study was in the way the tf-idf indexing was constructed, for which several papers have recommended a restricted vocabulary [7], [8], [10]. In this work, only GO terms were used for the indexing. Specifically, an index for yeast genes was constructed from 31,924 yeast-related MEDLINE abstracts. Gene expression data set was generated from cultures synchronized in cell cycle by three independent methods and consisted of measurements of 720 genes over 77 experimental conditions [2].

3 Experimental Results

3.1 Evaluating Clustering Outcomes

We used the C-index to compare the performance of the four clustering methods: K-means clustering of expression data, K-means clustering of text data, K-means clustering of the feature-level integrated expression and text data, and the MSC algorithm

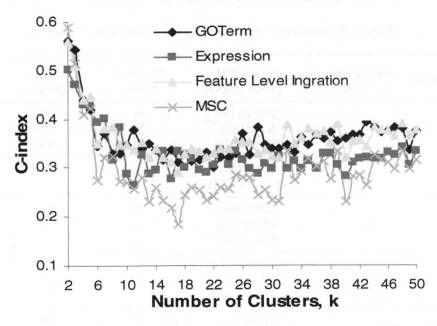

Fig. 1. Clustering results from expression, text (using Go Terms), expression-text feature level integration, and multi-source clustering. The horizontal axis shows the number of clusters desired, and the vertical axis shows C-index.

applied to expression and text data. Equal weights were used for the expression and text data in both the two multi-source algorithms, although the weights could be specified using expert knowledge to specify the importance of each data source. The expression data consisted of 720 genes under 77 experimental conditions and the text data consisted of 720 genes and 213 GO related terms. The C-indices were plotted against the number of clusters, k, for all values of k from 2 to 50. The results are shown in Figure 1. Using C-index as a criterion, the results from the multi-source data clustering exhibited the best performance for about 70% of values of k, implying that for a range of cluster sizes, the MSC algorithm has superior performance. The results from the feature-level integration were comparable to the methods that used only a single data source, suggesting that a simple combination of features and distance functions may not be the best approach to improve the quality of clustering, and that the semantic level integration does add value to the clustering outcomes.

C-index could also be used to choose the optimal number of clusters. Figure 1 indicates that C-index with k equal to 17 is smallest for MSC clusters. In the next subsection, we will explore transcription factor enrichment analysis on those 17 clusters.

3.2 Transcription Factor Enrichment

To assess the classification capability of the clustering algorithms, known information on binding sites (TFBSs) were used to evaluate whether the clusters have significant enrichment of being regulated by one or more TFs. A software package written in Java takes a list of genes as input and produces a ranked (by P-values) list of the TFs whose TFBSs are significantly over-represented in promoter regions of the genes in

Table 1. TF enrichment of clusters generated from Multi-Source Clustering

Cluster	# of Genes in Cluster	Enriched TF (Total genes)	Clustered Genes	-log10 (p-value)
1	61	SWI4(115)	31	27
		STB1(88)	23	17
		SWI6(125)	24	13
2	36	HAP1(49)	11	9
		HAP2/3/4(38)	4	7
3	76	MBP1(69)	25	24
		SWI6(125)	35	18
		MAT1(54)	13	7
4	18	MET31(11)	6	11
		CBF1(41)	9	41
		PHO4(46)	7	13
5	58	SWI6(125)	31	20
		MBP1(69)	23	19
		SWI4(115)	19	8

the list. Such significant TFs could be candidates regulating the corresponding set of genes. Each query gene set is composed of the genes from each cluster in a clustering (in this case, 17 clusters from MSC clustering were used). Table 1 shows details of 5 typical clusters with enriched transcription factors.

For example, cluster 1 in Table 2 contains 61 genes, 31 of which share TFBSs regulated by TF SWI4. Since only 115 genes are known to be regulated by this TF, this is considered statistically significant (P-value = 10-27). These P-values take into account the ratio of the number of genes within a cluster in comparison to that in the whole genome. As can be seen in the examples in Table 1, there are several transcription factors significantly enriched in a cluster. (Details of all clusters from our experiments are provided in a supplemental website [http://biorg.cs.fiu.edu/TFF].)

4 Discussion

The repositories of biomedical literature are increasing at a dramatic rate and should play an increasingly important role in exploratory analyses of genes. Vector space models were used to convert textual domain knowledge into numeric data (term vector space). Tailored term vocabulary (GO terms), which reflects the knowledge of this domain, was used to reduce the noise in the information.

A new approach based on knowledge extracted from TRANSFAC (a database of gene regulatory information) is used to assess the quality of clustering. Effectively, a new data source is used for evaluation. The C-index was used to compare results from four different clustering approaches and showed that MSC algorithm (with semantic integration of gene expression and biomedical text data) outperformed three other approaches. Also, the clusters from the MSC algorithm (with 17 clusters) were used to explore significant TFBSs, which could be potentially responsible for regulating the genes in that cluster. The software is available from the authors upon request.

Acknowledgements

ELZ was supported by a Florida International University Presidential Graduate Fellowship. The research of GN was supported in part by NIH Grant P01 DA15027-01.

References

1. Eisen, M. B., Spellman, P. T. et al. (1998). "Cluster analysis and display of genome-wide expression patterns." Proc Natl Acad Sci U S A 95(25): 14863-8.
2. Spellman, P. T., Sherlock, G. et al. (1998). "Identification of cell cycle regulated genes in yeast by DNA microarray hybridization." Mol Biol Cell 9: 371a-371a.
3. Sherlock, G. (2000). "Analysis of large-scale gene expression data." Curr Opin Immunol 12(2): 201-205.
4. Sharan, R., Elkon, R. et al. (2002). "Cluster analysis and its applications to gene express-data." Ernst Schering Res Found Workshop(38): 83-108.
5. Altman, R. B. and Raychaudhuri S. (2001). "Whole-genome expression analysis: challenges beyond clustering." Curr Opin Struct Biol 11(3): 340-7.

6. Shatkay, H., Edwards, S. et al. (2000). "Genes, themes and microarrays: using information retrieval for large-scale gene analysis." Proc Int Conf Intell Syst Mol Biol 8: 317-28.
7. Stephens, M., Palakal, M. et al. (2001). "Detecting gene relations from Medline abstracts." Pac Symp Biocomput: 483-95.
8. Chiang, J. H. and Yu, H. C. (2003). "MeKE: discovering the functions of gene products from biomedical literature via sentence alignment." Bioinformatics 19(11): 1417-1422.
9. Raychaudhuri, S., Chang, J. T. et al. (2003). "The computational analysis of scientific literature to define and recognize gene expression clusters." Nucleic Acids Res 31(15): 4553-60.
10. Glenisson, P., Mathys, J. et al. (2004). "Meta-Clustering of Gene Expression Data and Literature-based Information." SIGKDD Explorations 5(2): 101-112.
11. Yang, C., Zeng, E. et al. (2005). "Clustering Genes using Gene Expression and Text Literature Data. " To Appear, Proc. Of Computational Systems Bioinformatics CSB2005.
12. Ihmels, J., Friedlander, G. et al. (2002). "Revealing modular organization in the yeast transcriptional network." Nat Genet 31(4): 370-7.
13. Adryan, B. and Schuh R. (2004). "Gene-Ontology-based clustering of gene expression data." Bioinformatics 20(16): 2851-2.
14. Tanay, A., Sharan, R. et al. (2004). "Revealing modularity and organization in the yeast molecular network by integrated analysis of highly heterogeneous genomewide data." Proc Natl Acad Sci U S A 101(9): 2981-6.
15. Becker, S. (1996). "Mutual information maximization: Models of cortical self-organization." Network: Computation in Neural Systems 7(1): 7-31.
16. Segal, E., Yelensky, R. et al. (2003). "Genome-wide discovery of transcriptional modules from DNA sequence and gene expression." Bioinformatics 19 Suppl 1: 273-82.
17. Gibbons, F. D. and Roth, F. P. (2002). "Judging the quality of gene expression-based clustering methods using gene annotation." Genome Res 12(10): 1574-1581.
18. Ashburner, M., Ball, C. A. et al. (2000). "Gene ontology: tool for the unification of biology. The Gene Ontology Consortium." Nat Genet 25(1): 25-9.
19. Bolshakova, N., Azuaje, F. et al. (2005). "A knowledge-driven approach to cluster validity assessment." In Press, Bioinformatics.
20. Jain, A. K. and Dubes, R. C. (1988). Algorithms for clustering data, Prentice Hall.
21. Dempster, A. P., Laird, N. M. et al. (1977). "Maximum likelihood from incomplete data via the em algorithm." Journal of the Royal Statistical Society 39: 1-38.
22. Wingender, E., Chen, X. et al. (2000). "TRANSFAC: an integrated system for gene expression regulation." Nucleic Acids Res 28(1): 316-9.
23. Hubert, L. and Schultz, J. (1976). "Quadratic assignment as a general data-analysis strategy." British Journal of Mathematical and Statistical Psychologie 29: 190-241.
24. Baeza-Yates, R. and Ribeiro-Neto B. (1999). Modern Information Retrieval, Addison Wesley Longman Publishing Co. Inc.

Understanding Protein Structure Prediction Using SVM_DT

Jieyue He[1,2], Hae-Jin Hu[2], Robert Harrison[2,3,4], Phang C. Tai[3],
Yisheng Dong[1], and Yi Pan[2,*]

[1] Department of Computer Science,
Southeast University, Nanjing 210096, China
jieyuehe@seu.edu.cn
[2] Department of Computer Science
[3] Department of Biology,
Georgia State University, Atlanta, GA 30303-4110, USA
[4] GCC Distinguished Cancer Scholar
pan@cs.gsu.edu

Abstract. The explanation of a decision made is important for the acceptance of machine learning technology, especially for such applications as bioinformatics. Support vector machines (SVM) have shown strong generalization ability in a number of application areas, including protein structure prediction. However, it is a black box model. On the other hand, a decision tree has good comprehensibility. In this paper, a novel approach to rule generation for understanding protein secondary structure prediction by integrating merits of both support vector machine and decision tree is presented. This approach combines SVM with decision tree into a new algorithm called SVM_DT. The results of the experiments of protein secondary structure prediction on RS126 data sets show that the comprehensibility of SVM_DT is much better than that of SVM. Moreover, the generalization ability of SVM_DT is better than that of decision tree and is similar to that of SVM. Hence, SVM_DT can be used not only for prediction, but also for guiding biological experiments.

1 Introduction

The explanation of a decision made is important for the machine learning technology acceptance, especially for such applications as bioinformatics. The reasonable interpretation is not only useful to guide the "wet experiments", but also the extracted rules for interpretation are helpful to integrate computational intelligence with symbolic AI systems for advanced deduction. These years, there have been many studies focused on the accuracy of the prediction of protein structure using support vector machine, and there have been many good results [Sikder, 2005][Chandonia, 1999][hua, 2001][Casbon, 2002][Kim, 2002]. In spite of this, these methods do not explain the process of how a learning result was reached and why a decision was being made.

The support vector machine (SVM) method is a new and promising classification and regression technique proposed by Vapnik and his co-workers [Vapnik, 1998,

---

* Corresponding author.

G. Chen et al. (Eds.): ISPA Workshops 2005, LNCS 3759, pp. 203–212, 2005.
© Springer-Verlag Berlin Heidelberg 2005

Cortes et al, 1995]. SVM is recently of increasing interest due to developments in statistical learning theory. It is not only well-founded theoretically, but also superior in practical applications. SVM has been successfully applied to a wide variety of application domains [Cristianini, 2000] including handwriting recognition, object recognition, speaker identification, face detection, and text categorization. It is especially important for the field of computational biology [Noble, 2004]: because it is used for pattern recognition problems including protein remote homology detection, microarray gene expression analysis, recognition of translation start sites, protein structure prediction, functional classification of promoter regions, prediction of protein-protein interactions, and peptide identification from mass spectrometry data. Nevertheless, like the neural networks, the SVMs are black box models. They do not have the ability to produce comprehensible models that account for the predictions they make. It is important to have an ability of explaining why a decision is being made for the acceptance of the machine learning technology, especially for applications such as bioinformatics.

Some researchers have started to address the issue of improving the comprehensibility of SVM. Rule-extraction from technology IPOs in the US stock market [Mitsdorffer, 2002] and learning-based rule-extraction from support vector machines technique [Barakat, 2004] are two examples of pedagogical method. Nahla Barakat et al introduced an approach that handles rule-extraction as a learning task consisting of two steps. First they used the labeled patterns from a data set to train an SVM. Second, they applied the generated model to predict the label (class) for a different, unlabeled extended data set. The resulting patterns are then used to train a decision tree learning system and to extract the corresponding rule sets. However, the accuracy of decision tree may be much lower of SVM due to the limited learning ability of the SVM: because rules in this approach are generated by using a part of data set produced with the same attributes but modified values and label classified by SVM. Núñez et al [Núñez, 2002] proposed another approach to rule-extraction from SVM. First, prototype vectors are determined by means of k-means. Then, these vectors are combined with the support vectors using geometric methods to define ellipsoids in the input space, which are later translate to if-then rules. This approach does not scale well: in case of a large number of patterns and an overlap between different attributes, the explanation capability suffers.

In this paper, a novel approach of rule-extraction for understanding secondary protein structure prediction is presented. This approach combines SVM with decision tree into a new algorithm SVM_DT, which proceeds in three steps. First, this algorithm trains a SVM. Then a new training set can be generated by selecting from the result of SVM. This new data set for training decision tree will be better then the original data set due to using the advantage of SVM. Finally, this new training set is used to train a decision tree learning system and to extract the corresponding rule sets. The rules produced by combining SVM and decision tree are then annotated based on encoding schemes and verified in the original data set according to the explanation of biological meaning. From this we can get the rules accuracy. The results of the experiments for protein secondary structure prediction on the RS126 data set [Rost, 1993] show that the comprehensibility of SVM_DT is better than that of SVM. Moreover, the generalization ability of SVM_DT is better than that of C4.5 decision trees. The most important is that the explanation of the rules is very useful in biology. These rules with biological meaning not only indicate what a prediction is made and how. They also guide the "wet experiments" because when we want to get certain structure, we can try to satisfy the sequence condition to create the situation. Because we use SVM as a pre-process of decision tree to select strong instances to generate rules, the accuracy of SVM_DT is not much lower than that of SVM due to the limited learning ability of the decision tree.

This paper is organized as follows. Section 2 describes SVM_DT and provides the brief introduction of support vector machine and C4.5 decision tree. Section 3 presents an experiment of protein secondary structure prediction on RS126 data sets. Section 4 discusses some issues of SVM_DT that should be further investigated. Finally section 5 summarizes the main contribution of this paper.

2 SVM_DT

SVM represents novel learning techniques that have been introduced in the framework of structural risk minimization (SRM) inductive principle and in the theory of VC (Vapnik Chervonenkis) bounds. SVM has a number of interesting properties, including effective avoidance of over fitting, the ability to handle large feature spaces, and information condensing of the given data set, etc.

The basic idea of applying SVM for solving classification problems can be stated briefly as first: transform the input space to a higher dimension feature space through a non-linear mapping function. Secondly, construct the separating hyperplane with maximum distance from the closest points of the training set [Burges, 1998]. Suppose a binary classification task with the training data set ($\vec{x}_i$, y_i) i=1...N, $\vec{x}_i \in R^m$, $y_i = \{-1,+1\}$, The hyperplane decision function can be written as:

$$f(\vec{x}) = sign(\sum_{i=1}^{sv} \alpha_i y_i \langle \vec{x}, \vec{x}_i \rangle + b) \qquad (1)$$

In cases where the decision function is not a linear function of the data, the SVM first maps the input space to another Euclidean space. Thus, the decision function is formulated as:

$$f(\vec{x}) = sign(\sum_{i=1}^{sv} \alpha_i y_i K(\vec{x}, \vec{x}_i) + b) \qquad (2)$$

Notice that in the equation (1) and (2) there is a Lagrange multiplier α_i for every training point. Just a few of the points have a non-zero α_i. Those points for which $\alpha_i > 0$ are called "support vectors" (SV), and lies on the hyperplanes. The support vectors are the critical elements of the training set.

Decision tree learning [Mitchell, 1977] is a means for approximating discrete-valued target functions, in which the learned function is represented by a decision tree. Learned trees can also be re-represented as sets of if-then rules to improve human readability. Suppose, in a set of records, each record has the same structure, consisting of a number of attribute/value pairs. One of these attributes represents the category of the record. The problem is to determine a decision tree that, on the basis of answers to question about the non-category attributes, predicts correctly the value of the category attribute. In the decision tree, each node corresponds to a non-categorical attribute and each arc to a possible value of that attribute. A leaf of the tree specifies the expected value of the categorical attribute for the records described by the path from the root to that leaf. There are many decision tree algorithms. The results of the experiment [Lim, 2000] show the C4.5 [Quinlan, 1993, Quinlan, 1998] tree-induction algorithm provides good classification accuracy.

Rule sets are generally easier to understand than trees since each rule describes a specific context associated with a class. Furthermore, a rule set generated from a tree usually has fewer rules than the tree has leaves, another plus for comprehensibility. Finally, rules are often more accurate predictors than decision trees.

SVM claims to guarantee generalization, i.e. its decision model reflects the regularities of the training data rather than the incapability of the learning machine. SVM reveals the classification by looking at the critical cases. On the other hand, the advantage of the Decision Trees algorithm is easily comprehensible; it describes what attributes are important for classification [Lin, 2003]. Thus, the motivation of combining SVM and decision tree to classify is the desire of combining the strong generalization ability of SVM and the strong comprehensibility of rule induction. Specifically, our new algorithm SVM_DT employs SVM as a pre-process of decision tree.

Suppose we are given a training data set $S=\{(x_1,y_1),(x_2,y_2),....,(x_m,y_m)\}$, where x_i is the feature vector and and y_i is the expected class label or target of the i-th training instance. At first, SVMs are trained using N-fold cross validation. That is, for data set S, we divided it into N subsets with similar sizes (k) and similar distribution of classes. We perform the tests for the N runs, each with a different subset as the test set $(Te\_svm^i, i=1...N)$ and with the union of the other N-1 subsets as the training set $(Tr\_svm^i, i=1...N)$. Then, from each test set $(Te\_svm^i, i=1...N)$, based on the result of prediction, we select cases that are correctly predicted by SVM into new data set $(S^i\_svm, i=1...N)$. Finally, we use the original test data $(Te\_svm^i, i=1...N)$ as test data set $(Te\_dt^i, i=1...N)$ and the union of the other N-1 subsets S^i_svm as the training set $(Tr\_dt^i, i=1...N)$ to train a decision tree and induce the rule sets. Since support vector machine usually has strong generalization ability and we select the new data set from the correct result of SVMs as our inputs to DT, we believe that some bad ingredients of S, such as the noise, may be reduced by the process of SVMs, and some weak cases may be sieved by SVMs. It is indicated that new data set S^i_svm data is better than the original training data set S for rule induction based on our experiment results as shown later. This is the reason why we use support vector machine as a pre-process of decision tree.

After using SVM_DT algorithm, we can get rule sets. When we classify a case by using the rule sets, it may happen that several of the rules are applicable if all their conditions are satisfied. If the classes of applicable rules prediction are different, there are two ways to resolve the implicit conflict: select the rule with the highest confidence as a final result, or aggregate the predictions of the rules to reach a verdict. The latter strategy is usually better since it make use of decision fusion (combining rules) and usually this method produces better results according to literature [Gorgevik, 2002]. In this strategy, each applicable rule votes for its predicted class with a voting weight equal to its confidence value, the votes are tallied up, and the class with the highest total vote is chosen as the final prediction.

3 Experiments

These years, there have been many studies focused on the accuracy of the prediction of protein structure using support vector machine, and there have been many good results. However, there is an inability to explain the process by which a learning result was reached and why a decision is being made. Therefore, we apply the method of SVM_DT to the prediction of protein secondary structure. On one hand, the method is used to generate the rule sets for explaining how a secondary structure can be classify, and one the other hand, it is applied to evaluate the performance of the algorithm. We use RS126 [Rost, 1993] as a data set which was proposed by Rost & Sander. Based on their definition, it is a non-homologous set. This set was used in many researches on protein secondary structure prediction such as the experiments by Hua [Hua, 2001] and Kim [Kim, 2002].

The protein secondary structure prediction can be analyzed as a typical classification problem where the class (secondary structure) of a given instance is predicted based on its sequence features. The goal of secondary structure prediction is to classify a pattern of adjacent residues as helix (H), sheet (E) or coil(C, the remaining part) based on the idea that the segments of consecutive residues prefer certain secondary structure. In this study, firstly, we combined orthogonal matrix and BLOSUM62 matrix [Henikoff, 1992] as encoding schemes [Hu et al, 2004]. The orthogonal encoding scheme is the simplest profile which assigns a unique binary vector to each residue, such as (1, 0, 0...), (0, 1, 0...), (0, 0, 1...) and so on. The BLOSUM62 matrix is a measure of difference between two distantly related proteins. Namely, the values in the BLOSUM62 matrix mean "log-odds" scores for the possibility that a given amino acid pair will interchange with each other and it contains the general evolutionary information among the protein families. This BLOSUM62 matrix was applied as an encoding scheme by converting its data range to [0,1]. In the encoding schemes, the information about the local interactions among neighboring residues can be embedded as a feature value, because the feature values of each amino acid residue in a window mean the weight of each residue in a pattern. Therefore, the optimal window length 13 was adopted by testing different window lengths from 5 to 19. We construct three one-versus-one binary classifiers (H/~H, E/~E, and C/~C).

Secondly, to train the SVM, we selected the kernel function $K(x, y) = e^{-\lambda \|x-y\|^2}$ based on the previous studies [Hua, 2001; Kim, 2002], and the parameter of the kernel function λ and the regularization parameter C were optimized based on tests [Hu, 2004]. With the data set, we ran 7-fold cross validation in the experiments. That is, we divided the data set into seven subsets with similar sizes and similar distribution of classes. Then, we performed the tests for the seven runs, each with a different subset as the test set and with the union of the other six subsets as the training set. In this experiment, we used SVM^{light} [Joachims, 2002] software. In each run, we fed the training data into SVM^{light} to get the model and used test data as validation.

Thirdly, in order to compare the prediction result from SVM on test data to the original data set, and to see if they were consistent, we selected the instance into a new data set which was used later for building rules. We repeat the process until 7 sets of new data have been finished. Then, combining 6 of them as a training data and original test data as test data to train decision tree of C4.5 and C4.5 rules, we get 7 group rule sets. For comparison, we also applied the original train data and test data directly into C4.5 and C4.5 rules. All the average accuracy of binary classifier by three methods is shown as Table 1, respectively. From Table 1 we can see that the accuracy of binary classifier by SVM (SVM [light]) is better than that of binary classifier by the decision tree (C4.5), but the accuracy of binary classifier by SVM_DT is better than that of binary classifier by the decision tree. We believe that this is a benefit from the generalization ability of SVM.

Table 1. Comparison of accuracy of E/~E,H/~H and C/~C binary_classifier with three methods

Binary_classifier	SVM (%)	DT (%)	SVM-DT (%)
E/~E	80.7	78.4	79.6
H/~H	77.6	70.4	72.8
C/~C	70.5	67.1	69.3

The average number of rules produced by DT and SVM_DT are shown in Table 2. From Table 2, we can see SVM_DT generated more rules than DT.

Table 2. Comparison of number of rules with DT method and SVM_DT method

Binary_classifier	DT (average number of rules)	SVM-DT (average number of rules)
E/~E	21.7	91.7
H/~H	18.3	148.1
C/~C	22.1	98.1

Although the accuracy of the binary classifier by SVM_DT is not better than that of the binary classifier by the SVM, we have gotten the rule sets. Thus, finally, based on the encoding schemes, we decoded the rules. We obtained a group of logical rules which have biological meaning and then we checked them in the original sequence data according to the logical rules, to verify the accuracy of them. Some of the results are shown in Tables 3. There are four rows in Table 3. In the fourth row there are examples which are selected from the original sequence according to the logical rule of the second row and the explanation in the third row. For example, Rule 253 is produced by SVM_DT, and the description of rule is as follows:

IF

        A177>0

   and   A228<=0.035

   and   A300>0

THEN

        E [93.3%]

Table 3. Rule 253 for prediction for 'E' of protein secondary structure produced by SVM_DT, and explanation and examples in RS126 which match up to the explanation

Implicit rule produced by SVM_DT	IF
	    A177>0 and A228<=0.035 and A300>0
	THEN
	    E [93.3%]

Explicit rule with biological meaning	IF
	    Sq[1]= T
	    and Sq[2] in {C, I, L, M, F, Y, V}
	    and Sq[4]= V
	THEN
	    St[3]= E [93.3%]

Rule explanation	If the two amino acids before the target are T and followed by one of {C, I, L, M, F, Y, V}, and at the same time, the one following the target is V, then the secondary structure of the target is E with a 93.3% confidence. When verified with test data, it achieves an 88.9% prediction accuracy.
Validation examples using original data set	>1FDL: Sequence Length: 218 rule 253: the position is:22 TCTV EEEE rule 253: the position is:112 TLTV EEEE rule 253: the position is:198 TCNV EEEE

This means that Rule 253 has the confidence of 93.3%. By the encoded schemes, the logical expression of this rule with biological meaning is as follows:

IF
    Sq[1]= T
and Sq[2] in {C, I, L, M, F, Y, V}
and Sq[4]= V
THEN
    St[3]= E [93.3%]

It indicates that if the two amino acids before the target are T and followed by one of {C, I, L, M, F, Y, V}, and at the same time, the one following the target is V, then the secondary structure of the target is E. It has an 88.9% prediction accuracy which was obtained through verification of the original data according to the explanation derived from the rule. There are some examples shown in the fourth rows: in the protein 1FDL, the length of this protein is 218, and on position 22 we can see that two of the amino acids before position 22 are T and C and at the same time the amino acids following position 22 is V, therefore, no matter what the amino acid of position 22 is, then the secondary structure of this amino acid is 'E' with an 88.9% accuracy.

We also found that the rules generated have strong biological meaning. For example, in Rule 253 (Table 3), the first position is the weakly hydrophilic amino acid threonine (T), followed by a hydrophobic amino acid (C, I, L, M, F, Y, or V), then by any amino acid and finally by another hydrophobic amino acid valine (V). If this forms a sheet (E), then the two hydrophobic amino acids (C, I, L, M, F, Y, or V) and the V will point in the same direction (possibly into the core of the protein), and the hydrophilic amino acid threonine (T) could then point into the solvent.

4   Discussion

Experiments presented in section 3 show that although the accuracy of SVM_DT is similar to that of SVM, it is better than that of the decision tree. The most important thing is that we have created rule sets that show how the decisions are made through SVM_DT. Now remains three problems to solve.

First, the algorithm produces a large amount of rules. In the experiment, shown in Table 2, the average size of each rule set is about 100. Therefore, an intelligent criterion for selecting the more trustworthy rules has to be made and evaluated. If several of the rules are applicable for classifying a case and the classes of applicable rules predictions are different, we can resolve the implicit conflict by voting based on totaling up the confidence. This is a decision fusion problem. Which decision fusion method should be used still needs to be researched in the future.

Secondly, we fed SVM with the training data which was encoded. When we generated rules produced by SVM_DT, we needed to decode them so that we could get the rules with biological meaning. In addition, more importantly, the most commonly used amino acid encoding method has a drawback that leads to large computational cost and recognition bias [Yang, 2004]. One of the method researchers used was to replace kernel functions of SVMs with amino acid similarity measurement matrices [Yang, 2004]. How to use it and which matrix is suitable to be used as a kernel function for protein secondary structure prediction is our further work.

Thirdly, we have gotten some rule sets by SVM_DT. How to make use of the extracted rules to integrate computational intelligence with symbolic AI systems for advanced deduction to generate new rules needs to be studied.

Acknowledgement

The authors would like to thank Professor Thorsten Joachims for making SVM[light] software available. This research was supported in part by a scholarship under the State Scholarship Fund of China, and the U.S. National Institutes of Health (NIH) under grants R01 GM34766-17S1, P20 GM065762-01A1, and the U.S. National Science Foundation (NSF) under grants ECS-0196569, and ECS-0334813. This work was supported by the Georgia Cancer Coalition and computer hardware used was supplied by the Georgia Research Alliance. This work was also supported by the

National '863' of China (#2002AA231071) and Foundation of High Tech Project of JiangSu (BG2004034).

References

1. A.R. Sikder and A.Y. Zomaya.: An overview of protein-folding techniques: issues and perspectives. Int. J. Bioinformatics Research and Applications, Vol.1, issure 1,pp.121-143. (2005).
2. Barakat,N., Diederich, J. :Learning-based Rule-Extraction from Support Vector Machine. The third Conference on Neuro-Computing and Evolving Intelligence (NCEI'04) (2004).
3. Burges, C.J.C.: A tutorial on support vector machines for pattern recognition. Data Mining and Knowledge Discovery,2(2):121-167(1998)
4. Casbon, J.: Protein Secondary Structure Prediction with Support Vector Machines. (2002)
5. Chandonia, J.M., Karplus, M.: New Methods for accurate prediction of protein secondary structure. Proteins (1999)35, 293-306.
6. Cortes, C. , Vapnik, V.: Support-Vector Networks. Machine Learning, Kluwer Academic Publisher, Boston (1995) 20, 237-297
7. Cristianini, N., Shawe-Taylor, J.: An Introduction to Support Vector Machines and other Kernel-based Learning Methods. Cambridge University Press, Cambridge, UK (2000)
8. Gorgevik, D., Cakmakov, D.,Radevski, V.: Handwritten Digit Recognition Using Statistical and Rule-Based Decision Fusion. IEEE MELECON 2002,May 7-9
9. Henikoff, S., Henikoff, J.G.: Amino Acid Substitution Matrices from Protein Blocks. PNAS 89, 10915-10919(1992)
10. Hu, H., Pan, Y., Harrison, R., and Tai, P. C.: Improved Protein Secondary Structure Prediction Using Support Vector Machine with a New Encoding Scheme and an Advanced Tertiary Classifier. IEEE Transactions on NanoBioscience, Vol. 3, No. 4, Dec. 2004, pp. 265- 271.
11. Hua, S., Sun, Z.: A Novel Method of Protein Secondary Structure Prediction with High Segment Overlap Measure: Support Vector Machine Approach. J.Mol. Biol (2001) 308: 397-407
12. Joachims, T.: SVMlight . http://www.cs.cornell.edu/People/tj/svm_light/ (2002)
13. Kim, H. and Park, H.: Protein Secondary Structure Prediction Based on an Improved Sup port Vector Machines Approach.(2002)
14. Lim, T.S., Loh, W.Y., and Shih, Y.S.: A Comparison of Prediction Accuracy, Complexity, and Training Time of Thirty_Tree Old and New Classification Algorithm. Machine Learning, Vol.40, no.3, pp.203-228, Sept.2000
15. Lin, S., Patel, S., Duncan, A.: Using Decision Trees and Support Vector Machines to Classify Genes by Names. Proceeding of the Europen Workshop on Data Mining and Text Mining for Bioinformatics, 2003.
16. Mitchell, M.T.: Machine Learning. McGraw-Hill,US(1997).
17. Mitsdorffer, R., Diederich, J.,Tan, C.: Rule-extraction from Technology IPOs in the US Stock Market, ICONIP02, Singapore, 2002.
18. Noble, W. S..: Kernel Methods in Computational Biology. B. Schoelkopf, K. Tsuda and J.-P. Vert, ed. MIT Press (2004) 71-92
19. Núñez, H., Angulo, C., Catala, A.: Rule-extraction from Support Vector Machines. The European Symposium on Artifical Neural Networks, Burges, ISBN 2-930307-02-1, 2002, pp.107-112.

20. Quinlan, J.R.:Improved Use of Continuous Attributes in C4.5. J. Artificial Intelligence Research, vol. 4, pp. 77-90, 1996.
21. Quinlan, J.R.:C4.5:Programs for Machine Learning. San Mateo, Calif: Morgan Kaufmann, 1993.
22. Rost, B. and Sander, C.: Prediction of protein Secondary Structure at Better than 70% Accuracy. J. Mol. Biol. (1993)232, 584-599
23. Vapnik,V. :Statistical Learning Theory. John Wiley&Sons, Inc.,New York (1998)
24. Yang, Z.R., Chou, K.: Bio-support Vector Machines for Computational Proteomics. Bioinformatics 20(5),2004.

Various Features with Integrated Strategies for Protein Name Classification

Budi Taruna Ongkowijaya, Shilin Ding, and Xiaoyan Zhu

State Key Laboratory of Intelligent Technology and Systems (LITS),
Department of Computer Science and Technology, Tsinghua University,
Beijing, 100084, China
wwx01@mails.tsinghua.edu.cn, dingsl@gmail.com
zxy-dcs@tsinghua.edu.cn

Abstract. Classification task is an integral part of named entity recognition system to classify a recognized named entity to its corresponding class. This task has not received much attention in the biomedical domain, due to the lack of awareness to differentiate feature sources and strategies in previous studies. In this research, we analyze different sources and strategies of protein name classification, and developed integrated strategies that incorporate advantages from rule-based, dictionary-based and statistical-based method. In rule-based method, terms and knowledge of protein nomenclature that provide strong cue for protein name are used. In dictionary-based method, a set of rules for curating protein name dictionary are used. These terms and dictionaries are combined with our developed features into a statistical-based classifier. Our developed features are comprised of word shape features and unigram & bi-gram features. Our various information sources and integrated strategies are able to achieve state-of-the-art performance to classify protein and non-protein names.

1 Introduction

Biomedical literature has become a vast dataset that is in urgent requirement for automatic knowledge discovery to improve the effectiveness and efficiency of knowledge use. Nowadays, Named Entity Recognition (NER) is proved to be fundamental in information extraction and understanding in biomedical domain. Based on the method, the NER system can be roughly split into three categorizes: rule-based methods [1-2], dictionary-based methods [3], and statistical-based methods [4-7], although there are also combination of dictionary-based and rule-based method [8].

Dictionary based method is intuitive and effective in building annotated corpus, but it is in direct correlation with the completeness of dictionaries and fails to handle inconsistency in naming. Rule-based method relies on a set of expert-derived rules and has a high precision. But, it is domain-specific and usually hard to maintain and adapt to other areas. Statistical-based method is an alternative to those dictionary and rule based methods. This method is more flexible in environment adaptation but needs a large annotated corpus.

In this paper, we investigate the extent to which different feature sources and strategies contribute towards the task of classifying protein name and non-protein name. The classification task is the second task after named entity has been identified.

G. Chen et al. (Eds.): ISPA Workshops 2005, LNCS 3759, pp. 213–222, 2005.

Separating NER into two tasks provides a more accurate and efficient system because strategies and the relevant sources used in classification task is different than in identification task. Another reason for considering the classification task independently is that information extraction needs not to be limited to protein-protein interaction. Other types of information extraction also require name recognition. By only adjusting its feature sources environment, system architecture can be modified to classify another type of name. In addition, because classification task exploits various features and strategies, it can improve the performance of the entire process.

This paper is organized as follows. Section 2 briefly introduces feature sources for classification. Section 3 presents the idea of integrated strategies and approaches in detail. Section 4 describes our experimental results. Conclusion is presented in section 5.

2   Feature Sources for Protein Name Classification

To classify a protein name, both internal and external information should be considered [7]. Internal information is the information within the named entity, while the external information is information outside the named entity like nearby words and context occurrences. In addition, we also present our own feature sources including Fuzzy Word Shapes, Unigram and Bi-gram which contribute a lot to the classification task.

2.1   Internal and External Information

Compared to external information, internal information is a stronger factor to distinguish named entity. This feature can be collected using the most commonly occurred words from biomedical corpora. Words like "protein", "kinase", "alpha", "receptor" and "factor" usually indicate the possible presence of protein names. These words are described as functional terms (f-terms) features, which we borrowed from Fukuda *et al* [1]. In addition, suffix and prefix are also good indications of the presence of protein and non-protein names, like "-ase" in "alkaline phosphatase".

External information is provided in case of failure in extracting features from internal information. This information has been used for the task of word sense disambiguation (WSD), and is called contextual information. Observed on many researches, words that are close-by in location tend to have stronger predictive power for WSD. Therefore we include the external information by limiting the distance of the words. In addition we limit the external information to only nouns and adjectives.

2.2   Our Additional Sources

To improve the poor performance of above information when dictionary inquiries failed, unigram and bi-grams features which are calculated based on their statistical probability of training data to predict how strong they are related to protein name are used. These features are aimed to provide statistical information which is rarely captured in previous features. These unigram and bi-gram features significantly boost up our system performance.

In other hand, we introduce another surface feature, named *fuzzy word shape* features, to provide additional word shape information. This fuzzy word shape features implement simple fuzzy set [9] for computing the confidence score. Fuzzification process brings ascender/descender information, position of digit, position of capital, number of intersection in center words, number of vowels in word, number of consonants in word. Each character which appears in [bdfhkl] will be counted as ascender and each character appears in [gjpqy] will be counted as descender. Other characters than those which are in range of [a-z] will be counted as middle character. For each special character which appears in our shape focus, we calculate according to their position (Pos_{begin}, Pos_{middle}, and Pos_{end}) in word. Pos_{begin} is a first character based on the category. For instance: In category "ascender", then Pos_{begin} is the first position of ascender in the given name. The definition of Pos_{middle} and Pos_{end} is similar to Pos_{begin}:

$$Pos_{begin} = \underset{c_i \in type}{Min} (Pos(c_1), Pos(c_2), ..., Pos(c_n)) \tag{1}$$

$$Pos_{end} = \underset{c_i \in type}{Max} (Pos(c_1), Pos(c_2), ..., Pos(c_n)) \tag{2}$$

$$Pos_{middle} = \underset{c_i \in type}{Avg} (Pos(c_1), Pos(c_2), ..., Pos(c_n)) \tag{3}$$

where $Pos(Z)$ is a function returning position of character Z in word starting at 0. *Type* is our special character type {ascender, descender, capital, digit, symbol}. In addition, geometric features which calculate number of ascender, descender, middle, digit, symbol and intersection in word are also presented. After being extracted, these features are then normalized relatively to the length of the word. Finally, we got f in [0.0..1.0]. For calculating number of intersection, we use Table 1 to indicate number of intersection for each character.

Table 1. Intersection number in character

a	b	c	d	e	f	g	h	i	j	k	l	m
3.0	2.5	1.0	3.0	2.0	2.0	3.0	3.0	1.0	1.0	3.0	1.0	5.0
n	o	p	q	r	s	t	u	v	w	x	y	z
3.0	2.0	3.0	3.0	2.0	1.0	1.0	3.0	2.0	3.0	2.5	3.0	1.0

To clarify our word shape feature extraction, we take the word "Interleukin 2" as example. Table 2 shows our word shape feature representation of "Interleukin 2".

There are three areas in Figure 1 (Begin, Middle, and End). Once the special character hits on the beginning of the word, it will get a high score in the "Begin" area. Similar rules are applied to "Middle" and "End" area. These positional rules are applied for special characters which are defined using knowledge of protein nomenclature principles. Theses principles reveal that positional information of special cha-

Table 2. Word Shape Features for word "Interleukin 2"

Type Features	Pos	Val	Type Features	Pos	Val
Num Capital	-	0.07	Pos Capital	Begin	1.00
Num Vocal	-	0.38		End	0.00
Num Consonant	-	0.46		Middle	0.00
Num Ascender	-	0.23	Pos OtherChar	Begin	0.00
Num Descender	-	0.00	(not in range [a-z])	End	0.68
Num Middle	-	0.61		Middle	0.32
Num Digit	-	0.07	Pos Ascender	Begin	0.70
Num OtherChar	-	0.07		End	0.22
Num Intersection	-	0.52		Middle	0.76
Pos Digit	Begin	0.00	Pos Descender	Begin	0.00
	End	1.00		End	0.00
	Middle	0.16		Middle	0.00

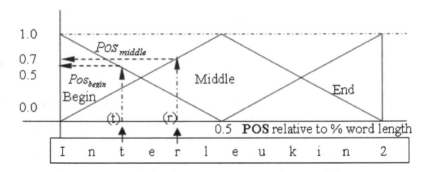

Fig. 1. Fuzzy Membership Position for 't' and 'r' in "Interleukin 2"

racters (ex. capital, digit, dash) has a special contribution to the classification task. Rules on position can be formulized into formula as follows:

$$PosNew_{begin} = FMember(Pos_{begin}, -\infty, 0.0, 0.5) \tag{4}$$

$$PosNew_{end} = FMember(Pos_{end}, 0.5, 1.0, \infty) \tag{5}$$

$$PosNew_{mddle} = FMember(Pos_{middle}, 0.0, 0.5, 1.0) \tag{6}$$

where Pos_{begin}, Pos_{end}, and Pos_{middle} are computed from formula (1, 2, and 3). In "Middle" case, function $FMember(pos, left, middle, right)$ returns a value of ~1.0 if the "pos" value is near to middle value; otherwise it will return a value of ~0.0 if "pos" value is near to "left" or "right". This function is a simple implementation of fuzzy membership function. After applying these fuzzy rules, we have position features

PosNew which provides better representation of features. The word shape feature extraction result can be seen on Table 2.

3 Methods

Stated in previous section, we try to incorporate the advantages of three methods and various features in our integrated strategies. In rule-based method, terms and knowledge of protein nomenclature are used. In dictionary-based method, rules to preserve dictionary list are used. For statistical-based method, SVM classifier which has been proved outstanding in biomedical domains for NER systems is used. Through the integrated strategies, a high performance can be achieved for classification task. Consider classification as a second task, which a score from identification task will be propagated into this task, hence a high confidence score is eagerly needed on this classification task.

3.1 Construction of Dictionaries

Ten dictionaries are constructed for classification tasks. They are one f-terms dictionary, one suffixes/prefixes dictionary, two external feature dictionaries (left context words dictionary and right context words dictionary), one in-context words dictionary, one protein names dictionary, one –in words with negative ending dictionary from NLProt (Mika *et al* [4]), two unigram dictionaries and two bi-grams dictionaries.

F-terms are taken into normalization by lower casing. This dictionary is manually collected on many papers using knowledge of experts. Words which are positively tied to classify class of protein names and non-protein names are used. Some of our f-term dictionary is shown in Table 3:

Table 3. Example of our f-term dictionary lists

Example of f-term dictionary lists					
factor~	receptor~	site~	vitamin~	region~	cell~
system~	sequence~	virus~	messenger~	element~	portion~
events~	system~	state~	motif~	particle~	kinase~
activit~	promot~	pathway~	complex~	protein~	enzym~

Morphological features as suffix and prefix are considered as important terminology cue for classification and have been widely used in biomedical domain. Similar to Zhou *et al* [5], we use statistical method to get the most frequent suffixes and prefixes from training data as candidates. Then, each of those candidates is sorted using formula below:

$$Morph - score(X) = (IN(X) - OUT(X))/(IN(X) + OUT(X)) \qquad (7)$$

where IN(X) is number of candidate X appearing in protein names and OUT(X) is number of candidate X in non-protein names. Then we manually selected the candidates over a threshold using expert knowledge.

Our external features dictionaries are taken from left context and the other is taken from right context. Both dictionaries are collected from training data as candidates which are limited only in adjective and noun words. Tokenization rules described in section 3.2 are used to extract these candidates. For these features we limit the number of words from environment to only 5 from left and 5 from right.

In-context features dictionary is similar to the work of Lee *et al* [6]. The most right 3 words from name in the training data are collected as candidates. These candidates are normalized using tokenization rules which are described in section 3.2.

Protein names dictionary is also collected from training data as candidates. This dictionary is merged with protein name dictionary we have extracted from SWISSPROT. Both dictionaries (generated from training data and SWISSPROT) are tokenized using tokenization rules in section 3.2

For unigram and bi-gram dictionaries, we apply differently with other dictionaries which we have described above. We only filter out the stop words and normalize white space in candidates. Tokenization step using tokenization rules on the candidates is not applied because of consideration on original shape information of candidates. For unigram we have two dictionaries. One contains protein names and the other does not contain protein names. Similar to our unigram dictionary, our bi-gram dictionaries are constructed.

3.2 Curating Dictionary

We curate all words in dictionary and provide a protein names curate-dictionary using tokenization rules. These tokenization rules consider the variability in writing such as hyphen, white space, capital, bracket, slash, numeral digit and special word like alpha, beta, gamma, kappa, etc. An example of tokenization process is shown below:

Sentence: IL-2 gene expression and NF-kappaB activation through CD28 requires reactive oxygen production by 5-lipogenase

Tokens: [il] [<N>] [gene] [express] [nf] [<M>] [b] [activation] [cd] [<N>] [require] [reactive] [oxygen] [production] [<N>] [lipogenase]

3.3 Simple Dynamic Matching

Our simple matching based on regular expression is implemented to search sub-string matching in a word or a sentence. This matching algorithm uses dynamic programming technique and is more flexible. It tries to search all combination which matches a source word/sub-word with a destination word/sub-word. The '~' symbol implements the '*' symbol in Regular Expression (RE) on Finite Automata, and means there can be none or some of characters to fill the '~' symbol. The details of this RE matching can be seen in example below:

Examples of match word:	Details of our RE models:	Curation process:
"inter~" → Interleukin	Observed word :	
"inter~in~ → Interleukin	"Interleukin-2"	Interleukin-2
"~ase" → kinase	Valid RE:	→ interleukin <N>
"~cept~" → receptor	inter~in~<N>	

Our experiment shows that using this model is better than using relaxed string matching algorithm. The result of relaxed string matching can be seen in Table 4, which contains $sm(x)$ function.

3.4 System Design

Because we only classify protein and non protein names, we employ one vs. rests classifier which is the basic model of SVM. For our external information, we use 10 tokens (5 from left environment, and 5 from right environment) which have been already filtered using our tokenization rules. For environment tokens, we put a weight value based on their distance to our "observed name". On features which are related to dictionaries, only f-terms and suffixes/prefixes features are extracted using our simple matching algorithm, the rests are using exact matching. Fuzzy word shape features are extracted using procedure described in section 2.2.

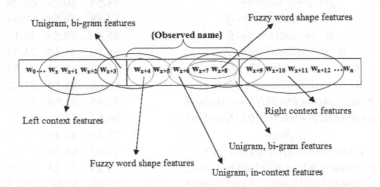

Fig. 2. Sequence words based on their feature extraction type

Figure 2 shows from which words these features are extracted. For example, *fuzzy word shape* features are extracted from first word and the last two words in the name. For those features which are related with environment (<left-contexts, right-contexts, in-context, fuzzy word shapes, unigrams, bi-grams>) we employ our weighting feature method that consider the distance between the name and the target word. After all features have been extracted, we assign a value based on the following formula:

$$feature_{type_i} = \begin{cases} X & \text{, if exist/computable} \\ 0 & \text{, otherwise} \end{cases} \tag{8}$$

where $feature_{type_i}$ is a type of features, and i refers to the specific element in each type. There are only 3 types. The first is feature which is related with dictionary. The X value for this type is 1.0 if the word is inside the word list in the dictionary, otherwise 0.0. The second type is fuzzy word shape feature. The X value for this type is discussed in 2.2. The last is unigram/bigram feature type. These features are taken into SVM classifier to train our model.

4 Experimental Setup

The experiments were conducted using Genia Corpus 3.02 developed by University of Tokyo. We use SVM [light] developed by Joachims, T. as our classifier. We are reporting all of our experiment results which influence us to design such features extraction models. Each step of our research is shown in following table:

Table 4. Experiment in adjusting and adding features on 25% Genia corpus

Experiments	Acc	Prec	Rec	F-sco
Baseline -> ft+in+lf+rf	83.57	77.41	69.88	73.45
ft+sp	77.45	73.60	97.71	83.96
ft+sp+in+lf+rf	84.27	78.71	70.42	74.33
ft+sp+in+lim(lf+rf)	84.54	80.23	69.29	74.36
ft+sp+tok(in)+lf+rf	84.38	79.54	69.64	74.26
ft+sp+tok(in+lf+rf)	85.46	79.56	74.11	76.74
ft+sp+tok(in+lim(lf+rf))	86.10	81.14	74.31	77.57
ft+sp+tok(in+lim(fill(lf+rf)))	85.89	80.41	74.56	77.37
ft+sp+tok(in+lim(lf+rf))+fws1	86.08	81.50	73.72	77.42
ft+sp+tok(in+lim(fill(lf+rf)))+fws1	87.45	81.86	78.64	80.22
ft+sp+tok(in+lim(fil2(lf+rf)))+fws1	86.85	81.21	77.21	79.16
fws3	79.59	82.46	84.08	83.26
ft+sp+in+lim(fill(lf+rf))+fws3	87.07	85.30	72.54	78.40
ft+sp+tok(in)+lim(fill(lf+rf))+fws3	88.25	84.23	78.35	81.18
ft+sp+in+tok(lim(fill(lf+rf)))+fws3	88.06	82.91	79.48	81.16
ft+sp+tok(in+lim(fill(lf+rf)))+fws3	88.84	84.93	79.63	82.19
fws3+ix	79.61	82.49	84.08	83.28
ft+sp+tok(in+lim(fill(lf+rf)))+fws3+ix	88.89	85.03	79.68	82.27
sm(ft)+sp+tok(in+lim(fill(lf+rf)))+fws3+ix	87.90	84.83	76.23	80.30
ft+sp+fws3+ix	84.20	85.89	88.34	87.10
ft+sp+tok(in+lim(fill(lf+rf)))+fws3+ix+ug	95.84	94.12	92.96	93.54
ft+sp+tok(in+lim(fill(lf+rf)))+fws3+ix+bg	91.93	89.53	84.99	87.20
ft+sp+tok(in+lim(fill(lf+rf)))+fws3+ix+ug+bg	96.74	94.85	95.08	94.96
sm(ft)+sp+tok(in+lim(fill(lf+rf)))+fws3+ix+ug+bg	96.60	95.00	94.44	94.72
ft+sp+tok(in+lim(fill(lf+rf)))+fws3+ix+ug+bg+dic	94.86	96.21	87.55	91.68

Table 4 experiments are important sources. We analyze those experiments to formulate decision for our features model. Within our expectation, the introduction of unigram and bigram features can greatly improve the performance by 7.8%. That the single use of bigram is of little effect may be due to the simplicity of our smoothing algorithm. However, the fuzzy word shape features boosted the classification task slightly. We attribute this phenomenon to the interference of other features.

Table 5. Description of symbol in Table 4

Description	Functions
ft = fterms	ug = unigram features
sp = suffixes/prefixes	bg = bi-gram features
in = inword features	tok(x) = tokenize x features
lf = left context features	lim(x) = limited window size (-5 and +5)
rf = right context features	fil1(x) = limited to noun and verb in extraction
fws1 = word shape features on the last name	on dictionary features
fws3 = word shape features on the first word and last	fil2(x) = limited to noun and verb both in extrac-
two words of name.	tion on dictionary features and feature extraction
ix = -in negative features from NLProt	process
dic = dictionary of protein names	sm(x) = using relaxed string matching for x

By looking at the system performance, our method without using any protein names dictionary as features performs better than using protein names dictionary as features. For this phenomenon, the only reason is the SVM classifier. Because in training task all of the protein names in dictionary are available, therefore SVM classifier which has the tendency to be outfitted to training samples has tied too much to protein name dictionary features than other features. However, in the testing task, protein names dictionary covers less instances of testing samples than it would do in training task. The possibility that no entry of our protein name dictionary appears in testing samples is also relatively high. For this reason, we also extract our protein names from various resources such as SWISSPROT.

Compared to other systems that have been developed, our system achieves better performance by integrating all of the relevant features. Torii *et al* [7] used name-internal and contextual features and implemented a context-based method in their classification task. Their system got f-score 91.00% on the protein class (while our system achieves 98.23% without the dictionary). Lee *et al* achieved 88.90% in their system which is combined with positional features, suffixes, orthographical character-istics and outside context. Therefore, it is clear that our integrated strategies with the relevant features are of great importance to the classification task.

5 Conclusions

In this paper, we present various feature sources with integrated strategies which achieve high performance to classify protein names. We introduce our new fuzzy word shape features, unigram and bi-gram features combined with all advantages of rule-based, dictionary-based, and statistical-based method. We have shown that our model is robust and capable of covering disadvantages from other models using fuzzy word shape features and our statistical based features. It is reasonable because noise words are pre filtered during features extraction. With additional source features, it is capable to cover leak of tokenization rules and also provide shape for words which are not in dictionaries. In case of words in list of dictionary, unigram and bi-gram features based on statistics will strengthen the information for classifying the name. Formulating more flexible fuzzy word shape positional model will be an attractive project. Besides, formulizing good smoothing method is promising for our statistical-based unigram and bi-grams features.

Acknowledgments

We thank to the members of the GENIA project at the University of Tokyo for making the corpus available. This work was supported by Chinese Natural Science Foundation under grant No.60272019 and 60321002.

References

1. K. Fukuda, T. Tsunoda, A. Tamura and T. Takagi, "Toward Information Extraction: Identifying Protein Names from Biological Papers", Proceedings of the 3rd Pacific Symposium on Biocomputing (PSB'1998), 3:705-716, 1998.
2. M. Narayanaswamy, K.E. Ravikumar, and K. Vijay Shanker. 2003. A Biological Named Entity Recognizer. In Proc. Of PSB 2003.8
3. A Simple and Practical Dictionary-based Approach for Identification of Protein in Medline Abstracts Sergei Egorov, PhD, Anton Yuryev, PhD, and Nikolai Daraselia, PhD (2004, American Medical Informatics Association).
4. Sven Mika and Burkhard Rost, "Protein names precisely peeled off free text."
5. GuoDong Zhou, Jie Zhang, Jian Su, Dan Shen, and ChewLim Tan. "Recognizing names in biomedical texts: a machine learning approach". Bioinformatics Vol. 20 no. 7. 2004, pages 1178-1190.
6. Ki-Joong Lee, Young-Sook Hwang and Hae-Chang Rim, "Two-Phase Biomedical NE Recognition based on SVMs". Proceeding of the ACL 2003 Workshop on Natural Language Processing in Biomedicine, pp. 33-40.
7. Manabu Torii, Scahin Kamboj, K. Vijay-Shanker, "Using name-internal and contextual features to classify biological terms".
8. S.Mukherhea, et al. "Enhancing a biomedical information extraction with dictionary mining and context disambiguation. ". IBM J. RES. & DEV. VOL 48 No. 5/6
9. L.A. Zadeh. "Fuzzy sets." Inform. Contr., 8, 574-591 (1965)
10. Nabota C, Collier N, Tsujii J. "Automatic term identification and classification in biology text", Proc Natural Language Pacific Rim Symposium 1999:369-75

Uniform Authorization Management in ChinaGrid Support Platform[*]

Hai Jin, Chuanjiang Yi, Song Wu, Li Qi, and Deqing Zou

Cluster and Grid Computing Lab.,
Huazhong University of Science and Technology, Wuhan, 430074, China
hjin@hust.edu.cn

Abstract. Users in grid computing environments typically interact with a lot of computing resource, storage resources and I/O devices. Different users are allowed to access different subsets of services, resources. These permissions should be executed correctly to guarantee the security of grid computing.

In *ChinaGrid Support Platform* (CGSP), there are large numbers of users, services, and resources. To ensure the security of CGSP, we build a user management mechanism to identify every entity, assign different rights based on user role and the properties of services and resources to ensure containers, services and resources in CGSP being used in a right way, and return the results to the correct user. We also consider the access control of files. These are designed in a uniform authorization management mechanism in CGSP.

1 Introduction

Grid computing is a resource sharing and coordinated problem solving in dynamic, multi-institutional virtual organizations [7, 8]. Users in grid computing environments typically interact with a lot of computing resource, storage resources, and I/O devices. Different users are allowed to access different subsets of services, resources. These permissions should be executed correctly to guarantee the security of grid computing.

In *ChinaGrid Support Platform* (CGSP) [1, 2, 3], there are large numbers of users, services, and resources. To ensure the security of CGSP, we build a user management mechanism to identify every entity, assign different rights based on user role and the properties of services and resources to ensure containers, services and resources in CGSP being used in a right way, and return the results to the correct user. We also consider the access control of files. These are designed in a uniform authorization management mechanism in CGSP.

The uniform authorization management mechanism includes three functionalities: (1) User management. User management offers the identity certification, proxy credentials management and identity mapping. (2) Authorization management. Authorization management offers multi-level access control based on *GlobusToolkit* (GT) [5] security and dynamic authorization mechanism. (3) File-level access control. We design the file-level access control based on the files metadata information.

[*] This paper is supported by ChinaGrid project from Ministry of Education, National Science Foundation of China under grant 60125208 and 90412010.

G. Chen et al. (Eds.): ISPA Workshops 2005, LNCS 3759, pp. 223–231, 2005.
© Springer-Verlag Berlin Heidelberg 2005

2 Architecture of Uniform Authorization Management

The modules of uniform authorization management include user management module, authorization management module and file-level access control, shown in Fig.1.

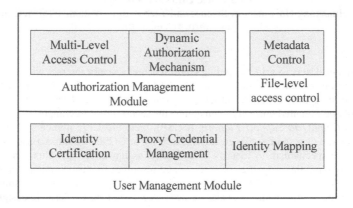

Fig. 1. Architecture of Uniform Authorization Management

User management module offers the identity certification, proxy credentials [11] management and Identity mapping.

1. Identity certification. Every entity in ChinaGrid gets X.509 certificate [10] and uses their certificate to verify each other.
2. Proxy credentials management. We introduce the proxy mechanism through saving a limited proxy certificate signed by user in proxy certificate management server. In this way, user need not use his own certificate every time and implement the single-sign-on.
3. Identity mapping. When user logins, domain manager get user information from user's register information. Domain server uses rule set to transfer user id to a domain id.

Authorization management module includes two parts:

1. Multi-level access control. CGSP inherits WSRF (*Web Services Resource Framework*) [17] security. Through implementing GSI Secure Conversation and GSI Secure Message, CGSP ensures the job submitted is legal and provide the security of job during execution.
2. Dynamic authorization mechanism. It predicts the probability of the success of task execution, and makes a decision to limit the user's right based on the prediction result.

File-level access control mechanism is designed based on the files metadata information. The files metadata information related to security includes owner, access privilege, authorization object, and so on.

3 Designing Uniform Authorization Management

3.1 User Management

The user management module is closely related to domain manager because the domain manager is responsible to manage the user identity and identity mapping. So the domain manager is the place to implement user management.

3.1.1 Identity Certification

We build a ChinaGrid CA (*Certificate Authority*) center. The CA gets the certificate request files submitted by CGSP entity and stores these files in local database. CA core software imports request files from database and signs these request files a X.509 certificate file. Entities in ChinaGrid get X.509 certificate and use their certificate to verify each other.

There are three types of users in CGSP: system administrator, service provider, and common user.

1. System administrator. System administrator is the user in the highest level. It manages the platform and monitors user state, service information, and resource state in the whole grid. It can also stop user service calling, repeal service issued and modify service describing from virtual service provider.

2. Service provider. Service provider is the actual supplier of real service. They register their service, computing resource, storage resource, and so on. The resource is encapsulated into a certain kind of service. And then the service description is submitted via service issuing portal to register this service. When service provider issues a service, it should submit its own *security descriptor file* to information server, which is important to Service-level Access Control.

3. Common user. The common users search the service using information center and submit their job requests via portal. The portal calls service and returns the result of service.

3.1.2 Proxy Credentials Management

After a user submits a job to CGSP, CGSP may invoke several modules to finish this job and these modules maybe invoke each other. Each module usually has different access control policy. In this situation, if entity A does not trust entity B but only trust user, user must use his certificate to notify entity A that the request from entity B is act as user's will to finish user's job. If a user uses his certificate every time, it will increase the complexity of job execution and also the risk of exposure of user's certificate information. So we introduce the proxy mechanism through saving a limited proxy certificate signed by user in proxy certificate management server. As mention above, module B can access the user proxy certificate from the proxy server and use the proxy to verify entity A. In this way, user need not use his own certificate every time and implement the single-sign-on. The working flow of signing a proxy and proxy server are shown in Fig. 2 and Fig. 3.

In CGSP, the proxy server produces proxy certificate request and related private key. Only proxy certificate request file is sent to common user to sign it, which avoids

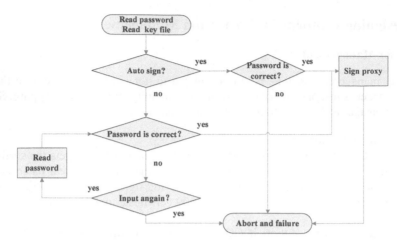

Fig. 2. Working Flow of Signing a Proxy

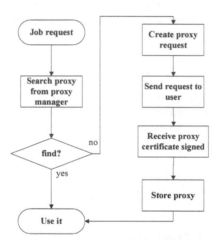

Fig. 3. Working Flow of Proxy Server

private key to be propagated in internet. After proxy client receives proxy certificate request from portal, and signs the request of proxy certificate by user's private key, the client will send back proxy certificate to proxy server. We choose the MyProxy [13] tool to manage these proxy credentials.

3.1.3 Identity Mapping

Domain manager is a management module in a CGSP domain [1]. It manages all the services and resources in its domain and set the access privileges for every CGSP entity. Considering the multi-domain situation and a large number of users in a domain, it is impossible to assign an access privilege for every CGSP user. So the domain manager just controls the users in local domain and offers a user identity mapping mechanism to map the outside user identity to local user identity when outside user wants to access the local services and resources.

Based on the identity certificate, the domain manager maps the outside credential to several limited and predefined local credentials. After the CGSP users register by using the interface of *addUser* and *updataUser*, the system will verify the identity and set the privilege by using the interface *queryUserList* and *mappingUser*.

3.2 Authorization Management

As the CGSP is developed based on GT 3.9.1, we inherit the GT security. We use some GT's security attributes to enhance the CGSP security. The multi-level access control is implemented based on the container and service security of GT.

3.2.1 Multi-level Access Control

CGSP inherits GT container and service level security. Through GSI Secure Conversation and GSI Secure Message, CGSP ensures the job submitted legal and provides the security of job during execution. Using security descriptor file, CGSP can supply container and service properties control mechanism including authentication and authorization. The container and service security descriptor type include credentials, gridmap, authentication methods, run-as mode, and authorization mechanism.

By using service security descriptor, we assign the access privilege when the users inquire usable service. The dynamic authorization mechanism is achieved based this.

3.2.2 Dynamic Authorization Mechanism

Dynamic authorization mechanism is closely related with information center in CGSP. All the service and resource information must be registered to information center. The information center can get all the attributes of services and resources, including the security descriptor. When the users inquire the available service and resource from information center, the information center can submit the services' security descriptor to the authorization module. The access control policy can be created before the job is executed according to the security descriptor and the user identity.

Dynamic authorization mechanism is provided to avoid blindly scheduling user's service requests and improve service efficiency. It can also record circumstance of service with the grid logging module.

3.3 File-Level Access Control

File-level access control mainly considers the security of data management in CGSP. To provide a uniform logical view of heterogeneous storage resources, the data management uses the metadata mechanism. The metadata refers to the data used to describe the physical data [4] including file length, file type, accessing privilege, logical file name, global identifier, and so on. We use the attribute of access privilege in metadata to achieve the file-level access control. The schema is described below:

```
#ACL
attributetype (8.2.6.3
        NAME  'ACL'
        DESC  'ACL control list'
        EQUALITY  caseIgnoreMatch
        SYNTAX  1.3.6.1.4.1.1466.115.121.1.15)
```

4 The Working Flow of Security in CGSP

Fig. 4 shows the working flow of security in CGSP.

The detail of each step is described as below:

1. User uses CA client software to create a certificate request file and a private key file and uploads the request file to CA. After CA signs the user's request, user can download his X.509 certificate.
2. After import user certificate to web browser, user connects CGSP portal by using https. Portal verifies the user id. If the information of user certificate is legal, user registers successfully. And then portal will send user's name and password to domain manager.
3. Domain manager maps user certificate DN to a domain id and sets the suitable privilege to user. After that, domain manager send user' username and password to proxy server.
4. Proxy server creates proxy request and proxy key. Proxy server sends proxy request to proxy client running on user host. After receiving proxy certificate signed by user, proxy server notifies proxy manager to manage the proxy certificate and proxy key.
5. Proxy client receives the request from proxy server and signs it, then returns the signed proxy certificate to proxy server.
6. Proxy manager saves the user proxy and proxy key. CGSP entity can access proxy manager to get user proxy. If proxy accessed does not exit, proxy manager will inform proxy server to execute step 4 and 5. If system does not need proxy mechanism, step 3~6 can be ignored.
7. After identity mapping, user can require information from information center and submit job to job manager. Job manager uses exiting service and resource to execute user's job if this session has enough rights.
8. If security descriptor mechanism permits, container and server can serve the user.

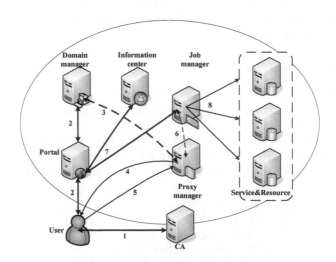

Fig. 4. Working Flow of Security

5 Performance Evaluation

The performance evaluation here ties to address three issues: 1) the performance of user login with or without certification; 2) the time of creating proxy credential; and 3) the response time of authorization policy created. The experimental environment is in local network, so we do not consider the latency effect in wide area network.

Fig. 5 shows the performance of user login with or without certification. We test 10 users' login time, and find the login time with certification is approximately 2 to 3 seconds more than the time without certification, due to the TLS connection dealing with the X.509 credentials.

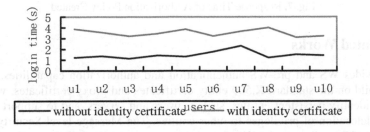

Fig. 5. Login Time with vs. without Certification

Fig. 6 shows the time of creating proxy credential. It is simple and the time just lie on the performance of computer. The experimental machine is a PC with a P4 2.4GHz CPU, 512 DDR266 RAM, and 100Mbps network adapter.

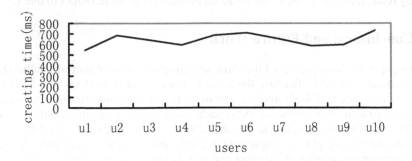

Fig. 6. Time of Creating Proxy Credential

Fig. 7 shows the response time of authorization policy created for a single service. The experimental machines are two PC with a P4 2.4GHz CPU, 512 DDR266 RAM, and 100Mbps network adapter. One is an information center and the other is authorization node. They connect each other with 1000M local network.

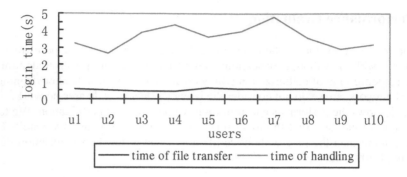

Fig. 7. Response Time of Authorization Policy Created

6 Related Works

GT provides WS and pre-WS authentication and authorization capabilities. Both of them build on the standard X.509 entity certificates and proxy certificates, which are used to identify persistent entities, such as users and servers, and to support the temporary delegation of privileges to other entities. The Message-level Security mechanisms of GT implement the WS-Security standard and the WS-SecureConversation specification to provide message protection for SOAP messages. The Transport-level Security mechanisms use *transport-level security* (TLS) [16] mechanisms to protect the transport-level data transfer.

UNICORE [12, 15] addresses security on all levels. User authentication is performed using X.509 certificates. A public–key infrastructure has been established for the German HPC centers that enforces rigorous control of certificates. User authorization is handled by the participant sites using their proven mechanisms. UNICORE sites completely retain their autonomy to authorize users and to allocate resources to them.

7 Conclusions and Future Work

In this paper we have presented the three key functionalities of uniform authorization management for CGSP. Because the security issue is relate to the whole CGSP system, each module of CGSP must cooperate with uniform authorization management module. From the job's point of view, authorization management module, including the GT's security mechanism, ensures the security of job execution in CGSP.

In the future, we plan to implement security mechanism to guarantee the secure transfer in data management. Another research is how to predict the probability of the success of task execution and make a decision to limit the user's right based the prediction result.

References

1. CGSP Working Group, *Design Specification of ChinaGrid Support Platform*, Tsinghua University Press, Beijing, China, 2004.
2. ChinaGrid, http://www.chinagrid.edu.cn.

3. ChinaGrid Support Platform, http://www.chinagrid.edu.cn/CGSP.
4. E. Deelman, G. Singh, M. P. Atkinson, A. Chervenak, N. P. C. Hong, C. Kesselman, S. Patil, L. Pearlman, and M. Su, "Grid-Based Metadata Services", *Proceedings of 16th International Conference on Scientific and Statistical Database Management (SSDBM'04)*, June 2004.
5. Globous Toolkits, http://www.globus.org.
6. H. Jin, "ChinaGrid: Making Grid Computing a Reality", *Digital Libraries: International Collaboration and Cross-Fertilization - Lecture Notes in Computer Science*, Vol.3334, Springer-Verlag, December 2004, pp.13-24.
7. I. Foster and C. Kesselman, "Globus: A Metacomputing Infrastructure Toolkit", *International J. Supercomputer Application*, 11(2), 115-128, 1997.
8. I. Foster, C. Kesselman, and S. Tuecke, "The Anatomy of the Grid: Enabling Scalable Virtual Organization", *International J. Supercomputer Applications*, 15(3), 2001.
9. I. Foster, C. Kesselman, J. Nick, and S. Tuecke, "The Physiology of the Grid: An Open Grid Services Architecture for Distributed Systems Integration", *Open Grid Service Infrastructure WG*, Global Grid Forum, June 22, 2002.
10. Internet X.509 Public Key Infrastructure Certificate and CRL Profile, http://www.ietf.org/rfc/rfc2459.txt.
11. Internet X.509 Public Key Infrastructure (PKI) Proxy Certificate Profile, http://www.ietf.org/rfc/rfc3820.txt.
12. M. Romberg, "The UNICORE Architecture: Seamless Access to Distributed Resources",. *Proceedings of The Eighth IEEE International Symposium on High Performance Distributed Computing, Washington*, 1999.
13. MyProxy, http://grid.ncsa.uiuc.edu/myproxy/.
14. Open Grid Services Architecture (OGSA), https://forge.gridforum.org/projects/ogsa-wg, or http://www.globus.org/ogsa/.
15. S. Haubold, H. Mix, W. E. Nagel, and M. Romberg, "The unicore grid and its options for performance analysis", *Performance Analysis and Grid Computing*, January 2004. Kluwer Academic Publishers, 275-288.
16. The TLS Protocol Version 1.0, http://www.ietf.org/rfc/rfc2246.txt.
17. Web Service Resource Framework (WSRF), http://www.globus.org/wsrf/.

Introduction to ChinaGrid Support Platform*

Yongwei Wu[1], Song Wu[2], Huashan Yu[3], and Chunming Hu[4]

[1]Department of Computer Science and Technology,
Tsinghua University, Beijing, 100084, China
[2]Cluster and Grid Computing Lab, School of Computer,
Huazhong University of Science and Technology, Wuhan, 430074, China
[3] School of Electronics Engineering and Computer Science,
Peking University, Beijing, 100871, China
[4]School of Computer Science,
Beihang University, Beijing, 100083, China

Abstract. ChinaGrid aims at building a public service system for Chinese education and research. ChinaGrid Support Platform (CGSP) is a grid middleware developed for the construction of the ChinaGrid. Function modules of CGSP for system running are Domain Manager, Information Center, Job Manager, Data Manager, Service Container and Security Manager. Developing tools for gird constructor and application developers consist of Service Packaging Tool, Job Defining Tool, Portal Constructor and Programming API. CGSP architecture is introduced first. Then, CGSP function modules and developing tools are described. At last, job executing flow in CGSP is also put forward in the paper.

1 Introduction

As an important new research field, Grid [5,6] mainly focuses on resource sharing and coordinated problem solving in dynamic, multi-institutional virtual organization over the Network. In these several years, grid computing has been paid more and more attention all over the world. Many nation-wide grid projects have being constructed, such as TeraGrid [14], UK e-Science Program [12], NASA Information Power Grid (IPG) [13], K*Grid [16], ChinaGrid [1,2], CNGrid [15] and so on.

As the kernel of grid construction, grid middlewares are developed to shield heterogeneities and dynamic behaviors of all kinds of grid low-level resources. All grids described above put much more efforts on their grid middlewares. Corresponding achievement includes OGSI [20], WSRF [9], WSI [10] and Globus Toolkits (GT) series [7,11], Open Middleware Infrastructure Institute (OMII) [17], Tinghua Grid (TG) [18], CROWN [19].

ChinaGrid [1,2] aims at constructing public service system for Chinese education and research. ChinaGrid Support Platform (CGSP) [3,4] is a grid middleware

* This Work is supported by ChinaGrid project of Ministry of Education of China, Natural Science Foundation of China under Grant 60373004, 60373005, 90412006, 90412011, and National Key Basic Research Project of China under Grant 2004CB318000.

G. Chen et al. (Eds.): ISPA Workshops 2005, LNCS 3759, pp. 232–240, 2005.

developed for building of the ChinaGrid. It integrates all sorts of heterogeneous resources, especially education and research resources distributed over China Education and Research Network (CERNET), to provide transparent and convenient grid services for science research and high education.

In moving towards this end, CGSP is developed based on following motivations:

- Provide a platform for grid construction from the top portal to the integration of bottom resources of grid. Not only does CGSP support the uniform management of heterogeneous resources, but it also supply the portal building, job defining, service packaging, and grid monitoring.
- Support secondary development of grid service and improve the flexibility of the system. Parallel programming interface and its running environment supply the complicated application development based on deployed services in grid.
- Follow latest grid standard and integrate existing advanced technology to avoid reduplicated works.
- Provide an extensible and reconfigurable grid framework, in order to fit the purpose of ChinaGrid to cover top 100 universities of China in the near future, and satisfy the autonomy of each ChinaGrid application or unit.
- Avoid unnecessary data delivery over grid. Data required by the computing job not stream with the job description file. It is delivered to the personal data space in data manager first and real computing nodes could get it directly when the job begins to be executed.

2   CGSP Architecture

CGSP is designed to provide grid toolkits for ChinaGrid application developers and specific grid constructors. It aims to reduce development cost of ChinaGrid as greatly as possible. It follows WSRF specification and is developed based on the core of GT3.9.1.

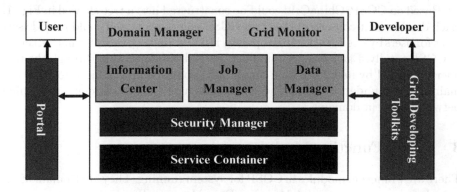

Fig. 1. CGSP Architecture

In CGSP, domain is an independent grid, which could provide service for users by itself. Each domain has the same logical structure and consists of same CGSP function modules. ChinaGrid consists of multiple domains which are constructed into a tree structure based on CGSP. Fig. 1 shows the architecture of one domain in CGSP.

There are two types of users for CGSP. Normal end-users define, submit and monitor computing job through CGSP Portal. Others construct grid or develop complicated application by using high-level Grid Developing Toolkits.

Besides CGSP Portal and Grid Developing Toolkits, the kernel of CGSP can be divided into 4 layers shown as Fig. 1. Service Container produces a basic environment for the installation, deployment, running and monitoring of CGSP service in all kernel component nodes. Security manager focuses on the user identity authentication, identity mapping, service and resource authorization, and secure message passing between CGSP nodes. Information Center, Job Manager and Data Manager are composed to shield the heterogeneity of CGSP real computing nodes. Domain manager is in charge of the user management, log and accounting, and user identity mapping between different CGSP domains. Grid monitor mainly focuses on the monitoring of CGSP resources load, quality of services, user actions, job status and network, to ensure system running normally, and enhance grid perform as well.

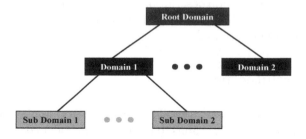

Fig. 2. CGSP Tree Structure

Based on CGSP, ChinaGrid could be constructed into a tree showed in Fig. 1. Each domain in it consists of the same CGSP components and could provide services for users by itself. Such a tree topology is maintained by the information center of CGSP totally. Each domain could get the global information through the tree query initiated by its information center and submit computing jobs to other domains directly under the help of the domain manager for the user identity mapping between different domains.

3   CGSP Function Module

There are 7 function modules in CGSP for system running. They are Domain Manager, Information Center, Job Manager, Data Manager, Service Container and Security Manager.

3.1   CGSP Portal

The CGSP Portal is an extended Tomcat web server that can be run independently. In the ChinaGrid System, each domain contains one Portal and the grid applications should be deployed as a web component (Portlet, JSP/Servlet etc.) in the Portal and interacts with the end users with these components. Through portal, normal CGSP users could define, submit and monitor computing jobs easily, and manage personal data as well.

3.2   Domain Manager

Domain Manager is the management module of domains. Its functions include user database maintenance and processing request for user registration, authentication, user information query and modification. Cross-domain identity mapping, user behavior logging and accounting are also involved in this manager. Furthermore, CGSP component monitoring is used to make sure that each CGSP component (such as Job Manager, Information Center) are working normally.

3.3   Grid Monitor (GM)

ChinaGrid is a complex system and therefore, monitoring is essential for understanding their operation, debugging, failure detection, scheduling policy decision and for performance optimization. GM could provide information about the current state of various grid entities as well as to provide notification when certain events (e.g., system failures, performance problems, etc.) occur.

3.4   Information Center (IC)

IC provides service registration, publish, metadata management, service searching, service matching and resources status collection for the CGSP services in a uniform way. Each domain has its own IC. Multiple ICs in ChinaGrid are organized in a tree structure. Based on it, searching a service in multiple domains becomes available. It is also used for fault tolerance of service manager. IC plays a key role in service detection and the system status monitoring of the ChinaGrid. Its main functions include:

- Organizing and monitoring software and hardware resources
- Registering and publishing grid services
- Updating and monitoring service status
- Discovering and retrieving service

To balance its function and performance, IC is designed to store relatively static or long-standing information. When necessary, information could be collected and maintained via a "push/pull" way between Service Container and IC.

3.5   Job Manager (JM)

JM focus on the job scheduling and execution management in CGSP. JM accepts users' requests in the form of SOAP message, and then interacts with IC to select and invoke relevant service according to "job description". Meanwhile, JM supports the work flow. JM is in charge of the process control of the work flow job, including parsing and compiling work flow description. The "rules" of the process of execution, including the process information, parallel distribution strategy and exception disposing rules, are described with the Grid Job Description Language (GJDL) customized based on BPEL by ourselves. In addition to controlling job's work flow, JM also monitors the status of jobs. The execution of the job in JM is completed through general running service deployed on the real computing nodes.

3.6   Data Manager (DM)

The main responsibilities of DM are to manage the storage resources and user data in the Grid and provide data service for users. In the view of system, DM is divided to three levels: data service access interface, metadata manager and storage resources. The function of it is to shield from users the heterogeneous underlying storage resources through the uniform data transfer protocol. And it provides a uniform storage resource access mode. The data service provided by metadata manager can shield the physical data storage path from users and organize the data space for them. So the users get a transparent data access. The targets of DM are as follows:

− Uniform data view based on user
− Uniform storage resource access mode
− Extendable storage architecture
− Data replica management
− High effectual and reliable data transfer mechanism

3.7   Security Manager (SM)

This module provides security functions, including identity authority, proxy certificate management, container and service level security and user access control. The Certificate Authority signs certificates for ChinaGrid entities to provide the basic security protection. Proxy management allows credential transferring among user, JM and CGSP services. Through implementing GSI Secure Conversation and GSI Secure Message, CGSP ensures the job submitted is legal and provides the security of job during job execution.

3.8   Service Container (SC)

SC is a basic runtime environment of the services and supply "service oriented facilities for computing", and it will be deployed on every node which supports the services. SC achieves core functions of the services including deployment, runtime, management, service status monitor. Besides acting as the basic Web Service Container, it also supports the life cycle management, asynchronous notification, remote deployment and hot deployment, batch job process etc.

The implementation of the SC is based on the core of Globus Toolkit 3.9.1, which includes the implementation of Web service core component because of the limited time and can not supply the necessary high level services for WSRF. Considering the requirement of CGSP, we extend and enhance the implementation of GT3.9.1 WSRF Core, and supply the necessary services properties for the running of ChinaGrid, such as remote and automatic deployment, hot deployment and general running service.

4   CGSP Developing Tools

The CGSP Grid Development Toolkits includes the CGSP Service Package Tool, Job Definition Tool, Portal Development Tool, Programming API (GridPPI) [21] and the corresponding running environment, visual administration/monitoring software, CGSP Installation Tool for remote service deployment and configuration. This package hides the underlying implementation of the CGSP's major functions and provides simple visual tool and programming interfaces, which makes the development of professional grid application easier. The major objectives of the software package for development are list as follows:

- Provide a set of visual resource packaging tool for developers to encapsulate the computing resources, software into CGSP services following ChinaGrid service specification
- Supply visual user interface to complete the design of work flow and generate XML job description files that satisfy with the GJDL and submitted to the job management for execution
- Provide a portal development framework
- Give out a programming specification and programming APIs which are used for grid user to develop grid applications with the support of services in grid system. The applications can run in the grid system
- Implement a graphics user interface for administrator to manage the grid system
- Provide a CGSP installation tool to ease and guide the installation of CGSP

5   CGSP Job Executing Flow

Fig. 3 shows the running flow of CGSP in a domain. Generally a grid application can be classified into three parts: resources (including computing resources, storage resources, software and legacy resources, data resources, etc.), jobs and interactions. First of all, the grid service containers should be deployed into the resources, and the resources will be extracted through service packaging tool, then these services should be deployed in the Service Containers (as depicted in figure 3, S1, S2, S3 represent respectively command-line style software, legacy program and service).

For the special resource–storage, data manager is used to provide logical storage space for users.

Then, we need to use job defining tool for modeling a typical work flow into a job described by the GJDL, which in turn will be sent to the Job Manager. Because the job requests are via SOAP, the Job Manager is deployed over the Service Container which is responsible for the essential service processes. Job Manager is responsible for job request analysis, service selection, job scheduling and execution management, etc.

Thirdly, each domain needs to deploy Service Manager which collects service information from containers to support other software modules. Besides, each domain has to deploy Domain Manager to implement the functions of user management and other issues.

Lastly, one or more grid portals can be deployed to satisfy specific needs of different specialties. Portal developing tool can help users to develop web applications satisfy the requirement of interaction and can be deployed in the portal.

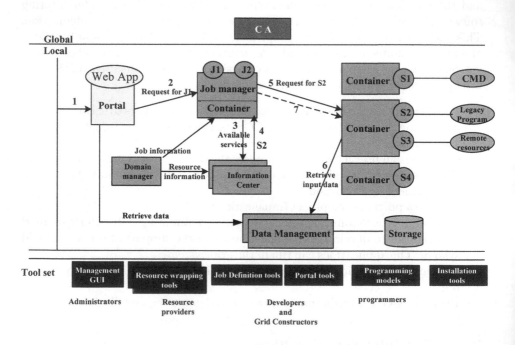

Fig. 3. CGSP Job Executing Flow

After an application is deployed, the steps of process are:

1. Firstly, a user should register and acquire the certificate signed by ChinaGrid. Then, the user logins the grid portal through a certain security protocol (such as HTTPS) and accomplishes the interaction with grid system through web applications deployed in the Portal.

2. If necessary, user should upload the input data required by the computing job/request to the personal data space in data manager through Portal. Then, user could define a job (such as J1) by using job defining tool in Portal. At last the GJDL file generated by the Portal will be sent to the Job Manager.
3. According to the job process rule of J1 which is stored locally, the Job Manager queries available services from Information Center and contribute to the accomplishment of job J1.
4. Information Center collects the service information using the "Push/Pull" model. It maintains resource view in time, and so could return an available service list sorted by a certain rule. In principle, Information Center will return local available services. If necessary, it will query other Information Centers for more available services if it can not find any service satisfying the requirement in its own domain.
5. Job Manager selects service S2, and sends the service query to corresponding real computing node.
6. After Service Containers receive the requests, they need to invoke the access interfaces provided by the Data Manager in order to get the data by logical file path in the unified data space. Then the Service Containers execute the services.
7. Job Manager continuously collects the services status in the execution processes to report to the user through Portal in time.
8. At last, when the job is completed, the service container will put the computing results to personal data space in Data Manager.

6   Conclusion

CGSP provides a platform for ChinaGrid construction from the top portal to the bottom computing nodes. Not only does it support the uniform management of heterogeneous resources, but it also supplies the portal building, job defining and service packaging. Support secondary development of grid service and improve the flexibility of the system. In addition to supply the portal to ChinaGrid normal users, CGSP achieves parallel programming interface based on deployed services in CGSP for developing complicated applications.

CGSP satisfies the expansion, autonomy and localization of ChinaGrid. It consists of 7 function modules for system running and 4 application developing and programming tools.

This paper has given a high-level overview and snapshot summary of the current state of CGSP. Readers are warned that much detailed and important information has been omitted, and the new releases and previews represent significant changes. These considering using CGSP are therefore encouraged to obtain up-to-date and full information from the website www.chinagrid.edu.cn/CGSP.

Acknowledgement

We wish to express our sincere appreciation to the Prof. Hai Jin, Prof. Weimin Zheng, Prof. Xiaomin Li, Dr. Xiaowu Chen and other ChinaGrid experts for extending their generous support for the successful conduct of the CGSP. Special thanks to CGSP working group members for providing materials for this paper.

References

1. ChinaGrid, http://www.chinagrid.edu.cn.
2. H. Jin, *ChinaGrid: Making Grid Computing a Reality*, Proceedings of ICADL 2004, Lecture Notes of Computer Science, (2004), 3334, 13-24
3. ChinaGrid Support Platform, http://www.chinagrid.edu.cn/CGSP.
4. CGSP Work Group, *Design Specification of ChinaGrid Support Platform*, Tsinghua University Press, Beijing, China, 2004
5. I. Foster, C. Kesselman, S. Tuecke, *The Anatomy of the Grid: Enabling Scalable Virtual Organization*, International J. Supercomputer Applications, 15(3), (2001)
6. I. Foster, C. Kesselman, *The Physiology of the Grid: An Open Grid Services Architecture for Distributed Systems Integration*, J. Nick, S. Tuecke, (2002)
7. I. Foster, C. Kesselman, *Globus: A Metacomputing Infrastructure Toolkit*, International J. Supercomputer Application, (1997), 11(2), 115-128
8. Open Grid Services Architecture (OGSA), https://forge.gridforum.org/projects/ogsa-wg, or http://www.globus.org/ogsa/
9. Web Service Resource Framework (WSRF), http://www.globus.org/wsrf/ and http://www.ggf.org/documents/GFD.30.pdf
10. Web Services Interoperability (WSI), http://www.ws-i.org/
11. Globous Toolkits, http://www.globus.org.
12. UK e-Science Program, http://www.rcuk.ac.uk/escience/;
13. NASA Information Power Grid, http://www.ipg.nasa.gov/;
14. TeraGrid, http://www.teragrid.org/;
15. China National Grid, http://www.cngrid.cn;
16. K*Grid, http://gridcenter.or.kr/
17. Open Middleware Infraxtructure Institute, http://www.omii.ac.uk/
18. Dazheng Huang, Fei Xie, Guangwen Yang, *T.G.: a Market-oriented Computing System with Fine-grained Parallelism*, 9th Workshop on Job Scheduling Strategies for Parallel Processing Seattle, Washington, (2002)
19. China Research and Development environment Over Wide-area Network, http://www.crown.org.cn
20. Tuecke, S., Czajkowski, K., Foster, I. , et.al.: *Open Grid Services Infrastructure (OGSI) Version 1.0*, Global Grid Forum Draft Recommendation. (2003).
21. Yongwei Wu, Guangwen Yang, Qing Wang, Weiming Zheng, *Coarse-grained Distributed Parallel Programming Interface for Grid Computing*, Lecture Notes in Computer Science, (2004), 3032, 255-258

A Microeconomics-Based Resource Assignment Model for Grid Computing[*]

Xingwei Wang, Nan Jiang, Jialin Wang, and Min Huang

School of Information Science and Engineering,
Northeastern University, Shenyang, P.R. China
wangxw@mail.neu.edu.cn

Abstract. In this paper, a microeconomics-based resource assignment model for grid computing is presented. In the proposed model, demand and supply relationship of gird resource affects its usage price and the price adjusts the amount of grid resource to be used by the user, so that the both-win between the user and the provider interests is achieved. The proposed model provides two schemes of grid resource assignment. When the available resource is abundant, the gaming scheme is used; based on the Nash equilibrium and Pareto optimality, the optimal usage amount of the resource by the user and the optimal usage price of the resource for the provider are determined. When the available resource is scarce, the biding scheme is used to assign resource to the user. Simulation results have shown that the proposed model is feasible and effective with good performance.

1 Introduction

The concept of grid computing derives from electrical power grid [1]. Through the high speed Internet, it can couple a wide variety of geographically distributed computing resource, such as CPUs, memories, databases, etc and make them fully shared in order to provide capacities of high performance computing, storage and various kinds of services to the users without caring where they come from.

Grid resource providers get their benefits from supplying their resource to their users and the users pay for their resource usage to fulfill their tasks. Thus, the providers need to price their resource. If the available resource is insufficient, the price can be increased properly; otherwise, the price can be lowered. Consequently, the users should only occupy a reasonable amount of resource in view of their requirements and finance budgets. So when assigning grid resource, both the interests of the users and the providers should be considered. Only when their both-win is achieved, can the transaction between them be made [2-8].

In this paper, a microeconomics-based resource assignment model for grid computing is proposed. It determines the usage price based on the resource demand/supply rela-

[*] This work was supported by the National Natural Science Foundation of China under Grant No.60473089, No.60003006 and No.70101006; the Natural Science Foundation of Liaoning Province under Grant No.20032018 and No.20032019; the China Education and Research Grid (ChinaGrid); the Modern Distance Education Engineering Project by China MoE.

G. Chen et al. (Eds.): ISPA Workshops 2005, LNCS 3759, pp. 241–248, 2005.

tionship between the user and the provider with both-win supported. The rest of this paper is organized as follows: in section 2, the proposed model is introduced; in section 3 and 4, the gaming and biding schemes of the proposed model are described respectively; in section 5, performance evaluation of the proposed model is done; finally, the conclusions are drawn.

2 Design of the Microeconomics-Based Resource Assignment Model for Grid Computing

2.1 Related Concepts

In microeconomics, resource assignment involves two basic entities: resource consumer and provider. The provider own resource and assign it to the consumer according to certain rules, and the consumer pays for its resource usage to fulfill its tasks. One consumer may submit its task to one or more providers. When one consumer requests certain amount of resource to one or more providers, a transaction is initiated, during which these players have their own interests respectively.

In this paper, the so-called Nash equilibrium means that the strategies chosen by the players of the game are in such a state: no player can benefit more by changing its strategy while the other keeps its strategy unchanged [7, 9]. Pareto optimality means that the result of a game satisfies that no player can increase its utility without decreasing the other's utility. When the result of a game is Pareto optimal under Nash equilibrium, both of these players in this game get maximum utilities simultaneously [10, 11].

2.2 Model Design

The proposed microeconomics-based resource assignment model for grid computing in this paper combines the concepts of Nash equilibrium, Pareto optimality and biding [12, 13] together with the following two schemes adopted. When the available resource is abundant, the gaming scheme for resource assignment is taken. Benefits of the provider and the consumer are represented by their utilities. With demand on resource increasing, the provider should increase its resource usage price to improve its utility and the consumer should only occupy a rational amount of resource to obtain its suitable utility; otherwise, the provider should lower its resource usage price to attract more consumers and thus obtain more utilities. In the course of the game, the two players affect each other's decision-making based on the demand/supply relationship. Finally, an equilibrium price is found, making these players' utilities reach Pareto optimality under Nash equilibrium. Therefore, the fair transaction between the provider and the consumer and their both-win are achieved. However, when the available resource is scarce, the biding scheme is taken.

In this paper, the basic unit of grid resource is used to measure the amount of its usage. Here, one basic unit is the minimum charging unit for the paid usage of grid resource. For example, the basic unit for memory and CPU can be M byte and MIPS respectively.

Suppose one consumer c requests R_c units of resource to one provider p and the finance budget of c is B_c. The resource requirement of a consumer could be flexible (that is, it is better to get R_c units of resource, however, more or less than R_c is still acceptable.) or rigid (that is, only R_c can be accepted).

Assume the current amount of the available resource of p is P_R basic units. When doing resource assignment, p compares P_R with a pre-set threshold Δ at first. If $P_R \geq \Delta$, consider the available resource to be abundant and the gaming scheme for resource assignment is initiated; otherwise, consider the available resource to be scarce and the biding scheme is initiated. p determines its Δ value dynamically based on its resource usage history records.

3 Gaming Scheme for Resource Assignment

Under this scheme, the resource assignment process can be considered as a game between the consumer and the provider. Its aim is to determine a reasonable amount of resource usage for the consumer and a suitable usage price for the provider, helping to achieve Pareto optimality under Nash equilibrium and reach both-win between them.

3.1 Playing Strategy for the Game Player

In this paper, the consumer and provider are two players in the game. The consumer's playing strategy is the amount of resource for it to use, that is, how much it will actually get from the provider. Suppose the consumer can choose one from m levels of resource usage $(O_1, O_2, \cdots O_m)$ according to its requirement and its finance budget. O_i is measured by the basic unit of the resource $(i = 1, 2, \cdots, m)$. The provider's playing strategy is the usage price per basic unit. Suppose the provider can choose one from n levels of usage price per unit $(S_1, S_2, \cdots S_n)$ according to the current resource demand/supply relationship.

3.2 Utilities for the Players

Under the strategy-pair (O_i, S_j), that is, when the consumer occupies O_i basic units of resource and the provider's usage price is S_j, the consumer's utility is defined as follows:

$$Uc_{ij} = \alpha \cdot \frac{B_c}{O_i \times S_j} \cdot g(O_i) . \tag{1}$$

$$\alpha = \begin{cases} 0 \ (rigid\ consumer\ requirement) \wedge O_i < R_c) \vee (O_i \cdot S_j > B_c) \\ 1 \ otherwise \end{cases} . \qquad (2)$$

$$g(O_i) = e^{-\sigma(O_i - R_c)^2} . \qquad (3)$$

From the definition of α in formula (2), it can be seen that if the consumer's requirement is rigid and can not be satisfied or the cost exceeds its finance budget, its utility is 0. From the definition of g in formula (3), it can be seen that the larger the difference between the actual amount of the consumer resource usage and its requirement, the lower its utility .

Under the strategy-pair (O_i, S_j), the provider's utility is defined as follows:

$$Up_{ij} = \frac{S_j - C_t}{C_t} \cdot f(O_i, S_j, C_A, P_R) . \qquad (4)$$

$$f(O_i, S_j, C_A, P_R) = (S_j + 1)^{\lambda \left(\frac{C_A \cdot O_i}{P_R - \Delta}\right)^K \cdot k} . \qquad (5)$$

$$k = \begin{cases} 1 & \dfrac{C_A \cdot O_i}{P_R - \Delta} > \delta \\ -1 & \dfrac{C_A \cdot O_i}{P_R - \Delta} \leq \delta \end{cases} . \qquad (6)$$

Here, C_t is the cost of the resource; $\lambda > 0$; C_A is the amount of consumers; $P_R - \Delta$ is the distance between the amount of current available resource and the pre-set threshold Δ, the smaller the distance, the more consumers, and thus the more demanding the resource. $\dfrac{C_A \cdot O_i}{P_R - \Delta}$ is the demand/supply factor, indicating the resource demand/supply relationship between the consumer and the provider;

When the demand/supply factor is bigger than a pre-set threshold δ, it is considered that the supply falls short of the demand. In this case, let $k = 1$ and f is an increasing function with S_j, that is, the provider's utility can be increased by increasing the price, and thus the more demanding the resource is (namely the larger the demand/supply factor is), the more sharply the provider's utility increases. Otherwise, when the demand/supply factor is smaller than the δ, it is considered that the supply exceeds the demand. In this case, let $k = -1$ and f is a decreasing function with S_j, that is, the provider's utility can be increased by decreasing the price, and thus the more abundant the resource is (namely the smaller the demand/supply factor is), the more sharply the provider's utility increases.

Define utility matrix $U_{m\times n} = \left((Uc_{ij}, Up_{ij})\right)_{m\times n}$, and the value of its element (Uc_{ij}, Up_{ij}) is the utility-pair of the consumer and the provider under the strategy-pair (O_i, S_j).

3.3 Gaming

According to the resource requirement of the consumer and the current status of the available resource of the provider, calculate those utility-pairs under different strategy-pairs, that is, get each element value of the utility matrix $U_{m\times n}$. Then, find out the optimal utility-pair (Uc_{i*j*}, Up_{i*j*}) from $U_{m\times n}$, which corresponds to the optimal strategy-pair (O_{i*}, S_{j*}).

As described in section 2.1, the optimal utility-pair is the Pareto optimal one under Nash equilibrium. In terms of the definition of Nash equilibrium, the utility-pairs under Nash equilibrium meet with the following conditions:

$$\begin{cases} Uc_{i*j*} \geq Uc_{ij*} & i = 1,2,\cdots,m \\ Up_{i*j*} \geq Up_{i*j} & j = 1,2,\cdots,n \end{cases} \tag{7}$$

However, not only the pure strategy Nash equilibrium solution may not exist, but also there may exist multiple Nash equilibrium ones [7]. Therefore, when two utility-pairs are both or neither under Nash equilibrium, their Pareto efficiencies defined as follows are compared to determine which one is better.

$$Pe_{ij} = 1 \Big/ (\alpha \cdot \frac{1}{Uc_{ij}} + \beta \cdot \frac{1}{Up_{ij}}) . \tag{8}$$

Here, $\alpha > 0, \beta > 0$. From the formula (8), only when the utilities of both the consumer and the provider are larger, are the values of their Pe_{ij} bigger. Thus, the specific utility-pair, which makes the value of the corresponding Pe_{ij} bigger, is more Pareto efficient.

The gaming process is described as follows:

Step1. Determine the consumer's strategies $(O_1, O_2, \cdots O_m)$ and the provider's strategies $(S_1, S_2, \cdots S_n)$.

Step2. Calculate the value of each element (Uc_{ij}, Up_{ij}) of the utility matrix $U_{m\times n}$.

Step3. If there exist one or more Nash equilibrium utility-pairs in $U_{m\times n}$, go to Step4; otherwise, go to Step5.

Step4. Compare its Pareto efficiency Pe'_{i*j*} of each Nash equilibrium utility-pair (Uc'_{i*j*}, Up'_{i*j*}) to get the Pareto optimal one (Uc_{i*j*}, Up_{i*j*}), go to Step6.

Step5. Compare its Pareto efficiency Pe_{ij} of each utility-pair (Uc_{ij}, Up_{ij}) in utility matrix $U_{m \times n}$ to get the Pareto optimal one (Uc_{i*j*}, Up_{i*j*}).

Step6. The strategy-pair corresponding to the optimal utility-pair (Uc_{i*j*}, Up_{i*j*}) is the optimal one (O_{i*}, S_{j*}), the gaming process ends.

4 Biding Scheme for Resource Assignment

When the current available resource of the provider is scarce, the biding scheme is taken. Its procedure is described as follows:

Step1. The provider advertises the base-biding price B_P of its resource to all consumers.

Step2. If $R_c \cdot B_P \leq B_c$, the consumer replies to the provider that it would like to accept this price; otherwise, it replies to the provider that it would reject this price.

Step3. After it has received replies from all consumers, the provider calculates the amount N_A of the consumers who would like to accept the current biding price. If $N_A > 0$, $BP = BP + \varepsilon$ (ε is the price increasing step), and the provider advertises this new biding price to all consumers, go to Step2, otherwise go to Step4.

Step4. The provider sorts these known biding prices that all consumers would like to accept, $B_{P1}, B_{P2}, \cdots$, in descending order, and thus get the following sequence: $B_P^{\,1}, B_P^{\,2}, \cdots$.

Step5. Let $i = 1$.

Step6. Assign R_c^i units of resource to the consumer whose biding price is $B_P^{\,i}$.

Step7. If $P_R > 0$, namely there are still some available resource left, $i = i + 1$, go to Step6.

Step8. For any consumer whose resource requirement is rigid, if its need is not met with, negotiate with the provider. If failed, the consumer quits from the biding process.

Step9. Calculate the actual payment of each consumer according to its resource usage and its acceptable highest biding price, the procedure ends.

5 Simulation Research

The proposed model has been implemented by simulation based on NS2 (Network Simulator 2) [14] and its performance evaluation has been done. Figure 1 shows the influence of the resource demand/supply relationship on the resource price when $\delta = 0.6$ under the gaming scheme. It can be seen that when the demand/supply factor is smaller than 0.6, the resource price changes slowly with it, while it is bigger

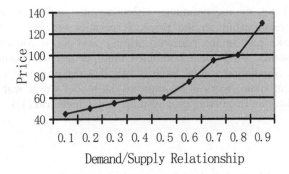

Fig. 1. Demand/Supply Relationship and Price

than 0.6, the resource price changes sharply with it. Thus, under gaming scheme, the influence of the resource demand/supply relationship on the resource price is rather sensitive.

Figure 2 shows the influence of the resource demand/supply relationship on the consumer utility and the provider utility under the gaming scheme. It can be seen that although the resource price increases with the demand/supply factor, the consumer utility and the provider utility do not change sharply. Therefore, under the gaming scheme, both the consumer utility and the provider utility are considered with both-win supported.

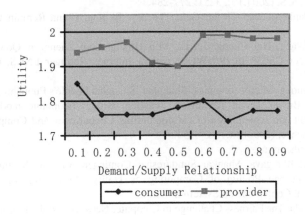

Fig. 2. Demand/Supply Relationship and Consumer/Provider Utility

6 Conclusion

In the view of microeconomics, the process of resource assignment for grid computing can be regarded as the procedure of coordination on the consumer utility and the provider utility. The interests of the two players should be taken care of with both-win achieved. In this paper, a resource assignment model for grid computing is proposed based on microeconomics, reflecting the influence of the resource demand/supply relationship on the price. It permits the involved parties of the transaction to take part in the resource pricing, and the introduction of the dual schemes for resource assignment combines multiple microeconomic concepts and means together. Simulation results have shown that the proposed model is feasible and effective. Our future work is to improve the model's practicability further and promote its application in existing grid systems (e.g. ChinaGrid [1]).

References

1. Hai Jin: "ChinaGrid: Making Grid Computing a Reality", *Digital Libraries: International Collaboration and Cross-Fertilization - Lecture Notes in Computer Science, Vol.3334,* Springer-Verlag, (2004.12), pp.13-24
2. Wang Xingwei, Liu Cong, Huang Min, Cao Jiannong: Research on soft-computing-based intelligent multi-constrained wavelength assignment algorithms in IP/DWDM optical Internet, Springer LNCS, (2004.12), 3358: 866-874
3. Zou Rui, Li Zhitang, Yang Dezhi: Research on Economic Models in Grid Computing. Application Research Of Computers, (2005), 2:82~84
4. J.F. Nash: The Bargaining Problem. Econometrica. (1950),18:155~162
5. M. Probst: Utility computing: Determining when the price is right. The IT Journal, First Quarter, (2002.4): 66–73
6. Wang Xingwei, Chen Minghua, Wang Qiang, Huang Min, Cao Jian-Nong: Research on the virtual topology design methods in grid-computing-supporting IP/DWDM-based NGI, Springer LNCS, (2004.10), 3251: 277-284
7. Drew Fudenberg, Jean Tirole: Game Theory, Beijing, China Renmin University Press, (2002).
8. Xingwei Wang, Hui Cheng, Jia Li, Min Huang, Ludi Zheng: A QoS-based multicast algorithm for CSCW in IP/DWDM optical Internet, Springer LNCS, (2003.12), 3033: 1059-1062
9. Zhou Huizhong: Microeconomics. Shanghai, Shanghai People's Publishing House, (2003)
10. Rajkumar Buyya, David Abramson, Jonathan Giddy: Economic models for resource management and scheduling in Grid computing. Concurrency and Computation: Practice and Experience, (2002),14:1507~1542
11. www.gametheory.net
12. Hemant K. Bhargava, Shankar Sundaresan: Contingent Bids in Auctions: Availability, Commitment and Pricing of Computing as Utility. Proceedings of the 37th Hawaii International Conference on System Sciences
13. Robert Denda: The Fairness Challenge in Computer Networks. Reihe Informatik, (2000), 6
14. The VINT Project: The ns Manual (formerly ns Notes and Documentation). http://www. isi.edu/nsnam/ns/ns-documentation.html. (2005), March.

The Campus Resource Management Based on Constellation Model in the ChinaGrid

Xiaoshe Dong, Yinfeng Wang, Xiuqiang He, Hua Guo,
Fang Zheng, and Weiguo Wu

School of Electronics and Information Engineering,
Xi'an Jiaotong University, Xi'an, 710049, China
{wangyf, hexqiang, guohua}@mailst.xjtu.edu.cn

Abstract. Based on the analysis of the physical feature of grid resources and the demands of resource organization and management in grid environment, this paper proposes a constellation model, which could manage the grid resources dynamically based on the Integrated Service Capabilities (ISC) of grid nodes. The higher logical layer of the grid system based on the constellation model can reflect the topology of the underlying practical organizations. The constellation model defines the minimum resource management unit in grid, which is called Solar system. The resources in grid system are classified according to the application category. By the approaches, the constellation model could reduce the complexity of organizing and managing the grid resources. This model also has good scalability. Uniform resource management can be realized in grid system based on the constellation model.

1 Introduction

In essence, the Grid resources are heterogeneous, dynamic and distributed. The resources are difficult to organize and manage in a dynamic manner. The complexity increases the cost of managing resource and the probability of errors. Two problems need to be resolved to efficiently organize and manage the grid resources: (1) the heterogeneous resources should be encapsulated, and abstracted into the uniform logical services to decrease the management complexity; (2) To improve the efficiency of resource management and usage, the grid resources should be abstracted into logical organizations that must match the topology of the underlying practical organizations. Only if the above two problems are resolved, can efficiently managing the resources in a dynamic manner be realized. Dynamically managing grid resources are prerequisite to implementing the scalability, security and QoS assurance for the grid system.

The campus resources are also heterogeneous, dynamic and distributed. In addition, different schools in the campus usually adopt different resource management policies according to the demands of their specialty, which further increases the heterogeneity of the campus resources. The complexity of resource sharing and usage exasperates the resource island problems. Resources are isolated in separate resource island and difficult to share, increasing the cost of computing.

G. Chen et al. (Eds.): ISPA Workshops 2005, LNCS 3759, pp. 249–256, 2005.

With the publishing of the OGSA/OGSI, and later the WS-Resource Framework (WSRF), service becomes a more and more important concept in grid. The service-oriented solutions to the grid problems have been the common realization in the field of grid. In the constellation model, each resource is encapsulated as a standard WSRF service, with the assistance of the Globus Toolkit 4(GT4). The services can be accessed through uniform and standard interfaces, which makes the heterogeneous resources easy to integrate. The grid nodes are classified into different categories, such as planet node, fixed star node, according to their ISC properties. The constellation model proposed in this paper can guarantee that the logical topology matches the underlying physical organizations. The model is easy to apply to the resource management of campus grid, and has been successfully applied in the campus grid platform of Xi'an JiaoTong University in the ChinaGrid [1] environment.

2 Definitions

Definition 1. *Planet* is the node that resides in a steady physical location, encapsulates self-resources and can provide service.

Definition 2. *Meteor* is the node that lies on the instable physical location, can provide service, and may be mobile computing objects.

Definition 3. *Integrated Service Capabilities* (ISC) *value* is the overall evaluation criterion of a node's service capabilities, including the node's computation resources, the network bandwidth and the availability (Mean Time To Failure MTTF). The ISC value metric Φ can be defined as the weighed average for these values as in the equation 1.

$$\Phi = \sum_{i=0}^{m-1} w_i \times \frac{r_i}{rs_i} + w_m \times \frac{b}{bs} + w_{m+1} \frac{t_{MTTF}}{ts} \tag{1}$$

r_i: the available node's computing resources, such as a single CPU speed, number of CPUs, memory, disk capability and so on,$0 \leq i \leq$ m-1;
b: network bandwidth;
t_{MTTF}: node's Mean Time To Failure;
rs_i: benchmark for different computation resources, the units adopt Gflops, Gbit and so forth;
bs: benchmark network bandwidth, the unit adopts Mbps or Gbps;
ts: benchmark MTTF, unit is hour;
w_i: weight factor; $\sum_{i=0}^{m+1} w_i = 1$, administrator can define each object's weight factor according to its relative significance.

Definition 4. *Fixed star* is the node that has the maximum ISC value in Solar system, or a fixed star can be designated by selecting one from the nodes whose ISC value exceed the criterion. Fixed star manages the planets, meteors around. The management includes registering, scheduling, monitoring, discovery, controlling, and accounting, etc.

Definition 5. *Solar system* owns one fixed star at most, the numbers of Planets and Meteor is x and y respectively, and then x, y≥0. The system obeys the same sharing and management rules. It can be represented as a fourtuple:

Solar system={Fixed star, Planet [x], Meteor [y], Rule}.

The Rule means Solar system can be organized according to geographical dispersal or service types.

Community Authorization Service (CAS) [2] or PKI, Certification Authority (CA) can be used in the Solar system. To avoid single points of failure and improve scalability, a node whose ISC value exceeds the criterion should be appointed as the standby of the fixed star, and it is necessary for the standby fixed star to keep updating to make sure of consistency.

3 Construction of Constellation Model

Definition 6: one or more (x≥1) Solar systems constitute a **Constellation**, which can be denoted by a fourtuple:

Constellation= {Solar system [x], Configuration-policy, Network, QoS-Radius}.

Configuration-policy: The constellation can be organized according to the geographic dispersal or the service types. The policies used in each Solar system can be composed for the constellation, either may be the main one. A Solar system could belong to multiple constellations. The constellations organized according to the geographic dispersal are similar to the TeraGrid[3], and those which are organized according to the service types of the Solar system are similar to the DataGrid[4].

Network: Solar systems in the constellation could be interconnected together using the P2P-like overlay network. [5] shows that the performance of the P2P system is very sensitive to the topology variation, even with a small number of peer arrivals/departures(≤2% of the total peers). Virtual links are built to provide multiple

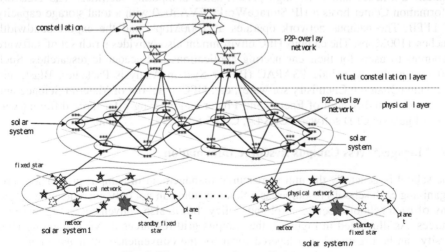

Fig. 1. The structure of constellation model

backup connections between the Solar systems. Hence the frequency of that the Solar systems join/leave the grid system resulted by the unsteady network can be decreased greatly, and therefore the performance of the constellation can be improved. When the constellation scale is relatively small, the *full-interconnection* can be used among Solar systems. Figure 1 shows the structure of constellation model.

QoS-Radius: QoS assurance in the constellation includes but is not limited to the following aspects: availability, security, and performance. QoS announced by the constellation could be ranged by the expression $<a_i^{min}, a_i^{max}>$. The range is relative to the status of nodes and the policies of the constellation. For example, if the allowed maximum response time is T_{max}, while the maximum delay is not allowed to exceed 50 percents, then the corresponding QoS range $<a_i^{min}, a_i^{max}>$ could be expressed as $<0, 1.5\times(estimated\ response\ time)>$. Through monitoring, scheduling, and tuning the running services, The SLMs[6] deployed on the fixed star negotiate a SLA within the QoS range to realize the Service level attainment.

4   Organization and Management of Campus Grid Resources

4.1   Campus Grid Resources

There are affluent computation and service resources in the campus grid environment, such as computers, storage, network, data, software and services, all of which are dynamic, distributed and heterogeneous. The static information of these resources is the environment in which tasks are executed, while the dynamic information, which is time-dependent, includes sharing policies, status of load on resources, and changes of network topology, etc. The campus grid resources in Xi'an Jiaotong University physically constitute a constellation according to the geographical dispersal.

Xi'an Jiaotong University's campus high performance computing environment is equipped with a Dawning3000 Supercomputer, an IBM RS6000 Cluster, an Intel® Itanium®2 Cluster and other high performance computing facilities. The Network Information Center hosts a HP StorageWorks EVA5000 with a total storage capacity of 11TB. The campus network operates at 1000Mbps, and the export bandwidth reaches 1100Mbps. The campus HPC environment also provides a rich set of software resources to users for their engineering applications and academic researches. Such software packages include PSAPAC (Power System Analysis Package), Blast, and Gaussian (Quantum Chemistry software), etc. HPCC, School of Material Science and Engineering, and School of Energy and Power Engineering offer three different versions of generic CFD software: CFX4.4, CFX5.5, and FLUENT 6.0, etc.

4.2   Manage/Access Campus Resource Information

The school is generally the unit of resource management in campus grid. Therefore, organizing each school's resources as a Solar system can not only guarantee the autonomy of each school's local control and policy, but is also convenient to organize resources. As illustrated in Figure 2, the campus grid resources in Xi'an Jiaotong University can be organized in a layered form for the convenience of management and usage.

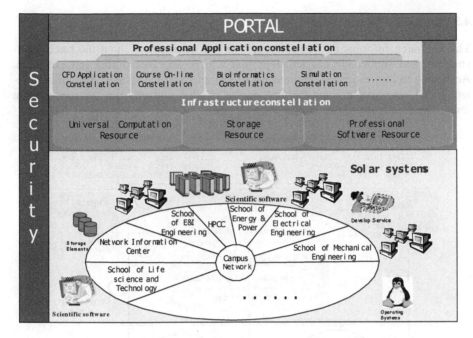

Fig. 2. Architecture of constellation model for organizing campus resource

Every school of Xi'an Jiaotong University determines the criterion of resources' ISC value according to the demands of its own administrative domain. Every school's resources are added into the campus grid environment as a Solar system (shown in Figure 2).

Resources provided by each Solar system can be registered to the following three infrastructure constellations: Universal Computation Resource, Storage Resource and Professional Software Resource. Resources managed by infrastructure constellations can be accessed through the grid portal. Professional application constellations, for example, CFD Application Constellation, Course On-line Constellation, Bioinformatics Constellation, and Simulation Constellation, can be constructed above infrastructure constellations. These constellations divide resources into different categories, avoiding repeatedly organizing resources for similar requests.

The dynamicity of resource organization includes the organization of resources across administrative domains and changes of resource sharing policies. Professional application constellations can aggregate resources in multiple administrative domains. Changes of resource sharing policies are constrained within a single Solar system and thus have no influence on the sharing policies of the whole constellation.

Each constellation within a Constellation-Model-based campus grid can have its own portal. According to the policies of security, user management, and semantic rules, the portal could implement such works as authenticating users and verifying tasks' validity. User authentication & authorization and other security issues in resource organization and management must be guaranteed at every layer of the model.

4.3 Executing Management

The Resource Information Center caches all the information about the basic infrastructure and application constellations that will be accessed during job execution. According to the resources requirements of the jobs and the scheduling policies, Selector and Scheduler execute the resources allocation uniformly in the constellation level. The details are shown in figure 3:

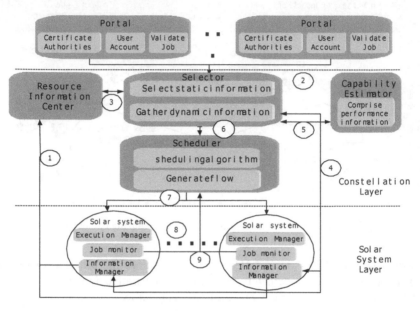

Fig. 3. The course of the resource allocation and scheduling in constellation

1). Each Solar system registers its information to the corresponding professional application constellation. The constellations' static information is kept in the Resource Information Center. Once the resources' static information changes (e.g. the software update), the Information Manager on each fixed star will send the update information to the Resource Information Center. Moreover, when the sharing policies are changed, it judges whether it should leave the constellation and which constellation it will join.

2). The users submit their jobs through the grid portal. The portal gets the detailed resources requirements from their job descriptions and transfers the requirements to the Selector.

3). Selector checks the Resource Information Center to see if the resource requirements can be satisfied by any available constellations. If so, it organizes the required resources of the satisfied constellation for job execution. Otherwise, Selector transfers the requirements to other constellations and probably get the satisfied resources from several other constellations.

4). Selector begins to require the satisfied resources' dynamic information from the Information Managers they belong to and wait for the response.

5).Selector transfers the information of all the available resources to the Capability Estimator to choose the most suitable resources according to the performance, work load, communication delay, and location information and so on. After the estimation, a resources list sorted by priority is returned to the Selector.

6). Selector selects the most suitable resources from the resource list, and transfers the information to the Scheduler to process.

7). Users can customize their desired scheduling algorithms to extend the scheduling policies. Scheduler produces the scheduling flow based on the scheduling algorithms and resources.

8). The jobs are scheduled to the involved constellations and the flow is managed by the Execution Manager to avoid the conflict of concurrent requests for the same resources. Job Monitor is responsible for monitoring the executing jobs. Once it detects any problem, it notifies the Scheduler. The jobs or Execution Manager can set the checkpoints periodically and save the information to the fixed star or the specified location to confirm the reliability of the data and avoid the repeated executions.

9). The result is returned after job execution is done.

The layers of the constellation model are independent of each other, and standard interfaces are well defined between neighbored layers, which facilitates the layer-by-layer implementation of the resource management software.

4.4 Scalability

The scalability requires that with the expansion of the scale of the grid resources, the response time of the tasks will not increase, moreover, the system can process more tasks.

In the constellation model, the newly-joined resources are firstly registered in the fix-star node of a Solar system, and then the Solar system could join in an appropriate constellation according to the type of the new resources. In this way, a layered resource management model is formed, which is adaptive to the expansion of the scale of the resources. New constellations can be created to aggregate the related Solar systems that contain the resources of the same new application type. The infrastructure and application-specific constellations could be interconnected together through the China Education and Research Network (CERNET) to form higher-level constellations platform. The Solar systems in a constellation and the constellations in the grid system are both aggregated in the P2P-like mode. The grid users can access all the resources in the entire grid system by issuing resource request to the portal of any constellation.

To decrease the system delay, the cache mechanism is applied in the Resource Information center that caches static information of its neighbor constellations. The system response time will not increase much with the expansion of the system scale, and the system efficiency is greatly improved.

5 Conclusions and Future Work

Based on the analysis of the physical feature of grid resources and the demands of resource organization and management in grid, this paper proposes the constellation model, which could manage the grid resources dynamically based on the Integrated Service Capabilities (ISC) of grid nodes. The constellation model has been applied in the campus grid system. The campus grid resources are organized in the infrastructure constellation and some application-specific constellations. The advantages of the model are summarized as follows: (1) Through defining the minimum resource management unit in grid for uniform management, this architecture lets users care about self-application and let constellation model responsible for the underlying resource management. (2) The resource discovery could be accelerated by caching the related resource information, i.e. the discovery process could be handled locally.(3) The constellation model defines standard interfaces between different layers, which benefit the development of new application by integrating the existing services. (4) Various types of applications can be adopted by introducing corresponding application-specific constellations. (5) The P2P-like interconnection mode is used in the model, making the constellation model scalable.

There are several aspects in which constellation model could be advanced. Security functionality should be strengthened at all layers, the model should be more scalable and the QoS guarantees need to be improved. We will do some research in these issues in the future.

Acknowledgments

This research is supported by China Education and Research Grid (Grant No.CG2003-CG008) and 863 projects of China (Grant No.2002AA104550)

References

1. Hai Jin.: ChinaGrid: Making Grid Computing a Reality, Digital Libraries: International Collaboration and Cross-Fertilization - Lecture Notes in Computer Science, Vol.3334, Springer-Verlag, December 2004, pp.13-24.
2. L. Pearlman, V. Welch, I. Foster, C. Kesselman, and S. Tuecke.: A Community Authorization Service for Group Collaboration. Presented at IEEE 3rd International Workshop on Policies for Distributed Systems and Networks, 2002.
3. Charlie Catlett. : The TeraGrid: Progress and Applications. February 2004.
4. http://lcg.web.cern.ch/LCG/.
5. J. Nabrzyski, J.M. Schopf, J. Weglarz (Eds): Grid Resource Management chapter: Xiaohui Gu, Klara Nahrstedt " QoS-Aware service composition for large-scale P2Psystem", Kluwer Publishing, Fall 2003, http://www.globus.org.
6. I. Foster, Argonne & U.Chicago (Editor): Open Grid Services Architecture GWD-I. http://forge.gridforum.org/projects/ogsa-wg.

Grid Computing Methodology for Protein Structure Prediction and Analysis*

Shoubin Dong [1], Pengfei Liu [1], Yicheng Cao [2], and Zhengping Du [2]

[1] School of Computer Science and Engineering,
South China University of Technology,
510640 Guangzhou, China
{sbdong, pfliu}@scut.edu.cn
[2] School of Bioscience and Bioengineering,
South China University of Technology,
510640 Guangzhou, China
{yccao, zhpdu}@scut.edu.cn

Abstract. In the post-genomics era, the protein structure prediction and analysis based on the amino acids sequence is becoming an essential part of biological research. The protein structure prediction belongs to CPU-intensive and memory demanding jobs. We have developed a prediction and analysis system named ProteinSPA, which employs the workflow under the grid environment to integrates multiple bioinformatics analytical tools and perform on huge volumes of data. In this paper, we explain the design, architecture, and implementation of ProteinSPA.

1 Introduction

The gap between the number of amino acids sequences and the number of solved protein sequences continues to widen rapidly in the post-genomics era due to the limitations of the current processes for solving structures experimentally, hence computational prediction of protein structures has come to play a key role in narrowing the gap. These methods have made such rapid progress in the past several years that they now can provide valuable information and insights for unknown proteins, so the method is becoming an essential part of biological research and even among the first tools applied in a biological research prior to experiments to generate premise to guide the design of experiments. We can even suppose that one day the computational structure prediction will mostly substitute for the experiment.

On account of the broad application, many research institutions have developed pipelines for the protein structure prediction [1-3]. Admittedly, the protein structure prediction jobs belong to the CPU-intensive and memory demanding ones; it always cost users long time to wait for the prediction result (And many systems don't support real-time mode just because the limitation of the computation capability). Some systems may accelerate the prediction process and curtail some optional steps that

---

* This research was jointly funded by the Natural Science Foundation of China under agreement No. 90412015 and ChinaGrid Project (project No. CG2003-GA002 and CG2003-CG005).

G. Chen et al. (Eds.): ISPA Workshops 2005, LNCS 3759, pp. 257–266, 2005.
© Springer-Verlag Berlin Heidelberg 2005

indeed reduce the time but cause the prediction result less precise. From above the necessary of the new design of the protein prediction pipeline is obvious.

The protein structure prediction and analysis involves several complex steps, including sequence homologous searching, multiple sequence alignment, comparative modeling, structure alignment, evaluation and measurement, and three-dimensional visualization etc. Thus it may require testing multiple analytical tools and performing on huge volumes of data to search for the right targets. Life science researchers traditionally chain together analytical tools and database searches, using either complex scripts, or by manually copying between web pages. The emergence of Grid [4] technologies has provided a new solution for integrating bio-informatics analytical tools and deal with huge volumes of data.

It has been generally recognized that both bioinformatics and post genomic are good opportunities for distributed high performance computing and collaboration applications. A large number of biologist projects are investing in Grid environments, and many computer scientists are developing Bioinformatics applications on Grid (also known as BioGrid). GGF (Global Grid Forum) Life Science Research Group (LSG) [5] focuses to establish related standards. The Asia Pacific BioGRID [6] attempted to build an environment for designing and managing Grid, comprising well tested installation scripts, avoiding dealing with Globus [7] details. The Bio-GRID work group of European Community Grid Project [8] developed an access portal for bimolecular modeling resources, while myGrid [9] is a large e-Science project of United Kingdom to develop open source data-intensive bioinformatics application on the Grid. Recently, Bioinformatics Grid (BG) of ChinaGrid [10], one of largest grid project of China, is to provide bioinformatics services for bioinformatics researchers, and allow them to submit work to high performance computing facilities, while hiding grid programming details.

As part of work of Bioinformatics Grid of ChinaGrid, this paper presents a generic and extensible service-oriented system -- Protein Structure Prediction and Analysis (ProteinSPA) based on the grid middleware. In Section 2, we describe the design of protein structure prediction. Section 3 introduces the workflow management in ProteinSPA. Section 4 demonstrates the utility and efficiency of ProteinSPA. Section 5 gives the conclusion.

2   The Design of Protein Structure Prediction and Analysis

Protein structure prediction is to seek a mapping from the protein's amino acids linear sequence to the three-dimensional coordinate of the atoms of protein. The typical protein contains more than 100 amino acids; while big protein contains more than 4500 amino acids. The number of all mapping from possible sequences to the structure increased with the number of the protein's amino acid residue will grow to be an astronomical figure. Luckily, the proteins exist in the nature are restricted, there also exist big number of the homology sequences, the relation between that and whose structure follows some rules, so it is possible to predict the proteins' structure. We can arrive at the conclusion after the analyzing the protein databank PDB [11] that, any pair of proteins, if their sequences' homologous part goes beyond 30% then they will have the similar three-dimensional structure. This is the guarantee of the success in structure prediction by homology modeling. Based on this basic idea, we propose a schematic diagram for protein structure prediction and analysis, which is illustrated in figure 1.

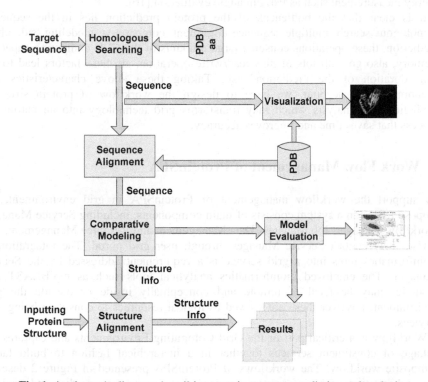

Fig. 1. A schematic diagram describing protein structure prediction and analysis

The sequence homologous searching is to search the protein structure databank and find the protein which has the known structure that is homologous to the target sequence by certain arithmetic or grading criterion. This job can be done by using some homologous searching tools such as Blast or its MPI version -- mpiBLAST [12] for parallel searching.

Multiple sequence alignment always follows the homologous searching, it compares the target sequence with the searching result of the homologous sequence to make the target sequence's amino acid residue mapping to the known protein's residue. Through the multiple sequence alignment it can shape the core of the protein structure model. At present the commonly used tool for multiple sequence alignment is ClustalW [13], it is a method that base on the progressive alignment concept. The popular tool used for homologous modeling is Modeller [14,15]. Before the Modeller can start homologous modeling, there should be some files contain the protein structure as template, such files always stored in the PDBaa (proteins from the Structure Protein Database) databank. The PDBaa file contains the basic remark information and also present the data that relate with the structure.

Finally, in order to support structure analysis, the system provides the structure alignment, which compares the predicted protein structure with some existing structure to find its possible functions, and do the prediction evaluation, based on energy measurement such as Psi, Phi angle evaluation [16].

It is clear that the bottleneck of the protein prediction lies in the sequence homologous search, multiple sequence alignment, comparative modeling, side chain prediction, these operations consume large amounts of the CPU computing capacity, memory, also go with lots of disk read/write operation, all these factors lead to the long duration of the prediction task. Taking these above characteristics and phenomena into account, we have to design the workflow of protein structure prediction and analysis which may transforms grid technology into an automated process that saves time and improves accuracy.

3   Work Flow Management of ProteinSPA

To support the workflow management of ProteinSPA in grid environment, we propose to design a system consists of main components, including Service Manager, Workflow Manager, Job Manager, Data Management and Resource Management.

User may contact Service Manager through user grid portal. The integration of bioinformatics tools into a grid service is a requirement addressed by the Service Manager. The employed bioinformatics analytical tools such as mpiBLAST and Modeller may be local or remote and conceptually inside or outside the grid environment, however these are viewed as logical resources to constitute being grid services.

Workflow is a critical part of the Grid Computing Environments and captures the linkage of constituent services together in a hierarchical fashion to build larger composite workflow. The workflows of ProteinSPA presented in Figure 2 describe the orchestration of bioinformatics services that are used to predict and analysis protein structure.

The workflow management system (Figure 3) generates the workflow definition in XML format according to predefined schema, and need to ensure that any output can be associated with the corresponding inputting records and the associated data of workflow. In this way, the detail of how an output is related to its inputs is available when required.

The Job Manager is responsible for performing resource discovery, scheduling, and dispatching jobs to computational nodes according to the predefined workflow, which is configured through ProteinSPA's administrator portal, starting the execution of the protein prediction task on the assigned nodes, and collects and results from the computational nodes. Processes are deployed to grid computing nodes dynamically at runtime based on Job Manager's instruction.

The Data Manager is responsible for the access, integration and storage of bioinformatics data, while Resource Management is the key to the smooth operation and expandability of grid environment. An agent resides on the computing node, performs a simple Node Monitoring Service on resource usage. As well the agent is responsible for setting up the execution environment on the assigned resource, starting the execution of the job, monitoring the job execution, getting the job running status information and sending that information back to the Resource Manager, finally it sends back the computing result to Job Manager by the way of Resource Manager.

```
                        ProteinSPA XML Workflow Document

<?xml version="1.0" encoding="UTF-8"?>
<workflow workflowId="20050703115573233">
<wfDescription> ProteinSPA workflow document. </wfDescription>
<a Task taskName="Homologous Searching" taskId="1" dependsOn="no">
< Homologous Searching >
<!-- ********** Homologous Searching specific commands -->
</ Homologous Searching >
</a Task>
<a Task taskName="Sequence Alignment" taskId="2" dependsOn="Homologous
Searching">
< Sequence Alignment >
<!-- ********** Sequence Alignment specific commands -->
</ Sequence Alignment >
</a Task>
<a Task taskName="Visualization" taskId="3" dependsOn="Homologous Searching">
< Visualization>
<!-- ********** Visualization specific commands -->
</ Visualization>
</a Task>
<a Task taskName="Comparative Modeling" taskId="4" dependsOn="Sequence
Alignment ">
< Comparative Modeling >
<!-- ********** Comparative Modeling specific commands -->
</ Comparative Modeling >
</a Task>
<a Task taskName="Structure Alignment" taskId="5" dependsOn="Comparative
Modeling">
< Structure   Alignment >
<!-- ********** Structure Alignment specific commands -->
</ Structure   Alignment >
<a Task taskName="Model Evaluation" taskId="6" dependsOn="Comparative
Modeling">
< Model Evaluation>
<!-- ********** Model Evaluation specific commands -->
</ Model Evaluation>
</a Task>
<a Task taskName="StoreResult" taskId="7" dependsOn=" Structure Alignment, Model
Evaluation">
< StoreResult >
<!-- ********** Store Results specific commands -->
</ StoreResult >
</a Task>
</workflow>
```

Fig. 2. XML representation of the ProteinSPA workflow

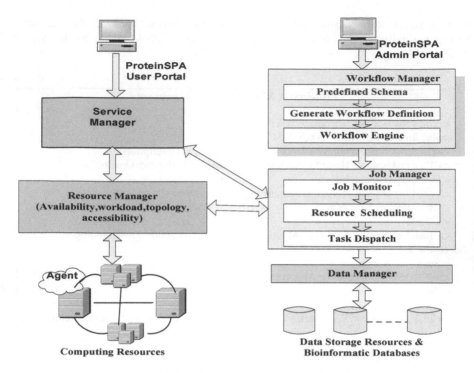

Fig. 3. Workflow management in ProteinSPA

The following describe the concrete workflow of the grid-enabled protein prediction pipeline: The user input the target sequence via grid portal, then the Workflow Manager contacts job manager according the workflow defined. The Job Manager collect the available computational nodes from Resource Manager, then it assigns the job to the enabled computational nodes belong to the grid environment, each computational node fetches its corresponding part of PDB data file via Data Manager. The Data Manager hold a lot of data storage nodes and each node has a segment of the PDB database, that is to say the PDB databank is divided into several segments on each data storage nodes. Sequence homologous search process runs on each computational node using one part of PDB database segments. After all runs finished, all the results returned by computational nodes are collected and presented to Job Manager, the Job Manager takes out the suited homologous sequence from the collected results and present them to the user, the user can choose one or more of the returned homologous sequences, if more than one, the Job Manager will assign each homologous sequence modeling task to multiple computational nodes to let them process the multiple sequence alignment and homologous modeling to generate the protein structure files. Finally the Job Manager gathers the results returned by each node and presents them to the user. After all process finished, all the results returned by computational nodes are merged and presented to end-user. By using data parallelism, very little network communication is needed, and the communication is not order dependant between the computational nodes and Job Manager.

4 Implementation and Evaluation

We implement ProteinSPA on top of CGSP (ChinaGrid Supporting Platform) [17], which is a grid middleware based on the Open Grid Services Architecture (OGSA) model [18] of Globus. Figure 4 shows the user interfaces and interactive results pages of ProteinSPA. Users may access ProteinSPA via the Grid Portal. This is a web based portal built on top of CGSP framework and executable on any suitably enabled web browser. The Grid Portal performs a number of roles; it provides an easy way to use interface to ProteinSPA for end users. Transcending the roles listed above the Grid Portal implements the Security Policy based on the Globus Grid Security Infrastructure (GSI) X.509 certificates to authenticate all users before granting access. Subsequently user credentials are forwarded on as required to other ProteinSPA services where further stages of access restriction and control are implemented. Thus end users should have no knowledge of the underlying services and architecture of ProteinSPA.

To demonstrate the efficiency and effective of ProteinSPA, we compared our prediction results with the test results from world famous protein space structure prediction server SWISS-MODEL [3], the ProteinSPA present high quality prediction results when the suitable template are selected.

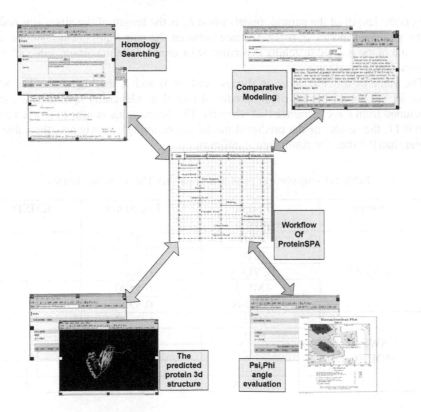

Fig. 4. User interfaces and results pages according to workflow management

We use two kinds of the data to evaluate the quality of the predicted model; they are TM-Score [19] value and RMSD (root mean square deviation) value from the prediction model and nature model (that is measured by the biological experiment). RMSD is a method to calculate the average error; it is used here to calculate the root mean square of α carbon atom between the computed prediction model and nature model. This value is the sum of the square root of the distance of every position α carbon atoms when the predicted model overlaps the nature model. The quality of the predicted model is poorer when the value is bigger.

TM-Score is a new kind of arithmetic used to calculate the homology. TM-Score is one variation of the LG (Levitt Gerstein) [20] grading standard which is the first method used to evaluate the sequence aliment. Of the twos protein structure models' topological structure, it can be used to estimate the quality of the predicted structure model in number. It is improved by extending the GDT [21] (Global Distance Test) and MaxSub [22].

$$TM - Score = MAX \left[\frac{1}{L_N} \sum_{i=1}^{L_T} \frac{1}{1 + \left(\frac{d_i}{d_0} \right)^2} \right] \tag{1}$$

L_N is the length of the natural model, while L_T is the length of the alignment residue in the predicted model, d_i is the distance between the pair i alignment residues, d_0 is the scale of the normal matching diversity; MAX denotes the maximum value after the optimal space overlapped.

The value of the TM-Score is always between 0 and 1, the bigger the TM-Score value is, the higher quality of the predicted model is. Generally speaking, it can be concluded from the experience that when the TM-Score value is near to or even lower than 0.17, the results of the predicted model are meaningless, whereas the value are bigger than 0.4 then the results are significant.

Table 1. Comparison of prediction results on TM-Score and RMSD

Server	Target Sequence	TM-Score	RMSD
ProteinSPA	1CHJ	0.2158	1.9
	1CIE	0.2165	1.8
	1UVQ-A	0.9685	1.0
	1MLU	0.5590	1.3
	1IW2-A	0.3327	2.5
SWISS-MODEL	1CHJ	0.2042	1.7
	1CIE	0.2099	1.6
	1UVQ-A	0.9624	1.0
	1MLU	0.5504	1.3
	1IW2-A	0.1189	2.9

To make the testing results bear more stringency, the test randomly select the following five items of the structure-known protein sequences and to predict these sequences' structure on the protein space structure prediction server SWISS-MODEL, then compare them with the predicted models from ProteinSPA

It can be seen from the above experimental results that the TM-Score value calculated from predicted model and the nature model are higher than the value from the SWISS-MODEL and nature model. Thus the quality of predicted results of ProteinSPA equals to the SWISS-MODEL or even better. It is mainly due to the advance design methods and the supporting of grid technology, the system is able to accomplish complete prediction and analysis tasks and gain the accuracy.

As the SWISS-MODEL system is not real-time, it does not support the instant resulting, it just sends the protein prediction result to the user via Email. So we can not compare the elapsed time of ProteinSPA with that of SWISS-MODEL. But it is observed that by using mpiBLAST to do the parallel scanning of PDB, the elapsed time of homology searching has been reduced with more computational nodes involved in the job.

5 Conclusion

In summary, we have developed a grid-enabled protein prediction and analysis system ProteinSPA based on conventional protein prediction tools and design methods. We integrate protein prediction design methodologies with grid technology which lets protein prediction system can run without any manual interception. By integrating with Grid technology, many other advantages are gained, including load balancing and time saving by searching parallel PDB database segments so to boost the efficiency. It indicates that grid computing methodology in our system provides an effective and efficient way for protein prediction and analysis.

We are now improving performance and functionalities of ProteinSPA by parallelizing the algorithms. Future works will regard the full implementation of ProteinSPA and its use for the advanced analysis of protein structure.

References

1. J. Guo, K. Ellrott1,W.J. Chung, D. Xu, S. Passovets and Y. Xu.: PROSPECT-PSPP: an automatic computational pipeline for protein structure prediction, Nucleic Acids Research, Vol. 32, Web Server issue (2004) 522-525
2. M. Shah, S. Passovets, D. Kim, K. Ellrott, L. Wang, I. Volkler, P. LoCascio, D. Xu, and Y. Xu.: A Computational Pipeline for Protein Structure Prediction and Analysis at Genome Scale, Bioinformatics 19 (2003) 1985-1996
3. SWISS-MODEL. http://swissmodel.expasy.org/
4. Foster, I., Kesselman, C.(eds.): The grid: blueprint for a new computing infrastructure. Morgan Kaufmann Publishers Inc., San Francisco, CA, USA (1999)
5. GGF, Life Science Grid Research Group. http://people.cs.uchicago.edu/dangulo/LSG/.
6. National Center for Biotechnology Information. http://www.ncbi.nlm.nih.gov/.
7. The globus project. http://www.globus.org/
8. EUROGRID Project. http://www.eurogrid.org/

9. myGrid. http://www.mygrid.org.uk/
10. China Research and Education Grid (ChinaGrid). http://www.chinagrid.edu.cn
11. PDB: Protein Data Bank. http://www.rcsb.org/pdb/
12. mpiBLAST. http://mpiblast.lanl.gov/
13. A. D. Baxevanis,B. F. F Ouellette. Bioinformatics: A Practical Guide to the Analysis of genes and Proteins (1998)
14. A. Fiser, R.K. Do, A. Sali. Modeling of loops in protein structures,Protein Sci. 9(2000)1753-1773
15. Modeller. http://salilab.org/modeller
16. PROCHECK. http://www.biochem.ucl.ac.uk/~roman/procheck/procheck.html
17. Globus: OGSA. http://www.globus.org/ogsa/
18. ChinaGrid Supporting Platform. http://www.chinagrid.edu.cn/CGSP/
19. Y. Zhang, J. Skolnick. Scoring function for automated assessment of protein structure template quality, Proteins (2004)
20. M. Levitt, M. Gerstein. A unified statistical framework for sequence comparison and structure comparison, Proc. Natl. Acad. Sci. USA 95 (1998): 5913–5920
21. A. Zemla, C. Venclovas, J. Moult, K. Fidelis. Processing and analysis of CASP3 protein structure predictions, Proteins 3 (1999): 22–29
22. N. Siew, A. Elofsson, L. Rychlewski, D. Fischer. MaxSub: an automated measure for the assessment of protein structure prediction quality, Bioinformatics 16 (2000): 776–785

Applying Service Composition in Digital Museum Grid

Xiangxu Meng, Shijun Liu, Rui Wang, Chenglei Yang, and Hai Guo

School of Computer Science and Technology, Shandong University, Jinan, 250100, China
{mxx, lsj, chl_yang}@sdu.edu.cn

Abstract. Digital museum is an effective method of protecting and using resources stored in museums. Digital museum grid was present to efficiently and effectively organize, present and share the resources over heterogeneous digital museum systems. In a service-oriented digital museum grid, by composing the services published to be entire applications dynamically, more interesting and individual applications would be created upon the massive and various collections. This paper present a three-phases service composition model includes functional modeling, service selecting and dynamic binding, in which all outputs of the three phases are reusable and express the service composition in different abstract levels. A service selection framework put forward in the paper presents a feasible method for service selecting. And a dynamic binding method based on service composition template and compositive evaluating is discussed which enhances the flexibility of service composition.

1 Introduction

A Web service is a software system designed to support interoperable machine-to-machine interaction over a network. Web service composition is an emerging paradigm for enabling application integration within and across organizational boundaries by taking several component products or services, and bundling them together to meet the needs of a given customer [1].

Recently, the grid is evolving to the Open Grid Service Architecture (OGSA)[2], which brings together various distributed application-level services to a 'market' for clients to request and enable the integration of services across distributed heterogeneous dynamic virtual organization [3].

Aimed at building grid-based massive information processing environment on a common grid support platform, the Massive Information Processing Grid (MIPGRID) project of ChinaGrid [4] has started, which organizes the computing resource, storage resource and information resources of different organizations effectively to support high performance computing and resource sharing.

In the past several years, 18 universities participate in the National Collegiate Digital Museum Project of china have established digital museum with much digital information of collections in these digital museum, but the digital resources of these museums are isolated, heterogeneous, geographically distributed and difficult be shared effectively. How to discovery and use these resources? How to extend application upon these resources? University Digital Museum Grid (UDMGrid), an application of the MIPGRID was set up in 2004 to solve the problems. With over 10 thousands of digital collections of various types including still images, text, video, 2D

G. Chen et al. (Eds.): ISPA Workshops 2005, LNCS 3759, pp. 267–275, 2005.

graphics and charts, 3D models, animations, etc. Archaeological Digital Museum of Shandong University [5] participates in the project and has been one of the first four nodes of UDMGrid.

The proposed system is service-oriented. By encapsulating each resource as a grid service and unifying the format of these above types of information, we could easily expand our system by inserting heterogeneous resource. Besides presenting the exhibitions dynamically, composing the services to be an entire application dynamically is another challenge of our project, which would enhance the interests of the visitors.

2 Related Works

Seamless composition of Web services has enormous potential in streamlining business-to-business or enterprise application integration [6]. Composition in Service-Oriented Architectures has been the focus of much research recently.

From the view of composition mode, service composition can be broadly classified into three categories: manual, semi-automated and automated composition. Manual composition frameworks expect the user to generate workflow scripts either graphically or through a text editor, which are then submitted to a workflow execution engine. Semi-automated composition techniques are a step forward in the sense that they make 'semantic suggestions' for service selection during the composition process; the user still needs to select the service required from a shortlist of the appropriate services and link them up in the order desired. Automated composition techniques automate the entire composition process by using AI planning or similar technology [7].

From the view of agility, service composition techniques can be categorized into two types: static service composition, and dynamic service composition. Static service composition is an approach in which application designers implement a new application manually by designing a workflow or a state chart describing the interaction pattern among components. Dynamic service composition composes an application autonomously when a user queries for an application. The dynamic service composition has the potential to realize flexible and adaptable applications by properly selecting and combining components based on the user request and context [8]. To realize high automated and dynamic composition, many semantics-based service composition methods are presented by both describing the semantic of services as well as the service composition mechanism must support semantics. Such as a semantics-based service composition system including Component Service Model with Semantic (CoSMoS), Component Runtime Environment (CoRE), and Semantic Graph based Service Composition (SeGSeC)[8]. There are many other methods of service composition such as constraint Driven Web Service Composition [9], which reduces much of the service composition problem to a constraint satisfaction problem and uses a multi-phase approach for constraint analysis, allows the process designers to bind Web Services to an abstract process, based on business and process constraints and generate an executable process. Some researches address the automated composition problem by proposing an agent-based services composition framework [1][10].

3 A Three-Phase Service Composition Model

An application of UDMGrid is composed by several actual services according to the workflow and executing rule of a specific requirement.

We do this by designing an abstract workflow from a high-level objective. Then, select suitable service for every activity from service registry in UDMGrid and implement the job by invoke these services according to the flow. We call it a three-phase service composition model, which is a semi-automated composition method actually, but enhances the flexibility by adopting more agile service selecting and dynamic binding.

We divide the application creating procession into functional modeling, service selecting and dynamic service binding. The output of preceding phase is the input of successive phase. All outputs of the three phases are reusable and express the service composition in different abstract levels: abstract flow template, service composition template, service composition instance, which is shown in Fig 1□□

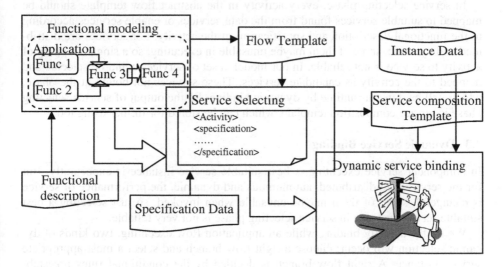

Fig. 1. Three-phase service composition model

3.1 Functional Modeling

At beginning, an application is initiated by the composer who knows what the application behaves. In our model, the composer designs an abstract flow firstly, which only include the functional description and specification of activities and the logic of application flow.

Many workflow systems use template in flow defining for its simple, intuitionistic, easy to use, and reusable, which reduce the repeated work in flow defining. Template is composed of nodes and arcs, where nodes stand for activities and arcs stand for relations between activities. We use template in expressing abstract flow too, the template is stored in a file and can be reused again.

For the functionality of whole process has defined, the functional flow model could be evaluated by simulation and be stored as a template file.

3.2 Service Selecting

To establish an application from several services, we get the functional description of the application from the abstract flow, select suitable service for every activity, and submit it to the workflow engine to execute. How to select the best suit services is the main matter should be considered.

We encapsulate each resource as a grid service called Data Service to hide the heterogeneity of resources. The enable services such as data gathering, scene constructing and rendering facilitate the application creating. These two kinds of services were registered into the service register in our system through Information service, and can be found and selected by the functionality supported by the Manager service. The Information service and the Manager service are two core services provided by our system.

In service selecting phase, every activity in the abstract flow template should be mapped to suitable services found from the data services or enable services according to the functional description and specification of the activity. For services are distributed and dynamic, some of them maybe unusable in executing, so a single mapping of activity to service is not reliable. In our model, a set of services could be selected and mapped to the activity as candidate services. These services not bound at the phase, which will be done in runtime by dynamic binding. So the output of service selecting phase is service composition template, which can be stored for further using too.

3.3 Dynamic Service Binding

In component service executing, a best suitable service instance is expectantly. But for the services are distributed, autonomous and dynamic, the performance of service is changeful, some of them maybe unusable when invoked, so just selecting a best suitable service instance in service selecting phase is not very reliable.

We do the actually binding while an application flow executing, two kinds of dynamic selection will occur: choose a right flow branch and select a most appropriate service instance. A right flow branch is decided by the conditional rules preestablished in the flow logic. A service instance will be dynamic selected from the candidate services by matching, which will be discussed in section 5.

4   Service Selection Framework

Like Fig 2 shows, there are four types of service in this framework: manager service, information service, data service and enable service. The first two are the core services of system responsible for the service discovery and invoking. The invoked Data Services search their relative heterogeneous resource and get the satisfying information including textual information and multimedia information, which is the main service in our system. And the enable services are a series of services to facilitate the applications creating in digital museum grid.

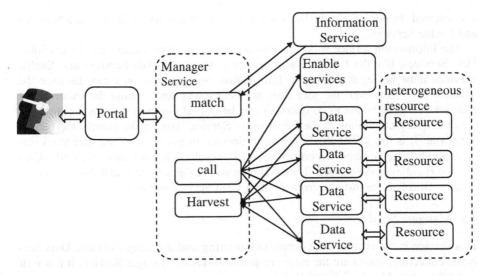

Fig. 2. Service selection framework

4.1 Data Service

The resources that can be used are from various types of sources like RDBMS systems including SQL Server, Oracle, and so on, relevant web pages and flat files. Also the format of the information is quite different from each other. For example, we have different types of media types including still images, text, video, 2D graphics and charts, 3D models, animations in our system. To access these heterogeneous resources with great efficiency, we encapsulate each resource as a grid service called Data Service to hide the heterogeneity of resources. User accesses the resource by calling the Data Service.

Although the resources are heterogeneous, we design these Data Services with the same calling interface to ensure the coherent processing of the user-submitted queries. This is helpful to easily use different resources. If there are some resources to be used, the only thing is to develop a Data Service to encapsulate the accessing the resources and unify the format of the services. So this ensures the expansibility of the system. Sharing is base on the uniform format. The queries are routed to all the working service providers in the same way and the response data would be also formatted coherently.

Because of the variety of the types of the resources, the queries would have to be transformed into the corresponding query format of each cooperative data service provider. Then the returned query results would be reformatted in the uniform format described by the metadata.

4.2 Information Service

Resource discovery is a key issue in Grid environments, since applications are usually constructed by composing hardware and software resources that need to be discovered and selected. In our system the key issue is how to discovery available Data Services and Enable Services.

The Information service is designed to register and support query for the available Data Services, like the UDDI in web services. All of the Data Services and Enable Services must be registered in the Information Service. The user can discover the resource here. However, the user does not necessarily know about the existence of each service. If he wants to do queries over the digital museum systems, he just submits the query conditions to the Information Service through the search interface at the portal. It is the job of the Information Service to query all of the registered services and have to combine the coincident query results. Then it returns the GSH (Grid Service Handle) of the service. The GSH tells where the service is and distinguishes a specific Grid Service instance from all other Grid Service instances.

4.3 Manager Service

This service is the core of the system. Discovering and invoking available Data Services, collecting results are the major responsibilities of Manager Service. It has four parts: Searcher, Match, Call and Harvest.

The Match module and Information Service realize organizing and managing resources with great efficiency. All information of resources is stored in Information Service. The responsibility of Match module is to discovery available resources from Information Service. When receiving the request, the Manager Service activates the Match module. And the Match module invokes the Information Service with the requirements. Then it gets the handles of the Data Services which match the requirements and transfers the handles to the Call module for use.

5 Dynamic Binding

Service composition template can be executed instantly after defined or it can be executed by retrieved from the template repertory.

For several services would satisfy an activity, which one should be selected to invoke is done automatically by an evaluating mechanism. The evaluating mechanism based on a compositive evaluating of specific attributes of a group of services acting the approximate functionality. The attributes be evaluated can be specified by the composer who know the requirements. The best service in compositive evaluating be selected and bound in the service composition.

To execute the service composition, each activity should mapped to a service, and all the component services should bound before the service composition initiated. In actual applications, a confirmation of service binding should made with the service providers before the service composition initiated, which ensures no service would unusable or unaccessible in executing. But if some bound services failure for some reason while the service composition executing, alternative service instance could be selected from service set in the service composition template.

A service composition be executed successfully is a service composition instance, which can be stored as a super service for further direct execution, just like a general web service, which suitable for some unchangeable and complex business process.

If initiate a service composition template again, evaluating of services set should be done again, because the specifications and states of service instance maybe have changed.   If all the component services have been bound successfully, the service composition could be initiated. Otherwise, if any component service could not be bound, which means the service composition template is unusable, must fall back on the abstract flow template, to do the service selecting again.

6   Implementation

The UDMGrid has established with the first four nodes distributed in four universities in China: Beihang university, Shandong university, Nanjing university and Kunming university of science and technology. Through the supporting of UDMGrid system, the heterogeneous collections can be integrated and shared easily, and many interesting applications can be built upon the massive and various collections.

Data service is the foundation of many other applications. Moreover, by retrieving heterogeneous resources directly from different repertories, the relations of different collections can be mined. For example, while searching "horse", the horse as an animal, "wild horse" fighter plane, ancient carriage of china, even gem like horse could obtained from different sources, which helpful in expanding the view of visitor.

In our service oriented digital museum grid system, the service composition is an important technique used in dynamic creating applications by a series of services

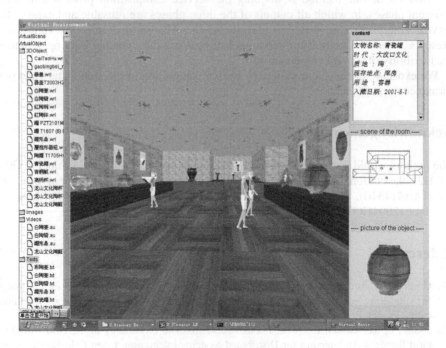

Fig. 3. Virtual museum demonstration

published. Virtual museum is one of these applications. A virtual museum mainly is composed of an empty indoor scene (the building) and collections. The empty indoor scene can be projected to 2D plane polygon. In reverse, we can easily get the building's 3D model by Sweep operation on this polygon. After the empty indoor scene's model has been built, users need to lay out collections (items on display) such as cultural relics with small volumes according to actual requirements, like Fig 3 shows. These jobs are implemented by data services who responsible for retrieving collections from heterogeneous resources, scene service who responsible for designing the 2D plane polygon and generating 3D model and rendering, deploy service who responsible for placing the collections in the scene, interactive service who responsible for interactive walkthrough and some other services.

To create the application, several enable services and data services were selected according to the functional requirement of the application, and were composed in a specific sequence defined in the abstract flow. The data services were bound dynamically according to the specific collections wanted from different data services associated with different resources.

7 Conclusion

In this paper, we mainly discuss the service composition application creating in the Grid-Enabled digital museum system utilizing cooperative Grid services. The main contribution of our method is dividing the service composition process into three different phases, in which all outputs of the three phases are reusable and express the service composition in different abstract levels. The service selection framework presents a feasible method for service selecting. And the dynamic binding enhances the flexibility of service composition.

We expect to enhance our system by further elaboration of the architecture and performance improvement.

Acknowledgement

The authors would like to acknowledge the support by the ChinaGrid Project (CG03-GF012), the National High Technology Research and Development Program of China (2003AA414310), the Science & Technology Development Projects of Shandong Province (2004GG1104011, 2004GG1104017).

References

1. Chris Preist, Andrew Byde, Claudio Bartolini: Agent-Based Service Composition Through Simultaneous Negotiation in Forward and Reverse Auctions. Approved for External Publication EC-03. Proceedings 4th ACM Conference on E-Commerce. San Diego. (2003)
2. Foster, I., Kesselman, C., Nick, J. and Tuecke, S.: The Physiology of the Grid: An Open Grid Services Architecture for Distributed Systems Integration. Open Grid Service Infrastructure WG. Global Grid Forum. (2002)

3. Hanhua Chen, Hai Jin, Xiaoming Ning, Zhipeng Lv: Q-SAC:Toward QoS Optimized Service Automatic Composition. Proceedings of the 5th International Symposium on Cluster Computing and Grid Cardiff, Wales, UK (2005)
4. Hai Jin: ChinaGrid: Making Grid Computing a Reality. Digital Libraries: International Collaboration and Cross-Fertilization - Lecture Notes in Computer Science. Vol.3334. Springer-Verlag. December (2004) pp.13-24
5. Xiang Hui, Meng Xiangxu and Yang Chenglei: Design and Implementation of Digital Archaeology Museum of Shandong University. Journal of System Simulation.15(3). (2003)
6. Biplav Srivastava & Jana Koehler: Web Service Composition - Current Solutions and Open Problems. ICAPS 2003 Workshop on Planning for Web Services (2003)
7. Majithia S., David W., Gray W. : A framework for automated service composition in service-oriented architectures. In Proceedings of t he 1st European Semantic Web Symposium. Heraklion. Greece. (2004) 269-283
8. Keita Fujii, Tatsuya Suda: Dynamic Service Composition Using Semantic Information, ICSOC'04. November 15–19. New York. USA. (2004)
9. Rohit Aggarwal, Kunal Verma, John Miller, William Milnor: Constraint Driven Web Service Composition in METEOR-S. Services Computing. 2004 IEEE International Conference on (SCC'04). September 15 – 18. Shanghai. China (2004)
10. McIlraith, S. and Son, T.C.: Adapting golog for composition of semantic web services. In Proc. of the 8th International Conference on Knowledge Representation and Reasoning (KR '02). Toulouse. France. (2002)

Grid Supporting Platform for AMS Data Processing

Junzhou Luo, Aibo Song, Ye Zhu, Xiaopeng Wang,
Teng Ma, Zhiang Wu, Yaobin Xu, and Liang Ge

Department of Computer Science & Engineering,
Southeast University, Nanjing 210096, P. R. China
{Jluo, Absong, Tonyzhuye, Xiaopeng, Mateng,
Zawu, Xuyaobin1983, Heavenbuyer}@seu.edu.cn

Abstract. The purpose of AMS experiment is to look for the source of the dark matter, source of the cosmic ray and the universe made of antimatter. The characteristics of AMS experiment are massive data and complicated computing. The data are frequently transmitted, retrieved and processed among the computing nodes located in USA, Europe and China. This paper introduces the grid platform at Southeast University, called SEUGrid, for the AMS data processing and analysis. Some key technologies such as the scheduling strategy, data replica management and semantic access control, which SEUGrid adopts to fit the AMS data processing, are described in the paper.

1 Introduction

The AMS（Alpha Magnetic Spectrometer）experiment, led by Nobel Prize winner Professor Samuel C. C. Ting, is large-scale international collaborative project. More than 300 scientists from 15 countries and regions including USA, Russia, Germany, France and China participate in the AMS experiment. Among them, there are a lot of world-famous scholars and universities such as American Massachusetts Institute of Technology, Swiss Geneva University and Italian Perugia University, etc. The project has got great attentions of each participating nation and region. AMS experiment is the only large physics experiment on the international space station. It is the first time in an experiment that human measures high-energy electric atom and particle accurately in space. The purpose of the AMS experiment is to look for the source of the dark matter, source of the cosmic ray and the universe made of antimatter.

AMS01 took the American space shuttle Discovery and succeeded in lifting off and carrying on the first experiment on June of 1998. Having flied for 10 days in the space, it has discovered a lot of new phenomena of earth track cosmic ray. AMS02 will be launched with the American space shuttle Atlantis, and put in the international space station. AMS data is divided into raw data, ESD formatted data, tagged data and Monte Carlo data, etc. A large number of raw data (probably 420T) pass through special-purpose communication facility of NASA to the ground. Among American MIT, Swiss CERN, Chinese Southeast University, French and Italian national nuclear physics research institute, etc, AMS ground data in the center SOC are transmitted, stored, computed and analyzed. The research work is featured in massive data amount, and complicated computing. With regard to calculating in MC simulation of AMS: in Intel Pentium 4, to finish one 1 million simulation of random chance event

G. Chen et al. (Eds.): ISPA Workshops 2005, LNCS 3759, pp. 276–285, 2005.
© Springer-Verlag Berlin Heidelberg 2005

calculation task needs 200G magnetic disc space and 1000 hours processor calculate time. In order to improve the computational efficiency and reduce the size of storage space, existing calculation resources need to be integrated, which means to integrate machinery equipments and software tools that each computer center has, so that they can work in coordination. As a result, the complicated analysis task can be handled in coordination. To achieve this, the grid platform dealing with AMS-02 magnanimity data needs setting up.

There are already some grid platforms at home and abroad now. Some famous ones are as follows: Science Grid of American of Ministry of Energy, EUROGRID, Data-Grid, TeraGrid of NSF and Vega grid of Institute of Computing Technology, etc. Though the common goal of these grid plans is to set up the extensive distributed computing infrastructure and offer the support for the data intensive computing, the application of every plan has clear direction. For example DataGrid provides service for three kinds of complicated calculations: high-energy physics, biomedical pattern process and the earth observes. The data processing of AMS has its own characteristics, the data more than 420TB will be frequently retrieved, transmitted and processed among MIT, CERN , Southeast University, France and Italy, etc. on Internet. Therefore it is impossible to use distributed database that deposits all data replica to accelerate retrieve speed. There is a need to develop some fast data-access technology and data-storage technology. Internet bandwidth and delay must be considered in scheduling strategy. At the same time, Internet high openness and share also brings security problems. As a result, grid platform being developed must be suitable for AMS experiment data processing which has its own features in access control, data management and strategy of task scheduling.

2 SEUGrid Architecture

A new grid platform SEUGrid has been developed for AMS data processing and analysis. This platform is now mainly used for AMS-02 MC production. Users can submit AMS MC jobs to SEUGrid from Grid web portal and the job scheduler module will decompose the jobs and deliver them to the Grid computing nodes to execute. Users can also check the status of the job processing and get the final results on Grid web portal.

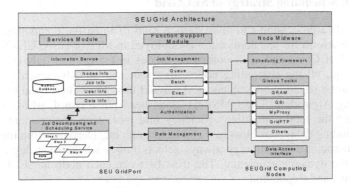

Fig. 1. SEUGrid Architecture

SEUGrid is composed of two comparatively independent parts, the Gridport and the Grid computing nodes. The Gridport's functions are managing Grid users' information, submitting computing jobs, checking job status, decomposing and delivering jobs, collecting computing results, etc. The Grid computing nodes receive MC jobs from the Gridport and produce the middle computing results. Gridport is structured with service module and function support module. In service module, there're two services. The information service based on the MySQL database offers Grid users the status of the computing nodes and the job processing, and it also accepts job submitting and information query for Grid users and data storage. The job decomposing and scheduling service firstly transfers the job into formal description, and then decomposes it into several small sub jobs. These sub jobs then are passed to the job management module for scheduling in the form of queue, batch and execs, and finally they are executed by Grid computing nodes. The authentication module is to validate the identity of the Grid users and authorize the job requests according to the dynamic attributes of the Grid resources and policies. And the data management module is used to organize and manage distributed data SEUGrid uses or produces. It also offers data transfer and storage services for the Grid users and applications. The Grid middleware that consists of the scheduling framework, the Globus toolkit and common data access interface is deployed on every Grid computing nodes. The scheduling framework is to schedule computing resources locally and interact with the job management module of the Gridport, and the Globus toolkit provides a universal Grid computing environment. The detail architecture of SEUGrid and the relationship between each component are shown in Figure 1.

3   Key Technologies in SEUGrid

According to the characteristics of AMS data processing, SEUGrid adopts some technologies such as task scheduling strategy, data replica management and semantic access control, which are different from the existing grid technologies, so that the efficiency of the AMS data processing on the platform of SEUGrid can be greatly improved.

3.1   Task Scheduling Strategy of SEUGrid

As AMS data processing and analysis is a kind of intensive computing application, the Grid Platform for this application is deployed in MIT of USA, CERN of Switzerland, SEU of China and other computing nodes in France and Italy etc. In this grid environment, all the computing nodes may join and quit dynamically, which may produce some negative consequences. To avoid this, Trust-Based and QoS-Measured Scheduling Algorithm (TB&QMSA)[1,2]has been put forward, whose purposes are to enhance the total computing efficiency and meet QoS requirements of the grid users including delay, cost, loss rate and bandwidth etc. Deriving from the trust model of human society, this strategy always selects nodes whose trust degree is high to improve the dynamic efficiency. The trust between each node in SEUGrid includes Direct Trust and Reputation.

Definition 1. Direct Trust $Trust_{(i,j)}^{D}$ from source node i to target node j can be

shown as follows: $$Trust_{(i,j)}^{D} = (\sum_{k=1}^{N} \alpha_{k}^{D} p_{k}^{j}) \times \rho_{i}^{j} \qquad (1)$$

Here, p_{k}^{j} is the statistic parameter of node j ; N is the total number of parameters ;

α_{k}^{D} is the weight ; ρ_{i}^{j} is the systematic crash rate of target node j. Direct Trust is the

trust brought by direct interaction and cooperation between source node and destination node, obtained directly from the source node.

Definition 2. The reputation of node j $Reputation_{j}$ can be defined as:

$$Re\,putation_{j} = \sum_{\substack{k=1 \\ k \neq i,j}}^{N-1} (\beta_{k}^{R} \times Trust_{(k,j)}^{D}) \qquad (2)$$

Here, N = total number of non-source nodes, β_{k}^{R} is the measure of relationship

between node i and non-source node k, such as the successful cooperation-rate. We
must point out that the measure of relationship can be dynamically adjustable, and

$\sum \beta_{k}^{R} = 1, \beta_{k}^{R} = \dfrac{1}{M}$ initially. Actually, reputation is the trust brought by direct

interaction and cooperation between source node and destination node, which will be
recommended to the source node by other non-source nodes.

Since trust between source node i and target node j form their direct trust,

$Trust_{(i,j)}^{D}$, and the reputation of target node j, $Reputation_{j}$, the definition of trust be-

tween source node i and target node j, $Trust_{(i,j)}$, can be shown as follows:

$$Trust_{(i,j)} = \alpha \times Trust_{(i,j)}^{D} + \beta \times Re\,putation_{j} \qquad (3)$$

Here, α and β are the weights of direct trust, $Trust_{(i,j)}^{D}$, and reputation, $Reputa-$

$tion_{j}$, respectively. By setting these two parameters, we can emphasize these two aspects of the trust easily.

TB&QMSA evaluates computing nodes primarily from three aspects: direct trust
integrating processing efficiency, scheduling efficiency and pre-assured service estimate; reputation of target computing nodes recommended by other Virtual Organizations and QoS constraints provided by grid users such as delay, cost and bandwidth
etc. So the evaluation expressions of node i can be simplified as :

$$w_{i}^{'} = [\alpha_{i}^{w1}(d_{i}^{'})^{T} + \alpha_{i}^{w2}(c_{i}^{'})^{T} + \alpha_{i}^{w3}(lr_{i}^{'})^{T} + \alpha_{i}^{w4}(bw_{i}^{'})^{T}] + \beta_{i}^{w}(t_{i}^{'})^{T} \qquad (4)$$

Here, $\alpha_i^{wj}\,(1 \leq j \leq 4)$ are the weight of grid user's QoS requirements such as delay, cost, loss rate and bandwidth etc. β_i^w is the weight of trust which integrates processing efficiency, scheduling efficiency and pre-assured service estimate.

TB&QMSA computes evaluation vector on QoS requirements w_i base on expressions (4), and sorts w_i in ascending order. Then the task can be decomposed and located to computing node with smallest w_i.

In order to verify the TB&QMSA, we have made simulations and comparisons between TB&QMSA and Non-QoS constraints Scheduling Algorithm (NSA). As fig. 2-3 shows, the task processing and scheduling of TB&QMSA is more efficient than NSA in instable grid environment. The reason is that trust mechanism is adopted so that the algorithm can make statistical trust for all virtual organizations in computational grid. By doing this, TB&QMSA may avoid non-trusted virtual organizations to enhance the total computing efficiency in instable grid environment. Meanwhile, TB&QMSA can also select virtual organization which satisfies user's QoS requirements, by which the total computing efficiency on the constraints of QoS requirements can be raised. The result of simulations indicates that: TB&QMSA can achieve good performance in large scale computational grid.

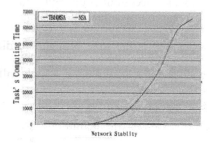 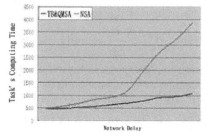

Fig. 2. Comparisons between TB&QMS and NSA in instable network environment

Fig. 3. Comparisons between TB& QMS and NSA in delaying network environment

3.2 Data Replica Management in SEUGrid

In distributed environment, the best method of improving the access data rate is to store all data copies in each node. But due to the restriction of Storage node capacity, preserving all data copies is unrealistic, especially for data processing of AMS for the total amount has reached 420T. SEUGrid adopts replica replacing algorithm, which only keeps part of copies and not only improves the speed of accessing but also saves the storage space.

There are some traditional replacement algorithms such LFU, LRU, etc. LFU algorithm replaces the least accessed replica with the new replica in a time window. This algorithm is based on access status of the recent time window, so it cannot strictly show a long-term access status. LRU algorithm replaces the replica that is not used for the longest time recently. This algorithm is beneficial for the latest replica. However, just the same problem with LFU algorithm, it cannot predict the hot spot replica in time window. It is a discrimination algorithm that discriminates the earlier arriving replica. In SEUGrid, the data management service mainly adopts the predict-based and cost-based replica replacement algorithm[3].

First, we introduce the concept of content similarity.

Definition 3.   Define the replica space {R} as the set of all the replicas and the replica-ID space {r} as a set of replica identifiers. Replica identifiers are assumed to be integer positive numbers. Content similarity can be defined as a mapping between {R} and {r} as follows. The smaller the difference |r1-r2|, the bigger is the content similarity between replica R1 and R2.

Based on the assumptions above, the history of replica requests can be seen as a random step in space of replica identifiers. Assuming replica access starts from replica identifier r0. So access event can be seen as series of random steps $(s_i, i>0)$ in which $s_i = r_i - r_{i-1}, i>0$.

According to spatial and time locality, files close in file space are more likely to be requested close together in time. We only consider a situation that a single user submits a batch of work onto data grid. The replica requests from a user have a correlation each other. After reasoning, we conclude:

$$f_n = \sum_{k=-n}^{n} \binom{n}{\frac{n+k}{2}} q^{\frac{n+k}{2}} (1-q)^{\frac{n-k}{2}} *k) + f_0 \tag{5}$$

We assume:

f_T: measured value at Tth (identifier of access replica at T time)
T: historical time window
T': predicted time window
M: the number of event s=1 in historical time window
N: the number of event s=-1 in historical time window
q=M/(M+N)   (6)   1-q=N/(M+N)   (7)
N=(M+N)*T/T '   (8)   f0=fT   (9)
fn can be computed by (5) –(9)

Assuming f(k, M+N,n) represents the access number of the replica whose identifier is the positive integer k in the future n replica accesses, and this number is predicted based on the historical information of M+N times of replica accesses.

f(k, M+N,n) is computed as follows:
C[k] =0 in which C[k] is the counter of replicas whose identifier is k.
For i=M+N+1 to i=M+N+n
if k<=fi<(2k+1)/2, C[k]=C[k]+1;
if (2k+1)/2<=fi<k+1, C[k+1]=C[k+1]+1;
in which, fi is computed according to (5)-(9).
f(k, M+N,n) =C[k]
f(k, M+N,n) represents the popularity of this replica in T' time window.

Because of the difference of replica size and bandwidth between CE (Computing Element) and SE (Storage Element), the cost of each replica replacement is different. For example, the replacement cost of a 1GB size of replica is absolutely bigger than that of a 100MB size. It is because the replacement of bigger replica will cause high network consumption. So, we should introduce the cost factors such as replica size or bandwidth into replacement metrics function including prediction factor.

We call cost factor as C. C is defined as following:

$$C=Sr / (Bce\text{-}se* Sce) \tag{11}$$

Sr: Size of the replica
Bce-se: Bandwidth between CE and SE that has this replica
Sce: The size of SE in CE.

Given prediction and cost factors, we introduce a PC-based algorithm.

$$F(k)= f(k, M+N,n)*(Sk/(Bce\text{-}se*Sce)) \tag{12}$$

F(k) is the replacement metrics of replica of the identifier k. f(k, M+N,n) is computed as before. Sk/(Bce-se*Sce) is computed as (11). For Bce-se when there are many SE that have Rk (the replica whose identifier is k) connecting to the CE site, we only consider   bandwidth that is largest is assigned to Bce-se.

By comparing with LRU and LFU algorithms in simulation experiments(as Fig. 4), we conclude that the PC-based algorithm has better average job time and rescues the consumption of network bandwidth.

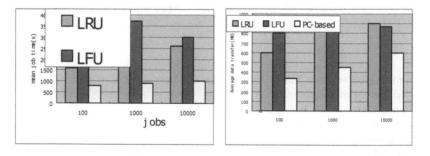

Fig. 4. The simulation results of LRU、LFU and PC-based algorithms in mean job time and bandwidth consumption

3.3 Semantic Access Control in SEUGrid

As far as AMS vast data processing is concerned, the computing nodes and Grid users are distributed all over the world, so access control and authentication based on integrating and balancing each entity's security requirements dynamically is very important. To address this issue, we present a new access control method that is called Semantic Access Control (SAC). According to the semantic descriptions of the policies, requests, resources and other entities, SAC uses machine reasoning at a semantic level to deduce authorization decision.

The use of Semantic Web technology in SAC mainly consists in the following three courses:

(i)   **Semantic Description of Entities.** Describe the semantics of all the entities involved in the access control scenario, especially the semantic of the request and the resources requested.

(ii)   **Semantic Description of Policies.** All the policies should be described or presented in semantic way which would require a universal policy markup language to be used. As in heterogeneous distributed Grid environment, it is unrealistic to use only one policy language, so the necessary translations are demanded.

(iii)   **Semantic Reasoning and Conflicts Resolving.** Based on the semantic descriptions of all the entities and policies, an efficient semantic reasoning mechanism should be taken to get the last result. This mechanism must also have the capabilities of identifying conflicts between polices and resolving them. In addition, it can reason about the current context of the process and what are the allowed interactions given that context.

Following this outline, a framework for semantic description of Grid entities is designed and a formal semantic policy language for semantic reasoning is defined. Then, machine reasoning can be quickly carried out by mapping the security policies to logic expressions. Based on these researches, we designed a new semantic access control model for Grid services. In this model, we use a policy enforcement point (PEP) to actually execute the access control for the requests, and set a policy decision center (PDC) behind to do semantic reasoning and make access decisions. The policies of TO and VO are collected and managed in the policy administrator center (PAC) and can be submitted to PDC when needed. Fig. 5 shows the architecture of the semantic access control model and its work flow.

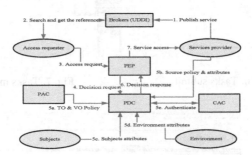

Fig. 5. Semantic Access Control Model

Compared with classical access control methods[4,5,6] and Grid access control existing solutions, SAC is more scalable, more applicable to different environments with heterogeneous and complex access criteria and avoids the need of a registration phase. So it can perfectly meet the Grid computing requirements. Further more, the facilities implementing the SAC model can work corporately with traditional firewalls on traditional network edges in a higher network layer. It offers a cheap way for organizations to apply their Grid systems without entirely modifying or weaking their underline network security systems.

4   Deployment and Application of SEUGrid

Now SEUGrid has been deployed in Southeast University and Shandong University. The Shandong University computing node is a node of Langchao Cluster, while the Southeast computing node is composed of two Intel Xeon 64bit servers, two HP 32bit servers and several PCs. The fig. 6-8 show the MC simulation task's submitting, monitoring and results retrieving, respectively.

Several computing tasks of MC simulation (three kinds of dataset – C, He and E (Electron)) obtained from CERN has been successfully running on this platform. Judging from the efficiency and quality when the computing tasks are completed, using grid is able to fully employ the Monte Carlo simulation features of AMS data, which is good at parallel computing, so that highly efficient distributed computing can be implemented. SEUGrid uses open gird computing standard and open sources as much as possible, by which system is fairly scalable and suitable in different environments. Besides the MC computing tasks, similar scientific computing tasks can also be handled on the platform.

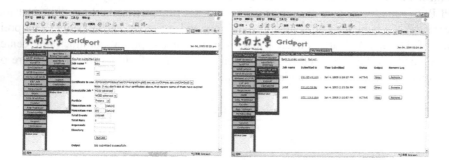

Fig. 6. Tasks submit   **Fig. 7.** Tasks monitor

Fig. 8. Results retrieve

5   Conclusions

SEUGrid provides the computing environment for AMS data processing, which includes computing tasks submission, scheduling, monitoring, raw data storage, and data replica management. Still it is primary, experimental system and the reliability and user-friendly needs improving. The current upper layer application of SEUGrid is mainly about the simulation of AMS-02, which, however, is only one aspect of AMS data processing. AMS data processing includes data reconstruction, physical analyses, etc. Application software based on SEUGrid will also be developed.

SEUGrid will be transplanted onto CGSP(ChinaGrid[7] Support Platform) in future. CGSP is the key network grid middleware for the ChinaGrid construction and development. It can integrate all kinds of resources in the education and research systems and shield the heterogeneity and dynamics of all the gird resources. In this way grid services that are transparent, highly efficient, reliable, convenient can be offered to all the scientific computing and engineering research. SEUGrid has been deployed in the millimeter wave national lab, Southeast University campus network center, Southeast University library, CERNET network center of Northeast China. After deployment, SEUGrid interconnects all the campus networks and integrate their resources, shaping the computing environment featured in 19TB repository and nearly 100 billion instructions per second. In this way SEUGrid provides computing service for AMS data processing, analysis and various grid applications in Southeast University. Meanwhile, it connects ChinaGrid using a special 100Gbps line to offer computing service for ChinaGrid. AMS data processing, analysis and storage are therefore implemented based on ChinaGrid.

Acknowledgement

This work is supported by ChinaGrid Project of Ministry of Education of China and by National Natural Science Foundation of China under Grants No. 90412014.

References

1. Peng Ji, Junzhou Luo."A Trust-Based Scheduling of Tasks on Grid Computing Systems", the International Conference on Computer, Communication and Control Technologies (CCCT '03) and the 9th International Conference on Information Systems Analysis and Synthesis (ISAS '03), Volume III, page 132-137.
2. Peng Ji, Junzhou Luo. "A QoS Demands Evaluation Based Classified Admission Control Algorithm", Proc. 7th International Conference on Computer Supported Cooperative Work in Design, 2003
3. Ma Teng, Junzhou Luo. "A Prediction-Based and Cost-Based Replica Replacement Algorithm Research and Simulation", Advanced Information Networking and Applications, 2005. AINA 2005. Volume: 1 page 935 - 940 ISSN: 1550-445X.
4. B. W. Lampson. "Protection", Computer Networks, 8(1):18–24, 1974.
5. X. Qian, T. Lunt. "A mac policy framework for multilevel relational databases", IEEE Transactions on Knowledge and Data Engineering, 8(1):1–14, 1996.
6. D. Ferraiolo, D. Kuhn. "Role based access control", 15th NIST-NSA National Computer Security Conference, 1992.
7. Hai Jin. "ChinaGrid: Making Grid Computing a Reality", Digital Libraries: International Collaboration and Cross-Fertilization - Lecture Notes in Computer Science, Vol.3334, Springer-Verlag, pp.13-24, 2004

A CGSP-Based Grid Application for University Digital Museums[*]

Xiaowu Chen, Xixi Luo, Zhangsheng Pan, and Qinping Zhao

The Key Laboratory of Virtual Reality Technology, Ministry of Education,
School of Computer Science and Engineering, Beihang University,
Beijing 100083, P.R. China
chen@buaa.edu.cn

Abstract. In order to effectively integrate and share the enormous dispersed resources of various digital museums, University Digital Museum Grid (UDMGrid) has been developed to provide one-stop information services about kinds of digital specimens in the form of grid services, based on ChinaGrid Support Platform (CGSP), which is a generic grid middleware serves well in various grid applications. This paper not only presents the overall architecture of CGSP-based UDMGrid, but also the ontology and its services, heterogeneous database access and integration, the logging and monitoring in UDMGrid, which are indispensable to UDMGrid, but not yet contained by CGSP, and can be easily incorporated to CGSP.

1 Introduction

There are eighteen featured university museums having already been digitized in different universities in 10 cities of China, which mainly relate to Geology & Geography, Archaeology, Humanities & Civilization, Aeronautics & Astronautics, and include 100,000 digital specimens [1]. These university digital museums play very important roles in the fields of education, scientific research, as well as digital specimen collection, preservation, exhibition, and intercommunication. However, these university digital museums dispersed on different nodes in CERNET (China Education and Research Network) lack sufficient interconnection, and only connected by web links. This brings problems on storage resource management, information resource sharing, information service quality and manner, since the information resource is isolated in so-called information island, which makes it difficult to effectively intercommunicate and share resource among digital museums.

About 3 years ago, China Ministry of Education (MoE) launched a grid computing program in China, named ChinaGrid program, aiming to provide the nationwide grid computing platform and services for education and research purpose among 100 key universities in China. The underlying common grid computing platform for ChinaGrid program is called ChinaGrid Supporting Platform (CGSP) [2]. In the first stage of ChinaGrid program, five ongoing main grid computing application platforms are under

---

[*] This paper is supported by China Education and Research Grid (ChinaGrid)(CG2003-GA004 & CG004), National 863 Program (2004AA104280), Beijing Science & Technology Program (200411A), National Research in Advance Fund (51404040305HK01015).

G. Chen et al. (Eds.): ISPA Workshops 2005, LNCS 3759 , pp. 286–296, 2005.

development, which include bioinformatics grid [3], image processing grid [4], computational fluid dynamics grid [5], course online grid [6], and massive information processing grid (MIPGrid) [7].

ChinaGrid brings new ways to solve the problems above of the dispersed university digital museum, since grid technology is good at resource sharing, information management and information service. Thus, University Digital Museum Grid (UDMGrid) [8] is proposed to using the grid technology to integrate and share the distributed digital museum information resources. UDMGrid, a typical application of MIPGrid, is an information grid, which has been developed to provide one-stop information service about kinds of digital specimens in the form of grid services. From the user's perspective, UDMGrid performs as a virtual digital museum, in which various digital specimens of all these 18 museums are preserved appropriately, and it also brings effective grid services on kinds of digital specimens in a simple and convenient way. For a simple example, users can browser the digital specimen information in multiple manners on only one UDMGrid portal instead of eighteen separate homepages, without rushing about among these digital museums. At present, UDMGrid has already involved four typical university digital museums including the Aeronautics and Astronautics Digital Museum of Beihang University (BUAA) [9], the Archaeological Digital Museum of Shandong University (SDU) [10], the Geosciences Digital Museum of Nanjing University (NJU) [11], and the Mineralogical Digital Museum of Kunming University of Science & Technology (KMUST) [12], and the based-CGSP integration of other 14 featured university museums are under way.

This paper presents the UDMGrid, which is a CGSP-based grid application for University Digital Museums. Besides the existing modules in CGSP 1.0, such as Portal, Job manger, Data manger .etc, which provide potent support for UDMGrid environment construction, there are three main indispensable specific modules including the Ontology and its services, heterogeneous database access and integration, and the logging and monitoring. These modules are indispensable to UDMGrid, but not yet contained by CGSP, and can be easily incorporated to CGSP.

The remainder of this paper is organized as follows. Section 2 discusses the overall architecture of the CGSP–based UDMGrid. In order to meet specific requirements of UDMGrid, the key research work of this paper includes the ontology and its services, heterogeneous database access and integration, and the logging and monitoring, which are being separately elaborated in section 3, 4, and 5. Section 6 shortly discusses the application workflow. Section 7 introduces a walkthrough of UDMGrid by an example. Section 8 ends this paper with conclusions and future work.

2 CGSP–Based UDMGrid Architecture

CGSP 1.0, is based on the core of Globus Toolkit 3.9.1, and is compatible with WSRF [13] and OGSA [14]. CGSP 1.0 provides both ChinaGrid service portal, and a set of development environment for deploying various grid applications. Also it provides potent support for UDMGrid as Fig.1 shows.

Portal: it is an entrance for the end user to access grid. In UDMGrid, portal provides one-stop digital specimen information services, and assists administer to monitory the grid and the status of its resources.

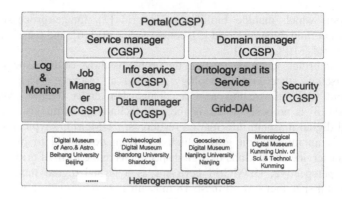

Fig. 1. The framework and function modules of CGSP–based UDMGrid

Information service: it provides a global view of grid information services, which is the foundation of job scheduling. At present, there are three kinds of grid services in UDMGrid, these services can be scheduled to combine various super services with the information provided by information service, it makes the grid services can be reused.

Data manager: in UDMGrid the information retrieved results about digital specimens are stored by Data manager, which is responsible for the management of various storage resources and data files in grid environment.

Job manager: based on information services and data management, it provides support for job management, scheduling, and monitoring for end users' computational task, so that data and resources can be accessed transparently within grid and cooperative working among distributed resources.

Domain manager: ChinaGrid is organized in domain, and each domain refers to an independent grid system to provide services to the others. UDMGrid is a typical grid system using domain method, which might be helpful to contribution statistic.

Security: In UDMGrid, users can be divided into two types, one is Administrator who is responsible for job definition and service management, the other is common user who can only submit job request and get job result.

Besides the existing modules in CGSP 1.0, the specific modules (gray parts) are indispensable to UDMGrid, but not yet contained by CGSP, and can be easily incorporated to CGSP, and have been implemented in form of web services. Through Job Manager's scheduling, these three modules can collaborate with the modules of CGSP to complete corporate tasks

Ontology and its services are used to present information resource from heterogeneous domains in a unified view, and it serves as a bridge for application to utilize digital museum resource in UDMGrid. Ontology services can make the mapping between different ontology available.

Grid-DAI (Grid Database Access and Integration) is a middleware to assist with access and integration of data from heterogeneous database sources in a grid application, and it makes the data access in a transparent way to user.

Logging and Monitoring is used to monitor real-time status of UDMGrid's resources. It can assist the administrator with performing adjusting according to logging and monitoring information.

3   Ontology and Its Services in UDMGrid

The information resources of digital museums are constructed by different domain experts, who use special metadata to describe information. The heterogeneity among these metadata brings difficulties for users to locate, organize and integrate the information resources. Therefore, shared concepts for these digital museums are indispensable.

Ontology defines a set of representational terms called concepts, among which the interrelationship describes a target world. In grid environment, Ontology becomes increasingly crucial to operations about the analysis and integration of information resources.

3.1   Ontologies in UDMGrid

There are two kinds of ontology to describe information resources of UDMGrid. One is global ontology, which can be tailored to suit the needs of users who share a common vocabulary [15]; the other is local ontology (source-specific ontology), which resides in the local resource repository. Each digital museum should publish its information with local ontology in order to support search, access and explanation. Fig.2 shows the UDMGrid ontology hierarchy structure.

Global ontology consists of generic ontology and domain-dependent ontology, which are both stored in global ontology repository. Generic ontology is information-rich and flexible, CYC [16], WordNet [17], and Sensus [18] are typical ontology of this kind, actually we choose some of them as generic ontology of digital museums; the other is domain ontology, which is more specific and professional, and requires domain expert's involvement. Just as Fig.3 shows, global ontology of UDMGrid categorizes concepts in a hierarchically structure that is divided into three layers: GO_Top, DO_Specimen, DO_Domains (The terms "GO" means generic ontology, "DO" means domain ontology). The top class is GO_Top, which contains the most generic attributes to describe an object, such as "Title", "Date" and so on; the class below is DO_Specimen, which contains the necessary attributes to describe specimens in digital museum, such as "Collection Time", "Creator" and so on; The bottom classes are DO_Domains, each attribute of which describes the specific domain's information resources, for example, "Voyage" is to describe specimens in aviation domain.

There are mainly three kinds of local ontology in UDMGrid: access metadata, database resource metadata and web resource metadata. Access metadata contains information on the location, structure, access rights and ownership of the distributed data sources; database resource metadata and web resource metadata separately describe the information of database resource and web resource, which are the main types of information resources of digital museums.

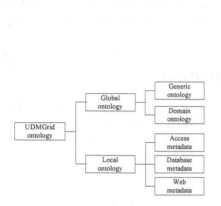

Fig. 2. UDMGrid ontology hierarchy structure

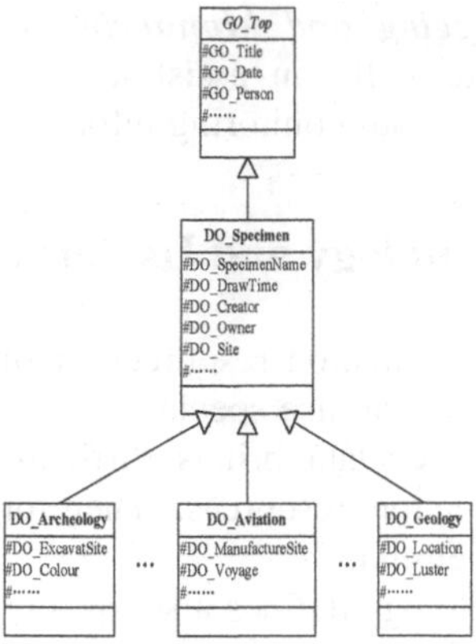

Fig. 3. UML for relationship of global ontology in UDMGrid

3.2 Ontology Services

Ontology and its services are used for information retrieval by mapping global concepts to underlying local concepts. As shown in Fig.4, users select interested terms in global ontology from portal, and then query agents construct an abstract query clause with these parameters, which is comprehensible but can not be executed on local data source. Therefore, it is required for ontology service to transform the abstract query clause to executable query clauses on relevant data source which is comprised of local ontology metadata. Then the retrieval agent can utilize the executable query clauses to collect desirable information resources.

4   Grid–DAI

Database is the main carrier of information resource in university digital museums. Therefore, to eliminate the information island among the digital museums, it is the key to access and integrate the heterogeneous database resources. Grid data access requires a flexible framework for handling data requests to a data resource that is to be integrated within a grid fabric [19]. UDMGrid introduced a solution for the database access and integration, Grid-DAI (Grid-Database Access and Integration), which is a middleware to assist with access and integration of data from heterogeneous database sources in the grid [20].

Recently the research about database (or data) access and integration is booming in grid and related application field. DAIS (Data Access and Integration Services Working Group) of GGF (Global Grid Forum) seeks to promote standards for the development of grid database services, focus principally on providing consistent access to databases [21]. OGSA-DAI (Open Grid Services Architecture Data Access and Integration) [22] provides the ability to access the separate databases and text file by the consistent web services interface.

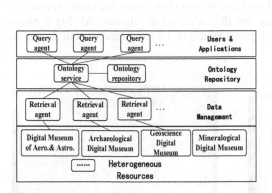

Fig. 4. The collaboration of ontology-modules in UDMGrid

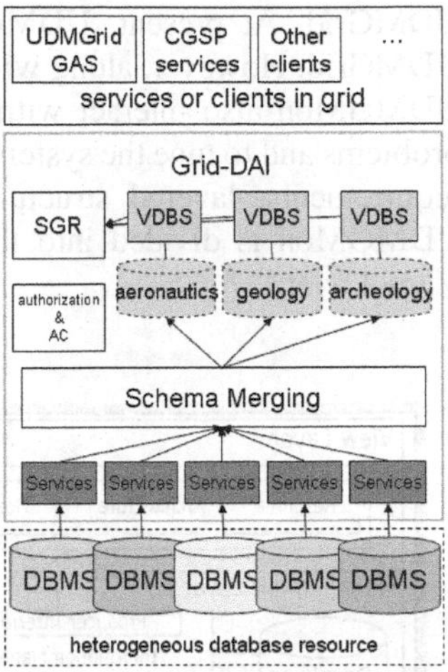

Fig. 5. Grid-DAI framework and relations with resources and application service

Compare to OGSA-DAI, the Grid-DAI not only enable accessing the data from heterogeneous database, but also merge decades of heterogeneous database into several virtual databases of special domains, such as geology, archaeology or esthetics. Thus the application services of UDMGrid can utilize the heterogeneous database resources via consistent interface and logic view.

Fig.5 describes the relations of Grid-DAI, heterogeneous database resources and application services in UDMGrid. It also illustrates the main framework of Grid-DAI: The bottom parts – DBMS are heterogeneous database resources of university digital museums, in which various database types are exists, such as MS SQL Server, Oracle, MySQL, Postgresql, DB2 and Xindice; Data access services (gray parts) provide consistent access to different databases; By schema merging, one or several databases belong to the same special domains can be integrated to one virtual database; Virtual Database Services (VDBS, blue rectangles) provide the consistent interface to access the "virtual database"; The developer of application services can query the VDBS from the Grid-DAI SGR (Service Group Registry), and then, access the virtual database which has integrated the information resource from several tangible databases via the VDBS.

5 UDMGMon: A Grid Monitoring System for UDMGrid

Monitoring module is very important for the robustness of UDMGrid. In order to provide grid resource information to UDMGrid administrators, decision support to other modules of UDMGrid, and reference for the data statistics and future construction, UDMGMon has been designed and implemented.

UDMGMon is a simple but extensible grid monitoring system, based on the Global Grid Forum's Grid Monitoring Architecture (GMA) [23], and designed especially for

UDMGrid. At present, UDMGMon is designed to interact with administrators of
UDMGrid. However, along with the development of UDMGrid, it is possible to make
UDMGMon also interact with applications to determine the source of performance
problems and to tune the system, and the like. With a view to the potential expansibility
requirements, layered structure may be the appropriate choice. As Fig.6 shows,
UDMGMon is divided into three layers: Detection Layer, Management Layer and
View Layer.

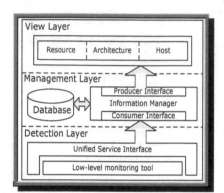   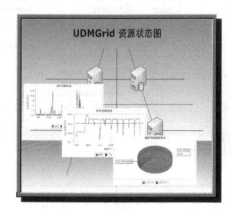

Fig. 6. The Architecture of UDMGMon   **Fig. 7.** The resource status view of UDMGrid

Detection Layer: This layer consists of several WSRF services which have unified
interfaces to upper layer. Existing low-level host or network monitoring tools, such as
SIGAR, are packaged in these services. By this means, no matter what low-level
monitoring tool is, the upper layer can acquire useful information in homogeneous
ways (that is, the different monitoring tools are transparent to information manager).
When new kinds of characteristics need monitoring, we can simply package relevant
measuring tools into a service without modifying the upper layer.

Management Layer: Information manager is the implementation of the intermediary
mentioned in GMA specification. The consumer interfaces collect data from detecting
service, use that data to generate visualized information, and then store both the raw
data and the visualized results into databases. When requests from the view browsers
come, the information manager will load visualized information and necessary raw data
from databases, and makes them available through a producer interface. In addition,
this layer maintains a dynamic list in databases to register which node is alive.

View Layer: This layer should provide three views: resource view, architecture view
and host view. The resource view tells the administrator which of the digital museum is
available at any particular time. The architecture view indicates whether the main nodes
of the grid work normally. The host view displays detail information about main nodes
of the grid including OS type, real-time CPU load, disk size, and so forth.

Two interaction modes have been implemented to transfer data between information
manager and detecting services: publish / subscribe and query / response. The query /

response interaction aims at acquiring static information whose lifetime is much longer than the detecting services' such as OS type, CPU main frequency, whereas, the publish / subscribe interaction directs at obtaining dynamic information which mainly consists of performance information (CPU load, for example). With UDMGMon, administrators can monitor real-time status of UDMGrid; moreover, they can do some performance adjusting according to information stored in databases. Fig.7 is the views' snapshot.

6 Grid Application Services

Kinds of grid application services have been designed and developed, such as AbstractSQLService, OntologyService and DoSearchService. AbstractSQLService is to form an abstract query clause based on the users' request parameters which are shown on the portal, and it is important to note that the definition of users' request parameters is according to the definition of global ontologies. OntologyService is responsible to transform the abstract query clause to a few executable ones, and during the process of transformation, OntologyService completes the mapping between global ontologies and local ontologies using the mapping information in ontology repository. The grid service DoSearchService has two functions. One is to execute these executable query clauses with the assist of Grid-DAI to get information resources stored in database, and the other function is to get information resource from webs, and both of the two functions need to transfer the retrieved result to the CGSP Portal. And some grid services can be scheduled to combine various super services with the service information provided by information center, it makes the grid services can be reused. For example, three kinds of grid services above can be combined to a kind of super services to complete a cooperative information retrieval task.

As Fig.8 shows, in the top layer is Authentication Centre, which provides authentication and authorization to the user, the bottom layer is the toolkit that provides necessary support to the development of UDMGrid. The middle layer is the core of CGSP-based UDMGrid, including the CGSP modules and UDMGrid specific modules in the form of grid services, based on which a workflow has been developed:

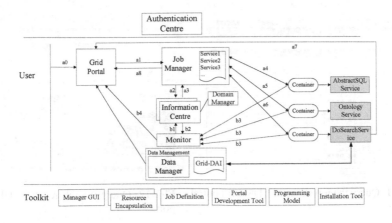

Fig. 8. The workflow of CGSP-based UDMGrid

a0. The User submits his/her request by portal.

a1. Portal packs the user's request as soap message and sends it to the Job manager module.

a2. Job manager module asks information center for services that can do the task.

a3. Information centre returns service list that can do the task. By the service list, Job manager will visit each service sequently to complete the corporate task.

a4. Job manager invokes the AbstractSQLService, and get the abstract query clause as result.

a5. Job manager invokes OntologyService, and get the executable query clauses as result.

a6. Job manager invokes DoSearchService, and get the information retrieval results.

a7. The information retrieval results are returned to the portal, and shown to the user.

7   A "Walkthrough": The UDMGrid in Operation

It's shown as follows for a user to require a grid service about the information of "horse" with the portal of UDMGrid integrating and sharing the resources of university digital museums.

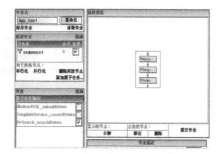

Fig. 9. Define the job in UDMGrid portal

Fig. 10. Submit the job in UDMGrid portal

Fig. 11. Query the job status in UDMGrid portal

Fig. 12. Query the job result in UDMGrid portal

In order to deal with the requirements and provide the information from various museums in the form of grid service, a job should be defined firstly. As shown in Fig.9, job defined "App_Gas1" is composed of a sequence named "sequence1" that is serialized by three grid application services including AbstractSQLService, OntologyService and AbstractSQLService. The output of the third service AbstractSQLService is chosen as the output of the whole job. Then, the job need be submitted in the UDMGrid portal, Fig.10 shows the page to fill in a form of requesting information, and "horse" is the input keyword both of the first service AbstractSQLService and of that job. Thirdly, after job is submitted to the grid, users may want to query job status from portal in order to find whether the job is finished or which step the job is processing. Fig.11 shows that now four jobs are finished and one job is running at step "3". The job results are transferred to the portal after the job is finished, and then user can browse the result from the portal. Finally, as Fig.12 shows, this job totally retrieved 1304 specimens from three digital museums except for the Mineralogical Digital Museum of Kunming University of Science & Technology, and 65 of which are from databases, 1249 from webs. In Fig.12, the left part is a picture of an aircraft named "wild horse" in the Aeronautics and Astronautics Digital Museum, and the right picture is about some 2000 years ago carriage equipments in the Archaeological Digital Museum of Shandong University. Moreover users can download the results from portal.

8 Conclusion and Future Work

In this paper, the CGSP-based UDMGrid indicates how to provide one-stop information services by incorporating the UDMGrid specified modules to CGSP. Much research and development has been done on these specific modules, which are indispensable to UDMGrid, but not yet contained by CGSP, and can be easily incorporated to CGSP. Ontology and its services are suggested to retrieve information by mapping global concepts to underlying local concepts; The Grid-DAI, a middleware, is assisting with access and integration of data from heterogeneous database sources in grid; for the robustness of UDMGrid, UDMGMon is designed and developed to monitor real-time status of UDMGrid's resources.

More and more users would like to enjoy the grid services with UDMGrid as well as the amount of digital specimens incredibly increasing, which might be coming from not only the other 14 university digital museums but also some additional digital museums in kinds of ways. Meanwhile, the security of UDMGrid needs to be improved since some digital specimens must be protected specially, and the research on the data mining technology in UDMGrid is one of the key topics of study work in the future.

Reference

[1] University Digital Museums. http://www.edu.cn/20020118/3018035.shtml.
[2] Hai Jin. ChinaGrid: Making Grid Computing a Reality. Digital Libraries: International Collaboration and   Cross-Fertilization - Lecture Notes in Computer Science, Vol.3334. Springer-Verlag, December 2004, pp.13-24.
[3] ChinaGrid Bioinformatics Grid. http://166.111.68.168/bioinfo/tools/index.jsp.

[4]   ChinaGrid Computational Fluid Dynamics (CFD) Grid. http://grid.sjtu.edu.cn:7080/grid/.

[5]   ChinaGrid Course Online Grid. http://realcourse.grids.cn.

[6]   ChinaGrid Image Processing Grid. http://grid.hust.edu.cn/ImageGrid/.

[7]   ChinaGrid Massive Information Processing Grid. http://athena.vrlab.buaa.edu.cn/gcc/.

[8]   Xiaowu Chen, Zhi Xu, Zhangsheng Pan,Xixi Luo. UDMGrid: A Grid Application for University Digital Museums. Grid and Cooperative Computing (GCC 2004), pp. 720~728, Wuhang, China, 2004.

[9]   The Digital Museum of Aeronautics and Astronautics (Beihang University, BUAA). http://digitalmuseum.buaa.edu.cn/.

[10] The Archaeological Digital Museum (Shandong University). http://museum.sdu.edu.cn/index/index.asp.

[11] The Geoscience Digital Museum (Nanjing University). http://202.119.49.29/museum/default.htm.

[12] The Mineralogical Digital Museum (Kunming Univ. of Sci. & Technol.). http://www.kmust.edu.cn/dm/index.htm.

[13] The Web Services Resource Framework. http://www.globus.org/wsrf/.

[14] Open Grid Services Architecture. http://www.ggf.org/Public_Comment_Docs/Documents/draft-ggf-ogsa-specv1.pdf.

[15] Jaime Reinoso-Castillo. Ontology-driven information extraction and integration from Heterogeneous Distributed Autonomous Data Sources. M.S. Thesis, Department of Computer Science, Iowa State University, 2002.

[16] D. B. Lenat. Cyc: A Large-scale investment in Knowledge Infrastructure. communications of the ACM, Nov 1995, pp. 33-38, Volume 38, no. 11.

[17] G. Miller. WordNet: A Lexical Database for English. In Proc. of Communications of CACM, Nov 1995.

[18] B. Swartout, R. Patil, K. Knight, and T. Ross. Toward Distributed Use of Large-Scale Ontologies. In Proc. of The Tenth Workshop on Knowledge Acquisition for Knowledge-Based Systems, Banff, Canada, 1996.

[19] Data Access and Integration Service. https://forge.gridforum.org/projects/dais-wg/.

[20] Zhangsheng Pan, Xiaowu Chen, Xiangyu Ji. Research on Database Access and Integration in UDMGrid. ISPA2005.

[21] Rob Vrablik, Melissa Hyatt. The information grid. IBM developerWorks.

[22] What is OGSA-DAI?. http://www.ogsadai.org.uk.

[23] B. Tierney, R. Aydt, D. Gunter, W. Smith, M. Swany, V. Taylor, R. Wolski. A Grid Monitoring Architecture. http://www.gridforum.org.

FleMA: A Flexible Measurement Architecture for ChinaGrid*

Weimin Zheng[1], Meizhi Hu[1], Lin Liu[1], Yongwei Wu[1], and Jing Tie[2]

[1] Department of Computer Science and Technology,
Tsinghua University, Beijing 100084, China
{zwm-dcs, wuyw}@tsinghua.edu.cn
{hmq02, 1199}@mails.tsinghua.edu.cn
[2] Internet and Cluster Computing Center, College of Computer,
Huazhong University of Science and Technology, Wuhan, 430074, China
tiejing@gmail.com

Abstract. Grid technologies are becoming more and more mature in recent years. In contrast to this trend, the resource measurement landscape in Grids looks rather dismal. As part of ChinaGrid SuperVision project, a **F**lexible **M**easurement **A**rchitecture (FleMA) for ChinaGrid is presented. In FleMA, business logic at application level is separated from the primary measurement issues at resource level to well adapt to various grid applications of ChinaGrid. A multi-level structure is exploited to generate compound metrics from raw measurements. FleMA also features open WSRF-compliant services and "plug-in" measurement pattern, making it possible to achieve and deploy advanced functions synchronously on top of the unique measurement substrate.

1 Introduction

Grid computing devotes to integrate miscellaneous distributed heterogeneous resources into a super coordinated aggregation to supply universal and transparent services. Recently both scientific and business communities are beginning to regard Grids as problem solving mechanisms [1].

Numerous infrastructure and software projects are being undertaken to realize various visions of Grids, of which ChinaGrid [2] is an ongoing one. Founded by the Ministry of Education of China, ChinaGrid project aims to provide the nationwide grid computing platform and services for research and education purpose among 100 key universities in China. The underlying common grid computing platform for ChinaGrid named ChinaGrid Supporting Platform (CGSP) is developed for the ambitious goal. By offering a whole set of tools for developing and deploying various grid components, such as Grid development toolkits, Job Manager, Information Service etc., CGSP integrates all kinds of resources in education and research environments, makes the heterogeneous and dynamic nature of resource transparent to the users. More information about ChinaGrid and CGSP can refer to [2, 3].

---

* This work is supported by ChinaGrid project of Ministry of Education of China, Natural Science Foundation of China under Grant 60373004, 60373005, 90412006, 90412011, and Nation Key Basic Research Project of China under Grant 2004CB318000.

G. Chen et al. (Eds.): ISPA Workshops 2005, LNCS 3759, pp. 297–304, 2005.

Grids are highly complicated distributed system. In order to better serve end users, most grid middleware manage to hide the underlying complicated implementation specification, which is appreciated when everything runs correctly. However, this advantage turns trouble when something behaves wrongly or awkwardly. Therefore, monitoring is essential for understanding their operation, failure detection and for performance optimization. Although several grid monitoring solutions have been proposed, such as MDS [7], R-GMA [6], Mercury [9], etc., they shared few common agreements, and poor interoperability is achieved.

ChinaGrid SuperVision (CGSV) is the right program launched to handle monitoring-related issues for ChinaGrid. CGSV utilizes WSRF [4] and WSDM [5] to keep in accordance with the latest efforts in grid community. Both measurement and control functionalities are intended in the roadmap of CGSV, and the former is the first attempt to satisfy the requirements from ChinaGrid community at current stage.

FleMA is the measurement framework designed for the implementation of CGSV. It can be well adaptive to various grid applications over ChinaGrid. In FleMA, application business logic is separated from the primary measurement issues at resource level. It features open WSRF-compliant services, flexible multi-level structure and "plug-in" measurement pattern. All open functionalities of components are XML-format remarked and implemented WSRF-compliant, which makes it interoperable with other monitoring facilities conveniently. The multi-level layout of diverse components is exploited to generate compound metrics from raw measurements. With "plug-in" pattern, special issues like measurement policy and event dissemination scheme can be customized and inserted dynamically. Multiple measurement policies work independently for different occasions may coexist at resource level. Furthermore, the flow and process model of performance data can also be tailored. These characters would be depicted elaborately in Sect. 2.2.

The remainder of this paper is organized as follows. The overview of FleMA is brought forward in Section 2.1. And primary software building blocks and crucial characteristics are covered in Section 2.2. Numbers of representative use cases of FleMA in ChinaGrid community are shown in Section 3. Section 4 examined related work and current status briefly, and Section 5 concludes the paper.

2 Architecture

2.1 Overview

FleMA aims not only to satisfy the special measurement requirements of ChinaGrid, but to provide a more general measurement framework for grid computing. Figure 1 pictures the vertical structure of FleMA, which is separated into two groups:

- Resource-focus: It comprises Sensor, Adapter, Monitor Service and Message Service. **Sensor**s are the actual entities collecting performance data of resources. Third-party monitoring tools could be connected in the manner of **Adapter**s. **Monitor Service** manages local deployed sensors/adapters and exports uniform WSRF-compliant services. **Message Service** is used to record local history information at resource level and disseminate events accurately from local to remote consumers subscribe topics to fulfill publish/subscribe semantics.

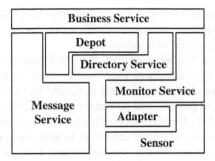

Fig. 1. Application Construction Structure of FleMA

- Application-focus: Directory Service, Depot and Business Service belong to this group. In an application scenario, **Directory Service** is somewhere well-known to publish and query information; **Depot** is similar to Message Service in information storage whereas distinguishes itself by business-logic oriented instead; **Business Service** here refers to business modules developed by application developers.

By orchestrating above components ingeniously, complex multi-level structures and advanced functions might be achieved in actual scenarios. These will be exemplified with several use cases in Sect. 3.

2.2 Software Building Blocks

In this section not all components shown in figure 1 are described. Sensor and Adapter act the same with corresponding peers in many other monitoring systems, while Directory Service achieves equal functions as GMA proposed, and Business Service itself is beyond FleMA in a sense. Therefore, to address the characteristics of FleMA only left three components are covered: Monitor Service, Message Service, and Depot. Figure 2 shows their software building blocks respectively.

Monitor Service. Monitor Service acts as the "producer" defined in GMA and therefore, is responsible for publishing all local monitoring metrics to public-known. It is implemented as a set of WSRF-compliant services. Consumers can make their own policies on measurement issues, such as "notify when CPU_LOAD is greater than 50 percent", "stop collecting free memory", "change the probing frequency of network throughout to 15 times slower than the previous", etc. Based on that, an interesting peculiarity of Monitor Service is: it maintains so-called "*personal measurement policy session*" for individual respectively, which means the policies made by a consumer would be effective until the next modification. Furthermore, it is desired that local deployed physical measurement facility would serve different logic upper applications. To achieve the ambitious goals, three correlative modules are designed:

- *Sensor Environment.* It manages local deployed sensors and/or adapters. Two parts are comprised: *Sensor/Adapter management* and *Actuate Trigger*. The former keeps the membership of measurement sensors/adapters through a soft-state mechanism. The latter is responsible to modify the basic action properties of sensors/adapters, such as setting "on/off" attributes of metrics, changing the minimal measurement unit of a metric, etc.

- *Measurement Policy Management.* All "personal measurement policy sessions" are maintained here. Consumers may modify their measurement policies dynamically at runtime. Isolation mechanism should be exploited to keep the independence of different policies and ensure them not to influence each other.
- *Restriction Control.* In FleMA, access restriction verification is the first step in handling requests. Only when the consumer is turned out to have corresponding restrictions, the execution would continue. Such kind of access control seems preferable when a resource plays different roles in multiple independent VOs use the unique monitoring facility local deployed.

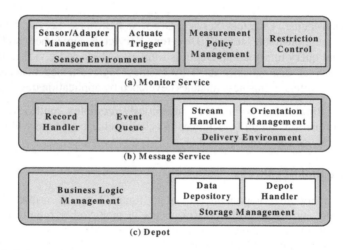

Fig. 2. Software Building Blocks of Monitor Service, Message Service and Depot

Message Service. It also follows WSRF and is designed to fulfill two purposes: One is to record performance data collected by local sensors/adapters with specified precisions; the other is to deliver topic events accurately to remote consumers subscribe topics subscribers, acting as an event dissemination proxy. (As proposed by GMA, metric measurements are denoted as events.) In the case of mass subscriptions originated from numbers of consumers, this is a promising effort to shift notification costs from usual system load. It consists of:

- *Event Queue.* Events, no matter to be recorded, disseminated, or discarded, are all sent to Event Queue. The speed difference between event arrival and event disposal might be fine-tuned by means of queues.
- *Record handler.* This module takes charge in the event storage at resource level, which intends to keep local meaningful performance data ignorant of upper special applications. It is from Event Queue that Record Handler picks correct events to deal with. Access interfaces like history events retrieval, deletion are open to users.

- *Delivery Environment*. The "stream" approach whose orientation is decided at runtime is used to distribute events to multiple consumers. Events to different consumers are picked from Record handler or Event Queue and organized in some order so that a balanced network cost and efficiency could be achieved. Two parts are involved: *Stream Handler* and *Orientation Management*. Orientation Management examines all measurement policies kept in Monitor Service to makes suitable stream directions. There may come out several stream directions at one time, to each of which Stream Handler will fork a process to operate on.

Depot. This component shares some similarities with Message Service in information storage, but focuses on application-level business issues, such as application-related performance data process over raw events. It implies Depot targets a special business while Message Service works at physical level to serve numbers of businesses. It comprises:

- *Business Logic Management*. It is used to manage all data process principles, such as application-specific aggregation and filter.
- *Storage Management*. Useful data process results under the contents in Business Logic Management are preserved by this module. Two parts are contained: Data Repository is the place to store results actually and Depot Handler is the real entity to perform the business logic on raw input data and store the results in Data Repository with certain formats.

3   Use Case

In ChinaGrid, a resource aggregation may supplying transparent services independently is termed as a domain, an alias of VO in a sense. Different domains might cover common physical resources. Every domain is conceived to be deployed with all CGSP components to make it independent from others.

CGSV is launched as the monitoring system of ChinaGrid. In its first stage, visualization and accounting storage utilities are intended besides the basic measurement facilities. Visualization aims to reveal current states and brief history information of resources; Accounting utilities mainly are prepared for the coming accounting program of ChinaGrid. Each of them all needs performance data of grid entities, consequently, considered as the application visions of FleMA.

3.1 Visualization

This application aims at friendly user interfaces and underlying supporting visualization-storage utilities. Visualization deployment follows the same philosophy of CGSP. Figure 3 is an example scenario of visualization based on FleMA, involving two domains with one common resource (Sensors/Adapters are omitted for brief).

As shown in figure 3, components in the resource-focus group of FleMA are uniquely deployed on every resource physically; while atop of them multiple visualizations are developed. Base on Message Service, different Depots configured with different business logic may retrieve right performance data independently. For instance, the Depot of Domain A only retrieve memory information of all resources, while in Domain B, the Depots are supposed to get CPU information of all resources and disk information of certain resources. It is Monitor Service that ensures the separation at physical level of different measurement roles of local resource in different domains. In each domain, there might be multiple-level layouts of Depots or Directory Services, making it convenient to generate compound metrics, e.g. the average CPU load of all resources.

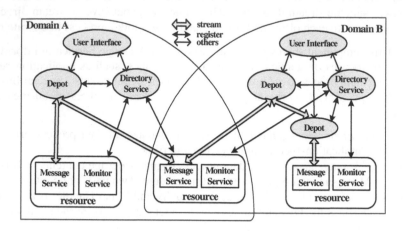

Fig. 3. An Example Scenario of Visualization

3.2 Accounting Storage Utilities

In our current consideration, resource usages of grid jobs are key items to be recorded. According to the design philosophy of CGSP [3], computational tasks are scheduled and managed by Job Manager deployed in a domain. Therefore, a special kind of monitor services is conceived to fetch the job information from CGSP components. For discrimination we call it CGSP Monitor Service.

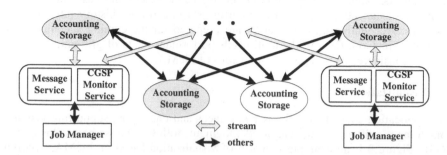

Fig. 4. An Example Scenario of Accounting Storage

Although there are various accounting fashions, only two primary cases are considered at present: application-domain and geographic-domain. The former can cross geographic domains and the latter may cover several application ones. Also it is imaginable that an application domain comprises common resources with a geographic one. The business logic of accounting storage mainly involves user identity, resource identity, domain identity, resource usage of jobs submitted to this domain's Job Manager, etc. Figure 4 gives an example scenario of accounting storage, in which gray-colored and colorless ellipses correspond to accounting storage utilities of application domain and geographic domain, or vice versa.

4 Related Work and Current Status

Resource monitoring is not new. There have been a number of research and commercial efforts, such as Ganglia [12], Log4J, etc. These range from source codes instruments to measurements of system information, and can be well integrated into grid monitoring frameworks. Several existing solutions are available for grid monitoring, e.g. MDS [7], NWS [8], R-GMA [6], Mercury [9], SCALEA-G [13], etc. Compared to these solutions, FleMA mainly differs itself in separating business logic from primary measurement issues at resource level. FleMA shares common ideas with JMS [10] and WSN [11] in message/notification mechanism, but distinguishes in that the dissemination orientation is customized dynamically and content-sensitive.

FleMA is the measurement architecture of the ongoing CGSV project. Currently, a suit of sensors whose behavior attributes can be tuned have been developed for general system information collection. The adapter to Ganglia is under construction. Monitor Service and Message Service are nearly finished, with the limitation of free access for any user to any metrics. However, Measurement Policy Management and Delivery Environment should be further revised. As for Directory Service and Depot, MDS4 and relational database technologies are being surveyed for them.

5 Conclusion

In this paper a **Fle**xible **M**easurement **A**rchitecture (FleMA) for ChinaGrid is presented. To adapt to various grid applications over ChinaGrid, the business logic at application level is separated from the primary resource-level measurement issues. The architecture is discussed in detail as well as application visions in ChinaGrid. Key features include open WSRF-compliant services, multi-level structure, plug-in measurement pattern, etc. FleMA makes it possible to achieve and deploy diverse advanced functions synchronously on top of the unique measurement substrate.

So far, FleMA focuses on the measurement of grid entities and the ability to satisfy requirements from ChinaGrid community of current stage. In the future, universal control of grid entities is one of the most important new functions. Another extension is to strengthen the support to diverse upper application-level frameworks, e.g. accounting service, performance forecast, system management automation, etc.

References

1. Ian Foster, Carl Kesselman. The Grid 2: Blueprint for a New Computing Infrastructure. San Francisco: Morgan Kaufmann Publishers Inc., 2003
2. ChinaGrid project, http://www.chinagrid.edu.cn

3. Hai Jin, ChinaGrid: Making Grid Computing a Reality. International Conference on Asian Digital Libraries ICADL 2004: 13-24
4. Web Services Resource Framework (WSRF). http://www.oasis-open.org/committees/tc_home.php?wg_abbrev=wsrf
5. Web Services Distributed Management (WSDM). http://www.oasis-open.org/committees/tc_home.php?wg_abbrev=wsdm
6. R-GMA: Relational Grid Monitoring Architecture. http://www.r-gma.org
7. MDS: Monitoring and Discovery System. http://www.globus.org/mds/
8. R. Wolski, N. Spring, and J. Hayes. The Network Weather Service: A Distributed Resource Performance Forecasting Service for Metacomputing. Future Generation Computing Systems, 15:757-768, 1999
9. Mercury Monitor. http://www.gridlab.org/WorkPackages/wp-11/
10. Java Message Service (JMS). http://java.sun.com/products/jms/
11. Web Service Notification (WSN). http://www.oasis-open.org/committees/tc_home.php?wg_abbrev=wsn
12. Matthew L. Massie, Brent N. Chun, and David E. Culler. The Ganglia Distributed Monitoring System: Design, Implementation, and Experience. Parallel Computing, Vol. 30, Issue 7, July 2004
13. Hong-Linh Truong, Thomas Fahringer, SCALEA-G: A Unified Monitoring and Performance Analysis System for the Grid. Scientific Programming, 12(4):225-237, IOS Press, 2004

A Resource Scheduling Strategy for the CFD Application on the Grid

Minglu Li, Chuliang Weng, Xinda Lu, Yong Yin, and Qianni Deng

Department of Computer Science and Engineering,
Shanghai Jiao Tong University, Shanghai 200030, China
{li-ml, weng-cl}@cs.sjtu.edu.cn

Abstract. In this paper, we focus on the scheduling issue for one kind of high performance computing applications, that is, computational fluid dynamics applications. Firstly, we focus on studying the characteristic of the CFD applications, and model this kind of applications that can be decomposed into multiple sub-jobs (tasks), which evolve to be represented by a DAG. Then, a hierarchical infrastructure for resource organization in the computational grid environment is proposed. Thirdly, we discuss the scheduling strategy in the presented scenario, and propose a task scheduling framework and analyze a corresponding algorithm with simulation experiments. Finally, we discuss the implementation with the related project.

1 Introduction

Computational Grid [1] provide a potential and promising platform for Computational Fluid Dynamics (CFD) applications. With the grid technology, the integration of computational resources belonging to the different organization becomes practical. However, one pending problem is how to organize and schedule the distributed, heterogeneous computational resources, meanwhile, the characteristic of the specific high performance application should be considered.

Considering the characteristic of WAN (wide area network), it is not suitable to schedule jobs among different distributed resource control domains, which need frequent communication with each other. There are different kinds of computers in a computational grid, and the variety includes different computation architectures, different operating systems and different compile environments, etc. Furthermore, some scientific computing problems need specific scientific and engineering library, which is owned by the specified resource control domain.

So we argue that the computational grid is suitable for one kind of the scientific computing problem that can be divided into multiple sub-problems, which can be solved through these distributed scientific and engineering softwares with the small communication frequency. Correspondingly, we assume that a series of sub-problems derived from one large-scale CFD application could be solved as sub-jobs in parallel by deploying them to the grid context. Meanwhile, the dependence among these sub-jobs should be considered.

G. Chen et al. (Eds.): ISPA Workshops 2005, LNCS 3759, pp. 305–314, 2005.

In this paper, we focus on the scheduling issue for large-scale CFD applications on the grid, and propose a scheduling strategy, and refer to its implementation.

2   Related Works

There are some research efforts on building grid platforms for CFD applications. The FlowGrid system [2] allows Computational Fluid Dynamics (CFD) simulations to be executed in Grid environments, and users can observe online the progress of their simulations by looking at intermediate results. The Cambridge CFD Grid [3] is a distributed problem-solving environment for large-scale CFD applications set up between the Cambridge eScience Centre and the CFD Laboratory in the Engineering Department at the University of Cambridge. Our previous work, Genetic Optimized Algorithm Grid System [4] focuses on the aircraft geometry designing, such as the controlling and monitoring over the designing progress and the cooperation for multi-designers around the world. In addition, there are some research efforts on scheduling algorithms in the grid environment. An extended version of Sufferage [5], Qsufferage is presented to schedule tasks in grid environments [6], which is a semi-online algorithm for scheduling tasks in combination with QoS.

The background of this research is ChinaGrid project [7], founded by Ministry of Education of China. ChinaGrid project is a scientific attempt to achieve the goals of constructing a virtual single image of heterogeneous, distributed, and dynamic computational resources, and providing a uniform application interface, by exploring various resources on the existing internet infrastructure, CERNET (China Education and Research Network).

3   The CFD Application Model

Firstly, let consider an example, that is, the integration simulation of the aircraft [8]. The simulation can be decomposed into multiple sub-jobs according to the principle of function decomposition, such as one input module, one airframe computing module, two aerofoil computing modules, one vertical tail computing module, and one tail plane computing module. For improving the computing performance, two different modules can be executed in parallel if no data dependence exists between two modules. This is an effective method in the parallel computing.

Similarly, a series of sub-jobs derived from one large-scale CFD application could also be solved in parallel by deploying them to the grid context. However, these sub-jobs are generally dependent on each other, and we assume that the dependence among the solving of these sub-jobs derived from the same CFD application, is that the output of one sub-job is the input of the other sub-job. Solving a large-scale CFD application can be represented by a set of computational tasks, which execute these sub-jobs derived from the large-scale CFD application.

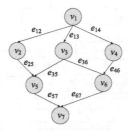

Fig. 1. The task graph

In the following, we adopt the term "task" to represent the sub-job derived from one CFD application, which is executed respectively on the distributed resource as the corresponding specific computational application instance in the computational grid.

Formally, these derived tasks can be organized using a directed acyclic graph (DAG), $G = (V, E)$, illustrated as Fig. 1. The set of vertices $V = \{v_1, v_2, ..., v_n\}$ represents of the tasks to be executed for solving the corresponding sub-jobs, and the set of weighted, directed edges E represents communication between tasks, which can be divided into two classes, one class represents transferring the large data file and the other class is the message for transferring parameters. $e_{ij} = (v_i, v_j) \in E$ indicates communication from task v_i to v_j, and $|e_{ij}|$ represents the volume of data sent between the two tasks.

4   Hierarchical Infrastructure

In this section, we discuss the resource organization infrastructure for the CFD application on the grid, which is based on the concept of service. For facilitating the application scheduling in the grid context, there are three components in the middleware infrastructure, illustrated as Fig. 2. We will discuss the three parts as follows, respectively.

4.1   Grid Portal

One component is the grid portal, by which the end users can easily query the service information such as computing power, scientific and engineering library, system load, etc., and initialize the parameters, invoke the computational service, monitor the intermedian computational result, and download the final computational result, and so on. Grid portals provide the well-suited interface for grid end users to co-schedule the large-scale application on the grid system.

Generally, end users use a simple graphical or Web interface to supply application specific parameters and simple execution configuration data. Many engineering experiences show that end users are best served by grid portals, which are web servers that allow users to configure or run a class of applications. The server is then given the task of authenticating the user with the grid and invoking the needed web services required to launch the user's applications.

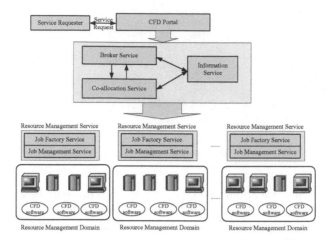

Fig. 2. The hierarchical infrastructure

4.2   Global Resource Management

After the customized request of end users sent to the global middleware that implements the global resource management (or control) and scheduling in the grid environment, it will be analyzed and decomposed in accordance with the characteristic of the request. In this paper, we assume that solving a large-scale CFD problem requested by the end user can be decomposed into a set of sub-jobs that are dependable on each other.

One component of the global middleware is the broker service, which resolves the request outputted by the grid portal and adopts different decomposition strategies for different problems. The decomposition strategy is dependent on the specific CFD application type. As described above, a large-scale application can be decomposed and evolved into a series of sub-jobs, which illustrated as a DAG. It is the co-allocation service that retrieves the real-time information of computational services from the information service, and decides how to assign the multiple computational tasks to distributed computational services with effective scheduling strategies.

4.3   Local Resource Management

As solving a CFD application can be decomposed into multiple sub-jobs, the sub-jobs can be solved across distributed computational resources with the benefit of the grid computing. There are two kinds of services to manage the local computational resources. One kind is the job factory service, and the other is the job management service.

The job factory service is responsible for creating the service instance for the CFD sub-job request, and allocating the corresponding computational resource, including hardware computing resources and the appropriate softwares or engineering libraries. Also it provides the local resource information to the outside, including the hardware information such as the computer architecture, and the software information such as the computational software package and library.

The job management service is responsible for managing the created service instances, and forms the *resource-service pair* (hereafter referred to as RS) based on the determined computational hardware and software resources for the specific request, which may be implemented according to WSRF [9]. Also it provides the intermedial status of running jobs to the outside.

4.4 Computational Fluid Dynamics (CFD) Grid Application Platform

According to the above principle of the hierarchical infrastructure, we have implemented Computational Fluid Dynamics (CFD) Grid Application Platform [10], which is based on ChinaGrid General Support Platform (CGSP) [11] and integrates different CFD applications from distributed organizations with the different engineering background in a grid context.

In the CFD platform, there are varied computational resources, including hardware resources and software resources, distributed in the individual resource control domains. It is the local resource management component that encapsulates the physical resources into virtual CFD services, which can correspondingly solve the one kind of CFD applications or one kind of sub-jobs derived from a CFD application. The global resource management component provides the broker services, information services and co-allocation services. The part touched by the end users is the CFD grid portal, through which users can submit the specific request, upload the initialization data, observe the intermedian processing status, download the final result, etc.

5   Scheduling Strategy

In this section, we focus on the scheduling strategy for CFD applications on the grid, which consists of the scheduling framework and the scheduling algorithm.

5.1   Task Scheduling Framework

Generally, the CFD problems discussed in the paper are computation-intensive rather than communication-intensive, so each specific software package is limited to execute one copy on one computer at a time. Correspondingly, the RS (the resource-service pair, section 4.3) modelling one specific CFD function component only executes one task at a time.

A CFD grid can be defined as a number of RS distributed in different resource control domains, where one RS consists of one kind of CFD software package and the specific hardware resource. One RS can solve one kind of sub-jobs derived from the CFD application. Formally, $R = \{R_1, R_2, ..., R_m\}$ denotes the set of the resource-service pairs. The cost function $C : V \times R \rightarrow \mathbf{R}$, represents the cost of each task executing on each available RS. The cost of executing task v_i on

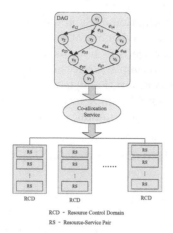

Fig. 3. The scheduling framework

resource-service pair R_j can be denoted by $C(v_i, R_j)$. For a particular task that cannot be executed on a RS, the function value will be infinity.

Based on the above assumption, a task scheduling framework for the CFD application on the grid is proposed as Fig. 3. The problem to be solved is how to assign tasks in a DAG to multiple available RS belonging to different resource control domains, so the next section will focus on this issue.

5.2   Scheduling Algorithm

For scheduling tasks of one large-scale CFD application effectively, we extend the DLS (Dynamic Level Scheduling) algorithm [12] to the grid context, and present a modified DLS algorithm, which will be described in details as follows.

Similar to the list scheduling algorithm, the DLS algorithm operates by assigning a priority to each task in the task graph, which is called as a level. The priority is used to choose among the set of tasks, which are ready to be scheduled at that time. The DLS algorithm differs from previous algorithms in that the level of a task depends upon the tasks that have already been assigned, and the dynamic level, denoted by $DL(v_i, R_j, \sum(t))$, reflects how well task v_i and the resource-service pair R_j are matched at state $\sum(t)$, where $\sum(t)$ encompasses both the state of the resource-service pair and the state of the communication resources at time t.

However, one task can only be scheduled to some specific resource-service pairs in the grid context, which is different from the situation where a majority of tasks can be scheduled to all processors in paper [12]. The value of a majority of DLs in the grid scenario is negative infinite, and cannot be solved even with the "generalized" dynamic level. So the definition of the modified dynamic level is proposed as follows.

$$MDL(v_i, R_{j|j \in A(v_i)}, \sum(t)) = SL(v_i) - \max(t_d(v_i, R_j), t_a(R_j)) + \Delta(v_i, R_j) \quad (1)$$

Where, $A(v_i)$ denotes the set of the available resource-service pairs that can execute task v_i. And $SL(v_i)$ is defined as the largest sum of execution times along any available directed path from v_i to the end of the graph. $t_d(v_i, R_j)$ denotes the earliest time that all data required by task v_i is available at the resource-service pair R_j at state $\sum(t)$, and $t_a(R_j)$ denotes the time at which R_j will be idle. $\Delta(v_i, R_j) = \bar{C}(v_i) - C(v_i, R_j)$, where $\bar{C}(v_i)$ denotes the median execution time of a task over all available resource-service pairs.

Assigning tasks in a DAG is to find out the ready task and the idle resource-service pair, in order to maximize the value of MDL. The detailed algorithm is shown as Table 1.

Table 1. The scheduling algorithm

---

1. Retrieve the real-time information about available resource-service pairs $\{R_j\}$;
2. Determine the ready tasks $\{v_i\}$ in the DAG;
3. Calculate the $MDL(v_i, R_{j|j \in A(v_i)}, \sum(t))$;
4. Determine the resource-service pair R_J and the task v_I, for maximizing the MDL;
5. Assign v_I to R_J;
6. Wait for the next scheduling event, and repeat the procedure.

5.3 Experiment

In the discribed scenario, one sub-job derived from a CFD application cannot execute as a task on each RS in the grid context. For testing the feasibility of the presented scheduling algorithm, we perform a series of simulation experiments with a customized, event-based simulator, in order to analyze the impact of resource usability ratio on the scheduling performance.

Firstly, we define the resource usability ratio r as the number of available resource-service pairs for one task divided by the total of all resource-service pairs in the system, that is, $r = m_a/m$, where m_a denotes the number of available resource-service pairs for one task, and m denotes the total of all resource-service pairs in the grid.

Our scheduling goal is to minimize the makespan, that is, the scheduling length for a large-scale CFD application. Through experiments, we will examine the impact of the resource usability ratio r on the performance of the presented algorithm, and estimate the feasibility of the proposed strategy.

There are two experiments with different parameters as follows, and the experimental results are shown as Fig. 4.

- Experiment 1. $m = 8$. One large-scale CFD application can be decomposed into 32 sub-jobs (tasks). The size of tasks is uniformly distributed in the range [1000, 5000], and the communication volume between tasks is uniformly distributed in the range [0, 500]. The processing capability of resource-service pairs is uniformly distributed in the range [100, 500], and the communication speed is uniformly distributed in the range [10, 50]. The experimental result is the average value of the 1000 simulation runs, where one task can be executed randomly on relative resource-service pairs according to the value of the resource usability ratio r.

– Experiment 2. $m = 12$, and the size of tasks is uniformly distributed in the range [10000, 50000]. The other parameters are the same with Experiment 1.

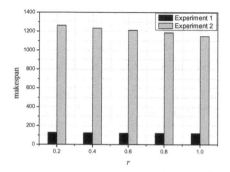

Fig. 4. The result of experiments

According to the Fig. 4, we can find that the makespan of one CFD application does not increase very quickly as the value of the resource usability ratio r decreases. That is to say, even if the fact that sub-jobs derived from one CFD application cannot be solved on each resource-service pair exists, the proposed strategy for assigning CFD tasks on the grid can also operate effectively. And it indicates that the dependence between different tasks in a DAG has more significant impact on the makespan. So the grid platform is also an effective way as previous parallel computing for improving the performance of high performance computing applications, except that the computing granularity is different between the two computing modes.

6   Implementation

In this section, we will give a brief profile of Computational Fluid Dynamics (CFD) Grid Application Platform [10], which is developed by us.

The CFD Grid Application Platform is one important part of the ChinaGrid Grid Platform, and provides an infrastructure to integrate different CFD applications across distributed CFD resource control domains into a virtual single image. Through its portal shown as Fig. 5, end users can easily access distributed and heterogenous CFD resources.

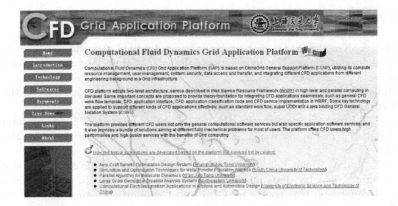

Fig. 5. The portal of the CFD Grid Application Platform

Currently, five typical applications are built based on the platform, which include Aerocraft Genetic Optimization Design System, Simulation and Optimization Techniques for Metal Powder Figuration Processing, Parallel Algorithm for Molecular Dynamics, Large Scale Geological Disaster Analysis System and Computational Electromagnetism Applications in Airplane and Automobile Design.

7   Conclusion

In this paper, we focus on resource scheduling for the CFD application on the grid. For analyzing the scheduling issue in the grid context, we firstly model the CFD application. Then a hierarchical infrastructure is proposed and the implementation in the CFD Grid Application Platform is discussed. Based on the application model and the resource organization means, we propose a scheduling strategy for the CFD application in the computational grid environment. Experimental results validate the effectivity of the presented strategy. At last, we refer to Computational Fluid Dynamics (CFD) Grid Application Platform, which is developed by us.

Acknowledgements

This research was supported by the ChinaGrid Program of MOE of China, the National 863 Program of China (No.2004AA104340 and No.2004AA104280), the grand project (No.03dz15027) of the Science and Technology Commission of Shanghai Municipality, and the National Natural Science Foundation of China (No. 60173031 and No. 60473092).

References

1. Foster, I., Kesselman, C., Tuecke, S.: The anatomy of the grid: enabling scalable virtual organizations. The International Journal of High Performance Computing Applications **15** (2001) 200–222
2. Wendler, J., Schintke, F.: Executing and observing CFD applications on the Grid. Future Generation Computer Systems **21** (2005) 11–18
3. Yang, X., Hayes, M., Jenkins, K., Cant, S.: The Cambridge CFD grid for large-scale distributed CFD applications. Future Generation Computer Systems **21** (2005) 45–51
4. Sun, X., Lu, X., Deng, Q.: The implementation of the genetic optimized algorithm of air craft geometry designing based on grid computing. In: Proceedings of The 2nd International Conference on Grid and Cooperative Computing(GCC 2003). Volume 3032 of LNCS. (2003) 164 – 167
5. Bartal, Y., Fiat, A., Karloff, H., Vohra, R.: New algorithms for an ancient scheduling problem. Journal of Computer and System Science **51** (1995) 359–366
6. Weng, C., Lu, X.: Heuristic scheduling for bag-of-tasks applications in combination with QoS in the computational grid. Future Generation Computer Systems **21** (2005) 271–280
7. Jin, H.: ChinaGrid: Making grid computing a reality. In: Digital Libraries: International Collaboration and Cross-Fertilization. Volume 3334 of LNCS. (2004) 13–24
8. Sun, J., Zhang, L., Chi, X., Wang, D.: Network Paralel Computing and Distributed Programming Environement (Chinese). Science Press, Beijing, China (1996)
9. Czajkowski, K., Ferguson, D., Foster, I., Frey, J., Graham, S., Sedukhin, I., Snelling, D., Tuecke, S., Vambenepe, W.: The WS-Resource Framework. http://www-106.ibm.com/developerworks/library/wsresource/ws-wsrf.pdf (2004)
10. ChinaGrid Project: (The CFD Grid Application Platform) http://grid.sjtu.edu.cn:7080/grid/.
11. ChinaGrid Project: (ChinaGrid General Support Platform) http://www.chinagrid.edu.cn/CGSP/index.jsp.
12. Sih, G., Lee, E.: A compile-time scheduling heuristic for interconnection-constrained heterogeneous processor architectures. IEEE Transactions on Parallel and Distributed Systems **4** (1993) 175–187

A Robust Coalition-Resistant Threshold Signature Scheme with Anonymous Signers

Ming-wen Wang, Qing-xin Zhu, and Li Qing

School of Computer Science and Engineering, UEST of China, Chengdu, 610054, China
sohuwmw@sohu.com, qxzhu@uestc.edu.cn, qingli_new@163.com

Abstract. In this paper we present a novel robust coalition-resistant (t, n) threshold signature scheme with anonymous signers. Only t or more group members can generate signatures on behalf of a group with n members, while any t-1 or fewer members cannot do the same thing. We construct the scheme based on a modified RSA digital signature scheme and Shamir's secret sharing scheme. The signature process consists of four phases: system setup, individual signature generation and verification, sign and verify. The designated signature combiner can verify the partial signature from the auxiliary value of the partial signature, and the scheme can resist the coalition attack from more than t malicious group members due to the use of shadow partial signature. Compared with the existing threshold signature schemes, the scheme is robust and secure, and convenient to implement.

Keywords: threshold scheme, group scheme, digital signature, coalition attack, robust scheme.

1 Introduction

Along with the rapid developments of telecommunication and computer network, the security problem seems to be more and more important. Digital signature techniques, which allow transferring message and user identity authentication, begin to play a very important role in the network communication. In addition to the ordinary digital signature scheme, a lot of special signature schemes have been proposed in the past years. Threshold signature is one of them, in which only t or more group members can generate signatures on behalf of a group with n members, while any $t-1$ or less members cannot do the same thing. On the other hand, anyone can use a group public key to verify the group signature. This kind of signature schemes has many potential applications such as decision-making, e-voting et al.

Desmedt firstly introduced the concept of group-oriented cryptography in 1987 [1]. According to whether a verifier can trace back the signers of a threshold signature, there are two kinds of threshold signature schemes: with anonymous signers and with traceable signers. In the case with anonymous signers, nobody can reveal the identities of the detailed signers. In 1991, Desmedt and Frankel proposed the first threshold digital signature scheme based on RSA system [2]. Inspiring by Desmedt et al's initial work, a lot of research has been done on the threshold signature. Harn constructed two group-oriented (t,n) threshold digital signature schemes in [4], one needs the

G. Chen et al. (Eds.): ISPA Workshops 2005, LNCS 3759, pp. 315–322, 2005.
© Springer-Verlag Berlin Heidelberg 2005

mutually trusted center and the other needs not. However, Li et al. pointed out that above schemes [2, 4] cannot resist coalition-attack and the secret parameters can be revealed with high probability [5]. In order to trace the signers, Wang et al. proposed two (t,n) threshold digital signature schemes in 1998 [11]. Unfortunately, their schemes are insecure under a forgery attack [9]. To overcome the weakness of previous threshold digital signature schemes, Li et al. proposed two group-oriented (t,n) threshold digital signature schemes with traceable signers in [6]. One of their schemes needs the assistance of a mutually trusted center, while the other does not. In 2003, Wang et al. show that Li et al's schemes are actually untraceable. They also demonstrate an attack to show that their second threshold signature scheme is insecure [10]. In 2000, Shoup [8] has also presented a (k,l) threshold signature scheme with t' corrupted players, but the scheme has the requirements that $k \geq t'+1$ and $l-t' \geq k$.

Based on a modified RSA signature scheme, Xu presented a (t,n) threshold signature scheme with anonymous signers in [13]. Xu's scheme circumvents the problem of calculating inverses when $\varphi(N)$ must remain secret to the shareholders, so it is efficient and convenient to implement. Unfortunately, Wang and Qing pointed out in [12] that Xu's scheme cannot resist the coalition attack from more than t malicious group members. That is, more than t malicious group members can work together to get the secret parameters of the system with high possibility. Thereafter the danger of leakage of the system secret becomes larger and anyone who has the system secret can forge the signatures on behalf of the group. In addition, Xu's scheme lacks for robustness in that the designated signature combiner cannot verify the individual signature. So the protocol maybe fail and it is hard to find out the wrong partial signatures. The above two problems are very important for threshold signature scheme, so we try to improve Xu's threshold signature scheme in these two aspects. Gennaro et al. have proposed some elegant protocols to enhance the robustness of RSA functions in [3], we will adopt some of their techniques into our scheme.

The rest of the paper is organized as follows. Section 2 reviews Xu's modified RSA digital signature scheme. In section 3 we propose a robust coalition-resistant threshold signature scheme with anonymous signers. Section 4 presents our security analysis on the scheme. The conclusion is drawn in the last section.

2   Modified RSA Digital Signature Scheme

Given a one-way, strongly collision-free hash function H, Xu introduced a modified RSA signature scheme and proved that the security level of this scheme was the same as the security level of the original RSA scheme in [13]. Xu's modified RSA scheme consists of the following three phases.

Setup: Firstly, the dealer selects two safe large primes p, q and calculates $N = pq$. Secondly, the dealer selects $e \in [1, \varphi(N)-1]$ with $\gcd(e, \varphi(N)) = 1$ and calculates $d \in [1, \varphi(N)-1]$ satisfying $de \equiv 1 \bmod \varphi(N)$. Thirdly, the dealer selects a positive integer k and an appropriate hash function h, defines H as $H(m) = h^k(m) \bmod N$. At last, the dealer declares n, e, k, h as public key and d as secret key, sends d to the signer and destroys p and q.

Sign: For message m, the signer calculates the signature as $S = H^d(m) \bmod N$.

Verify: For received message m and its signature S, the verifier accepts S if $S^e \equiv H(m) \bmod N$ holds.

3 Proposed Threshold Signature Scheme

Denote the total number of the individuals in the group by n and let the threshold value be t, where $t \leq n$. Let $IN = \{1, 2, ..., n\}$ denote the index set. Let $U = \{u_i \mid i \in IN\}$ denote the identities of the group members while their pseudonyms are denoted by $X = \{x_i \mid i \in IN\}$. Our proposed scheme consists of the following phases.

3.1 System Setup

The trusted dealer chooses appropriate safe hash function h and RSA parameters e, d, $N = pq$. Note that p and q are large safe primes with $p = 2p'+1$ and $q = 2q'+1$, where $p' < q'$ and p', q' are large primes too.

The dealer randomly chooses a polynomial $f(x) \in Z_{\varphi(N)}[x]$ of degree $t-1$, with $f(0) = d$. For each $i \in IN$, the dealer randomly chooses small and different number $x_i \in Z_{\varphi(N)}$ as the pseudonym of the group member u_i. Then the dealer randomly chooses $t_i \in Z_{\varphi(N)}$ with $\gcd(t_i, \varphi(N)) = 1$ and calculates

$$y_i = f(x_i) \bmod \varphi(N) \tag{1}$$

$$\hat{y}_i = t_i y_i \bmod \varphi(N) \tag{2}$$

$$\hat{t}_i = t_i^{-1} \bmod \varphi(N) \tag{3}$$

For the purpose of individual signature verification, the dealer chooses three secure parameters $0 \leq k_1, k_2, k_3 = k_1 + k_2 + \log N$, chooses $b_i \in [1, 2^{k_1}]$ and $c_i \in [1, 2^{k_3}]$ randomly with uniform distribution. Then calculates w_i over the integers

$$w_i = c_i + b_i \hat{y}_i \tag{4}$$

In the end, for each $i \in IN$, the dealer publishes h, n, e, x_i, and sends $\hat{y}_i$ and w_i to u_i secretly, sends $\hat{t}_i, b_i, c_i$ to the designated signature combiner C secretly, then destroys the secret parameters $p, q, \varphi(N), t_i$ and y_i.

3.2 Individual Signature Generation and Verification

Without loss of generality, we denote the t members who signed the message m by $U(B) = \{u_1, u_2, ..., u_t\}$ and their pseudonyms by $X(B)$, where $B = \{1, 2, ..., t\} \subseteq IN$. For each $i \in B$, individual u_i calculates $h(m)$ and

$$S_i = h(m)^{\hat{y}_i} \bmod N \tag{5}$$

$$\xi_i = h(m)^{w_i} \bmod N \tag{6}$$

S_i is the partial signature and ξ_i is the auxiliary value. Then u_i sends (x_i, ξ_i, S_i) to C. Thereafter, the designated signature combiner C checks

$$S_i^{b_i} h(m)^{c_i} \overset{?}{=} \xi_i \tag{7}$$

If the equation holds, C concludes $S_i = \pm h(m)^{\hat{y}_i} \bmod N$ and accepts the individual partial signature, otherwise the partial signature will be rejected.

3.3 Sign

The signature combiner C firstly calculates

$$\pi = \prod_{i, j \in B \wedge i > j} (x_i - x_j) \tag{8}$$

Note that $\prod_{j \in B \setminus \{i\}} (x_i - x_j) \mid \pi$, so C can calculate

$$a_i = \frac{\pi}{\prod_{j \in B \setminus \{i\}} (x_i - x_j)} \prod_{j \in B} (-x_j) \tag{9}$$

For accepted partial signature S_i, C calculates

$$\hat{S}_i = S_i^{\hat{t}_i} \bmod N \tag{10}$$

And the signature of m signed by $U(B)$ is $(S_m, X(B))$, where

$$S_m = \prod_{i \in B} \hat{S}_i^{a_i} \bmod N \tag{11}$$

3.4 Verify

Using publicly available $X(B)$, the verifier calculate π and furthermore calculate

$$H(m) = h(m)^\pi \mod N \tag{12}$$

Then check

$$S_m^e \overset{?}{\equiv} H(m) \mod N \tag{13}$$

If the equality holds, the verifier accepts the signature S_m of the message m, otherwise rejects S_m.

4 Security Analysis

In this section, we will discuss the security and feature of our proposed robust coalition resistant threshold signature scheme. First, we will prove the correctness of the scheme.

Theorem 1. If all the players follow the protocol, the correct signature of message m can surely be generated. In another word, $S_m \equiv H^d(m) \mod N$ holds, so $S_m^e \equiv H(m) \mod N$ holds.

Proof. We will give our proof in two steps.

(1) To prove that the partial signature verification equation $S_i^{b_i} h(m)^{c_i} = \xi_i$ holds.

For $i \in B$, after u_i issued the correct partial signature S_i, we get from (5) $S_i^{b_i} h(m)^{c_i} = h(m)^{b_i \hat{y}_i + c_i}$. So from (4) and (6), we get $S_i^{b_i} h(m)^{c_i} = h(m)^{w_i} = \xi_i$.

(2) To prove that $S_m^e \equiv H(m) \mod N$ holds after signing.

From (2), (3), (5), (10), we get

$$\hat{S}_i = h(m)^{y_i} \mod N \tag{14}$$

From (11) and (14), we get

$$S_m = \prod_{i \in B} h(m)^{y_i a_i} = h(m)^{\sum\limits_{i \in B} y_i a_i} \mod N \tag{15}$$

Let $Y_i = f(x_i), (i \in B)$ over the rational number field. From Langange interpolation polynomials we get

$$f(x) = \sum_{i \in B} Y_i \prod_{j \in B \setminus \{i\}} \frac{x - x_j}{x_i - x_j} \tag{16}$$

Due to $f(0) = d$ and $Y_i \equiv y_i \bmod \varphi(N)$, we get

$$\pi d \equiv \sum_{i \in B} y_i \frac{\pi}{\prod\limits_{i \in B \wedge j \neq i}(x_i - x_j)} \prod_{j \in B \setminus \{i\}}(-x_j) \equiv \sum_{i \in B} y_i a_i \bmod \varphi(N) \tag{17}$$

Assuming it is infeasible to factor N, we can think $h(m) \in Z_N^*$. Hence from (16), (17) we get

$$h(m)^{\sum\limits_{i \in B} y_i a_i} \equiv h(m)^{\pi d} \equiv H^d(m) \bmod n \text{, thus } S_m^e \equiv H^{de}(m) \equiv H(m) \bmod N. \quad \square$$

Theorem 2. For each $i \in B$, u_i can convince C to accept the partial signature S_i where $S_i \neq \pm h(m)^{\hat{y}_i} \bmod N$, with possibility $\leq 1/p' + 1/2^{k_1} + 1/2^{k_2}$.

Proof. Our proof is similar to the proof process in reference [3]. Due to space limitation, please see [3] for details. $\square$

Theorem 3. By means of coalition attack from more than t malicious group members, the probability of the scheme being frustrated is no more than $(4p'q')^{-t-1}$.

Proof. Assume the malicious group members construct the set $X(B)$, where $B = \{1, 2, \ldots, t+1\}$. For each $i \in B$, if u_i can get y_i, there exists a type of coalition attack as follows:

Firstly, the members of $X(B)$ send their y_i to the attacker A. Now $\forall l \in B$, the attacker can calculates $t+1$ polynomials:

$$F_l(x) = \sum_{i \in B \setminus \{l\}} y_i \pi_l \prod_{j \in B \setminus \{i\}} \frac{x - x_j}{x_i - x_j} = \pi_l f(x) \bmod \varphi(N)$$

$$\text{where } \pi_l = \prod_{i,j \in B \setminus \{l\} \wedge i > j}(x_i - x_j) \tag{18}$$

Consequently for arbitrary $k, l \in B(k \neq l)$, we have

$$F_{k,l}(x) = \pi_k F_l(x) - \pi_l F_k(x) = 0 \bmod \pi_k \pi_l \varphi(N) \tag{19}$$

$F_{k,l}(x)$ is the polynomial over the integral ring. From (19) we know all coefficients of $F_{k,l}(x)$ are multiple of $\pi_k \pi_l \varphi(N)$, and the value of $F_{k,l}(x)$ for arbitrary x is the multiple of $\pi_k \pi_l \varphi(N)$ too. By solving the greatest common divisor of the coefficients and values of $F_{k,l}(x)$, A can acquire the secret information $\varphi(N)$ at high possibility, and further get the secret $f(x)$ of the system. Thereafter A can compute $y_i(i \in IN)$ from publicly available x_i, hence A can forge signature on behalf of the group.

From the above analysis we know that in order to prevent the coalition attack, the key point is to prevent u_i from knowing y_i. In our proposed scheme we have $y_i = \hat{t}_i \hat{y}_i \bmod \varphi(N)$. And u_i only knows $\hat{y}_i$. Since $\hat{t}_i = t_i^{-1} \bmod \varphi(n)$ and t_i is chosen at random from $Z_{\varphi(n)}^*$, the probability for u_i to guess y_i successfully is $1/\varphi(N) = (4p'q')^{-1}$. For (t, n) scheme, the attacker A needs at least $t+1$ correct y_i, so the successful probability is no more than $(4p'q')^{-t-1}$.   □

The above analysis focuses on the robustness and coalition resistant properties of the proposed scheme. In the following, we will discuss some other security properties of the scheme.

(1) We construct our scheme by combining a modified RSA signature scheme and Shamir's secret sharing scheme [7]. Assuming it is hard to solve the discrete logarithm problem, the individuals outside the group cannot issue the valid partial signature because they do not know the secret exponential $\hat{y}_i$. The secure properties of Shamir's scheme are preserved in that the attacker cannot acquire any valid information of d even if s/he gets $t-1$ secret share, hence the valid signature can only be generated by t or more group members.

(2) The verifier can check whether the signature $(S_m, X(B))$ is valid. Nevertheless s/he only knows the pseudonyms of $X(B)$, not the corresponding real identities $U(B)$, so the verifier cannot find out the detailed signers. In another word, the scheme is with anonymous signers.

(3) The signature combiner C can combine signature by calculating the shadow partial signature $\hat{S}_i$ of S_i. However C must solve discrete logarithm problem if s/he wants to obtain $\hat{y}_i$ from $S_i = h(m)^{\hat{y}_i} \bmod N$, $i = 1, 2, ..., t$. This is infeasible, so C cannot create the signature instead of other group members even in the later time. Other individual signers do not have the secret information $\hat{t}_i$ of C, so they cannot calculate the shadow partial signature $\hat{S}_i$. Hence clearly no one except C can generate the group signature.

5 Conclusions

In this paper we introduce a modified RSA digital signature scheme. Combining this RSA scheme with Shamir's perfect secret sharing scheme, we present a robust coalition-resistant (t, n) threshold signature scheme with anonymous signers and analyze it. The scheme has the common properties of ordinary threshold signature scheme. In particularly, the scheme is robust in two aspects. First, by introducing the auxiliary values the designated signature combiner can verify the individual partial signature. Second, by introducing shadow partial signatures the coalition attack from more than t malicious group members can be resisted. Furthermore, this scheme is efficient and convenient to implement for circumventing the problem of calculating inverses for arbitrary elements in structures.

References

1. Y Desmedt. Society and group oriented cryptography: a new concept. In CRYPTO 1987, LNCS 293, Berlin, Springer-Verlag(1988): 120-127.
2. Y Desmedt, Y Frankel. Shared generation of authenticators and signatures. In CRYPTO 1991, LNCS 576, Berlin, Springer Verlag(1991): 457-469.
3. R Gennaro, S Jarecki, H Krawczyk et al. Robust and efficient sharing of RSA functions. In CRYPTO 1996, LNCS 1109, Berlin, Springer-Verlag(1996): 157-172.
4. L Harn. Group-oriented (t, n) threshold digital signature scheme and multisignature. IEE proceedings– Computers and Digital Techniques, 141(5), 1994: 307-313.
5. C Li, T Hwang, N Lee. Threshold-multisignature schemes where suspected forgery implies traceability of adversarial shareholders. In EUROCRYPT 1994, LNCS 950. Berlin, Springer-Verlag(1995): 194-204.
6. Z C Li, J M Zhang, J Luo, et al. Group-oriented (t, n) threshold digital signature schemes with traceable signers. In Proceedings of Topics in Electronic Commerce: Second International Symposium, ISEC 2001. LNCS 2040, Berlin, Springer-Verlag(2001): 57-69.
7. A Shamir. How to share a secret. Communications of the ACM, 1979, 22(11): 612-613.
8. V Shoup. Practical threshold signatures. In EUROCRYPT 2000, LNCS 1807, Berlin, Springer-Verlag (2000): 207-220.
9. Y Tseng, J Jan. Attacks on threshold signature schemes with traceable signers. Information Processing Letters, 71(1999): 1-4.
10. G L Wang, X X Han, B Zhu. On the security of two threshold signature schemes with traceable signers. In the proceedings of Applied Cryptography and Network Security 2003, LNCS 2846, Berlin, Springer-Verlag (2003): 111-122.
11. C T Wang, C H Lin, C C Chang. Threshold signature schemes with traceable signers in group communications. Computer Communications, 21(8), 1998: 771-776.
12. G L Wang, S H Qing. Weaknesses of some threshold group signature schemes. Journal of Software. 2000, 11(10): 1326-1332.
13. Q L Xu. A modified threshold RSA digital signature scheme. Chinese Journal of Computers, 2000, 23(5): 449-453.

A Novel ID-Based Partial Delegation with Warrant Proxy Signature Scheme

Haifeng Qian and Zhenfu Cao[*]

Department of Computer Science, Shanghai Jiao Tong University,
Huashan road 1954, Shanghai 200030, China
{ares, zfcao}@cs.sjtu.edu.cn

Abstract. A novel ID-based proxy-protected signature scheme based on identity information is presented in this paper. We review the concept ID-Based signature introduced by Shamir, define the security notion of an ID-Based signature. We also improve the Shamir's ID-Based signature and prove its security under the proposed security notion. From the improved Shamir's ID-Based signature scheme we construct an ID-Based proxy signature scheme, the security is based on the underlying ID-based signature scheme. Our scheme is efficient and easy to implement. The scheme simplifies the public key as the user's id and can be easily applied to all the RSA-type cryptosystems.

Keywords: proxy signature, identity-based signature, provably secure, RSA, random oracle model

1 Introduction

In 1984, Shamir proposed a new model for public key cryptography in [10], called identity (ID)- based encryption and signature schemes, to simplify key management procedures of certificate-based public key infrastructures (PKIs). In ID-based cryptography an entity's public key is derived directly from its identity information, for example, name, e-mail address, or IP address of the user. The corresponding private key is generated for the user by a trusted third party called private key generation center (PKG) and given to the user through a secure channel.

The widely-accepted notion of security for signature schemes is unforgeability under chosen-message attacks [3]. While an ID-based signature scheme must add one other security consideration (unforgeability under chosen-ID attacks) to the notion of security besides unforgeability under chosen-message attacks. Under chosen-ID attacks Shamir's original ID-based signature exists forgery using the method 'blinding' in [2].

The concept of proxy signature was first introduced by Mambo *et al.* in 1996 [7,8]. A proxy signature scheme consists of three entities: original signer, proxy signer and verifier. If an original signer wants to delegate the signing capability to

---

[*] Corresponding Author

G. Chen et al. (Eds.): ISPA Workshops 2005, LNCS 3759, pp. 323–331, 2005.
© Springer-Verlag Berlin Heidelberg 2005

a proxy signer, he/she uses the original signature key to create a proxy signature key, which will then be sent to the proxy signer. The proxy signer can use the proxy signature key to sign messages on behalf of the original signer. The verifier can be convinced that the proxy signature is generated by the authorized proxy entity of the original signer. There are three types of delegation, full delegation, partial delegation and delegation by warrant.

After the concept of proxy signature was first introduced by Mambo et al. [7,8], many researchers have done a lot of work in this field, and several kinds of proxy signature schemes have been put forth [4,5,6] etc. Kim et al.in [5] gave a new type of delegation called partial delegation with warrant, which can be considered as the combination of partial delegation and delegation by warrant.

Being inspired of above ideas, we will give an ID-based version of partial delegation with warrant proxy signature scheme and the scheme is a simple efficient proxy-protected signature scheme which is mainly based on factoring. Of course, our scheme also satisfies the basic security properties.

The rest of the paper is organised as follows. In section 2, we review some important definitions of proxy signature and ID-based signature. Then we review and improve Shamir's ID-based signature scheme in section 3. In section 4 we propose our proxy-protected signature and section 5, we will analyze the scheme's security. Finally, concluding remarks are made in section 6.

2   Basic Definitions

2.1   Basic Definitions of ID-Based Signature

An IBS scheme can be roughly described using the following steps.

- **Setup:** The Private Key Generator (PKG), which is a trusted third party, creates its master (private) and public key pair, which we denote by ms and Pub respectively.
- **Extraction:** The signer Alice authenticates herself to the PKG and obtains a private key sk_{ID} associated with her identity ID.
- **Signature Generation:** Using the private key sk_{ID} , the signer creates a signature σ on her message M.
- **Signature Verification:** Having obtained the signature σ and the message M, the verifier checks whether σ is a genuine signature on M using the identity ID and the PKG's public key Pub. If it is, he returns "Accept". Otherwise, he returns "Reject".

A secure IBS can resist two kinds of attacks: (1) Chosen-message attack and (2) Chosen-ID attack. Chosen message attack implies the forger $\mathcal{F}$ can actively attack the IBS system and the signing oracle is provided, then the attacker $\mathcal{F}$ must output an valid signature not previously answered by the signing oracle. While Chosen-ID attack means that the attacker $\mathcal{F}$ is allowed to arbitrarily register an public key ID, and gets the corresponding secret key sk_{ID} in PKG, finally $\mathcal{F}$ must output any of the others' secret keys or the master key of the whole system.

Definition 1 (Secure IBS). *A secure Identity-based signature must be able to resist the Chosen-message attack and Chosen-ID attack under the corresponding cryptographical assumptions.*

2.2 Security Requirements of the Proxy Signature

Mambo *et al.* [7,8] pointed out that the proxy signature schemes should satisfy the following six properties: *Unforgeability, Verifiability, Undeniability, Distingishability, Proxy signer's deviation and Identifiability.*

In order to make a proxy signature scheme fairer to the original signer and the proxy signer in commercial circumstances, Lee *et al.* [6] somewhat enhanced the properties introduced by Mambo *et al.* The properties stated in [6] are described in the following.

Strong Unforgeability: A proxy signer can create a valid proxy signature on behalf the original signer. However, the original signer and any third party can't generate a valid proxy signature with the name of proxy signers.

Strong Identifiability: From a proxy signature anyone can determine the identity of the corresponding proxy signer.

Strong Undeniability: Once a proxy signer generates a valid proxy signature on behalf of the proxy signer, the proxy signer can't deny his signature generation against anyone.

Prevention of Misuse: It should be confident that proxy key pair can't be used for other purposes. In the case of misuse, the responsibility of proxy signature should be determined explicitly.

3 Shamir's ID-Based Signature and Its Improvement

This section reviews the original Shamir's ID-based signature, points out the insecurity under Chosen-ID attack. After that, we give a very small improvement which makes the signature scheme satisfy the security notion.

3.1 Review of Shamir's ID-Based Signature

Like all IBS schemes Shamir's ID-based signature also contains four algorithms: Setup; Extraction; Signature Generation; and Signature Verification. The scheme is set as follows:

Setup:
   (1) $n = pq$ where p, and q are two large primes;
   (2) e a random number satisfying $\gcd(e, \varphi(n)) = 1$ (e and n are public parameters for using by the system-wide users);
   (3) d an integer satisfying $ed \equiv 1 \mod \varphi(n)$ (d is the master-key of PKG);
   (4) $h : \{0,1\}^* \rightarrow Z_{\varphi(n)}$ (h is a strong one way function);
   The PKG keeps d as the master-key, and publicizes the public parameter $Pub = (n, e, h)$

Extraction: Given an identity $ID \in Z_n$, the algorithm generates the secret key $sk_{ID} = ID^d \mod n$ associated with ID

Signature Generation: Given a secret key sk_{ID} and a message m, the signer picks a random number $r \in Z_n$ and outputs a signature $\sigma = (R, S)$ where $R = r^e \mod n$, and $S = sk_{ID} \cdot r^{h(R\|m)} \mod n$.

Signature Verification: Given a message m and the signature $\sigma = (R, S)$, the verifier checks whether $S^{\ e} \equiv ID \cdot R^{h(R\|m)} \mod n$ holds by using the identity information ID, if it holds, the signature is valid, otherwise, invalid.

From Shamir's IBS we observe that the secret keys of users actually are the signatures of common RSA signature algorithm, thus common RSA signature can not resist the 'blinding' attack (the forger picks a random $t \in Z_n$ and sets $ID_0 = t^e \cdot ID \mod n$. He then asks the signer to sign ID_0. The signer may be willing to provide his signature S_0 on the innocent-looking ID_0. But recall that $S_0 \equiv ID_0^{\ d} \mod n$. The attacker now simply computes $S \equiv S_0 \cdot t^{-1} \mod n$ and obtains signature $S = ID^d$ on the original ID. Indeed he gets another user's secret key).

3.2   Improvement of Shamir's ID-Based Signature

With a very small improvement Shamir's IBS will turn to be secure, the method is to use FDH-RSA signature algorithm[1] to generate the secret keys of the users. The improved scheme is set as follows:

Setup: e is a prime number and n, d, h are the same as previous one, $H :$ $\{0,1\}^* \to Z_n$ is a cryptographical hash function.

Extraction: The PKG uses FDH-RSA signature algorithm to generate user's secret key $sk_{ID} = H(ID)^d \mod n$.

Signature Generation: the same as the Shamir's scheme, the signer picks a random number $r \in Z_n$ and output a signature $\sigma = (R, S)$ where $R = r^e \mod n$, and $S = sk_{ID} \cdot r^{h(R\|m)} \mod n$.

Signature Verification: the verification equation changes to $S^{\ e} \equiv H(ID) \cdot R^{h(R\|m)} \mod n$, others are the same.

The improved scheme is secure against Chosen-ID attack, for the FDH-RSA signature algorithm is secure in random oracle. However, whether it can resist the Chosen-message attack is not proved by Shamir. Here we will prove its security under RSA assumption.

Here we assume a user's public key is $y \equiv x^e \pmod{n}$ (where x is the secret key) and h is a random oracle. By using the proof technique of [9] we may prove the improved scheme and Shamir's IBS are secure. Before we present the security proof, Let's review the forking lemma first in [9].

Lemma 1 (the forking lemma). *Let A be a Probabilistic Polynomial Time Turing machine, given only the public data as input. If A can find, with non-negligible probability, a valid signature $(m; R; h_1; S_1)$, then, with non-negligible probability, a replay of this machine, with the same random tape and a different* *oracle, outputs two valid signatures* $(m; R; h_1; S_1)$ *and* $(m; R; h_2; S_2)$ *such that* $h_1 \neq h_2$ *(where* $h_1 = h_1(R||m)$ *and* $h_2 = h_2(R||m)$*).*

With the lemma above we can get the following theorem easily.

Theorem 1 (CMA-Secure). *The improved scheme is existentially unforgeable in random oracle model under RSA assumption.*

Sketch of proof. Here we assume a user's public key is $y \equiv x^e \pmod{n}$ (where x is the secret key). If an attacker $\mathcal{F}$ can break the improved IBS (Shamir's IBS) scheme, then by using the forking lemma, he can obtain two valid signatures $(m; R; h_1; S_1)$ and $(m; R; h_2; S_2)$ such that

$$
\begin{aligned}
S_1{}^e &\equiv H(ID) \cdot R^{h_1} \quad \mathrm{mod}\ n, \\
S_2{}^e &\equiv H(ID) \cdot R^{h_2} \quad \mathrm{mod}\ n, \\
h_1 &\neq h_2.
\end{aligned}
\tag{1}
$$

Thus

$$
\begin{aligned}
\left(S_1 \cdot S_2^{-1}\right)^e &\equiv R^{h_1 - h_2} \quad \mathrm{mod}\ n, \\
S_1 \cdot S_2^{-1} &\equiv r^{h_1 - h_2} \quad \mathrm{mod}\ n.
\end{aligned}
\tag{2}
$$

With a non-negligible probability $\gcd(h_1 - h_2, e) = 1$, there exist s, t such that

$$
s \cdot e + (h_1 - h_2) \cdot t = 1.
\tag{3}
$$

Then,

$$
\begin{aligned}
r &= r^{s \cdot e + (h_1 - h_2) \cdot t} \\
&= R^s \cdot \left(r^{h_1 - h_2}\right)^t \\
&\equiv R^s \cdot \left(S_1 \cdot S_2^{-1}\right)^t \quad \mathrm{mod}\ n.
\end{aligned}
\tag{4}
$$

So $\left(\frac{S_1}{r^{h_1}}\right)^e \equiv H(ID) \equiv y \mod n$, then we find $x = \left(\frac{S_1}{r^{h_1}}\right)$ and solve the RSA problem. $\qquad\square$

Now we conclude that the improved Shamir's Identity-based signature is a secure signature scheme.

4   The Proposed Scheme

In this section, we will propose our simple efficient proxy-protected signature scheme based on factoring. To illustrate it clearly, we divide it into five algorithms: *Setup, Extraction, Warrant generation, Signature generation, and Signature verification*. Without loss of generosity we assume that U_o is original signer and U_p is proxy signer, and they both register their public keys using their identities and get the corresponding private keys from the PKG.

Setup: In the similar way in section 3, the PKG setup the system parameters as follows:

    1. $n = pq$ where p, and q are two large primes;

2. e is a prime number satisfying $\gcd(e, \varphi(n)) = 1$ (e and n are public parameters for using by the system-wide users);
3. d an integer satisfying $ed \equiv 1 \mod \varphi(n)$ (d is the master-key of PKG);
4. $h : \{0,1\}^* \rightarrow Z_{\varphi(n)}$ (h is a hash function which can be viewed as a random oracle).

The PKG keeps d as the master-key, chooses H where $H : \{0,1\}^* \rightarrow Z_n$ is a cryptographical hash function, then publicizes the public parameter $Pub = (n, e, h, H)$.

Extraction: Suppose U_o is an original signer and U_p is a proxy signer with identity information ID_o and ID_p respectively.

1. We assume that the original signer U_o and the proxy signer U_p register their identity information ID_o and ID_p, then the PKG send to them their private keys $sk_{ID_o} = H(ID_o)^d$ (mod n) and $sk_{ID_p} = H(ID_p)^d$ (mod n) respectively through a secure channel.

Warrant Generation: When the original signer U_o delegates her signing capability to the proxy signer U_p, they will run the following steps:

1. The original signer U_o first makes a warrant m_w, which records the delegation policy including limits of authority, valid periods of delegation, the proxy signer's identity information *etc.* Then he publishes m_w.
2. U_o randomly chooses an $r_o \in Z_n$, then uses the improved Shamir's Identity-based signature scheme to generate a signature $\sigma_o = (R_o, S_o)$ on warrant m_w. Here

$$S_o \equiv sk_{ID_o} \cdot r_o^{h(R_o||m_w)} \mod n$$
$$R_o \equiv r_o^e \mod n \tag{5}$$

3. U_o sends the signature $\sigma_o = (R_o, S_o)$ on warrant m_w to proxy signer U_p via a public channel.
4. After receiving the the signature $\sigma_o = (R_o, S_o)$ on warrant m_w, the proxy signer U_p checks

$$S_o{}^e \equiv H(ID_o) \cdot R_o^{h(R_o||m_w)} \mod n \tag{6}$$

to verify its validity. If it holds, the proxy signer U_p confirms the warrant's validity; otherwise, the proxy signer U_p rejects the signature of the warrant.

Signature Generation: Assume the proxy signer U_p wants to sign on message m on behalf of the original signer U_o, he would follow the steps below:

1. Choose a random number r_p, and compute R_p, where

$$R_p \equiv r^e \equiv (r_p \cdot S_o)^e \mod n \tag{7}$$

2. Apply $h()$ to compute $h(R_p||m||m_w)$.
3. Use the improved Shamir's Identity-based signature scheme in section 3 and the proxy private key sk_{ID_p} to compute S_p as the proxy signature on message m, where

$$S_p \equiv (sk_{ID_p}) \cdot (r_p \cdot S_o)^{h(R_p||m||m_w)} \mod n, \tag{8}$$

4. Finally, send signature $\sigma = (R_o, R_p, S_p)$ to verifier associated with m_w, m.

Signature Verification: Any verifier or receiver can run the following steps to verify the proxy signature $\sigma = (R_o, R_p, S_p)$ associated with m_w, m.
1. Check the warrant m_w, confirm the delegation policy including limits of authority, valid periods of delegation, the proxy signer's identity information *etc.*
2. Apply $H()$ to compute the original signer's public key $H(ID_o)$ and proxy signer's public key $H(ID_p)$ with the identity information of the original and proxy signers.
3. Check

$$S_p{}^e \stackrel{?}{=} (R_o{}^{h(R_o||m_w)} R_p \cdot H(ID_o))^{h(R_p||m||m_w)} \cdot H(ID_p) \mod n. \quad (9)$$

If it holds, the signature σ's validity will be accepted, otherwise, it will be denied.

5 Security

In this section, we shall prove that the proposed scheme can work correctly and satisfy the basic security requirements.

Theorem 2. *The proposed proxy signature scheme is verifiability, strong undeniability, distingishability, proxy signer's deviation and strong identifiability if the original signer, proxy signer and verifier all follow the issuing protocol.*

Proof. From Equations.(5)-(9), it is obvious that the proposed scheme satisfies verifiability,strong undeniability, distinggishability, proxy signer's deviation and strong identifiability. The identities of the original signer and proxy signers' appear in Equation 9. Therefore, once the original signer and proxy signer generate a valid signature, they can't deny their signature and the signature is easy to be strongly distinguishable and identifiable. Deviation is also obvious to see in Equations (5)-(9). □

To prove the proposed scheme satisfies the strong unforgeability, we will prove two aspects. One is the original signer can't forge a proxy signature and the other is the proxy signer also can't get the original signer's private key or forge a valid signature of the original signer.

Theorem 3. *The proposed scheme is against existential forgery on adaptive chosen message attack in the Random Oracle model under RSA assumption.*

Proof Sketch. Suppose $\mathcal{A}$ is the original signer, From the point view of $\mathcal{A}$, $r = r_p \cdot S_o$ is uniformly distributed in Z_n since r_p is randomly chosen from Z_n. Therefore, (R_p, S_p) is standard signature of the improved ID-based signature. Since the improved Shamir's ID-based signature is CMA secure in random oracle model, thus we conclude that the original signer can't forge the proxy signature. □

Theorem 4. *In the proposed proxy signature scheme, the proxy signer can not get original signer's private key or forge a valid signature of the original signer.*

Proof Sketch. The original signer computes the signature $\sigma_o = (R_o, S_o)$ on warrant m_w and sends it to proxy signer. From the point view of the proxy signer the original signer has just given a signature on warrant. If the proxy signer can get original signer's private key or forge a valid signature of the original signer that means the improved Shamir's ID-based signature scheme is not secure, While it is impossible from theorem 1. Therefore, theorem 4 holds.   □

Corollary 1. *The proposed proxy-protected signature scheme, it has the properties of Strong unforgeablity and prevention of misuse and can work correctly.*

Remark 1. The proposed signature scheme ensures forward-secure property. As the proxy warrant m_w records valid period, when the valid period expires, the proxy private key will be invalid automatically.

6   Conclusions

We have proposed a simple efficient ID-based proxy-protected signature based on RSA trapdoor permutation and proved it is provable secure in the Random Oracle model. As the modulus of the original signer and proxy signer are same, it overcomes the problems caused by different moduli of the users. The public key here is the identities of the users, so we do not need them to be certificated by Certificate Authority (CA), thus it is obviously against the public key substitution attack. The main computations of the proposed scheme is efficient and easy to implement because of only a few exponentiation computations. Besides, the scheme can be easily applied to all the RSA-type cryptosystems.

Acknowledgments

The authors would like to thank anonymous referees and reviewers for their suggestions to improve the paper. Besides, this article is supported by the National Science Fund for Distinguished Young Scholars under Grant No. 60225007, the National Research Fund for the Doctoral Program of Higher Education of China under Grant No. 20020248024 and the Science and Technology Research Project of Shanghai under Grant Nos. 04JC14055 and 046407067.

References

1. Bellare, M., Rogaway, P.: The exact security of digital signatures: How to sign with RSA and Rabin, In: Proceedings of Eurocrypt'96, Lecture Notes in Computer Science, vol.1070, Springer-Verlag, 1996, pp.399-416.
2. Boneh, D.: Twenty years of attacks on the RSA cryptosystem. In: Notices of the American Mathematical Society (AMS), 46(2): 1999, pp.203–213.
3. Goldwasser, S., Micali, S. and Rivest, R.: A digital signature scheme secure against adaptive chosen-message attacks. SIAM J. Computing, 17(2): (1988), pp.281–308.

4. Kim, H., Baek, J., Lee, B. and Kim, K.: Secret Computation with secrets for mobile agent using one-time proxy signature. The 2001 Symposium on Cryptography and Information Security, Oiso, Japan.
5. Kim, S., Park, S. and Won, D.: Proxy signatures, revisited, In: Pro. of ICICS 97, Lecture Notes in Computer Science, vol. 1334, Springer-Verlag, (1997) pp. 223–232.
6. Lee,B., Kim, H. and Kim, K.: Strong proxy signature and its application. in: Proc. of ACISP2001, 11B-1: (2001) pp.603–608.
7. Mambo, M., Usuda, K. and Okmamoto, E.: Proxy signatures: delegation of the power to sign message, IEICE Transaction Functional E79-A(9) (1996) pp.1338–1354.
8. Mambo, M., Usuda, K. and E. Okmamoto.: Proxy signatures for delegation signing operation,in: Proceedings of the Third ACM Conference on Computer and Communication Security, New Delhi, India, January 1996, pp.48–57.
9. Pointcheval, D., Stern, J.: Security proofs for signatures. In: Proceedings of Eurocrypt'96. Lecture Notes in Computer Science, vol. 1070, Springer-Verlag, (1996) pp.387–398.
10. Shamir, A.: Identity-based cryptosystem and signature schemes. Advances in Cryptology-CRYPTO'84, Lecture Notes in Computer Science, vol. 0196, Springer-Verlag, (1984) pp.19–22.

An Efficient Proxy-Protected Signature Scheme Based on Factoring*

Yuan Zhou, Zhenfu Cao, and Zhenchuan Chai

Department of Computer Science and Engineering,
Shanghai Jiao Tong University, Shanghai 200030, P. R. China
zhouyuan@sjtu.edu.cn, zfcao@cs.sjtu.edu.cn

Abstract. Proxy signature is an active cryptographic research area, and a wide range of literature can be found nowadays suggesting improvement and generalization of existing protocols in various direction. However, most of previously proposed schemes in these literatures are based on discrete logarithm problems. To our best knowledge, there still doesn't exist an indeed proxy signature scheme based on factoring. The paper present a new proxy signature scheme based on factoring, along with a complete proof of security in the Random Oracle model. The proposed scheme does not need a secure channel to transmit proxy private key.

1 Introduction

The notion of proxy signature scheme introduced by Mambo et al. in 1996 [1]. A proxy signature scheme allows a entity called original signer to delegate his signing capability to another entity, called proxy signer. After that, the proxy signer can sign some messages on behalf of the original signer.

So far, most proxy signature schemes [3,4,5,6,7,8,9] are based on discrete logarithm problems. In [10], Shao present a proxy scheme, which based on RSA assumption. However, no security proof was given. The security notions of proxy signature primitive were first prosed by Boldyreva, Palacio, and Warinschi [3].

Recently, mobile computation environments have been paid great attentions. Many low-powered and resource-constrained small devices have arisen, such as smart cards, cell phones and pagers. To adapt to these devices, Kim et al. [4] proposed a one-time proxy signature based on discrete logarithm problem. In Asiacrypt 2003, Huaxiong Wang and Josef Pieprzyk also presented an efficient one-time proxy signature based on one-way functions without trapdoors [5]. As one-time proxy signature is much efficient and can be easily implemented, it is particularly fir for mobile computation environments. However, just as its name suggests, one-time proxy signature cannot sign an unlimited number of messages.

---

* This research is partially supported by the National Natural Science Foundation of China for Distinguished Young Scholars under Grant No. 60225007, the National Research Fund for the Doctoral Program of Higher Education of China under Grant No. 20020248024 and Grant-in-Aid for Scientific Research (C) under Grant No. 14540100.

G. Chen et al. (Eds.): ISPA Workshops 2005, LNCS 3759, pp. 332–341, 2005.

Being inspired of above ideas, in this paper, we would like to propose a simple efficient proxy-protected signature scheme, which is based on factoring and can be applied in mobile computation environments.

In this paper, we first propose security notions for warrant-based proxy-protected signature schemes. At the same time, we present a warrant-based protected-proxy signature based on integer factorization. The proof security of it is under the proposed security notions. Moreover, our scheme does not need a secure channel to transmit proxy private key.

The rest of this paper is organized as follows. Section 2. gives the security notions for warrant-based proxy-protected signature schemes. Section 3. presents our proposed scheme and corresponding proof of security.

2 Security Notions of Warrant-Based Proxy-Protected Signature Schemes

In this section, we first recall the syntax of the warrant-based proxy-protected signature [3].

Definition 1. Warrant-based proxy-protected signature.

Let warrant-based proxy-protected signature $PS=(\mathcal{G}, \mathcal{K}, (\mathcal{D}, \mathcal{P}), \mathcal{PS}, \mathcal{PV})$ be defined as follows:

- *The parameter generation algorithm $\mathcal{G}$ takes input 1^k where k is the security parameter, and outputs some global parameters **params**.*
- *The key generation algorithm $\mathcal{K}$ takes input global parameters **params** and outputs a original signer' key pair (pk_{os}, sk_{os}) and a proxy signer's key pair (pk_{ps}, sk_{ps}).*
- *$(\mathcal{D}, \mathcal{P})$ is a pair of interactive randomized algorithms which form the two-party proxy-delegation protocol. The input to each algorithm includes two public keys pk_{os}, pk_{ps} and the the proxy signer's warrant M_w respectively. $\mathcal{D}$ also takes as input the secret key sk_{os} of original signer , and $\mathcal{P}$ also takes as input secret sk_{ps} of the proxy signer. As result of the interaction, the output of $\mathcal{P}$ is a proxy signing key s_P, which the proxy signer uses to produce proxy signatures on behalf of the original signer.*
- *The randomized proxy signing algorithm $\mathcal{PS}$ takes as input s_P, sk_{ps} and a message $M \in \{0,1\}^*$, and outputs a proxy signature $p\sigma$.*
- *The (usually deterministic) proxy verification algorithm $\mathcal{PV}$ takes input $(pk_{os}, ps_{ps}, M, p\sigma)$, and outputs a bit. We say that $p\sigma$ is a valid information for M relative to pk_{os} and pk_{ps} if $\mathcal{PV}(pk_{os}, ps_{ps}, M, p\sigma)=1$.*

In the course of implementing the two-party proxy-delegation protocol (i.e. implement the interactive randomized algorithms $\mathcal{D}$ and $\mathcal{P}$), some schemes need secure channel (call this case SC), the other ones does not need it (call this case NSC). According to the two cases, we construct two model of warrant-based proxy-protected signature schemes.

Model 2.1 (SC). Let PS=$(\mathcal{G}, \mathcal{K}, (\mathcal{D}, \mathcal{P}), \mathcal{PS}, \mathcal{PV})$ is a warrant-based proxy-protected signature scheme.

- The description of the algorithms $\mathcal{G}$ and $\mathcal{K}$ are the same as the corresponding parts in definition 1.
- The original signer sends to the designated proxy signer an appropriate warrant M_w in a public channel and a signature s_w for M_w under the secret key sk_{os} in a secure channel. The warrant M_w includes the public key, identity of the designated proxy signer, etc. When receiving the warrant M_w and its signature s_w, by using his key pair (pk_{ps}, sk_{ps}) and s_w, the proxy signer generates the proxy signing key s_P.
- When the proxy signer want to generate proxy signature $p\sigma$ on some message M, he simply executes ordinary signing operation with the proxy signing key s_P.
- To verify the proxy signature, the verifier first computes the proxy public key p_P using the warrant M_w, the original signer's public key pk_{os}, the proxy signer's public key pk_{ps} and some information involved in the proxy signature $p\sigma$, then carries out the verification by the same checking operation as in the ordinary signature scheme.

Model 2.2 (NSC). Let PS=$(\mathcal{G}, \mathcal{K}, (\mathcal{D}, \mathcal{P}), \mathcal{PS}, \mathcal{PV})$ is a warrant-based proxy-protected signature scheme.

- The description of the algorithms $\mathcal{G}$ and $\mathcal{K}$ are the same as the corresponding parts in definition 1.
- The original signer sends to the designated proxy signer an appropriate warrant M_w together with a signature s_w for M_w under the secret key sk_{os} in a public channel. The warrant M_w includes the public key, identity of the designated proxy signer, etc. The proxy signing key s_P is $\{M_w, s_w, pk_{os}, sk_{ps}\}$.
- When the proxy signer want to generate proxy signature $p\sigma$ on some message M, he simply executes ordinary signing operation on message $M\|s_w$ with his secret key sk_{ps}.
- To verify the proxy signature, the verifier simply executes two ordinary signature verifying operation. That is, whether S_w is a valid signature of M_w and whether $p\sigma$ is a valid signature of the message $M\|s_w$.

Informally, the proxy-protected signature satisfies the following three basic security properties.

Verifiability: From a proxy signature, any verifier can be convinced of the original signer's agreement on the signed message.

Unforgeability: Only a designated proxy signer can create a valid proxy signature for the original signer (even the original signer cannot do it).

Undeniability: A proxy signer cannot repudiate a proxy signature he created.

Now, we will give the formal security notions for the above two models respectively. First, we consider the **SC** model.

SC Model: Let PS=$(\mathcal{G}, \mathcal{K}, \mathcal{S}, \mathcal{V} (\mathcal{D}, \mathcal{P}), \mathcal{PS}, \mathcal{PV})$ is a warrant-based proxy-protected signature scheme, where **S**=$\{\mathcal{G}, \mathcal{K}, \mathcal{S}, \mathcal{V}\}$ is a standard signature scheme. In **PS**, the secure channel is used. We consider the following game between a challenger $\mathcal{C}$ and an forger $\mathcal{F}$:

- **Setup.** The challenger $\mathcal{C}$ runs algorithm $\mathcal{G}$ and $\mathcal{K}$ to obtain a key pair (pk_U, sk_U). The adversary $\mathcal{F}$ is given pk_U.
- **Queries.**
  - Delegation query (pk_{ps}). When the adversary $\mathcal{F}$ runs algorithm $\mathcal{G}$ and $\mathcal{K}$ to obtain a key pair (pk_{ps}, sk_{ps}), and sends pk_{ps} to the challenger, the challenger $\mathcal{C}$ generates an appropriate warrant M_w for pk_{ps} and a signature s_w for M_w using the secret key sk_U, then responds s_w.
  - Signature query (M). The challenger $\mathcal{C}$ runs the algorithm $\mathcal{S}$ to generate the proxy signature σ and sends it to the adversary.
  - Proxy signature query (M, M_w, s_w, pk_{os}). The challenger $\mathcal{C}$ runs the algorithm $\mathcal{PS}$ to generate the proxy signature $p\sigma$ and sends it to the adversary.
- **Output.**
  1. $\mathcal{F}$ outputs a pair (M, $p\sigma$) and a public key pk_{ps}, and wins in the game, if (1) the public key pk_{ps} was not queried in delegation queries, (2) $\mathcal{PV}(p_P, M, p\sigma)$=1. Here p_P is defined as model 2.1.
  2. $\mathcal{F}$ outputs a pair (M, σ) and wins the game if (1) M was not queried in signature queries, (2) $\mathcal{V}(pk_U, M, \sigma)$=1.
  3. $\mathcal{F}$ outputs a tuple (M, $p\sigma$, M_w, s_w, pk_{os}) and wins in the game, if (1) the entity for M, M_w and pk_{os} was not queried in proxy signature queries, (2) $\mathcal{PV}(p_P, M, p\sigma)$=1. Here p_P is defined as model 2.1.

Using the above game, we can define the security notion of the **SC** model. Let us define $\mathbf{Adv}^{\mathbf{SC}}_{\mathbf{PS},\mathcal{F}}(k)$ to be the probability that $\mathcal{F}$ wins the game.

Definition 2. Security of the SC model.
*We say a warrant-based proxy-protected signature scheme of **SC** model is secure if for any polynomial probabilistic time adversary $\mathcal{F}$ $\mathbf{Adv}^{\mathbf{SC}}_{\mathbf{PS},\mathcal{F}}(k)$ is negligible.*

We describe the security notion of **NSC** model.

NSC Model: Let PS=$(\mathcal{G}, \mathcal{K}, \mathcal{S}, \mathcal{V} (\mathcal{D}, \mathcal{P}), \mathcal{PS}, \mathcal{PV})$ is a warrant-based proxy-protected signature scheme, where **S**=$\{\mathcal{G}, \mathcal{K}, \mathcal{S}, \mathcal{V}\}$ is a standard signature scheme. In **PS**, the secure channel is not used. We consider the following game between a challenger $\mathcal{C}$ and an forger $\mathcal{F}$:

- **Setup.** The challenger $\mathcal{C}$ runs algorithm $\mathcal{G}$ and $\mathcal{K}$ to obtain a key pair (pk_U, sk_U). The adversary $\mathcal{F}$ is given pk_U.
- **Queries.**
    - Delegation query (pk_{ps}). When the adversary $\mathcal{F}$ runs algorithm $\mathcal{G}$ and $\mathcal{K}$ to obtain a key pair (pk_{ps}, sk_{ps}), and sends pk_{ps} to the challenger, the challenger $\mathcal{C}$ generates an appropriate warrant M_w for pk_{ps} and a signature s_w for M_w using the secret key sk_U, then responds s_w.
    - Signature query (M). The challenger $\mathcal{C}$ runs the algorithm $\mathcal{S}$ to generate the proxy signature σ and sends it to the adversary.
    - Proxy signature query (M, M_w, s_w, pk_{os}). The challenger $\mathcal{C}$ runs the standard signature algorithm $\mathcal{S}$ to generate the proxy signature $p\sigma$ for message $M\|s_w$, and sends it to the adversary.
- **Output.**
    1. $\mathcal{F}$ outputs a pair $(M, p\sigma)$ and a public key pk_{ps}, and wins in the game, if (1) the public key pk_{ps} was not queried in delegation queries, (2) $\mathcal{PV}(pk_U, pk_{ps}, M\|s_w, p\sigma)=1$.
    2. $\mathcal{F}$ outputs a pair (M, σ) and wins the game if (1) M was not queried in signature queries, (2) $\mathcal{V}(pk_U, M, \sigma)=1$.
    3. $\mathcal{F}$ outputs a tuple $(M, p\sigma, M_w, s_w, pk_{os})$ and wins in the game, if (1) the entity (M, M_w, s_w, pk_{os}) for M, M_w and pk_{os} was not queried in proxy signature queries, (2) $\mathcal{PV}(pk_{os}, pk_U, M\|s_w, p\sigma)=1$.

Let us define $\mathbf{Adv}_{\mathbf{PS},\mathcal{F}}^{\mathbf{NSC}}(k)$ to be the probability that $\mathcal{F}$ wins the game.

Definition 3. Security of the NSC model.

*We say a warrant-based proxy-protected signature scheme of **NSC** model is secure if for any probabilistic polynomial time adversary $\mathcal{F}$ $\mathbf{Adv}_{\mathbf{PS},\mathcal{F}}^{\mathbf{NSC}}(k)$ is negligible.*

3   Our Proposed Scheme

In this section, we will propose a warrant-based proxy signature scheme, whose security is based on integer factorization. Moreover, the scheme is under **NSC** model, i.e. our scheme needs no secure channel to transmit proxy private key. The scheme comprises six phases: key generation phase, (standard) signing phase, (standard) verification phase, delegating phase, proxy signing phase, and proxy verification phase. Improved Rabin signature scheme is proposed in [12], which will be applied in our scheme.

3.1   Improved Rabin Signature Scheme

Generate an Rabin key pair $\{(N, a), (p, q)\}$ with $N = p \cdot q$, $p \equiv q \equiv 3(\mathrm{mod}4))$, and $a \in Z_N^*$ satisfying Jacobi symbol $\left(\frac{a}{N}\right) = -1$ where (N, a) is public key and (p, q) is private key. The scheme requires an hash function $H : \mathcal{M} \to Z_N^*$.

Signature Algorithm: For some message $M \in \mathcal{M}$, First compute c_1 and c_2 as follows:

$$c_1 = \begin{cases} 0, & \text{if } \left(\frac{H(m)}{N}\right) = 1 \\ 1, & \text{if } \left(\frac{H(m)}{N}\right) = -1 \end{cases}.$$

$$c_2 = \begin{cases} 0, & \text{if } \left(\frac{l}{p}\right) = 1 \\ 1, & \text{if } \left(\frac{l}{q}\right) = -1 \end{cases}.$$

where $l = a^{c_1} \cdot H(M)$.
Then compute s from the following equation:

$$s^2 \equiv (-1)^{c_2} \cdot a^{c_1} H(m) (\bmod N).$$

The signature on M is (s, c_1, c_2).

3.2 The Proposed Scheme

Key Generation Phase: The original signer generates a Rabin key pair $\{(N_o, a_o), (p_o, q_o)\}$ with $|p_o| = |q_o| = k/2$. Here k is an system security parameter. A proxy signer has Rabin key pair $\{(N_p, a_p), (p_p, q_p)\}$. Our scheme requires two hash functions:

$$H_1 : \{0, 1\}^* \rightarrow Z_{N_o}^*;$$
$$H_2 : \{0, 1\}^n \times \{0, 1\}^* \rightarrow Z_{N_p}^*$$

The security analysis will view H_1 and H_2 as random oracles

Signing Phase: To sign a message $M \in \{0, 1\}^n$, the original signer applies the improved Rabin signature proposed in section 3.1.

Verification Phase: When receiving a signature (s, c_1, c_2) on message M, the verifier checks if $s^2 \equiv (-1)^{c_2} \cdot a^{c_1} H_1(M) \bmod N_o$. If the equation does not hold, verifier rejects the signature. Otherwise, he accepts it.

Delegating Phase: When the original signer delegates his signature capability to the proxy signer, they will run the following steps:

1. The original signer first makes a warrant M_w, then publishs it.
2. The original signer uses the improved Rabin signature scheme on M_w to generate proxy key (s_w, c_1^w, c_2^w), and send it to the designed proxy signer publicly. Here

$$s_w^2 \equiv (-1)^{c_2^w} \cdot a_o^{c_1^w} H_1(M_w) \bmod N_o \tag{1}$$

3. After receiving the proxy certificate (M_w, s_w, c_1^w, c_2^w), the proxy signer verifies the proxy certificate by checking if the equation (1) holds. If it holds, the proxy key will be accepted.

Proxy Signing Phase: To sign a message $M \in \{0,1\}^n$ on behalf of the original signer, the proxy signer does the follows:

Use the improved Rabin signature scheme to compute (γ, c_1, c_2) such that

$$\gamma^2 \equiv (-1)^{c_2} \cdot a_p^{c_1} \cdot H_2(M, s_w) \bmod N_p.$$

The signature for M is given by $\sigma_P = (M_w, s_w, \gamma, c_1^w, c_2^w, c_1, c_2)$.

Proxy Verification Phase: When receiving a proxy signature $\sigma_P = (M_w, s_w, \gamma, c_1^w, c_2^w, c_1, c_2)$, the receiver has to run the following steps:

1. Check if $s_w^2 \equiv (-1)^{c_2^w} \cdot a_o^{c_1^w} H_1(M_w) \bmod N_o$. If this condition does not hold, reject the signature.
2. Compute $h = H_2(M, s_w) \bmod N_p$ and then check if $\gamma^2 \equiv (-1)^{c_2} \cdot a_p^{c_1} \cdot h \bmod N_p$. If this condition does not hold, reject the signature. Otherwise, accept it.

4   Security Analysis

In this section, we will prove that our scheme is secure (i.e. verifiable, unforgeable, and undeniable) in the random oracle model.

Theorem 1. *If integer factorization problem is hard then the proposed scheme is secure in the random oracle model.*

Proof: We show that for any adversary $\mathcal{F}$ with non-negligible advantage $\mathbf{Adv}^{\mathbf{NSC}}_{\mathbf{PS},\mathcal{F}}(k)$, we can construct an algorithm $\mathcal{B}$ with non-negligible advantage $\mathbf{Adv}^{\mathbf{IF}}_{\mathcal{B}}$ to solve the integer factorization problem in a polynomial time. Let $N = p \cdot q$ be a random instance of the integer factorization problem. Here, p and q are two large primes and $p \equiv q \equiv 3 \bmod 4$. $\mathcal{B}$' job is to take as input N and try to work out p and q.

Here is how $\mathcal{B}$ is constructed.
$\mathcal{B}$ simulates $\mathcal{F}$'s challenger in the following game:

H_1**-Oracle Queries.** The algorithm $\mathcal{B}$ maintains a list of tuples $\langle M_w^i, N_o^i, s_w^i, S_w^i \rangle$ as explained below. We refer to this list as H_1^{list}. The list is initially empty. When the algorithm $\mathcal{F}$ queries the oracle H_1 at a point $\langle M_w^i, N_o^i \rangle$, the algorithm $\mathcal{B}$ first checks if the query $\langle M_w^i, N_o^i \rangle$ already appeared on the list H_1^{list} in a tuple $\langle M_w^i, N_o^i, s_w^i, S_w^i \rangle$. If it did, $\mathcal{B}$ responds with $H_1(M_w^i) = S_w^i \in Z_{N_o^i}^*$. Otherwise, $\mathcal{B}$ picks a random $s_w^i \in Z_{N_o^i}^*$, computes $S_w^i \equiv (s_w^i)^2 \bmod N_o^i$ and adds the tuple $\langle M_w^i, N_o^i, s_w^i, S_w^i \rangle$ into H_1^{list}, then responds with $H_1(M_w^i) = S_w^i \in Z_{N_o^i}^*$.

H_2**-Oracle Queries.** The algorithm $\mathcal{B}$ maintains a list of tuples $\langle M_i, s_w^i, N_p^i, w_i, W_i \rangle$ as explained below. We refer to this list as H_2^{list}. The list is initially empty. When the algorithm $\mathcal{A}$ queries the oracle H_2 at a point $\langle M_i, s_w^i, N_p^i \rangle$, the algorithm $\mathcal{B}$ first checks if the query $\langle M_i, s_w^i, N_p^i \rangle$ already appears on the list H_2^{list} in a tuple $\langle M_i, s_w^i, N_p^i, w_i, W_i \rangle$. If it was, $\mathcal{B}$ responds with $H_2(M_i, s_w^i) = W_i \in Z_{N_p^i}^*$. Otherwise, it selects a random $w_i \in Z_{N_p^i}^*$, computes $W_i = (w_i)^2 \bmod N_p^i$ and adds the tuple $\langle M_i, s_w^i, N_p^i, w_i, W_i \rangle$ into list H_2^{list}, then responds with $H_2(M_i, s_w^i) = W_i \in Z_{N_p^i}^*$.

Delegation-Oracle Queries. The algorithm $\mathcal{B}$ maintains a list of tuples $\langle N_p^i, M_w^i, s_w^i, c_1^{w_i}, c_2^{w_i} \rangle$ as explained below, where $c_1^{w_i} = c_2^{w_i} = 0$. We refer to this list as D^{list}. The list is initially empty. When the algorithm $\mathcal{A}$ asks for a delegation for a public key N_p^i, the algorithm $\mathcal{B}$ does it as follows: it first checks if the query $\langle N_p^i \rangle$ already appears on the D^{list} in the tuple $\langle N_p^i, M_w^i, s_w^i, c_1^{w_i}, c_2^{w_i} \rangle$. If it was, respond with the proxy certificate $\langle M_w^i, s_w^i, c_1^{w_i}, c_2^{w_i} \rangle$. Otherwise, it runs the above algorithm for responding to H_1-oracle queries to obtain a $s_w^i \in Z_N^*$ such that $H_1(M_w^i) = S_w^i$. Let $\langle M_w^i, N, s_w^i, S_w^i \rangle$ be the corresponding tuple on the H_1^{list}. Then respond with the proxy certificate $\langle M_w^i, s_w^i, c_1^{w_i}, c_2^{w_i} \rangle$.

Proxy Signing Queries. Let $\langle M_i, M_w, s_w, c_1^w, c_2^w, N_o^i \rangle$ be a signature query issued by $\mathcal{F}$. The algorithm $\mathcal{B}$ responds to this query as follows:

- It checks if the query $\langle M_w, N_o^i \rangle$ already appears on the H_1^{list} in a tuple $\langle M_w, N_o^i, s_w, S_w \rangle$. If it was not, $\mathcal{B}$ returns the symbol $\perp$. Otherwise, $\mathcal{B}$ checks if M_w is a valid warrant for N and if $\langle s_w, S_w \rangle$ satifies $s_w^2 \equiv S_w \bmod N_o^i$. If these conditions do not hold, $\mathcal{B}$ returns the symbol $\perp$.
- It runs the above algorithm for responding to H_2-oracle queries to obtain a $W_i \in Z_N^*$ such that $H_2(M_i, s_w^i) = W_i$. Let $\langle M_i, s_w^i, N, w_i, W_i \rangle$ be the corresponding tuple on the H_2^{list}. Then, it computes $\gamma = w_i$.

The proxy signature is given by $\sigma_P^i = (M_w, s_w, \gamma, c_1^w, c_2^w, c_1^i, c_2^i)$, where $c_1^{w_i} = c_1^{w_i} = c_1^i = c_2^i = 0$.

Output.

1. Assume $\mathcal{F}$ produces a tuple $\langle \sigma_P, N_p \rangle$ satisfying the following condition: (1) The delegation query $\langle N_p \rangle$ has not been made, (2) (M, σ_P) is a valid proxy signature. The algorithm $\mathcal{B}$ tries to translate this forge into factor N as follows: $\mathcal{B}$ first checks if the query $\langle M_w, N \rangle$ already appears on the list H_1^{list} in a tuple $\langle M_w, N, s_w', S_w \rangle$. If it was not, $\mathcal{B}$ return 0. Otherwise, $\mathcal{B}$ checks if $s_w' \equiv \pm s_w \bmod N$, where s_w is involved in σ_P. If it was, $\mathcal{B}$ return 0. Otherwise, $\mathcal{B}$ computes $p = \text{GCD}(s_w' - s_w, N)$, and returns 1. The probability that $\mathcal{B}$ return 1 is denoted by $\mathbf{Adv}_{\mathcal{F},1}^{\mathbf{NSC}}(k)$. Here, k is an security parameter.
2. Assume $\mathcal{F}$ produces a tuple $\langle \sigma, N_s \rangle$ satisfying the following condition: (1) The signing query $\langle M \rangle$ has not been made, (2) (M, σ) is a valid signature. The algorithm $\mathcal{B}$ tries to translate this forge into factor N as follows: $\mathcal{B}$ first checks if the query $\langle M, N_s \rangle$ appears on the list H_1^{list} in a tuple $\langle M, N_s, v, V \rangle$. If it was not, $\mathcal{B}$ return 0. Otherwise, $\mathcal{B}$ checks if $\gamma \equiv \pm v \bmod N$. If it

was, $\mathcal{B}$ return 0. Otherwise, $\mathcal{B}$ computes $p=\mathrm{GCD}(\gamma - v, N)$, and returns 1. The probability that $\mathcal{B}$ return 1 is denoted by $\mathbf{Adv}_{\mathcal{F},2}^{\mathbf{NSC}}(k)$. Here, k is an security parameter.

3. Assume $\mathcal{F}$ produces a tuple $\langle \sigma_P, N_o \rangle$ satisfying the following condition: (1) The proxy signing query $\langle M, M_w, s_w, c_1^w, c_2^w, N_o \rangle$ has not been made, (2) (M, σ_P) is a valid proxy signature. The algorithm $\mathcal{B}$ tries to translate this forge into factor N as follows: $\mathcal{B}$ first checks if the query $\langle M, s_w, N \rangle$ appears on the list H_2^{list} in a tuple $\langle M, s_w, N, w, W \rangle$. If it was not, $\mathcal{B}$ return 0. Otherwise, $\mathcal{B}$ checks if $\gamma \equiv \pm w \bmod N$. If it was, $\mathcal{B}$ return 0. Otherwise, $\mathcal{B}$ computes $p=\mathrm{GCD}(\gamma - w, N)$, and returns 1. The probability that $\mathcal{B}$ return 1 is denoted by $\mathbf{Adv}_{\mathcal{F},3}^{\mathbf{NSC}}(k)$. Here, k. Here, k is an security parameter.

Suppose up to q_{H_1} H_1-oracle queries and q_{H_2} H_2-oracle queries were issued. We denote $\max\{q_{H_1} \cdot 2^{-k}, q_{H_2} \cdot 2^{-k}\}$ by F. It is easy to see that the relation $\mathbf{Adv}_{\mathcal{F}}^{\mathbf{NSC}}(k) \geq \max\{\mathbf{Adv}_{\mathcal{F},1}^{\mathbf{NSC}}(k), \mathbf{Adv}_{\mathcal{F},2}^{\mathbf{NSC}}(k), \mathbf{Adv}_{\mathcal{F},3}^{\mathbf{NSC}}(k)\}$ is hold. So we have the relation $\mathbf{Adv}_{\mathcal{B}}^{\mathbf{IF}} \geq \mathbf{Adv}_{\mathcal{F}}^{\mathbf{NSC}}(k)$ - F. Since $\mathcal{F}$ are polynomial algorithm, it is easy to see q_{H_1} and q_{H_2} are polynomial functions of security parameter k and $\mathcal{B}$ is polynomial function of security parameter k. Thus the theorem is proved.

5 Conclusion

In this paper, we proposed a new proxy-protected signature scheme, which is based on factorization assumption and needs no secret channel to transmit proxy private key. Moveover, the security of our scheme was proved in the random oracle model. Compared to the other schemes, our scheme reduces the mount of time-consuming computations. Therefore, in the mobile computation environments, our schemes can be applied in many low-computation devices, such as cell phones, pages, smart cards etc.

References

1. Mambo, M., Usuda, K. and Okamoto, E.: Proxy signatures for delegating signing operation. In Proceedings of the 3rd ACM Conference on Computer and Communications Security (CCS), New Delhi,India, pp. 48-57, 1996.
2. Mambo, M., Usuda, K. and Okamoto, E.: Proxy signatures delegation of the power to sign message. IEICE Transaction Functional E79-A(9) 1338-1354, 1996.
3. Boldyreva, A., Palacio, A. and Warinschi, B.: Secure proxy signature schemes for delegation of signing rights. http://venona.antioffline.com/2003/096.pdf.
4. Kim, H., Baek, J., Lee, B. and Kim, K.: Secret Computation with secrets for mobile agent using one-time proxy signature. The 2001 Symposium on Cryptography and Information Security, Oiso, Japan.
5. Wang, H.X., Pieprzyk, J.: Efficient one-time proxy signatures. Proceedings of Asiacrypt'2003, LNCS 2894, pp.507-522, Springer-Verlag, 2003.
6. Sun, H.M., Lee, N.Y., Hwang, T.: Threshold proxy signatures. IEE Proc-Comput. Digit. Tech. 146(5) 259-263, 1999.

7. Zhang, K.: Threshold proxy signature schemes. in:1997 Information Security Workshop, Japan , pp.191-197, September 1997.
8. Kim, S., Park, S., Won, D.: Proxy signatures, revised. ICICS'97, LNCS vol.1334, pp.223-232, Springer-Verlag, 1997.
9. Yi, L., Bai, G., Xiao, G.: A new type of proxy signature scheme. Electronic Letters, 36(6), pp.527-528, 2000.
10. Shao, Z.: Proxy signature schemes based on factoring. Information Processing Letter, Vol.85, No.3, pp.137-143, 2003.
11. Ballare, M. and Rogaway, P.: Random oracles are practical: a paradiam for designing efficient protocols. In first ACM Conference on Computer and Communication Security, ACM, 1993.
12. Rabin, M.O.: Digitalized signatures. Foundations of Secure Communication, Academic Press, pp.155-168, 1978.

Security of an Efficient ID-Based Authenticated Key Agreement Protocol from Pairings

Shengbao Wang[1,2], Zhenfu Cao[1], and Haiyong Bao[1]

[1] Department of Computer Science and Engineering,
Shanghai Jiao Tong University, 1954 Huashan Road,
Shanghai 200030, P.R. China
[2] Center of Computing , Paobing Academy,
451 Huangshan Road, Hefei 230031, P.R. China
{shengbao-wang, cao-zf, bhy}@cs.sjtu.edu.cn
http://tdt.sjtu.edu.cn

Abstract. Authenticated key agreement protocols are essential for secure communications in open and distributed environments. In 2004, Ryu et al. proposed an efficient two-party identity-based authenticated key agreement protocol based on pairings. However, in this paper, we demonstrate that their protocol is vulnerable to a key-compromise impersonation attack. The attacking scenario is described in details. Furthermore,we point out that their protocol provides the property of deniability and at the same time it is the mechanism used to achieve deniability that allows the key-compromise impersonation attack.

1 Introduction

Key agreement protocol allows two or more communication parties to establish a secret session key over an open network. In key agreement protocols, both parties contribute information to the generation of the shared session key. The session key is usually subsequently be used to achieve some cryptographic goal, such as confidentiality or data integrity. Diffie and Hellman [5] first proposed an efficient two-party key agreement protocol in 1976. However, it does not provide the two parties to authenticate each other. Afterwards, many key agreement protocols were proposed to provide mutual authentication among communication parties. If in a protocol one party is assured that no other party aside from the specially identified party (or parties) may gain access to the particular established secret key, then the key agreement protocol is said to provide *implicit key authentication (IKA)*. A key agreement protocol that provides mutual IKA between (or among) parties is called an *authenticated key agreement (AK)* protocol [3]. Key agreement protocols employ private or public key cryptography. In this paper, we shall only consider two-party key agreement protocols in the public-key setting.

In the past, some desired security attributes for AK protocols have been identified in [3,7,8]. We briefly explain the security attributes as follows (refer to [3,7] for a detailed discussion):

G. Chen et al. (Eds.): ISPA Workshops 2005, LNCS 3759, pp. 342–349, 2005.
© Springer-Verlag Berlin Heidelberg 2005

- **Known-key Secrecy.** Suppose an established session key between two entities is disclosed, the adversary is unable to learn other established session keys.
- **Perfect Forward Secrecy.** If both long-term secret keys of two entities are disclosed, the adversary is unable to derive old session keys established by that two entities.
- **Key-Compromise Impersonation (K-CI) Resilience.** Assume that entities A and B are two principals. Suppose $A's$ secret key is disclosed. Obviously, an adversary who knows this secret key can impersonate A to other entities (e.g. B). However, it is desired that this disclosure does not allow the adversary to impersonate other entities (e.g. B) to A.
- **Unknown key-Share (UK-S) Resilience.** Entity A cannot be coerced into sharing a key with entity B without $A's$ knowledge, i.e., when A believes that the key is shared with some entity $C \neq B$, and B (correctly) believes the key is shared with A.
- **No key Control.** Neither A nor B can predetermine any portion of the shared session key being established between them.
- **Deniability.** Each party of the protocol should be able to deny having taken part in a particular protocol run.

The main desirable *performance attributes* of AK protocols include a minimal number of passes (the number of messages exchanged in a run of the protocol), low communication overhead (total number of bits transmitted), and low computation overhead.

The idea of *identity (ID)-based cryptography* was first introduced by Shamir in 1984 [9] . The basic idea behind an ID-based cryptosystem is that end users can choose an arbitrary string, for example email addresses or other online identifiers, as their public key. This eliminates much of the overhead associated with key management. In traditional PKI settings, key agreement protocols relies on the parties obtaining each other's public-key certificates, extracting each other's public keys, checking certificate chains (which may involve many signature verifications) and finally generating a shared secret. The technique of identity-based cryptography greatly simplifies this process [6].

In 2001, Boneh and Franklin [1] gave the first feasible solutions for ID-based encryption (IBE) using the Weil pairing on elliptic curves. Since then many ID-based AK protocols using pairings have been suggested. In particular, Smart [10] proposed an ID-based AK protocol based on the idea of the IBE scheme of Boneh and Franklin. Later, Shim [11] and Chen and Kudla [4] independently pointed out that Smart's protocol does not provide the *full* forward secrecy which is an important security requirement for an AK protocol. Shim [11] further proposed an efficient ID-based AK protocol to provide the full forward secrecy. He also gave more security analysis to show that the proposed protocol provides other attractive security properties for an AK protocol as listed above, such as known-key security, K-CI resilience, and UK-S resilience. However, it was pointed out by Sun and Hsieh [12] that Shim's AK protocol suffers from an important security flaw because it is not protected from a man-in-the-middle attack. Most recently,

Ryu et al. [8] introduced an efficient ID-based AK protocol using pairings in which computation and communication overheads for establishing a session key are significantly reduced. Ryu et al. also argue that their protocol has the properties of know-key security, perfect forward secrecy, no key control, and especially, K-CI resilience.

In this paper, we show that Ryu et al.'s protocol is still insecure against the K-CI attack. Furthermore, we point out that their protocol provides the property of deniability [2] and give a discussion on the relationship between the property of K-CI resilience and deniability for the protocol. The rest of this paper is structured as follows. In the next section, we give the definition of pairings and some related mathematical problems. Section 3 briefly reviews Ryu et al.'s ID-based AK protocol from pairings. We show that Ryu et al.'s protocol is vulnerable to a K-CI attack in Section 4. In Section 5, some further discussions are given. Finally, we draw our conclusion in Section 6.

2   Technical Backgrounds

2.1   Pairings

In this section, we describe in a more general format the basic definition and properties of the pairing: more details can be found in [1].

Let G_1 be a cyclic additive group generated by an element P, whose order is a prime q, and G_2 be a cyclic multiplicative group of the same prime order q. We assume that the discrete logarithm problem (DLP) in both G_1 and G_2 are hard. An *admissible pairing* e is a bilinear map $e : G_1 \times G_1 \to G_2$, which satisfies the following three properties:

1. *Bilinear*: If $P, Q \in G_1$ and $a, b \in Z_q^*$, then $e(aP, bQ) = e(P, Q)^{ab}$;
2. *Non-degenerate*: There exists a $P \in G_1$ such that $e(P, P) \neq 1$;
3. *Computable*: If $P, Q \in G_1$, one can compute $e(P, Q) \in G_2$ in polynomial time.

We note that the modified Weil and Tate pairings associated with supersingular elliptic curves are examples of such admissible pairings.

2.2   Bilinear Diffie-Hellman Problem

The security of the ID-based authenticated key agreement protocol discussed in this paper is based on the Computational Diffie-Hellman (CDH) and Bilinear Diffie-Hellman (BDH) assumptions [1,4]:

1. **A Diffie-Hellman (DH) Tuple in G_1**
   $(P, xP, yP, zP) \in G_1^4$, for some x, y, z chosen at random from Z_q^* satisfying $z = xy \bmod q$.
2. **Computational Diffie-Hellman (CDH) Problem**
   Given the first three elements from the four elements in a DH tuple, compute the fourth element.

3. **CDH Assumption**

   There exists no algorithm running in expected polynomial time, which can solve the CDH problem with non-negligible probability.

4. **Bilinear Diffie-Hellman (BDH) Problem**

   Let P be a generator of G_1. The BDH problem in $< G_1, G_2, e >$ is that given $(P, xP, yP, zP) \in G_1^4$ for some x, y, z chosen at random from Z_q^*, compute $W = e(P, P)^{xyz} \in G_2$.

5. **BDH Assumption**

   There exists no algorithm running in expected polynomial time, which can solve the BDH problem in $< G_1, G_2, e >$ with non-negligible probability.

3   Review of Ryu et al.'s Protocol

In this section, we briefly review the ID-based AK protocol due to Ryu et al. [8]. This protocol involves there entities: two users (say Alice and Bob) who wish to establish a shared secret session key, and a *private key generator (PKG)* from whom they each acquire their own private key (Note that the PKG is a common setting in all kinds of ID-based cryptosystems). The ID-based AK protocol consists of two stages: system setup and authenticated key agreement.

3.1   System Setup

Suppose we have an admissible pairing $e : G_1 \times G_1 \rightarrow G_2$ as described in the preceding section, where G_1 and G_2 are two groups with the same prime order q. The PKG follows the following steps:

1. picks an arbitrary generator $P \in G_1$, a secret master key $s \in Z_q^*$;
2. chooses a cryptographic hash function $H_1 : \{0, 1\}^* \rightarrow G_1$;
3. publishes the system parameters $params =< G_1, G_2, e, P, H_1 >$;
4. computes the private key $S_{ID} = sQ_{ID}$ for a user with the identity information ID, in which the user's public key is $Q_{ID} = H_1(ID)$;
5. distributes the private key S_{ID} to the user with the identity information ID via a secure channel.

Thus, each user's ID-based public/private key pair is defined as (Q_{ID}, S_{ID}) where $Q_{ID}, S_{ID} \in G_1$.

3.2   Authenticated Key Agreement

We denote user Alice and Bob's public/private key pairs as (Q_A, S_A) and (Q_B, S_B), respectively. To establish a shared session key, Alice and Bob each firstly generate an ephemeral private key (say a and $b \in Z_q^*$), and compute the corresponding ephemeral public keys $T_A = aP$ and $T_B = bP$. They then exchange T_A and T_B as described in Figure 1(M_i denotes the i-th message flow).

$$M_1 : \text{Alice} \to \text{Bob} : T_A$$
$$M_2 : \text{Bob} \to \text{Alice} : T_B$$

Fig. 1. Ryu et al.'s ID-based AK Protocol

After the message exchange, the two users do the following:

1. Alice computes the shared secret K_{AB} as follows (after receiving T_B):

$$K_{AB} = kdf(\text{Alice}, \text{Bob}, V_{AB}, aT_B),$$

in which $V_{AB} = e(S_A, Q_B)$ and $kdf()$ is a predetermined key derivation function of the two users.

2. Bob computes the shared secret K_{BA} as follows (after receiving T_A):

$$K_{BA} = kdf(\text{Alice}, \text{Bob}, V_{BA}, bT_A),$$

in which $V_{BA} = e(S_B, Q_A)$.

It is easy to see $aT_B = bT_A = abP$. And, by the bilinearity of the pairing, we can easily get the following equation:

$$\begin{aligned}
V_{AB} &= e(S_A, Q_B) \\
&= e(sQ_A, Q_B) \\
&= e(Q_A, Q_B)^s \\
&= e(Q_A, S_B) \\
&= V_{BA}.
\end{aligned}$$

Thus, the two secret keys computed by Alice and Bob (K_{AB} and K_{BA}) are equal to each other, i.e., the two users successfully established a shared secret session key after running an instance of the protocol.

We note that Ryu et al.'s ID-based AK protocol actually makes use of the ID-based non-interactive static authenticated key agreement protocol due to Sakai et al. [13]. In Sakai et al.'s scheme, two parties can share a common static secret without any interaction between them. We refer the readers to [13] to see how this "magic" result is achieved.

In [8], Ryu et al. showed that their protocol is more efficient than Chen and Kudla's protocol while at the same time enjoys all the security properties. In particular, they also claimed that their protocol is secure against the K-CI attack. However, contrary to their claim, in the next section we will show that Ryu et al.'s protocol is still vulnerable to the K-CI attack.

4   K-CI Attack on Ryu et al.'s Protocol

Assume that Alice's private key S_A is compromised. Obviously, an adversary Eve who knows this private key can impersonate Alice to any other entity, since S_A is the only private key of Alice which exactly identifies her. As previously stated, it is desired that this compromise does not allow the adversary Eve to impersonate other entities to Alice.

In this section, we give the following scenario to show that Ryu et al.'s ID-based AK protocol is insecure against the K-CI attack. In our scenario, the two users Alice and Bob are about to run an instance of the AK protocol as described in Section 3. As in the same section, we denote the ID-based non-interactively shared static key of Alice and Bob as V_{AB}. With the knowledge of Alice's private key S_A, Eve tries to impersonate Bob to Alice. Notice that Eve can easily compute $V_{AB} = e(S_A, Q_B)$ exactly in the same way as Alice does. The K-CI attack launched by Eve against Alice and Bob is described as follows:

1. Eve first generates a random $b' \in Z_q^*$, and computes $T'_B = b'P$, then he intercepts T_B from Bob to Alice while sends T'_B to Alice instead;
2. Upon receiving T'_B, Alice computes the session key as follows:

$$K'_{AB} = kdf(\texttt{Alice}, \texttt{Bob}, V_{AB}, aT'_B),$$

where $V_{AB} = e(S_A, Q_B)$;
3. After intercepting T_A from Alice to Bob, Eve computes the session key similarly as follows:

$$K_{EA} = kdf(\texttt{Alice}, \texttt{Bob}, V_{AB}, b'T_A).$$

Thus the shared session key established by Eve and Alice is as follows:

$$\begin{aligned}
K'_{AB} &= kdf(\texttt{Alice}, \texttt{Bob}, V_{AB}, aT'_B) \\
&= kdf(\texttt{Alice}, \texttt{Bob}, V_{AB}, ab'P) \\
&= kdf(\texttt{Alice}, \texttt{Bob}, V_{AB}, b'T_A) \\
&= K_{EA}.
\end{aligned}$$

Therefore, when Alice wants to create a secure communication with Bob, Eve can always impersonate Bob to Alice. The above K-CI attacking scenario is presented graphically in Figure 2.

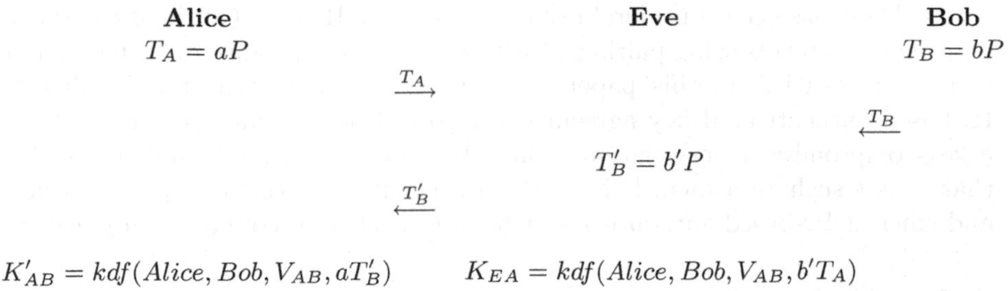

Alice		Eve		Bob
$T_A = aP$				$T_B = bP$

$$\xrightarrow{\quad T_A \quad}$$

$$\xleftarrow{\quad T_B \quad}$$

$$T'_B = b'P$$

$$\xleftarrow{\quad T'_B \quad}$$

$K'_{AB} = kdf(Alice, Bob, V_{AB}, aT'_B)$ $K_{EA} = kdf(Alice, Bob, V_{AB}, b'T_A)$

Fig. 2. K-CI Attack on Ryu et al.'s ID-based AK Protocol

5   Further Discussions: Deniability Versus K-CI Resilience

In short, as for Ryu et al.'s protocol, the properties of deniability and K-CI resilience may seem in conflict with each other. In their protocol, the mechanism used to provide deniability allows K-CI attack.

Deniability. On one hand, as electronic communications become a part of everyday life, privacy protection for communication parties has become more and more important. Deniability is one of the most desirable features for privacy protection in key agreement protocols. Borrowing the definition of *deniable encryption* by Canetti et al. [2], we may say that a two-party key agreement protocol is *deniable* for one party, if the other party could have simulated the protocol without the presence of him.

As has been pointed out in Section 3, Ryu et al.'s protocol adopted the mechanism of Sakai et al. [13] to enable each party of the protocol to compute the ID-based static shared secret $V_{AB} = V_{BA} = e(Q_A, Q_B)^s$ without any interaction with the other party. Thus, Ryu et al.'s protocol can be simulated perfectly by either party. Therefor, the protocol can be seen to provide deniability to both of the two communication parties.

K-CI Resilience. On the other hand, the property of K-CI resilience is essential for AK protocols: compromise of a short-term secret affects only that particular session, whereas compromise of a long-term secret to allow K-CI attack is fatal to the security of future sessions, and therefore must be remedied immediately.

As has been illustrated in Section 4, Ryu et al.'s protocol doesn't provide K-CI resilience. Once again, it is due to the adoption of Sakai et al.'s non-interactive key agreement mechanism [13]. In fact, when an adversary knows one party Alice's secret key, he is able to compute all the static shared secret values (denoted as $V_{Ai} = V_{iA} = e(Q_A, Q_i)^s$) non-interactively shared between her and any other entity i. As a result, in Ryu et al.'s protocol the adversary can impersonate any entity i to Alice.

6   Conclusion

In the area of secure communications, key agreement is one of the most important issues. There has been considerable recent interest in ID-based authenticated key agreement protocols using pairings. However, few of them achieve all the desired security properties. In this paper, we have shown that Ryu et al.'s efficient ID-based authenticated key agreement protocol from pairings is vulnerable to a key-compromise impersonation attack. We have also investigated the reason that causes such an attack. It is an important future work to propose a secure and efficient ID-based authenticated key agreement protocol based on pairings.

Acknowledgments

The authors would like to thank Rongxing Lu for valuable discussions, and the anonymous reviewers for their helpful comments that improved the presentation of this paper. This work was partially supported by the NSFC under Grant No. 60225007 and the NRFC under Grant No. 20020248024.

References

1. D. Boneh, M. Franklin. Identity-based encryption from the Weil pairing. In *Proc. of CRYPTO 2001*, LNCS vol. 2139, pp. 213-229. Springer-Verlag, 2001.
2. R. Canetti, C. Dwork, M. Naor, and R. Ostrovsky. Deniable encryption. In *Proc. of CRYPTO 1997*, LNCS vol. 1294, pp. 90-104. Springer-Verlag, 1997.
3. S. Blake-Wilson, A. Menezes. Authenticated Diffie-Hellman key agreement protocols. In *Proc. of SAC 1998*, LNCS vol. 1556, pp. 339-361. Springer-Verlag, 1999.
4. L. Chen, C. Kudla. Identity based key agreement protocols from pairings. In *Proc. of the 16th IEEE Computer Security Foundations Workshop*, pp. 219-213. IEEE Computer Society, 2002.
5. W. Diffie, M.E. Hellman. New directions in cryptography. *IEEE Trans. Inf. Theory* 22(6), pp.644 - 654, 1976.
6. N. McCullagh, P.S.L.M. Barreto. A new two-party identity-based authenticated key agreement. In *Proc. of CT-RSA 2005*, LNCS vol. 3376, pp. 262-274. Springer-Verlag, 2005.
7. A. Menezes, P. van Oorschot and S. Vanstone. Handbook of Applied Cryptography, pp. 237-238. CRC Press, 1997.
8. E.K. Ryu, E.J. Yoon, and K.Y. Yoo. An efficient ID-based authenticated key agreement protocol from pairings. In *Proc. of NETWORKING 2004*, LNCS vol. 3042, pp. 1458-1463. Springer-Verlag, 2004.
9. A. Shamir. Identity-based cryptosystems and signature schemes. In *Proc. of CRYPTO 1984*, LNCS vol. 196, pp. 47-53. Springer-Verlag, 1984.
10. N. Smart. An ID-based authenticated key agreement protocol based on the Weil pairing. *Electron. Lett.*, 38(13), pp. 630-632, 2002.
11. K. Shim. Efficient ID-based authenticated key agreement protocol based on Weil pairing. *Electron. Lett.*, 39(8), pp. 653-654, 2003.
12. H. Sun, B. Hsieh. Security analysis of Shim's authenticated key agreement protocols from pairings. IACR Cryptology ePrint Archive, Report 2003/113, 2003.
13. R. Sakai, K. Ohgishi, and M. Kasahara. Cryptosystems based on pairing. In *Proc. of SCIS 2000*. Okinawa, Japan, 2000.

Encryption Based on Reversible Second-Order Cellular Automata*

Zhenchuan Chai, Zhenfu Cao, and Yuan Zhou

Department of Computer Science and Engineering,
Shanghai Jiaotong University, 1954 Huashan Road,
Shanghai 200030, P.R.China
{zcchai, zfcao, Yzhou}@cs.sjtu.edu.cn

Abstract. In this paper, we present a novel cryptosystem based on reversible second-order cellular automata. The cryptosystem is featured by its large key space and high speed due to cellular automata's parallel information processing property. Moreover, the encryption and decryption devices share the identical module, which preserves the merit of local connection of cellular automata in both encryption and decryption devices. So the scheme could be implemented in hardware efficiently. We also apply such system in message and image encryption.

1 Introduction

With the ever-increasing growth of data communication, the need for strong data security and easy implementation of the cryptosystem has become a basic necessity. Cellular automaton (CA), first introduced by John Von Neumann in the 1950s, has been accepted as a good dynamical system for simulation of complex physical systems and the development of complexity in biology. The advantage of its simple parallel-structure but complex behaviors also makes CA a promising encryption device in favor of hardware implementation. We exploited some features of CA to implement a cryptosystem in this paper.

1.1 Encryption with Cellular Automata

Over decades of years, cellular automata have been used as encrypting devices in both symmetric systems and public-key systems. In 1985, Stephen Wolfram [1] first used iterations of a CA with rule 30 to generate key stream in stream cipher cryptography. Then, a lot of researches have been done on how to generate a high quality pseudorandom key stream using CAs [2,3,4]. And it has been stated that, with fewer gate delays and higher implementation efficiency, maximum-length

---

* Supported by the National Natural Science Foundation of China for Distinguished Young Scholars under Grant No. 60225007, the National Research Fund for the Doctoral Program of Higher Education of China under Grant No. 20020248024, the Science and Technology Research Project of Shanghai under Grant No. 04JC14055 and 04dz07067.

G. Chen et al. (Eds.): ISPA Workshops 2005, LNCS 3759, pp. 350–358, 2005.

CA [3] could generate the key stream equivalent to that output by linear feedback shift register (LFSR). CAs were also used in block cipher cryptography. S.Nandi et al [2] implemented a block cryptosystem based on additive CAs with group properties. Kari[5] proposed a cryptosystem with reversible CA. And in 2002, Zhang [6] presented a new method of encryption based on reversible CA that has a large key space. However, all these block schemes use CA rules with specific properties that constitute only a small fraction of the CA rule space[9], so could not exploit other potential CA rules that show good qualities for cryptology. Moreover, zhang's scheme has an asymmetric implementation of encryption and decryption in hardware, because the inverse of a reversible CA is usually not equal to itself. And the inverse of selected reversible CA usually breaks the merit of locality of CA, i.e. the neighbors of a cell may be far from it, which is not desirable for implementation in hardware. CAs were proposed for public-key systems by Guan[7] and Kari [5], but none of which seemed to be successful enough to be put into practical use.

In this paper, we present a new symmetric cryptosystem based on reversible second-order CA, which overcomes all the shortcomings mentioned above. Our system could exploit, in theory, any one-order CA to be part of secret key, so the key space is enormously large. Our scheme is efficient due to the parallel structure of CA. And the encryption/decryption modules share the same structure that is easy for implementation in hardware.

1.2   Cellular Automata

Cellular automata are dynamic systems in which space and time are discrete. A cellular automaton consists of a large collection of cells, each of which can be in one of a set of states, updated synchronously in discrete time steps, according to the states of neighbor cells.

In order to define a CA, one has to specify at least four parameters: the *dimension d*, the *state set S*, the *neighborhood vector N* and the *local rule f*.

A d-dimensional CA consists of a d-dimensional array of identical cells, each of which is indexed by Z^d, the set of d tuples of integers. Each cell is always in one state from a finite state set S. For example, a k-state CA may have state set $S = \{1, ..., k\}$. The neighborhood vector N tells where the neighbors of a specified cell are situated. Given a neighborhood vector $N = \{\overrightarrow{x_1}, \overrightarrow{x_2}, \cdots, \overrightarrow{x_m}\}$, $\overrightarrow{x_i} \in Z^d$, a cell indexed by $\overrightarrow{x}$ can work out its m neighbors' indexes by calculating $\overrightarrow{x} + \overrightarrow{x_i}$ for $i = 1, 2, \cdots, m$. The local rule f is a function mapping from S^m to S that updates a cell's state according to its m neighbors' states, i.e. $a_{\overrightarrow{x}}^{t+1} = f(a_{\overrightarrow{x}+\overrightarrow{x_1}}^t, a_{\overrightarrow{x}+\overrightarrow{x_2}}^t, \cdots, a_{\overrightarrow{x}+\overrightarrow{x_m}}^t)$, where $a_{\overrightarrow{x}}^t \in S$ means the state of a cell indexed by $\overrightarrow{x}$ at time step t.

A *configuration* $C \in S^n$ (n is the number of cells of CA) is all the states of the cells in the CA, and *neighborhood configuration* is all the neighbors' states of a cell.

Elementary CA [10] is a 1-dimensional 2-state 3-neighborhood CA with neighborhood vector $N = \{-1, 0, 1\}$, where each cell is indexed by an integer *i*. The elementary CA updates its cells with $a_i^{t+1} = f(a_{i-1}^t, a_i^t, a_{i+1}^t)$. There are 2^3 possible distinct neighborhood configurations (the states of $a_{i-1}^t, a_i^t, a_{i+1}^t$) in elementary CA. If each of these neighborhood configurations is assigned with a boolean value (0 or 1), then the number of such possible assignments could total up to 2^{2^3}. Actually, each assignment defines a local rule f, which is a mapping from neighborhood configuration to next state, and the local rule f is numbered by the decimal version of the assignment (8 bits). For example, rule 90 (01011010), rule 150 (10010110), and rule 102 (01100110) assigns each possible neighborhood configurations as in Table 1:

Table 1. Rule 90, rule 150, and rule 102

	$(a_{i-1}^t, a_i^t, a_{i+1}^t)$:111	110	101	100	011	010	001	000	
Rule 90	$(a_i^{t+1} = f(\bullet))$: 0	1	0	1	1	0	1	0	Decimal 90
Rule 150	$(a_i^{t+1} = f(\bullet))$: 1	0	0	1	0	1	1	0	Decimal 150
Rule 150	$(a_i^{t+1} = f(\bullet))$: 0	1	1	0	0	1	1	0	Decimal 102

A CA is called *uniform* if the same rule applies to all the cells, otherwise the CA is called *hybrid*.

In a finite CA, extreme cells, i.e., cells located at the boundary, may have their neighbors missing. It is called null boundary if the values of the missing neighbors are assumed to be 0 and cyclic boundary if the extreme cells are assumed to be adjacent. A CA has input boundary, if the values of missing neighbors are determined by input[6].

A CA is called additive if its rule could be expressed with EXOR and/or EXNOR operation. And such CA could be characterized by a characteristic matrix. Complete characterization of additive CA based on matrix algebraic could be found in [8].

Note, the rule 102,150,90 could be expressed in combinational logic (readers are referred to table 1):

$$\text{Rule 102: } a_i^{t+1} = f_{102}(a_{i-1}^t, a_i^t, a_{i+1}^t) = a_i^t \oplus a_{i+1}^t$$
$$\text{Rule 150: } a_i^{t+1} = f_{150}(a_{i-1}^t, a_i^t, a_{i+1}^t) = a_{i-1}^t \oplus a_i^t \oplus a_{i+1}^t$$
$$\text{Rule 90: } a_i^{t+1} = f_{90}(a_{i-1}^t, a_i^t, a_{i+1}^t) = a_{i-1}^t \oplus a_{i+1}^t$$

So the CA could easily be implemented in hardware as Fig 1(a).

2 Reversible Second-Order CA(RCA²)

In this section, we give a brief introduction to reversible (one-order) cellular automata and reversible second-order cellular automata, which is the building block of our schemes.

At each time step, by applying local rule (or rules) to every cells of a CA, one obtains a new configuration C^{t+1} from the CA's old configuration C^t called

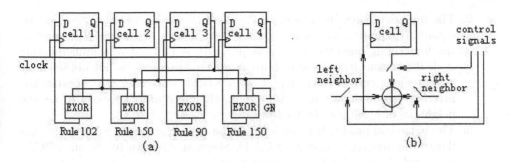

Fig. 1. (a)Hybrid elementary CA with input boundary. (b) Programmable CA with three control signals.

C^{t+1}'s predecessor. Thus, the local rule (or rules) defines a mapping from C^t to C^{t+1}, called the global map $F(\cdot)$, i.e. $C^{t+1} = F(C^t)$. And such CA is called one-order CA because its "next" configuration is only derived from its "current" configuration.

A CA is called second-order CA (CA²) if its "next" configuration is a function of both the "current" and the "previous" one [9].

For instance, a one-order CA could be characterized by $C^{t+1} = F(C^t)$, where C^t denotes CA's configuration at time step t, and $F(\cdot)$ is a global map determined by local rule (or rules). Then a second order CA could be characterized as

$$C^{t+1} = G(C^t, C^{t-1}) \tag{1}$$

where $G(\cdot)$ is a global map defined by some time and space relations between the cells.

If given C^{t+1} and C^t, there is only one configuration C^{t-1} that satisfies equation (1), then such CA is called reversible CA² (RCA²).

Now, let's consider a special second-order CA, described as follows:

$$C^{t+1} = G(C^t, C^{t-1}) = F(C^t) - C^{t-1} \tag{2}$$

where $F(\cdot)$ is a global map of some one-order CA.

It could easily be seen that the CA² of equation (2) is reversible with its reverse CA² described as follows:

$$C^{t-1} = F(C^t) - C^{t+1} \tag{3}$$

We strength that the RCA² constructed in equation(2) has the following properties:

1: Whether the underlying one-order CA characterized by $F(\cdot)$ is reversible (i.e. $F(\cdot)$ is injective[9]) or not, such RCA² could be constructed from it. So the number of RCA² is at least as many as that of one-order CA, much more than that of RCA.

2: The inverse of such RCA^2 and RCA^2 itself in fact share the same dynamic equation (equation (2) and (3)), and both inherit the merit of locality of the underlying one-order CA. This property is preferable in implementing such RCA^2 and its inverse in hardware. This property is not obtained by any previous cryptosystem based on reversible one-order CA, because the inverse of a one-order CA usually breaks the merit of locality of CA, i.e. the neighbors of a cell may be far from it.

3: The behaviors produced by such RCA^2 have been showed qualitatively similar to the underlying one-order CA by Stephen Wolfram[10]. So such RCA^2 is suitable for constructing cryptosystem.

4: Given a configuration pair (C^t, C^{t+1}), no one could trace back the initial configuration pair (C^0, C^1) without any information about local rules or $F(\cdot)$.

We will construct our scheme using this basic RCA^2 in the next section.

3 RCA^2 Based Block Cipher Scheme

In this section, we first present our basic scheme, and then enhance the basic scheme to a more strong one by employing RCA^2 with input boundary.

3.1   Basic Scheme

Our basic scheme is straightforward form Eq2.2. A block of plaintext $M(= M_a || M_b)$ could be fed into the RCA^2 as initial configuration pair $\langle C^0 = M_a, C^1 = M_b \rangle$. Then the RCA^2 runs for p rounds, and outputs the cipher, a configuration pair$\langle C^p, C^{p+1} \rangle$. To decode the cipher, $\langle C^{p+1}, C^p \rangle$ is put back into the RCA^2 as initial configuration pair, and is processed with $p$iterations to recover the plaintext M.

In this basic scheme, the secret key consists of the global map $F(\cdot)$ of underlying one order CA and the number of iteration p. The cipher and the plain text are pairs of configurations of the RCA^2.

3.2   Experiment on Enhanced Basic Scheme

In order to increase the difficulty of cryptanalysis, we could make a tradeoff between security and extension of cipher. For instance, $C^0$of the initial configuration pair $\langle C^0, C^1 \rangle$ could be plaintext M while C^1 is a random chosen vector. The following example illustrates the enhanced scheme.

In the example, we use a 1-dimensional 2-state hybrid RCA^2 that consists of 50 cells. The secret $F(\cdot)$ is the underlying elementary CA's global map determined by a mixture of rules 54,90,150, i.e., each cell is applied with rule 54,90 or 150. The number of iteration p is set to 100. We encrypt two 50-bit messages m1 and m2 with only one bit difference and the same random configuration C^1. Fig 2 shows the results.

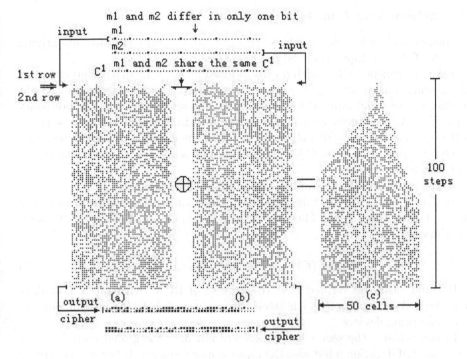

Fig. 2. Time and space diagrams of encryption processes

Fig. 3. Image encryption with 2-dimensional RCA^2

In the diagram (a), the first row is the plaintext m1 to be encrypted. The second row is a random configuration C^1. The m1 and C^1 constitute the initial configuration pair $\langle m1, C^1 \rangle$ which the RCA^2 takes to iterate 100 rounds and outputs the cipher. The whole process of iterations was recorded as a sequence of configurations that forms the time-space diagram of (a). So the last two rows of the diagram is the output cipher. In order to show the effect of one-bit change of plaintext on the cipher, we flipped only one bit in the m1 to obtain m2. With other settings the same as that of m1's encryption process, including the same random configuration C^1, we obtain the m2's encryption time-space diagram (b). Then we overlap the diagram (a) and (b) with EXOR operation to form diagram (c). Diagram (c) illustrates clearly the difference between (a) and (b), thus we could see the avalanche effect of one bit change in plaintext on the cipher.

3.3   Scheme Based on RCA^2 with Input Boundary

We modify our basic scheme into a stronger one by employing the underlying one order CA with input boundary.

Take an elementary CA with n cells indexed by $i(i = 1, \cdots, n)$ as an example, the extreme cells a_1 and a_n have their neighbors (a_0 and a_{n+1}) missing. So at our choices, we could input the values of assumed a_0 and a_{n+1} at the boundary of the CA. Alternatively, we could compose a n dimensional vector $v = (v_1 = a_0, 0, \cdots, 0, v_n = a_{n+1})^T$ with all zero except for the extreme elements, and have it taken module 2 with the CA's configuration. Such CA is regarded as having input boundary.

In the modified scheme, we have an input vector sequence $I = \{V^t = (v_1^t, 0, \cdots, 0, v_n^t)^T, t = 1, 2, \cdots, p\}$ taken module 2 addition with configurations of the RCA^2 at each time steps. Then the transition equation of RCA^2 with input boundary is:

$$C^{t+1} = F(C^t) + C^{t-1} + V^t \quad t = 1,\ 2,\ \cdots \tag{4}$$

It could easily be verified that the reverse of RCA^2 with input boundary characterized by equation (4) is itself. So we use such RCA^2 as our encryption/decryption devices.

In this scheme, the secret key consists of not only the global map $F(\cdot)$ and the number of iteration p but also the input vector sequence I. For an encryption process with p iterations, the number of possible input vector sequence I would be 4^p. Compared with basic scheme, this modified scheme multiplies the key space enormously.

3.4   Image Encryption with 2-Dimensional RCA^2

So far, we have discussed cryptosystem based on 1-dimensional RCA^2, i.e., the cells of such RCA^2 are arranged in line. Informally, a RCA^2 is called 2-dimensional if its cells are arranged in grid. A 2-dimensional RCA^2 is suitable for performing image encryption because its cells map exactly to the pixels in the image.

The encryption scheme based on 2-dimensional RCA^2 is similar to that described above, except that the neighbors of a cell may locate "around" it.

Here, we just give an visualized effect of image encryption in Fig.3. The black and white image of size 100×150 was set as an initial configuration, and it took 100 rounds of iteration to output the ciphers. We adopted " von Neumann neighborhood" in this experiment, i.e. the neighbors of a cell consist its immediate "up", "down", "left", and "right" cells.

4   Discussion

In our scheme, the secret key is composed of three sub-keys: the local rules that determine the global map $F(\cdot)$, the number of iteration p, and the input vector sequence I. The key space is the multiplication of these three individual sub-key spaces, which is formidably large for a brute –force attacker. For instance, if we confine the underlying CA to be elementary CA with 50 cells, and limit the usable additive rules to be (51,102,90,150), then the number of possible underlying CA is 4^{50}, because each cell could take one of the four rules. In practice, there are much more CAs to choose. A n-cell 2-state CA with each cell having m neighbors has $(2^{2^m})^n$ possible candidates. At first glance, the number of iteration p should not be too small to have the avalanche effect of one bit difference to take place over the whole RCA^2, but the random vector in the initial configuration pair guarantees that the cipher seems random even when p is a small number. For a modified scheme, the input vector sequence I extends the key space greatly. If we confine the p of elementary CA to be in [30,130], then the number of possible I is $\sum_{p=30}^{130} 4^p$.

Differential cryptanalysis is a potent chosen plaintext/ chosen ciphertext cryptanalytic attack introduced by Biham and Shamir. So one might expect our scheme to yield to such attacks. Yet, due to probabilistic nature, our scheme resists such attacks. Differential cryptanalysts might choose pairs of plaintexts with specified difference between members of pair. Then they can study the differences between members of the corresponding pair of ciphertexts. But the random vector of initial configuration pair in our scheme makes the statistics of the plaintext-pair/ciphertext-pair differences yield no information about the key used in encryption.

In theory, our schemes could employ all possible one-order CA in the CA space. However we suggest that the local rules with maximum output entropy is preferable, i.e., local rules that have equal probability of outputting 1 and 0, such as 150,90. Such rules may have better chance of possessing good quality of permutation. Still no evidence shows that choices of other kinds of CA may lead to compromise of the secret keys.

Our scheme could be implemented efficiently with programmable CA (PCA) [2]. In a PCA, a cell's neighbor dependence could be controlled by control signals as shown in Fig 1(b). Then control signals for all cells act as part of secret key. Because the RCA^2 and its reverse share the same equation, the encryption and decryption devices may use identical circuit. One might argue that when implemented in hardware, the underlying CA may be confined to additive CA in favor of hardware implementation, thus the possible key space may be reduced. So it is worth pointing out that even if the underlying CA is confined to additive CA, the key space is still large enough to resist brute force attack.

5   Conclusion

We present a new block cipher cryptosystem based on reversible second-order cellular automata. The encryption and decryption devices share the same mod-ule, and could be implemented efficiently in hardware due to the simple structure of CA. The scheme has high speed due to the parallel information processing property of CA. And our scheme has larger key space than any other existing CA-based block schemes because all one-order CA are possible candidates for the underlying CA. So, the complex behaviors of underlying one-order cellular automata and the tremendous large key space make it very hard to attack.

References

1. Wolfram,S.: Cryptography with cellular automata. in: Advances in Cryptology, 1985, 429-432
2. Nandi,S.: Kar,B.K. and Pal,P. Chaudhuri, Theory and application of cellular automata in cryptography, IEEE Trans, Compu., 43(12) (1994), 1346-1356
3. Taejoo Chang, Iichho Song et al: Maximum length cellular automaton sequences and its application, Signal Processing 56 (1997) 199-203
4. Zomaya,A.Y., Seredynski,F., Bouvry,P.: Secret key cryptography with cellular automata, in: Proc. Of the International Parallel and Distributed Processing Symposium, 2003
5. Kari,J.: Cryptosystems based on reversible cellular automata, personal communication, (1992)
6. Zhang Chuanwu, Peng Qicong, Li Yubo: Encryption based on reversible Cellular Automata, in: Communications, Circuits and Systems and West Sino Expositions, IEEE 2002 International Conference Vol. 2 (2002) 1223-1226
7. Guan,P.: Cellular automaton public key cryptosystems, Complex Syst. 1 (1987) 51-56
8. Das,A.K., A.Ganguly, A.Dasgupta, S.Bhawmik and P.P.Chaudhri: Efficient characterisation of cellular automata, IEE Proc., Part E, 37 (1990) 81-87
9. Toffoli,T., and Margolus,N.: Invertible cellular automata: A Review, Physica D.45 (1990) 229-253
10. Wolffram,S.: Statistical mechanics of cellular automata, Review Modem Phys.,55(3) (1983) 601-644

ID-Based Proxy Signature Using Bilinear Pairings

(Extended Abstract)

Jing Xu[1], Zhenfeng Zhang[2], and Dengguo Feng[3]

[1] State Key Laboratory of Information Security, P.R. China
[2] Graduate School of Chinese Academy of Sciences, Beijing 100039, P.R. China
[3] Institute of Software, Chinese Academy of Sciences, Beijing 100080, P.R. China
{xujing, zfzhang, feng}@is.iscas.ac.cn

Abstract. Identity-based (ID-based) public key cryptosystem can be a good alternative for certificate-based public key setting, especially when efficient key management and moderate security are required. A proxy signature scheme permits an entity to delegate its signing rights to another entity. But to date, no ID-based proxy signature scheme with provable security has been proposed. In this paper, we formalize a notion of security for ID-based proxy signature schemes and propose a scheme based on the bilinear pairings. We show that the security of our scheme is tightly related to the computational Diffie-Hellman assumption in the random oracle model.

Keywords: ID-based signatures, proxy signatures, bilinear pairings, provable security.

1 Introduction

The paradigm of proxy signature is a method for an entity to delegate signing capabilities to other participants so that they can sign on behalf of the entity within a given context (the context and limitations on proxy signing capabilities are captured by a certain warrant issued by the delegator which is associated with the delegation act). For example, Alice the executive might want to empower Bob the secretary to sign on her behalf for a given week when Alice is out of town. Such proxy capability transfer may be defined recursively to allow high flexibility in assigning limited entitlements.

Proxy signatures have found numerous practical applications, particularly in distributed computing where delegation of rights is quite common. Examples discussed in the literature include distributed systems, Grid computing, mobile agent applications, distributed shared object systems, global distribution networks, and mobile communications. The proxy signature primitive and the first efficient solution were introduced by Mambo, Usuda and Okamoto [1]. Since then proxy signature schemes have enjoyed a considerable amount of interest from the cryptographic research community. Furthermore, various extensions of the basic

G. Chen et al. (Eds.): ISPA Workshops 2005, LNCS 3759, pp. 359–367, 2005.

proxy signature primitive have been considered. These include threshold proxy signatures [2], blind proxy signatures [3], proxy signatures with warrant recovery [4], nominative proxy signatures [5], one-time proxy signatures [6], and proxy-anonymous proxy signatures [7].

Unfortunately, the extensive cryptographic research on the topic has brought developers more confusion than guidance because almost every other paper breaks some previously proposed construction, and proposes a new one. Very few schemes were left unbroken, and none of them has provable-security guarantees. Typically, security of these schemes is argued by presenting attacks that fail, which provides only very weak guarantees. The first work to formally define the model of proxy signatures, is the work of Boldyreva, Palacio, and Warinschi [8]. Recently, Malkin, Obana and Yung develop the first formal model for fully hierarchical proxy signatures and prove that proxy signatures are equivalent to key-insulated signatures [9].

In a certificate-based public key system, before using the public key of a user, the participants must verify the certificate of the user at first. As a consequence, this system requires a large storage and computing time to store and verify each users public key and the corresponding certificate. In 1984 Shamir [10] proposed ID-based encryption and signature schemes to simplify key management procedures in certificate-based public key setting. Since then, many ID-based encryption and signature schemes have been proposed. The main idea of ID-based cryptosystems is that the identity information of each user works as his/her public key, in other words, the user's public key can be calculated directly from his/her identity rather than being extracted from a certificate issued by a certificate authority (CA). ID-based public key setting can be a good alternative for certificate-based public key setting, especially when efficient key management and moderate security are required.

The bilinear pairings, namely the weil-pairing and the tate-pairing of algebraic curves, are important tools for research on algebraic geometry. They have been found various applications in cryptography recently [11],[12],[13],[14]. More precisely, they can be used to construct ID-based cryptographic schemes.

In the area of provable security, the last couple of years saw the rise of a new trend consisting of providing tight security reductions for asymmetric cryptosystems : the security of a cryptographic protocol is said to be tightly related to a hard computational problem if an attacker against the scheme implies an efficient algorithm solving the problem with roughly the same advantage. But up to now, no one proposes an ID-based proxy signature scheme providing tight security reductions.

Our current work is aimed at filling this void. Based on the work of [8] and [9], we define a formal model for the security of ID-based proxy signature scheme. Then we propose an efficient ID-based proxy signature scheme whose security can be proved tightly related to computational Diffie-Hellman (CDH) problem in the random oracle model. Unlike [8], we do not rely on the forking lemma in our security reduction, hence the advantage relation can be shown to be linear, which is almost the best possible.

The rest of the paper is organized as follows. In Section 2 we give formal definitions of presumed hard computational problems from which our reductions are made. In Section 3 a formal security model of ID-based proxy signature scheme is given. In Sections 4 , we present an ID-based proxy signature scheme and analyze its security. And we end with concluding remarks in Section 5.

2   Definitions

2.1   The Bilinear Pairing

Let G be a cyclic additive group generated by P, whose order is a prime q, and V be a cyclic multiplicative group of the same order. Let $\hat{e} : G \times G \to V$ be a pairing which satisfies the following conditions:

1. Bilinearity: For any $P, Q, R \in G$, we have $\hat{e}(P + Q, R) = \hat{e}(P, R)\hat{e}(Q, R)$ and $\hat{e}(P, Q + R) = \hat{e}(P, Q)\hat{e}(P, R)$. In particular, for any $a, b \in \mathbf{Z}_q$,

$$\hat{e}(aP, bP) = \hat{e}(P, P)^{ab} = \hat{e}(P, abP) = \hat{e}(abP, P).$$

2. Non-degeneracy: There exists $P, Q \in G$, such that $\hat{e}(P, Q) \neq 1$.

3. Computability: There is an efficient algorithm to compute $\hat{e}(P, Q)$ for all $P, Q \in G$.

The typical way of obtaining such pairings is by deriving them from the weil-pairing or the tate-pairing on an elliptic curve over a finite field.

2.2   Gap Diffie-Hellman (GDH) Groups

Let G be a cyclic group of prime order q and P be a generator of G.

1. The decisional Diffie-Hellman (DDH) problem is to decide whether $c = ab$ in Z/qZ for given $P, aP, bP, cP \in G$. If so, (P, aP, bP, cP) is called a valid Diffie-Hellman (DH) tuple.

2. The computational Diffie-Hellman (CDH) problem is to compute abP for given $P, aP, bP \in G$.

Definition 2.1 The advantage of an algorithm $\mathcal{F}$ in solving the computational Diffie-Hellman problem on group G is

$$AdvCDH_{\mathcal{F}} = Pr[\mathcal{F}(P, aP, bP) = abP : \forall a, b \in Z_q]$$

The probability is taken over the choice of a, b and $\mathcal{F}$'s coin tosses. An algorithm $\mathcal{F}$ is said (t, ε)-breaks the computational Diffie-Hellman problem on G if $\mathcal{F}$ runs in time at most t, and $AdvCDH_{\mathcal{F}}$ is at least ε.

Now we present a definition for a gap Diffie-Hellman (GDH) group.

Definition 2.2 A group G is a (t, ε)-gap Diffie-Hellman (GDH) group if the decisional Diffie-Hellman problem in G can be efficiently computable and there exists no algorithm (t, ε)-breaks computational Diffie-Hellman on G.

If we have an admissible bilinear pairing $\hat{e}$ in G, we can solve the DDH problem in G efficiently as follows:

(P, aP, bP, cP) is a valid DH tuple $\Leftrightarrow \hat{e}(aP, bP) = \hat{e}(P, cP)$

Hence an elliptic curve becomes an instance of a GDH group if the Weil (or the Tate) pairing is efficiently computable and the CDH is sufficiently hard on the curve.

2.3   ID-Based Setting from Bilinear Pairings

The ID-based public key systems allow some public information of the user such as name, address and email *etc.*, rather than an arbitrary string to be used as his public key. The private key of the user is calculated by a trusted party, called PKG and sent to the user via a secure channel.

ID-based public key setting from bilinear pairings can be implemented as follows:

Let G be a cyclic additive group generated by P, whose order is a prime q, and V be a cyclic multiplicative group of the same order. A bilinear pairing is the map $\hat{e} : G \times G \rightarrow V$. Define cryptographic hash function $H : \{0,1\}^* \rightarrow G$.

- $\mathcal{G}$: PKG chooses a random number $s \in Z_q^*$ and sets $P_{pub} = sP$. He publishes system parameters $params = \{G, V, \hat{e}, q, P, P_{pub}, H\}$; and keeps s secretly as the *master-key*.
- $\mathcal{K}$: A user submits his/her identity information ID and authenticates him to PKG. PKG computes the user's private key $d_{ID} = sQ_{ID} = sH(ID)$ and sends it to the user via a secure channel.

3   ID-Based Proxy Signature

Based on the work of [8] and [9], we give formal definition for ID-based proxy signature schemes.

3.1   Syntax of ID-Based Proxy Signature Schemes

Definition 3.1   An ID-based proxy signature scheme is a tuple $(\mathcal{G}, \mathcal{K}, \mathcal{S}, \mathcal{V}, (\mathcal{D}, \mathcal{P}),$
$\mathcal{PS}, \mathcal{PV}, \mathcal{ID})$, where algorithms $\mathcal{G}$ and $\mathcal{K}$ are the same as in section 2.3, and the others are defined as follows.

- $\mathcal{S}$: The signing algorithm, which takes a signing key d_{ID} of original designator and a message m_ω as input, outputs a signature ω called warrant on m_ω. The message m_ω contains the identity(ID) of the designated proxy signer and, possibly, restrictions on the message the proxy signer is allowed to sign.
- $\mathcal{V}$: The verification algorithm, which takes ID of original designator, a message m_ω, and a warrant ω as input, outputs "*accept*" if the signature is valid, or "*reject*" otherwise.
- $(\mathcal{D}, \mathcal{P})$: (interactive) Proxy-designation algorithms (where $\mathcal{D}$ and $\mathcal{P}$ are owned by the designator ID_i and the proxy signer ID_j, respectively). The input to each algorithm includes ID_i, ID_j. $\mathcal{D}$ also takes as input the secret key d_i of

the designator, a message m_ω and a warrant ω. $\mathcal{P}$ also takes as input the secret key d_j of the proxy signer. As result of the interaction, the expected local output of $\mathcal{P}$ is the warrant ω and skp, a proxy signing key that user ID_j uses to produce proxy signatures on behalf of user ID_i. $\mathcal{D}$ has no local output.

- $\mathcal{PS}$: The proxy signing algorithm, which takes a proxy signing key skp, a message m and a warrant ω as input, outputs a proxy signature $psig$.
- $\mathcal{PV}$: The proxy verification algorithm, which takes the identity of the original designator(ID), a message m, a warrant ω and a proxy signature $psig$ as input, outputs "*accept*" if the proxy signature is valid, or "*reject*" otherwise.
- $\mathcal{ID}$: The proxy identification algorithm, which takes a warrant ω and a proxy signature $psig$ as input, outputs an identity of the designated proxy signer.

Correctness. We require that for all message m and all users $i, j \in \mathbb{N}$, if the proxy signing key skp and the warrant ω are the output of consecutive executions of $(skp, \omega) \leftarrow [\mathcal{D}(ID_i, ID_j, d_i, m_\omega, \omega), \mathcal{P}(ID_i, ID_j, d_j)]$, then $\mathcal{PV}(ID_i, m, \omega, \mathcal{PS}(skp, m, \omega)) = 1$, $\mathcal{ID}(\omega, \mathcal{PS}(skp, m, \omega)) = ID_j$ and the message m does not violate the warrant ω.

3.2   ID-Based Proxy Signature Security

We first informally describe some of the features of our adversarial model.

We model a seemingly extreme case in which the adversary is working against a single honest user, say ID_1, and can extract the private keys of all other users. Since any attack can be carried out in the presence of more honest users, our assumption is without loss of generality. The adversary can play the role of user $ID_i(i \neq 1)$ in executions of the $(\mathcal{D}, \mathcal{P})$ protocol with ID_1, as designator or as proxy signer. In both cases, the adversary may behave dishonestly in an attempt to obtain information from ID_1. The adversary also can request ID_1 to run the $(\mathcal{D}, \mathcal{P})$ protocol with himself, and see the transcript of the execution. We emphasize that we do not assume the existence of a secure channel between a designator and a proxy signer.

We model chosen-message attack capabilities by providing the adversary access to two oracles: a standard signing oracle and a proxy signing oracle. The first oracle takes input a message m, and returns a standard signature for m by user ID_1. The second oracle takes input a tuple (i, l, m), and, if user ID_1 was designated by user ID_i at least l times, returns a proxy signature for m created by user ID_1 on behalf of user ID_i, using the l-th proxy signing key.

The goal of the adversary is to produce one of the following forgeries: (1) a standard signature by user ID_1 for a message that was not submitted to the standard signing oracle, (2) a proxy signature for a message m, such that no query (i, l, m) was made to the proxy signing oracle, or (3) a proxy signature for a message m by some user ID_i on behalf of user ID_1, such that user ID_i was never designated by user ID_1.

ID-based proxy signature security is formally defined as follows.

Definition 3.2 Let **PS**= $(\mathcal{G}, \mathcal{K}, \mathcal{S}, \mathcal{V}, (\mathcal{D}, \mathcal{P}), \mathcal{PS}, \mathcal{PV}, \mathcal{ID})$ be an ID-based proxy signature scheme. Consider an experiment $\mathbf{Exp}_{PS,\mathcal{A}}^{ps-uf}(k)$ related to scheme **PS**, adversary $\mathcal{A}$, and security parameter k. First, system parameters **params** are generated by running $\mathcal{G}$ on input 1^k. Then the private key d_1 of user ID_1 is generated by $\mathcal{K}$. The empty arrays **skp$_i$** of each user and an empty set D are created. Adversary $\mathcal{A}$ can make the following requests or queries,in any order and any number of times.

- (**Extraction Queries**) Given an identity $ID_i(i \neq 1)$, the challenger returns the private key d_i corresponding to ID_i.
- (ID_1 **Designates** ID_i **Requests**) $\mathcal{A}$ can request to interact with user ID_1 running $\mathcal{D}(ID_1, ID_i, d_1)$, for some $i \neq 1$, and play the role of userID_i running $\mathcal{P}(ID_1, ID_i, d_i)$; after a successful run, D is set to $D \bigcup \{ID_i\}$.
- (ID_i **Designates** ID_1 **Requests**) $\mathcal{A}$ can request to interact with user ID_1 running $\mathcal{P}(ID_i, ID_1, d_1)$, for some $i \neq 1$, and play the role of userID_i running $\mathcal{D}(ID_i, ID_1, d_i)$. The private output skp of $\mathcal{P}$ is stored in the last unoccupied position of **skp$_i$**. We emphasize that $\mathcal{A}$ does not have access to the elements of **skp$_i$**.
- (ID_1 **Designates** ID_1 **Requests**) $\mathcal{A}$ can request that user ID_1 run $(\mathcal{D}, \mathcal{P})$ protocol with itself, and see the transcript of the interaction. The private output skp of ID_1 is stored in the next available position of **skp$_1$**. $\mathcal{A}$ does not have access to the elements of **skp$_1$**.
- (**Standard Signature Queries**) $\mathcal{A}$ can query signatures with respect to identity ID_1 on messages of his choice.
- (**Proxy Signature Queries**) $\mathcal{A}$ can query proxy signatures by ID_1 on behalf of ID_i using the l-th proxy signing key, i.e. query (i, l, m). If key **skp$_i$**$[l]$ has already been defined, we say the query is valid and the challenger returns $\mathcal{PS}(\mathbf{skp_i}[l], m)$; if **skp$_i$**$[l]$ has not been defined, the query is said to be invalid and the challenger returns $\perp$.

Eventually, $\mathcal{A}$ outputs a forgery (m, sig) or $(m, psig, ID)$. The output of the experiments is determined as follows:

1. If the forgery is of the form (m, sig), where $\mathcal{V}(ID_1, m, sig) = 1$, and m was not queried to standard signature oracle, then return 1.[forgery of a standard signature]

2. If the forgery is of the form $(m, psig, ID)$, where $ID = ID_i$ for some $i \neq 1$, $\mathcal{PV}(ID_i, m, psig) = 1$, $\mathcal{ID}(psig) = ID_1$, and no valid query (i, l, m) was made to proxy signature oracle, then return 1. [forgery of a proxy signature by user ID_1 on behalf of user ID_i]

3. If the forgery is of the form $(m, psig, ID_1)$, where $\mathcal{PV}(ID_1, m, psig) = 1$ and $\mathcal{ID}(psig) \notin D \cup \{ID_1\} \cup \{\perp\}$, then return 1. [forgery of a proxy signature by user ID_i on behalf of user ID_1; user ID_i was not designated by user ID_1]

4.Otherwise, return 0.

We define the advantage of adversary $\mathcal{A}$ as

$$\mathbf{Adv}_{PS,\mathcal{A}}^{ps-uf}(k) = Pr[\mathbf{Exp}_{PS,\mathcal{A}}^{ps-uf}(k) = 1].$$

Adversary $\mathcal{A}$ is said $(t, q_H, q_E, q_S, q_{PS}, \varepsilon)$-breaks a proxy signature scheme if: $\mathcal{A}$ runs in time at most t; $\mathcal{A}$ makes at most q_H queries to the hash function H, at most q_E queries to the key extraction oracle, at most q_S queries to the standard signing oracle and at most q_{PS} queries to the proxy signing oracle; and $\mathbf{Adv}_{PS,\mathcal{A}}^{ps-uf}(k)$ is at least ε. We say a proxy signature scheme is $(t, q_H, q_E, q_S, q_{PS}, \varepsilon)$-secure if no adversary $(t, q_H, q_E, q_S, q_{PS}, \varepsilon)$-breaks it.

4   Our Proxy Signature Scheme

Our proxy signature scheme is based on SOK-IBS (Sakai-Ogishi-Kasahara Identity Based Signature)[15].The constituent algorithms of our proxy signature scheme $\mathbf{PS}= (\mathcal{G}, \mathcal{K}, \mathcal{S}, \mathcal{V}, (\mathcal{D}, \mathcal{P}), \mathcal{PS}, \mathcal{PV}, \mathcal{ID})$ are defined as follows.

- $\mathcal{G}$: Assume k is a security parameter.G is a GDH group of prime order $q > 2^k$ generated by P, and $\hat{e} : G \times G \to V$ is a bilinear map. Pick a random master key $s \in Z_q^*$ and set $P_{pub} = sP$. Choose hash functions $H_1, H_2, H_3 : \{0,1\}^* \to G$, and hash function $H_4 : \{0,1\}^* \to Z_q^*$

- $\mathcal{K}$: Given a users identity ID, compute $Q_{ID} = H_1(ID) \in G$ and the associated private key $d_{ID} = sQ_{ID} \in G$.

- $\mathcal{S}$: Given the private key d_i of original designator ID_i, in order to sign a message m_ω,

  1. Randomly pick $r_\omega \in Z_q^*$ and compute $U_\omega = r_\omega P \in G$ and then put $H_\omega = H_2(ID_i, m_\omega, U_\omega) \in G$.
  2.Compute $V_\omega = d_i + r_\omega H_\omega \in G$.

  The signature on m_ω is the warrant $\omega = \langle U_\omega, V_\omega \rangle$

- $\mathcal{V}$: To verify a signature $\omega = \langle U_\omega, V_\omega \rangle$ on a message m_ω for an identity ID_i, the verifier first takes $Q_i = H_1(ID_i) \in G$ and $H_\omega = H_2(ID_i, m_\omega, U_\omega) \in G$. He then accepts the signature if $\hat{e}(P, V_\omega) = \hat{e}(P_{pub}, Q_i)\hat{e}(U_\omega, H_\omega)$ and rejects it otherwise.

- $(\mathcal{D}, \mathcal{P})$: In order to designate user ID_j as a proxy signer, user ID_i sends user ID_j a message m_ω and an appropriate warrant ω. The user ID_j verifies this signature ω,and if it is valid, he computes a proxy signing key as

$$skp = H_4(ID_i, ID_j, m_\omega, U_\omega)d_j + V_\omega.$$

- $\mathcal{PS}$: Given proxy signing key skp, in order to sign a message m on behalf of user ID_i,
  1. Randomly pick $r_p \in Z_q^*$ and compute $U_p = r_p P \in G$ and then put $H_p = H_3(ID_j, m, U_p) \in G$.
  2.Compute $V_p = skp + r_p H_p \in G$.

  The proxy signature for message m on behalf of user ID_i produced by user ID_j is $psig = (m_\omega, ID_j, U_\omega, U_p, V_p)$

- $\mathcal{PV}$: To verify a proxy signature $psig = (m_\omega, ID_j, U_\omega, U_p, V_p)$ for message m with the original designator's identity ID_i, the verifier first takes $Q_i = H_1(ID_i) \in G$, $Q_j = H_1(ID_j) \in G$, $H_\omega = H_2(ID_i, m_\omega, U_\omega) \in G$ and $H_p = H_3(ID_j, m, U_p) \in G$. He then accepts the signature if

$$\hat{e}(P, V_p) = \hat{e}(P_{pub}, Q_j)^{H_4(ID_i, ID_j, m_\omega, U_\omega)}\hat{e}(P_{pub}, Q_i)\hat{e}(U_p, H_p)\hat{e}(U_\omega, H_\omega)$$

and rejects it otherwise.

– $\mathcal{ID}$: Given a proxy signature $psig = (m_\omega, ID_j, U_\omega, U_p, V_p)$ for message m, the proxy identification algorithm is defined as $\mathcal{ID}(psig) = ID_j$.

Correctness. The proxy signature scheme is correct because of the following.

$$\hat{e}(P, V_p)$$
$$= \hat{e}(P, skp + r_p H_p)$$
$$= \hat{e}(P, H_4(ID_i, ID_j, m_\omega, U_\omega)d_j + V_\omega + r_p H_p)$$
$$= \hat{e}(P, H_4(ID_i, ID_j, m_\omega, U_\omega)d_j + d_i + r_\omega H_\omega + r_p H_p)$$
$$= \hat{e}(P_{pub}, Q_j)^{H_3(ID_i, ID_j, m_\omega, U_\omega)} \hat{e}(P_{pub}, Q_i)\hat{e}(U_p, H_p)\hat{e}(U_\omega, H_\omega).$$

Security. The following theorem formally relates the security of our scheme to computational Diffie-Hellman assumption in the random oracle model.

Theorem 1. *Given a security parameter* k, *let* G *be a* (t', ε')-*GDH group of prime order* $q > 2^k$. P *be a generator of* G, *and* $\hat{e} : G \times G \to V$ *be a bilinear map. Then the ID-based proxy signature scheme on* G *is* $(t, q_H, q_E, q_s, q_{PS}, \varepsilon)$-*secure against forgery for any* t *and* ε *satisfying*

$$\varepsilon \geq 4e(q_E + 1)\left(1 - q_s(q_{H_2} + q_s)2^{-k}\right)^{-1}\left(1 - q_{PS}(q_{H_3} + q_{PS})2^{-k}\right)^{-1}\varepsilon'$$

$$t \leq t' - C_G(q_{H_1} + q_{H_2} + q_{H_3} + q_{H_4} + 5q_s + 7q_{PS} + 4)$$

where e is the base of natural logarithms, and C_G is the time of computing a scalar multiplication and inversion on G.

Proof can be found in the full version of this paper [16].

5   Conclusion

ID-based public key cryptosystem can be an alternative for certificate-based public key infrastructures. In this paper we formalized a notion of security for ID-based proxy signature scheme and proposed an scheme from bilinear pairings. The security of our scheme is tightly related to Computational Diffie-Hellman (CDH) problem in the Random Oracle model. Furthermore, we showed that optimal security reductions are also achievable for ID-based proxy signatures.

Acknowledgements

This work is supported by the National Grand Fundamental Research Program of China under Grant No. G1999035802, the National Natural Science Foundation of China under Grant No. 60373039, and the Youth Foundation of the National Natural Science of China under Grant No. 60025205. The authors would like to thanks the anonymous referees for their helpful comments.

References

1. M. Mambo, K. Usuda, and E. Okamoto. Proxy signatures for delegating signing operation. In Proceedings of the 3rd ACM Conference on Computer and Communications Security (CCS), 48-57. ACM, 1996.
2. J. Herranz and G. Sez. Verifiable secret sharing for general access structures, with application to fully distributed proxy signatures. In Proceedings of Financial Cryptography 2003, LNCS. Springer-Verlag, 2003.
3. S. Lal and A. K. Awasthi. Proxy blind signature scheme. Cryptology ePrint Archive, Report 2003/072. Available at http://eprint.iacr.org/, 2003.
4. S. Lal and A. K. Awasthi. A scheme for obtaining a warrant message from the digital proxy signatures. Cryptology ePrint Archive, Report 2003/073. Available at http://eprint.iacr.org/, 2003.
5. H.-U. Park and L.-Y. Lee. A digital nominative proxy signature scheme for mobile communications. In ICICS 2001, volume 2229 of LNCS, 451-455. Springer-Verlag, 2001.
6. H. Kim, J. Baek, B. Lee, and K. Kim. Secret computation with secrets for mobile agent using one-time proxy signature. In Cryptography and Information Security 2001, 2001.
7. K. Shum and V.-K. Wei. A strong proxy signature scheme with proxy signer privacy protection. In Eleventh IEEE International Workshop on Enabling Technologies: Infrastucture for Collaborative Enterprises , 2002.
8. A. Boldyreva, A. Palacio and B. Warinschi, Secure Proxy Signature Scheme for Delegation of Signing Rights, IACR ePrint Archive, available at http://eprint.iacr.org/2003/096/, 2003.
9. T.Malkin, S.Obana and M.Yung. The Hierarchy of Key Evolving Signatures and a Characterization of Proxy Signatures. Eurocrypt 2004, LNCS 3027, 306-322, Springer-Verlag, 2004.
10. A. Shamir, Identity-based cryptosystems and signature schemes, Advances in Cryptology-Crypto 1984, LNCS 196, 47-53, Springer-Verlag, 1984.
11. D. Boneh and M. Franklin, Identity-based encryption from the Weil pairing, Advances in Cryptology-Crypto 2001, LNCS 2139, 213-229, Springer-Verlag, 2001.
12. D. Boneh, B. Lynn, and H. Shacham, Short signatures from the Weil pairing, Advances in Cryptology-Asiacrypt 2001, LNCS 2248, 514-532, Springer-Verlag, 2001.
13. A. Joux, The Weil and Tate Pairings as Building Blocks for Public Key Cryptosystems, ANTS 2002, LNCS 2369, 20-32, Springer-Verlag, 2002.
14. D.Boneh and X.Boyen, Short Signatures Without Random Oracles. Eurocrypt 2004, LNCS 3027, 56-73, Springer-Verlag, 2004.
15. M.Bellare, C.Namprempre and G.Neven. Security Proofs for Identity-Based Identification and Signature Schemes, Advances in Cryptology-Eurocrypt 2004,LNCS 3027,268-286,Springer-Verlag, 2004.
16. J.Xu, Z.F.Zhang and D.G.Feng . ID-Based Proxy Signature Using Bilinear Pairings. Available from http://eprint.iacr.org/2004/206.
17. B.Libert, and J.J.Quisquater. The Exact Security of an Identity Based Signature and Its Applications. Available from http://eprint.iacr.org/2004/102.

Efficient Fair Certified E-Mail Delivery Based on RSA

Zhenfeng Zhang and Dengguo Feng

State Key Laboratory of Information Security,
Institute of Software, Chinese Academy of Sciences,
Beijing 100080, P.R. China
zfzhang@is.iscas.ac.cn

Abstract. Certified e-mail delivery (CEMD) has become one of the basic requirement in performing business transactions over the Internet securely. How to construct fair protocols for certified e-mail delivery based on the RSA cryptosystem is of great interest.

Recently, Nenadic etc. proposed a novel RSA-based method for the *verifiable and recoverable encrypted signature* (VRES), and utilized it to construct a security protocol for certified e-mail delivery, which are claimed to provide strong fairness to ensure that the recipient receives the e-mail if and only if the sender receives the receipt. However, as a building block, their RSA-based VRES is totally breakable. This papers shows that an adversary can generate a valid VRES which cannot be recovered by the designated TTP, and hence the proposed certified e-mail delivery protocol cannot guarantee the required fairness.

Based on probabilistic signatures, we proposed a novel fair CEMD protocol which works with the RSA cryptosystem and guarantees strong fairness. Moreover, there is no need for a registration phase between a party and TTP, and the proposed protocol is more computation and communication efficient.

Keywords: Fair exchange, RSA, E-mail, Security protocol.

1 Introduction

Communication by e-mail has become a vital part of everyday business and has replaced most of the conventional ways of communicating. The basic e-mail security services include the provision of privacy (only the intended recipient can read the message) and authentication (the recipient can be assured of the identity of the sender). Cryptographic mechanisms for providing these security services have been applied in Internet mail systems, such as S/MIME [16] and PGP [17]. In addition to sender authentication and message privacy, S/MIME can also provide a signed receipt service. A signed receipt from the recipient (requested by the sender) serves as a non-repudiable proof of receipt for a specific e-mail. However, the return of this receipt relies on the willingness of the recipient to honor the sender's request and provides no protection to the sender if the recipient chooses not to sign and return the acknowledgement after having read the

G. Chen et al. (Eds.): ISPA Workshops 2005, LNCS 3759, pp. 368–377, 2005.

message. In other words, this technique does not truly provide non-repudiation of the receipt security service.

Important business correspondence may require certified e-mail delivery service, analogous to that provided by conventional mail service. For a viable certified e-mail service, the following security properties are needed:

- Non-repudiation of origin - the recipient must have a way of proving that a specific e-mail indeed originates from the sender;
- Non-repudiation of receipt - the sender must have a way of proving that the recipient has indeed received a specific e-mail;
- Strong fairness for the exchange - the recipient should obtain a specific e-mail if and only if the sender obtains a receipt for it.

By now, certified e-mail delivery (CEMD) has become one of the central problems in performing business transactions over the Internet securely and can be applied in numerous e-commerce transactions. Briefly speaking, this is the problems of how two mutually distrustful parties can fairly exchange a sender's valuable e-mail for a receiver's digital signature representing a proof of reception. A CEMD protocol [10,12] shall provide strong fairness to ensure that the recipient receives the e-mail if and only if the sender receives the receipt.

The most practical and efficient approach to the fair exchange problems is to make use of an off-line trusted third party (TTP) to help the participants with the exchange. By this approach, the exchanging parties attempt to exchange their respective items themselves, i.e. without any involvement of the TTP. Should any dispute arise during the exchange process due to a party's misbehavior or a network failure, TTP is invoked to recover the disputed items and restore fairness.

Recently, a new category of off-line TTP-based fair exchange protocols has been proposed based on a cryptographic primitive called Verifiable and Recoverable Encryption of a Signature (VRES) [1,2,3,4,5,7,8,11]. The VRES represents a digital signature encrypted in such a way that a receiver of the VRES can verify that it indeed contains the correct signature without obtaining any information about the signature itself. The receiver can also verify that a designated TTP can help to recover the original signature from the VRES, in case the original signature sender refuses to do so.

In SAC'04, Nenadic, Zhang and Barton [14] proposed a new RSA-CEMD protocol for the two communicating parties to fairly exchange an e-mail message for an RSA-based receipt, which is claimed to provide strong fairness to ensure that the recipient receives the e-mail if and only if the sender receives the receipt. The main contribution of their work is a novel RSA-based method for the *verifiable and recoverable encrypted signature* (RSA-VRES), which is utilized as a crucial primitive to construct their RSA-CEMD protocol. The proposed protocols has been used as a main cryptographic primitive in the Fair Integrated Data Exchange Services (FIDES) project [15] provided for E-commerce transactions. However, as a building block, their VRES scheme is totally breakable. This papers shows that an adversary can easily generate an VRES which cannot be recovered by the designated TTP, and hence the proposed certified e-mail delivery protocol can not guarantee the claimed fairness.

Since fairness is impossible to be achieved in a deterministic two-party signing protocol, as proved by Even and Yacobi [9], we consider verifiable and recoverable encryption of probabilistic signatures in this paper. Based upon this idea, we proposed a novel fair certified e-mail delivery protocol, which work with the RSA cryptosystem and is more computation and communication-efficient. In our protocol, there is no registration between a party and TTP, which makes our protocol much concise and easy to implementation. In fact, TTP only needs to generate a trapdoor permutation as the system parameter, while the trapdoor kept secret by TTP is only used in the recovery phase to ensure fairness.

The rest of the paper is organized as follows. In section 3, we briefly review Nenadic etc.'s VRES scheme, and give a cryptanalysis using the Chinese Remainder Theorem. Then we present our RSA-based fair certified e-mail delivery protocol and analysis its security and efficiency in section 4.

2   Notations and Assumptions

The following notation will be used in the remaining part of the paper.

- $E_{pk}(x)$ and $E_{sk}(x)$ express a ciphertext or a signature of an item x created with a public key pk or a private key sk, using the RSA cryptosystem.
- $h(\cdot)$ and $H(\cdot)$ are collision-resistant one-way hash functions.
- $x\|y$ denotes the concatenation of data items x and y.

The following assumptions are used in the design of the RSA-CEMD protocol.

- P_a wishes to send an e-mail message M to P_b in exchange for P_b's receipt on M.
- P_a and P_b have agreed to employ an off-line TTP P_t to help them with the exchange if they cannot reach a fair completion of the exchange themselves.
- Every party P_i ($i \in \{a, b, t\}$) has a pair of public and private keys, expressed as $pk_i = (e_i, n_i)$, $sk_i = (d_i, n_i)$, where n_i is a product of two distinct primes p_i and q_i of length $\frac{k}{2}$, and $e_i d_i \equiv 1 \bmod ((p_i - 1)(q_i - 1))$. The public key pk_i is certified by a Certification Authority and known by all the other parties.

3   Security Flaws of Nenadic et al.'s Verifiable and Recoverable Encrypted Signature

In [14], party P_b's receipt for a message M in a CEMD protocol is represented by P_b's RSA signature on a message M, i.e., $receipt_b = h(M)^{d_b} \bmod n_b$. Moreover, the following notations are used:

Party P_b has obtained a certificate $C_{bt} = (pk_{bt}, w_{bt}, \sigma_{bt})$, issued by P_t prior to the exchange, for an additional RSA-based public key pk_{bt}. The pk_{bt} and its corresponding private key sk_{bt} are denoted as $pk_{bt} = (e_{bt}, n_{bt})$ and $sk_{bt} =$

(d_{bt}, n_{bt}), where n_{bt} is a product of two distinct large primes chosen by P_t and is approximately the same size as n_b, and e_{bt} is required to be the same as e_b, i.e. $e_b = e_{bt}$. The w_{bt} is defined as $w_{bt} = h(sk_t, pk_{bt})^{-1} \times d_{bt} \bmod n_{bt}$, where sk_t is P_t's private key. The σ_{bt} is P_t's RSA signature on $h(pk_{bt}, w_{bt})$, that is, $\sigma_{bt} = E_{sk_t}(h(pk_{bt}, w_{bt}))$. P_t only needs to issue one certificate C_{bt} for P_b, when party P_b registers with P_t.

In the following we describe the generation, verification and recovery process of Nenadic et al.'s VRES scheme.

VRES Generation: To generate a verifiable and recoverable encryption of his signature $receipt_b$, denoted as (y_b, x_b, z_b), P_b randomly chooses a prime number $r_b < n_b$ and computes:

$$y_b = r_b{}^{e_b} \bmod (n_b \times n_{bt}), \tag{1}$$
$$x_b = r_b \times h(D_a)^{d_b} = r_b \times receipt_b \bmod n_b, \tag{2}$$
$$z_b = r_b \times h(y_b)^{d_{bt}} \bmod n_{bt}. \tag{3}$$

Here, y_b is a slightly modified RSA encryption of the number r_b, and x_b represents the "encryption" of signature $receipt_b$ with the random number r_b. Note that

$$y_b \bmod n_b = r_b{}^{e_b} \bmod n_b = E_{pk_b}(r_b),$$
$$y_b \bmod n_{ht} = r_b{}^{e_{bt}} \bmod n_{bt} = E_{pk_{bt}}(r_b).$$

So, the r_b can be recovered from y_b using either of the private keys sk_b or sk_{bt}.

VRES Verification: To verify P_b's verifiable and recoverable encrypted signature (y_b, x_b, z_b), P_a does the following:

(a) Checks the correctness of P_t's signature σ_{bt} in C_{bt}.
(b) Confirms that

$$x_b{}^{e_b} = \left(r_b \times (h(M))^{d_b}\right)^{e_b} = y_b \times h(M) \bmod n_b. \tag{4}$$

(c) Confirms that

$$z_b{}^{e_b} = \left(r_b \times (h(y_b))^{d_{bt}}\right)^{e_b} = y_b \times h(y_b) \bmod n_{bt}. \tag{5}$$

In detail, verification (a) makes sure that C_{bt} is a valid certificate issued by P_t. Verification (c) together with (b) ensures that P_t can decrypt y_b with key sk_{bt} to obtain r_b for the recovery of P_b's signature $receipt_b$ from x_b.

VRES Recovery: To recover $receipt_b$ from the VRES (y_b, x_b, z_b), P_t first derives the private key $sk_{bt} = (d_{bt}, n_{bt})$ from P_t's certificate $C_{bt} = (pk_{bt}, w_{bt}, \sigma_{bt})$ using its private key sk_t, as $d_{bt} = h(sk_t, pk_{bt}) \times w_{bt} \bmod n_{bt}$. P_t then uses the derived sk_{bt} to decrypt $y_b \bmod n_{bt} = E_{pk_{bt}}(r_b)$ to recover r_b, i.e., P_t computes $r_b = (y_b \bmod n_{bt})^{d_{bt}} \bmod n_{bt}$. The r_b can then be used for P_a to compute P_b's signature from x_b as

$$receipt_b = (r_b{}^{-1} \times x_b) \bmod n_b.$$

3.1   Cryptanalysis of the RSA Based VRES

From the VRES verification process we see that the correctness of a verifiable and recoverable encrypted signature (y_b, x_b, z_b) is actually ensured by checking (4) and (5). In [14,15], the authors then claim that, a designated semi-trusted third party P_t, who holds the private key sk_{bt}, can decrypt y_b as

$$r_b' = y_b^{d_{bt}} \bmod n_{bt}, \tag{6}$$

and, for this extracted r_b', the $receipt_b$ can then be recovered from (2) as

$$receipt_b = (r_b'^{-1} \times x_b) \bmod n_b.$$

In fact, from (4) we see that $receipt_b = h(M)^{d_b} = x_b \times y_b^{-d_b} \bmod n_b$. Therefore, the fairness of their VRES scheme is essentially ensured by the fact that the recovered r_b' from (6) satisfies

$$r_b' = y_b^{d_b} \bmod n_b. \tag{7}$$

However, as $y_b \in \mathbf{Z}_{n_b \times n_{bt}}$ is a modified RSA encryption of r_b, the verification conditions (4) and (5) do not guarantee (7). That is, P_b can generate a VRES which satisfies (4) and (5) but doesn't satisfy (7).

In fact, holding the private keys $sk_b = (d_b, n_b)$ and $sk_{bt} = (d_{bt}, n_{bt})$, for any y_b, P_b can always compute x_b and z_b as

$$x_b = (y_b \times h(M))^{d_b} \bmod n_b, \tag{8}$$
$$z_b = (y_b \times h(y_b))^{d_{bt}} \bmod n_{bt}. \tag{9}$$

In view of $e_b = e_{bt}$, the resulting triplet (y_b, x_b, z_b) definitely satisfies (4) and (5), and is a valid VRES on $h(M)$.

Moreover, P_b can choose a particular $\tilde{y}_b$ such that (7) does not hold. For this purpose, P_b randomly chooses two distinct prime numbers $r_b < n_b$ and $r_b' < \min\{n_b, n_{bt}\}$, and computes

$$y_{b1} = r_b^{e_b} \bmod n_b, \quad y_{b2} = r_b'^{e_{bt}} \bmod n_{bt}.$$

Now, using the Chinese Remainder Theorem, P_b can compute a value $\tilde{y}_b \in \mathbf{Z}_{n_b \times n_{bt}}$ efficiently such that

$$\tilde{y}_b \equiv y_{b1} \bmod n_b, \; \tilde{y}_b \equiv y_{b1} \bmod n_{bt}.$$

And, for this very $\tilde{y}_b$, P_b computes $\tilde{x}_b$ and $\tilde{z}_b$ using (8) and (9). Then the triplet $(\tilde{y}_b, \tilde{x}_b, \tilde{z}_b)$ is a valid VRES and will certainly pass P_a's verification.

Noting $\tilde{y}_b \equiv y_{b1} \equiv r_b^{e_b} \bmod n_b$ we have $\tilde{y}_b^{d_b} = r_b \bmod n_b$. Since $\tilde{y}_b \equiv y_{b2} \equiv r_b'^{e_{bt}} \bmod n_{bt}$ and $r_b' < n_{bt}$, the value computed from (6) is definitely r_b'. Because r_b and r_b' are two distinct primes less than n_b, i.e. $r_b \not\equiv r_b' \bmod n_b$, the resulting r_b' extracted by TTP cannot satisfy (7), and thus the $receipt_b'$ computed by P_a as $receipt_b' = (r_b'^{-1} \times x_b) \bmod n_b$ cannot be a valid signature of P_b on $h(M)$.

This is totally unfair for P_a. As Nenadic et al.'s CEMD [14] protocol is constructed based on the VRES, and their security relies on the fairness of the VRES, their CEMD protocol *cannot* provide the required fairness.

From the above cryptanalysis we see that the security flaw of their VRES is due to the arbitrariness of y_b. To overcome such an attack, some kind of proof such as [2,6] shall be provided together with a VRES (y_b, x_b, z_b) to ensure that y_b has the correct form (1) for some unknown $r_b < \min\{n_b, n_{bt}\}$. Then by the Theorem of Cross-Decryption [13], the r_b' extracted by TTP from (6) will definitely satisfy (7). However, such a proof will make the protocols [12-15] more complex and inefficient.

4 Our RSA-CEMD Protocol

In our protocol, instead of generating an RSA public-private keys, TTP P_t generates a public key $PK = N$ and publishes it as a system parameter, and keeps $SK = (P, Q)$ secret, where $N = PQ$ and P, Q are distinct strong primes of length $\frac{k}{2}$, i.e., $P = 2P' + 1$ and $Q = 2Q' + 1$, while P' and Q' are also primes. Denote by $H'(\cdot) = H(\cdot)\|1$, which maps any string to an odd integer.

Considering $\varphi(N) = 4P'Q'$, with only three prime factors $2, P, Q$, the probability of the output from H' being co-prime to $\varphi(N)$ is overwhelming, because finding an odd integer not co-prime with $4P'Q'$ is equivalent to find P' or Q' or $P'Q'$ and consequently factoring N.

Party P_b's receipt for a message M, denoted as $receipt_b = (\delta, r)$, is represented by P_b's probabilistic signature on M, i.e.

$$\delta_b = H\left(h(M)\|r_b^{H'(ID_{P_b}\|pk_b)} \bmod N\right)^{d_b} \bmod n_b.$$

The RSA-CEND protocol consists of two protocols: the exchange protocol and the receipt recovery protocol.

4.1 The Exchange Protocol

In the exchange protocol, parties P_a and P_b attempt to exchange a message M for its receipt, without any involvement of the TTP. The exchange protocol comprises steps (E1)-(E4), as shown in Table 1.

Table 1. The RSA-CEMD Protocol

(E1): $P_a \rightarrow P_b : h(M), E_{sk_a}(h(M))$
(E2): $P_b \rightarrow P_a : \delta_b, y_b$
(E3): $P_a \rightarrow P_b : M$
(E4): $P_b \rightarrow P_a : r_b$

(**E1**): P_a transfers to P_b the hash value $h(M)$ and its digital signature $E_{sk_a}(h(M))$. The signature will serve as a non-repudiable proof of origin of the message M.

(**E2**): Upon receipt of the two items, P_b verifies P_a's signature by decrypting the signature $E_{sk_a}(h(M))$ with P_a's public key pk_a to gain a hash value $h(M)'$, and confirming that $h(M)' = h(M)$.

If the verification is negative, P_b may either ask P_a to re-send message (E1) or terminate the protocol execution. Otherwise, P_b produces a *verifiable and recoverable encryption* of its receipt for message M, denoted as (δ_b, y_b). Precisely, P_b first randomly chooses $r_b \in \mathbf{Z}_N^*$ and computes $y_b = r_b^{H'(ID_b\|pk_b)} \bmod N$, where ID_b is P_b's identity or identifier information. Then P_b computes

$$\delta_b = H(h(M)\|y_b)^{d_b} \bmod n_b.$$

Now (δ_b, y_b) is P_b's VRES on M and is delivered to P_a.

(**E3**): Upon receipt of these items, P_a performs the following verification to check the correctness of P_b's VRES (δ_b, y_b). Confirm that

$$H(h(M)\|y_b) = \delta_b^{e_b} \bmod n_b,$$

and accept (δ_b, y_b) as a valid VRES only if the above equation holds. If this verification is negative, P_a may either ask P_b to re-send message (E2) or terminate the protocol execution. Otherwise, P_a transfers the message M to P_b.

(**E4**): Upon receipt of M, P_b performs the following verification to ensure the correct message M was received: Confirm that message M received generates the hash value identical to that received in step (E1), i.e. calculate the fresh hash value $h(M)''$ of the received message M and compare it with the hash value $h(M)$ received from P_a in step (E1).

If the verification is negative, P_b may either ask P_a to re-send message (E3) or terminate the protocol execution. Otherwise, P_b transfers r_b to P_a.

Upon receipt of r_b, P_a uses it to check that $y_b = r_b^{H'(ID_b\|pk_b)} \bmod N$. If this verification is positive, the certified e-mail delivery is completed successfully, i.e. P_a has obtained P_b's $receipt_b = (\delta_b, r_b)$ and P_b has obtained P_a's message M together with its proof of origin $E_{sk_a}(h(M))$.

4.2   The Receipt Recovery Protocol

In case when P_a fails to obtain P_b's correct $receipt_b$ after handing over M to P_b, P_a may request P_t for the receipt recovery by invoking the recovery protocol.

(**R1**): P_a transfers the items M and (δ_b, y_b) to P_t, which performs the following verification. Confirm that $H(h(M)\|y_b) = \delta_b^{e_b} \bmod n_b$. If the verification is negative, P_t rejects P_a's request. Otherwise, P_t uses his knowledge of the factorization of N and hence $\varphi(N)$ to compute

$$r_b = y_b^{H'(ID_b\|pk_b)^{-1} \bmod \varphi(N)} \bmod N. \tag{10}$$

(**R2**): P_t then sends r_b to P_a, who then check that $y_b = r_b^{H'(ID_b\|pk_b)} \bmod N$.
(**R3**): P_t forwards M to P_b.

Table 2. The Recovery Protocol

$$
\begin{aligned}
&\text{(R1): } P_a \rightarrow P_t : M, \delta_b, y_b \\
&\text{(R2): } P_t \rightarrow P_a : r_b \\
&\text{(R3): } P_t \rightarrow P_b : M
\end{aligned}
$$

4.3 Security and Efficiency Analysis

We shall show that the proposed protocol is secure against various attempts of cheating by either P_a or P_b.

For a malicious P_b, he attempts to cheat by generating a VRES (σ_b, y_b) on the message M in (E2), which will pass P_a's verification, but the r_b cannot be recovered correctly by the designated TTP P_t in (R2). After getting the message M in (E3), P_b refuses to send r_b to P_a, or just send a wrong r_b. However, this is always not the case. In fact, for any y_b, the number $r_b \in \mathbf{Z}_N$ satisfying $y_b = r_b^{H'(ID_b\|pk_b)}$ mod N can always be extracted by P_t as (10) using the trapdoor $SK = (P, Q)$. And then (δ_b, r_b) is a valid receipt on the message M. Therefore, a malicious P_b cannot gain any advantage over P_a in our CEMD protocol.

P_a attempts to cheat by refusing to send M or sending an incorrect M' in step (E3). If P_b does not receive M before a timeout or detects the incorrect message M' through the verification in step (E3), P_b will consequently terminate the protocol. Note that it is computationally infeasible for P_a to compute r_b from y_b by himself, without the knowledge of $SK = (P, Q)$. This means that P_a will not receive r_b in step (E4), which is needed to compute P_b' $receipt_b$, so P_a gains no benefit from this misbehavior.

P_a attempts to cheat by requesting P_t to recover P_b's receipt after step (E2) without sending M to P_b in step (E3). One of the conditions for P_t to accept P_a's request is that P_a must provide message M that can pass the verification in step (R1). If the verification is positive, P_t forwards P_a's message M to P_b while passing r_b to P_a. Thus, P_a cannot benefit from this misbehavior, as message M will ultimately be delivered to P_b by P_t.

There is another attack we must take into consideration: colluding attack. That is, P_a may attempt to collude with another user P_c, and try to have P_t recover r_b from y_b. From (10) we see that the exponent $H'(ID_b\|pk_b)$ is explicitly bound with a user's identity and public-key. Therefore, P_a and P_c need to generate a number $y_c = r_b^{H'(ID_c\|pk_c)}$ mod N. However, as the output of the function $H'(\cdot)$ is of a fixed length such as 160-bit, it is infeasible to generate such a y_c with the only knowledge of y_b.

Finally, we remark that our trust on P_t is minimal: it is only semi-trusted, which means that P_t cannot generate a valid receipt (δ_b, r_b) without getting the corresponding VRES (δ_b, y_b). From P_t's point of view, a VRES is actually equivalent to a receipt since he has the trapdoor of the permutation $y_b = r_b^{H'(ID_b\|pk_b)}$ mod N. Noting the underlying receipt (δ_b, r_b) is a probabilistic RSA signature, which is non-existential forgeable under adaptive chosen-message attacks, a malicious P_t cannot generate a valid receipt (δ_b, r_b) himself. So, our protocol is also secure against a malicious TTP.

Efficiency Analysis: In [14], it is shown that their protocol requires less computation and communication overhead, and places less security and storage requirements on the TTP. So we compare our protocol with that in [14].

In Nenadic et al.'s CEMD protocol, it requires an initialization phase for a party and a TTP to agree on a shared secret, which is then used by TTP for possible receipt recovery. In our protocol, there is no need for such a registration between a party and TTP.

In the CEMD protocol of Nenadic et al.'s, both the VRES generation and the VRES verification require 3 modular exponentiations, and a VRES requires $4k$-bits; whereas our VRES requires 2 modular exponentiation in the generation phase and 1 exponentiation in the verification phase, and a VRES is of $2k$-bits. And, both recovery protocols require 2 modular exponentiations.

5   Conclusions

Certified e-mail delivery over Internet is an important e-commerce application. Recently, Nenadic, Zhang and Barton proposed a novel security protocol for certified e-mail delivery, which are claimed to provide strong fairness to ensure that the recipient receives the e-mail if and only if the sender receives the receipt. The proposed protocols are designed based upon a novel and efficient scheme enabling the *verifiable and recoverable encrypted signature* (VRES) for the RSA cryptosystems. However, as a crucial building block for these protocols, their VRES is totally breakable. This papers shows that an adversary can easily generate an RSA-based VRES which cannot be recovered by the designated TTP. As a result, the proposed certified e-mail delivery and certified e-good delivery protocols do not satisfy the required fairness.

Based upon probabilistic signatures, we proposed a novel fair CEMD protocol, which works with the RSA cryptosystem and is more computation and communication efficient. Moreover, there is no registration between a party and TTP, which makes our protocol much concise and easy to implementation.

Acknowledgement

The work is supported by National Natural Science Foundation of China under Granted No.60373039, and National Grand Fundamental Research Project of China under Granted No.G1999035802.

References

1. N.Asokan, V.Shoup, M.Waidner. Optimistic fair exchange of digital signatures. IEEE Journal on Selected Areas in Communications, 18(4): 593-610, 2000.
2. G. Ateniese. Verifiable encryption of digital signatures and applications, ACM Transactions on Information and System Security, 7, 1 (2004), 1-20.

3. G. Ateniese, C. Nita-Rotaru. Stateless-recipient certified E-mail system based on verifiable encryption. Proc. RSA Conference-Topics in Cryptology, LNCS 2271, pp.182-199, Springer-Verlag, 2002.
4. F. Bao, R. Deng and W. Mao. Efficient and practical fair exchange protocols with off-line TTP. Proc. IEEE Symposium on Security and Privacy, pp.77-85, 1998.
5. C. Boyd, E. Foo. Off-line fair payment protocols using convertible signatures. ASIACRYPT'98, LNCS 1514, pp.271-285, Springer-Verlag.
6. J. Camenisch and M. Michels. Separability and efficiency for generic group signature schemes. Proc. Crypto'99, LNCS 1666, pp.106-121, Springer-Verlag.
7. L. Chen. Efficient Fair Exchange with Verifiable Confirmation of Signatures. Proc. ASIACRYPT'98, LNCS 1514, pages 286-299, Springer-Verlag, 1998.
8. R. H. Deng, L. Gong, A. A. Lazar, and W. Wang. Practical Protocols for Certified Electronic Mail. J. of Network and System Management, 4(3): 279-297, 1996.
9. S. Even and Y. Yacobi. Relations among public key signature schemes. Technical Report 175, Computer Science Dept., Technion, Israel, 1980.
10. M. Franklin, M. Reiter. Fair exchange with a semi-trusted third party. Proc. ACM conference on computer and communications security, Zurich, pages 1-5, 1997.
11. J. A. Garay, M. Jakobsson, and P. MacKenzie. Abuse-free optimistic contract signing. Proc. Advances in Cryptology - CRYPTO'99, LNCS 1666, pages 449-466, Springer-Verlag, Berlin, Germany, 1999.
12. B.Schneier and J.Riordan. A certified E-mail protocol. Proc.13th Computer Security Applications Conference, pp.347-352. ACM Press, 1998.
13. I. Ray and I. Ray. An optimistic fair exchange E-commerce protocol with automated dispute resolution, Proc. International Conference on E-Commerce and Web Technologies (EC-Web). LNCS 1875, pp. 84-93, Springer-Verlag, 2000.
14. A. Nenadic, N.Zhang and S.Barton. Fair certified E-mail delivery, Proc. ACM Symposium on Applied Computing (SAC 2004) - Computer Security Track, Nicosia, Cyprus, pages 391-396, 2004.
15. A. Nenadic, N. Zhang, S. Barton. FIDES-A middleware E-commerce security solution, Proc. 3rd European Conference on Information Warfare and Security (ECIW 2004), London, UK, pp. 295-304, 2004.
16. S/MIME. *Secure Multipurpose Internet Mail Extensions*. Available at http://www.rsasecurity.com/standards/smime/.
17. OpenPGP, *An Open Specification for Pretty Good Privacy*. Available at http://www.ietf.org/html.charters/openpgp-charter.html.

Appendix

The following is well-known as the Chinese Remainder Theorem, and is extremely useful in §3.1.

Theorem (Chinese Remainder Theorem). *Let* $n_1, \cdots, n_k$ *be pairwise relatively prime, positive integers. For any integers* $a_1, \cdots, a_k$, *there exists an integer* z, *unique modulo* $n := \prod_{i=1}^{k} n_i$, *such that*

$$z \equiv a_i \pmod{n_i} \quad for \quad i = 1, \cdots, k.$$

Moreover, if we let $n = n_i m_i$ *and* $m_i' m_i \equiv 1 \bmod n_i$ *for* $i = 1, \cdots, k$, *then the solution* z *can be computed as* $z \equiv m_1' m_1 a_1 + m_2' m_2 a_2 + \cdots + m_k' m_k a_k \pmod{n}$.

Intrusion Tolerant CA Scheme with Cheaters Detection Ability

Liwu Zhang and Dengguo Feng

State Key Laboratory of Information Security (Institute of Software of Chinese Academy of Sciences), Beijing, 100080, P. R. China
zlw@is.iscas.ac.cn

Abstract. In this paper, we put forward a practical intrusion tolerant CA scheme with the ability of cheater detection. Compared to the scheme of ITTC's project[1], the scheme has built-in ability of detecting cheaters, and has ability to generate signature without specifying one group of servers in the serial mode. We also present shares proactive refresh protocol to prevent key shares from gradually exposed or corrupted. Our scheme can be changed from (t, n) scheme to $(t, n + 1)$ scheme.

Keywords: Intrusion Tolerance, Threshold Signature, CA, Proactive

1 Introduction

In a PKI system, the compromise of CA's private keys is fatal, which can result in potentially devastating financial losses, legal liabilities or disruption of business activities. One common way to protect CA's private key is to store it in a hardware security module(HSM). A HSM protects the private key from reading access. However, if HSM is stolen, the whole PKI system is corrupted, which is called the single point failure.

Recently, threshold cryptography has been adopted to CA system to obtain intrusion tolerant ability. With threshold cryptography technology, the functions of private key are distributed among several servers, and a predetermined number of servers must cooperate in order to generate signature correctly. In a particular (t, n) scheme, sign functions are distributed among n servers, and t of servers must cooperate to generate a signature. If less than t servers are controlled by the adversary, the security of ITCA system just degraded instead of key compromised or system corrupted.

RSA is the most widely used signature algorithm in CA systems, and many schemes have been put forward on implementing RSA threshold. In this paper, we put forward an intrusion tolerant CA scheme. Compared to the ITTC's scheme[1], our scheme has built-in ability of detecting cheaters and it can generate a signature without specifying a group.

G. Chen et al. (Eds.): ISPA Workshops 2005, LNCS 3759, pp. 378–386, 2005.

1.1 Related Works

Thomas Wu, Michael Malkin, Dan Boneh [1] introduced ITTC's project. The project implemented an intrusion tolerant system that can be embedded into web server and CA. Adi Shamir[7] gives the classical secret sharing scheme based on LaGrange Interpolation. V. Shoup[8] gives a practical threshold signature scheme based on Shamir's secret sharing. Yair Frankel, Philip D.MacKenzie, Moti Yung[9] present a robust distributed RSA-Key generation method. Michael Malkin, Thomas Wu, Dan Boneh[2] present a practical way to implement shared generation of RSA keys. Pierre-Alain Fouque and Jacques Stern[5] present a fully distributed RSA scheme. Dan Boneh, Glenn Durfee, Yair Frankel[3] give analysis on affects of RSA keys when exposing small fraction of its bits. Tal Rabin[4] analyzed a simplified approach to implement threshold and proactive RSA. Amir Herzberg, Markus Jakobsson, Stanislaw Jarecki, Hugo Krawczyk, Moti Yung[10] present a proactive protocol of public key and signature systems.

1.2 Notations and Definitions

- N is RSA modulus, e is public key, d is private key.
- n denotes the total number of servers, and t is the threshold number.

ITCA: An intrusion tolerant CA system that has features as follows: a) CA keys are distributed among n servers. b) Any qualified subset can generate signature correctly and efficiently. c) Any non-qualified subset can't forge signature. Practical ITCA system is always (t, n) threshold scheme, where $(1 \leq t \leq n)$.

1.3 Organization of Paper

Section 2 gives the architecture and components of our ITCA system. Section 3 gives our way of shares distribution and its security analysis. Section 4 gives the signature work mode and performance analysis of our ITCA system. Section 5 gives the protocol based on built-in ability of cheater detection. Section 6 gives shares proactive refresh protocol that prevent shares from gradually exposed and corrupted. Section 7 gives protocol to extend (t, n) scheme to $(t, n + 1)$ scheme. Section 8 gives a shared RSA key generation protocol to remove the trusted dealer. Section 9 gives the conclusions.

2   Architecture and System Components

Our ITCA system composed of a trusted dealer, n share servers, several combiners and several RA agents(as shown in Fig 1). *Share Server* - key component of an ITCA system, it holds shares of the signature private key. A share server can manage multiple keys. *Trusted Dealer*- generate RSA key parameters, and split it into shares. *RA Agent* - the interface between RAs and CA, which responsible for handle request from RAs and dispatch tasks to share servers. *Combiner* - responsible for combine partial results to a signature, but it has no private key shares.

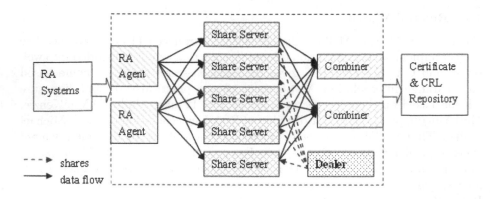

Fig. 1. Architecture and Components of Intrusion Tolerant CA

3   Shares Distribution

Additive form secret sharing allows for strait forward implementation of RSA threshold. Suppose the message formatted by PKCS#1 is M, the standard signature would be $Sig = M^d \mod N$, and verification is $M = Sig^e \mod N$.

3.1   Shares Distribution of Usually Adopt

To implement (t, n) scheme, the common additive form secret sharing scheme split d into $m = \binom{n}{t}$ groups. Each group corresponds to a combination, and it has no relationship with others. The equation array shown as follows:

$$d = \; d_{11} + d_{12} + \cdots + d_{1t}$$
$$d = \; d_{21} + d_{22} + \cdots + d_{2t}$$
$$\vdots$$
$$d = d_{m1} + d_{m2} + \cdots + d_{mt}$$

ITTC's scheme[1] adopted an optimized shares distribution. The system reuse one group of shares, and this effectively reduced the number of shares to $t\lfloor \binom{n}{t}/2^{n-t} + 1 \rfloor$, and each server stored $\lfloor \binom{n}{t}/2^{n-t} + 1 \rfloor$ shares.

3.2   Shares Distribution of Our Scheme

In our scheme, private key is split once instead of being split into $\binom{n}{t}$ groups. The shares satisfy $d = d_1 + d_2 \cdots + d_k$, where $k = \binom{n}{n-t+1}$. Shares are distributed as follows:

1) The trusted dealer generates RSA key parameters and publish (N, e).
2) The trusted dealer splits private key d into a form $d = d_1 + d_2 \cdots + d_k$, where $k = \binom{n}{n-t+1}$.

3) The trusted dealer distribute each share to share servers through secure channel according to the following rules: Each share is corresponding to a combination of $\binom{n}{n-t+1}$, and the share is distributed into all $n - t + 1$ share servers of the combination, so there are total $k = \binom{n}{n-t+1} = \binom{n}{t-1}$ shares, and each share server stores $r = (n - t + 1)k/n$ shares. The trusted dealer publishes g^{d_i}.

Comparable Example of Shares Distribution

Suppose $n = 4, t = 3$. Table 1 a) shows the original scheme. It needs $k = \binom{4}{3} = 4$ groups of shares, and each group has 3 shares, totally 12 shares. With optimized shares distribution, the scheme just need reuse 2 group of shares. Optimized shares distribution scheme is adopted by ITTC's project, as shown in Table 1 b).

In our scheme, private key is split into $k = \binom{n}{n-t+1} = \binom{4}{2} = 6$ shares, and shares satisfy $d = d_1 + d_2 + d_3 + d_4 + d_5 + d_6$, as shown in Table 1 c).

Table 1. Shares Distribution Method

a) Original

	S1	S2	S3	S4
1	d_{11}	d_{12}	d_{13}	
2	d_{21}	d_{22}		d_{23}
3	d_{31}		d_{32}	d_{33}
4		d_{41}	d_{42}	d_{43}

b) ITTC's Project

	S1	S2	S3	S4
1	d_{11}	d_{12}	d_{13}	d_{13}
2	d_{21}	d_{21}	d_{22}	d_{23}

c) Our Scheme

	S1	S2	S3	S4
1	d_1	d_1		
2	d_2		d_2	
3	d_3			d_3
4		d_4	d_4	
5		d_5		d_5
6			d_6	d_6

3.3 Security Analysis

Theorem 1. The scheme is t secure in secret sharing$(1 \leq t \leq n)$.

Proof: Due to the distribution method, private key d is split in a form $d = d_1 + d_2 \cdots + d_k$, where $k = \binom{n}{n-t+1}$. Each share is distributed into $n - t + 1$ servers of a combination $\binom{n}{n-t+1}$.

1) Any t servers can recover the private key d.
   To a certain share $d_i(1 \leq i \leq k)$, excluding t servers that specified, there are $n - t$ servers left. Due to shares distribution, d_i is distributed into $n - t + 1$ servers, but there are only $n - t$ positions left, according to *pigeon hole principle*, at least one of the specified t servers have d_i. So, every share of private key d can be found in the specified t servers.
2) Any $t - 1$ servers cannot get any useful information about d.
   Each share is distributed into all $n-t+1$ servers of a combination of $\binom{n}{n-t+1}$, to any $t - 1$ servers specified, there are $n - t + 1$ servers left, and this a combination of $\binom{n}{n-t+1}$, so, there must be one share (suppose d_j) corresponding to the combination that only be distributed in this group of servers, and the $t - 1$ servers left must short of share d_j.

RSA is sensitive to bits exposure(for details see [3]). Let shares be the same size of secrets d, our scheme can be information theoretic secure in secret sharing, but introduce of negative numbers brings a little trouble.

For simplicity, we choose $d_i(1 \leq i \leq k)$ in positive numbers, where $k = \binom{n}{n-t+1}$. Let shares $d_i(1 \leq i \leq k-1)$ be a random number in the range $(\lfloor d/2k \rfloor, \lfloor d/k \rfloor)$, and $d_k = d - d_1 \cdots - d_{k-1}$. Because shares are select in positive numbers, the information-leak is about $\log k$ bits(suppose $n = 5, t = 3, k = 10, \log 10 < 4bits$), and which is negligible compared to the size of private key d. The scheme published g^{d_i}, when adversary computes d_i from g^{d_i}, they face the discrete logarithm problem.

3.4   File Format of ITCA

Our ITCA system manages four types of key files: (1)Standard RSA public key consists of (N, e). (2) Private share files stored on each share server. Each share server holds r private shares $(d_1, \cdots, d_r)$ and its ID, where $r = (n - t + 1)\binom{n}{n-t+1}/n$. (3) Public key parameters stored on RA agents and combiners. (4) Mapping between private shares and share server.

4   Signature Process

In ITTC's project, the ITCA system requires client to specify one group of shares before performing signature process. Our ITCA system provides two signature modes: one is the parallel mode, the other is the serial mode.

4.1   Compute Signature in Serial

1) The RA agent arbitrarily chooses a share server and sends M to it.
2) The share server i receives M from RA agent(or previous share server), then excludes share that already participated the signature from the shares it has, then computes the sum of shares (suppose d_i). Then share server i computes $pSig_i = M^{d_i}$, and sends $pSig_i$ to another share server(message shown in Table 2).
3) Repeat step 2 till the last share server(e.g. number t server). The last server excludes shares that participated sign process(suppose d_t), and computes $pSig_t = M^{d_t} \mod N$. Then it sends result to the combiner.
4) The combiner computes $Sig = pSig_1 \cdot pSig_2 \cdots pSig_t \mod N$, and verify the signature with public key. If valid, accept the signature, or else run cheaters detection protocol.

Note: $ProT$ identify the type of protocol. $RaaID$ identify the RA agent. $TaskID$ identify the task by a serial number. $keyID$ identify the key in case that server manage multiple keys. k is the number of shares, where $k = \binom{n}{n-t+1}$. sID_i $(1 \leq i \leq k)$ identify the shares. $SevID_i$ identify the share server. Request message M. Partial result $pSig_i$.

Table 2. Message format of compute signature in serial

Type	INT	INT	INT	INT	INT	INT	INT	$\cdots$
Words	$ProT$	$RaaID$	$TaskID$	$keyID$	k	sID_1	$SevID_1$	$\cdots$

$\cdots$	INT	INT	BitString	INT	INT	BitString	$\cdots$	INT	BitString
$\cdots$	sID_k	$ServerID_k$	M	t	$SevID_1$	$pSig_1$	$\cdots$	$SevID_t$	$pSig_t$

4.2   Compute Signature in Parallel

1) The RA agent specifies one group of share servers to generate signature, then sends M and ID of shares to all t share servers in the group through secure channel(request message shown as Table 3 a).
2) The share server i in the specified group receives request message, and knows shares that it should signed with. Share server computes sum of specified shares and got sum d_i, then computes partial result $pSig_i = M^{d_i} \mod N$, and send $pSig_i$ back to RA agent through secure channel(response message shown in Table 3 b).
3) The RA agent receives t partial result that signed with the specified shares from specified t share servers, combines it and get the standard signature. E.g. Computes $Sig = pSig_1 \cdot pSig_2 \cdots pSig_t \mod N$.
4) The combiner verifies signature with the standard public key. If the signature valid, combiner accepts the signature, otherwise the system starts cheaters detection protocol.

Table 3. Message format of compute signature in parallel

a) Request from RA agent

Type	INT	INT	INT	INT	INT	INT	INT	$\cdots$	INT	INT	BitString
Words	$ProT$	$RaaID$	$TaskID$	$keyID$	k	sID_1	$SevID_1$	$\cdots$	sID_k	$SevID_k$	M

b) Response from share server

Type	INT	INT	INT	INT	INT	INT	BitString	BitString
Words	$ProT$	$SevID$	$RaaID$	$TaskID$	$keyID$	k	M	$pSig_i$

4.3   Performance Analysis

Because shares in ITTC's scheme and our shcme are approximately the size of private key d, so the time that share server computes a partial signature cost approximately the time of a standard signature. In ITTC's scheme, all the t specified share servers compute partial signatures simultaneously, the responding time is the same as a standard signature, but total cost is t times of a standard signature.

In our scheme, when work in the parallel mode, all the t share servers compute sum of specified shares, then computes partial result cost the time of a standard signature. Compared to ITTC's scheme, our scheme do extra add operation at most $r - 1$ times in parallel mode, which can be negligible compared to the cost of computing partial signatures.

In our scheme, when work in serial mode, share servers compute sum of shares and compute partial signature one by one, totally t share servers took part in the signature, and do modulus multiply for $t - 1$ times. So, the total cost is approximately t times the cost of a standard signature. But for a single task, the signature responding time approximately t times of that in parallel mode.

5   Detection of Corrupted Shares and Cheaters

Share servers may be controlled by the adversary, so system should make sure that shares are not corrupted. Our system has built-in ability to detect corrupted servers. The protocol is shown as follows:

1) RA agent broadcast M that signed error last time.
2) After received M, each share server sign M with every share it has, and got partial signature result M^{d_i} (for $1 \leq i \leq r$), where $r = \binom{n}{n-t+1}(n - t + 1)/n$. The server fill the response message with r partial result, and sends it to the combiner.
3) The combiner compares partial results that signed with the same share (known from ID) from each share server to detect the different one.
4) The combiner combines partial results from each share server($Sig = M^{d_1}M^{d_2}\cdots M^{d_k} \mod N$, where $k = \binom{n}{n-t+1}$), then verify it with standard public key to detect the corrupted servers.

6   Proactive Refresh of Shares

Hardware failure may cause shares losses, and shares can be gradually exposed or compromised. In such cases, we need to renew existing shares without changing the secret. The protocol is shown as follows:

1) For each share d_i, share server split it into $k = \binom{n}{n-t+1}$ new shares, satisfy $d_i = d_{i1} + \cdots + d_{ik}$, then share server publishes $g^{d_{i1}}, \cdots, g^{d_{ik}}$.
2) Then share server distribute shares d_{ij} to all $n - t + 1$ share servers of the combination of $\binom{n}{n-t+1}$ through secure channel.
3) Each share server checks if $g^{d_{i1}}g^{d_{i2}}\cdots g^{d_{ik}} = g^{d_i}$ hold. If the equation hold, all share servers agree on the same group of d_i, else it broadcast a complain.
4) If there is no accuse, each server generate new shares by equation $d_i^{new} = \sum_{j=1}^{k} d_{ji}$ for each number i share it has.

7   Change from (t, n) Scheme to $(t, n + 1)$ Scheme

1) For every shares d_i, share server u split it into $r = \binom{n+1}{n-t+2}$ new shares that satisfy $d_i = d_{i1} + \cdots + d_{ir}$, and publishes $g^{d_{i1}}, \cdots, g^{d_{ir}}$.

2) The server u distribute d_{ij} to all the $n-t+2$ share servers of the combination $\binom{n+1}{n-t+2}$ through secure channel.
3) Each share server checks if $g^{d_{i1}}g^{d_{i2}}\cdots g^{d_{ir}} = g^{d_i}$ hold. If it doesn't hold, the server broadcast a complain. Else, all share servers agree on a same group of shares. Each server generates new shares by $d_i^{new} = \sum_{j=1}^{k} d_{ji}$.
4) Each share server publishes $g^{d_1^{new}}, \cdots, g^{d_r^{new}}$, and verifies if the equation $g^{d_1^{new}}g^{d_1^{new}}\cdots g^{d_k^{new}} = g^{d_1}g^{d_2}\cdots g^{d_k}$ hold. If it doesn't hold, system run cheaters detection protocol.

8   Shared Generation of RSA Keys

We use protocols in [2], and adapt shares to the form our scheme need.

1) Each server picks 2 random numbers p_i , q_i and keep them as secrets.
2) n servers shared compute $N = (p_1 + \cdots + p_n)(q_1 + \cdots + q_n)$.
3) n servers engage in a distributed computation to test that N is the product of two primes. If test fails, the protocol restart from step 1.
4) Given a public key e, servers shared generate private key d.

With this protocol, server i got shares d_i and $d = \sum_{i=1}^{n} d_i$. It is easy to adapt shares to the form needed in our scheme. The protocol is as follows:

1) For every share d_i, Share Server u split it into $k = \binom{n}{n-t+1}$ new shares, satisfy $d_i = d_{i1} + \cdots + d_{ik}$, then server u publishes $g^{d_{i1}}, \cdots, g^{d_{ik}}$, and distributes shares d_{ij} to $n - t + 1$ Share Servers of combination $\binom{n}{n-t+1}$ through secure channel.
2) Each server verify if $g^{d_{i1}}g^{d_{i2}}\cdots g^{d_{ik}} = g^{d_i} \mod N$ hold. If it doesn't hold, the server broadcast a complain.
3) Server u generate new shares by $d_i^{new} = \sum_{j=1}^{k} d_{ji}$ for each share it has(d_i^{new} satisfy $d = \sum_{i=1}^{r} d_i^{new}$).

Follow above steps, we get $d = d_1^{new} + \cdots + d_k^{new}$, where $k = \binom{n}{n-t+1}$.

9   Conclusions

Our ITCA scheme is simple and practical. The private key of our ITCA system is t secure in secret sharing, and components will not disclose useful information of private shares while sign a certificate. One feature of our scheme is that it has built-in ability to detect cheaters. Another feature is that the scheme need not specify a group in the serial mode.

We provide shares proactive refresh protocol to prevent shares from gradually exposed or corrupted. We also present protocol to extend scheme from (t, n) to $(t, n + 1)$, and makes our scheme scalable and flexible. The trusted dealer is an optional component in our ITCA scheme, which can be removed by shared generation of RSA keys.

References

1. Thomas Wu, Michael Malkin, Dan Boneh. Building Intrusion Tolerant Applications. In the 8th USENIX Security Symposium. August,23-24,1999
2. Michael Malkin, Thomas Wu, Dan Boneh. Experimenting With Shared Generation of RSA keys. In proceedings of the Internet Society's 1999 Symposium on Network and Distributed System Security, pp.43-56.
3. Dan Boneh, Glenn Durfee, Yair Frankel. Exposing an RSA Private Key Given a Small Fraction of its Bits. In Advances in Cryptology - ASIACRYPT '98, LNCS,vol.1514, pp. 25-34. Springer-Verlag, 1998.
4. Tal Rabin. A Simplified Approach to Threshold and Proactive RSA. Proceedings of the 18th Annual International Cryptology Conference on Advances in Cryptology. LNCS, pp.89-104, Springer-Verlag,1998.
5. Pierre-Alain Fouque, Jacques Stern. Fully Distributed RSA under Standard Assumptions. In ASIACRYPT 2001, vol. 2248 of LNCS, pp. 310–330, 2001.
6. J. Benaloh and J. Leichter. Generalized secret sharing and monotone functions. In "Advances in Cryptology – CRYPTO '88", S.Goldwasser, ed., Lecture Notes in Computer Science 403 (1989), 27-35
7. Adi Shamir. How to share a secret. Communications of ACM,22(11):612-613,Nov1979.
8. V. Shoup. Practical Threshold Signatures. In Eurocrypt'00, LNCS 1807, pp.207-220. Springer-Verlag, 2000.
9. Yair Frankel, Philip D.MacKenzie, Moti Yung. Robust Efficient Distributed RSA-Key Generation. The Thirteenth Annual ACM Symposium on Theory of Computing – STOC '98.
10. Amir Herzberg, Markus Jakobsson, Stanislaw Jarecki, Hugo Krawczyk, Moti Yung. Proactive Public Key and Signature Systems. ACM Conference on Computer and Communications Security,1996.

Improvement of Protocol Anomaly Detection Based on Markov Chain and Its Application[*]

Zheng Qin[1], Na Li[2], Da-fang Zhang[1], and Nai-Zheng Bian[1]

[1] College of Software, Hunan University,
410082, ChangSha, China
[2] College of Computer and Communication, Hunan University,
410082, ChangSha, China
qz88@263.net, ln1314@21cn.com, dfzhang@hnu.cn

Abstract. As we know, a lot of network attacks come from abusing different network protocols and several new attacks violate the protocol standard. Kumar Das first presented the concept of the protocol anomaly detection. The idea of protocol anomaly detection is not new but interesting. It aims to set up models for proper use of protocols and any behavior that departs from the models will be regarded as an intrusive or suspicious one. In this paper, we made some improvements that aim at the lack of stochastic protocol models based on Markov Chain and made some evaluations for that presented by Juan M. Some necessary states are added to the protocol model. Furthermore, the initial and transition probabilities are more precise. Also, we propose to combine Chi-Square Distance into Markov Chain method to detect protocol anomaly. The experimental results show that SYN Flooding attack can be detected efficiently by the new approach.

Keywords: Intrusion Detection, Protocol Anomaly Detection, Markov Chain, Chi-Square Distance, DARPA Evaluation Dataset.

1 Introduction

The system that uses the intrusion detection techniques is generally called IDS. The principle approaches of intrusion detection include misuse detection, anomaly detection and specification-based detection [1]. There are some previous studies about protocol anomaly detection. Kumar Das first presented the concept of protocol anomaly detector, which builds models of TCP/IP protocols using their specification [2], known as RFC [3]. Juan M.Estevez-Tapiador proposed a stochastic protocol modeling for anomaly-based network intrusion detection [4]. Also, E. Lemonnier presented the concept of Protocol Anomaly Filter [5]. As to cryptographic protocol, Sachi P.Joglekar and Stephen R.Tate presented the design of ProtoMon (Protocol Monitor), which was capable of detecting the attack using the defect of cryptographic protocols [6].

Our approach is different from the previous research work. We build models of Application layer protocols and transport layer protocol, mainly about FTP and TCP,

---

[*] This paper is supported by the National Natural Science Foundation of China under Grant No.60273070, the Sci & Tech. Project of Hunan under Grant No. 04GK3022.

G. Chen et al. (Eds.): ISPA Workshops 2005, LNCS 3759, pp. 387–396, 2005.
© Springer-Verlag Berlin Heidelberg 2005

using the attack-free datasets, which is intrusion detection evaluation dataset of Year 1999, issued in public by Lincoln Laboratory of Massachusetts Institute of Technology in U.S.A [7]. The dataset is also called DARPA evaluation dataset. The models of protocols are an improvement of previous research. Then, we go on to put forward a new evaluation measure based on Chi-square Distance to detect attacks. The experimental results verify the validity of the new measure by detecting SYN Flooding attacks.

The rest of this paper is organized as follows. In Section 2, we introduce how to set up protocol models based on Markov Chain. Then, we propose a new method based on Chi-Square Distance to evaluate the protocol models in section 3. Also, we verify the efficiency of Chi-Square Distance by detecting SYN Flooding in section 4. Finally, we summarize the paper by presenting our conclusions and future research work in section 5.

2   Protocol Model Based on Markov Chain

In this section, relevant knowledge of Markov Chain is introduced first. Then, we make some improvements for protocol models based on Markov Chain presented by Juan M.Estevez-Tapiador. The space of the dataset used in Juan M.Estevez-Tapiador'experiments for the construction of protocol models was too small [4], so the statistical results may have some differences with the actual [8]. Since we adopt the authorized DARPA datasets [7], our protocol models can efficiently reflect the actual use of protocols in the network.

2.1 Markov Chain

We first introduce the Markov Hypothesis: the state at time t+1 only depends on the state at time t. Let the value of state X_{m+k} at time m+k be a_j, the value of state X_m at time m be a_i, and the value of state X_{s_i} at time S_i be a_{s_i}, $s_1 < s_2 < \ldots \ldots < s_l < m < m+k$. Markov Chain is defined as below [9]:

$$P\{X_{m+k} = a_j \mid X_{s_1} = a_{s_1}, \ldots \ldots, X_{s_l} = a_{s_l}, X_m = a_i\} \tag{1}$$
$$= P\{X_{m+k} = a_j \mid X_m = a_i\} = p_{ij}(m, m+k)$$

$p_{ij}(m, m+k)$ is called k-step transition probability, which describes the probability of $X_{m+k} = a_j$ when $X_m = a_i$ .Another definition of Markov Chain can be found in formula (2)[9]. $p_{ij}(m, m+1)$ is the one-step transition probability. The initial probability of $X_m = a_i$ can be seen in formula (3) and transition probability of $X_n = a_j$ when $X_m = a_i$ can be seen in formula (4).

$$P\{X_{m+1} = a_j \mid X_{s_1} = a_{s_1}, \ldots \ldots, X_{s_l} = a_{s_l}, X_m = a_i\} \tag{2}$$
$$= P\{X_{m+1} = a_j \mid X_m = a_i\} = p_{ij}(m, m+1)$$

$$P_j(n) = P\{X_n = a_j\} \tag{3}$$

$$P_{ij}(m,n) = P\{X_n = a_j \mid X_m = a_i\} \tag{4}$$

2.2 The Models of Application Protocols and TCP Based on Markov Chain

Many researchers have built models of system calls based on Markov Chain and Hidden Markov Chain [10-13]. If the model of analysis object is correct, the method based on Markov Chain is robust enough [14]. We will set up models for application layer protocols and TCP protocol of TCP/IP network based on Markov Chain.

2.2.1 Application Protocol Model

Here, we will introduce how to set up models of FTP based on Markov Chain. The experimental data is from 1999 DARPA evaluation dataset. It is composed of two-week traffic without attacks and one-week traffic including labeled attacks [7]. Firstly, we use the incoming traffic filtered by destination port as training sequence with the tool of TCPDUMP [15]. The corresponding order is below:

tcpdump –r inside –w ftp_inside.tcpdump tcp port 21

From the above order, we can obtain the FTP traffic. Secondly, we quantize the flags of TCP header to label each TCP packet. Seen from figure 1, if the flag is 000010, which means SYN=1. Then, we can transfer the binary number into decimal number 2. After labeling, we can get a sequence of decimal numbers. Such sequence

URG	ACK	PSH	RST	SYN	FIN

Fig. 1. The Flags in TCP Header

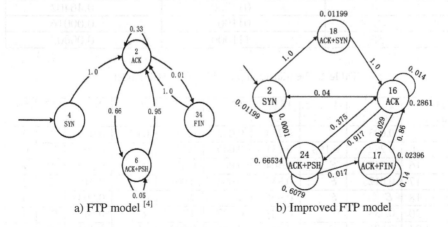

a) FTP model [4]

b) Improved FTP model

Fig. 2. The FTP model and the Improved FTP model based on Markov Chain

satisfies the Markov Hypothesis. The range of the decimal numbers mentioned above is $0\sim2^6-1$, but not all the numbers in this range is legal[3]. The model of FTP protocol based on Markov Chain in Juan M.Estevez-Tapiador's paper is shown in figure 2a) [4]. The model of FTP in this paper is shown in figure 2b), which uses the sequence of these decimal numbers mentioned above as inputs. Every circle in figure 2b) represents state and the number in the circle represents the decimal number mentioned above. The numbers outside the circles represent initial probabilities of very state and the numbers on the arrows are transition probabilities between states. From the above two figures, we find that the decimal number of very state in figure 2b) is different from figure 2a), that is because the author adjusted every binary bit in TCP flags [4]. At the same time, compared to figure 2b), figure 2a) is lack of necessary states and transitions between states, and the transition probabilities are different from figure 2b). The experimental data is from DARPA evaluation dataset without attacks and the sample space is large, about 3G-4G and 10 days [7], so the results are more convictive.

2.2.2 TCP Model

Here, TCP model based on Markov Chain is built with the same method mentioned in 2.2.1. The corresponding TCP model is not showed because of the complexity of TCP protocol. Every emerged flag value of TCP packet and initial probability of each state

Table 1. The flag values and initial probabilities of TCP model

Flag Values	Flags in TCP Header	Initial Probabilities
2	000010	0.02974
4	000100	0.00011
16	010000	0.41835
17	010001	0.05794
18	010010	0.02914
20	010100	0.00052
24	011000	0.46402
25	011001	0.00016
56	111000	0.00002

Table 2. The transition probabilities of TCP model

Flag Values	2	4	16	17	18	20	24	25	56
2	0.003	ε	0.254	0.002	0.678	0.035	0.028	ε	0
4	0.292	0.198	0.131	0.049	0.139	0	0.191	0	0
16	0.047	ε	0.304	0.069	0.018	ε	0.562	ε	ε
17	0.012	ε	0.857	0.003	0.001	ε	0.019	ε	0
18	ε	ε	0.996	ε	ε	0	0.004	0	0
20	0.233	0	0.183	0.037	ε	ε	0.547	0	0
24	0.005	ε	0.437	0.065	0.002	ε	0.491	ε	ε
25	0	0	0.962	ε	0.001	0	0.036	0	0
56	0.007	0	0.868	0.005	0	0	0.12	0	0

by means of statistical method can be seen in Table 1. Table 2 shows the transition between each state, $\varepsilon = 10^{-3}$. If the transition probabilities by means of statistical method are lower than a given value ε, they are set to ε. The value of zero in the table shows no transition between states.

3 Model Evaluation Based on Chi-Square Distance

In this section, we use the TCP model based on Markov Chain and evaluate the model according to expressions (6) and (7) [4]. MAP is the abbreviation for Maximum A-posteriori Probability. Let $A = \left[a_{ij} \right]$ be the matrix of transitions between states. The computation of a_{ij} is defined in formula (5). $\Pi = (\pi_i)$ is the vector of initial probability of every state. $O = \{o_1, o_2, \cdots, o_T\}$ is a sequence of TCP flag values. From expression (6), we can see that the value of MAP(t) approaches zero quickly. Therefore, sometimes it is more useful to use a representation in a logarithmic scale.

$$a_{ij} = \frac{P[q_t = o_j, q_{t-1} = o_i]}{P[q_{t-1} = o_i]} \tag{5}$$

$$MAP(t) = \pi_{o_t} \cdot \prod_{t}^{T-1} (a_{o_t o_{t+1}}) \tag{6}$$

$$\log MAP(t) = \log(\pi_{o_t}) + \sum_{t}^{T-1} \log(a_{o_t o_{t+1}}) \tag{7}$$

Here, We choose a sample window W and calculate the absolute value of Log-MAP(t) for every W packets. Then, we calculate the Chi-Square Distance of |LogMAP(t)| to measure the deviation of the observed activities from the normal activities. The methods based on Chi-Square Distance are Average and EWMA methods. In the following, the two methods will be introduced respectively.

3.1 Average Method

Let $X_i = (X_{i,1}, X_{i,2}, \ldots, X_{i,p})$ denotes the ith observation, which is a vector and has p attributes. If data sample size is n, let

$$\overline{X} = (\overline{X_1}, \overline{X_2}, \ldots, \overline{X_p}) \tag{8}$$

$$\overline{X_k} = \frac{1}{n} \sum_{i-1}^{n} X_{i,k}, k = 1, 2, \ldots, n \tag{9}$$

Generally, the statistical distance of an observation, X_i from $\overline{X}$ is given by formula (10) and (11) [16]:

$$T^2 = (X_i - \overline{X})^T S^{-1}(X_i - \overline{X}) \tag{10}$$

$$S = \frac{1}{n-1}\sum_{i=1}^{n}(X_i - \overline{X})(X_i - \overline{X})^T \tag{11}$$

S is a sample covariance matrix. If the space of data is very large, the calculation cost of S and S^{-1} will become very high. So a more scalable distance measure of X_i from $\overline{X}$ called Chi-Square Distance is proposed in formula (12)[16]. Formula (12) can simplify the computation of distance and the corresponding cost is much lower than that of formula (10).

$$X_i^2 = \sum_{k=1}^{p}\frac{(X_{i,k} - \overline{X}_k)^2}{\overline{X}_k} \tag{12}$$

3.2 EWMA Method

EWMA is the abbreviation for exponentially weighted moving average. The method of EWMA has function of prediction, and the ith observation relies on the $(i-1)^{th}$ observation. One-step EWMA method is shown as follow [16]:

$$\hat{X}_i = \hat{X}_{i-1} + w(X_{i-1} - \hat{X}_{i-1}) \tag{13}$$

Generally, the EWMA method estimates the value of the ith observation by adding some weight w to the previous one. The choosing of w is an important factor in EWMA method. Chi-Square Distance is defined below [16]:

$$X_i^2 = \sum_{k=1}^{p}\frac{(X_{i,k} - \hat{X}_{i,k})^2}{\hat{X}_{i,k}} \tag{14}$$

4 Application of Chi-Square Distance in Detecting SYN Flooding

The attack of SYN Flooding exploits three-way handshake mechanism of TCP protocol and its limitation in maintaining half-open connections [17]. It can be considered as an instance of protocol anomaly. It is a kind of Denial of Service, which consumes a large amount of resources, thus preventing legitimate users from receiving services, so detecting such attacks is meaningful in reality. In previous research work, there are some methods to detect such attack. The two algorithms are an adaptive threshold algorithm and a particular application of the cumulative sum (CUSUM) algorithm [17, 18]. SYN Flooding attacks can't be detected by Juan M.Estevez-Tapiador'method[19]. We use the model of TCP protocol based on Markov Chain to detect this kind of attack with the methods of Average and EWMA methods separately.

This experiment chooses the first 10000 TCP packets both under the normal condition and when SYN Flooding attack occurs. Here are two sample windows, one is 100 and the other is 1000. Figure 3 shows the |LogMAP(t)| values in the two sample windows. From that figure, we can learn that there are big differences in the value of |LogMAP(t)| between normal condition and the moment of attack. In order to scale these differences, we adopt the measure based on Chi-Square Distance (CSD for short).

Firstly, we adopt the average method. The CSD calculation method is shown in formula (12) and the CSD values are shown in figure 4 and 5. Figure 4 shows the CSD under the normal condition. From this figure we can see that when the sample window is 100, the max value of CSD is 10, and when the window is 1000, the max value of CSD is 25. Although the CSD value under normal condition has an abrupt value, yet this is very small so we can still take it as normal. Then, we analyze the CSD while SYN Flooding happens. From figure 5, we can learn that when the sample window is 100, the minimum value of CSD is about 40 and the max value is about 200, which is much larger than the normal max value 10, and when the sample window is 1000, the minimum value of CSD is about 800 and the max value is about 1200, which is much larger than the normal value 25. So we can detect the SYN Flooding through Average method.

Now, we analyze the EWMA method with formula (13) and (14). In this experiment we only analyze the condition while the sample window is 1000. Seen from figure 6, when w=0.2, the max normal CSD is about 20; when w=0.4, the max normal value is about 12. But when the SYN Flooding occurs, the CSD value goes down quickly. Also, we can see that the CSD value under w=0.4 goes down more quickly than the CSD value under w=0.2. So we can conclude that the selection of w has a great influence on CSD value.

In the Average method, if the CSD value has great difference with the one under normal condition we can say that the attack has happened. In the future, we will study more datasets to determine the max value. If the sample space is not big enough, it is easy to bring the problem of high false positive rate in this method.

In the EWMA method, if the CSD value drops sharply we can say that the SYN Flooding attacks is happening. The exact value of w should be determined by large amounts of experiments. Yet from this experiment, we can tell that the larger w, the sharper the CSD drops. If the attackers find this rule they may slow down the attack speed in order to delay the dropping speed of CSD curve. So we can make a concept of *CSD dropping speed* to scale it. The EWMA method doesn't rely on the normal max value. So, it can avoid the problem of high false positive rate, which lies in the Average method. Meanwhile, this method has certain learning characteristics [16].

In the following, we will analyze the influence of sample window to CSD values. We can learn from figure 4 and figure 5 that the larger the window, the larger the value we can get in the disparity of CSD value between normal condition and that under SYN Flooding attacks. Referring to the anomaly detection, we hope that there is great difference between normal and abnormal condition. But if the sample window is very big, it will be difficult to confirm attacks quickly, and if the window is small, it will bring the high cost of calculations.

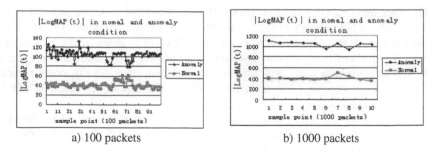

a) 100 packets   b) 1000 packets

Fig. 3. |LogMAP(t)| in normal and anomaly condition

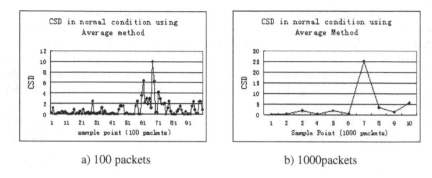

a) 100 packets   b) 1000packets

Fig. 4. CSD in normal condition using Average method

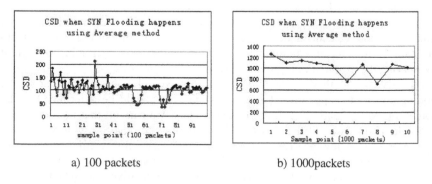

a) 100 packets   b) 1000packets

Fig. 5. CSD when SYN Flooding happens using Average method

So we can conclude that both the Average method and EWMA based on Chi-Square Distance can detect the SYN Flooding effectively. But the Average method may cause high false positive rate while the EWMA method won't. Meanwhile, the EWMA method has its learning characteristic. So we can say that the EWAM method is better than the Average method. In the experiment, we have only taken 10000 TCP packets as data for analysis, but the sample window W, the threshold and the value of *w* should be determined by large amounts of experiments. Here, we only verify the validity of Chi-Square Distance when detecting the SYN Flooding attacks.

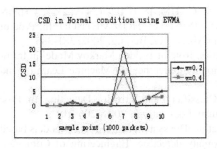
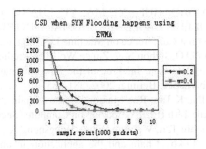

a) Normal condition   b) SYN Flooding happens

Fig. 6. CSD in normal and SYN Flooding using EWMA (1000 packets)

5 Conclusion

In this paper, we first build protocol models based on Markov Chain, using the DARPA evaluation dataset of 1999. Besides the improvement of protocol models, another contribution is the use of Chi-Square Distance for detecting protocol anomaly, such as SYN Flooding attack. The method presented in the paper simplifies the calculation of distance and the corresponding cost is very low. In the future, we will adjust the value of w, ε and the sample window W to get their optimum values. Also, we will build models for other protocols based on Markov Chain, such as SSH, and detect other attacks using the method of Chi-Square Distance.

Reference

1. Karl Levitt. Intrusion Detection: Current Capabilities and Future Directions. In: Proc of 18th Annual Computer Security Applications Conference. 2002, 365-370
2. Kumar Das. Protocol Anomaly Detection for Network-based Intrusion Detection. http://www.sans.org/rr/whitepapers/detection/349.php, 2004-1-16
3. J. Postel. "Transmission Control Protocol". RFC 793. http://www.faqs.org/rfcs/rfc793.html, 1981-9
4. Juan M. Estevez-Tapiador, Pedro Garcia-Teodoro, Jesus E.Diaz-Verdejo. Stochastic Protocol Modeling for Anomaly Based Network Intrusion Detection. In: Proc of the First IEEE International Workshop on Information Assurance (IWIA'2003). 2003, 3-12
5. E. Lemonnier. Protocol Anomaly Detection in Network-based IDSs. http://erwan.lemonnier.free.fr/exjobb/report/protocol_anomaly_detection.pdf, 2001-6
6. Sachi P.Joglekar, Stephen R.Tate. ProtoMon: Embedded Monitors for Cryptographic Protocol Intrusion Detection and Prevention. In: Proc of the International Conference on Information Technology: Coding and Computing (ITCC'04). 2004, 81-86
7. MIT Lincoln Laboratory. Intrusion detection evaluation web site. http://www.ll.mit.edu/IST/ideval, 2003-04-01
8. Na Li, Zheng Qin, Da-fang Zhang, et.al. Protocol Anomaly Detection Model Based on Markov Chain. Computer Science, 2004, 31(10): 66-68
9. Shuqing Zhao, Wei Deng. The analysis of stochastic signal. The first edition, 1999, 153-159

10. BO GAO, HUI − YE MA, YU − HANG YANG. HMMS (HIDDEN Markov CHAIN MODELS) BASED ON ANOMALY INTRUSION DETECTION METHOD. In: Proc of the First Conference on Machine Learning and Cybernetics. Beijing, 2002, 381-385
11. Fei GAO, Jizhou Sun, Zunce Wei. The Prediction Role of Hidden Markov Model in Intrusion Detection. In: Proc of the First International Conference on Machine Learning and Cybernetics. Beijing, 2002, 381-385
12. S. Jha, K.Tan, R.A Maxion. Markov Chains, Classifiers, and Intrusion Detection. In: Proc of the 14th IEEE Workshop on Computer Security Foundations. 2001, 206-219
13. Xiaobin Tan, Weiping Wang, Hongsheng Xi, et al. The system call sequence models based on Markov Chain and the application in anomaly detection. Engineering of Computer, 200228(12): 189 − 191
14. N. Ye, Y. Zhang, C. M. Borror. Robustness of the Markov chain model for cyber attack detection. IEEE Transactions on Reliability, 2003, 52(3): 116-123
15. TCPDUMP public repository. TCPDUMP. http://www.tcpdump.org/, 2004-6-12
16. Nong Ye, Qiang Chen, Connie M. Borror. EWMA Forecast of Normal System Activity for Computer Intrusion Detection. IEEE TRANSACTIONS ON RELIABILITY, 2004, 53(4): 557-566
17. Haining Wang, Danlu Zhang, Kang G.Shin. Detecting SYN Flooding Attacks. In Proc of IEEE INFOCOM, 2002, 1530–1539
18. V. Siris, F. Papagalou. Application of Anomaly Detection Algorithms for Detecting SYN Flooding Attacks. In: Proc of IEEE Global Telecommunications Conference. 2004, 14-20
19. Na Li. The research of Protocol Anomaly Detection Based-on Markov Chain. Master thesis. Hunan University, 2005.

Research and Implementation of Workflow Interoperability Crossing Organizations

Dingsheng Wan[1], Qing Li[1], and Guihai Chen[2]

[1] College of Computer & Information Engineering,
Hohai University, Nanjing 210098, China
dshwan@hhu.edu.cn
[2] State Key Laboratory of Novel Software Technology,
Nanjing University,Nanjing 210093, China
gchen@nju.edu.cn

Abstract. In order to resolve the shortcomings of traditional workflow interoperation and realize more flexible workflow interoperation, this article describes a new workflow interoperating model based on web services and interoperating agents to realize workflow interoperation. We also developed a prototype workflow system to realize the new model. The new model is more general, flexible, and capable of crossing all kinds of platforms and can be applied to a wider range.

1 Introduction

In order to support the interoperation and integration of the business workflow between two organizations using workflow management system, workflow management system of the organization needs workflow interoperation and integration [3][5]. The integration of web services and agents technology raises a new way to realize workflow interoperating. This article describes a new workflow interoperating model based on web services and interoperating agents to realize workflow interoperation. Based on the new model we have developed a prototype workflow system to realize workflow interoperating.

2 The Framework of the New Workflow Interoperating Model

In order to resolve the defects of traditional workflow interoperation and realize more flexible workflow interoperation, this article describes a new workflow interoperating model, in which workflow management system uses web services as basic inter-operation module [1]. Because of web services's standard describing, publishing, finding and integrating abilities [4], the new interoperating model is more general and flexible. The model uses a special interoperating agent to separate the interoperating logic from the internal business workflow process, which means the internal business workflow process only focuses on the business logic of the organization, without considering the interoperating relationship outside. The interoperating agent manages the interoperating relationship to support a more flexible and stable workflow

G. Chen et al. (Eds.): ISPA Workshops 2005, LNCS 3759, pp. 397–402, 2005.

interoperating between organizations. The two interoperating sides supply necessary web services to each other [6]. The figure 1, figure 2 and figure 3 show the whole new interoperating workflow model.

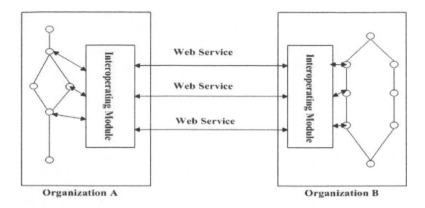

Fig. 1. The macroscopical interoperating model

The figure 1 shows every workitem of workflow process which wants to interoperate with others. Instead of interoperating with other organization's internal workflow process, it should interoperate with its interoperating agent firstly. Then the interoperating agent communicates with the other interoperating agents of the other organizations. The two interoperating agents of two organizations publish some web services, and then they interoperate with each other using web services.

The figure 2 shows an interoperating module which comprises of several interoperating agents, an agent helper and a Web container which includes many servlets.

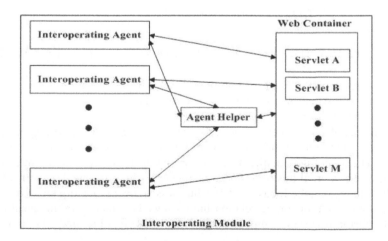

Fig. 2. The interoperating module

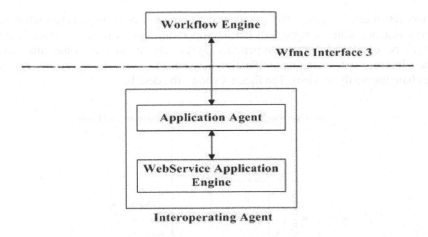

Fig. 3. The interoperating agent

The figure 3 shows an interoperating agent which comprises of an application agent and web services application engine. The workitem which wants to interoperate with other external workitems uses application agent to start the web services application engine through WFMC interface 3 [2], [7]. Then the web services application engine communicates with other using web services.

From outside of the organization, only some services can be seen, which means the internal workflow process is not disclosed. The internal workflow process only sends interoperating requests to the interoperating agent which decides to interoperate with its interoperating partner, and the internal workflow process does not know the interoperating partner. When the interoperating relationship has been changed, we need only change the interoperating module instead of changing the internal workflow process.

3   The Implementation of Workflow Process Level Interoperation

As described as above, there are 8 workflow services registered in the UDDI registry, there are 7 workflow process level interoperating services and only one workflow workitem level service. Workflow process level interoperating service means the target which requests interoperation is another workflow management system, and workflow workitem interoperating service means the target which requests interoperation is a workflow workitem of another workflow management system.

In a given crossing organization workflow example, a workitem named **Pa** in organization A's workflow process instance needs to start a workflow process definition instance in organization B when organization A's workflow process instance is running, then it gets special information from organization B. That means the workitem **Pa** needs to read all the workflow processes definitions in organization B(listing process definition service); then create a instance of the required workflow process definition(creating process instance service).when the new process instance is running, some attributes of the instance maybe need to be obtained(getting process instance attributes service); the instance states maybe need be changed(changing process instance states service); all the interoperating agents of the instance maybe need to be obtained(listing interoperating agent service) and at some time some process instance state changing notification may need to be received(process instance state changing notify service). The figure 4 shows the details.

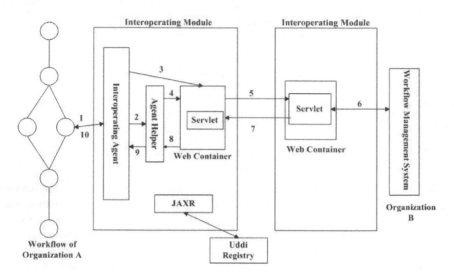

Fig. 4. Workflow process level interoperation

4   The Implementation of Workflow Workitem Level Interoperation

Workflow Workitem level interoperation is an interoperation between two workitems of two workflow processes running in the two different organizations. It realizes the information communication between two workitems. Figure 5 shows the details.

In a given crossing organization workflow example, we need to register the 8 workflow services of every workflow management system to UDDI registry. When the workitem **Pa** of the running workflow process instance is being executed, it needs to get some external information and then it starts an interoperating agent and sends the request information to the interoperating agent. After the interoperating agent of organization A has received the instruction of the workitem **Pa**, it stores the request information into the agent helper. The interoperating agent of organization A sends a request starting information to the local sending servlet in order to start the servlet. After the local sending servlet of organization A has started, it gets the request interoperating information stored into the agent helper temporarily. According to some querying information, the sending servlet in organization A looks for the started corresponding workflow process instance of the organization B in the UDDI registry(using the listing process instance service).

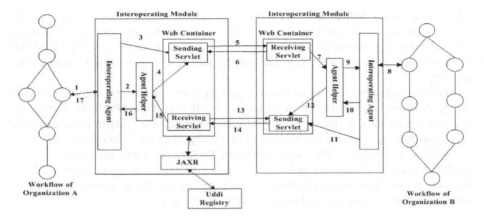

Fig. 5. Workflow workitem level interoperation

If there is not any stored corresponding workflow process instance, it starts a new workflow process instance; then gets all the interoperating agent's name of the instance in order to look for a given interoperating agent. If the given interoperating agent can't be found, it waits for a while and then continues to search. If the given interoperating agent is found, it encapsulates request interoperating information, the name of request interoperating agent of organization A and the name of reply interoperating agent of organization B into a request SOAP message, then sends the message to the receiving servlet in organization B using SAAJ technology. At the same time, it waits for the ACK message of the partner. After a given time, if it does not get the ACK message, it sends the SOAP request message again. After repeating several times, if it still cannot get the ACK message, it queries the UDDI registry again to looks for new web services which supply the same service. After the receiving servlet of the organization B receives the SOAP request message, it returns a ACK to the sender. The receiving servlet of organization B gets the request interoperating information from the SOAP request message and stores it into the agent helper in organization B temporarily. The agent helper of organization B checks up the request interoperating information's type and content. If the corresponding workflow process instance of the organization B does not start, it starts a new given workflow process instance.

When the internal workflow process instance of organization B has been executing the given workflow workitem, it starts the corresponding interoperating agent. After the interoperating agent of organization B is started, it gets the information stored in the agent helper of organization B, and then gets the corresponding reply information from the workflow process instance's context according to the request interoperating information in organization B. The interoperating agent of organization B stores the reply information which gets from the internal workflow process instance's context in organization B into the agent helper of organization B. The interoperating agent of organization B sends a request to ask for information to the local sending servlet in order to start the local sending servlet. After the local sending servlet is started, it gets the reply information and the URL of organization A's receiving servlet from the agent helper of organization A. The local sending servlet of organization B encapsulates the reply information into a SOAP reply message, and then sends the reply message to the receiving servlet of organization A and waits for the ACK from the partner. After a while if it does not receive the ACK, it repeats sending again. After receiving the SOAP reply message, it returns a ACK to the sending servlet of organization to confirm the receving.

The receiving servlet of organization A gets the reply information and stores it into the agent helper of organization A temporarily. After workitem **Pa** 's interoperating agent of organization A finds the reply information, it gets the reply information from the agent helper. The interoperating agent of organization A transfers the reply information to workitem **Pa** , then workitem **Pa** sets the reply information to the workflow relevant data of internal workflow process instance in organization A. Then the internal workflow process instance continues to execute the next workitem. Thus a whole workflow interoperation has completed successfully.

5 Conclusion

This paper describes a new workflow interoperating model based on web services and interoperating agent. According to the new workflow interoperating model, we have developed a workflow interoperating prototype system based on Enhydra-Shark project. It resolves the problem that we must open a internal workflow of organization A to organization B. Because it adopts the web services as basic interoperating cell, it is more general, flexible, and capable of crossing all kinds of platforms. Because it transfers the information from web services to the workflow engine through the WFMC interface 3, it can be applied to a wider range of applications.

References

1. Aissi, S., Malu, P., Srinivasan, K.: E-Business Process Modeling: The Next Big Step. IEEE Computer 35(5):55-62, May 2002
2. Hayes, J.G., Peyrovian, E., Sarin, S., Schmidt, M.T., Swenson, K.D., Weber R.: Workflow Interoperability Standards for the Internet. IEEE Internet Computing. 4(3):37-45, 2000
3. Jablonski, S., Bussler, C.: Workflow Management –Modeling, Concept, Architecture and Implementation. International Thomson Computer Press, 2001
4. Kim, Y., Kang, S., Kim, D., Bae, J., and Ju, K.: WW-Flow: Web-Based Workflow Management with Runtime Encapsulation. IEEE internet computing, 4(3):56-64, 2000
5. Li, Q., Lochovsky, F.H.: ADOME: an Advanced Object Modelling Environment. IEEE Transactions on Knowledge and Data Egnineering, 10(2):255-276, 1998
6. Li, H.X., FAN, Y.S.: Web Service-Based Integration and Interoperation of Heterogeneous Workflow Management System. Information and Control, vol.32, No.3, June, 2003
7. Workflow Management Coalition: The Workflow Standard - Interoperability Abstract Specification. WFMC-TC-1012, Version1.0, October 1996.

LSBE: A Localization Scheme Based on Events for Wireless Sensor and Actor Networks

Peng Han, Haiguang Cheng, Bo Yu, Dan Xu, and Chuanshan Gao

Department of Computer Science and Engineering, Fudan University,
200433 Shanghai, China
{041021070, hgchen, 031021070,
032021218, cgao}@fudan.edu.cn

Abstract. Due to the hardware constraint of sensors, the nodes' localization is a difficult problem in WANs. Many localization schemes have been proposed in WANs and Ad Hoc, but most of them are not energy-efficient and unsuitable to WSANs. The appearance of another kind of heterogeneous nodes, actors, in WSANs presents us a good chance to solve this problem in more effective methods. In this paper, we analyzed why the localization schemes in WSNs and Ad Hoc are not adaptive to WSANs and then according to the unique features and application requirements of WSANs, we designed a novel localization schemes, LSBE, which is characterized by new ideas such as event-driven, limited beacons, signal strength level and actors cooperation. In additional, via simulation experiments, we proved that the positioning error of the LSBE doesn't exceed 0.5m and the energy consumption of the system can be limited to a lower level compared with other existing localization schemes.

1 Introduction

The skill and technology advance in microelectronics and computer field has led emergence of WSANs (wireless sensor and actor networks) [1] recently. In WSANs, most applications will depend on position information of the sensor nodes. For example, in the case of fire, sensors which sensed fire must report their positions to water sprinkler actors so that these actors can go there and extinguished the fire before the fire spread uncontrollable. Similarly, in battlefield, robot soldier actors must immediately set out to the place where sensors report to find enemies. So how to acquire position information of sensors is one of the most important research fields in wireless sensor and actor networks.

Researchers have proposed many localization schemes for WSNs or Ad Hoc, such as APIT[2], DVBS[3] or GLCOL[4]. However, there are several drawbacks for these schemes. Firstly, in order to position sensors, additional reference nodes knowing their position must be added into the network, which rise the hardware burden of the WSNs; secondly, in these schemes, all sensors will take part in each time localization operation, which will use up rare energy of sensors especially when the localization were operated frequently.

There are two main reasons leading us to propose our novel localization scheme for WASNs. The first is that the main objective for users to construct a WSANs is to watch the environment and take actions to deal with gusty events. So in a large area,

G. Chen et al. (Eds.): ISPA Workshops 2005, LNCS 3759, pp. 403–411, 2005.

only the small part of sensors sensed events needs to be located. We need a localization method that only requires the part of sensors around the event to take localization operations. We refer it as a localization scheme based on events. Secondly, there appears another kind of nodes, actors, in WSANs, which are resource-unconstraint comparing with normal sensors. In new localization scheme, we should consider how to make the best of actors in order to save limited energy of sensors.

This paper discusses several kinds of localization schemes in localization field, analyzes why they are not suitable for WSANs and then presents a novel localization scheme called LSBE, which is based on events and effectively utilizes the specialties of WSANs. We help such a study to serve as a guide for future research and present research challenges in this field.

The remainder of the paper is organized as follows: In section 2, we give brief descriptions to previous work in localization field. In section 3, we will give a detailed description of LSBE. In section 4, we describe our simulation and evaluate its performance. In section 5, we investigate challenges in localization for WSANs. Finally, the paper is concluded in section 6.

2. State of Art

With regard to the mechanisms used for estimating location, the existing schemes can be divided into two categories: accurate and approximate. The former is defined by protocols that use absolute point-to-point distance estimates or angle estimates for calculating location. The latter gets the objective' position not by on accurate calculation but by imprisoning the objective into a small area and then use the center of the area as the objective' position.

2.1 TDOA Localization Scheme

The Time Difference of Arrival (TDOA) technology has been widely proposed as a necessary ingredient in localization solution for wireless sensor networks. While many infrastructure-based systems have been proposed that use TDOA [5][6][7], additional work such as AHLos[8] has employed such technology in infrastructure-free sensor networks. But TDOA depends on extensive hardware that is expensive and energy consuming, such as complex transceivers and time synchronization devices. Due to the hardware constraints of sensors, TDOA is not a suitable localization schemes for WSANs.

2.2 DV-HOP

DV-HOP[3] assumes a heterogeneous network consisting of sensing nodes and landmark. Instead of single hop broadcasts, landmarks flood their location throughout the network maintaining a running hop-count at each node along the way. Nodes calculate their position based on the received landmark locations ,the hop-count from the corresponding landmark, and the average-distance per hop, a value obtained through landmark communication. One landmark estimates its average per hop by communication with all other landmarks.

There are several drawbacks in DVBS. Firstly, Landmarks flood their positions information and all nodes in networks need to relay these packets, which induces tremendous energy consuming. Moreover, each node needs to assign fixed memory to save all landmarks' location information, hop counts to all landmarks and average per hop, which will take up precious memory resource of nodes. Secondly, because information doesn't be transmitted point-blank, computation based on large scale will lead to severe error.

2.3 APIT

APIT[1] is used to acquire approximate positions information of nodes. Reference nodes being aware of their own location beacon their position information. Nodes save the received position information and judge if it is inside triangles composing of three reference nodes whose localization information have been received by this node. Then the position of the node is estimated by the center of the lap part of all triangles which the node is inside (Figure 1).

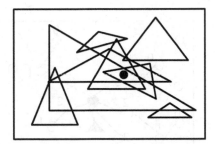

Fig. 1. The objective (dark point) judges which triangles it is in and then it takes the center of these triangle as its' position

In APIT, nodes not only spend costly energy on relaying flooding localization information of all reference nodes but also need large memory to save locations data of all reference nodes and strong computation ability to judge if it is in some triangles. What is most perishing is that its position accuracy is not very high and may not satisfy application requirement of WSANs.

3 LSBE Localization Scheme

In this section, we describe our novel localization schemes, LSBE. It is one kind of localization scheme based on event and only localize the position of the node detecting the wanted event and if there is no event taking place, the localization operation don't occur.

In WSANs[1], Another kind of nodes---actors bring us a good chance to solve the localization problem. Since actors are resource-unconstrained, they can get their own real-time localization information via GPS or some other mechanism. So, actors can replace the reference nodes in WSNs. Moreover, because actors are powerful and removable, they can cooperate to localize the position of the sensor reporting the event and then take actions to deal with the event.

There are three main novel ideas in LSBE. The first is limited beacons; The second is distance estimate based on signal strength; The third is actors cooperation.

3.1 Limited Beacons

This idea limits the transmit range of beacons by setting lifetime of them. We present three different kinds of limited beacons

LB1) Each time the packets passes one node, the lifetime is subtracted one and then is relayed until its' lifetime equals to 0;

LB2) When the packet arrives at an actor, it is discard even its' lifetime is not 0. Otherwise, it is transmitted according to the method 1.

LB3) When the packet arrives at an actor, the actor immediately broadcasts a "stop" signal to ask other nodes to stop relaying the packet. After the packet arrives at nodes which have received the "stop" signal, it is discarded. Otherwise, it is transmitted according to method 2.

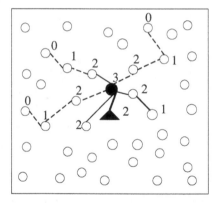

Fig. 2. The broken line, the thick real line and the thin real line present the beacon transmission by LB1, LB2, LB3 respectively

3.2 Distance Estimate Based on Signal Strength Level

There have been many research about the distance estimate between nodes in sensor network, such as technology based on hop counts in DVBS[3] or technology based on gradient in OGCS[6]. In this paper we suggest a distance estimation method based on radio signal strength level. We assume that the RF of all actor can reach any sensors in the network and sensors can apperceive signal strength of RF. In the following, we will describe our idea in detail.

As we all know, RF will attenuate during transmission. So, we can estimate the distance between sensors and actors via the strength of RF signal. We divide the RF signal into many levels according to the accuracy requirement of applications. One level is mapping to a special signal strength range and also mapping to a distance

Table 1. Distance estimate demonstration

Level	Signal strength(W)	Distance(m)
10	0.50~0.45	1
9	0.45~0.35	2
8	0.35~0.30	3
7	0.30~0.24	4
6	0.24~0.15	5
5	0.15~0.8	6
...	...	...

range. Sensor saves a form that includes the level-distance pairs (e.g. table 1). When sensors receive RF signal from actors, they look up this form and estimate their distance to actors.

3.3 Actors Cooperation

As we all know, in order to locate one point in two dimension space, we need three reference points at least. If there is only one actor received the event beacon, the actor need immediately communicate with other actors and asks them to help to locate the objective. By this cooperation, the event sensor can be located even the event reports beacons arrives at only one actor. For example, in the figure 3, the event reports only arrives at the actor A and then the actor A asks for helps of the actor B and actor C so the event sensor can receive localization information from the three actors to calculate its position.

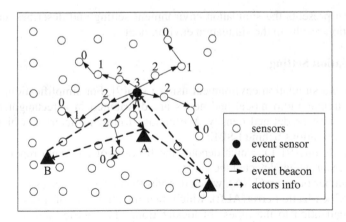

Fig. 3. In the lifetime, the event report beacon of the event sensor only arrived at actor A, so the actor A ask actor B, C to send out their localization information to assist to locate

3.4 Main Algorithm

The LSBE Algorithm can be broken down into four steps:

1) The event sensor beacons its reports based on one of limited beacons methods.

2) The actor received the event reports sends out its' location information composed of its position information and original signal strength value and contacts others actors asking them to assist to locate the event node.

3) After the event sensor received location information from actors, it estimates distances to these actors according to the level-distance form and then calculates its average position based on acquired distances and localization information of actors by the triangle calculation:

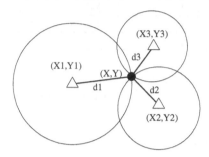

Fig. 4. The sensor(X,Y) calculate its' position using (X1,Y1), (X2,Y2), (X3,Y3), d1, d2 and d3

When the sensor receives more than 3 actors, it can calculates its' position in many times and then get their average value as its final estimated position.

4   Simulation

This section presents the simulation environment setting and describes and analyzes the simulation results in the simulation environment.

4.1   Simulation Setting

We establish a simulation environment using j-sim[9]. For simplification, we assume a perfect circular radio model and nodes are distributed in a rectangular terrain in accordance with predefined density. We choose following metrics, which underpin the major motivations behind LSBE:

Reports lifetime(RLT), which denotes the lifetime of the event reports beacon of the event sensor which detected the event.

Total number of actors(TNA), which denotes the density of actors in network.

Average localization error(ALE), which measures the ratio of the sum of errors in n times localization to the times of localization. This metric indicates the location accuracy of our scheme.

Average sensors ratio(ASR), which measures the ratio of the number of sensors participating in one time localization operations to the total number of sensors in network. This metric examines the effect of limited beacons and indicates the energy consumption of the system.

Average the number of actors(ANA), which measures the average number of actors received the event reports and indicates what lifetime the event reports should be set in order to insure at least one actor can receive the event reports when varying the total number of actors.

Table 2. The parameters used in our study

Area of sensor field	$100*100 \text{ m}^2$
Number of sensor nodes	10201
Radio range of sensor nodes	1m
Radio range of actors	200m

4.2 Simulation Results

In this section, we present and analysis simulation results of experiments.

4.2.1 The Number of Actors Received the Event Report (ANA) When Varying the Lifetime of the Event Reports (RLT) and the Total Number of Actors (TNA)

In this experiment, we analyze the effect of varying the total number of actors and the preset lifetime of the event reports to determine their effect on the number of actor received the event reports.

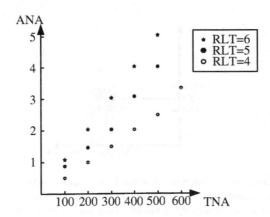

Fig. 5. When TNA is not large, for example, equal to 100, the event reports should be set a lifetime over 6 in order to arrive at a actor at least. When there are enough actors, for example over 600, even the lifetime is 3, the reports still can arrive at over 3 actors.

4.2.2 Average Sensors Ratio (ASR) When Varying the Event Report Lifetime (RLT)

In this experiment, we analyze ASR in one time localization operation to test the effect of the limited beacons method. Figure 6 shows the results when the limited beacon adopt the method LB2 the method LB3 respectively.

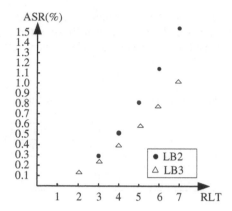

Fig. 6. ASR keeps increasing and the increasing speed becomes more quickly along with the increasing of RLT in two limited beacon methods. But even the reports lifetime reaches 7, ASR is only about 1.5% in the LB2 and also we can find the use of "stop" signal in the LB3 decreases ASR comparing with the LB2. This experiment proves that our limited beacons scheme controls the transmitting scope of the event reports and can save the energy of the system.

4.2.3 Average Localization Error

In this experiment, we run our localization scheme for 100 times to find its' positioning accuracy and the factors to affect it when varying TNA, ANA and RLT.

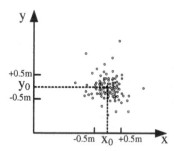

Fig. 7. Figure 7 presents simulation result when TNA equals to 400 and RLT equals to 4. Most of result is in 0.5m around the real position. We find the positioning accuracy is affected by TNA, ANA and RLT. Generally, more actors taking part in localization, higher the accuracy. We think that redundancy lead to the smaller error.

5   Research Challenge

In this section, we discuss some problems that we should continue to research about.

Adaptation to noisy environment: Our localization method is very effective in restricted domains, with idealized radio conditions. But, idealized radio conditions do not hold in noisy environment that are characterized by severe multipath phenomenon, fading, obstructions etc. in order to generalize our scheme to noisy environments, we are currently investigating techniques for empirical adaptation of actors.

Adaptation to real-time requirement: The event-driven localization scheme can save the rare energy of sensors, but it maybe have longer delay than those localization schemes which get sensors positions at the beginning. How to improve LSBE in this way? We are doing research in this field.

Collision avoidance: In actual situation, maybe there are multi-sensors detected the origination of the event. If these sensors send out reports about event, it will lead RF collision. So, in future works, we should study how to deal with this problem.

Adaptation to the mobile situation: In our scheme, only when there are events taking place, the localization operations will be launched. So LSBE is more suitable for the environment where location of nodes change frequently. But, in mobile environment, the situation is especially complex. In future works, we need to do painstaking and comprehensive analysis and experiments in mobile environments.

6 Conclusion

For the inherent limitation of sensors energy, we should decrease the energy consumption spending on localization schemes. Considering the application requirement and network characters of WSANs, we present our novel localization scheme, LSBE, which is event-triggered and energy-efficient. By simulation tests, we prove that LSBE is a feasible and suitable localization scheme. At the end, we introduce some problems and challenges in future works.

References

1. Ian F. Akyildiz, Ismail H. Kasimoglu, Wireless sensor and actor networks: research challenges, Ad Hoc Networks (2004)
2. Tian He, Chengdu Huang, Brian M.Blum, John A. Stankoivic and Tarek Abdelzaher, Range-Free Localization Schemes for Large Scale Sensor Networks, ACM MobiCom, San Diego, California, USA (2003)
3. D. Niculescu and B. Nath, DV Based Positioning in Ad hoc Networks, In Journal of Telecommunication Systems(2003)
4. N. Bulusu, J. Heidemann and D. Estrin, GPS-less Low Cost Outdoor Localization for Very Small Devices, IEEE Personal Communications Magazine (2000) 28-34
5. P.Bahl and V.N.Padamanabhan, RADAR: An In-Building RF-Based User Location and Tracking Systme, In Proceedings of the IEEE INFOCOM (2000)
6. A.Harter, A.Hopper and P.Steggles, A.Ward and P.Webster, The anatomy of a context-aware application, In Proceedings of MOBICOM'99, Seattle, Washington(1999)
7. N.B.Priyantha, A.Chakraborty and H.Balakrishnan, The Cricket Location-Support System, In Proceedings of MOBICOM'00, New York (2000)
8. A.Savvides,C.C.Han and M.B.Srivastaa, Dynamic Fine-Grained Localization in Ad-Hoc Networks of Sensors, In Proceedings of MOBICOM'01, Rome, Italy (2001)
9. The Network Simulator –j-sim, http://www.j-sim.org/

Crossing Effects Analysis Between Routing and MAC Protocol in Mobile Ad Hoc Networks

Panlong Yang and Chang Tian

Telecom Engineering Department of P.L.A University of Science and Technology
veron_yang@sina.com, tianchang@163.com

Abstract. Most of MANET routing protocol simulations haven't considered crossing effects of routing protocol and MAC protocol. In this paper, statistical method based on Multi-variance analysis is applied to evaluate the ad hoc network routing protocol performance results. Statistical results show that routing protocol and MAC protocol have different effect on different network metric, which will affect the overall network performance seriously. "Interactive effect" between routing layer and MAC layer will direct the protocol design in a "cross-layer" fashion instead of independent layered architecture. Mathematical performance evaluation model will be more effective and more accurate in performance comparison of newly built protocols than previous simple one without considering the "Crossing effect". To make further analysis, we set up a simulation environment of "Vertical" traffic, and analyze the crossing effects between routing layer and MAC layer. In "Vertical" traffic pattern, MAC layer dominates delivery ratio metric, but if the multi-path mechanism is used to avoid congestion in MAC layer, the network system performance improves accordingly.

1 Introduction

Mobile ad hoc networking is one of the most innovative and challenging areas of wireless networking and this technology promises to become increasingly present in everybody's life. With the distributed and self-configuring characteristics, mobile ad hoc networks can be fast deployed with moderately low cost [1].

Various routing protocols have been delivered for MANET. Some of them originated from traditional Internet-Based routing protocol, while some of parameters and routing mechanisms are revised in adaptation to MANET environment [2][5][6]. The rest of them adopting on-demand routing mechanism, this kind of protocol "reactively" find routes between source and destination. Other new methods also include hybrid routing, a routing method combining proactive routing and reactive routing, location information based routing, energy-efficient routing etc.

Based on traditional layering architecture of network protocol suit, MANET protocol stack is also layered. MAC protocols such as MACA, MACAW etc [7][9] are right below routing layer. In MANET simulation platform, there are many choices in building a MANET system. E. Royer [2] has found that choices of MAC protocols affect the relative performance of routing protocols. But their research work is roughly based on simple comparison of simulation results, and they haven't theoretically analyzed the

G. Chen et al. (Eds.): ISPA Workshops 2005, LNCS 3759, pp. 412–421, 2005.

results instead of raw data comparison. Simple comparison sometimes will lead to hazy results and even mistakes in protocol evaluation.

The goal of this research is to find an effective way in finding cross-layering effects between routing protocol and MAC protocol instead of rough comparison between different figures or tables. In this paper, different MAC protocols and routing protocols are simulated and evaluated in GlomoSim simulation platform. With multiple-variance analysis method, cross effects of MAC protocols and routing protocols are uncovered under reasonably statistical process. Multiple-variance analysis provides us a theoretical support on cross-layering design. Routing protocol considering MAC protocol properties would be of great beneficial in bandwidth saving, fast broken link detection and other routing factors.

2 Overview of Protocol Evaluation and Cross-Layering Design

Since mobile ad hoc network aims at being with higher reliability, better coverage and convergence, higher capacity, and mobility management, protocol evaluations are of great importance in newly built system with advanced mobility prediction, higher throughput, lower routing overhead etc. Most of these improvements in protocol are based on simulation. Since pure analytical methods are not general or detail enough to illustrate multi-hop network system, simulation results can effectively help protocol designer build new generation of efficient network protocols.

Among all these network scenarios, different network factor would affect network performance seriously. E. Royer [2] has found that, by simulation of three different routing protocols over different type of MAC protocols, network performance varies, which implies that MAC protocols would affect routing protocol in some extent. Sung [11] et al have simulated different routing protocol under the simulation platform GlomoSim from UCLA. Although Sung [11] have suggested a series of routing selection standards, and have some reasonable results in routing protocol performance evaluation, their results are lacking of compositive analysis based on statistical procedure.

Recent research has been focusing on cross-layering mechanism based on interaction between different layers in order to make further optimization. Although there is common awareness that different layer of protocols do not act in isolation, very little formal characterization of their interaction has been made. Our main contribution is simulation based experiments coupled with rigorous statistical analysis to characterize the interaction between the MAC protocol and routing protocol.

3 Brief Introduction of Routing Protocols and MAC Protocols

MANET routing protocols enable each wireless nodes working in a self-configuring and distributed way. They are generally categorized into two basic types according to the route finding method: Proactive and Reactive. In this paper, we cast most of our contractions on four routing protocols listed below.

● WRP (Wireless Routing Protocol)

WRP routing protocol maintains routing information through the exchange of triggered and periodical updates. WRP use the predecessor to destination listed in routing table in order to avoid routing loops.

ACK list for update messages can effectively improve protocol reliability in network with low quality wireless links or unidirectional wireless links.

● AODV (Ad Hoc on Demand Distance Vector)

AODV protocol is a reactive version of DSDV protocol. Due to loss of pre-maintained routing table, source nodes would broadcast RREQ message over the entire network. Destination node will reply with RREP messages and RERR messages are sent back to source nodes when wireless link becoming unreachable.

● FSR (Fisheye State Routing)

FSR is a layered structured in topology maintenance, as a scalable routing protocol, FSR do not flooding message over entire network. FSR routing update mechanisms are time-triggered, while in different topology layer, routing update interval varies. As network size increases, FSR has its merits in sparing routing overhead without losing accuracy of routing table entries.

● DSR (Dynamic State Routing)

DSR is a loop free source based on demand routing protocol, in which each node maintains route caches that contain the source routes learned by the node. Source node initiate route discovery process as its local cache has no route to destination. With the source route labeled in packet header, intermediate node can learn route messages and cache them into its local entry. DSR protocol also supports multi-path routing, which can be more efficient in traffic congested network. We present this simulation results in section 5.

The MAC protocols simulated in this paper are categorized into four types, which present technological improvements in MAC protocol.

● CSMA

A commonly known MAC protocol, in this paradigm, a node would not send a packet in its queue until it senses wireless channel is idle.

● MACA

Many protocols have been proposed to avoid the hidden terminal problems. Two notable examples are the MACA and MACAW protocols. MACA introduced a reservation system achieved with exchange of RTS-CTS pair of control packets. MACAW also has congestion avoidance mechanism.

● FAMA

FAMA builds upon MACA protocol by adding non-persistent carrier sensing to RTS-CTS messages exchange. The addition of carrier sense to the control packet exchange aids in the prevention of control packet collisions.

● IEEE802.11

IEE802.11 MAC standard was designed with a reservation system similar to MACA or MACAW. 802.11 also improve fairness characteristics comparing MACA and MACAW. ACK messages are also a good aiding in detecting hidden terminal if CTS packets are in collision.

4 Simulation and Protocol Evaluation

To illustrate the crossing effects in a more reasonable and obvious way, we adopt the same simulation environment as in paper of E. Royer [2]. Configuring parameters in GlomoSim platform are listed in Table 1:

Table 1. Configuring Parameters in GlomoSim Platform

Number of Nodes	100
Area	1500 × 1500
Mobility Model	RANDOM WAYPOINT Speed 0~10m/s
Propagation Model	Free Space
Channel Bandwidth	2Mbps
Traffic	20 Sessions, 512 bytes length, 1packet/s

Parameters of WRP, FSR, and AODV protocol in Glomosim platform are shown in Table 2:

Table 2. Simulation Parameters in Routing Protocol

	Maximum Interval of HELLO	1s
	Maximum HELLO message lost	4
WRP	Update Ack Time out	1s
	Retransmit Timeout Period	1s
	Retransmit times	4
	Threshold of routing zone	2 hops
	HELLO interval	5s
FSR	Max HELLO message lost	3
	Intra zone update interval	5s
	Inter zone update interval	15s
	HELLO Interval	1s
AODV	Maximum HELLO message lost	3
	Retransmit Time	750ms

In simulation platform, we have WRP, FSR and AODV as routing protocol, while we use CSMA, MACA and IEEE 802.11 as MAC protocol. Different combinations of routing protocol and MAC protocol are simulated in simulation platform.

We use statistical tool that is Multi-variance analysis to process simulation results. Multi-variance analysis method can effectively figure out cross-effects between factors from raw collected data. Without losing generality, we make assumptions according to multi-variance analysis method that:

(1) The i th level of factor A increase output value y to the amount of α_i, $\sum_{i=1}^{p} \alpha_i = 0$.

(2) The j th level of factor B increase output value y to the amount of β_i, $\sum_{i=1}^{p} \beta_i = 0$.

(3) Errors in different tests are normally distributed, with all expectations equal to zero, and variances are all the same;

(4) Errors in different tests are all statistically independent to each other.

We build the mathematical model of multi-variance analysis, as equation (1) shows.

$$y_{ij} = \mu + \alpha_i + \beta_j + \varepsilon_{ij}, \qquad i = 1,...,p; \; j = 1,...,q \tag{1}$$

In equation (1), $\sum_{i=1}^{p} \alpha_i = 0$, $\sum_{i=1}^{p} \beta_i = 0$, $\varepsilon_{ij} \sim N(0, \delta^2)$, and independent each other.

We aimed at judging equations listed below:

$H_{01}: \quad \alpha_1 = \alpha_2 = \alpha_3 = ... = \alpha_p \qquad H_{02}: \quad \beta_1 = \beta_2 = \beta_3 = ... = \beta_q$

$$\bar{y}_{i.} = \frac{1}{p} \sum_{j=1}^{q} y_{ij}, \qquad \bar{y}_{.j} = \frac{1}{p} \sum_{i=1}^{p} y_{ij}, \qquad \bar{y} = \frac{1}{pq} \sum_{j=1}^{q} \sum_{i=1}^{p} y_{ij},$$

It has been proved that: $\bar{y}_{i.}$ is a least square estimation of $\mu + \alpha_i$; $\bar{y}_{.j}$ is a least square estimation of $\mu + \beta_i$.

To describe the variance in a more clear way, in equation (2), sum of variance can be decomposed as follows:

$$S_T = \sum_{i=1}^{p}\sum_{j=1}^{q}(y_{ij} - \bar{y})^2 = q\sum_{i=1}^{p}(\bar{y}_{i.} - \bar{y})^2 + p\sum_{j=1}^{q}(\bar{y}_{.j} - \bar{y})^2 + \sum_{i=1}^{p}\sum_{j=1}^{q}(y_{ij} - \bar{y}_{i.} - \bar{y}_{.j} + \bar{y})^2 \tag{2}$$
$$= S_A + S_B + S_E$$

In equation (2), S_A represents variance of error between different groups. It is composed of p sum of squares. Since $\sum_{(\bar{y}_{i.} - \bar{y}) = 0}$ constrained, freedom of S_A is $p-1$, it represents the differences resulting from factor A. S_B represents variance of error between different groups resulting from factor B. Its freedom is also $q-1$; S_E is random error and is composed of pq sum of squares. It can be expressed in $p+q-1$ independent equations:

$$\sum_{i=1}^{p}(y_{ij} - \bar{y}_{i.} - \bar{y}_{.j} + \bar{y}) = 0 \qquad j = 1,..., q \qquad \sum_{i=1}^{q}(y_{ij} - \bar{y}_{i.} - \bar{y}_{.j} + \bar{y}) = 0 \qquad i = 1,..., p-1$$

If the assertion $H_{01}: \alpha_1 = \alpha_2 = ... = \alpha_p = 0$ is true, we have

$$F_A = \frac{S_A \big/ (p-1)}{S_E \big/ (p-1)(q-1)} \sim F(p-1, (p-1)(q-1)) \tag{3}$$

$$F_B = \frac{S_B \big/ q-1}{S_E \big/ (p-1)(q-1)} \sim F(q-1, (p-1)(q-1)) \tag{4}$$

From the F_A and F_B, we can make assertion whether H_{01} or H_{02} is true. This method is called F theorem.

Taking the simulation results as raw data inputs, use the equation (2) (3) (4), and the threshold is chosen as $F_{0.05}$, we can get the variance analysis of network delivery rate metric. It is shown in Table 3.

Table 3. Variance Analysis Results on Network Delivery Ratio

Variance Factor	Sum of Squares	Freedom	$F_{0.05}$	$Pr > F_{0.05}$
MAC Protocol	84.212358	3	9.1645	0.0117
Routing Protocol	15.225117	2	2.4853	0.1636
Random Error	19.37802	6		
Sum	117.81549	11		

From Table 3, we can see that, to network delivery ratio, MAC protocol has more effects on it than that of routing protocol. Value of $Pr > F_{0.05}$ is between 0.01~0.05. Simulation results in paper [2] also show that the simulation scenario with AODV and IEEE 802.11 has the maximum delivery rate among combinations of various routing protocol and MAC protocol. From the variance analysis in network delivery ratio, conclusion can be made that RTS/CTS/DATA/ACK packet sequences assure the reliability of data packets transferring in network. Since AODV is a reactive routing protocol, it relies heavily on IEEE 802.11 mechanism to inform the broken link. This mechanism helps AODV reducing large amount of routing overhead. Higher reliability in MAC layer also helps the "RREQ+RREP" messages interaction more efficient than CSMA and MACA. While FSR and WRP are traditionally proactive routing protocol, they are not very sensitive to MAC layer protocol considering the routing overhead. If using other kind of MAC protocol, reactive routing protocol like AODV or DSR must add link detection mechanism based on periodical hello or implicit feed back.

We can compute the variance analysis results according to equation (1) based on our simulation results, it is shown in Table 4.

Table 4. Variance Analysis Results on Network Routing Control Overhead

Variance Factor	Sum of Squares	Freedom	$F_{0.05}$	$Pr > F_{0.05}$
MAC Protocol	10.206767	3	2.0269	0.2117
Routing Protocol	51.010067	2	15.1943	0.0045
Random Error	10.071533	6		
Sum	71.288367	11		

From Table 4, we can conclude that routing protocols are predominant in routing overhead metric. The proactive routing protocol WRP has very great routing overhead. Comparing to routing protocol, MAC layer protocol has no obvious effect on routing overhead. It also reveals that most of routing protocols have not considered the MAC effects on routing protocol. Traditional protocol is layered and each layer is independent to each other. Variance analyses of normalized routing overhead metrics are shown in Table 5.

Table 5. Variance Analysis Results of Normalized Routing Overhead Metric

Variance Factor	Sum of Squares	Freedom	$F_{0.05}$	$Pr > F_{0.05}$
MAC Protocol	10281.896	3	7.0468	0.0216
Routing Protocol	2091.512	2	2.1502	0.1977
Random Error	2918.182	6		
Sum	15291.589	11		

We find that, in different network metrics, routing protocol and MAC protocol have different effects. But variance analysis listed above did not consider cross-layer effects, with various variance analyses of different metrics have been statistically processed, we are trying to find crossing effects between MAC protocols and routing protocols. By adding an assumption that:

Factor A_i combining with factor B_j will increase y by τ_{ij}, and we get

$$\sum_{i=1}^{p} \tau_{ij} = 0, \quad j = 1,..., q; \sum_{j=1}^{q} \tau_{ij} = 0, \quad i = 1,... p;$$

Thus, the output value can be expressed as:

$$y_{ijl} = \mu + \alpha_i + \beta_j + \tau_{ij} + \varepsilon_{ijl} \tag{5}$$

In equation (5), $\sum_{i=1}^{p} \alpha_i = 0, \sum_{j=1}^{q} \beta_j = 0$, and we can also have

$$\sum_{i=1}^{p} \tau_{ij} = 0, j = 1,..., q; \sum_{j=1}^{q} \tau_{ij} = 0, \quad i = 1,..., p; \cdot$$

And distribution of random error ε_{ijl} is $\varepsilon_{ijl} \sim N(0, \delta^2)$, each ε_{ijl} are independent each other.

$\{a_i\}$ is defined as main effects of factor A ; $\{\beta_j\}$ is defined as main effects of factor B ; $\{\tau_{ij}\}$ is defined as cross effects of factor A and factor B .

$H_{01}: \alpha_1 = \alpha_2 = ... = \alpha_p = 0$ $H_{02}: \beta_1 = \beta_2 = ... = \beta_p = 0$

$H_{03}: \tau_{ij} = 0$ $i = 1,..., p, j = 1,..., q$ $\bar{y}_{ij} = \frac{1}{k} \sum_{l=1}^{k} y_{ijl}$, $\bar{y}_{i.} = \frac{1}{q} \sum_{j=1}^{q} \bar{y}_{ij}$, $\bar{y}_{.j} = \frac{1}{p} \sum_{i=1}^{p} \bar{y}_{ij}$

Decompose variance into four parts as follows:

$$S_T \overset{\Delta}{=} S_A + S_B + S_{AB} + S_E$$ Especially, S_{AB} represents the cross-effects of factor A and factor B .Freedom of each of these variances are: $p-1, q-1, (p-1)(q-1)$ and $pq(k-1)$. If $H_{01}: \alpha_1 = \alpha_2 = ... = \alpha_p = 0$ is true:

$$F_A = \frac{S_A \Big/ (p-1)}{S_E \Big/ pq \, (k-1)} \sim F \, (p-1, \, pq \, (k-1)) \qquad (6)$$

If $H_{02} : \beta_1 = \beta_2 = ... = \beta_p = 0$ is true:

$$F_B = \frac{S_B \Big/ q-1}{S_E \Big/ pq \, (k-1)} \sim F \, (q-1, \, pq \, (k-1)) \qquad (7)$$

If $H_{03} : \tau_{ij} = 0 \quad i = 1,..., \, p, \, j = 1,..., \, q$ is true:

$$F_{AB} = \frac{S_{AB} \Big/ [(p-1)(q-1)]}{S_E \Big/ [pq \, (k-1)]} \sim F \, ((p-1)(q-1), \, pq \, (k-1)) \qquad (8)$$

If one of F_A, F_B, F_{AB} is bigger than threshold, main effects and cross-effects of factor A and B are accordingly increases.

Table 6. Cross Effects of MAC and Routing Protocol in Packet Delivery Ratio Metric

	Freedom	Sum of Squares	F	$Pr > F_{0.05}$
MAC	3	168.6120	1732.909	0.00006
Routing Protocol	2	30.16672	465.0574	0.0023
MAC*Routing	6	41.04484	210.9190	0.0075
Random Error	12	0.38920		
Sum	23	240.2128		

From Table 6, we can find that routing protocol and MAC protocol have great crossing effects on each other considering packet delivery ratio metric. Combination of AODV and IEEE 802.11 will achieve high packet delivery rate. The design paradigm of AODV protocol make fully use of the IEEE 802.11 MAC protocol, when using CSMA or MACA, AODV must use HELLO messages to maintain connectivity between neighbors. The control overhead is significant larger than that of IEEE 802.11. Combination of AODV and IEEE802.11 outperform other combinations, thus with the statistical analysis, we can draw the conclusion that, some assumption we've made on MAC layer before designing routing protocol will help improve overall performances.

In section 5, we will analysis cross-layering effects between routing protocol and MAC protocol considering the traffic pattern. With layered traffic pattern, traffic is concentrated to a small fraction of nodes, which will affect performance seriously.

5 Further Analysis of Crossing-Effects

In our simulation, "vertical" traffic pattern is different to the "identical" traffic pattern. "Vertical" traffic has bottleneck in the network while "identical" traffic has not. Since delivery ratio is a key factor in military environment.

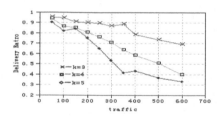

Fig. 1. Traffic layer Vs Delivery Ratio

From Fig 1, we can see that, network delivery ratio decreases as network traffic level k increases. Congestion and queue buffer overflow in MAC layer lead to the low delivery ratio in bottleneck link under "vertical" traffic scenario, while route error is not a key factor. An efficient MAC protocol dealing with high traffic load scenario such as adaptive TDMA or token-based algorithm will significantly improve the overall network performance.

We change our simulation scenario, and the network size grows from 750m × 750m into 1500m × 1500m, to ensure the same node density, number of nodes changed into 200. DSR (Dynamic Source Routing) supports multi-path routing and we randomly select routes for destination between multiple routes in the cache table. From Fig2, we can see that, if the network size grow larger, and traffic is somewhat balanced between the "bottleneck" routes, network performance improves, especially the delivery ratio of the congested bottleneck link. Due to lack of optimization on the multi-path scheduling algorithm, in very low traffic and very high traffic scenario, the multi-path routing performs worse than optimal path routing.

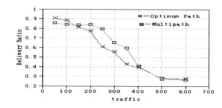

Fig. 2. Optimum Path routing VS multi-path routing

6 Conclusions

Statistical method of multi-variance analysis is a basic tool in exploring cross-layering effects between MAC and routing layer. It avoids inaccurate results comparison according to raw statistical results.

MAC layer and routing layer has significant cross-layering effects. Although traditional layered protocol architecture still separate MAC and routing layer, and functioned as two parts, we strongly recommend that MANET protocol design should cross-layered, before optimize routing protocol, characteristics of MAC layer must be seriously studied, it will help improve routing protocol efficiency.

References

[1] Paul Sass. Communications networks for the Force XXI Digitized Battlefield[C]. Mobile Networks and Applications 4 (1999) 139–155

[2] Elizabeth M. Royer, Sung-Ju Lee and Charles E. Perkins. The Effects of MAC Protocols on Ad hoc Network Communications. Proceedings of the IEEE Wireless Communications and Networking Conference, Chicago, IL, September 2000.

[3] Marco Conti, Silvia Giordano. Cross-Layering in Mobile Ad Hoc Network Design [J]. IEEE Computer Magazine February 2004 P48-51.

[4] Charles E. Perkins and Elizabeth M. Royer. Ad-hoc On-Demand Distance Vector Routing. Proceedings of the 2nd IEEE Workshop on Mobile Computing Systems and Applications, New Orleans, LA, February 1999, pp. 90-100.

[5] S.Murthy, and J.J. Garcia. An Efficient Routing Protocol for wireless networks[J]. Mobile Networks and Applications, pp183-197. October 1996.

[6] G.Pei, and M. Gerla. Fisheye State Routing: A Routing Scheme for Ad Hoc Wireless Networks[C]. Proceedings of IEEE International Conference on Communications. Page.70-74. New Orleans, LA. June 2000.

[7] L. Kleinrock, and F.A. Tobagi. Packet Switching in Radio Channels: Part 1-Carrier Sense Multiple-Access Models and Their Throughput-Delay Characteristics. IEEE Transactions on Communications. 23(12):1400-1416. December 1975.

[8] P. Karn. MACA- A New Channel Access Protocol for Packet Radio. Proceedings of the ARRL/CRRL Amateur Radio Ninth Computer Network Conference, pages 134-140, 1990.

[9] C.L.Fullmer, and J.J. Garcia. Floor Acquisition Multiple Access for Packet Radio Networks. Proceedings of the conference on Applications, Technology, Architecture and Protocols for Computer Communication (SIGCOMM). Pages 263-273. 1995

[10] IEEE Standards Department. Wireless LAN Medium Access Control (MAC) and Physical Layer (PHY) Specifications. IEEE standard 802.11-1997, 1994.

[11] Sung-Ju Lee, Julian Hsu, Russell Hayashida, etc Selecting a routing strategy for your ad hoc network. Computer Communication 26 (2003) p723-733

Low-Latency Routing in Ad Hoc Wireless Networks Using Finite Horizons

Amer Filipovic, Amitava Datta, and Chris McDonald

The University of Western Australia,
35 Stirling Highway,
Crawley, WA, 6009, Australia
{amer, datta, chris}@csse.uwa.edu.au

Abstract. An ad-hoc wireless network is a cooperative body of mobile wireless nodes that is capable of sustaining multi-hop communication. DSR is a well known routing protocol that has been proven to be robust and reliable in forming such networks. The protocol inherently has a large control packet and byte overhead, so it makes extensive use of its caching strategy to optimise its performance. However, large control packets severely restrict the protocol's ability to scale to larger networks. In addition, the source controlled routing paradigm introduces high latency when scaled. In this paper we address this problem by presenting a hybrid protocol, called Finite Horizon Routing (FHR), which improves upon the existing routing strategy of DSR and makes it more resilient to link failures in oversized networks. FHR partially removes the large control packet problem of DSR. Through our simulations we show that the reliability, total overhead, and latency can be improved by up to 10%, 23% and 53% respectively.

1 Introduction

An ad-hoc wireless network is a group of arbitrarily connected hosts that require no centralised control. These hosts form a collaborative body in which their individual limitations become less apparent. By relaying each other's messages, the nodes are capable of data aggregation and distribution across distances larger than their transmission radii. Cooperation also enables individual nodes to learn of the network connectivity and determine ways of establishing communication channels with one another. It is this learning property that makes ad-hoc networks versatile and attractive in disaster recovery situations, healthcare, academic institutions, and corporate conventions and meetings [8].

Dynamic Source Routing (DSR) [9] is one of the commonly used routing protocols in wireless ad-hoc networks. One of the main strengths of DSR is its aggressive caching strategy that results in accumulation of topology knowledge by each individual node. This allows DSR to choose optimal paths and maintain connectivity between source and destination pairs [11,9]. In addition, advanced decision-making schemes such as energy consumption balancing and link-stability modelling are supported by its well-informed cache [8]. At the same

G. Chen et al. (Eds.): ISPA Workshops 2005, LNCS 3759, pp. 422–433, 2005.

time, the source routing paradigm results in the use of large packet headers [2]. As the distance between the source and the destination increases, so does the size of every packet transmitted between the two. Long routes are harder to maintain at the source, since a slight movement by a single node along the route can initiate the need for new route discoveries. Hence, most DSR studies fall short of testing the protocol beyond a small number of hops [4, 9, 1].

In this paper, we propose a novel routing mechanism, called Finite Horizon Routing (FHR), that is based on DSR but without many of its associated scaling shortcomings — a claim that is confirmed by our results. Section 2 provides a brief outline of related work. We follow this with a formalisation of finite horizon routing in Sections 3 and 4. Sections 5 and 6 outline our method of approach and the results of our simulations, followed by a detailed discussion of the observed trends and drawn conclusions in Section 7.

2   Related Work

Dynamic Source Routing (DSR) is a source driven on-demand routing protocol [10, 9]. The source routing paradigm used by DSR dictates that all routing decisions are explicitly made by the source. Thus, each source node must maintain complete knowledge of the routes to the packet destinations. DSR does this by using route requests and replies that contain entire path information. It also employs promiscuous mode to observe the circulating packets and to aggressively cache the routing information stored within. Its detailed operation is well documented [10].

Hu and Johnson [7] have developed a natural extension to DSR called *flow state routing*. These flow states enable DSR to route a packet from a known source to a known destination using a known path with minimum overhead. Conceptually, this is a Dynamic Source Routing protocol with an additional header — a tuple ⟨source address, destination address, flow identifier⟩ used to identify the path that the packet will use. Studies have shown that using the flow-state can reduce the routing overhead without affecting the path optimality [7, 10]. However, the problems with maintaining long routes at the source are not helped by this extension, since it is still an explicitly source controlled process.

The Ad-hoc On-demand Distance Vector (AODV) [14] routing protocol is a competitor to DSR in terms of reliability and energy efficiency [1, 3]. AODV uses the same on-demand route discovery as DSR, but does not maintain a global topology knowledge. Instead, AODV only maintains next hop information. It therefore has a small overhead compared to DSR [2]. However, this also means that any advanced strategies depending on the knowledge of the topology beyond a single hop cannot be used. In addition, since less information is propagated throughout the network, AODV is more susceptible to using sub-optimal paths and exhausting *popular* nodes of their energy reserves [3, 4].

Zone Routing Protocol (ZRP) makes use of both, proactive and reactive, techniques to deliver faster response times for route requests, and to reduce the overhead of searching for routes [13, 5]. It tackles both the overhead and the route stability issues in oversized networks. The main idea behind ZRP is that there exist two tiers of topology knowledge: local neighbourhood within a defined routing zone r_{zone}, and a global topology outside r_{zone}. Each node attempts to pro-actively keep an up-to-date view of its routing zone, a technique which is both costly and inefficient [1, 4]. The global topology is maintained using on-demand protocols such as DSR. This allows ZRP to quickly route packets across the network and recover from remote link failures without explicitly informing the source.

Recent additions to ZRP include SHARP [15] and the closely related Independent Zone Routing (IZR) [16] in which nodes optimise the values of r_{zone} in an adaptive and distributed manner. Here the zone radius determination algorithm calculates the traffic ratios of local topology update packets to the global topology routing packets. r_{zone} is adapted to obtain the optimal combination of the two.

3   Routing Notation

In this section, we introduce a notation that describes the degree of control within a routing protocol. In particular, we are concerned with the decisions that are made by the source, and the decisions that are made by the intermediate nodes. We use three definitions:

- *Def I:* Let S denote the source node, and D denote the destination node.
- *Def II:* Let P_N define a path from one node to another, as constructed by node N. Hence, $P_{n_0} = \{n_0, n_1, n_2, n_3, \ldots, n_h\}$ defines a path from n_0 to n_h, where the two nodes are h hops apart.
- *Def III:* Let r and f denote the *intermediate router* and *finite horizon* respectively. These two parameters define the way a routing protocol relinquishes the responsibility of routing to its intermediate nodes. The finite horizon is the extent to which a node is prepared to control the path that a packet should take. Intermediate router is the node that is burdened with the responsibility of routing the packet beyond the finite horizon. Hence, a path from the node n_0 to the destination can be expressed as $P_{n_0} = \{n_0, \ldots, n_r, \ldots, n_f, \ldots, D\}$. It should be therefore noted that the condition $r \leq f \leq h$ must hold true.

Using these routing specifications, we can easily describe the manner in which routing is performed by DSR. A route constructed at the source can be represented as

$$P_S = \{S, n_1, n_2, \ldots, n_{h-1}, D\} \mid \{f = r = \infty\}. \tag{1}$$

ZRP, IZR and DSR with flow states make use a similar form of source routing and so can loosely fall under this category. At the other end of the spectrum, AODV's routing mechanism can be represented as

$$P_S = \{S, n_1\} \mid \{f = r = 1\}. \tag{2}$$

In AODV, the source does not specify where the packet should go after the next hop, and it burdens the next hop node with the task of routing the packet.

4 Finite Horizon Routing

Finite Horizon Routing (FHR) is a combination of the source routing paradigm and next-link based routing protocols. The idea behind finite horizons is that each node has the best knowledge of its immediate neighbourhood. Hence, we allow a source node to decide the initial direction of a packet, but not the entire route. As the packet gets closer to the destination, the more knowledgeable local nodes can determine the missing hops. We define the path constructed by a node S using FHR as

$$P_S = \{S, n_1, \ldots, n_r, \ldots, n_f\}. \tag{3}$$

The choice of f determines the distance to the horizon and the boundary of local knowledge, while the value of r can be modified to suit the application — for example, in an untrustworthy environment we may wish only to allow a small subset of nodes to make routing decisions. Such trustworthy node may or may not coincide with the one at the finite horizon. It should also be evident that FHR can be made to emulate AODV by reducing the finite horizon to one, and DSR by increasing the finite horizon beyond the network diameter.

4.1 Protocol Operation

A node that wishes to send a packet discovers the route to the destination using DSR's *route request* and *route reply* packets. These explicitly state the route between the two nodes. It is noted that this limits the number of hops to 63, since the route request and route reply packets have limits on the number of hops that they can contain. However, at this stage we are not scaling the network to such an extent, we are merely dealing with 12-hop networks that already exceed DSR's recommended network diameter of five to ten hops [10].

Once a route to the destination is found, the source initiates communication by specifying only the first few hops (defined by finite horizon, f). A node chooses its finite horizon based on the number of hops that it wishes to control and verify. Each node will ensure that the next hop is valid and respond with a route error if the link is broken. The source will also choose an intermediate router, r, whose responsibility is to provide the path beyond the finite horizon. There is no reason why r and f could not be the same node, however, there may be applications in which a node may want to control the route to one extent (finite horizon) and want to allow a node before that horizon to make some routing decisions. Hence, the values of f and r can be fixed or variable — selected by some application or routing specific set of rules.

As the packet progresses, each node will check the source route to see if it has been nominated as an intermediate router (further explained in Section 4.2). If so, it performs two main functions. One is to check that the path segment between itself and the finite horizon is valid by looking into its own cache. It should be noted that this step may not be necessary if the condition $r = f$ is true, ie if the intermediate router lies on the boundary of the finite horizon. The second function is to construct the path from the finite horizon to the destination. Prior to releasing the packet to the next hop, the intermediate router will choose its own values of r and f, again using its own metrics and set of rules. The source route header is truncated to the horizon and the packet forwarded.

4.2   The Algorithm

The algorithm outlined in this section specifies the exact procedure followed by each node upon receiving a packet with a source route. We make reference to the pseudocode provided in Figure 1.

If the node receiving the packet is specified in the path before the intermediate router, then it is only responsible for verifying that the next hop is available (Figure 1 lines 4–13). If there is a link failure, it must inform the previous intermediate router by sending a *link error* packet. It should then also attempt to salvage that packet by finding an alternate path to the destination.

ProcessReceivedPacket
1: $P \leftarrow$ ReceivedPacket
2: CheckLoops(P)
3: $(n_1, \ldots, n_r, \ldots, n_f) \leftarrow$ ExtractRouteHeader(P)
4: **if** $myAddress \in n_1, \ldots, n_{r-1}$ **then**
5:      $err_{link} \leftarrow$ Forward(P)
6:      **if** err_{link} **then**
7:          SendTo n_1 (LINK_ERROR, n_i, n_{i+1})
8:          SalvagePacket(P)
9:      **else**
10:         ForwardPacket(P)
11:     **end if**
12:     Return
13: **end if**
14: **if** $myAddress == n_r$ **then**
15:     $err_{link} \leftarrow$ CacheVerify($n_r, \ldots, n_f$)
16:     **if** err_{link} **then**
17:         SendTo n_1 (LINK_ERROR, $err_{link}.node1$, $err_{link}.node2$)
18:         SalvagePacket(P)
19:         Return
20:     **end if**
21:     $path \leftarrow$ CacheFindPath(n_f, n_{dest})
22:     **if** $path == NULL$ **then**
23:         SendTo n_1 (HORIZON_ERROR, n_f, n_{dest})
24:         $path \leftarrow$ CacheFindPath($myAddress, n_{dest}$)
25:     **else**
26:         $path \leftarrow$ JoinPaths($n_r \ldots n_f$, path)
27:     **end if**
28:     **if** $path == NULL$ **then**
29:         DropPacket(P)
30:     **else**
31:         $path \leftarrow$ TruncatePathToHorizon(path, f)
32:         ForwardPacket(P, path)
33:     **end if**
34: **end if**

Fig. 1. An abstract view of the processing required to facilitate finite horizons

If the node receiving the packet finds that it has been selected as an intermediate router then its responsibility increases. Firstly the router must ensure that any hops between itself and the finite horizon specified in the packet header are still in its cache (Figure 1 line 15). The previous router relies on the cache of this node to be more current than its own. Link errors are communicated back to the previous router using link error packets.

The next step is the path reconstruction. The router will attempt to put together a path to the destination using the route to the finite horizon as a starting point (Figure 1 lines 21–27). If this is not possible, a *horizon link error* is generated informing the previous router that a path between the horizon and the destination does not exist. The recipient of the horizon link error will then have to determine what information to remove from its cache, since it is likely to be more than one link that is in error. In addition, this intermediate router will also attempt to find any other path to the destination and use it instead. If no path is available, the packet is dropped. Otherwise, the node truncates the new route to a horizon of its choice, specifies the next intermediate router, and then forwards the packet.

4.3 Error Handling

When using FHR, there are several error handling operations that must be performed. Firstly, since the source node no longer explicitly controls the path, the possibility of loops is introduced. FHR handles this by using unique IDs for all packets. These IDs are monotonically increasing sequence numbers generated at the source, and left unchanged by forwarding nodes and routers. When a duplicate packet is received with a *time to live* field (from the IP packet header) lower than the one recorded earlier, a loop must have formed. The incorrect information is purged from the cache by exiting the FHR mode and using a complete source route — by not truncating the path to the finite horizon this time around (if a node is within a loop then it must have an incorrect path to the destination within its cache). This causes link confirmation at each hop and consequently generation of a *route error* that will break the loop.

Secondly, since the entire path is no longer stored in every packet, the opportunity to learn, and confirm, the existence of links is reduced. Hence each node will have different knowledge based on its location within the route. Nodes will generally have better knowledge of the downstream topology — topology in the direction of packet destinations.

Finally, a node receiving a *link* or a *horizon error* needs to purge its cache of erroneous data. Link removal is trivial, however, removing paths between the horizon and the destination may be difficult. FHR uses *mobi-cache*, a link-based cache with two tiers of knowledge [6]. The primary cache stores all the paths that are currently in use, whereas the secondary cache stores all the individual links of which this node is aware. Hence, when a node receives a horizon error, it can determine which links need to be removed by examining its primary cache.

5 Methodology

The results presented in this paper were simulated using *cnet* with wireless extensions [12] — a C-based discrete event network simulator. We used two simulation environments, a 1500m x 300m grid of 50 nodes, and a 3000m x 300m grid of 100 nodes. The former puts our algorithm under commonly simulated conditions [4, 1], while the latter tests its scalability, with a path length of up to (and in some cases over) 12 hops. The rectangular grids were chosen to highlight the differences between FHR and DSR — given that our goal was to optimise long-distance communication. In all simulations, there were 10 source nodes generating CBR traffic at a rate of 4 packets/second. The packet size was fixed at 512 bytes. Each node had a transmission range of 250m, and simulations were run for a total of 900 seconds. We used the waypoint model to simulate different levels of mobility. A *timeout* parameter specified the amount of time a node was stationary before choosing a random waypoint and random speed between 1m/s and 20m/s, for the smaller grid, and a random speed between 1m/s and 10m/s for the larger grid. The speed must be reduced for the large network since a path with a length of 12 hops cannot be established if nodes are moving at speeds of up to 20m/s. The probability of path remaining valid long enough so that it can be discovered and used becomes too slim and so the results would not be a true indication of the protocol performances.

6 Results and Analysis

In this section we present our results. Firstly, we analyse the throughput as any improvements must not come as a tradeoff to packet delivery. In the smaller grid shown in Figure 2(a) we see that FHR does not significantly affect the throughput, as there is no opportunity for it to use its finite horizons. However, Figure 2(b) demonstrates that in larger topologies, where the paths are generally longer, FHR is better equipped to handle mobile conditions. As the mobility increases (timeout drops below 300s), we see that FHR with lower finite horizon values deliver more packets than standard DSR. As topology changes, DSR requires every link on the initial path to be operational in order to deliver packets, whereas FHR does not. Instead, FHR allows the packets to travel to the *router* closer to the destination, which can then reroute them using its local knowledge. In the 3000m x 300m grid and at highest mobility (timeout of zero seconds), FHR can deliver 10% more packets than DSR. At other mobilities — between a zero timeout and a 300 second timeout, the improvement lies in the range of 5-8%.

At a timeout of 300 seconds where DSR and FHR have similar throughput, FHR with a horizon of three has a latency 53% lower than DSR. In completely mobile scenarios, a 36% reduction in latency is observed. These improvements can be attributed to FHR's delegation of responsibility for the packet to the intermediate routers. Whereas DSR must maintain paths of up to 12 hops, the intermediate routers only maintain the topology within their horizon, allowing

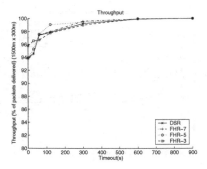

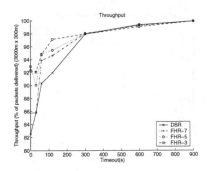

(a) Throughput in a small grid topology

(b) Throughput in a large grid topology

Fig. 2. In smaller topologies, FHR's throughput closely tracks to that of DSR. In larger topologies, FHR is faster in responding to topology changes, and hence has better performance in mobile conditions.

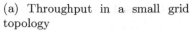

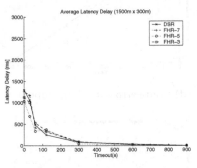

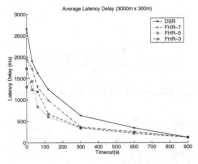

(a) Latency in a small topology

(b) Latency in a large topology

Fig. 3. As the information in the cache of FHR no longer contains up-to-date global knowledge, it is understandable that its path length is slightly affected in larger topologies, as shown in 3(a). However, as 3(b) shows, the latency delay in delivering the packets by FHR is still lower than that of DSR.

for a more distributed routing process. The result is a tradeoff — DSR will ensure that every link is valid, increasing latency, while FHR will näively forward the packet reducing the latency but increasing the risk that a route to the destination may not exist. We observe that values of horizons lower than three offer virtually no further benefit.

Finally we examine the issue of the large overhead found in DSR. Figures 4(a) and 4(b) depict the total number of control packets transmitted throughout the network, including retransmissions. In smaller networks, shown in Figure 4(a), both DSR and FHR quickly increase the number of control packets in mobile conditions, as is demonstrated for timeouts below 120 seconds.

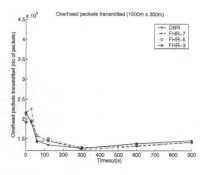

(a) Overhead in a small topology

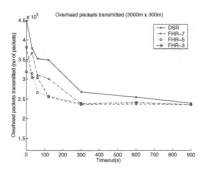

(b) Overhead in a large topology

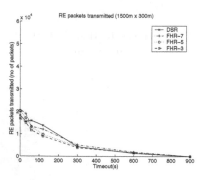

(c) Route errors in a small topology

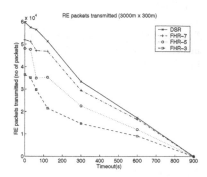

(d) Route errors in a large topology

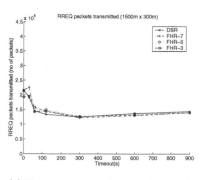

(e) Route requests in a small topology

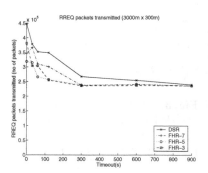

(f) Route requests in a large topology

Fig. 4. The overhead imposed by FHR and DSR under different topology sizes and mobilities shows that FHR is more efficient in terms of the overhead used

In the larger topology of 100 nodes, the Figure 4(b) shows that DSR exhibits a similar trend as in smaller topology. FHR's ability to contain topology changes to the local neighbourhood allows it to scale better. Hence FHR with a finite horizon of three will transmit anywhere between 3,538 and 93,708 fewer packets than DSR, amounting to savings between 2% and 27%. As expected, most of the improvement is made in the lower timeout range (more mobile conditions). When combined with the headers imposed on data packets, the reduction in the control byte overhead is equivalent to between 0.13MB at lowest mobility and 1.75MB at the highest mobility — 1.5% and 20%. The overhead reduction for FHR with a finite horizon of three peaked at 2.57MB (23%) and a timeout of 120m/s. The reasons for the lower overhead are twofold. Firstly, the topology changes cause a minimal number of cache updates through route errors, and secondly each source route header imposed on the data packet is smaller since it only contains the path segment that lies within the local finite horizon.

We further analyse the routing overhead by examining the number of *route error* and *route request* messages that are propagated throughout the network. Figure 4(d) shows that in a large network topology the number of *route errors* that are transmitted by DSR is proportional to the mobility level. FHR follows a similar pattern. However, any error caused by a link failure can be quickly and easily handled at the intermediate router which has the liberty of rerouting packets using alternative links, containing the route error propagation. In completely mobile conditions, FHR transmits 39% less packets.

It can be observed from Figure 4(e) and 4(f) that *route requests* comprise the majority of the overhead packets. Hence, both FHR and DSR expend most of their efforts rediscovering routes in mobile conditions. However in scenarios of higher mobilities and larger networks, DSR's susceptibility to route breakages becomes more apparent. FHR on the other hand, can concentrate on maintaining smaller route segments between the routers without attempting to discover distant topology changes.

7   Discussion and Conclusions

The results presented in previous section address two issues of scalability of DSR. The first is the size of the data packets. It is often argued that since source routes proportionally grow with the length of the path, DSR cannot be used in large networks. The overhead of DSR can grow to 50% of the data packets in networks of 5–7 hops [4]. FHR manages to keep the overhead low by reducing the number of needed route requests and by limiting the size of the source route of data packets through the finite horizon.

The second issue of scaling in DSR evident from our results is the rigid control of the source. When the routes are controlled by the source then any changes along the route must be communicated back to the (possibly distant) source which then has to find another path to the destination. Consider our scenario of a 12-hop network where the last few hops are constantly breaking. These route errors (REs) have to propagate all the way back to the source which has a time delay, T_{RE}. Unless the source has another valid path to the destination, its new route request (RREQ) and route reply (RREP) packets will incur a delay of their own, $T_{RREQ} + T_{RREP}$. So the total delay is quite significant, and by the time another route is established, in a mobile environment, there is a good chance that one of the other links in the new path will become invalid.

In FHR, the topology changes are more localised; the link breakages are not necessarily communicated to the source, but only to the last *intermediate router*. In the worst case, the intermediate router will not have another path to the destination, and so the route error will eventually have to go back to the source. Several points aid the cause of FHR. Firstly, an intermediate router is closer to the destination, so its knowledge of the destination whereabouts are almost guaranteed to be better than that of the more distant source. The only time this is likely not to be true is when there is only a single source-destination pair in the network and no other traffic exists. Having more than one source-destination pair increases each node's knowledge of its immediate neighbourhood. This is confirmed by our experiments. Secondly, if the intermediate router does have another path to the destination, then the delays of T_{RE} are reduced (since the route error only has to travel a few hops), and the T_{RREQ} and T_{RREP} are completely eliminated. Admittedly this does not happen all the time, but our tests do show that in a significant majority of the cases this holds true.

Both FHR and DSR have an ultimate limit of 63 hops which is imposed by the route request and route reply header size. However, DSR's specification recommends that it not be used in networks beyond 10 hops [10]. The simulations presented in this paper show that in a 12-hop network DSR's performance in terms of reliability, latency and routing overhead diminishes, whereas FHR maintains high delivery ratio with low latency and overhead. Thus the 63 hop limit is not the limiting issue at present.

The high level contribution of this work is specification of finite horizon routing, and its ability to emulate several competitive routing protocols through changes to finite horizon and intermediate router parameters. In addition, a working implementation of the algorithm has been tested against DSR with positive results. FHR exhibits greater throughput, lower latency and lower overhead than DSR in large topologies. In environments where long routes are not used, FHR regresses to the performance of DSR.

Acknowledgements

This work was supported by an Australian Postgraduate Award with Jean Rogerson Award and WAIDS.

References

1. Josh Broch, David A. Maltz, David B. Johnson, Yih-Chun Hu, and Jorjeta Jetcheva. A performance comparison of multi-hop wireless ad hoc network routing protocols. In *ACM/IEEE International Conference on Mobile Computing and Networking (MOBICOM)*, volume 4, pages 85–97. ACM Press, October 1998.
2. Laura Marie Feeney. An energy-consumption model for performance analysis of routing protocols for mobile ad hoc networks. *ACM Journal of Mobile Networks and Applications*, 6(3):239–249, June 2001.

3. Amer Filipovic. Energy efficiency of ad hoc routing protocols, November 2002. Honours Thesis, School of Computer Science & Software Engineering, The University of Western Australia.

4. Amer Filipovic and Amitava Datta. Building blocks of energy and cost efficient wireless sensor networks. In *European Workshop on Wireless Sensor Networks*, pages 218–233. Springer-Verlag, January 2004.

5. Zygmunt J. Haas. A new routing protocol for reconfigurable wireless networks. In *IEEE International Conference on Universal Personal Communications*, volume 2, pages 562–566, San Diego, CA, October 1997.

6. Yih-Chun Hu and David B. Johnson. Caching strategies in on-demand routing protocols for wireless ad hoc networks. In *Mobile Computing and Networking (MOBICOM)*, pages 231–242. ACM Press, August 2000.

7. Yih-Chun Hu and David B. Johnson. Implicit source routes for on-demand ad hoc network routing. In *International Symposium on Mobile Ad Hoc Networking and Computing*, pages 1–10, Long Beach, CA, USA, 2001. ACM Press.

8. Mohammad Illyas, editor. *The Handbook of Ad Hoc Wireless Networks*. CRC Press, 2003.

9. David B. Johnson and David A. Maltz. Dynamic source routing in ad hoc wireless networks. In Tomasz Imielinski and Hank Korth, editors, *Mobile Computing*, volume 353, chapter 5, pages 153–181. Kluwer Academic Publishers, 1996.

10. David B. Johnson, David A. Maltz, and Yih-Chun Hu. The dynamic source routing protocol for mobile ad hoc networks (DSR), July 2004. IETF Internet Draft.

11. Christine E. Jones, Krishna M. Sivalingam, Prathima Agrawal, and Jyn Cheng Chen. A survey of energy efficient network protocols for wireless networks. *ACM Wireless Networks*, 7(4):343–358, July 2001.

12. Chris McDonald. Cnet network simulator, August 2004. [Available at http://www.csse.uwa.edu.au/cnet] The University of Western Australia.

13. Marc R. Pearlman, Zygmunt J. Haas, and Syed I. Mir. Using routing zones to support route maintenance in ad hoc networks. In *IEEE Wireless Communications and Networking Conference (WCNC)*, volume 3, pages 1280–1285, Sept 2000.

14. Charles E. Perkins and Elizabeth M. Royer. Ad-hoc on-demand distance vector routing. In *IEEE Workshop on Mobile Computing Systems and Applications (WMCSA)*, volume 3, pages 90–100, New Orleans, LA, USA, February 1999.

15. Venugopalan Ramasubramanian, Zygmunt J. Haas, and Emin Gn Sirer. Sharp: A hybrid adaptive routing protocol for mobile ad hoc networks. In *International Symposium on Mobile Ad Hoc Networking & Computing (MOBIHOC)*, pages 303–314, Annapolis, Maryland, USA, June 2003. ACM Press.

16. Prince Samar, Marc R. Pearlman, and Zygmunt J. Haas. Independent zone routing: An adaptive hybrid routing framework for ad hoc wireless networks. *IEEE/ACM Transactions on Networking*, 12(4):595–608, August 2004.

Energy Usage in Biomimetic Models for Massively-Deployed Sensor Networks

Kennie H. Jones[1], Kenneth N. Lodding[1], Stephan Olariu[2], Larry Wilson[2], and Chunsheng Xin[3]

[1] NASA Langley Research Center, Hampton, VA 23681
{k.h.jones, Kenneth.n.lodding}@nasa.gov
[2] Old Dominion University, Norfolk, VA 23529
{olariu, wilson}@cs.odu.edu
[3] Norfolk State University, Norfolk, VA 23504
cxin@nsu.edu

Abstract. Promises of ubiquitous control of the physical environment by sensor networks open avenues that will redefine the way we live and work. Due to the small size and low cost of sensors, visionaries promise smart systems enabled by deployment of huge numbers of sensors working in concert. At the moment, sensor network research is concentrating on developing techniques for performing simple tasks with minimal energy expense, assuming some form of centralized control. Centralized control does not scale to large networks and simple tasks in small-scale networks will not lead to the sophisticated applications predicted. Recently, the authors have proposed a new way of looking at sensor networks, motivated by lessons learned from the way biological ecosystems are organized. Here we demonstrate that in such a model, fully distributed data aggregation can be performed efficiently, without synchronization, in a scalable fashion, where individual motes operate autonomously based on local information, cooperating with neighbors to make local decisions that are aggregated across the network achieving globally-meaningful effects.

1 Introduction

While futurists long dreamed of machines working with other machines, a giant step towards realization of this dream may be credited to the DARPA-sponsored *SmartDust* program [6]. The goal of SmartDust was to make machines with self-contained sensing, computing, transmitting, and powering capabilities so small and inexpensive that they could be released into the environment in massive numbers. These devices have come to be called *motes* and serve as nodes in a sensor network [15,16]. As the motes are severely energy-constrained, they cannot transmit over long distances, restricting interaction to motes in their immediate neighborhood. Much current research involves forming and managing multi-hop sensor networks where motes only transmit to nearby motes.

Since building massively-deployed sensor networks is prohibitively expensive under current technology, we have witnessed attempts at deploying small-scale sensor networks in support of a growing array of applications [2]. These prototypes provide

G. Chen et al. (Eds.): ISPA Workshops 2005, LNCS 3759, pp. 434–443, 2005.
© Springer-Verlag Berlin Heidelberg 2005

solid evidence of the usefulness of sensor networks and suggest that the future will be populated by pervasive sensor networks that will redefine the way we live and work [12]. However, current sensor networks are for the most part modeled after conventional computing networks under centralized control and involve a small number of motes. It is, therefore, not clear that they provide a credible approximation of the massive deployment envisioned by the proponents of sensor networks [1,4,6,7,15]. Rather than adapting conventional techniques of centralized computer control, new techniques dependent on local cooperation among network nodes will lead to self-sustaining communities of machines with emergent behavior that autonomously operate and adapt to changes in the environment. This evolution so parallels the development of life on Earth that living systems are likely to provide realistic models for sensor network design.

1.1 Our Contributions

Recently, Jones *et al* [2] proposed to look at sensor networks in a novel way, motivated by their belief that in order to scale to massive deployment, sensor networks can benefit from lessons learned from the way biological ecosystems are organized. Indeed in the presence of a *massive* deployment, sensor networks may benefit from behavior as a community of organisms, where individual motes operate based on local information, making local decisions that propagate across the network to achieve globally-meaningful effects. This differs greatly from the current direction of sensor network research. Rather that applying conventional techniques requiring centralized control and the establishment and maintenance of complicated infrastructure, our motes, upon deployment, will begin to operate autonomously without the establishment of any infrastructure. In this paper we take the work in [2] one step further. We demonstrate that in such a model, fully distributed data aggregation can be performed in a scalable fashion in massively deployed sensor networks, where individual motes operate based on local information, making local decisions that are aggregated across the network to achieve globally-meaningful effects. We then analyze the energy costs for this method of aggregation.

We will also show that memory of past experience and local cooperation among neighbors can lead to beneficial adaptive behavior. We do not claim that our examples here demonstrate much learning or intelligence. But again, we are arguing for a change in direction where local learning and cooperation is paramount in design leading to systems that adapt to environmental change without centralized direction.

The two important metrics of concern are time required to do work and the energy expended to do that work. If work must be done serially, then the time required to do that work will scale linearly (or worse) with the size of the network. The total energy consumption of the network is expected to increase with the size of the network, but a desirable property for scalability is for the energy consumption per mote to remain stable regardless of the size of the network. We will show that both desired characteristics are found in our examples: both the time required for our task and the energy required per mote to accomplish the task stabilizes as the size of the network grows. We believe consideration of these properties is crucial in the design of a scalable sensor network.

The remainder of this work is organized as follows. In Section 2, we present our model based on ecology where motes, like organisms, autonomously interact with their environment while cooperating communally with a local neighborhood. We also explain our use of cellular automata to model a sensor network. In Section 3, we present an algorithm for calculating an average across a distributed sensor network that adheres to our biological model. Section 4 surveys the problems facing current sensor motes in managing a small, fixed energy budget where motes must sleep as much as possible. In Section 5 we present a novel stochastic MAC protocol that proves through our simulations to efficiently facilitate the implementation of our averaging algorithm. In Section 6, we conclude by reviewing how our technique moves in a different direction for sensor network development and discuss future work.

2 An Ecological Model for Sensor Networks

We think of motes as *organisms* within a community. At *birth*, deployment time, the motes are endowed with *genetic material*, containing, among others, an initial *state* and *rules* by which they interact with the environment. The state and the rules may change as the motes interact with the environment, reflecting their dynamic adaptation to conditions in their neighborhood. Additionally, the motes may *remember* and *record* their interaction with the environment by storing information in their limited on-board memory. Memory and its use to change state or rules are considered learning. Changing state conditions or rules based on learning demonstrates some level of cognition.

One of the main goals of this work is to use learning and cognition to enable *local decisions* based on *local information* that effect *global* results. Limiting decisions to localities is important for reasons of scalability and autonomy. Local decisions allow distributed control. In turn, distributed control through local decisions provides a natural redundancy affording fault tolerance – as some motes exhaust their energy budget and expire others will continue to make decisions.

We propose to use *cellular automata* as a viable model for massively deployed sensor networks operating as organisms in an ecosystem. A cellular automaton represents, in most ways, a distribution of sensor motes throughout a geographic region. Each internal cell is surrounded by neighbor cells. Neighbor cells represent those motes that can receive a transmission from a cell. Thus, the regularity of the grid represents a logical indication of physical proximity. Visibly, the set of neighbors need not be limited to the eight adjacent cells. Increasing the number of cells that can receive transmissions from the selected cell is specified by the neighbor *radius*. One apparent limitation of this model is that the number of neighbors is fixed for a given radius; however, this can be changed by disabling some of the neighbors.

3 Aggregating Sensed Data: Average Calculation

One of the key contributions of this work is to show that fully distributed data aggregation can be performed in a scalable fashion in massively deployed sensor networks. Imagine a large-scale sensor network where individual sensors and/or actuators need to take action based on a perceived global threshold. For example, if the average temperature inside a building exceeds a certain temperature, individual actuators will operate on blinds that will block the sun from overheating the room.

In [2], centralized control of a sensor network was deemed unacceptable due to issues of scalability, single points of failure, and cost of constructing and maintaining complex infrastructure. Our objective is for the sensor network to calculate an average value across the network without any mote or any central authority having global knowledge of all mote values. The problem is for each mote to obtain and maintain the global average by iteratively using only data that is available locally.

In [2], we gave a detailed description of our algorithm for consensus on a majority binary value where motes within a neighborhood consult with each other and cooperate to make local decisions resulting in achievement of a global goal. Here we will use that same method to calculate the global average. Assume that a data value collected by each mote is converted to a real number, a *color*, in the range [0, 255]. Upon deployment, the motes are endowed with genetic material (see [9,14] for details): an activity *status*, and a *transmission time* within a specified *time period*.

When the algorithm begins, each mote independently starts its own clock. The time period is divided into one or more slots. The transmission time assigned to a mote is one of these time slots within a time period. Because the transmission time for each mote is a random number, there is no guarantee that two or more motes will never transmit at the same time. Simultaneous transmissions will cause collisions, thus a MAC layer protocol is assumed to decide cellular execution order. The transmission time is fixed at deployment (being part of the genetic material), but the execution order in each time slot is a "function of the environment" and may change at different times. Even with MAC layer negotiations, by this method each cell is acting *asynchronously* and *autonomously*.

When a cell reaches its transmission time within the time period, it is *selected* for action in which it queries its neighbors for their color value. If all are not equal, it calculates the average and sets all cells in the neighborhood to this average, else, the selected cell becomes inactive. When all cells are inactive, the simulation ends. Thus, only local information; no global control, is required. As these local neighbor cells are cooperating with each other, acting on local environmental information, and remembering information from one action that will affect a future action, we argue that this system demonstrates simple cognition.

It is important to understand that in this discussion, we are concerned only with functionality of the motes. When a cell is selected, several transmissions are made between the selected mote and its neighbors. MAC negotiations are assumed. In the next section, we will address implementation of a MAC to accomplish this task in an energy efficient manner. Also, in this discussion, time is discussed as unitless. A time slot need only be long enough for all transmissions to occur satisfying a transaction of the selected cell. Thus, we are concerned with reducing the time periods required for convergence and demonstrating that the time required does not largely increase with growth of the network size.

Figure 1 depicts an initial distribution in a cellular automaton with a 30 x 30 grid of cells showing a random distribution of colors. Figure 2 depicts the color change after the first time period. Notice that after only one iteration, the cells are much closer to the same color. Figure 3 illustrates the color change after 10 periods. The converged average is always equal to the average of the original distribution calculated prior to starting the algorithm. An interesting and valuable attribute of this algorithm is that the average color following each cell selection is also exactly equal to the initial calculated average.

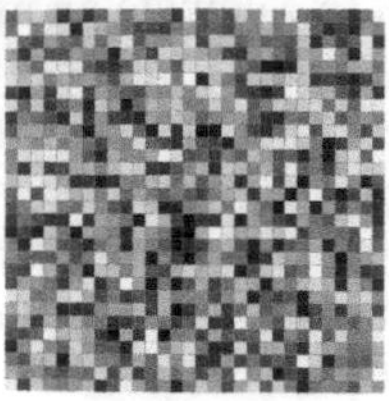

Fig. 1. Initial distribution of colors for color averaging

Fig. 2. Distribution of colors after the first time period

Fig. 3. Distribution of colors after 10 time periods

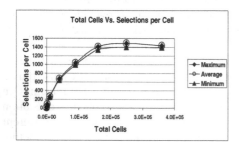
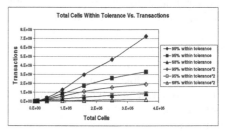

Fig. 4. Illustrating the minimum, average, and maximum number of cell selections

Fig. 5. Percentage of cells within tolerance

A greater advantage of our decentralized approach is in the distribution of energy expenditure. The "funnel effect" of multi-hop routing required for the centralized approach described above will deplete the energy of cells much faster when their distance to the sink is shorter. In our decentralized approach, the workload is not only evenly distributed, but the workload required of an individual mote actually decreases as the grid size increases, as shown in Figure 4. As stated earlier, some applications require a close agreement of common value, while others may tolerate a much larger divergence. We call the latter case "good enough computing" and show that, in such cases, a distributed consensus on a common value range can occur quickly with relatively few transactions. As an example, a 200 x 200 grid begins with a color distribution in which all 256 colors are represented in a fairly even distribution with a standard deviation of 73.74.

However, the algorithm comes close to the solution very quickly. The simulation takes 271 time steps to come to a solution where all cells are within the specified tolerance. After only 1 time step, the number of colors represented has been reduced to 55. By the 86th time step, there are only 3 colors represented. The standard deviation is within the tolerance of 0.5. Figure 5 shows that solutions with a large percentage of cells within the tolerance asymptotically slope towards zero as the grid size increases. Most importantly, solutions up to 95% within the tolerated average reach that asymptote quickly with few transactions regardless of grid size.

Although we have not modified our simulator for other functions, it follows that our approach could be used for some. As examples, if instead of calculating the average, a selected cell determines the minimum (or maximum) value and sets all cells in the neighborhood to this value, the simulation will converge where all cells are set to the minimum (or maximum) value.

Our model of "good enough computing" may be of great value in the presence of changing values. A centralized approach would require a snapshot state of all motes to be buffered as the average for that state is computed. Using our method, a close approximation of the average may be maintained without the need for such a snapshot. The quality of that "good enough" state is dependent upon the accepted tolerance.

4 Energy Considerations

The algorithm in Section 3 relies in a crucial way on a rather strong assumption, namely that any mote can contact any neighbor at any time. This could be accomplished if all motes constantly listen except for times when they need to transmit. But this does not work well in the energy-constrained environment of the sensor network. Because of limited on-board energy supply, the longevity of the networked would be severely curtailed if the motes remain in receive mode constantly. With energy conservation as a primary concern, it is unacceptably inefficient for motes to keep their receivers active when not needed [1,3,18]. The MICA2 mote currently available from Crossbow Technology, Inc. [18] is used in many sensor network implementations. When the radio receiver is active, it consumes 7 mA; when it is inactive (i.e., *sleeping*), it consumes only 0.002 mA. If used as Crossbow recommends, a 1:99 ratio of inactive to receiving the mote uses on average 0.24 mA and can operate 5.78 months on a 1000 mA-Hr battery. If the radio remains in active receiving mode constantly, and *no other functions are performed*, the motes will last only 6 days.

Clearly for required efficiency, the mote must alternate between sleeping and receiving with the large majority of the time sleeping. Then the challenge is, how does a mote that desires to communicate with a neighboring mote know when the brief receiving period begins? Transmission is more expensive than receiving and consumes 10 mA. Thus, wasting transmissions when the recipient mote is sleeping must be avoided. A centralized approach using a synchronized clock among all motes can be used, but this requires global communication and coordination. As our interest is in massively-deployed sensor networks, this approach is not attractive, as its complications escalate rapidly as the size of the network grows.

The problem of coordinating the transmission and receiving among motes is greatly exacerbated by the energy hole problem discussed in [2]. Not only are motes closest to the sink expending the vast majority of energy, they must be well coordinated and efficient when switching between receiving a message and forwarding that message. This management becomes more complicated the closer the mote is to the sink, as it receives more messages. We want our motes to be asynchronous and autonomous. We do not want them to have to coordinate clocks and schedules even with their neighbors, much less with the entire community.

5 An Energy-Efficient Approach to Averaging

Suppose that instead of asking questions of neighbors and expecting a response, the motes behave and act completely asynchronously and autonomously. Each mote maintains its own clock independent of every other mote. A sleeping period, the length of the receiving time within a sleeping period, and the number of times the mote will awaken to transmit during a sleeping period is assigned as genetic material upon deployment. Upon activation, each mote decides for itself when it will awaken to transmit and when it will awaken to listen during the sleeping period. Furthermore, each mote makes this decision anew each sleeping period. As a heuristic approach, regularity is an enemy to this process. If fixed choices are made and neighbor receiving and transmitting times are aligned, the process will succeed, but if they are not aligned, the process will fail completely.

Transmissions are brief: a single 8 bit packet representing the current color constitutes each transmission. The MICA2 mote transmits at a rate of 40 Kbits/sec. Thus, a transmission burst of a single packet expends 10 mA for 0.2 msec resulting in an energy cost of 5.56E-7 mA-Hr. Receiving periods are assigned in multiples of msec. Thus, any mote listening when a neighbor makes a 0.2 msec transmission will hear that transmission. Notice that the clocks do not need to be synchronized. If a transmission spans the msec boundary of the listening mote, the received message will be incomplete and will be discarded.

The work done is similar to our original process. The objective is for each mote to gather from its neighbors their color values and average these with its own color. It is different from our original process in two important respects. Motes are never guaranteed to hear from all of their neighbors. A mote listens for its receiving period and averages all values it receives during that period with its own current color. Any of its transmissions subsequent to its receiving period will broadcast the new averaged color to any motes that are listening. Because all neighbors are not queried and set to the new average, the desirable property of the previous algorithm whereby the average of the neighborhood always remains equal to the initial average of the community is lost. But as will be demonstrated, our property of "good enough computing" still holds.

In a sample simulation, a 10 x 10 grid of 100 motes are assigned the parameter, 20 msec, for duration of the sleep period. To access the optimal values for receiving duration and number of transmissions, these values are varied as in Table 1. The first pair designates that during each sleep period of 20 msec, 1 msec is randomly selected for receiving and during every other msec period, a single transmission is made. Only one transmission can be made during a msec period. However, there can be periods during the sleep period when no transmissions occur as exemplified by the pair, {3,5}. In this case, there are 17 potential transmission periods, but during 12 of these, the mote remains sleeping. It would seem intuitive that the optimal results would be

Table 1. Tested Transceiving Ratios

Rec. Period	#Trans.	Rec. Period	#Trans.
1	19	14	6
2	18	15	5
3	17	16	4
4	16	17	3
5	15	18	2
6	14	19	1
7	13	3	15
8	12	3	10
9	11	3	5
10	10	5	10
11	9	5	5
12	8	10	5
13	7	15	3

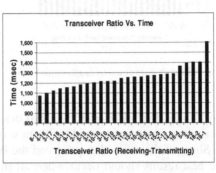

Fig. 6. Time required to reach consensus

obtained by transmitting every period when a mote is not receiving but this is not the case. It is of no value to transmit when no neighbor is listening. Because each mote reassigns the transceiving ratio anew with each sleep period, it is difficult to predict the results. The simulation ends when all cells have a color value within the specified tolerance of the converged average (i.e., all colors are *equal*).

Three metrics are of particular concern to reaching consensus: the overall time required, the energy consumed, and the variance between the converged average and the average of the initial distribution. Figure 6 compares the time required to reach consensus for all tested ratios.

Figure 7 compares the energy cost to reach consensus for all tested ratios. Ratios with short receiving times performed at substantially lower cost. A number of top performers had ratios with components that add to less than 20, most notably 3-5 and 5-5. Figure 8 compares the deviation of the converged average from the average of the initial distribution for all tested ratios.

A remarkable property of this approach is the even distribution of cost among the motes. All motes expended equal amounts of energy to perform the task. This attribute cannot be overemphasized. In this approach, the longevity of the network is maximized.

It is instructive to recall Crossbow's recommendation of a 1:99 ratio of transceiving to sleeping [18]. To test this recommendation, a simulation was executed using a sleep period of 100 with a receiving period of 1 and 1 transmission. The simulation ran for 12 hours and did not converge. It is understandable why this ratio did not work. If all motes within a neighborhood rarely transmit and rarely receive, it is unlikely that any will ever communicate. For all of the talk of the requirement for motes to sleep much of the time to save energy, it is not useful to sleep when there is

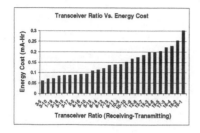

Fig. 7. Energy consumed to reach consensus   **Fig. 8.** Percent deviation of converged average from average of initial distribution

work to be done. The objective is to design a sleep/transceive ratio that will get the work done as soon as possible without wasted energy.

Some of the ratios that produced the best results were not expected. It seems that the best results should occur when all time periods are used for either receiving or transmitting. But this is not the case (e.g., 3-5, 3-10, 5-5). Although the transceiving periods are defined as genetic material, the choice of when these periods occur within the sleep period is made randomly at runtime. Thus, the choice of when transceiving periods occur by a mote is considered an environmental influence to its neighbors. This is an example of emergent behavior that produces such surprising results in living systems [17]. We define emergent behavior as that which is produced when genetic rules (known at deployment) are influenced by environmental events. If the set of all genetic rules and environmental events are known, then all behaviors should be able to be calculated. However, it is likely impossible to predict all possible environmental events. This prediction is exacerbated when learning is a factor. If environmental events are remembered over time, this memory may be used to learn new rules (i.e., to change the genetic rules) in unpredictable ways that may produce unpredictable interaction with future environmental events.

6 Concluding Remarks

We see the full potential of sensor networks only reached when there are massive numbers of heterogeneous motes acting asynchronously and autonomously, yet cooperating in a way that their local actions, based on local information, combine to affect a functional and sustainable network interacting with the environment. This is how living systems have evolved so successfully. Individual organisms operate by a combination of innate rules (i.e. genetics) and learned behavior in a local niche. The combination of the actions of the individual organisms results in a multifunctional, sustainable ecosystem.

In this work we have demonstrated a function completed by a sensor network acting as a society: autonomous motes functioning asynchronously cooperative to achieve a common goal. The function is carried out without centralized control and without any mote needing to know all information known within the society. We have also shown that the goal can be closely approached with few costs in time and resources compared with the much more costly final answer. Finally, we have analyzed the energy costs of this method and demonstrated that it is more efficient than a centralized approach.

References

1. F. Akyildiz, W. Su, Y. Sankarasubramanian, and E. Cayirci, Wireless sensor networks: A survey, Computer Networks, 38(4), 2002, 393-422.
2. K. H. Jones, K. N. Lodding, S. Olariu, L. Wilson, and C. Xin, Biology-inspired distributed consensus in massively-deployed sensor networks, *Proc. 4th International Conference on Ad hoc Networks and Wireless,* Cancun, Mexico, October 6-8, 2005.
3. D. Culler, D. Estrin and M. Srivastava, Overview of sensor networks, *IEEE Computer,* 37(8), 2004, 41-49.
4. N. A. Lynch, *Distributed Algorithms,* Morgan Kaufmann Publishers, San Francisco, California, 1996.
5. B. Hemingway, W. Brunette, T. Anderl and G. Boriello, The flock: Mote sensors sing in undergraduate curriculum, *IEEE Computer,* 37(8), 2004, 72-78.
6. J. M. Kahn, R. H. Katz, and K. S. J. Pister, Next century challenges: Mobile support for Smart Dust, *Proc. ACM MOBICOM,* Seattle, WA, August 1999, 271--278.
7. D. Lammers, *Embedded projects take a share of Intel's research dollars.* EE Times, August 28, 2001. Retrieved April 5, 2004, from http://today.cs.berkeley.edu/800demo/eetimes.html
8. K. Martinez, J. K. Hart and R. Ong, Environmental sensor networks, *IEEE Computer,* 37(8), 2004, 50-56.
9. S. Olariu, A. Wadaa, L. Wilson and M. Eltoweissy, Wireless sensor networks: leveraging the virtual infrastructure, *IEEE Network,* 18(4), 204, 51-56.
10. S. Olariu and Q. Xu, A simple self-organization protocol for massively deployed sensor networks, *Computer Communications,* to appear, 2005.
11. S. Park, I. Locher, A. Savvides, M. B. Srivastava, A. Chen, R. Muntz and S. Yue, Design of a wearable sensor badge for smart kindergarten, Proc. 6th International Symposium on Wearable Computers, Seattle, WA, October, 2002.
12. K. Ryokai and J. Cassell, StoryMat: A play space for collaborative storytelling, Proc. CHI'99, October 1999.
13. K. Sohrabi, J. Gao, V. Ailawadhi and G. Pottie, Protocols for self-organization of a wireless sensor network, *IEEE Personal Communications,* 7(5), 2000, 16-27.
14. A.Wadaa, S. Olariu, L. Wilson, M. Eltoweissy and K. Jones, Training a wireless sensor network, *Mobile Networks and Applications,* 10, 2005, 151-167.
15. B. Warneke, M. Last, B. Leibowitz and K. Pister, SmartDust: communicating with a cubic-millimeter computer, *IEEE Computer,* 34(1), 2001, 44-55.
16. V. V. Zhirnov and D. J. C. Herr, New frontiers: self-assembly and nano-electronics, *IEEE Computer,* 34(1), 2001, 34-43.
17. K. Kelly: *Out of Control: The New Biology of Machines, Social Systems, and the Economic World,* Perseus Books 1994.
18. MPR/MIB User's Manual, Crossbow Technology, Inc., Retrieved May 5, 2005, from http://www.xbow.com/Support/Support_pdf_files/MPR-MIB_Series_Users_Manual.pdf

Probabilistic Behavior of Sensor Network Localization[*]

Xun-Xue Cui[1,3], Zhan Zhao[2], and Qing Tao[3]

[1] State Key Laboratory for Novel Software Technology, Nanjing University,
Nanjing 210093, China
xxcui@tsinghua.org.cn
[2] The Institute of Electronics, Chinese Academy of Sciences, Beijing, 100080, China
[3] New Star Research Institute of Applied Technology, Hefei, 230031, China

Abstract. Positioning is a fundamental issue for wireless sensor network operation. Despite the recent proposals for the development of localization algorithms, the probabilistic behavior in position estimation using inaccurate measurements has not been analyzed. The paper focuses on two theoretical problems of localization from the viewpoint of probability analysis. First, it was proved that the position error in positioning is distributed by the χ^2. Secondly, we demonstrated that the sensor connectivity distribution converges to the Poisson. Experiments of connectivity distribution were performed, and some conclusions were given to conduct a sensor network deployment.

1 Introduction

There has been an increase of wireless sensor networks (WSNs) for monitoring environmental information. Localization of sensor nodes is a fundamental problem in the kind of networks. The problem of location estimation for all nodes given some anchors with known coordinates and relative distance between neighbors, is called the location discovery or localization problem. When endowed with the ability to know their positions, sensor nodes can support a rich set of geographically aware protocols, and can accurately report the positions of detected targets and events[1-3].

Usually the optimization objective in a localization problem is to minimize the error of coordinates to fit all the known distance or angular measurements. Unfortunately, those measurements and the final results computed from them are often inaccurate. In environments where inaccurate information is common rather than exceptive, the ability to detect inaccurate data and estimate the correctness of the solutions is an important part of network system. The accuracy of measurements varies widely with hardware technology and environmental conditions. In this paper we will analyze the localization characteristics by examining the error behavior and node connectivity. The significance of probabilistic behavior analysis of sensor network localization can offer a guide for designing a valuable localization algorithm, as a sensor network has its speciality different from other networks. The node connectivity is to determine what should be met for connectivity requirements, when

---

[*] This project is partially supported by the Opening Foundation of State Key Laboratory for Novel Software Technology in Nanjing University, the Natural Science Foundation of Anhui Province of China (050420212) and the Excellent Youth Science and Technology Foundation of Anhui Province of China (04042069).

G. Chen et al. (Eds.): ISPA Workshops 2005, LNCS 3759, pp. 444–453, 2005.

nodes are deployed in a field to implement the sensing and positioning function correctly. The study of the node connectivity provides a universal principle to understand the feasible behavior of localization. The novel research contributions of our work presented in the paper are:

1) Linear transformation of position estimation is distributed by the χ^2 distribution.
2) We also prove that node connectivity distribution converges to the Poisson.

Through error investigation we can improve the correctness of location discovery. Many designs of sensor networks can benefit from the conclusions. For example, correct predictions of network performance with the presence of error can improve resource management in sensor networks. If location modeling generates node locations with appropriate error distribution, it would be a help for sensor network simulations. On the other hand, the success of a localization algorithm also depends on connectivity. An indication has to be obeyed on the percentage of anchor nodes required by a statistical study of connectivity.

This paper is organized as follows. The next section gives an overview of the related work. Section 3 describes the probabilistic distribution of position error. We discuss the properties of node connectivity in Section 4. Section 5 concludes the paper.

2 Background and Related Work

2.1 Background

In the paper we study the sensor network localization problem, which is defined as follows. We are given m anchor nodes $a_1, \ldots, a_m \in \mathbf{R}^d$ whose positions are known (e.g. via GPS), and n sensor nodes $x_1, \ldots, x_n \in \mathbf{R}^d$ whose positions we wish to determine. Furthermore, we are given the Euclidean distance $\overline{d}_{kj}$ between a_k and x_j for some k, j, and d_{ij} between x_i and x_j for some $i<j$. Specially, let Na={(k, j): $\overline{d}_{kj}$ is specified} and Nx={(i, j): i<j, d_{ij} is specified}. The localization problem is then to find a realization of $x_1, \ldots, x_n \in R_d$ from the view of mathematical model such that:

$$\| a_k - x_j \|^2 = \overline{d}_{kj}^2 \quad \forall (k, j) \in N_a \tag{1}$$

$$\| x_i - x_j \|^2 = d_{ij}^2 \quad \forall (i, j) \in N_x \tag{2}$$

Distance measurements are the input parameters of a location discovery algorithm as the main source of error. As a sensor network is intended to be used in a remote and inhospitable region, where the error characteristic of distance measurements cannot be examined in advance, the quality prediction of a network greatly depends on the error model. There have been three most frequently adopted measuring technologies: Received Signal Strength Indicator (RSSI), Time Difference of Arrival (TDoA) and acoustic-based ranging. For the localization problem with measurement noises, usually noises are randomly generated according to the following formula,

$$d_{kj} = \hat{d}_{kj}(1 + \rho) \tag{3}$$

where $\hat{d}_{kj}$ represents the true distance between nodes i and j, $\rho \in N(u, \sigma^2)$ is a Gaussian random variable.

If two nodes can communicate with each other to exchange information such as their coordinates, they are called neighbors. The connectivity of a node is the average number of its neighbors. It is an important parameter that has an impact on the accuracy of many localization algorithms. Coverage is a key goal in localization, defined as the percentage of non-anchor nodes for which a position is able to be determined after self-configure computation.

2.2 Related Work

Despite there being a plenty of positioning papers, comparatively little has been published on the theoretical issues of localization [4]. Patwari et al. [5] proved that Cramer-Rao Bounds (CRBs, i.e. location estimate variance bounds) decrease as more devices are added to a network. They derived CRBs and maximum-likelihood estimators under Gaussian and log-normal models. Sasha et al. [6] proved that the distribution of location error could be approximated with a family of Weibull distribution, and that the distribution parameters may be unequivocally determined from the inconsistencies in position and distance measurements. The authors selected four models of continuous distribution whose parameters are determined using maximum likelihood estimates. The Weibull model is the best one to fit the random samples through Kolmogorov-Smirnov tests. Savvides et al. [7] derived the Cramer-Rao Bound for Gaussian error for localization using distance and angular measurements, and used these bounds on a carefully controlled set of scenarios to study the trends in the error induced by measurement, network density and beacon uncertainty. The authors declare it is the first effort to construct an analytical framework to characterize the trends error behavior for multihop localization. The key difference between this paper and these related works is that the latter were analyzed for a given application background by statistical modal, and the former will be discussed based on the fine-drawn process of operational mathematics. The conclusions in the paper will give several guide rules for general applications.

On the error problem in a localization algorithm, there have been several methods proposed to deal with this problem from different aspects. Early Zangl et al. [8] derived probability density functions of the expected distance between two nodes by considering the number of joint neighbors, and used those functions for positioning. Savvides et al. [9] also discussed the connectivity requirements with probabilistic analysis, and performed a statistical test to obtain an indication on the percentage of beacons required. They directly took the connectivity distribution as the Poisson without a proof. A detailed proof for this perspective is provided in the paper, thus we give a theory contribution to the connectivity aspect. Yinyu Ye et al. [10, 11] proposed a famous semidefinite programming (SDP) relaxation method for localization. Since the distance measurements contain random errors, the solution to the SDP problem was discussed to constitute error management with probabilistic analysis. Recently a time-based positioning scheme (TPS) is presented for location discovery [12], in which a statistical error analysis of coordinate estimation was given, and the major sources of errors affecting TPS's position accuracy were identified. Simulation results show that localization error strongly depends on the variance of TDoA measurements used in positioning. All of those works are limited on improving localization precision in a special application background via a detailed algorithm on the basis of probability. We study the general probabilistic behavior of localization error and discuss the probabilistic distribution principle of position error. Thus the research motivations of error behavior are different.

3 Error Probability of Position Coordinates

Position error is crucial for the localization problem. Common methods for developing a position use atomic multilateration as their main primitive, which makes up the basic case where an unknown node could estimate its location if it is within ranges of at least three anchors. From the estimated distances (d_i) and the known positions (x_i, y_i) of the anchors, we derive the following equations:

$$(x_1 - x)^2 + (y_1 - y)^2 = d_1^2$$

$$......$$

$$(x_n - x)^2 + (y_n - y)^2 = d_n^2$$

(4)

where the unknown position is denoted by (x, y). The equations can be linearized by subtracting the last equation from the first $n-1$ equations.

$$x_1^2 - x_n^2 - 2(x_1 - x_n)x + y_1^2 - y_n^2 - 2(y_1 - y_n)y = d_1^2 - d_n^2$$

$$......$$

$$x_{n-1}^2 - x_n^2 - 2(x_{n-1} - x_n)x + y_{n-1}^2 - y_n^2 - 2(y_{n-1} - y_n)y = d_{n-1}^2 - d_n^2$$

(5)

Reordering the terms gives a proper system of linear equations in a form $Ax=b$, where

$$A = \begin{bmatrix} 2(x_1 - x_n) & 2(y_1 - y_n) \\ ...... & ...... \\ 2(x_{n-1} - x_n) & 2(y_{n-1} - y_n) \end{bmatrix}$$

(6)

$$b = \begin{bmatrix} x_1^2 - x_n^2 + y_1^2 - y_n^2 + d_n^2 - d_1^2 \\ ...... \\ x_{n-1}^2 - x_n^2 + y_{n-1}^2 - y_n^2 + d_n^2 - d_{n-1}^2 \end{bmatrix}$$

(7)

The equations are solved using minimum mean square estimate (MMSE) approach: $\hat{\mathbf{x}} = (\mathbf{A}^T\mathbf{A})^{-1}\mathbf{A}^T\mathbf{b}$. In exceptional cases the matrix inverse cannot be computed. In most of the cases we are able to get the position estimation ($\hat{\mathbf{x}}$). We will discuss the probabilistic distribution resulted from this computation process in the following. The order of a matrix is $2*1$ according to the product: $(\mathbf{A}^T_{2\times(n-1)}\mathbf{A}_{(n-1)\times2})^{-1}\mathbf{A}^T_{2\times(n-1)}\mathbf{b}_{(n-1)\times1}$, thus the solution can be represented as a quadratic equation where the coefficients are k_i, k_i' ($i=1, 2, ..., n$), respectively, and the distance vector is $d=(d_1, ..., d_n)^T$:

$$\hat{\mathbf{x}} = \begin{bmatrix} \mathbf{x} \\ \mathbf{y} \end{bmatrix} = \begin{bmatrix} k_0 + k_1 d_1^2 + k_2 d_2^2 + ... + k_n d_n^2 \\ k_0' + k_1' d_1^2 + k_2' d_2^2 + ... + k_n' d_n^2 \end{bmatrix} \tag{8}$$

The ranging error could be considered as a Gaussian random variable based on some research results reported in [13, 14]. The localization precision will be improved when several times of ranging are carried out for an anchor. If $D_1 \sim N(\mu_1, \sigma_1^2)$ and $D_2 \sim N(\mu_2, \sigma_2^2)$ are the two consecutive measurements, the new combination measurement $D \sim N(\mu, \sigma^2)$ is computed as: $\mu = \dfrac{\mu_1\sigma_2^2 + \mu_2\sigma_1^2}{\sigma_1^2 + \sigma_2^2}$, $\sigma = \dfrac{\sigma_1\sigma_2}{\sqrt{\sigma_1^2 + \sigma_2^2}}$. The empirical formula is derived from the process that the combination of estimation (D) is determined with $D = \alpha_1 D_1 + \alpha_2 D_2$, where $\alpha_1 = \dfrac{\sigma_2^2}{\sigma_1^2 + \sigma_2^2}$, and $\alpha_2 = \dfrac{\sigma_1^2}{\sigma_1^2 + \sigma_2^2}$.

The weight of α_1, α_2 is such determined that the larger the variance of a variable, the smaller its weight in the combination formula. The treatment accords with usual experiences. Thus μ and σ can be obtained by the plus rule of independent Gaussian distribution. For many times of ranging results, the formula should be computed cumulatively. Suppose that the final estimation between a node and an anchor is calculated as $d_i \sim N(\mu_i, \sigma_i^2)$, and all d_i variables are normal random ones with the identical deviation, i.e. $d_i \sim N(\mu_i, \sigma^2)$, and $u_i \geq 0$. We can take the following proposition.

Proposition 1: A linear transformation of position estimation of a node in sensor network is distributed by the χ^2 distribution under a certain conditions.

Proof: Consider the transformation of x in the coordinates (x, y) from equation (8):

$$\mathbf{x}' = x - k_0 = k_1 d_1^2 + k_2 d_2^2 + ... + k_n d_n^2 \tag{9}$$

Assume that $\mathbf{K} = \begin{bmatrix} k_1 & 0 & 0\cdots0 \\ 0 & k_2 & 0\cdots0 \\ \cdots\cdots & & \cdots \\ 0 & 0 & 0\cdots k_n \end{bmatrix}$, $\mathbf{d} = (d_1, d_2, ..., d_n)^T$, and $\mathbf{M} = (\mu_1, \mu_2, ..., \mu_n)^T$.

Let $Q = \mathbf{d}^T\mathbf{K}\mathbf{d}/\sigma^2$, then

$$Q = (d_1,...,d_n) \left(\begin{bmatrix} k_1 & 0 & 0\cdots0 \\ 0 & k_2 & 0\cdots0 \\ \cdots\cdots & & \cdots \\ 0 & 0 & 0\cdots k_n \end{bmatrix} \begin{pmatrix} d_1 \\ \cdots \\ d_n \end{pmatrix} \right) / \sigma^2 = (k_1 d_1^2 + k_2 d_2^2 + ... + k_n d_n^2)/\sigma^2 = (x\text{-}k_0)/\sigma^2 \quad (10)$$

If k_i equals zero or one, then $\mathbf{K}$ is an idempotent matrix, i.e. $\mathbf{K}^2 = \mathbf{K}$. According to linear algebra theory in Ref. [15], if $Q = \mathbf{X}^T \mathbf{A} \mathbf{X}/\sigma^2$ exists for an idempotent matrix, then $Q \sim \chi^2(n, \delta)$ where n=rank(A), $\delta = \sigma \mathbf{M}^T \mathbf{A} \sqrt{\mathbf{M}}$. Thus for $Q = d^T \mathbf{K} d/\sigma^2$, there is $Q \sim \chi^2(n', \delta)$ where n'=rank(K) and $\delta = \sigma \mathbf{M}^T \mathbf{K} \sqrt{\mathbf{M}}$, i.e.

$$\frac{x - k_0}{\sigma^2} \sim \chi^2(n', \delta)$$

On the other hand, the similar result of the identical formation can be obtained on the estimate y in the coordinates (x, y). Therefore we have our proposition.

The importance of the above conclusion for sensor network localization is obvious. The bound can be found for central χ^2 distribution through looking for the relative table. Furthermore some perfect statistical rules of χ^2 distribution could be used to guide an error examination. The linear transformation of a node's position estimation is distributed by the χ^2 distribution, if the elements in $\mathbf{K}$ are 0/1. This result helps us to explore some deeper research issues in localization. For example, if there is $k_i=0$, it means that the node's position is independent of this kind of distance estimation, and the existing of d_i^2 is redundant in the computation of equations. In the meaning of physics, it shows that the item of distance measurement could be canceled so as to save energy in that node.

Note that the analysis result from the paper is different from Ref. [6], which considered the values of residuals between distance estimate and position error as Weibull distribution. Statistical experiments and hypotheses test were done for supporting their viewpoint in that paper. The two papers provide different research route and conclusion of probabilistic characteristic in localization.

4   Node Connectivity Analysis

Consider a region for network, denoted by A whose area is S_A. Suppose that N nodes are randomly distributed with the density Φ over the deployed region, and they have equal properties. A subarea (D) has an area of S_D, represented by biases in the Figure 1. Now analyze the number of nodes surrounded by the subarea D. N_1 and N_2 are nodes with R radius range, and their distance is d with C as the intersection.

Proposition 2: Suppose that a sensor network is uniformly distributed with the 2-dimensional node density Φ, if there is a subarea (D) with the area S_D and X nodes inside it, the probabilistic distribution of the random variable X is given by

$$P\{X = m\} = \frac{(\Phi \cdot S_D)^m \cdot e^{-\Phi \cdot S_D}}{m!} \quad (11)$$

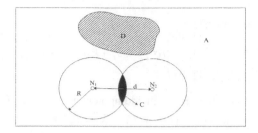

Fig. 1. A region example of sensor network scenario

Proof: The probability p that a node is located within the subarea D is calculated as $p = S_D/S_A$. The probability of m nodes within D is determined by binomial distribution:

$$P\{X = m\} = C_n^m \cdot p^m (1-p)^{n-m} \tag{12}$$

Consequently, the node density is $\Phi = n/S_A$. The above equation is calculated with p and Φ We have

$$P\{X = m\} = C_n^m \cdot (\frac{\Phi \cdot S_D}{n})^m (1 - \frac{\Phi \cdot S_D}{n})^{n-m} \tag{13}$$

$$P\{X = m\} = C_n^m \cdot (\frac{\Phi \cdot S_D}{n})^m (1 - \frac{\Phi \cdot S_D}{n})^{n-m} = \frac{n!}{(n-m)!m!} \cdot \frac{(\Phi \cdot S_D)^m}{n^m} \cdot \frac{(1 - \frac{\Phi \cdot S_D}{n})^n}{(1 - \frac{\Phi \cdot S_D}{n})^m} \tag{14}$$

$$= (1 - \frac{\Phi \cdot S_D}{n})^n \cdot \frac{(\Phi \cdot S_D)^m}{m!} \cdot \frac{n!}{(n-m)!(n - \Phi \cdot S_D)^m}$$

As $n \to +\infty$, the three parts in the above equation can be independently computed:

1) According to the definition of exponent distribution, $\lim\limits_{n \to +\infty} (1 - \frac{\Phi \cdot S_D}{n})^n = e^{-\Phi \cdot S_D}$.

2) The second part is independent of n, $\lim\limits_{n \to +\infty} \frac{(\Phi \cdot S_D)^m}{m!} = \frac{(\Phi \cdot S_D)^m}{m!}$.

3) The third item can be calculated below, we perform a normative deduction:

$$\lim\limits_{n \to +\infty} \frac{n!}{(n-m)!(n - \Phi \cdot S_D)^m} = \lim\limits_{n \to +\infty} \frac{n}{n - \Phi \cdot S_D} \cdot \frac{n-1}{n - \Phi \cdot S_D} \cdots \frac{n-m+1}{n - \Phi \cdot S_D} = 1.$$

Combining the above three equations, we obtain: $P\{X = m\} = e^{-\Phi \cdot S_D} \cdot \frac{(\Phi \cdot S_D)^m}{m!}$.

Therefore, for large value of N tending to infinity, the binomial distribution of the number of nodes converges to the Poisson.

This proposition provides a universal principle and a guide for sensor network localization with an integral process on the basis of mathematical deduction. It can be referenced in many algorithm designs and performance evaluations, although some papers had assumed its legitimacy without the detailed validation process.

The node connectivity corresponds to the number of nodes inside a subarea. We can also derive two corollaries on connectivity from Proposition 2.

Corollary 1: The connectivity of a node and the number of its neighbors is distributed by the Poisson.

Proof: The node connectivity is the number of its neighboring nodes within its wireless sensing range. Considering the idealized case, the sensing range in Figure 1 is within a circle with the radius R. If the number of the total nodes within the circle is m, then the node connectivity is $m-1$ except itself. According to Proposition 2, the connectivity is still distributed by the Poisson.

To discuss the connectivity influence on positioning farther, we conduct several important standards to statistical tests for different connectivity: $P\{X = 0\}$, $P\{X = 2\}$, $P\{X = 3\}$, $P\{X = 4\}$, $P\{X >= 3\}$ and $P\{X >= 4\}$. The calculation method of $P\{X >= 3\}$ and $P\{X >= 4\}$ is given below:

$$P\{X >= m\} = 1 - \sum_{i=0}^{m-1} P\{X = i\} \tag{15}$$

We consider that a network scenario is characterized by the radio range $R=30m$, and the network coverage area is $1km*1km$. The number of the total nodes (n) is uniformly random among [0, 3000], then the node's density $\Phi=n/1000000$, $S_D=900*\pi$. The results in Figure 2 show the probabilities of a node with 0, 2, 3, 4, and more than 3 and 4 neighbors, respectively.

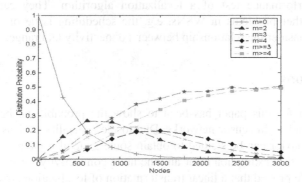

Fig. 2. Distribution probability of several connectivity cases

Figure 2 shows that the node density should not be too low. For example, in this experiment the number of nodes cannot be below 1000, which means that the probability of $m=0$ equals about 7% from the result of the figure. The communications between nodes would not be connected resulted from this condition, as the connectivity is zero and no neighbor exists. When the number of nodes increases, the probability will tend to be stable if the connectivity is larger than either three or four. It is known that the node connectivity is at least three when atomic multilaterations are used for localization [9]. The probability could not be converged to one by increasing solely the number of nodes. The connectivity is always less than three with a certain probability. Therefore we believe that when the localization process is completed only using atomic multilaterations, its positioning coverage is limited and the positions of some nodes may not be estimated. If you expect to get a higher coverage, you have to choose other localization algorithm. Discuss of connectivity also facilitates us identify the performance of localization algorithms.

Corollary 2: If two nodes have an equivalent sensing radius R, the distance between them is d ($0 \leq d \leq 2R$), and the number of nodes (X) inside the radio range intersection of the two nodes, then the probability of variable X is specified with:

$$P\{X = m\} = e^{-\Phi \cdot S_C} \cdot \frac{(\Phi \cdot S_C)^m}{m!} \tag{16}$$

where $S_C = 2R^2 \cos^{-1}(\frac{d}{2R}) - \frac{d}{2}\sqrt{4R^2 - d^2}$.

Proof: Assume that there are two nodes N_1 and N_2 shown in Figure 1. In the idealization condition, they have an equivalent sensing radius R. If $0 \leq d \leq 2R$, the intersection between them is shown by black spot denoted by C. According to geometry knowledge, the area (S_C) of part C can be deduced as the result. Due to the space of the paper, we omit the detailed process in the paper. The correlative conclusion can be made based on the result of Proposition 2.

The probabilistic model of Corollary 1 and 2 will provide instructions for the design and performance test of a localization algorithm. They can be used for reference on other problems in WSNs, e.g. the scheduling issue of on-duty nodes, which has to consider the relationship between connectivity and range.

5   Conclusions

The motivation for this paper has been to show the probabilistic behavior for the localization problem in sensor networks. Due to the speciality of sensor network, its localization behavior can be studied to obtain some general principles by probability theory. The position estimation error and the node connectivity issues were analyzed in the paper. We proved that a linear transformation of localization error is distributed by the χ^2 distribution. The number of nodes in a deployed area and node connectivity is distributed by the Poisson, if a sensor network is configured in a uniform fashion over the whole field. Some connectivity requirements should be met to accomplish successfully localization according to the result of simulation experiments. Understanding of localization characteristics is of importance while implementing localization process and evaluating localization methods.

References

1. J. Hightower and G. Borriello, "Location Systems for Ubiquitous Computing," *IEEE Computer*, vol. 34, pp. 57-66, 2001.
2. M. Tubaishat and S. Madria, "Sensor networks: an overview," *IEEE Potentials*, pp. 20-23, APRIL/MAY 2003.
3. I. F. Akyildiz, W. Su, Y. Sankarasubramaniam, and E. Cayirci, "Wireless sensor networks: a survey," *Computer Networks*, vol. 38, pp. 393-422, 2002.
4. K. Langendoen and N. Reijers, "Distributed localization in wireless sensor networks: a quantitative comparison," *Computer Networks*, vol. 43, pp. 499-518, nov. 2003.
5. N. Patwari, A. O. H. III, M. Perkins, N. S. Correal, and R. J. O'Dea, "Relative Location Estimation in Wireless Sensor Networks," *IEEE Transactions On Signal Processing*, vol. 51, pp. 2137-2148, 2003.
6. S. Slijepcevic, S. Megerian, and M. Potkonjak, "Characterization of Location Error in Wireless Sensor Networks: Analysis and Applications," *Second International Workshop Information Processing in Sensor Networks (IPSN03)*, Palo Alto, CA, USA, 2003.
7. A. Savvides, W. Garber, S. Adlakha, R. Moses, and M. B. Srivastava, "On the Error Characteristics of Multihop Node Localization in Ad-Hoc Sensor Networks," *Proceedings of the 2nd International Workshop on Information Processing in Sensor Networks (IPSN03)*, PARC Palo Alto, 2003.
8. J. Zangl and J. Hagenauer, "Large Ad-Hoc Sensor Networks with Position Estimation," *Proc. of the 10th Aachen Symposium on Signal Theory*, Aachen, Germany, 2001.
9. A. Savvides, C. Han, and M. B. Strivastava, "Dynamic Fine-Grained Localization in AdHoc Networks of Sensors," *International Conference on Mobile Computing and Networking (MobiCom) 2001*, Rome, Italy, July 2001.
10. P. Biswas and Y. Ye, "Semidefinite Programming for Ad Hoc Wireless Sensor Network Localization," *Proceedings of the third international symposium on Information processing in sensor networks*, Berkeley, California, USA, 2004.
11. A. Man-Cho So and Y. Ye, "Theory of Semidefinite Programming for Sensor Network Localization," *SODA05*, 2005.
12. X. Cheng, A. Thaeler, G. Xue, and D. Chen, "TPS: A Time-Based Positioning Scheme for Outdoor Wireless Sensor Networks," *IEEE INFOCOM 2004-The Conference on Compute Communications*, HongKong, 2004.
13. V. Ramadurai and M. L. Sichitiu, "Localization in Wireless Sensor Networks: A Probabilistic Approach," *Proc. of the 2003 International Conference on Wireless Networks (ICWN 2003)*, Las Vegas, NV, June 2003.
14. L. Girod and D. Estrin, "Robust Range Estimation Using Acoustic and Multimodal Sensing," *IEEE/RSJ International Conference on Intelligent Robots and Systems (IROS 2001)*, Maui, Hawaii, 2001.
15. G. Strang, *Linear Algebra and its Applications*, Third edition: Harcourt College, 1988.

Hybrid Authentication and Key Management Scheme for WSANs

Xiaomei Cao[1], Maolin Huang[2], Yuequan Chen[1], and Guihai Chen[1]

[1] National Laboratory of Novel Software Technology,
Nanjing University, 210093, China
xmcao@dislab.nju.edu.cn
[2] Faculty of Information Technology University of Technology,
Sydney Broadway NSW 2007, Australia

Abstract. Wireless Sensor and Actor Networks (WSANs) consist of three types of nodes with different capabilities and functions. Because of these heterogeneities, current network security mechanisms would be hard to satisfy the security/cost requirements of all types of nodes. In this paper, we propose an integrated security approach, called Hybrid Security Scheme (HSS). It splits a WSAN into two layers, the sink-actor layer and the actor-sensor layer, according to nodes' functionalities and capacities. Different security mechanisms are provided to achieve the security services at corresponding levels. Furthermore, an adaptive switching mechanism is provided to satisfy the dynamic topology of network, and several methods are also used to reduce the system costs.

1 Introduction

WSANs have been proposed by Akyildiz and Kasimoglu in 2004 [1]. In WSANs, sensors gather information about the physical world, while actors make decisions and then perform appropriate actions upon the environment. Therefore, WSANs can not only monitor the physical events occurred in the sensing field, but also react to the events in real-time. These capabilities give WSANs a great practical value in many real-world applications. However, the security issues, which are actually even more crucial than wireless sensor network(WSN), have not been exploited in WSANs.

Many security protocols have been proposed for mobile ad hoc networks (MANETs) [6, 9, 10], and wireless sensor networks(WSNs) [2, 3, 4, 12]. Considering both the limitation of device and the complexity of encryption algorithm, most security protocols of MANETs use asymmetric encryption approach or mix-key encryption approach, while most security protocols of WSNs are based on symmetric encryption approach [5]. However, due to the diversity and heterogeneity of WSANs, these existing protocols are not suitable for WSANs [1]. Therefore, in this paper, we propose a new Hybrid Security Scheme (HSS), especially for its entity authentication and key management. The major contributions are summarized as follows:

G. Chen et al. (Eds.): ISPA Workshops 2005, LNCS 3759, pp. 454–465, 2005.

a) Based on node functionalities and capacities, a new integrated security approach, called Hybrid Security Scheme (HSS) is proposed. HSS splits the WSAN into two layers, the sink-actor layer and the actor-sensor layer, where each layer provides different security services.
b) According to the dynamic feature of WSANs, a mechanism is designed to allow a quick and smooth swapping between the centralized key management and the decentralized key management.
c) Due to threats during the key management process, secret key refresh, as well as the update and the revocation of certificates are designed based on the requirements and capacity of particular nodes.

The remainder of the paper is organized as follows: Section 2 reviews some background knowledge and main features of WSANs, and some related work. Scheme statements are presented in section 3. Section 4 describes the authentication and key management in the sink-actor layer. Section 5 describes the authentication and key management in the actor-sensor layer. In Section 6, we give the analysis and evaluation of the hybrid scheme with respect to the security and cost efficiency measurements. Finally, conclusion is given and the future work is also pointed out in section 7.

2   Background

2.1   The Physical Structure and Characteristics of WSANs

There are three types of nodes in a WSAN, including sinks, actors and sensors, with different distribution densities and different capacities in terms of battery, computation, storage, and communication capabilities. Figure 1 illustrates the physical architecture of WSANs. The major characteristics of a WSAN network can be presented as follows:

a) *Differences among nodes of various types*: The main differences between WSANs and WSNs are clear distinctions among nodes of various types. Particularly, these can be described in two aspects as follows: In WSANs, the number of sink, actors and sensors in WSAN increases significantly from small to large. However, the capacities and cost of these three different kinds of nodes decrease accordingly. On the other hand, in WSANs, the effects and scopes of functions performed by various types of nodes decrease in the order of sink, actors and then sensors.Obviously, higher level security services should be provided to those nodes which take higher responsibility and perform more powerful functionalities.
b) *The dynamic characteristic of network topology*: There are two issues in the dynamic feature of WSAN's topology. First, when certain conditions occur, most of nodes including sinks, actors and even sensors can move their positions in specific areas. For example, there are several types of common actors described in [1]. These actors, such as smart Robots, can move quickly and smoothly. Second, the nodes can be added in or moved out dynamically.

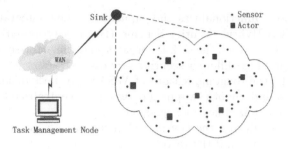

Fig. 1. The architecture of WSANs

2.2   Related Work

Distributed CA scheme [9, 10] use a (k, n) threshold scheme to distribute the service of CA to some or all nodes in MANETs. Each of these nodes is capable of generating a partial certificate using their share of the certificate signing key SK_{CA}, but only by combining k such partial certificates can a valid certificate be obtained. Hubaux et al. [6] propose a peer-to-peer authentication protocol based on public-key certificates. Both distributed CA scheme and certificate repository scheme are based on asymmetric encryption and thus require that all nodes are capable of performing the necessary computations, which may not be feasible for energy-limited sensor nodes.

Perrig et al. proposed the SPINS scheme [12], which is a security architecture specifically designed for WSNs. In SPINS, each sensor node shares a secret key with the base station. The drawback of this architecture is that the base station is responsible for managing keys of each sensor, which reduces the scalability and self-organizing ability of the sensor networks. A solution called selective key distribution scheme is proposed in [2, 4] to save energy consumption in WSNs. It relies on probabilistic key sharing among the nodes of a random graph and uses a simple shared-key discovery protocol for key distribution and re-keying. One drawback of this scheme is that some wireless links may not be keyed and thus a node may need to use a multi-link path to communicate with one of its neighbor nodes. More recently, Dutertre et al. proposed a lightweight protocol [3] that achieves the authentication and key management through the leverage of the initial trust in WSNs. However, since each sensor should generate and then store pairwise keys shared with all its neighbors immediately after deployed, the communication and storage cost are huge.

3   Scheme Statement

3.1   Assumption

HSS is based on some assumptions. First, before all nodes are deployed into the network, the initial keys and certificates are already pre-distributed by the off-line Trusted Third Party (TTP). Then, actors can move freely within part of the entire monitoring region, while the sensors are stable once they are deployed. Finally, the sink and the actors in network have a certain degree of capacity for intrusion detection. They can monitor and perceive the invasions in the given sub-regions.

3.2   Overview of HSS

To accommodate the differences of nodes and provide efficient and flexible security services, HSS splits the WSAN network into two layers: sink-actor layer and actor-sensor layer. And it includes an integrated cryptography mechanism and a combined key management method:

a) *An integrated cryptography mechanism*: In sink-actor layer, a mix-key cryptography mechanism is used for entity authentication and key management. In actor-sensor layer, on the other hand, HSS employs the ordinary symmetric encryption scheme. A light-weight key management method is also used in this layer to reduce the number of keys stored in sensor nodes and simplify the process of key update.

b) *A combined key management method*: In sink-actor layer both the centralized and the distributed key management methods are available for use. At any given time the choice of a specific method is depends on the existence of sink nodes. HSS also provides mechanisms which can collaborate with these two methods by smooth switch. In actor-sensor layer, a centralized key management approach in each local region let each actor manage keys of all nodes in its sub-region. If one actor is removed or disabled, another actor will be coordinated to take the responsibility of managing keys in that sub-region.

3.3   Notations

The notations that are frequently used in the paper are summarized in Table 1.

4   Authentication and Key Management in Sink-Actor Layer

HSS uses mix-key cryptography mechanism in sink-actor layer. It includes pre-distribution, revocation, verification and refresh of certificates, as well as the generation of session keys.

4.1   Pre-distribution of Keys and Certificates

In sink-actor layer, each actor A is pre-distributed with PK_A, SK_A, $CERT_A$ and PK_{CA} by an off-line TTP. The certificate of node A can be expressed as: $CERT_A = E_{SK_{CA}}[A \| PK_A \| T_{sign} \| T_{expire}]$, where T_{sign} is the publish time

Table 1. Notation List

Notation	Meaning
A, B, . . .	Label of nodes
$M1\|M2$	Message that combines $M1$ and $M2$
$A \to B : M$	A send a message M to B
$CERT_A$	A's public key certificate
K_{AB}, K_s	Key that shared by A and B, or by several nodes
PK_A, SK_A	A's public key and private key
N_A, N_B	Nonce produced by A, B
$F(K_{OLD})$	One way hash functionused for updating keys
$H(M)$	Hash function, return digest of the message M
$E_{Kx}[M]/D_{Kx}[M]$	Use secret key K_x to encrypt and decrypt message M

of this certificate, and T_{expire} is the expiration time of this certificate. Each certificate has the same period of validity, i.e, $T_{expire} - T_{sign}$. The sink, on the other hand, is pre-distributed with $PK_{CA}, SK_{CA}, CERT_{CA}$, as well as a public key binding table, which consists of IDs and public key of all actors in the network.

4.2   Revocation of Certificates

The certificate held by the compromised nodes is revoked upon intrusion detections. HSS adopts the mechanism from [7] for the revocation of certificates. Practically, each actor maintains a certificate revocation list (CRL) to record the revoked certificates respectively. If one actor A perceives a wrong behavior taken by actor B, it will label B as a suspect actor and then flood an accusation about B to the network. When another actor C in the network receives this accusation, it will first check its CRL table to see whatever A is a revoked actor. If so, the accusation will be ignored. Otherwise C will also label B as a suspect node. When C has received $k1$ accusations about B, C will put the certificate of B in its CRL. When this certificate reaches its expiration time, C will clear this certificate from its CRL.

Since each certificate is only effective in a limited time period, an accusation only need to be flooded a limited number of hops to prevent the accused nodes to update their certificates before the expiration of certificates. The number of the hops for flooding an accusation is calculated as: $TTL \geq [(T_{expire} - T_{sign}) * 2S_{max}/d]$, where S_{max} is the maximum transmission speed of a actor, and d is the transmission area of a single hop through the wireless medium.

4.3   Authentication of Certificates and Generation of Session Keys

Before a normal communication between any pair of nodes in the sink-actor layer, it is essential for both nodes to authenticate the certificate and obtain the public key of them. Then they will generate and distribute a secret session key for this communication. Here a node could be either a sink or an actor. Suppose that node A want to communicate with node B. A will first pass $CERT_A$ to B. If $CERT_A$ is not appeared in the CRL maintained by B, then B will use PK_{CA} to decrypt the certificate for verifying the validation of certificate. If the decryption of certificate is done successfully and the certificate has not yet expired, then B will obtain PK_A. After that, B will pass $CERT_B$ to A and let A to authenticate it. If the verification is passed, A will then also obtain PK_B.

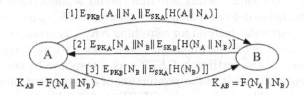

$$[1] E_{PK_B}[A \| N_A \| E_{SK_A}[H(A \| N_A)]]$$

$$[2] E_{PK_A}[N_A \| N_B \| E_{SK_B}[H(N_A \| N_B)]]$$

$$[3] E_{PK_B}[N_B \| E_{SK_A}[H(N_B)]]$$

$$K_{AB} = F(N_A \| N_B) \qquad K_{AB} = F(N_A \| N_B)$$

Fig. 2. Key generation and distribution in sink-actor layer

Figure 2 illustrates the process of generating and distributing session key between nodes A and B. During the message transmission, HSS provides security services in multiple directions based on the powerful capabilities of nodes. Particularly, the confidentiality is provided by public key encryption to prevent message eavesdropping. Authentication and non-repudiation services are provided by digital signature technique to prevent malicious deny. Integrity is provided by message digest for preventing unauthorized modification of message. Finally, freshness is provided the check of the nonce to prevent message replay attacks. When steps 1 to 3 of the message exchange has completed, nodes A and B may obtain the session key K_{AB} through the implementation of one-way hash function F in the local region. Then K_{AB} is used to encrypt data for the consequent transmission. After the transmission between A and B is complete, K_{AB} will be disabled immediately.

4.4 Refresh of Certificates

To refresh certificates, a parameter $T_{refresh}$ is predefined for bounding the valid time of all certificates. That is, $T_{expire} \leq (T_{sign} + T_{refresh})$, a certificate holder must refresh its certificate within $T_{refresh}$.

If the sink node exists, the traditional PKI model [11] is used to refresh actors' certificates. The sink acts as CA. If the old certificate sent by any actor is not in the CRL of the sink, a new certificate signed with SK_{CA} will be generated by the sink.

When an actor could not receive any beacon signal from the sink for a certain period of time, it will assume that the sink has left the network. In these cases, full distributed CA method [9,10] is used to refresh actors' certificates. To achieve distributed certificate refresh, each actor is pre-distributed with a part of CA's secret key $SK_{CA}^i (1 \leq i \leq n, n$ is the total number of actors when first deployed) by TTP. Each of these actors is capable to generate a part of the new certificate using its shared secret key SK_{CA}. The complete certificate can only be obtained by merging k such partial certificates into one.

When actor A receives the signal from the sink again, the method of updating certificates is switched to centralized mechanism. Since in both situations the same keys SK_{CA} and PK_{CA} are used for the verification and signature of certificates, the none-stop switching is achieved.

There are two additional points here that should be mentioned: First, because actors can be added or deleted dynamically, therefore SK_{CA}^i have to be refreshed periodically. A particular method for refreshing SK_{CA}^i is given in [9, 10]. Second, it is possible that an individual malicious node uses a wrong SK_{CA}^i to generate an incorrect part of the certificate $CERT_A$ as a response to node A's request. This could eventually result in the production of a wrong certificate. Therefore, some methods should be used to verify $CERT^i (1 \leq i \leq k)$ generated by k nodes. In [8] some mechanisms for this kind of verifications are described.

5   Key Management in Actor-Sensor Layer

In actor-sensor layer, symmetric encryption is used to implement the entity authentication and secret key management. Each actor is responsible for the centralized management of keys in its assigned sub-region. Based on the mobility feature of actors, it is impossible that one sub-region has no actor for a long time. If an actor is removed or disabled, another actor will be coordinated to take the responsibility of managing keys in that sub-region.

5.1   Authentication and Key Management Between Actor and Sensor

HSS uses a light-weight key management method by adopting the concept of initial trust mentioned in [3], and we modify it technically to reduce the number of keys to be stored in sensor nodes and simplify the process of updating keys. The concept of initial trust is based on the assumption that there is a time delay T_{resist} for capturing a sensor and obtaining the secret key from it. Therefore those sensors and actors which are set up at the same time must be reliable in the time period of T_{resist}.

Authentication and key generation between actor and sensor will occur at two occasions: the bootstrapping phase and the addition of new nodes.

a) *Bootstrapping phase*

Before the bootstrap, all sensors and actors are pre-distributed with an initial secret key K_s^1. This key is used in the initial stage for the entity authentication, and the generation and distribution of keys that are shared between sensors and actors. In the bootstrapping phase, HSS will use K_s^1 to establish shared secret keys between sensors and actor within the time window T, where $T \leq T_{resist}$. Suppose that an actor A has broadcasted its ID and its existence state to all sensors in a given sub-region, and B is a sensor in the sub-region. Figure 3 illustrates the process of generation and distribution of secret key K_{AB} between actor A and sensor B. When a secret key K_{AB} is

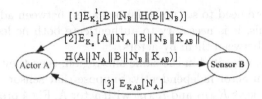

Fig. 3. Key generation and distribution between actor and sensor

generated, the security link between actor A and sensor B is established. The new key K_{AB} will be stored in sensor B, while the actor A maintains a binding table. The binding table contains all the secret keys that are shared by sensors and actor A of a give sub-region.

b) *Addition of new nodes*

If it is necessary, a group of new nodes can be added into the WSAN network. We assume that there is a secret key K_s^i that has been set up to be shared by these added new nodes before deployed, where i indicate the number of that group. Through the establishment of security links, K_s^i will be transferred from task management node to every actor. Each actor will work with the new added sensors in a particular sub-region. They quickly generate shared secret keys in the same way as used in the bootstrapping phase and append these keys and their IDs into the binding table.

There are two additional points need to be mentioned: first since sensors do not have the capability of preventing the release of secret data, when a predefined time window T runs out, sensors will delete secret key K_s^i immediately. Second after time window T expires, a security link between actor A and sink is established, and a copy of the binding table maintained by A has been sent to the sink. Therefore, when a new actor is going to be moved to the same sub-region, it only need to be authenticated and obtain the copy of the binding table from the sink.

Since sensors are unable to prevent the release of confidential data, it is necessary for a sensor to periodically update the secret key which is shared with an actor. HSS sets up a time period T_{update} as the update cycle time. When T_{update} expires, the actor will broadcast an update request to the sensors in the sub-region. The sensors and the actor will use the previous session keys separately as the inputs to implement the one way hash function F and then will use the outputs of F as new session keys, that is, $K_{NEW} = F(K_{OLD})$. After these processes, the sensor will replace the old session key with this new session key. The actor will also update its binding table accordingly, and then establish a security link by sending a copy of its binding table to the sink node for backup purpose.

5.2 Authentication and Key Management Between Sensor and Sensor

In some cases, there need to set up communication between adjacent sensors in WSANs. To do this, it is necessary to authenticate both nodes and generate a shared secret key between them by actors.

If two sensors are located in the same sub-region, then they have established secret keys with an actor independently. Suppose that sensors B1 and B2 have their shared secret keys K_{AB1} and K_{AB2} with actor A, Fig 4 presents the process of generating a session key K_{B1B2} shared between B1 and B2.

If actor A finds out that it does not have a secret key shared with B2 while checking the request sent in step 1, then it means that B2 and B1 are not located in the same sub-region in which a particular actor A manages. To finding out the corresponding actor of B2, actor A will broadcast a request to other actors. This request can be expressed as:

$$A \to * : A||N_A||CERT_A||B2||H(A||N_A||CERT_A||B2)$$

When a particular actor C receives the request, it will first verify A's certificate $CERT_A$. If the certificate is not in CRL and has not yet expired, C authenticates the identity of A and obtains PK_A, then actor C will check its binding table and try to match B2 in the table. If B2 is matched, then C will generate a session key K_{B1B2} which is to be shared between B1 and B2, and send back a reply message to A. The format of reply message can be expressed as:

$$C \to A : [C||N_A||B2||K_{B1B2}||[H(C||N_A||B2||K_{B1B2})]]$$

After that, A and C will encrypt the session key K_{B1B2} by using their secret keys shared with B1 and B2 independently, and send their encrypted session keys to B1 and B2. On the other hand, if $CERT_A$ is illegal or expired, then C ignores the request.

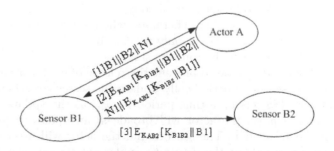

Fig. 4. Key generation and distribution between sensors

6 Security and Performance Analysis

Security and performance are always a trade-offthat is, a higher degree of security service is always based on the higher cost of the system. When there are different types of nodes mixed in the network, the key problem that needs to be addressed in the design of security service is to investigate security requirements required by different nodes and the resources that the nodes can provide. We now analysis the objects and costs for providing security services in different layers of WSAN network:

6.1 Analysis of Security Issues in Sink-Actor Layer

The nodes in sink-actor layer usually possess rich resources and require high degree of security. Therefore, it is necessary to use asymmetric encryption mechanism to generate session keys. This solution can provide general security services, such as confidentiality, integrity, freshness, non-repudiation and authentication. Although a complex asymmetric encryption algorithm RSA is usedin practice it does not affect the speed and the overall process of the encryption since the size of key management messages that need to be processed are relatively small. Furthermore, HSS reduces the computational complexity by restricting the use of digital signature only on the digest of messages, rather than on the original messages.

It is not avoidable that the maintenance of certificates also costs system resources, especially when using a distributed method to update the certificates. The threshold $k1$ for distributed certificate revocation and the threshold k for distributed certificate refresh are critical parameters of the layer. If the attacker manages to capture and compromise $k1/k$ actors before being detected by their neighbors, the attacker can generate false messages from these $k1/k$ compromised actors against intact actors. The result is decided by a temporal competition between the intact community and the compromised but not-yet-revoked actors. There is at least one advantage available to the intact community: the attacker will experience a non-trial delay to compromise the captured devices, and then issue false messages. Adding various tamper resistance mechanisms [13] to wireless devices can further increase the delay, thus minimize the winning chance of the compromised nodes. To obtain a unique security class, HSS sets up a unique value for k1 and k. At the same time, CA can modify the period of validity of certificate, the certificate update cycle time $T_{refresh}$, as well as the value of $k1/k$ based on the current situation of network security (e.g. the percentage of revoked certificates excesses a certain threshold) during the update of certificates.

6.2 Analysis of Security Issues in Actor-Sensor Layer

The majority of nodes in the actor-sensor layer are sensors which possess limited resources. Therefore, how to reduce computational cost spent on security services is a key problem. Since sensors are unable to prevent the release of information, the number of secret keys stored in sensors should be minimized, especially the information that could affect the privacy of other nodes. Finally, since sensors are the nodes with the highest distribution density in the network, the problem of extensibility of the network need to be considered.

In HSS, symmetric encryption mechanism is used as the basis for providing security services in the actor-sensor layer. The main advantage of this approach is the less cost in both the computation and the storage. Each sensor permanently keeps only one secret key shared with the actor. This not only saves the memory space for sensors, but also limits the damage (or lost) caused by the release of data from a node. Besides, when refreshing the shared secret keys, the simple one way hash function is used to calculate these keys locally without requiring any data transmission or data exchange. This also reduces the computational and communication cost. The actor takes the responsibility of generating and maintaining all session keys used by sensors in a given sub-region, whereas the sink only periodically receives the binding table of a sub-region sent from the actor and conducts some adjustments if necessary. This significantly enhances the scalability of the network.

The main problem of updating secret keys is that the intensity of the new key is equal to the old one after the transaction made by the one way hash function. If an attacker obtains the old key as well as the updating function, then the attacker could easily complete the update of keys. Therefore, to provide better quality of security, we may set up an updating cycle time T_{update} which is shorter than T_{resist}. However, it would possibly reduce the performance of a node if the updating of keys is too frequent. Therefore, in HSS key updating strategy, the sink is allowed to adjust the value of T_{update} according to the current security/performance situation of network.

7   Conclusion

In this paper, we propose a new Hybrid Security Scheme (HSS) for WSANs based on WSAN's characteristics, especially for its entity authentication and key management strategy. In the sink-actor layer, where the nodes usually possess rich resources, HSS employs mix-key cryptography. Based on the existence of sink node, either a centralized strategy or a decentralized strategy is used for node authentication and the generation and distribution of keys. In the actor-sensor layer, where the nodes usually possess limited resources, HSS adopts the ordinary symmetric key cryptosystem, which is to implement centralized management of authentications and key management through the actor node assigned to each sub-region. After the analysis of function and performance of the security scheme, it shows that HSS can effectively prevent the active attacks and passive attacks during the process of node authentication and key management. In comparison with other security solutions, HSS has stronger flexibility, adaptability and scalability, and also provides a better foundation for supporting other security services. When multiple sinks are deployed in a WSAN, there will be some new problems, such as coordination among sinks. Thus we will consider HSS in the case of multiple sink nodes in the future work.

Acknowledgement

This work is supported by the China NSF grant, the China Jiangsu Provincial NSF grant (BK2005208) , the China 973 project (2002CB312002) and TRAPOYT award of China Ministry of Education.

References

1. I. F. Akyildiz and I. H. Kasimoglu. Wireless Sensor and Actor Networks: Research Challenges. Ad Hoc Networks Journal (Elsevier) Vol. 2, No 4, pp. 351-367, October 2004.
2. H. Chan, A. Perrig, and D. Song. Random Key Pre-distribution Schemes for Sensor Networks. Proc. of 2003 IEEE Symposium on Research in Security and Privacy, pp. 197-213, May 2003.
3. B. Dutertre, S. Cheung, and J. Levy. Lightweight Key Management in Wireless Sensor Networks by Leveraging Initial Trust. SDL Technical Report SRI-SDL-04-02, April 6, 2004.
4. L. Eschenauer and V.D. Gligor. A key-Management Scheme for Distributed Sensor Networks. CCS-02, Washington, DC,USA, November 2002.
5. F. Hu and N. K. Sharma. Security Considerations in Ad Hoc Sensor Networks. Ad Hoc Networks 3 (2005) 69-89.
6. J.P. Hubaux, L. Buttyan, and S. Capkun. The Quest for Security in Mobile Ad Hoc Networks. Proceedings of the ACM Symposium on Mobile Ad Hoc Networking and Computing (MobiHOC), Long Beach, CA, USA, October 2001.
7. J. Kong, H. Luo, K. Xu, D. Lihui Gu, M. Gerla, and S. Lu. Adaptive Security for Multi-layer Ad-hoc Networks. Special Issue of Wireless Communications and Mobile Computing, Wiley Interscience Press, 2002.
8. J. Kong, P. Zerfos, H. Luo, S. Lu, and L. Zhang. Providing Robust and Ubiquitous Security Support for Mobile Ad-Hoc Networks. IEEE ICNP, 2001.
9. H. Luo and S. Lu. Ubiquitous and Robust Authentication Services for Ad Hoc Wireless Networks. Technical Report 200030, UCLA Computer Science Department, 2000.
10. H. Luo, P. Zerfos, J. Kong, S. Lu, and L. Zhang. Self-Securing Ad Hoc Wireless Networks. Seventh IEEE Symposium on Computers and Communications (ISCC '02), 2002.
11. R. Perlman. An Overview of PKI Trust Models. IEEE Network, 13(6):38-43, 1999.
12. A. Perrig, R. Szewczyk, V. Wen, D. Culler, and J. D. Tygar. SPINS: Security protocols for sensor networks. MobiCom 2001, pp. 189-199 July 2001.
13. E. Suh, D. Clarke, B. Gassend, M. van Dijk, and S. Devadas. AEGIS: Architecture for Tamper-Evident and Tamper-Resistant Processing, 17th International Conference on Supercomputing(ICS '03), 2003.

Storage-Optimal Key Sharing with Authentication in Sensor Networks

Jian Wang[1], Z.Y. Xia[1], Lein Harn[2], and Guihai Chen[3]

[1] Nanjing University of Aeronautics and Astronautics, China
Wangjian@nuaa.edu.cn
[2] University of Missouri, Kansas City, USA
[3] State Key Lab of Novel Software Technology, Nanjing University, China

Abstract. Wireless Sensor Networks are edging closer to widespread feasibility with recent research showing promising results in developing and adapting new mechanisms to suit their environment. Secure communication between these distributed wireless devices is a desired characteristic, especially in scenarios where these sensors will be exploited for military and other mission-critical operations. This paper highlights some of the research challenges for extending secure communications over these resource-constrained devices and points out why current protocols do not scale well in this unique application realm. Then, a storage-optimal key sharing scheme with authentication is proposed in this paper. This scheme requires each sensor node to hold one secret key and hash functions only, and is optimal in terms of memory consumption which is more rigorous constraint factor than computation and communication resources limit.

1 Introduction

Recent advances in electronic and computer technologies have paved the way for the proliferation of wireless sensor networks (WSNs). Sensor networks usually consist of a large number of ultra-small autonomous devices. Each device, called a sensor node, is battery powered and equipped with integrated sensors, data processing capabilities, and short-range radio communications. In typical application scenarios, sensor nodes are spread randomly over the terrain under scrutiny so as to collect sensing data. Examples of sensor network projects include SmartDust [1] and WINS.

Sensor networks are being deployed for a wide variety of applications [2], including military sensing and tracking, environment monitoring, patient monitoring and tracking, smart environments, etc. When sensor networks are deployed in a hostile environment, security becomes extremely important, as these networks are prone to different types of malicious attacks. For example, an adversary can easily listen to the traffic, impersonate one of the network nodes, or intentionally inject misleading information to other nodes, and even severe, make DoS attacks, e.g. exhausting the battery power by continuously broadcasting meaningless messages.Additionally, adversary can capture the nodes to get secret information stored in them, including secret keys. Due to the fact that communication among sensors is via wireless links,

G. Chen et al. (Eds.): ISPA Workshops 2005, LNCS 3759, pp. 466–474, 2005.
© Springer-Verlag Berlin Heidelberg 2005

sensor networks are highly vulnerable to security attacks [3,4,5]. To provide security, communication should be encrypted and authenticated. The task of securing WSNs is an open research problem. A solution must strike a tradeoff between the security provided and the consumption of energy, computing and communication resources in the nodes.

Security is an important issue for wireless sensor networks. Similar to the wired networks, there are five main attributes of security for a wireless sensor network, i.e. confidentiality, integrity, authentication, non-repudiation and availability. Confidentiality ensures that information is secretly passed only to authorized members. Integrity is to guarantee that a message is transferred without being corrupted. Authentication is to enable a node to identify the peer node it is communicating with, and is thus a useful property to detect isolated or compromised nodes. Non-repudiation is to ensure that a node cannot deny having sent/received the message. Availability is to ensure that the network services survive despite denial of service attacks which could be invoked at any level of the sensor network, e.g., jamming the frequency to interfere with communication. Key management service could be certainly a target of attack of this kind too.

The key problem of securing WSNs is how to bootstrap secure communications between sensor nodes, i.e. to set up secret pair-wise keys between communicating nodes in the communication range. This problem is known as the *key agreement* or *key sharing* problem, which has been widely studied in general network environments. There are three types of general key agreement schemes: trusted-server schemes, public-key schemes, and key pre-distribution schemes. *Trusted-server* schemes depend on a trusted server for key agreement between nodes; an example is Kerberos. This type of scheme is not suitable for sensor networks because this kind of schemes can't scale well and this central server will also be an attacking target and thus a point of failure. *Public-key* schemes depend on asymmetric cryptography and require some sort of public-key infrastructure to be in place; an example of such schemes is an authenticated key agreement protocol using public-key certificates. However, as pointed out by Perrig, et al.[6], the limited computation and energy resources of sensor nodes often make it undesirable to use public-key algorithms in WSNs. A third way to establish keys pair-wise is via *Key Pre-Distribution* (KPD), where (secret) key information is distributed to all sensor nodes prior to deployment. Such schemes seem most appropriate for WSNs.

Sensor network is usually constrained in memory, computation and communication resources. Thus, key sharing approaches are always measured by overloads of memory, computation and communication. And, operations of communication are more consuming than that of computation. Therefore, most schemes by now have been focusing on reducing the round number of communication. In fact, communication is usually constrained by one-hop so that the overhead of communication is relatively moderate. Memory resources are more rigorous constrained factor, because all employed keys, programs, sensing data, and etc are compulsorily reserved altogether in the memory which is definitely only some hundreds of kilobyte in most cases. Thus, this paper intends to advance a storage-optimal authenticated key sharing scheme.

1.1 Our Main Contribution

1. Highlight definitely the contradiction between connectivity and resilience in KPD schemes. This shows the proposed KPD schemes improper to be applied in real scenario.
2. Propose a novel storage-optimal authenticated key sharing scheme. Each node need to hold a private key and two one-way hash functions only and additionally it can pair-wisely authenticate with other node.

1.2 Structure of This Paper

This paper is organized as following. Key pre-distribution is narrated and analyzed in section 2, and at the same time the contradiction between connectivity and robustness is highlighted there. Section 3 gives some unique characteristics of wireless sensor network and some assumptions employed later. We describe the proposed scheme, and analyze its security and performance in section 4 and 5 respectively. Section 6 discusses previously proposed related works. And finally, section 7 concludes this paper.

2 Key Pre-Distribution (KPD)

Up to now, there are two kinds of KPDs employed in the scenarios of sensor networks, i.e. deterministic KPDs [7,8] and random KPDs[9,10,11,12]. Deterministic KPDs can certainly guarantee the connectivity and the exclusive key pairing, but it requires each node keep more keys (usually $O(\sqrt{N})$, N is the number of sensor nodes in a sensor network). On the contrary, random KPDs often emplys smaller key ring assigned to each sensor node compared with deterministic KPDs, but it only assures connectivity in high probability, and even worse, it makes the exclusive key pairing to be a difficult and exhaustive task.

In order to enhance the resistance against node capture in the some degree of connectivity, some types of multi-space schemes are proposed, e.g. Blom's key pre-distribution based schemes, secret-sharing based schemes and hash-chain based schemes. In fact, they gain higher resilience with the moderate cost of memory.

KPD is some sort of resource consumption and security tradeoff. And more public message transmitted which means more information it discloses, more prone to node-capture it is. For example, with disclosed information (e.g. key id), attacker can adaptively choose a node which holds the most unknown keys as next target. In order to avoid uncovering the key ids, only node ids are exchanged in some schemes (e.g. [11]), which necessitates some mapping from node id to key ids it holds so that nodes can know the key ids of other node with its id. The mapping undoubtedly expense extra memory, and if it is known by attacker, he then still is capable to choose the most valuable target.

In addition, the contradiction between connectivity and resilience exists in the random KPDs exists. High connectivity usually requires more keys assigned to each node. Attacker can get more keys upon success in compromising node each time if we assume the attacker is smart enough to choose the most valuable target to attack. In another extreme, each node keeps few keys so that attacker is required to compromise more significant number of nodes before he can successfully destroy whole network. But, fewer key in each node means lower probability of connectivity.

3 Unique Characteristics of Wireless Sensor Network and Some Assumptions

WSNs had attracted much more attentions and been extensively studied recently. WSNs own some unique characteristics as followings

1. Power constraint. Usually, batteries which usually can not be recharged are utilized to provide power for sensor nodes after sensor networks are deployed.
2. Low volume of computation, communication, and memory capability. Sensor network is comprised of large quantities of sensor nodes, and thus sensor node should be in low cost. In a Wireless Sensor Network (WSN for short), individual sensor nodes, or sensors, are constrained in energy, computing, and communication capabilities. Typical sensor node contains a 4MHz CPU, 200kByte RAM, 64kByte ROM, and 19.2kbps wireless transmitter.
3. No topology infrastructure is known prior to deploy. A large amount of sensor nodes are randomly spread in a sensed region. Thus, it is difficult to determine a node's neighborhood before deployment. Typically sensors are mass-produced anonymous commodity devices that are initially unaware of their location. Once deployed, sensors should self-organize into a network that works unattended.
4. Vulnerability. Due to the fact that individual sensor nodes are anonymous and that communication among sensors is via wireless links, sensor networks are highly vulnerable to security attacks [4,7,12,13]. Communications between sensor nodes is easily intercepted by adversary. Attacker can also intentionally modify or inject some false data into the message between sensor nodes to mislead the user who uses the sensor network. And furthermore sensor node is also vulnerable to node capture. Due to cost constraint, sensor node usually don't have secure hardware, such as tamper resistant part, thus secret information embedded in captured sensor node may be obtained by attacker. Moreover, adversary can launch a DoS (Denial of Sevices) attack by sending a lot of meaningless packet or jamming the frequency to interfere with communication.

In order to implement key sharing with authentication, we also give some assumptions as

1. No tamper-resistance. Due to cost limit, sensor node doesn't possess tamper-resistance capability, which means secret information embedded in captured sensor node may be obtained by attacker.
2. An attacker can intercept those communications in its transmission range only, but not whole communication.
3. Sensor node has the same range of wireless transmission.
4. A secure window exists in the phase of initial deployment. During such window, sensor node can securely transmit small volume of message in the plaintext, even if it is very short.

4 Proposed Scheme

4.1 Notations

$H(x)$ One-way hash function
$H^i(x)$ Run i times of hash function
$E(k,m)$ Secure encryption function which means to encrypt message m with key k.
$f(k_1,k_2)$ One-way hash function

4.2 Our Proposal

Our scheme is comprised of 3 phases sequentially, i.e. initialization pre-deployment phase, key sharing phase, and authentication phase, described briefly in the following.

Initialization pre-deployment phase
Each node is assigned a private key. And a one way hash function, H, is chosen and public. In addition, choose another one way hash function f which can guarantee $f\left(k_i, H^2\left(k_j\right)\right) = f\left(k_j, H^2\left(k_i\right)\right)$, $H^2(k)$ means invoking 2 times of H in k.

Key sharing phase
After deployment, each node firstly broadcast $H^2(k_i)$ (k_i is its private key) as its public key. And after receiving the public key of its neighbor (one hop), say j, node i can compute a shared key k_{ij} which is used to securely communicate with node j as

$k_{ij} = f\left(k_i, H^2\left(k_j\right)\right)$. Node j can compute the sharing key k_{ij} in the same way.

Authentication phase
After computing k_{ij}, node i transmits authentication message $E\left(k_{ij}, H\left(k_i\right)\right)$ to node j.
After receiving authentication message from i, node j can decrypt it with k_{ij} to get h'. Then, it can check if $H^2(k_i)=H(h')$. If so, it means $H^2(k_i)$ comes from node i that possesses k_i. Node i can check the authenticity of $H^2\left(k_j\right)$ in the same way.

4.3 Considering the Function f and H

Function, H, must be one-way. Otherwise, adversary can easily get the secret key k_i of a node with intercepting $H^2\left(k_i\right)$. And, function, f, must also be one-way. Otherwise, node j can easily know the secret key k_i of another neighbor node i one-hop away with known sharing key between them. In addition, they must meet the special property, i.e. $f\left(k_i, H^2\left(k_j\right)\right) = f\left(k_j, H^2\left(k_i\right)\right)$. Bilinear mapping can be employed to construct such functions, described as follows.

Suppose a $GF(p)$ (p is a prime) finite field. Suppose G_1 is a cyclic group of $GF(p)$ with primitive element g and order $p-1$. And, suppose $k \in G_1$, then $k = g^t \bmod p$

$(t \neq 0)$ and define $H(k) = k^m = g^{tm} \bmod p \in G_1$, here $m \neq 0$ is a predefined parameter.

Define f a bilinear mapping $f: G_1 \times G_1 \rightarrow G_2$ (G_2 is also a multiplicative group) as,

$$f(g_1, g_2^a) = f(g_1, g_2)^a = f(g_1^a, g_2), \quad g_1, g_2 \in G_1$$

If $\quad k_i = g^{t_i} \bmod p \in G_1 \quad$ and $\quad k_j = g^{t_j} \bmod p \in G_1 \quad$, $\quad$ then

$H^2(k_i) = g^{2t_i m} \bmod p$ and $H^2(k_j) = g^{2t_j m} \bmod p$. We have

$$f(k_i, H^2(k_j)) = f(g^{t_i}, g^{2t_j m}) = f(g, g)^{2t_i t_j m}$$

$$f(k_j, H^2(k_i)) = f(g^{t_j}, g^{2t_i m}) = f(g, g)^{2t_i t_j m}$$

$$\therefore f(k_i, H^2(k_j)) = f(k_j, H^2(k_i))$$

But we know such Bilinear mapping with exponent is exhaustive to compute. If G_1 and G_2 are defined in elliptic curve, the overhead of computation may decrease some orders of magnitude with reserving similar security.

$$k_i = t_i \cdot g \in G_1, \quad k_j = t_j \cdot g \in G_1$$

$$H^2(k_i) = 2t_i m \cdot g, \quad H^2(k_j) = 2t_j m \cdot g$$

$$f(k_i, H^2(k_j)) = f(t_i \cdot g, 2t_j m \cdot g) = f(g, g)^{2t_i t_j m}$$

$$f(k_j, H^2(k_i)) = f(t_j \cdot g, 2t_i m \cdot g) = f(g, g)^{2t_i t_j m}$$

$$\therefore f(k_i, H^2(k_j)) = f(k_j, H^2(k_i))$$

Bilinear mapping based on elliptic curve is still computationally extensive relative to sensor network. Therefore, finding low-computation function f is still future work.

5   Security and Performance Analyses

5.1 Security Analysis

Secrecy of shared key
Due to the one-wayness of function H, attacker can not know k_j with knowing $H^2(k_j)$ transmitted from node j. Furthermore, attacker can not derive the sharing key $k_{ij} = f(k_i, H^2(k_j))$ without knowing the secret key k_i, due to the one-wayness of function f.

Resilience to node capture
Each node keeps one secret key and publishes its hash value of the key, and these secret keys are completely independent. Any node can impossibly know secret keys of nodes owing to one-wayness of function H. Thus, even a node is compromised and its secret key is known by attacker, secret keys of other nodes still keep secret. Furthermore, even attacker successfully captures many nodes, survival can still work securely. Our scheme can effectively deter the avalanche effect most proposed KPDs confront.

Resilience to Denial of Service (DoS) attacks
Our scheme can resist DoS attacks by authenticating each other. An attacker can record $H^2(k_j)$ legitimate node sent and then later broadcasts this fake value of $H^2(k_j)$ (in fact, he doesn't hold the corresponding secret key k_j), authenticating phase can find such attacker so as to avoid further-processing.

Resistance to impersonating
Attacker can probably impersonate as a fake node by producing a secret key k itself and sending $H^2(k_j)$ publicly. In order to mitigate such risk, it is a feasible way to tightly bind secret key of sensor node with sensor node id. For example, in the pre-deployment phase, the base station can firstly choose randomly secret key and then invoke the predetermined one-way hash function g (determined by the base station) on the 2-time hash value of the key to generate the corresponding node ID, and then assign a pair (k_i, id_i) to a node. During deployed, node can check each other if opponent is a fake node through validating if $g\left[H^2(k_i)\right] = id_i$.

5.2 Performance

In our scheme, each node needs only keep one secret key and two one-way hash functions H and f and possibly an extra one-way function to combine node id with its secret key, which is small and independent with network scale. And only two rounds of communication are needs for key sharing and authenticating, one for sharing and one for authenticating, which is still moderate and acceptable. And each node need invoking two times of one-way hash function H and one times of one-way hash function to produce a shared key between any two nodes, and invoking one symmetric encryption for authentication, which is reasonable.

Compared with deterministic KPDs ($O(\sqrt{n})$ storage requirement in each node, (n is the network scale)[8,9,10], our scheme outperforms in the storage requirement. Moreover, our scheme has advantageous over random KPDs [11,12,13] in that it can assure the connectivity with less storage.

In addition, our scheme doesn't need the exclusive testing, which is essential in many random KPD schemes and is an exhausted task. With reasonable resource-consumption, our scheme can guarantee both connectivity and resilience.

6 Related Works

If it is known which nodes will be in the same neighborhood prior to deployment, pair-wise keys can be established between these nodes (and only these nodes) *a priori*. However, most sensor network deployments are random; thus, such *a priori* knowledge about the topology of the network does not exist. A number of key pre-distribution schemes do not rely on prior knowledge of the network topology. A naive solution is to let all nodes store an identical *master* secret key. Any pair of nodes can use this master secret key to securely establish a new pair-wise key. However, this scheme does not exhibit desirable network resilience: if a single node is compromised, the security of the entire sensor network is compromised. Some existing studies suggest storing the master key in tamper-resistant hardware to reduce the risk, but this increases the cost and energy consumption of each sensor. Furthermore, tamper-resistant hardware might not always be safe.

At the other extreme, one might consider a key pre-distribution scheme in which each sensor stores $N-1$ keys, each of which is known to only one other sensor node (here, we let N denote the total number of nodes in the network). This scheme guarantees perfect resilience because any number of compromised nodes does not affect the security of any *un*compromised pairs of nodes. Unfortunately, this scheme is impractical for sensors with an extremely limited amount of memory because N could be large. Moreover, adding new nodes to a pre-existing sensor network is difficult when employing this scheme because the existing nodes do not have the new nodes' keys.

Recently, two key pre-distribution schemes suited for sensor networks have been proposed. Eschenauer and Gligor [13] proposed a random key pre-distribution scheme which may be summarized as follows: before deployment, each sensor node is assigned a random subset of keys from a large key pool; to agree on a key for communication, two nodes find a common key (if any) within their subsets and use that key as their shared secret key. Now, the existence of a shared key between a particular pair of nodes is not certain but is instead guaranteed only with some probability (which can be tuned by adjusting the parameters of the scheme).

Based on this scheme, Chan, Perrig, and Song [12] proposed a generalized "q-composite" scheme which improves the resilience of the network (for the same amount of key storage) and requires an attacker to compromise many more nodes in order to compromise any additional communication. The difference between this scheme and the previous scheme is that the q-composite scheme requires two nodes to find q (with $q > 1$) keys in common before deriving a shared key and establishing a secure communication link. It is shown that, by increasing the value of q, network resilience against node capture is improved for certain ranges of other parameters [12].

J. Wu and R. Wei [10] indicate the probabilistic method [9] can not yield practical CFF (Cover-free family) for key distribution. At the same time, among all known methods, this probabilistic construction provides the best sufficient conditions to ensure the existence of a CFF. That means based on the currently known methods, we can not construct or prove the existence of CFF that can provide satisfactory performance for ad hoc network key distribution.

7 Conclusion

Sensor network has been attracting much more concerns. Security is of sensor network very important component in many cases, especially when sensor network is employed in hostile environment. Key sharing, also known as bootstrapping, is a key component which is the base what other security functionalities will be implemented on. This paper surveys proposed Key Pre-distribution (KPD) schemes to be employed in the sensor network, and indicates the contradiction between connectivity and resilience to node-capture. A new scheme is proposed in this paper, which can guarantee both connectivity and resilience under the low consumption of memory, computation and communication. Further works include finding low-consuming function f which owns this special property, i.e. $f(k_i, H^2(k_j)) = f(k_j, H^2(k_i))$. In addition, we will try to find some one-way function to map a secret key to corresponding node id so as to validate the authenticity of secret key.

References

1. Warneke M., Last B., Leibowitz, and K. Pister, SmartDust: communicating with a cubic-millimeter computer, *IEEE Computer*, vol. 34, no. 1, January 2001.
2. I. Akyildiz, W. Su, Y. Sankarasubramanian, and E. Cayirci, Wireless sensor networks: A survey, *Computer Networks*, Elsevier Science, vol. 38, no.4, 2002.
3. D. Carman, P. Kruus, and B. Matt, "Constraints and Approaches for Distributed Sensor Networks Security," NAI Technical Report #00-010, Sep. 2000.
4. G. Jolly, M. Kuşçu, and P. Kokate, "A Hierarchical Key Management Method for Low-Energy Wireless Sensor Networks ", UMBC Online Document, Nov. 2002.
5. A. Wadaa, S. Olariu, L. Wilson, K. Jones, and Q. Xu, "On Training Wireless Sensor Networks," Proc. 3-rd International Workshop on Wireless, Mobile and Ad Hoc Networks, Nice, France, April 2003.
6. A. Perrig, J. Stankovic, and D. Wagner, "Security in Wireless Sensor Networks," Communications of the ACM, vol. 47, no. 6, pp. 53–57, June 2004.
7. M. Eltoweissy, H. Heydari, L. Morales, and H. Sudborough, "Combinatorial Optimization for Key Management in Secure Multicast Environments," Journal of Network and System Management, Kluwer Pobs, 2004.
8. S. A. Camtepe, B. Yener, Combinatorial Design of Key Distribution Mechanisms for Wireless Sensor Networks, ESORICS 2004: 293-308.
9. Aldar C-F. Chan, Distributed symmetric key management for mobile ad hoc networks, IEEE INFOCOM 2004.
10. J. Wu and R. Wei, Comments on "Distributed Symmetric Key Management for Mobile Ad hoc Networks" from INFOCOM 2004, eprint.iacr.org/2005/008.pdf
11. M. Ramkumar, N. Memon, HARPS-Hashed Random Preloaded Subset Key Distribution, Cryptology ePrint Archive, Report 2003/170, 2003, http://eprint.iacr.org/2003/170.
12. H. Chan, A. Perrig, and D. Song, "Random Key Pre-distribution Schemes for Sensor Networks," Proceedings of IEEE 2003 Symposium on Security and Privacy, Berkeley, CA, May 2003.
13. L. Eschenauer and V. Gligor, "A Key Management Scheme for Distributed Sensor Networks," Proceedings of the 9th ACM Conference on Computing and Communication Security, Nov 2002.

An Asynchronous Replica Consistency Model in Data Grid*

Jiafu Hu, Nong Xiao, Yingjie Zhao, and Wei Fu

School of Computer, National University of Defense Technology,
410073 Changsha, China
hjf0008@etang.com

Abstract. Data Grid is an emerging technology to provide uniform access and management of the large scale distributed scientific datasets. To enhance the accessing performance, replica is an ideal solution for the Data Grid. But in the wide-area network environment, to maintain the consistency of those replicas is not a simple task because of the resource's autonomy and the network's instability. In this paper, a new asynchronous model is proposed, which could avoid the inconsistency in spite of the possible network congestion and system failure. This model could be more suitable for the resource autonomy characteristic, putting fewer burdens on storage resources, and it is also easier to implement while providing more scalability for the grid system. And then a detailed implementation, use case and some further research plans are described.

1 Introduction

The Grid technology is intent to share the distributed and heterogeneous resources. In recent years, the volume of datasets in modern large-scale scientific researches, information services and digital media applications is growing explosively. The effective storage, distribution, management, processing, analyzing and mine of mass datasets with high performance I/O capability have become the main problems that many applications and scientists faced with. The Data Grid technologies are emerging efforts to solve this problem by connecting an aggregation of hundreds of heterogeneous computers and storage resources located in different places of the world to facilitate sharing and cooperating of data and correlative resources. Data Grids enable scientists from different universities and research organizations to collaborate with one another to solve large-scale scientific problems.

Ensuring efficient access to such huge and widely distributed data is really a challenge to Grid designers. The major barrier is the high latency of Wide Area Networks and the Internet, which impacts the scalability of Grid systems. To overcome this barrier, large amounts of data need to be replicated in multiple copies at several world-wide distributed sites. The replication of data can offer improved efficiency in a Grid network such as high data availability, low bandwidth consumption, reduced

---

* This paper is supported by the 973-2003CB317008, the National Hi-Tech R&D 863 Program of China (No. 2002AA131010), and National Natural Science Foundation of China (NO. 90412011,No. 60203016).

G. Chen et al. (Eds.): ISPA Workshops 2005, LNCS 3759, pp. 475–484, 2005.

data access latency, increased fault tolerance, load balancing, improved scalability and so on. Data created by one scientist may be modified by others, so how to keep those distributed copies consistent over the Data Grid is a big challenge.

The replica consistency is a traditional issue in distributed systems, but it introduced new problem in the Data Grid. The traditional consistency implementations such as invalidation protocols, distributed locking mechanism, the atom operation and two phase commit protocols are not very suitable for the Data Grid environment because of too long delays in the wide-area network and the high autonomy of the Data Grid resource. For example, in a Data Grid, the replicas for a file may be distributed over different countries. So if one node which holds the replicas is not available when the update operation working, the whole updating will fail.

SkyHawk serial grid software system not only integrates distributed heterogeneous computing and data resource with uniform management and scheduling, but also supports autonomous characteristic of local system. In the Sky Hawk system, replica is an important measure for performance. For the effective consistency of replica, this paper presents a novel model for replica consistency management in the Data Grid in following sections. Section 2 introduces some related works. The asynchronous consistency model will be proposed and discussed in detail in section 3.In section 4 the replica consistency service will be described in relation with other services in the grid. Section 5 will give some further research agenda to optimize the consistency model and in section 6 we will conclude the whole paper.

2 Related Work

The replica problem has been a traditional issue, and in many Data Grid projects the replicas are very important techniques for the consideration of performance and availability. But different projects adopted different methods for replica consistency problem. The consistency problem could be divided into the metadata replica consistency and the data content consistency. Here we mainly concern about the latter.

The Globus project provides tools for Grid computing like job scheduling, resource discovery, security, etc. Recently, Globus is also working on a Data Grid effort that enables fast and efficient file transfer, a replica catalogue for managing files and some more replica management functionality based on files. But the replica update synchronization is not addressed.

In the HEP community which can be found in two Data Grid projects PPDG and GriPhyN, they adopted the Primary-copy approach, which also known as the"master-slave" approach. In this way, only one well defined entity in the system (e.g. one user or a production team at one site) is allowed to modify a particular piece of data (e.g. a file). As a result, the replication is not symmetric any more in the system. The process of determining the most up-to-date version in the system is not required. Only the information "who is the owner" needs to be propagated to all slave replicas. In case of data access only one well defined node needs to be contacted to obtain the most recent version of the data.

In the EDG, a pilot project called the Grid Data Management Pilot (GDMP) also designed its own implementation for the replica consistency problem, which adopted the Subscription and relatively independent sites method. In its implementations, a site only wants to obtain data content and does not care about consistency at all. When any other site does updates on a particular file, only certain sites are notified. This follows a subscription model where a site subscribes explicitly to a data producing site. A site that has not subscribed is itself responsible to get the latest information from other sites. This allows a site to do local changes without the agreement of other sites. However, such a site has to be aware that the local data is not always up-to-date. So an export buffer, where the newest information of a site is stored, and an import buffer, where a local site stores all the information that needs to be imported from a remote site are provided. This approach allows more flexibility concerning data consistency and independence for a local site.

Based on all of these methods, and combined with the GridDaEn system which is a part of the Sky Hawk serial grid software system, this paper present a new method for the replica consistency problem. It could be more suitable for the resource autonomy characteristic, putting fewer burdens on storage resources, and it is also easier to implement while providing more scalability for the grid system.

3 Replica Consistency Model

In this section the proposed replica consistency service with respect to the updating problem is discussed. First, the replica consistency deployment will be presented.

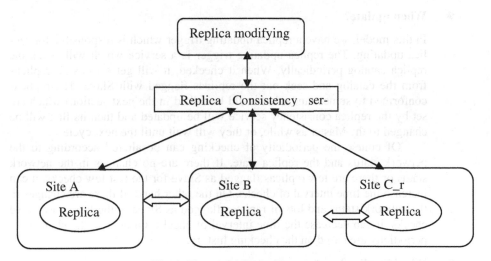

Fig. 1. The model for replica consistency

Here we propose an asynchronous model for the replica updating. In this model, every replica for a file could be flagged with these three states:

- **Master.** When a replica is flagged as Master, it means this replica has been successfully updated by the replica consistency service. So the Master state stands for a valid replica which could be accessed by the replica selection service for the user's request or be a source for other replica's updating.

- **Slave.** Once a replica is set as Slave, it means that this replica is not a valid replica, so it could not be accessed by the application or end-user and it also tells the replica consistency service that it need to be updated. But whether or not this replica could be updated is determined by the replica consistency services. Because the model is an asynchronous working mode, when a replica of file is modified, the application does not care about the other replica's updating. The work is left for the replica consistency service. In this model, the replica consistency service may choose not to update the replica data at once according to some policy, it just sets the that replica as Slave in the replica catalog
- **Free.** When a replica is flagged as Free, it means that this replica is been updating, so the replica consistency service does not have to update it anymore. And this replica can not be accessed because it's not a valid replica yet. When its updating process finished, its state will change to Master.

Replica Updating Policy

In the Data Grid environment, especially in the WAN condition, the resources are autonomous, the load are not balanced, and the network is unstable, so it's not reasonable for all the replicas be updated in a synchronous way. But we also need keep the replica consistent, so when the replica should be updated, which replica should be updated are our main focuses.

- **When update?**

  In this model, we have a replica updating trigger which is responsible for replica updating. The replica updating trigger is a service which will check the replica catalog periodically. When it checked, it will get a file's all replicas from the catalog and seek out the replicas flagged with Slave. The replicas conformed to some standards (would be talked in the next section) which are set by the replica consistency service will be updated and then its flag will be changed to the Master as while, or they will wait until the next cycle.

  Of course the periodicity of checking can be altered according to the network status and the replica state. If there are no changes in the network status or there are few replicas flagged as Slave for the last few checks, it can increase the time interval of checks. On the other hand, if there are changes in the network status and lots of replicas flagged as Slave in the last consecutive checks, it can decrease the time interval of checks. Of course, the changes of periodicity are based on the checking history.

- **Which replica?**

  As the discussed above, in an updating process, the replica consistency service query some standards to decide which replicas have the priority to be updated. Here, we will give the standards in details. When a set of replicas flagged as Slave is selected from the catalog, the replica consistency service will obtain the information about the locations of replicas from Resource Location Services. For each location, the replica consistency service will request the

Monitor service to get the following information: whether the node which holds the replica is available, the network condition for that node, the storage cost for the replica to be updated at that node, the system load on that node and even the number of request from that node. Bases on these information, we could calculate the cost and the advantage of updating the replica. Then we could compare all the cost/advantage of the replicas and then select some suitable replicas to be updated at this cycle. The proportion of the replicas be updated could be set by the system developer, for example we could set the first half of the replicas to be updated.

- **Optimization**

In our updating process, which replica could be the source for the Slave replicas? Of course, we could do some optimization work. When a replica flagged with Slave to be updated, the replica consistency service would choose the best replica from the replicas flagged with Master. The choosing process could be done by the replica selection service. Also when a replica is updated, its flag would be changed to Master, so it also could be used as source for updating other replica flagged with Slave.

User Case

Here we proposed a use case for better understanding for this model.

It is a common operation issued by a user or an application. The operation includes reading a data file from the grid, doing some modifying work and then writing it back.

t = t0: User submits a read operation for a file to the Data Grid.

t = t1: The replica selection service selects the "best" replica for that file which is has the lowest access cost from replica catalog, and return the location for that replica to the user.

t = t2: The user read the data from that replica location and processes the data.

t = t3: The user finishes his process and closes that file then the file data has to be written back to where it is from.

t = t4: After the successful writing, the replica which has been modified is flagged with Master and all other replicas are flagged with Slave in the replica catalog. Then the system will return a true value to the user.

t = t5: After a checking periodicity, the replica updating trigger will be run to check if any replica has been flagged with Slave.

t = t6: The replica updating trigger get the replica list which is flagged with Slave, then call the replica location service to get their physical location.

t = t7: The replica consistency service get all the replicas' updating cost and advantages based on the information provided by the monitor services.

t = t8: The replica consistency service selects the replicas with higher updating advantage/cost from all the replica physical locations.

t = t9: The replica consistency service selects the lowest accessing cost replica from the replica list which is flagged with Master.

t= t10: The replica consistency service calls the transportation service to transport the data between the source replica location to the destination and set the replica which is to be updated as Free.

t = t11: After the successful transportation, the replica which has just been updated will be flagged with the Master in the replica catalog.

t = t12:   From the operation at t5, the process repeats.

This use case presents basic mechanism that how the replica consistency service works. In this use case we just give a common situation and do not care about too many failure situations. So in the next section we will give some further research.

4   Replica Consistency Design

In this section, we will give a description of the replica consistency service in the Data Grid infrastructure. The relationships between the replica consistency service and other related services in the Data Grid are shown in the following figure.

This replica consistency is based on the premise that in the Data Grid environment the data modifying operation is not too frequent. If this condition is not satisfied, the replica is unnecessary.

From the end user or application's view, the replication consistency service is a single service entry which must interoperate with other services.

4.1 Replication Consistency Service

The replication consistency service which encapsulates the underlying systems and services and provides a uniform interface to the application or top services is mainly for the situation when a replica of a file is modified. The user of the Data Grid which may be application, common user or computing task may access the data through the Data Grid. Of cause, if their access is read-only, then we have no need to considerate about the consistency problem. Unfortunately quit proportions of accessing are modifying mode, so replica consistency service should be an indispensable component in the Data Grid.

The replica consistency service proposed here is for releasing the user from worrying about the inconsistency of replica. To some extent, the replica consistency service may be transparent to end-user for that that they don't have to pay any attention to the existence of many copies of the file; even the replica itself is transparent to end-user.

Because the Data Grid is deployed in the wide-area network, the network bandwidth may be unstable; the data-resource may unavailable, and so it may be incredible if we expect the Data Grid always update all the replicas in a real-time manner. So the replication consistency service proposed here is an asynchronous working model which allows the replicas not to be updated at the same time. And the replica consistency service must also provide the function that preventing the user from accessing the inconsistent or dirty data.

In the Data Grid environment, we try our best to abide by the OGSA architecture, so the replica consistency service is also a higher service building on some underlying services, in the next sections we will describe some services which may interact with or which provide service for the replica consistency service.

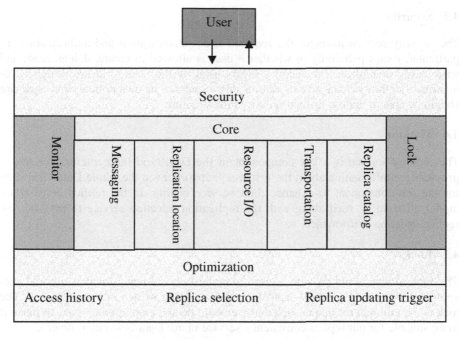

Fig. 2. The main components of the replica consistency service

4.2 Core

The main function of the replica consistency service, those of replica updating and the replica maintaining are provided through the core. The core is a set of APIs which are implemented through accessing some underlying or other services which are related to the replica consistency service:

- The messaging is used for the updating message communication, because the replica consistency service proposed here is a service which uses the asynchronous mode, so we must design a unique format for its message transportation and maintenance.
- The replica location service and the replica catalog both are used for managing the replicas which are distributed over the grid. And the replica location service is also built on the replica catalog. Here we list the replica catalog separately for that we must use it for recording the updating information for the replica.
- The *Transport* service provides the functionalities required for file transfer and may be implemented by means of different techniques, such as FTP, HTTP or GridFTP. If we want to implement the part of a file to be replicated, the third party controlled transferring, or just transfers the modified part of a file to the related replica, the GridFTP is recommended.
- Resource I/O is a resource accessing API which may have different implements such as the NFS, SMB, FTP, or even HPSS. These services implemented the data read/write in the physical resource.

4.3 Security

The security service manages the required user authentication and authorization; in particular, issues pertaining to whether a user is allowed to create, delete, read, and write a file or replica. The security layers used by the Data Grid are designed for maximal flexibility. Each VO should be able to enforce its own policies and each site should be able to impose its own security infrastructure.

4.4 Monitor

The monitor service is a key component in the Data Grid infrastructure for that it provides the information about the resource, network, even the whole Data Grid state for the top component to enhance their service quality. In the replica consistency model, it could be used along with the replication selection service to promote the replica updating performance.

4.5 Lock

The lock service could provide a grain granularity consistency for that it could prevent user from reading a dirty data when the data being written into the resource. The lock is a traditional technique such that we could do some optimizing work to make it more suitable for our replica consistency service in our Data Grid environment.

4.6 Optimization

The goal we set the replica in the Data Grid is to optimize the data accessing performance. And there are many services which are provided for top services, so we must set some mechanism to utilize these underlying services. Here we will focus on the optimization problems of replica selection and replica initiation.

The optimization component consists of the following three services: replica selection, access history and replica updating trigger which will be described in the following subsections.

- **Replica Selection Service.** The *Replica Selection* service requires the replica catalog service for translating a file to its physical location and then requires the *Monitoring Service* for estimating the file accessing time. In particular, a single file may have multiple replicas that are physically located on various Storage site all over the Grid. Based on the information provided by the monitoring service, the replica selection service selects the replica with the lowest estimated accessing time and calls the transportation service to execute the file transfer to the related Storage site. Here the replica selection also could be used for updating the best-suited replica.
- **Access History Service.** The access history service keeps track of accesses to replicas. Statistics may include time series about requests for a file and users who have initiated the file request. The access history serves as the main input for replica updating. For example, if request frequency for a file from a site is very high, but the replica at that has not been updated yet, then the replica consistency service should think about that replica's updating first. It can also be used for other purposes such as a replica creation.

- **Replica Updating Trigger.** This service may be a key service in this replica consistency model for that it could decide when to update the replica based on the replica selection and the access history service. This service could trigger the replica transport between different replicas.

5 Further Researches

In the discussion above, we give a simple model about the replica consistency problem, but we do not give too much consideration about the failure or exception situation in the processing such as operation failure, another user's request for the same file data when a user is just writing, etc. Here we give some further consideration.

- **Lock**
  We could design a lock mechanism to cooperate with the replica consistency service to get more accurate consistency. When a user is just doing a read/write operation, then the file could be set with a lock, so other user's concurrent read/write operations are prevented, which could effectively reduce the possible dirty data reading and further increasing the consistency.
- **Recover and Rollback**
  In the above use case, we ignored the possible failure the system may encounter, such as data transporting is break, an operation was stopped by some exception. So we need some mechanism to handle these situations, here we consider the recover and rollback methods as the strategies for these situations. But both methods need some extra information which records the system state. If an exception event broken, then the system could do the post-process based on this information.
- **Partial file updating**
  If one file is modified partly or is just appended, we could think about just transferring the part which be modified or the part which be appended when updating happed. This could effectively enhance the updating performance and reduce the network congestion. But this needs the replica catalog, application Meta-Data and transporting tools to cooperate with each other. So it is the possible further research point.

6 Conclusions

We have presented an overview of the model for the replica consistency service in the Data Grid. Due to the complexity of grid and the wide-area network, we put this service in a classical service infrastructure. We first studied its relationship with other service in the replica management service and its underlying service which provide support for it. Furthermore we give its design in details, and a use case in presented for detailed understanding. And at last we proposed some techniques which could better the performance and robust capability, which needs some more detailed research for applying in the real Data Grid deployment.

Reference

1. Chervenak, A., Foster, I., Kesselman, C., Salisbury, C., Tuecke, S.: The Data Grid: Towards an Architecture for the Distributed Management and Analysis of Large Scientific Data Sets. Journal of Network and Computer Applications, Vol. 23 (2001) 187-200
2. FU Wei, XIAO Nong : A Self-determinate Replica Management of Massive Scientific Data in Grid Environment. the 20th national database conference(2003)
3. D. Du¨ llmann, W. Hoschek, J. Jaen-Martinez, A. Samar, H.Stockinger, K. Stockinger, Models for replica synchronization and consistency in a data grid, in: Tenth IEEE Symposium on High Performance and Distributed Computing (HPDC-10), San Francisco, CA, August 7–9, 2001.
4. P. Kunszt, E. Laure, H. Stockinger, K. Stockinger, Advanced replica management with reptor, in: Fifth International Conference on Parallel Processing and Applied Mathematics, Czestochowa, Poland, September 7–10, 2003.
5. H. Stockinger, A. Domenici, F. Donno, G. Pucciani, K.Stockinger, Replica Consistency Service (RCS)—design principles and basic architecture v0.3, Technical report—Draft, August 21, 2003
6. Bill Allcock, Ann Chevernak, Ian Foster, Carl Kesselman, Chuck Salisbury, Steve Tuecke. The Data Grid: Towards an Architecture for Distributed Management and Analysis of Large Scientific Data Sets. to be published in the Journal of Network and Computer Applications.
7. 7.Yuri Breitbart, Henry Korth. Replication and Consistency: Being Lazy Helps Sometimes, 16th ACM SIGACT-SIGMODSIGART Symposium on Principles of Database Systems, Tucson,Arizona, May 12-14, 1997.
8. Heinz Stockinger, Data Replication in Distributed Database Systems, CMS Note 1999/046, July 1999.
9. [Golding92] Richard Golding. A weak-consistency architecture for distributed information services. Computing Systems 5(4), Fall 1992, pp. 179-405. Usenix Association.
10. Andrea Domeniciab, Flavia Donnocb, Gianni Pucciania, Heinz Stockingerc, and Kurt Stockingerc Replica Consistency in a Data Grid
11. XIAO Nong, LI Dongsheng, FU Wei, HUANG Bin, LU Xicheng.: GridDaen: A Data Grid Engine. 2nd International Conference on Grid and Cooperative Computing, (2003)
12. L. Guy, P. Kunszt, E. Laure, H. Stockinger, K. Stockinger "Replica Management in Data Grids", Technical Report, GGF5 Working Draft, Edinburgh Scotland, July 2002
13. W. H. Bell, D. G. Cameron, L. Capozza, A.P. Millar, K. Stockinger, F. Zini, OptorSim -A Grid Simulator for Studying Dynamic DataReplication Strategies, Int. J. of High PerformanceComputing Applications, Vol.17 (4),2003.
14. Heinz Stockinger. Distributed Database Management Systems and the Data Grid. 18th IEEE Symposium on Mass Storage Systems and 9th NASA Goddard Conference on Mass Storage Systems and Technologies, San Diego, April 17-20,2001.
15. Asad Samar, Heinz Stockinger. Grid Data Management Pilot (GDMP): A Tool for Wide Area Replication, IASTED International Conference on Applied Informatics (AI 2001),Innsbruck, Austria, 2001.

Distributed Access Control for Grid Environments Using Trust Management Approach[*]

Gang Yin[1], Huai-min Wang[1], Tao Liu[2],
Dian-xi Shi[1], and Ming-feng Chen[3]

[1] School of Computer Science,
National University of Defense Technology, China
jack_nudt@yahoo.com.cn
[2] School of Electronic Science and Engineering,
National University of Defense Technology, China
bravewendy@163.com
[3] China Xi'an Satellite Control Center,
cmf1968@sina.com

Abstract. In Grid environments, virtual organizations (VOs) often need to define access control policies to govern who can use which resources for which purpose over multiple policy domains. This is challenging, not only because the entities in VOs must collaborate with each other to share resources across administrative domains, but also because there usually exist a large amount of underlying sites (resource providers) and users in VOs. In this paper, we introduce to use trust management approach to address these problems in Grid environments. We propose a rule-based policy language (RPL) framework to describe the authorization and delegation policies related to VOs, sites and users. This paper also introduces the design of an enhanced community authorization service (ECAS) based on RPL framework, which can be seamlessly integrated with local authorization mechanisms. ECAS uses different kinds of delegation policies for flexible collaboration on authorization between entities in VOs. Compared with similar research works, ECAS enhances the flexibility and scalability of decentralized authorization in Grid environments.

Keywords: Grid, VO, Access Control, Trust Management

1 Introduction

Grid technologies [4] are increasingly becoming the platform of choice for developing and deploying distributed computation and data intensive applications across virtual organizations (VOs) [3]. VOs are collections of sites (resource providers) and users from different domains (organizations) that seek to share and use diverse resources in

---

[*] This work is supported by Grand Fundamental Research 973 Program of China (No.2005CB321804), National Natural Science Foundation under Grant No.90412011; the National High Technology Development 863 Program of China (No.2003AA115210; No.2004AA112020).

G. Chen et al. (Eds.): ISPA Workshops 2005, LNCS 3759, pp. 485–495, 2005.
© Springer-Verlag Berlin Heidelberg 2005

a collaborative fashion. Entities need to collaborate with each other to perform Grid tasks spanning across multi-domains or even different nations. The collaboration aspects of resource sharing in VOs require the access control models to be more flexible and scalable.

Grid Security Infrastructure [2] (GSI) and Community Authorization Service (CAS) [5] have progressed alongside the evolution of grids in the last few years. GSI is mainly an authentication infrastructure based on X.509 certificates, which provides identity based authentication across sites for VOs. CAS is built upon GSI and allows the sites to delegate some policy authority to the VO while maintaining ultimate control over their resources. However, GSI and CAS are essentially identity based and may not suit for the VOs that require flexible collaboration between entities. Furthermore, it will be even harder for CAS to control the dynamic delegation between users and sites.

Research work on trust management [1,6~9] attracts more and more attention in the field of information security. Trust management is an approach to access control in environments where entities that are not in the same administrative domains need to share resources. In this paper, we adopt the trust management approach to address the access control problems in Grid environments. Trust management is used to help automate authorization decisions rather than replacing the existing Globus security infrastructure. The rest of the paper is organized as follows. Section 2 presents a rule-based Grid policy language (RPL) for Grid environments, defines the main components and meta-rules in RPL. Section 3 describes the enhanced community authorization service (ECAS) using RPL language, together with comprehensive scenarios. Section 4 provides a brief discussion of other related works, and highlights the novel features of our approach. Section 5 presents the concluding remarks and future works.

2 Trust Management in Grid Environments

This section presents a rule-based policy language (RPL) framework for access control in Grid environments.

2.1 Syntax of Policies

RPL has four kinds of policy components: sets, rules, predicates and queries, as shown in table 1. The five fundamental sets give a precise description for variables and constants in RPL. Entities may be VOs, sites, users and user proxies. The syntax of RPL rules are the declarative language based on Datalog^C [10], which can be used to specify policies as well as semantic rules.

One important concept in RPL is session. To create a session, a user must log on the server to activate the roles that are to be used. The server makes a "role-activation-query" to determine whether the user can active the roles. If the query returns "TRUE", then the server will create a session, bind the user to the session and authorize the session with the activated roles. In RPL, a session can be held by the entity who is not the initiator of the session. This is critical for the dynamic delegation between users and sites in VOs.

Table 1. Rule-based Policy Language framework for Grids

The following is a list of fundamental sets: • E, R, P are sets of entities, local roles and permissions respectively. • DR $\subseteq$ E $\times$ R is a set of distributed roles; $A.r$ is an element of DR where A$\in$E and r$\in$R, which means the local role r is defined and interpreted by entity A. • S $\subseteq$ E $\times$ R is a set of sessions; $Sess(A, r)$ is an element of S where A$\in$E and r$\in$R.
Distributed Rules: A distributed rule has the form: A.H $\leftarrow$ $A_1.B_1$, $A_2.B_2$, ... , $A_n.B_n$, Ψ, where H and B_i are predicates, A and A_i are entities asserting the predicates, which are called *principals* of predicates. H is the *rule head*, A is the *issuer* of the rule. Ψ is a constraint.
Reserved Predicates[1, 2, 3]: • x.PRA(p, r): x assigns p to r. • x.ERA(y, r): x assigns y to be a member of r. • x.d-ERA(y, dr): x assigns y to be a member of dr. • x.PROXY(y): x asserts y to be its user proxy [2]. • x.ESM(y, s): x binds y to s. • x.DoA(y, r): x delegates the authority of r to y. • x.DoC(r, r'): x allows the users who are members of r to delegate their capabilities of r (activated by the members of r) to the members of r'. 1: The parameters of predicates have special types, where p$\in$P, r and r'$\in$R, dr$\in$DR, s$\in$S, x and y$\in$E. 2: The roles r and r' in predicates are local to the entity x, i.e., they are defined and interpreted by x. 3: RPL also support user-defined-predicates; this will largely improve the expressiveness of RPL.
Query Predicates: • **role-activation-query** predicate: canActivate(e, dr) where e$\in$E, dr$\in$DR. • **access-decision-query** predicate: accessAllowed(e, p) where e$\in$E, p$\in$P.

The constraints in RPL rules can express various security requirements. For example, a temporal constraint on authorizations can be expressed easily:

$$A.ERA(B, r) \leftarrow \text{time-ranges}(2005\text{-}4\text{-}30, 2005\text{-}7\text{-}1).$$

which means that A authorizes B to be a member of r between date "2005-4-30" and date "2005-7-1". The predicate "time-ranges" is a user defined predicate which checks whether the current date is between the dates specified in parameters. Distributed role hierarchy (DRH) is often used in coalition environments and has been supported in several trust management systems. DRH policies can be easily expressed using RPL. A DRH rule has the form:

$$A.ERA(?x, r) \leftarrow B.ERA(?x, r')$$

which means that entity A allows all members of B.r' to be the members of A.r. DRH implicitly expresses delegation of role authorities [9]. As demonstrated in section 3, DRH policies are very important for authorization in VOs.

2.2 Meta Rules

RPL use meta-rules to define the implicit semantics which can not be expressed by policy predicates. The syntax of meta-rules is similar to the distributed rules. But the parameters and principals of the predicates in meta-rules are usually variables, and this is the reason why meta-rules can express policies with more general meanings. RPL has following meta-rules:

[MR-1]   ?x.canActivate(?y, ?r) ← ?z.PROXY(?y), ?x.ERA(?z, ?r).

[MR-2]   ?x.ERA(?y, ?r) ← ?x.DoA(?y, ?r), ?y.d-ERA(?z, ?x.?r).

[MR-3]   ?x.canAccess(?y, ?p) ← ?x.ERA(?y, ?r), ?x.PRA(?p, ?r).

[MR-4]   ?x.canAccess(?y, ?p) ← ?z.ESM(?y, Sess(?u, ?r)), ?x.canAccess(?u, ?p).

[MR-5]   ?x.ERA(?z, ?r) ← ?x.ESM(?y, Sess(?z, ?r)).

The meaning of above meta-rules is easily read based on the interpretations in table 1. Here we give further explanation on some rules. MR-1 is an entry to answer role-activation-queries. The predicate "PROXY" at right side of the rule indicates that only user proxies can make role activation requests. "?x" is a variable representing a VO entity. When "?x" deduces "?x.ERA(?z, ?r)", it may need some ERA policies defined by the home site of the user "?z" because of the use of DRH policies. It is the responsibility of "?z" to submit the ERA policies related to the current role-activation-query. MR-3 and MR-4 are the entries to answer access-decision-queries. MR-3 is the entry to access decision for local requests within the site "?x", while MR-4 is the entry for VO requests. Note that MR-4 contains a recursive predicate "canAccess", which ensures the entity "?y" to share the access capabilities of the session "Sess(?u, ?r)". MR-5 maps the binding of the requesting entity "?y" and the session "Sess(?u, ?r)" to a distributed ERA predicate, which will be used by the local inference process.

3   Enhanced Community Authorization Service

We now introduce an enhanced community authorization service (ECAS) based on RPL. The access control mechanisms in ECAS can be clearly divided into two parts: authorization components and authentication components. Authorization components include policy databases (predicates and rules), access control algorithms and facilities for integration with local authorization mechanisms. The security administrators of VOs and sites can use authorization components to express VO policies and achieve seamless integration between VO authorization and local authorization of sites. Authentication components mainly include two protocols: session creation protocol (SCP) and session delegation protocol (SDP). The two protocols implicitly transfer credentials (signed rules) from VOs to intermediate or target sites. The basic concept in the two protocols is *session certificate* which is expressed by *ESM* predicate in RPL. A *session certificate* binds an identity to a session (see section 2.1). More detailed description of SCP and SDP will be introduced in section 3.3.

3.1 Integration with Local Authorization Mechanisms

It is not easy for VOs to integrate with the local authorization mechanisms of underlying sites, not only because of the heterogeneous technologies used by local systems, but also because of the fact that each site may each have different capabilities for enforcing the policy. In this paper, we make the assumption that each local authorization mechanisms has following capabilities:

- Support identity based access control;
- Simple role-based access control, which complies with RBAC0 [11].

Now we show how to integrate these legacy policies with ECAS. Table 2 shows an access control list (ACL) at Grid-site1.

The first two lines in table 2 are identity-based policies. The authentication of identities maybe based on X.509 certificates or UNIX user accounts. The third line is a simple role-based policy (we put these inhomogeneous policies into one ACL just for convenient) which defines the permissions held by the Professor role. The last three lines in table 2 are added for the mapping between VO roles and local permissions. For example, the role VO1-PJ1-User is assigned the permissions required by a user of Project-1 in VO1.

Table 2. Local Authorization Policies Defined by Grid-site1

	Subject	Subject Type	Permission
1	Alice	Identity	*Read* gridftp://Grid-site1/mydir/*
2	Bob	Identity	*Write* gridftp://Grid-site1/myfile
3	Professor	Role	*Read* gridftp://Grid-site1/mydir/* *Write* gridftp://Grid-site1/myfile
4	VO1-PJ1-User	Role	*Read* gridftp://Grid-site1/mydir/* *Write* gridftp://Grid-site1/myfile1
5	VO1-PJ2-User	Role	*Read* gridftp://Grid-site1/mydir/* *Write* gridftp://Grid-site1/myfile2
6	VO2-PJ3-User	Role	*Read* gridftp://Grid-site1/mydir/* *Write* gridftp://Grid-site1/myfile3

When a site (e.g. Grid-site1) receives a request, first it will decide which roles the requesting entity can hold according to VO policies (this process will be described in next section). Then the site will ask the local authorization mechanism what permissions these roles can hold, through following function:

Boolean LocalAuthorized(String subject, String permission);

We use the function *LocalAuthorized* to "wrap" the local authorization mechanism in a site who is a member of a VO. This function has two parameters *subject* and *permission*, both have the type of String. *LocalAuthorized* obtains the permission list authorized to *subject*, and then check whether *permission* is in the permission list. The *subject* parameter may be an "Identity" subject or "Role" subject, as shown in table 2. This function can be easily implemented if the local authorization mechanism supports identity-based or simple role-based authorization policies, which are now widely used in most information systems. We integrate the function into the logic engine by following rule:

$$?x.PRA(?p, ?r) \leftarrow p\_LocalAuthorized(?r, ?p).$$

The logic engine dynamically maps the *LocalAuthorized* function to the predicate *p_LocalAuthorized* with same parameters (this mechanism is supported by most Prolog engines). If the function returns "TRUE", then the predicate is proved, otherwise the predicate fails.

3.2 Decentralized Authorization

ECAS uses two kinds of policies in RPL to express the delegation of policy authorities in a VO: (1) ECAS allows VOs and sites to express trust to each other using DRH policies; (2) ECAS also allows VOs to delegate their security administrative authorities to other entities, such as administrators or users.

Table 3. VO Policies Defined by Grid-site1

Policy Type	Policies & Certificates
Authorization	Grid-site1.ERA(Alice, Professor). Grid-site1.ERA(Bob, Researcher).
Distributed Role Hierarchy (DRH)	Grid-site1.ERA(?x, VO1-PJ1-User) ← VO1.ERA(?x, PJ1-User). Grid-site1.ERA(?x, VO1-PJ2-User) ← VO1.ERA(?x, PJ2-User).

Table 3 shows the VO policies defined by Grid-site1. The authorization policies defines the user-role assignment relation in Grid-site1, which are also called *role credentials* in this paper. Grid-site1 defines its trust to VO1 with DRH policies.

The sample policies of VO1 are defined in table 4. VO1 uses DRH to express trust to sites and achieves more scalable authorization. VO1 can also delegate some of administrative authority to individuals by DoA policies (as shown in table 4), such as the project managers or security administrators of VO. In this example, VO1 delegates the authorities over the roles PJ1-User and PJ2-User to Jack and Tom respectively. The DoA policies are stored at ECAS server of a VO.

Being assigned with role authorities, Jack and Tom can authorize the entities with the role managed by them, such as the d-ERA policies asserted by Jack as shown in table 4. ECAS allows VO to define more subtle policies to address the dynamic aspects of access control in VO environments. For example, VO1 can control the delegation between users and sites with DoC policies (as shown in table 4).

Similar to CAS, the access control policies are stored in a decentralized way in ECAS. CAS embeds the restriction policies for a user defined by VO into a restricted proxy certificate [5] and communicates the policies to sites. This is not appropriate for the VOs with large scale because there maybe various kinds of policies related to a user, and often only small part of the policies are relevant to the current task.

Table 4. VO Policies Defined by VO1

Policy Type	Policies & Credentials
Authorization	VO1.ERA(Grid-site1, CO-Site). VO1.ERA(Grid-site2, CO-Site). VO1.ERA(Grid-site3, CO-Site). Jack.d-ERA(Alice, VO1.PJ1-User). Jack.d-ERA(?x, VO1.PJ1-User) ← Grid-site1.ERA(?x, Professor).
Distributed Role Hierarchy (DRH)	VO1.ERA(?x, PJ1-User) ← Grid-site1.ERA(?x, Professor). VO1.ERA(?x, PJ2-User) ← Grid-site1.ERA(?x, Professor). VO1.ERA(?x, PJ1-User) ← Grid-site2.ERA(?x, Researcher).
Delegation of Authority (DoA)	VO1.DoA(Jack, PJ1-User). VO1.DoA(Tom, PJ2-User).
Delegation of Capability (DoC)	VO1.DoC(PJ1-User, CO-Site). VO1.DoC(PJ2-User, CO-Site).

By using *session certificates*, ECAS does not need to transfer policies between VOs and sites. The ECAS server binds a user to the activated roles in *session certificates*. The *session certificate* will be submitted to sites (i.e. resource providers) together with the access request by the user's proxy. The session certificate will be useful for sites to make access decision. The user may also delegate the capabilities in the session to other entities. The creation and delegation of *session certificates* will be fully discussed in the next section.

3.3 Authentication and Delegation of Capabilities

This section mainly explains the two protocols of ECAS, *session creation protocol* (SCP) and *session delegation protocol* (SDP). Firstly, we introduce the basic protocol for general user logon process, which serves as the foundation for the delegation of user capabilities.

In the original CAS paradigm [5], the users log on the VO server to obtain a restricted capability certificate before they can access Grid services, and this process is illustrated in figure 1-I. We extend this to SCP to support role activation, as shown in figure 1-II.

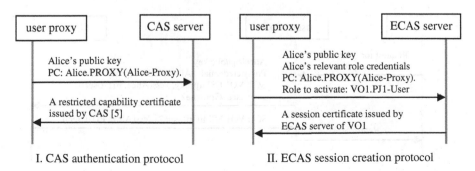

I. CAS authentication protocol   II. ECAS session creation protocol

Fig. 1. Compare of session creation process in CAS and ECAS

ECAS inherits the proxy mechanism of GSI [2]. The user proxy is represented by a new private-public key pair generated by Alice. Here the user proxy is identified by the name Alice-Proxy. In figure 1, the proxy credential "Alice.PROXY(Alice-Proxy)" essentially creates a short-term binding between the new key pair and Alice's identity. The logon process (and all the subsequent actions) is performed by Alice-Proxy on behalf of Alice. In SCP, Alice-Proxy needs to submit public key and some relevant credentials of Alice to ECAS server.

Suppose the ECAS server in figure 1 is managed by VO1. Alice needs to select the VO roles that she wants to use in current session. For example, if Alice wants to start a task of Project-1, she will need to activate the role VO1.PJ1-User. The VO1 server will check whether Alice can activate this role by raising the following query to the logic engine:

$$? \leftarrow VO1.canActivate(Alice\text{-}Proxy, VO1.PJ1\text{-}User).$$

According to the VO policies defined in table 4 and the submitted *role credentials* of Alice, the semantics of ROL will authorize Alice to activate the role VO1.PJ1-User, and then VO1 creates a session for Alice and return a *session certificate* binding the session to Alice:

$$VO1.ESM(Alice\text{-}Proxy, Sess(Alice, PJ1\text{-}User))$$

VO1 is the issuer of above *session certificate*. Alice-Proxy can use this certificate to access Grid resources authorized to the role of VO1.PJ1-User. The *session certificate* is also useful for two purposes: (1) The identity in session structure can be used for security auditing in target sites; (2) The *session certificate* implies a user-role assignment relation between the user and the role in the session structure (as shown by MR-5 in section 2.2).

Suppose Grid-site2 provides some functions for Project-1. However, while processing the request, Grid-site2 must retrieve data from Grid-site3. To simplify our discussion, we suppose Grid-site3 have similar policies with Grid-site1 (see table 3), which allows the entities entitled with VO1.PJ1-User to access local resources related to Project-1. According to the meta-rules of RPL, Grid-site2 will gain the access to resources in Grid-site3 if Alice will delegate the capabilities (i.e. the activated role VO1.PJ1-User) in the *session certificate* to Grid-site2. ECAS support this kind of delegation using a *session delegation protocol* (SDP), as shown in figure 2.

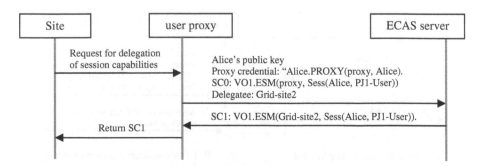

Fig. 2. Session delegation protocol between user proxy and ECAS server

SDP starts when the site receives a request from the user proxy to perform the Grid functions. The site will require the proxy to delegate the necessary capabilities to it. When the proxy receives the delegation request from the site, it will forward this request to ECAS server. In above example, Grid-site2 first send a delegation request to Alice-Proxy, then Alice-Proxy provides the VO1 ECAS server with the identity of delegatee and the *session certificate* obtained through the logon process, together with Alice's public key and the proxy credential, as shown in figure 2. The ECAS server will check whether this delegation should be allowed by raising the following query:

$$? \leftarrow \text{VO1.ESM(Grid-site3, Sess(Alice, PJ1-User))}.$$

According to the RPL semantics defined in section 2 and VO policies (especially DoC policies) defined in section 3.2, VO1 will authorize the delegation request by issuing another *session certificate* and return to Alice-Proxy:

$$\text{VO1.ESM(Grid-site2, Sess(Alice, PJ1-User))}.$$

Alice-Proxy will send it to Grid-site2 for future use (when Grid-site2 tries to access resources at Grid-site3). Grid-site2 will submit this *session certificate* to Grid-site3 when it need to access resources located at the latter. When Grid-site3 receives the credentials provided by Grid-site2, it will make access decision for the request coming from Grid-site2.

3.4 Access Decision

Target sites (i.e. resource providers) need to decide whether to allow the coming requests accessing their resources. For example, if Grid-site3 receives a request from Grid-site2 and the operations in request is mapped to permission p, then Grid-site2 will transfer the request to an access control query:

$$? \leftarrow \text{Grid-site3.canAccess(Grid-site2, p)}.$$

As we have mentioned, Grid-site2 will submit a *session certificate* together with the request: VO1.ESM(Grid-site2, Sess(Alice, PJ1-User)). Grid-site3 will use this *session certificate* and the local policies (include local VO policies and legacy policies) to prove the access control query. The request will be permitted if the query is proved to be "TRUE"; otherwise it will be rejected by Grid-site3.

4 Related Work

We have discussed Grid Security Infrastructure (GSI) and Community Authorization Service (CAS) developed by Globus [2~5]. In this section, we compare our work to some other efforts in the area of Grid security services and architectures.

GridAdmin [13] is an authorization system using KeyNote [8] to manage the trust relationships between Grid administrators and Grid users. GridAdmin also introduce trust metrics to help judge the merits and suitability of each request. SVE [12] collaboration infrastructure allows multiple sites to share their distributed application objects, while respecting organizational autonomy over local resources. SVE uses email address to identity an entity. However, GridAdmin and SVE adopt the peer model for authorization among enclaves (sites or organizations), which increase the cost to collaborative authorization. But they do not support automatic policy retrieval, nor do they touch the delegation between users and running servers.

A lot of trust management systems have been proposed in recent years, such as KeyNote [8], SPKI [1], Cassandra [6], etc. Credential discovery [9] is inherent to most trust management systems, which will incur communication and computation costs. ECAS adopts the push model of credential retrieval. The user submits related credentials to ECAS server, who will create a session certificates (sc) for user. The user submits the sc to target sits to gain access of resources. A session contains the activated VO roles, which eliminate the need for the target sites to search the certificates necessary to prove the membership of these activated roles (as shown by MR-5 in section 2.2).

5 Conclusion

This paper proposes a rule-based trust management language named RPL (Rule-based Policy Language) to express the access control policies for VOs in Grid environments. We also give a detailed description of the ECAS, an enhanced CAS based on RPL framework. Compared with similar research works, ECAS is more flexible and scalable for decentralized authorization in Grid environments.

References

1. C. M. Ellison, B. Frantz, B. Lampson, R. Rivest, B. M. Thomas, and T. Ylonen. SPKI Certificate Theory. IETF RFC 2693, 1998.
2. Foster, I., et al. A Security Architecture for Computational Grids. in Proceedings of the 5th ACM Conference on Computer and Communications Security. 1998.
3. Foster, I., Kesselman, C. and Tuecke, S. The Anatomy of the Grid: Enabling Scalable Virtual Organizations. International Journal of High Performance Computing Applications, 15 (3). 200-222. 2001.
4. Foster, I. and Kesselman, C., "Globus: A meta-computing infrastructure toolkit," The International Journal of Supercomputer Applications and High Performance Computing, vol. 11, no. 2, pp. 115-128, Summer 1997.
5. L. Pearlman, C. Kesselman, V. Welch, I. Foster, S. Tuecke, The Community Authorization Service: Status and Future, CHEP03, March 24-28, 2003, La Jolla, California.
6. Moritz Y. Becker, Peter Sewell, Cassandra: Flexible Trust Management, Applied to Electronic Health Records Proceedings of the 17th IEEE Computer Security Foundations Workshop (CSFW'04).
7. M. Blaze, J. Feigenbaum, and J. Lacy. Decentralized trust management. In Proceedings of 17th Symposium on Security and Privacy, pages 164-173, Oakland, 1996. IEEE.
8. M. Blaze, J. Feigenbaum, John Ioannidis, and Angelos D. Keromytis. The KeyNote trust-management system, version 2. IETF RFC 2704, September 1999.

9. Ninghui Li, William H. Winsborough, John C. Mitchell, Distributed Credential Chain Discovery in Trust Management, Journal of Computer Security, volume 11, number 1, pp. 35-86, February 2003
10. Paris C. Kanellakis, Gabriel M. Kuper, and Peter Z. Revesz. Constraint query languages. Journal of Computer and System Sciences, 51(1):26-52, August 1995.
11. Ravi S. Sandhu, Edward J. Coyne, Hal L. Feinstein, and Charles E. Youman. Role-based access control models. IEEE Computer, 29(2):38-47, February 1996.
12. Shands, D., et al., Secure Virtual Enclaves: Supporting Coalition use of Distributed Applications Technologies. ACM Transactions on Information and System Security, 2001. 4(2): p. 103-133.
13. Thomas B. Quillinan, Brian C. Clayton, and Simon N. Foley, GridAdmin: Decentralising Grid Administration using Trust Management. Proceedings of the ISPDC/HeteroPar 2004.

Research on Database Access and Integration in UDMGrid[*]

Zhangsheng Pan, Xiaowu Chen, and Xiangyu Ji

The Key Laboratory of Virtual Reality Technology, Ministry of Education,
School of Computer Science and Engineering, Beihang University,
Beijing 100083, P.R. China
chen@buaa.edu.cn

Abstract. UDMGrid (University Digital Museum Grid) is devoted to the integration and sharing of resources from various university digital museums whose main carriers of resources are heterogeneous databases dispersed throughout CERNET. This paper presents the UDMGrid-DAI for database access and integration in UDMGrid. It merges decades of various databases in UDMGrid into several virtual databases oriented some certain domains, and provide consistent access interface and uniform logic view of these databases for the developer of grid applications.

1 Introduction

The purpose of UDMGrid (University Digital Museum Grid) [1, 2], which supported by ChinaGrid [3], is to integrate the enormous dispersed resources of various digital museums, to share the resources effectively and eliminate the information island, to filter and classify the specimen information, and to provide appropriate information service to users according to their knowledge levels and motivation through unified grid portal [1]. The information resources of existing digital museum include heterogeneous databases, such as MS SQL Server, DB2, Oracle, MySQL, Postgresql, or XML database. Because UDMGrid is oriented to domain-intensive applications, and its various digital museums and grid users could be classified by kinds of subjects. It requires consistent interface for access and integration of heterogeneous database resource from isolated digital museums.

Usually, the requirements come from three import ways. First, the developer of GAS (UDMGrid Application Service) [1] often concerns the information on some certain domain, such as geology, archaeology or esthetics, and needs consistent interface to access the different resource. Second, the developer hopes access the resource just once and receive result including information from multiple databases, like visit a virtual database that contain data of several databases. Finally, to extend

---

[*] This paper is supported by China Education and Research Grid (ChinaGrid) (CG2003-GA004 & CG004 & GP004), National 863 Program (2004AA104280), Beijing Science & Technology Program (200411A), National Grand Fundamental Research 973 Program of China under the grant No. 2002CB312105.

G. Chen et al. (Eds.): ISPA Workshops 2005, LNCS 3759, pp. 496–505, 2005.
© Springer-Verlag Berlin Heidelberg 2005

functions of the current web application of digital museum, the UDMGrid need be able to obtain the domain-congener information for existing digital museums.

On the other hand, Information grid is a system using the grid technologies to achieve the sharing, and managing of information resources, and to provide information services [4]. And it is the key issue to access and integrate the heterogeneous database information. Data access means the retrieval, manipulation and insertion of data, which may be stored using a range of different formats and infrastructures [5]. Grid data access requires a flexible framework for handling data requests to a data resource that is to be integrated within a grid fabric [5]. And data integration interests the common external schema [6] of heterogeneous resource.

Recently the research about database (or data) access and integration is booming in grid and related application field. DAIS-WG (Data Access and Integration Services Working Group) of GGF (Global Grid Forum) seeks to promote standards for the development of grid database services, focus principally on providing consistent access to databases [5, 7]. The group had issued the draft of grid data service specification including WS-DAIR [8] and WS-DAIX [9]. The former is for relational database, and the latter is for XML repositories. The principal objective of OGSA-DAI (Open Grid Services Architecture Data Access and Integration) is to produce open source database access and integration middleware which meets the needs of the UK e-Science community for developing Grid and Grid related applications [10]. OGSA-DAI provide the ability to access the separate databases and text file by the consistent Web Services interface. However, it can't eliminate the semantic difference between the databases, merge the response from heterogeneous databases, and provide a uniform logic view to the request. Neither DAIS nor OGSA-DAI provides standard or ability to integrate several database related to one scientific domain into a virtual database which the UDMGrid requires. The Computer Network Information Center of Chinese Academy of Science has presented a reference framework to achieve collecting, storing and access database metadata, based on the Grid Service. The framework make it to support rational database background for storing static metadata, and make use of the Information Provider to get dynamic metadata [11]. The system provides the interface to access to metadata of hundreds of databases by grid service. But, it doesn't support the consistent access to dispersed databases.

UDMGrid introduced a solution for the database access and integration, UDMGrid-DAI (UDMGrid-Database Access and Integration). UDMGrid-DAI is a grid middleware to assist with access and integration of data from heterogeneous database sources within the grid. It integrates heterogeneous database resource into several domain-oriented virtual databases through schema merging. The GAS and other clients access the resource not only in consistent interface but also in consistent logic view of resource via the VDBS (Virtual DataBase Service).

The rest of this paper is organized as fallow. Section 2 describes the relationship between UDMGrid and UDMGrid-DAI. Section 3, 4, 5 and 6 respectively present the description and analysis of architecture, Domain Ontology, VDB & VDBS, and Req/Res Transform Service in UDMGrid-DAI. Section 7 illustrates the application of UDMGrid-DAI. Finally, Section 8 draws a conclusion and outlines the future work.

2 UDMGrid-DAI

The framework and function components of UDMGrid are shown as figure 1. The UDMGrid-DAI encapsulate the database resources underlying the UDMGrid. The users & Applications utilize the UDMGrid-DAI to access heterogeneous resource. The other components in UDMGrid, for example, ontology, resource representation & interactive management, logging management and GSI, will be invoked when the UDMGrid-DAI works.

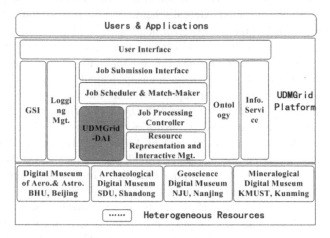

Fig. 1. Architecture of UDMGrid

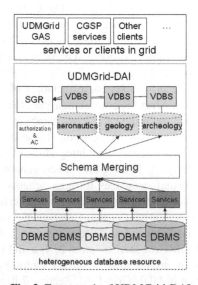

Fig. 2. Framework of UDMGrid-DAI

UDMGrid-DAI is a collection of services and deposits of resource. To meet the domain-intensive requirement of UDMGrid, UDMGrid-DAI concern the ability of information integration more than OGSA-DAI and DAIS, not the access ability. Compared to OGSA-DAI, the final propose of UDMGrid-DAI is to merge decades of heterogeneous databases into several virtual database related to special scientific domain, and then, provide consistent interface to visit them. The framework of UDMGrid-DAI and the relations between UDMGrid-DAI, heterogeneous and application services in UDMGrid are illustrated as figure 2.

As the figure 2 illustrated from bottom to up, DBMS are heterogeneous database resources in university digital museums. They are autonomously managed, and may be MS SQL Server, Oracle, MySQL, Postgresql, DB2 or XML database. The database resource provider should download and run ResInit Client (Resource Initialize Client) to initialize the local resource when registering to the grid. The data access services (gray part) of UDMGrid-DAI can provide consistent access to different databases for other service in UDMGrid-DAI, for example VDBS. It will return XML document or JDBC ResultSet to the request sender. Through schema merging, several databases on the same scientific domain can be integrated into one virtual database. The schema of virtual database is deposited in the Domain Ontology, and can be "read" by user through VDBS. The UDMGrid-DAI transforms the request aimed at virtual database to actual databases, and then integrates responses from the actual databases for consumer services, while these services visiting the VDBS (Virtual DataBase Service). The developer of application services or clients of the UDMGrid can query the VDBS from the UDMGrid-DAI SGR (Service Group Registry), and then, access the virtual database which has integrated the resource from several actual databases via the VDBS.

3   Architecture of UDMGrid-DAI

The design of UDMGrid-DAI makes reference to specification issued by DAIS-WG of GGF. UDMGrid-DAI is organized as a collection of loosely-coupled components. UDMGrid-DAI components contain services, clients and inner deposits, database or LDAP. All the services are built using GT4 (Globus Toolkit) [12].

The architecture of UDMGrid-DAI is illustrated as figure 3.

1) *Access agent* is a web service which can be deployed in UDMGrid-DAI or database resource client. It provides basic access service (query, update or insert) to actual database. The user (other service within UDMGrid-DAI, ResMonitor Service, for example) of Access Agent should submit SQL clause operable to database, and the agent will response XML document or ResultSet to request sender.

2) *Resource Metadata* preserves metadata of database resource that have been integrated into the grid. And ResMonitor Service (Resource Monitor Service) will check the status of database resource via the Access Agent periodically.

3) *Domain Ontology* database conserve ontology description of special domain, such as geology, archaeology and esthetics. The ontology is defined by experts from digital museums.

4) *VDBS* (Virtual DataBase Service). UDMGrid-DAI merge several databases belonging to the same scientific domain into one virtual database. GAS (Grid

Application Service) or other services within Grid can obtain information from several domain-congeneric databases by visiting VDBS once.

5) *VDB_SGR* Service provides interface of querying VDBS to GAS.

6) *Req/Res TranServ* (Request/Response Transform Service). The service transforms the request from VDBS and integrates the response from Access Agent.

7) *ResInit* (Resource Initialize) Client/Services are used to initialize a new database resource when the resource registering into grid environment.

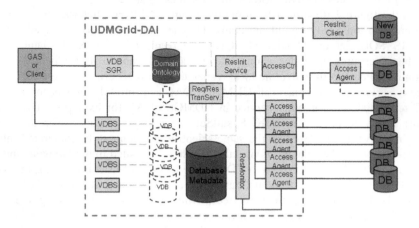

Fig. 3. Architecture of UDMGrid-DAI

4 Domain Ontology

Ontology is used to describe the concept and relations between concepts of some certain discipline [13, 14, 15]. It is required to describe the Domain Ontology in UDMGrid-DAI. There are two main kinds of global ontology in UDMGrid. One is generic ontology, which is information-rich and flexible. The other is domain

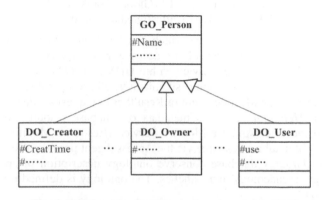

Fig. 4. Relationship of entities in domain ontology [16]

ontology, which is more specific and professional, and its construction requires domain expert's involvement [16]. The domain ontology describe the skeleton of a certain scientific domain in a hierarchically structure. As shown in figure 4, GO _Person is an entity in domain ontology, while it is the sup class of DO_Creator, DO_Owner, and DO_User which locates in other classes. Through this mechanism, the Domain Ontology has a better description ability and extensibility [16].

5 VDB and VDBS

UDMGrid-DAI merge several databases belonging to the same scientific domain into one virtual database. Each VDBS represent a virtual database, and will register into VDBSGR (Virtual DataBase Service Group Registry). The developer of UDMGrid application service can query the VDBSGR to find available VDBS.

Figure 5 is the GUI of virtual database manager. The hierarchy of virtual databases is organized as the left part of figure 5. In UDMGrid-DAI, the child virtual databases can extend the virtual tables of their parent virtual databases.

VDBS performs mainly two important functions. 1) As described above, Domain Ontology describes basic knowledge skeletons of some certain scientific domain. The skeletons are exposed to the GAS developer through VDBS. GAS and other clients can retrieval external schema of virtual database via the interface of VDBS. 2) GAS and other clients within grid access virtual database by invoking query interface of VDBS just like access to an actual existing database, and the response from VDBS will involve information from several actual databases.

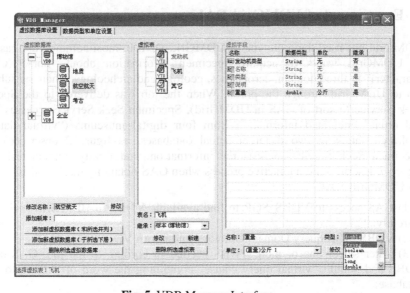

Fig. 5. VDB Manager Interface

6 Request/Response Transform Service

When application service in UDMGrid visits the VDBS to retrieve information, VDBS forwards the request to Req/Res TranServ. The services transform the request and integrate the response from Access Agent. On the one hand, while GAS submitting "virtual query clauses" to virtual database, TranServ transform the clauses to operable ones for the special actual database. And then, TranServ submits these operable clauses to actual databases via Access Agent. On the other hand, TranServ should combine the response from the Access Agent into one XML document including the query result from different databases and return to VDBS. While combining the query result, TranServ will eliminate the semantic difference between heterogeneous databases, converse the weight of specimen to the metric system, for example.

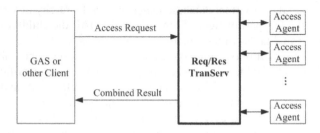

Fig. 6. Req/Res TranServ

7 Experiment of UDMGrid-DAI

UDMGrid has used the prototype of UDMGrid-DAI. In most common use case, user of UDMGrid wants to acquire specimen information about "horse (Chinese character)" in three domain, aeronautics, geology and archeology. Then, he submits a job to UDMGrid through the portal. When the job was delivered to the Specimen Seek Service (a sort of GAS in UDMGrid), Specimen Seek Service accesses VDBS and obtain integrated information from four digital museums ("virtual database" geology containing two different actual databases, as figure 2 described). Then Specimen Seek Service analysts the information, and finally outputs task result. Figure 7 describes the interactive process when GAS obtaining integrated information via UDMGrid-DAI.

1) GAS access to VDBS_SGR to find available VDBS in UDMGrid environment currently;

2) VDBS_SGR query Domain Ontology and return VDBS list to GAS;

3) After select one or more VDBS needed in cording to the job, GAS connect VDBS and submit "virtual query clause" containing the word of "horse" to virtual database;

4) VDBS invokes TranServ to transform "virtual query clause" to operable query clauses;

5) TranServ access to DB Metadata to finish the transformation;

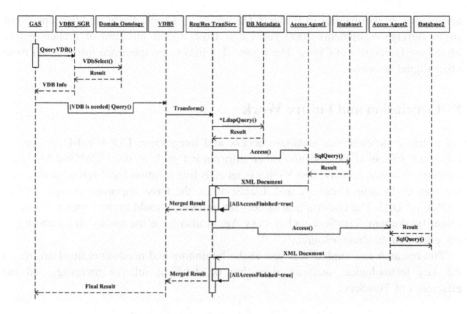

Fig. 7. Sequence Diagram of UDMGrid-DAI

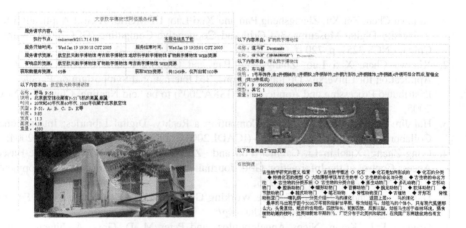

Fig. 8. Parts of grid service results about the parameter "horse"

6) TranServ forward query clauses to Access Agent;

7) Access Agent access databases and obtain the query result containing specimen information about horse;

8) TranServ merge the result from different database resources and return final result to GAS via VDBS.

Finally, GAS processes specimen information and return visual result to user. Figure 8 illustrates part result of the job. Left-bottom part is a photo of "P-51D Mastang fighter plane" (Chinese name is "wild horse") from digital museum of aeronautics & astronautics in Beihang University of China. Right-middle is photo of some carriage equipments 2000 years ago from digital museum of archeology in Shandong University of China. The figure also lists some specimen information from other digital museums.

8   Conclusion and Future Work

As a grid middleware for database access and integration, UDMGrid-DAI play an important role in UDMGrid and other information grid. In the UDMGrid-DAI, the concept of virtual database and VDBS is an effective solution for database access and integration. Domain Ontology and TranServ are the most important components in UDMGrid-DAI. The construction of domain ontology should invite experts of related scientific domain. TranServ and Access Agent also have the ability of extending to integrate non-database resource.

The research and impletion is just at the beginning and needs continued efforts on the key technologies, such as algorithm of database schema merging, and the efficiency of TranServ.

References

1. Xiaowu Chen, Zhi Xu, Zhangsheng Pan and Xixi Luo: UDMGrid: A Grid Application for University Digital Museums. 3rd Grid and Cooperative Computing (GCC2004), Wuhan China, LNCS 3251, p. 720 ff, Oct, 2004;
2. Xiaowu Chen, Xixi Luo, Zhangsheng Pan and Qinping Zhao: A CGSP-based Grid Application for University Digital Museums. 3rd International Symposium on Parallel and Distributed Processing and Applications (ISPA'2005) to be held Nanjing, China, 2-5 Nov, 2005;
3. Hai Jin: ChinaGrid: Making Grid Computing a Reality. Digital Libraries: International Collaboration and Cross-Fertilization (ICADL2004), LNCS 3334, pp. 13~24, Dec, 2004;
4. Gang Zhang, XiaoLin Li, Ganmei You and ZhiWei Xu: Research on the Role-Based Access Control of the Information Grid. Journal of Computer Research and Development, Vol.39, No.18 Aug, 2002, p952~956;
5. Data Access and Integration Service Working Group (DAIS-WG) of Global Grid Forum, https://forge.gridforum.org/projects/dais-wg/;
6. Graham J. L. Kemp, Nicos Angelopoulos, and Peter M. D. Gray: Architecture of a Mediator for a Bioinformatics Database Federation. IEEE Transactions on Information Technology in Biomedicine, VOL. 6, NO. 2, Jun 2002;
7. Malcolm P Atkinson, Vijay Dialani and Leanne Guy: Grid Database Access and Integration: Requirements and Functionalities. Global Grid Forum (GGF,http://www.ggf.org) GFD-I.13 Mar 13th 2003;
8. Mario Antonioletti, Brian Collins, Amy Krause and Simon Laws: Web Services Data Access and Integration - The Relational Realisation (WS-DAIR). DAIS-WG (Data Access and Integration Service Working Group) in Global Grid Forum (GGF http://www.ggf.org), https://forge.gridforum.org/projects/dais-wg, Feb 2005;

9. Mario Antonioletti, Shannon Hastings, Amy Krause, Stephen Langella, Simon Laws, Susan Malaika and Norman W Paton: Web Services Data Access and Integration – The XML Realization (WS-DAIX). DAIS-WG (Data Access and Integration Service Working Group) in Global Grid Forum (GGF http://www.ggf.org), https://forge.gridforum.org/projects/dais-wg, Feb, 2005;

10. Open Grid Services Architecture Data Access and Integration (OGSA-DAI). http://www.ogsadai.org;

11. Fei Zhang and Baoping Yan: A Database Metadata Management Framework Based on Grid Service. Computer Engineering and Applications, 2004, 29;

12. About the Globus Toolkit. http://www.globus.org/toolkit/about.html;

13. Hui Zhang and Liusheng Huang: A Design of Wrapper in Ontology Based Information Integration Framework. Computer Engineering and Applications, 2004.19;

14. Baisong Liu and Ji Gao: RDF Based Semantic Integration of Heterogeneous Information Sources. Journal of the China Society for Scientific and Technical Information, 2002.12;

15. Qi Gao and Huajun Chen: Comparison and Analysis of Web Ontology Languages and Reasoning, Computer Applications and Software, Oct.2004;

16. Xixi Luo and Xiaowu Chen: OOML-Based Ontologies and its services for information retrieval in UDMGrid. 6th International Workshop on Advanced Parallel Processing Technologies (APPT 2005) to be held Hong Kong, China, 27-28 Oct. 2005.

Resource Allocation Based on Pricing for Grid Computing Environments*

Jiadi Yu, Minglu Li, and Feng Hong

Department of Computer Science and Engineering,
Shanghai Jiao Tong University, Shanghai 200030, P.R. China
{jdyu, li-ml, hongfeng}@cs.sjtu.edu.cn

Abstract. Grid computing has been widely accepted as a promising paradigm for large-scale distributed systems in recent years. Mechanism based on economic models is an effective approach to solve the problem of grid resources management. The essence of this problem is how to allocate resources for achieving the goal of a highly efficient utilization of resources in response to current resource prices. In this paper, we present a method of resource allocation based on the pricing, and discuss the process of resource allocation and resource pricing algorithms for allocating resources to grid users in order to maximize the benefit for both grid providers and grid users.

1 Introduction

A grid computing environment is one in which applications can utilize multiple computational resources that may be distributed at widespread geographic locations [1][2][3]. Resource management and scheduling is a complex undertaking due to the large-scale heterogeneity present in the distributed resources, management policies, users, and application requirements in such environments [9]. Grid resources may be distributed at widespread geographic location, and are administrated and owned by different organizations. The resource providers and the resource consumers have different goals and demands, and often use different strategies to manage grid resources.

In a grid computing environment, the different characteristics of various resources result in many practical difficulties, such as heterogeneous resources that differ in many aspects, such as no uniform resource management strategy, etc. A promising solution to the problem of resource management in a grid environment is a procedure based on the market mechanism in economics: market mechanism is based on distributed self-determination, which is also suitable for resource management in the grid context; at the same time, variations in price reflect the supply and demand of resources; and finally, market theory in economics provides precise depiction for the efficiency of resource allocation [10]. Therefore pricing has been extensively used as a means to arbitrate resource allocation.

---

* This work is supported by a 973 project (No.2002CB312002) of China, a grand project (No.03dz15027) and a key project (No.025115033) of the Science and Technology Commission of Shanghai Municipality.

G. Chen et al. (Eds.): ISPA Workshops 2005, LNCS 3759, pp. 506–513, 2005.

Based on the above realization, we have developed a simple framework for a price-based resource allocation in [11]. In this paper, we analyzed this framework in detail, and GRB components. We further discuss the process of resource allocation in detail, and present a specific algorithm that can be used to compute the price. Finally, the a simulated experiment is presented and discussed.

2 Related Works

There are some published research on resource management for grid computing based on economics principles, and these economic models can be improved both conceptually and computationally.

The distributed pricing method is studied in [4], which is based on the equilibrium theory to realize an optimal allocation of grid resources by the market mechanism, and introduced an iterative algorithm of resource-agent. It is suitable for large-scale distributed systems.

In [5], 'G-commerce', which is computational economies for controlling resource allocation in Computational Grid settings, is investigated. This paper defines a hypothetical resource and resource producers, then measure the efficiency of resource allocation under two different market conditions: commodities markets and auctions. The results indicate that commodities markets are a better choice for controlling Grid resources than previously defined auction strategies.

In [6], a commodity market based approach is used to allocate resources, where resources are classified into different classes based on the hardware components, network connectivity, and operating systems. In a commodity market, the prices of the commodities ("resources") are fixed using individual supply and demand functions.

GRACE [7][8][9] (the Grid Architecture for Computational Economy) proposed by Buyya is a distributed computational economy-based resource allocation framework, which provides a mechanism for regulating the Grid resources demand and supply. GRACE offers incentive for resource owners to be part of the Grid and encourages consumers to optimally utilize resources and balance timeframe and access costs. It is built on the existing Grid middleware systems and offers an infrastructure for resource management and trading in the Grid environment.

A distributed group-pricing algorithm is presented for determining the price according to the general equilibrium theory in [10]. According to this algorithm, resources in the system are divided into multiple resource groups according to the degree of price correlation of resources. When the demand and supply of resources in the system changes, the price of one resource group will be adjusted simultaneously until the excess demand of all resources becomes zero. However, [10] didn't analyze how to allocate resources for achieving the goal of most efficient utilization of resources.

3   Resource Allocation Model

According to the economics principles, a fully competitive resource market is established for grid, which can trade grid resources, and provides the basic exchange function for grid resource users and providers. In grid resource market, the demand and supply should approach an equilibrium. Price of every resource traded is advertised to consumers and providers. According to the price of resources traded and resource pricing algorithm, users can order grid resources and providers also can sell grid resources.

In order to complete a user job, any grid resource user will consume a wide range of resources. However, a resource provider may only be interested in a relatively small subset of these resources for the purposes of deciding a price for the user, such as CPU, memory, Disc, etc. Users and providers can and only can bid and be asked for these resources.

Fig. 1 shows Resource Allocation Based on the Pricing Model. In our resource scheduling system, the whole grid system as a global grid is organized as resource domains. All resources are grouped into various resource domains according to their types. In this model, GR-Agents is the grid resource agents, which is used to manage local resource domains and represents the interests of the grid resource providers of the computational grid, and GU-Agents are the grid user agents, which is used to manage a job submitted by users and represent the interests of a grid user.

Grid Resource Broker (GRB) [9] is a mediator between the user and grid resources by using middleware services. It is responsible for identifying the available resources, negotiating for service costs, and performing resource selection. It has information about the locations of current resource providers in the grid and their prices. It is composed of RS-Agent, RF-Agent, RD-Agent and RP-Agent:

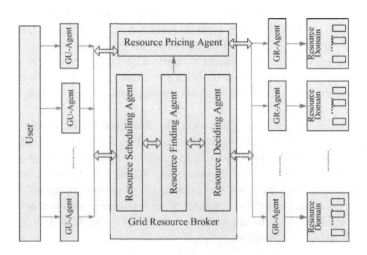

Fig. 1. Resource Allocation Model

Resource Scheduling Agent (RS-Agent) is used to recognize and analyze job requirements and originated from as defined by a user.

Resource Finding Agent (RF-Agent) is used to find the location of resources that can meet the requirements.

Resource Deciding Agent (RD-Agent) is used to store the information submitted by all existing GR-Agents.

Resource Pricing Agent (RP-Agent) is used to negotiate price between GU-Agent and GR-Agent.

In the grid, each GR-Agent publishes resources of their resources domain to RD-Agent. When the number, prices and processing power of the resources that are decided to sell are changed, GR-Agent will update the advertised information to RD-Agent. RD-Agent stores these information so that other GU-Agent can choose from these resources that can meet the user requirement. When a user prepares to submit a job, a new GU-Agent is created. GU-Agent denotes RS-Agent to analyze and recognize a submitted job, and then get demand resource information that can meet the requirement of a submitted job. RS-Agent orders RF-Agent to find the location of resource information according to demand resource information. Then, RF-Agent sends resource information that can meet the requirement to RP-Agent, and RP-Agent negotiates resource prices between GU-Agent and GR-Agent. At first, GU-Agent queries GR-Agent price information of the resource. If GU-Agent refuses the given price to make a purchase, new price may be set over again. When a GU-Agent purchases a portion of the resource, the price that GU-Agent pays is unable to be changed, and GR-Agent should continue to provide resource to the GU-Agent until the user job is completed. Interactions and negotiations between GU-Agent and GR-Agent are by the means of RP-Agent, and multi GU-Agents and GR-Agents can interact and negotiate simultaneously according to market supply and demand. RF-Agent select resources that meet the requirement of the submitted job to GU-Agent. Resource allocation algorithms are provided to complete resource price bargaining. In this algorithm an initial set of prices is set respectively by user and provider, and then is announced to GR-Agent and GU-Agent. GR-Agent and GU-Agent communicates their prices to RP-Agent, and RP-Agent may negotiate this price. If resource prices can't reach an agreement in RP-Agent, RP-Agent communicates with GR-Agent and GU-Agent to update their prices according to resource price algorithm respectively, and the cycle repeats itself until they arrive an acceptable price.

4   Resource Allocation Process and Pricing Algorithms

The whole grid system is made up of n Grid Domains, which is an autonomous, administrative and interactive entity consisting of a set of k resources units, and are managed by a GR-Agent$_i$. We define a $\xi = (\xi_{i,j})_{n \times k}$ as system processing power matrix, where $\xi_{i,j}$ specifies processing power of the ith Grid Domain for the jth type of resource, and define resources prices that is stored in a vector $P_t = \{P_t^1, P_t^2, \ldots, P_t^k\}$ with the range of prices being L to H, $P_t^k \in (L, H)$, for each member of the vector i = 1,.., k and each time period t, where L is lower limit on prices of resources, and H is the initial upper limit on prices asked. Each Grid Domain will produce a dualistic table $\Gamma_i(\xi, P_t)$ (the i index Grid Domains, $i \in (1, n)$). GR-Agent$_i$ holds this table and publishes it to RD-Agent in order to resources allocation. RD-Agent initializes $\Gamma(\Gamma_1, \Gamma_2, ..., \Gamma_n)$ according to the information submitted by all existing GR-Agents. All information of resources provided is stored in Γ. Γ should be updated by GR-Agents if the change happens within current Grid Domains. Otherwise, GR-Agents needn't update Γ.

A user submits a job to GU-Agent. GU-Agent denotes RS-Agent to analyze and recognize submitted job, and then get demand resources information $\Theta(\theta, \zeta, p)$ that can meet the requirement submitted job, where θ denotes type of requirement resource; ζ denotes processing power of requirement resource; p denotes prices that can be received by user. RS-Agent sent table $\Theta(\theta, \zeta, p)$ to RF-Agent in order to find the location of resources which can meet the requirement.

According to information of resources provided Γ and demand resources Θ, RF-Agent finds grid resources which can meet the requirement. If resources provided do not satisfy requirement resources (for example, any θ cannot be found in Γ, or $\zeta_\theta > \xi_\theta$ exists), GR-Agents will update Γ. If appropriate resources still cannot be satisfied after some times, RF-Agent informs RS-Agent that the job cannot be implemented. Then RS-Agent sends this message to RU-Agent, and RU-Agent will cancel this job and notify the user. If appropriate resource can be found, RF-Agent can get a quadruple $\Phi(\theta, GR_{i,j}, P_t, p)$, where$\theta, P_t, p$ are defined above; $GR_{i,j}$ denotes the ith Grid Domain for the jth type of resource. RF-Agent sent table $\Phi(\theta, GR_{i,j}, P_t, p)$ to RP-Agent in order to negotiate resource prices between GU-Agent and GR-Agent.

GR-Agent attempts to maximize grid resources provider income, and GU-Agent want to purchase resources by lowest price simultaneously. GR-Agent sells the grid resources, and the prices P_t in Φ are updated by using allocation algorithm. Thus GR-Agent decreases the price of any unit by a small amount ε after each negotiation. A GU-Agent represents the grid user to make trade decisions so that user can get maximized benefit. GU-Agents buy grid resources on the basis of price information p in Φ that it is willing to pay for resources. The price paid for resource should be as low as possible without failing to obtain the resource. Therefore GU-Agent decides respectively whether or not accepts this resource price to purchases for each resource. If a resource price was rejected, GU-Agent increases the price of any unit by a small amount μ, and then sends to RP-Agent at the next negotiation.

There are two pricing algorithms for GU-Agent (Fig. 2(a)) and GR-Agent (Fig. 2(b)). GU-Agent pricing function is $P_t = p + \mu \Delta t$, and GR-Agent pricing function is $P_t = P_0 - \varepsilon \Delta t$, where t is the time parameter, p and P_0 denotes base price that are set respectively by GU-Agent and GR-Agent ($p, P_0 \in (L, H)$, where L is lower limit on prices that provider can accept and is set by GR-Agent, and H is the upper limit on prices that user can accept and are set by GU-Agent). With time elapsing, GU-Agent pay with a higher price by increasing the price

```
Double price
If (not exist NegotiationPrice())
    price = P
Else {
        price=NegotiationPrice()
        If ((! PriceNegotiation ()) and (price < H))
                price = price+μ
        Else {
                If (price > H)
                price = 0
            }
    }
return(price)
```

(a)

```
Double price
If (not exist NegotiationPrice())
    price = P₀
Else {
        price=NegotiationPrice()
        If ((! PriceNegotiation ()) and (price > L))
                price = price – å
        Else {
                If (price < L)
                price = 0
            }
    }
return(price)
```

(b)

Fig. 2. Pricing Algorithm (a)GU-Agent Pricing Algorithm; (b)GR-Agent Pricing Algorithm

by a small amount μ as well as GR-Agent offer resource with a lower price by decreasing the price by a small amount ε after each negotiation. Two algorithms was made in respective agents, and then GR-Agent and GU-Agent negotiate resource prices in RF-Agent. If negotiation is successful, resources prices are set and stored in a prices vector $P_t = \{P_t^1, P_t^2, \ldots, P_t^\theta\}$; otherwise two functions must make again in GR-Agent and GU-Agent respectively. If any resource price exceed with the range of prices being L to H, we consider that this price negotiation is unsuccessful.

5   Experiments

The goal of this experiment is to compare the performance of the price-based resource allocation algorithm to other conventional resource allocation approach, which no pricing is used, and the incoming task queries are matched with the next available resource offer which meets the task's constraints. We simulate grid environment to evaluate experimentally the price-based resource allocation algorithm. We neglect the network topology and the communication costs associated with it. Instead, we assume that each of the users can submit jobs to any of the resources. However, it is still adequate for certain situations. This experiment is to study the schedule efficiency of price-based allocation algorithm in terms of resource allocation efficiency. In this experiment, we choose respectively 100, 200, 600, and 1000 resource domains to compare resource allocation efficiency of the price-based resource allocation algorithm to the conventional approach under various the number of resource domains. The experiment results are shown in Fig. 3 for resource allocation efficiency.

From the results in Fig. 3, when the number of resource domains is low, the difference in resource allocation efficiency between the two allocation methods is small, and both can achieve a good allocation efficiency, so using conventional

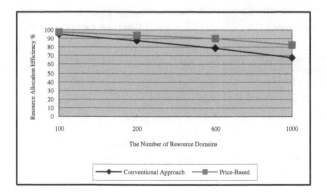

Fig. 3. Resource Allocation Efficiency

approach might be sufficient. When the number of resource domains increases, resource allocation efficiency of both methods will decrease. However, the resource allocation efficiency of price-based allocation algorithm decreases slower than that of the conventional approach. In other words, for a large number of resource domains, the conventional approach will not match the performance of the price-based allocation algorithm.From above performance comparisons, we can see that the resource allocation efficiency of the price-based resources allocation method is effective improved.

6   Conclusions

Resource allocation based on Pricing is an effective approach to manage resources of grid computing environment. In this paper, we analyzed a resource allocation method based a on pricing model in detail, which consists of GRB components and two economic agent types: GR-Agents that represent the economic interests of grid resource providers and maximize the profit for providers, and GU-Agents that represent the interests of grid resource and at the same time, achieve maximal benefit for grid users. Such a method should have broad applications in the management of various rid resources at high efficiency.

References

1. Foster, I., Kesselman, C.(eds.).: The Grid: Blueprint for a New Computing Infrastructure. Morgan Kaufmann (1999)
2. Foster, I., Kesselman, C., Tuecke S.: The Anatomy of the Grid: Enabling Scalable Virtual Organizations. International Journal of High Performance Computing Application, 15(3) (2001) 200-222
3. Foster, I., Kesselman, C., Nick, J., Tuecke, S.: The Physiology of the Grid: An Open Grid Services Architecture for Distributed Systems Integration.

4. Cao, H., Xiao, N., Lu, X., Liu, Y.: A Market-based Approach to Allocate Resources for Computational Grids. Computer Research and Development (Chinese), Vol.39, No.8 (2002) 913-916
5. R. Wolski, J. Plank, J. Brevik, and T. Bryan: Analyzing Market-based Resource Allocation Strategies for the ComputationalGrid. International Journal of High-performance Computing Applications, Sage Publications, 2001,Vol 15(3), 258-281
6. Subramoniam, K., Maheswaran, M., Toulouse, M.: Towards a Micro-Economic Model for Resource Allocation in Grid Computing System. Proceedings of the 2002 IEEE Canadian Conference on Electrical and Computer Engineering ,2002, 782-785
7. Buyya, R.: Economic-based Distributed Resource Management and Scheduling for Grid Computing. PhD Thesis, Monash University, Melbourne, Australia, April 12, 2002. Online at http://www.buyya.com/thesis/
8. Buyya, R., Abramson, D., and Giddy, J.: An Economy Driven Resource Management Architecture for Global Computational Power Grids. The 7th International Conference on Parallel and Distributed Processing Techniques and Applications (PDPTA 2000), Las Vegas, USA, June 26-29, 2000.
9. Buyya, R., Abramson, D., Giddy, J.: A Case for Economy Grid Architecture for Service Oriented Grid Computing. Proceedings of International Parallel and Distributed Processing Symposium: Heterogeneous Computing Workshop (HCW 2001), San Francisco, USA.
10. Chuliang Weng, Xinda Lu, Qianni Deng: A Distributed Approach for Resource Pricing in Grid Environments. In: Proceedings of the Second International Workshop on Grid and Cooperative Computing (GCC 2003), Shanghai, China, December 7-10, 2003, LNCS, Vol.3033,(2004) 620 - 627.
11. Yu Jiadi, Li Minglu, Li Ying, Hong Feng. A Framework for Price-Based Resource Allocation on the Grid. In: Proceedings of the 5th International Conference on Parallel and Distributed Computing, Applications and Technologies (PDCAT2004),Singapore, December 8-10, 2004, LNCS,Vol. 3320,(2004)339 - 342

CMSA: A Method for Construction and Maintenance of Semantic Annotations

Lixin Han[1,2,3], Guihai Chen[1], Linping Sun[2], and Li Xie[1]

[1] State Key Laboratory of Novel Software Technology, Nanjing University, China
[2] Department of Mathematics, Nanjing University, China
[3] Department of Computer Science and Engineering, Hohai University, China
lixinhan2002@yahoo.com.cn

Abstract. An important precondition for the success of the Semantic Web is founded on the principle that the content of web pages will be semantically annotated. In this paper, we propose a method, CMSA, of automatically acquiring semantic annotations. In the CMSA method, semantic annotations are acquired from semantic relationships. Class hierarchy is used to describe semantic relationships. One key feature of CMSA is that the hybrid algorithm of exploiting the desirable properties of both clustering algorithms and inference mechanism is proposed to construct semantic annotations. Another key feature of CMSA is that the k-nearest-neighbor query is introduced to maintain semantic annotations. The method can find more useful semantic information, improve precision, and manage semantic annotations easily.

1 Introduction

The success of the Semantic Web depends on the availability of ontologies as well as on the proliferation of web pages annotated with metadata conforming to these ontologies [1]. Therefore, how to improve the ability to annotate the content of web pages with semantic information is a critical issue.

Generally, there are three kinds of approaches for acquiring semantic annotations [2]. Firstly, semantic annotations are manually produced. For example, Annotea + Amaya, Yawas, Edutella, SHOE, OntoAnnotate, HTML-A, WebKB, Karina, Mangrove, and SMORE. In these systems, it is possible that humans provide extremely fine-grained semantic annotations but these systems overly depend on people's experience. Manual annotation is time consuming and expensive. In addition, it is difficult that millions of documents are annotated and therefore in this framework, annotation is meant mainly to be statically associated to the documents. Secondly, semantic annotations are semi-automatically produced. For example, MnM, Melita, OntoAnnotate, Teknowledge, and IMAT. Such systems presuppose a certain amount of manually annotated pages on which the system can be trained. However, even with the machine assistance, this is an arduous, time consuming and error-prone task. Thirdly, semantic annotations are automatically produced. For example, AeroDAML KIM, MnM, and Magpie. These systems overcome the burden of manual

G. Chen et al. (Eds.): ISPA Workshops 2005, LNCS 3759, pp. 514–519, 2005.
© Springer-Verlag Berlin Heidelberg 2005

training of the system. However, not all the annotation is reliable. There is an urgently need for solving robust problem with respect to noise.

We propose a method, CMSA (Construction and Maintenance of Semantic Annotations), for the construction and maintenance of semantic annotations. In the CMSA method, Class hierarchy is used to describe semantic relationships. The method manages semantic annotations easily.

2   CMSA Method

The CMSA method consists mainly of the CLCSA algorithms for the automatic construction of semantic annotations and TAMSA algorithm for the automatic maintenance of semantic annotations.

2.1   The Construction of Semantic Annotations

Different users determine different expectations for available information. Thus the identification of association relationships between concepts is very important. Hierarchical clustering techniques can find some existed patterns in the data. However, it is not possible to encode all the relevant relationships as rules, because they are not all usually known. The existed relationships in the knowledge base provide a scope for discovering new relationships. Based on some rules generated from the class hierarchy, new meaningful relationships can be discovered through an inferential process. Accordingly, based on the idea above, we propose the CLCSA (Introduce Complete-Link Clustering to Constructing Semantic Annotations) algorithm for automatically constructing semantic annotations. The CLCSA algorithm can exploit the desirable properties of both complete-link clustering algorithms and inference mechanism. The semantic annotations can be constructed from the Web resources.

The CLCSA algorithm is described as the following steps:

Input: a set of patterns
Output: a class hierarchy
{ i=0;
　　compute the proximity matrix D_i containing the distance between each pair of patterns. Treat each pattern as a cluster, that is, $D_{pq}=d_{pq}$.; // D_{pq} is the distance between each pair of clusters, d_{pq} is the distance between each pair of patterns
　　　while all patterns are not in one cluster
　　　{i=i+1;
　　　　find the most similar pair of D_{pq} in the proximity matrix,. Merge these two clusters C_p and C_q into one cluster C_r, , that is, $C_r=\{C_p,\ C_q\}$; // C_r, C_p, C_q is cluster
　　　　according to the formula $D_{rk}=\max\{D_{pk},\ D_{qk}\}$, calculate the proximity matrix D_i to reflect this merge operation;
　　　　generate some rules from the class hierarchy;
　　　　store these rules into the knowledge base;

the widely used Jena2's inference mechanism [3, 4] is used to infer semantic associations from the existing rules in the knowledge base in order to discover more meaningful association instances;}}

In contrast to the widely used complete-link clustering algorithm [2], the CLCSA algorithm provides the inference mechanism to find more useful association instances.

2.2 The Maintenance of Semantic Annotations

On the one hand, the maintenance of semantic annotations updates some parts of the semantic annotations. On the other hand, the maintenance of semantic annotations updates the automated modification of minor relations into the existed semantic annotations. This does not change major concepts and structures but makes the semantic annotations more precise. The TAMSA (The Automatic Maintenance of Semantic Annotations) algorithm is proposed to maintain semantic annotations using a k-nearest-neighbor query method [5]. We employ the B+-tree that basically becomes linear search for high dimensional data.

The TAMSA algorithm is described as the following steps:

Input: a class hierarchy, a class
Output: merge the class into the class hierarchy
{ the children of the root node is added to a queue;
    while the queue is not empty
        { a node is taken off the queue;
          the branch and bound algorithms [6, 7] is used to evaluate whether the node
          and any of its descendants are close enough to the class;
          if the node and any of its descendants are not close enough to the class
          then the subtree represented is discarded by this node;
          else if the node is not a leaf node
              then the children of this node is added to a queue;
              else { the class is inserted into the leaf node;
                      if there are "too many" classes in the leaf node
                      then {the leaf nodes are split;
                              some classes in the the leaf nodes is reassigned to the
                              other centers that may increase the least squared error;}}
      if   the class is farthest from any cluster center
      then a new cluster center is introduced;
      some new rules are generated from the updated a class hierarchy;
      these rules are stored into the knowledge base;
      the widely used Jena2's inference mechanism [3, 4] is used to infer
      semantic associations from the existing rules in the knowledge base in
      order to discover more meaningful semantic relationships;}}

3 Related Work

Handschuh et al. [8] refer to the framework as deep annotation, an original framework to provide semantic annotations for large sets of data. Deep annotation leaves semantic data in database systems. They incorporate the means for server-side markup that allows the user to define semantic mappings by using OntoMat-Annotizer. An ontology and mapping editor and an inference engine are then used to investigate and exploit the resulting descriptions.

Cimiano et al. [1] propose PANKOW, a novel approach towards the Self-annotating Web, which employs an unsupervised, pattern-based approach to categorize instances with regard to a given ontology. The approach combines the idea of using linguistic patterns to identify certain ontological relations as well as the idea of using the Web as a big corpus to overcome data sparseness problems. PANKOW has been conceived for their annotation framework CREAM [9] and has been implemented in OntoMat[4] using queries to the Web service API of Google[TM]. With regard to range, they have only covered the relationship between instances and their concepts, but not other relationships between instances.

Zhang et al. [10] address the problem of integrating objects from a source taxonomy into a master taxonomy. Their main contribution is to show that the implicit knowledge in the source taxonomy can be effectively exploited to boost taxonomy integration by marrying Cluster Shrinkage (CS) that can enhance the classification by exploiting such implicit knowledge and Transductive Support Vector Machines (TSVM) that extends SVM to transductive learning setting.

M. Vargas-Vera et al. [11] describe MnM, an ontology-based annotation tool which provides both automated and semi-automated support for annotating web pages with semantic contents. MnM integrates a web browser with an ontology editor and provides open APIs to link to ontology servers and for integrating information extraction tools. MnM can be seen as an early example of the next generation of ontology editors, being web-based, oriented to semantic markup and providing mechanisms for large-scale automatic markup of web pages. Within this work they have focused on creating a generic process model for developing semantically enriched web content. In addition, their process model is generic with respect to the specific ontology server and IE technologies used.

Dill et al. [12] describe Seeker, a platform for large-scale text analytics, SemTag, is built on the Seeker platform for large scale text analytics. SemTag is an application that performs automated semantic tagging. The Seeker platform can provide highly scalable core functionality to support the needs of SemTag and other automated semantic annotation algorithms. SemTag can tag very large numbers of pages, with terms from a standard ontology, in an automated fashion. In addition, since SemTag operates as a centralized application with access to the entire database and associated metadata, it has many advantages over a local, per-page tagger. They introduce a new disambiguation algorithm specialized to support ontological disambiguation of large-scale data.

Dingli et al. [13] propose a methodology to learn how to annotate semantically-consistent portions of the Web extracting and integrating information from different sources with minimum user intervention. The methodology is based on a combination of information extraction, information integration and machine learning techniques. Information is initially extracted by starting from structured sources and is then used to bootstrap more complex modules such as wrappers for extracting information from highly regular Web pages. In formation extracted by the wrappers is then used to train more sophisticated IE engines. All the training corpora for the IE engines are produced automatically. The user intervention is limited to provide an initial URL and to add information missed by the different modules when the computation is finished. No preliminary manual annotation is required.

In contrast to the above work, CMSA employs the hybrid algorithm of exploiting the desirable properties of both complete-link clustering algorithms and inference mechanism for the construction of semantic annotations. Further more, CMSA employs a k-nearest-neighbor query method and branch and bound method for the maintenance of semantic annotations.

4 Conclusion

With emergence of Semantic Web [14], Annotating web pages with ontology derived semantic tags plays an important role on the Semantic Web. In this paper, we propose a method called CMSA for the construction and maintenance of semantic annotations. In the CMSA method, the CLCSA algorithm is used to construct semantic annotations and the TAMSA algorithm is used to maintain semantic annotations.

Acknowledgements

This work is supported by the National Grand Fundamental Research 973 Program of China under No. 2002CB312002, China Postdoctoral Science Foundation under No. 2005037720, the State Key Laboratory Foundation of Novel Software Technology at Nanjing University under grant A200308, Jiangsu Planned Projects for Postdoctoral Research Funds, the Natural Science Foundation of Jiangsu Province of China under grant BK2005208, the Natural Science Foundation of Jiangsu Province of China under grant BK2004114 and the Key Natural Science Foundation of Jiangsu Province of China under grant BK2003001.

References

1. Philipp Cimiano, Siegfried Handschuh, Steffen Staab: Towards the Self-Annotating Web. In the Proceedings of the Thirteenth International World Wide Web Conference. New York, USA, May 17-22, 2004.
2. Faical Azouaou, Weiqin Chen, Cyrille Desmoulins: Semantic Annotation Tools for Learning Material. In the Proceedings of 3th International Conference on Adaptive Hypermedia and Adaptive Web-Based Systems. Eindhoven, The Netherlands, August 23-26, 2004.
3. Kevin Wilkinson, Craig Sayers, Harumi A. Kuno, Dave Reynolds: Efficient RDF Storage and Retrieval in Jena2. SWDB 2003: 131-150.
4. J. Carroll, I. Dickinson, C. Dollin, D. Reynolds, A. Seaborne, K. Wilkinson: The Jena Semantic Web Platform: Architecture and Design. HP Laboratories Technical Report HPL-2003-146.
5. N. Roussopoulos, S. Kelley, F.Vincent: Nearest Neighbor Queries. In the Proceedings of the 1995 ACM SIGMOD International Conference on Management of Data. San Jose, California, May 22-25, 1995.

6. E. L. Lawler, D. E. Wood: Branch-and-bound methods: A survey. Operations Research, 14: 699-719, 1966.
7. R. E. Moore: Global optimization to prescribed accuracy. Computers and Mathe-matics with Applications, 21(6/7): 25-39, 1991.
8. Siegfried Handschuh, Steffen Staab, Raphael Volz: On Deep Annotation. In the Proceedings of the Twelfth International World Wide Web Conference. Budapest, Hungary,May 20-24, 2003.
9. S. Handschuh, S. Staab: Authoring and annotation of web pages in CREAM. In the Proceedings of the 11th International World Wide Web Conference, May 7-11, 2002, Honolulu, Hawaii, USA.
10. Dell Zhang, Wee Sun Lee: Web Taxonomy Integration using Support Vector Machines. In the Proceedings of the Thirteenth International World Wide Web Conference. New York, USA, May 17-22, 2004.
11. M. Vargas-Vera, Enrico Motta, J. Domingue, M. Lanzoni, A. Stutt, F. Ciravegna: MnM: Ontology driven semi-automatic and automatic support for semantic markup. In the Proceedings of the 13th International Conference on Knowledge Engineering and Knowledge Management, EKAW02. Springer Verlag, 2002.
12. Stephen Dill, Nadav Eiron, David Gibson, Daniel Gruhl, R. Guha, Anant Jhingran, Tapas Kanungo, Sridhar Rajagopalan, Andrew Tomkins, John A. Tomlin, Jason Y. Zien: SemTag and Seeker: Bootstrapping the Semantic Web via Automated Semantic Annotation. In the Proceedings of the Twelfth International World Wide Web Conference. Budapest, Hungary,May 20-24, 2003.
13. Alexiei Dingli, Fabio Ciravegna, Yorick Wilks: Automatic Semantic Annotation using Unsupervised Information Extraction and Integration. In the Proceedings of 2th International Conference on Knowledge Capture October 23-25, 2003 Sanibel, Florida.
14. T. Berners-Lee, J. Hendler, O. Lassila: Semantic web. Scientific American, 1(1):68-88, 2000.

NDP2PSim: A NS2-Based Platform for Peer-to-Peer Network Simulations

Wu Kun, Dai Han, Yang Zhang, Sanglu Lu, Daoxu Chen, and Li Xie

State Key Laboratory for Novel Software Technology,
Department of Computer Science and Technology, Nanjing University,
210093, China
{wukun, daihan, zhangy,
sanglu, cdx, xieli}@dislab.nju.edu.cn

Abstract. Nowadays simulation is the major method to evaluate and analyze the performance of peer-to-peer systems. With the development of the research, more and more researchers point out that the underlying network highly impacts the performance of peer-to-peer systems. But most existing simulators are still based on some simplified models without considering the underlying network. Meanwhile, most simulators can only simulate some specific protocols on small scales. We designed and developed an integrated and generic simulation platform, NDP2PSim, built on NS2 to overcome these weaknesses. This platform can provide a realistic and generic simulation environment for almost all kinds of existing P2P protocols on large scales. And some common functions of P2P systems are also abstracted and provided as modules in order to make the platform easy to use. In this paper, we describe the structure of NDP2PSim in detail and compare it with other existing simulators.

1 Introduction

The rapid progress of computer and network technologies has increased the interests in and demand on a new kind of computing paradigm named Peer-to-Peer (P2P). In the field of P2P computing, a lot of new mechanisms on routing protocols, peer organizing strategies, resource distribution algorithms and etc are proposed to improve the performance of P2P systems. But the inspection of a new algorithm or protocol of P2P on an actual test bed system is a quite difficult and complicated task. So simulation with the testing model of P2P-system is regarded as a potential and feasible method to evaluate these new algorithms and protocols in a controlled environment.

Simulation is the process of designing a model of a real system and conducting experiments with this model for the purpose of understanding the behavior of the system and/or evaluating various strategies for the operation of the system [3]. And P2P simulation is a process to understand the behaviors, especially the dynamic network behaviors, of the P2P systems. Due to the complexity of P2P-system, modeling and simulating them are also not easy tasks. In most existing P2P simulators, such as CAN simulator [1], Gnutella simulator [7], Chord simulator [11] and etc, the underlying network characteristics are often ignored to simplify the model of P2P simulation. These simulators pay their all attentions to the characteristics of application-layer. But as is

G. Chen et al. (Eds.): ISPA Workshops 2005, LNCS 3759, pp. 520–529, 2005.
© Springer-Verlag Berlin Heidelberg 2005

known to all, the performance of P2P system is highly dependent on the underlying network characteristics [4]. Without taking into consideration of the impacts from the underlying network, the simulation model cannot be regarded as integrated and realistic.

In order to deepen researches on P2P-network more credible and more practical, we'd like to design and develop an integrated simulation platform, which includes both application layer network and a detailed underlying network model, called NDP2PSim. We choose NS2, a well-known generic network simulator, to provide the underlying network model, and construct a more credible, more usable and more powerful simulation platform for the simulation in P2P systems.

The rest of the paper is organized as follows. Section 2 describes the related works in P2P-network simulation. To overcome the weaknesses of these existing simulators, a novel simulation platform, named NDP2PSim, is presented and demonstrated in detail in section 3. In Section 4, we take Freenet simulation as a case study to illustrate the use of NDP2PSim. Section 5 displays qualitative evaluation of the platform. Finally, we conclude this paper and outline our future work in Section 6.

2 Related Works

Till to now, researchers have developed several specific P2P simulators. We observe that these simulators have following problems:

1) These simulators can only be used in one or two specific fields of P2P. Take Chord Sim as an example, it can only simulate the Chord protocols.
2) The influence from underlying network is always neglected in these simulators, which makes the simulations departure from the practical application.
3) In most P2P protocols, peers always dynamically join or leave the networks. But some existing P2P simulators don't support the simulations on the dynamic networks.
4) Many existing simulators can only support some or even one specific P2P systems. They are not the generic simulation tools for researching. If a comparison of two protocols is required, these simulators may not construct the environments for the both protocols.

NS2 [6], developed in VINT project, is a widely used generic and powerful network simulator that provides substantial support for simulation of local and wide area networks. To construct the both structured and unstructured P2P networks, some researchers introduce NS2 as a tool of P2P simulations.

With abundant components libraries, NS2 can simulate WAN, LAN, wireless networks, satellite networks and etc. As a generic network simulator, NS2 can be used in two ways: 1)using the existing modules for simulations, users just need to write a Tcl script; 2)expanding the existing modules or adding new modules into current systems, users have to rewrite or expand the current C++ and Otcl codes. The latter one is more useful in research but more complex. In the field of Internet research, NS2 is always regarded as a highly reliable simulator and the simulations results produced by NS2 are considered believable and acceptable.

Unlike commercial software, however, NS2 is lack of user-friendly documents and references. Therefore, it's quite difficult for new users to modify and expand the existing codes. It means that users, who plan to verify their mechanism, have to spend much time to get started. Another problem users must face is the lack of application-layer modules in NS2. It just provides few application-layer modules, such as ftp, telnet. This problem forces the P2P researchers to implement the application-layer parts for P2P simulations all by themselves.

All above weaknesses of the existing P2P simulators and NS2 spur us to develop a novel and more generic simulation platform -- NDP2PSim. Our main goal is to over-come the weaknesses of NS2 and packet-level simulation framework and provide a more usable, credible and generic simulation platform for P2P, or even all overlay networks.

3   NDP2PSim: A NS2-Based P2P Simulation Platform

In this section, we discuss the structure and implementation of NDP2PSim. To sup-port all kinds of network topologies, our simulation platform has a structure inherited from NS2. Moreover, the request for the underlying network models also inspires the introduction of a novel way to construct the simulation topologies. We first introduce the network topology used in NDP2PSim in subsection 3.1. Then, in subsection 3.2, we describe the structure of our NDP2PSim in detail.

3.1   The Virtual Network Topology

To produce the virtual network topologies used by NDP2PSim, users can manually write Tcl scripts by themselves. But it is a heavy and knotty job and will take too much time to produce a simple network topology. GT-ITM [8], designed by Getech, is a useful and widely used topology-producing tool. Using GT-ITM, users can get a complex network topology graph only by defining a few parameters. Here, in our NDP2PSim, we also use GT-ITM to simplify the network topology generation.

As Figure 1 shows, the peers (or nodes) of NDP2PSim topologies are classified into two categories, routing peers and application peers (or leaf peers). Routing Peers are produced by GT-ITM. They have no application component, and their only task is to forward the messages. Application peers, chosen from the routing peers or attached to the routing peers, have application components, events sponsors and handlers.

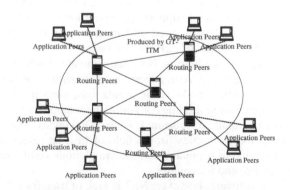

Fig. 1. The Virtual Topology of NDP2PSim

There are also two types of links in the virtual network. One is called physical link, which takes charge of IP packets transmission in the simulation. The other is called virtual link. Virtual links are dynamically built to connect the application peers during the simulation period. Each virtual link consists of several physical links. In other words, one hop in virtual link can has several hops of physical links.

3.2 The Structure of NDP2PSim

NDP2PSim inherits the structure of NS2 and also extends some existing modules in NS2. Because of the characteristics of NS2, our NDP2PSim includes an accurate underlying network model and can support large-scale simulation. As Figure 2 shows, our NDP2PSim can be viewed as a new kind of agent in NS2 (in fact, the NS2 only is a provider of the underlying network model). It mainly consists of five Modules: *Socket Module*, *Interface Module*, *P2P Application Module*, *Message Handler* and *Statistic Module*. We will describe the implementations and functions of each module in detail.

- *Socket Module*

The introduction of Socket Module aims to simulate the TCP socket actions more credibly and make the underlying network model more transparent to users. This module supports actual application message transmission across the peers and congestion control of TCP. Moreover, some necessary socket operations such as bind, listen, connect, send, recv and poll are provided to make the simulation closer to the actual TCP sockets. To convey the change of socket status to the Application Module, some functions with the prefix *upcall_* (e.g. upcall_recv, upcall_connected) are also defined in this module. With these upcall_s, the underlying modules can influence the status of Application Module.

- *Interfaces Module*

The Interface Module encapsulates some basic P2P application interfaces (message send and recv interfaces on application-layer), with which many complicated P2P application can be designed and set up in the P2P Application Module. Moreover, this module combined several Socket Modules into a socket map container (refers to C++ STL). The Application Module can get the corresponding socket through the address of the destination peer from this map. In fact, this module provides users with a list of basic application and socket interfaces needed in the communication simulation.

- *P2P Application Module*

There are a large number of specific applications in the P2P network. Here, we can abstract them into five main parts according to the different functions:

1) File Initiator. It can assign files to the peers according to certain distribution models in advance. So once joining the networks, the peers can immediately act as information providers.
2) Link Related Functions. They are invoked when logical links are established or destroyed.
3) File Store & Search Functions. They provide the necessary data structures and accessing implementation to simulate the file store and search. The search operation can be initiated according to some certain distribution models, such as Zipf.

4) Application Multicast Functions. They help the users to build simple multicast trees and application CBR so that users can conveniently construct the logical topologies to simulate the application-layer multicast.

5) CentralServer class. CentralServer acts like a central server during the simulation, but it is only an object, which isn't attached to any peers. The reason this class exists is that some algorithms require the support of out-of-band means [5] to choose peers' neighbors before the peers joining the network. Therefore, CentralServer is given to act as an optional out-of-band information provider in the P2P simulation networks.

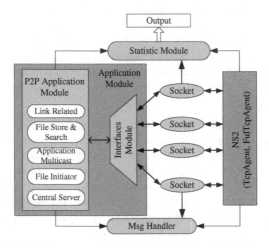

Fig. 2. The Structure of NDP2PSim (P2P Application Agent)

In the P2P Application Module, most functions are achieved by two classes cooperatively: SimAgent and SimApp. SimAgent is used to handle the message transmission according to different P2P protocols. By invoking the msg handler module, SimAgent can get the needed messages and deliver them to the destination peers. Users only need to implement the actions of peers as the protocol describing in some functions, such as upcall_recv. SimApp provides users some APIs to trigger the events (such as join, leave, query, insert, and etc.) or change the peers' states (online, offline and idle).

All these events should be triggered according some distributions. So we introduce a controller into this module as the input of the system. The controller dynamically generates the user actions based on some behavioral models. To master the generation of events, the controller provides an Tcl interface, called genop{}, to force the controller to generate corresponding event at specified time points.

Moreover, the P2P Application Modules provide some interfaces for extensibility. Some interfaces for implementation of the server actions, such as passive connection, are reserved in this module. This design make our platform can be used in some overlay network simulations. And in some protocols, such as Gnutella 0.6, peers can also act as ultrapeers to provide the partial information of the network.

- *Message Handler*

The main functions of Message Handler are to create and parse the application-layer messages. In this module, we define the format of common message header and message data used in application layer. Once receiving the messages, Socket Module invokes the Message Handler to parse the messages. It analyzes the header and informs the P2P Application Module to do the corresponding actions. The users can also define their own message types in this module if necessary.

- *Statistic Module*

The Statistic Model takes charge to collect three kinds data from P2P Application Module, Socket Module and NS2 (underlying layer network). The data collected here are presented in two different output files. One records the data of the P2P Application Module and the Socket Module, while the other one records the data from the underlying layer. The data of application and socket module include the degree of neighbors, the total number of control messages and data messages of each peer, the average delay of file search, the query/insert success rate, and the message queue length on each peer, etc. And the data from the underlying layer include the bottleneck bandwidth among IP links between two peers, the payload of underlying links, the packet loss rate, and etc. Users, who need these data, just need set the trace path in the Tcl scripts. The reason why we choose these data as NDP2PSim's standard statistic output is based on the P2P evaluation metrics proposed by some researchers [2, 10]. With these data, the performance of P2P systems can be evaluated comprehensively and extensively. If users require more data, they only need to add their own codes in this module.

4 Case Study: Freenet Simulation with NDP2PSim

To explain how to use NDP2PSim, we simulated the Freenet with it as an example. The Freenet is an adaptive peer-to-peer network application that permits the publication, replication, and retrieval of data while protecting the anonymity of both authors and readers [5]. The Freenet protocol is packet-oriented and uses self-contained messages. The requests for files, which are identified by binary file keys called transaction ID, are passed along from node to node. Each node independently makes local decisions about where to send the request next. Once received the requests, the node choose the nearest key in its routing table to forward the requests. Each request is given a hops-to-live limit, which is decremented at each node to prevent infinite chains, and a depth counter, which is incremented at each hop, to measure the path of the requests. When the requests are stopped at some destination, a backtracking message (request succeeded or request failed) should be returned to the initiator. The protocol details can be referred in [5].

The main actions of Freenet include Request.Data, Send.Data Request.Insert and Reply.Insert, and etc. We define all these messages in the message handler and add the corresponding message parsing sentences into the parsing function. Then the upcall_recv in SimAgent is rewritten to make sure that the SimAgent delivers the messages according to the Freenet protocol. As the protocol requires, we also altered the data structure of file storing in SimApp for data management. For the routing algorithm in the Freenet, a new data structure, route_table_, is introduced into SimAgent.

That table can help SimAgent decide where to send the requests next. Then an execution script is written conforming to the Tcl language syntax in order to construct the simulation environment and scenario. In the script, the function constructing the simulation topology is created by GT-ITM. The parameters of nodes and events, such as requests, inserts, etc. are also set in the script. Then run the script to do the simulation.

During the simulation, the data are collected by the statistic module and redirected into the files for future analysis. And the NDP2PSim also provides a trace file as the input for nam, which is a Tcl/TK based animation tool for viewing network simulation traces and real world packet tracedata[6].

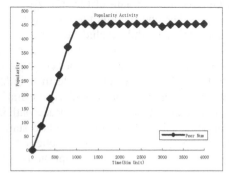
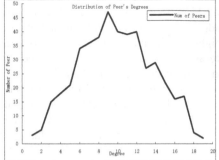

Fig. 3. Population Activity with Dynamic Arrivals and Departures

Fig. 4. Distribution of Peer's Degree in Freenet

In this paper, we selected some data of NDP2PSim's output to show the final simulation results. We simulated the Freenet with an about 480 peers virtual network topology generated by GT-ITM. To completely display the functions of NDP2PSim, we also use as more as provided distribution functions to configure the scenario the simulation. Figure 3, Figure 4 and Figure 5 demonstrate these data and illustrate the partial performance of Freenet. Figure 3 shows the activities of peers in the simulation, while Figure 4 shows the distribution of the peers' degrees. Both of these two figures are based on the data collected from the application layer. The Figure 3 plots the total number of active peers in the Freenet networks during the simulation. Because NS2 can stop the simulation at a certain time point set in the script, most peers are still up when the simulation finished. The degree of peers means the number of the neighbor peers.

In Figure 5, we can understand the evolution of the request path length over times. The App Depth represents the final value of the depth counter during the simulation. The IP Depth, from the underlying network model of NS2, is the IP hops that the messages passed by. And the value of Hops is calculated as follows:

$$Hops = (initial\ hops\text{-}to\text{-}live) - (hops\text{-}to\text{-}live)'$$

where (hops-to-live)' is the value of hops-to-live when the query arrives at the destination peer. This figure shows that the median request path-length drops as the network converges.

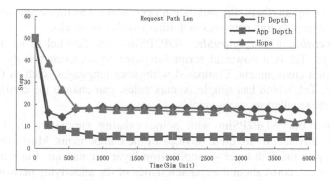

Fig. 5. Time Evolution of the Successful Query Path-Length

These figures reveal that NDP2PSim can simulate the P2P networks with the underlying network models and collect data from both application-layer and IP layer of the network (from the NS2 module). These data can help the users to do more precise analysis on the P2P network from not only the view of the overlay network but also the perspective of the TCP/IP layer of the Internet. The other kinds of P2P networks can be simulated in similar ways with the NDP2PSim.

5 Analysis and Evaluation

The structure described in section 3 brings NDP2PSim the following characteristics:

- *Generic.* NDP2PSim is applicable to most existing P2P systems, including both structured and unstructured P2P networks. Most common aspects of P2P systems are captured in this platform to accommodate the diversity of these P2P networks. We also extend the corresponding modules of NS2 to make NDP2PSim support the simulations of hierarchical networks. Furthermore, the platform can provide both large-scale and small-scale network simulations with the help of GT-ITM.
- *Highly Credible.* NDP2PSim focuses on not only the events happened on application layer but also the impacts of underlying network on P2P simulations. The underlying network provider, NS2 is a widely accepted generic simulator, and its results of underlying networks simulations are acceptable among scientific fields. So the results provided by NDP2PSim can also be credible.
- *Easy to Use.* NDP2PSim is designed with many application simulation modules and data collection interfaces. With these modules and interfaces, users can conveniently construct their own simulation scenarios and easily do the performance analysis.
- *Dynamic.* The population of peers in many P2P systems is dynamic for the peers joining and leaving the network. The variations of the network should be concerned in order to simulate the lifetime of the peers.
- *Extensible.* We have designed some interfaces in NDP2PSim for other fields, such as, some reserved interfaces for the actions of servers. By the implementa-

tion of these interfaces, the simulation peers can act as the servers and be used to simulate the C/S link networks and other overlay networks.

- **Interoperable & Configurable.** NDP2PSim uses Tcl/Otcl as its user interface language. Tcl is a powerful script language to comprehensively describe the simulation environment. Compared with other languages, such as C, C++, Java and etc, Tcl, which has simpler syntax rules, can change the configuration and re-run the simulations more quickly.

We compared our NDP2PSim with some existing simulators in Table 1, and NDP2PSim's advantages are quite obvious in the comparisons. Most existing simulators only support the fifth layer — application-layer simulations. But our NDP2PSim based on NS2, concerns about the characteristics of the underlying networks. With the help of NS2, NDP2PSim can be applicable for almost all kinds of P2P protocols, while other simulators always only can support one or two specific networks. Another advantage of NDP2PSim is the support of dynamic networks. Most P2P protocols consider the peers' action, such as join or leave, which makes the P2P topologies variable. The consideration of dynamic networks is quite significant.

With the above description and comparison, we can draw the conclusion that NDP2PSim are more practical and more generic than most existing P2P simulators.

Table 1. Comparisons Between NDP2PSim and Existing Simulators

Simulator	Simulated Layer	Supported protocol #	Dynamic Network Supported	Data Collection	Output
Chord Simulator	5	1	No	5	Text
Gnutella Simulator	5	1	No	5	Text
NeuroGird	5	2	Yes	5	Text
Freenet Simulator	5	2	Yes	5	Text
NDP2PSim	2-5	Many	Yes	2-5	Text & Graphics

6 Conclusion and Future Work

In this paper, we developed a generic, credible, NS2-based P2P simulation platform, named NDP2PSim, to overcome the weaknesses in existing simulators. In our platform, we paid more attention to the underlying-network characteristics and usability in P2P simulations. Compared with the existing P2P simulators or frameworks, our platform not only supports underlying network information collection, but also provides many frequently used application modules. Users can construct their own simulation environments by using existing modules or expanding the interfaces of application layer easily. We expect our NDP2PSim can effectively deepen the researches on P2P systems.

In the future, we hope to provide more complicated application modules to make NDP2PSim more powerful and easy to use. Also, we plan to implement our platform on the pdns, a parallel and distributed version of NS2, to support larger scale simulation.

Acknowledgements

This work is partially supported by the National Natural Science Foundation of China under Grant No.60402027; Jiangsu Natural Science Foundation under Grant No. BK2005411; the National High-Tech Research and Development Program of China (863) under Grant No.2004AA112090; the National Basic Research Program of China (973) under Grant No.2002CB312002.

References

1. S. Ratnasamy, P. Francis, M. Handley, R. Karp, S. Shenker. A Scalable Content-Addressable Network, 2001. *In Proceeding of the ACM SIGCOMM 2001 Technical Conference*, San Diego, CA, USA. Aug 2001.
2. N. Ting. A Generic Peer-to-Peer Network Simulator. *In Proceeding of the 2003-2004 Grad Symposium, CS, Dept, University of Saskatchewan*. April 7-8, 2003.
3. C. D. Pegden, R.E. Shannon, R. P. Sadowski. <Introduction to Simulation Using SIMAN>. *McGraw-Hill*. 1990.
4. M. Ripeanu, I. Foster, A. Iamnitchi. Mapping the Gnutella Network: Properties of Large-Scale Peer-to-Peer Systems and Implications for System Design. *Internet Computing Journal*. 2002.
5. I. Clarke, O. Sandberg, B. Wiley, T. W. Hong. Freenet: A Distributed Anonymous Information Storage and Retrieval System. *In Workshop on Design Issues in Anonymity and Unobservability, Berkeley, CA, pp. 46-66*. Jul 2000.
6. K. Fall, K. Varadhan. The ns Manual (formerly ns Notes and Documentation). *The VINT Project*. Oct 30, 2001.
7. M. Portmann and A. Seneviratne. Cost-Effective Broadcast for Fully Decentralized Peer-To-Peer Networks. *Computer Communications Journal, Special Issue on Ubiquitous Computing*, 2002.
8. K. Calvert, M. Doar, E. W. Zegura. Modeling Internet Topology. *IEEE Communication Magazine*. 1997.
9. K. Calvert, E. Zegura. GT Internetwork Topology Models (GT-ITM). *College of Computing, Georgia Institute of Technology*, 1996.
10. S. Merugu, S. Srinivasan, E. Zegura. p-sim: A Simulator for Peer-to-Peer Networks. *MASCOTS 2003*. Orlando, FL, USA.
11. Chord Internet Website. *URL: http://www.pdos.lcs.mit.edu/chord/*. 2003.

Resource Scheduling Scheme for Grid Computing and Its Petri Net Model and Analysis[*]

Yaojun Han[1], Changjun Jiang[2], and Xuemei Luo[1]

[1] College of International Business Administration,
Shanghai International Studies University, Shanghai 200083, China
[2] Department of Computer Science & Engineering, Tongji University,
Shanghai, 200092, China
Jimmy_hans@sohu.com

Abstract. The resource scheduling problem becomes complex, as resources are distributed, heterogeneous, dynamic and autonomous. A resource scheduling scheme with three-level for grid computing is proposed in this paper by analyzing present resource scheduling scheme. Petri net is a powerful graphical and mathematics tool for describing the concurrent, asynchronous and dynamic events. This paper models and analyzes the resource scheduling scheme of grid computing using hierarchical Petri net. Different Petri net models for resource scheduling of different layers are given in this paper. Petri model for different layer has different behavior, which represents heterogeneous and autonomous features of grid computing resources. Finally, we get some important results such as throughput, load balance and makespan on resource scheduling by analyzing reachability of Petri nets.

1 Introduction

In grid computing[1] environment, effective resource scheduling scheme is important to optimize the use of resource. Three scheduling schemes were discussed in [2]. They are centralized, hierarchical and distributed scheme. The centralized scheme is not very scalable because the grid scheduler must maintain a lot of detailed information about the constituent sites. This scheme also does not facilitate the use of different priority schemes at the different constituent centers. Unlike the centralized scheme, tasks are not maintained in the grid scheduler queue until dispatch time in hierarchical scheme. Once submitted to a local scheduler, the grid scheduler has no further direct influence on the scheduling on the task, and the task cannot be moved to another site even if the load at the other site becomes lower at some time in the future. Distributed scheme is similar to the hierarchical scheme except that there is a grid scheduler at every site and tasks are submitted to the local grid scheduler where the task originates.

[*] This work is support partially by projects of National Basic Research Program of China(973 Program)(2003CB316902, 2004CB318001-03), National Natural Science Fund (60125205, 90412013, 60473094), Shanghai Science & Technology Research Plan (04XD14016), and Science Research Funds of Shanghai International Study University.

G. Chen et al. (Eds.): ISPA Workshops 2005, LNCS 3759, pp. 530–539, 2005.

Since all tasks are submitted locally, the distributed scheme is more scalable than the hierarchical scheme. But, the performance of distributed scheme is poorer than one of central and hierarchical scheme according to [2].

Based on the hierarchical scheme and distributed scheme, we propose a three-level scheduling scheme. The differences between three-level scheduling scheme and present scheme are: (a) all tasks are submitted to home scheduler in stead of grid scheduler at themselves sites in the framework, which shows the autonomy of grid resource and is convenient for user to submit and supervise tasks; (b) the framework adds local scheduler between home scheduler and grid scheduler, which not only lightens the pressure of grid scheduler, but also makes tasks be possibly executed in local area.

Because of the complexity of resource scheduling in grid computing environment, the need arises in resource scheduling for powerful graphical and analytical tools. Although some resource scheduling heuristics were proposed in grid computing environment [3], graphic representation and formal description for resource scheduling in grid computing have not given more attention.

Petri nets are promising tools for modeling and analysis information processing systems that are characterized as being concurrent, asynchronous, parallel and distributed [6]. So it has received increasing application in modeling and analyzing resource scheduling. W.M.P. van der Aalst modeled and analyzed scheduling problems using timed Petri nets in [4]. To support the modeling of scheduling problems, it provided a method to map tasks, resources and constraints onto a timed Petri net. But it is very complex and difficult for low-level Petri net to model a big and complex system. In order to settle this problem, one method is to use synthesis of Petri nets. Another method is to introduce hierarchical Petri net. We gave a resource scheduling model for grid computing based on sharing synthesis of Petri nets in [9]. A hierarchical Petri net (HPN) model for the scheduling problems was given in [5]. But the resources that they discussed are homogeneous and single. So it is not suitable to the heterogeneous and multi-resources scheduling in grid computing environment. This paper models and analyzes the resource scheduling scheme of grid computing using hierarchical Petri net. Different Petri net models for resource scheduling of different layers are given in this paper. Finally, we get some important results such as throughput, load balance and makespan on resource scheduling by analyzing reachability of Petri nets.

The rest of this paper is organized as follows. The concepts of Petri nets related to this paper were reviewed in section 2. In section 3, we give resource scheduling framework for grid computing environments. Different Petri net models for resource scheduling of different layers (home scheduler, local scheduler and grid scheduler) are given in section 4. Some results about resource scheduling are gotten by analyzing reachability of Petri nets in section 5. In section 6, we give an example. The conclusions of the paper are given in section 7.

2   Concepts of Petri Nets Related to the Paper

In this section, we simply review some concepts of Petri nets related to this paper. See references [6],[7] and [8] for the details of the definitions of Petri nets.

Definition 1. A Petri Net is a bipartite directed graph represented by a four-tuple PN = $(P,T;F,M_0)$, where,

(1) N=$(P,T;F)$ is a net,

(2) $M: P{\rightarrow}Z$ is marking function, where M_0 is an initial marking, Z={0, 1, 2, …} is non-negative integer set,

Definition 2. Let PN = $(P,T;F,M_0)$ be a Petri net. For $x{\in}P{\cup}T$, $x{\bullet}=\{y{\in}P{\cup}T|(y,x) \in F \}$ and $\bullet x=\{y{\in}P{\cup}T|(x,y) \in F\}$ are called the pre-set and post-set of x respectively.

Definition 3. Let PN = $(P,T;F,M_0)$ be a Petri net.

(1) A transition $t{\in}T$ is enabled in M iff $\forall p{\in}{}^\bullet t: M(p){\geq}1$,

(2) A transition t enabled in M can fire and yield a new marking $M'(p)=M(p)-1$ for any $p{\in}$ pre-set of t and $M'(p)=M(p)+1$ for any $p{\in}$ post-set of t.

Definition 4. A colored Petri net (CPN) is a seven-tuple CPN=$(P,T; F, M_0, I-,I_+,C)$, where,

(1) $(P,T;F,M_0)$ is a Petri net,

(2) C is a function: $P{\cup}T{\rightarrow}\rho(D)$, where $\rho(D)$ is a power set of color set D, such that: for any $p{\in}P,C(p)$ is a set of all possible colored tokens in place p; for any $t{\in}T,C(t)$ is a set of all possible colors occurred in transition t,

(3) $I-$ and I_+ are negative function and positive function of $P{\times}T$ respectively, such that: for any $(p,t){\in} P{\times}T$, $I-(p,t) \in [C(t)_{MS}{\rightarrow}C(p)_{MS}]_L$ and $I-(p,t)=0$ iff $(p,t){\notin} I$; $I_+(p,t) \in [C(t)_{MS} \rightarrow C(p)_{MS}]_L$, and $I_+(p,t)=0$ iff $(p,t){\notin} O$, $M_0: P{\rightarrow}D_{MS}$ is an initial marking that satisfies $\forall p{\in}P: M_0(p) \in C(p)_{MS}$.

For $t_j{\in}T$, let $C(t_j)$ be a color set associated to t_j, $c_k{\in} C(t_j)$, M is current marking of CPN, then t_j is enabled with respect to c_k in a marking M (hereinafter represented by t_j /c_k iff $M(p_i){\geq} I-(p_i, t_j/c_k)$ for any input place p_i of c_k. A transition t_j enabled with respect to c_k in a marking M can fire and yield a new marking $M'(p_i)$:

$$M'(p_i) = \begin{cases} M(p_i)+I_+(p_i,t_j/c_k) & if & p_i \in t_j^\bullet-{}^\bullet t_j \\ M(p_i)-I_-(p_i,t_j/c_k) & if & p_i\in{}^\bullet t_j - t_j^\bullet \\ M(p_i) & others \end{cases}$$

Definition 5. A timed Petri net (TDPN) is a five-tuple TDPN = $(P,T; F, M_0,D)$, where,

(1) $(P,T; F, M_0)$ is a Petri net,

(2) $D: T{\rightarrow}R$ is a firing time delay, where R is a real set.

In a TDPN defined in this paper, the time delay associated with transition t is a function of color token of input places of transition t.

Definition 6. A hierarchical colored Petri net (HCPN) is a nine-tuple HCPN=(S,SN, SA, PN, PT, PA, FS, FT, PP), where,

(1) S is a finite set of pages such that:

(a) Each pages $s{\in}S$ is a non-hierarchical colored Petri net:

$(\Sigma_s, P_s, T_s, A_s, N_s, C_s, G_s, E_s, I_s)$.

(b) The set of net elements are pairwise disjoint:

$$\forall s_1, s_2 \in S: [s_1 \neq s_2 \Rightarrow (P_{s_1} \cup T_{s_1} \cup A_{s_1}) \cap (P_{s_2} \cup T_{s_2} \cup A_{s_2}) = \phi].$$

(2) $SN \subseteq T$ is a set of substitution nodes.

(3) SA is a page assignment function. It is defined from SN into S such that: no page is a subpage of itself:

$$\{s_0 s_1 \dots s_n \in S^* | n \in N_+ \wedge \forall k \in 1..n: s_k \in SA(SNs_{k-1})\} = \phi.$$

(4) $PN \subseteq P$ is a set of port nodes.

(5) PT is a port type function. It is defined from PN into {in, out, i/o, general}.

(6) PA is a port assignment function. It is defined from SN into binary relations such that :

(a) Socket nodes are related to port nodes: $\forall t \in SN: PA(t) \subseteq X(t) \times PN_{SA(t)}$.

(b) Socket nodes are of the correct type: $\forall t \in SN \; \forall (p_1, p_2) \in PA(t)$:

$$[PT(p_2) \neq general \Rightarrow ST(p_1, t) = PT(p_2)] \square$$

(c) Related nodes have identical color sets and equivalent initialization expressions :

$$\forall t \in SN \; \forall (p_1, p_2) \in PA(t): [C(p_1) = C(p_2) \wedge I(p_1) = I(p_2)].$$

(7) $FS \subseteq P_s$ is a finite set of fusion sets such that : Members of a fusion set have identical color sets and equivalent initialization expressions :

$$\forall fs \in FS \; \forall p_1, p_2 \in fs: [C(p_1) = C(p_2) \wedge I(p_1) = I(p_2)].$$

(8) FT is a fusion type function. It is defined from FS into {global, page, instance} such that: Page and instance fusion sets belong to a single page:

$$\forall fs \in FS: [FT(fs) \neq global \Rightarrow \exists s \in S: fs \subseteq P_s].$$

(9) $PP \in S_{MS}$ is a multi-set of prime pages.

3   Resource Scheduling Scheme for Grid Computing Environments

3.1   Resource Scheduling Scheme

Based on the hierarchical scheme and distributed scheme given in [2], we give a three-level scheduling scheme shown in Figure 1. In three-level scheduling scheme, the resources are connected via a three-level hierarchical network. The first level is a wide-area network (WAN) that connects local area networks (LANs). The second level is a LANs that connects computing resources (personal computers and high performance computers), storage resources and other resources at the third-level. Unlike hierarchical scheme and distributed scheme, all tasks are submitted to home scheduler in stead of grid scheduler at themselves sites in the three-level scheduling scheme, which shows the autonomy of grid resource and is convenient for user to submit and supervise tasks. In addition, the three-level scheduling scheme adds local scheduler between home scheduler and grid scheduler, which not only lightens the pressure of grid scheduler, but also makes tasks be possibly executed in local area.

The three-level scheduling scheme has following main functions.

The function of home scheduler includes: (1) receives tasks submitted by user and assigns them to resources, (2) sends tasks to local scheduler, (3) receives subtasks assigned by local scheduler and assigns them to resources, (4) provides information of home machine to the local scheduler.

The function of local scheduler includes: (1) receives tasks and information about home machine submitted by home schedulers, (2) sends tasks to grid scheduler, (3) receives tasks assigned by grid scheduler and assigns subtasks to home schedulers, (4) provides information of local area network to grid scheduler.

The function of grid scheduler includes: (1) receives tasks and information about local area network submitted by local schedulers, (2) assigns tasks to local schedulers.

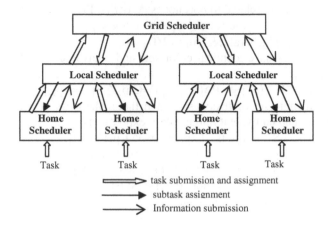

Fig. 1. Three-level task scheduling scheme

3.2 Process of Task Submission and Assignment

Each task with its processing requirements such as estimated processing time, estimated communication time, deadline and parallel degree is submitted to its home scheduler by user. The process of task submission and assignment is as follows.

(1) A task is submitted to home scheduler by user through home machine. The home scheduler analyzes the submitted task. If the task can be completed within its deadline in home machine, then the task is executed on the home machine. Otherwise, the task is sent to the local scheduler.

(2) When local scheduler receives the task submitted by home scheduler, it decides if the task is can be completed within its deadline in the local area network. If so, the local scheduler assigns subtasks of the task to some machines in the local area network according to some algorithm. Otherwise, the task is sent to the grid scheduler.

(3) When grid scheduler receives the task submitted by local scheduler, it inserts the task into the queue of tasks.

Based on the queue of tasks and the information about all local area network, the grid scheduler assigns task to some local area network according to some algorithm.

4 Hierarchical Petri Net Models for Resource Scheduling in Grid Computing Environment

Definition 7. The extended colored timed Petri net model for home scheduler is a ten-tuple H-ECTDPN= $(P, T, F, W, M_0, C, D, R, IN, OUT)$, where,

- $P = \{p_j | j =1,2, \dots ,8\}$ is a finite set of places.
- $T = \{t_j | j =0,2, \dots ,10\}$ is a finite set of   transitions.
- $F \subseteq (P \times T) \cup (T \times P)$ is a finite set of arcs.
- $C = \{(id, dt)\} \cup \{(ET, CT)\} \cup \{(a) \cup (info)\}$ is a set of colors, where id is ID number of a task, dt is the deadline of a task, ET is the expected execution time matrix of all subtasks of a task on all machines, CT is the expected communication time of a task, a is the arrival time of a task, $info$ is information of a machine, including available processor's number, time that is ready for executing next task, etc.
- $W = f(F) = \{f_j | j =1,2, \dots ,24\}$ is a finite set of weighted functions of arcs, where, $f_0 = f_1 = (pd, dt, ET, CT, a)$, $f_2 = (info)$, $f_3 = f_6 = f_7 = f_1 + f_2$, $f_4 = f_2$, $f_5 = (info)$, $f_8 = f_9 = f_{10} = f_{12} = f_1$, f_{11}: the task selected by home scheduler according to some algorithm, f_{13}: the task completed by home machine, f_{14}: the subtasks selected by local scheduler according to some algorithm, f_{15}, f_{20}, f_{21}: the remote subtask completed by home machine, f_{16}, f_{23}, f_{24}: the current information of the machine, f_{17}: f_{19} the task completed by remote machine, f_{18}, f_{20}: the remote subtasks assigned to the machine.
- $M_0(p_2) = (info)$. Other places have no tokens in initial marking.
- D: $T \rightarrow R$ is a firing time delay, where, $D(t_0)$ is a random number, $D(t_1) = D(t_2) = D(t_3) = D(t_7) = D(t_9) = D(t_{10}) = 0$, $D(t_4) = D(t_5) =$ communication time of task or subtask, $D(t_6) = D(t_8) =$ execution time of task or subtask.
- $R = \{(p_3, t_6)\}$ is an inhibit arc. Its function is to give home task higher priority than remote tasks.
- $IN = \{pn_2, pn_4\}$ is input units.
- $OUT = \{pn_1, pn_3, pn_5\}$ is output units.

The graphical representation of H-ECTDPN is shown in figure 2. The table 1 gives the descriptions for figure 2.

Definition 8. The colored timed Petri net model for local scheduler is a nine-tuple L-CTDPN = $(P, T; F, W, M_0, C, D, IN, OUT)$, where, explanation of each element is similar to one of definition 7. The graphical representation of L-CTDPN is omitted.

Definition 9. The colored timed Petri net model for grid scheduler is a nine-tuple G-CTDPN = $(P, T; F, W, M_0, C, D, IN, OUT)$, where, explanation of each element is similar to one of definition 7. The graphical representation of L-CTDPN is omitted

Definition 10. The hierarchical colored Petri net model for grid resource scheduling system is a seven-tuple HCPN = $(P, T, S; F, W, M_0, C)$, where,

(1) $P = \{P_1, P_2, P_3, P_4, P_5\}$, where,

    (a) $P_1 = \{p_{11}, p_{12}\}$ is a finite set of input unit and output unit for grid scheduler.

    (b) $P_2 = \{p_{2i} | i=1,2,\dots, n$, where n is the number of LAN$\}$ is a finite set of input units for local schedulers.

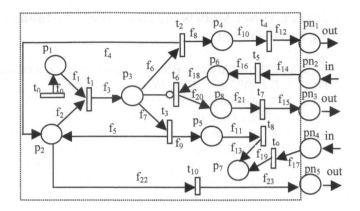

Fig. 2. H-ECTDPN model

Table 1. Description for Fig. 2

Place	Description	Transition	Description
p_1	Tasks Submitted by user	t_0	Submitting task to home machine
P_2	Resources	t_1	Getting task and machine info.
p_3	Ready for scheduling task	t_2	Cann't complete task within deadline
p_4	Ready for submitting task	t_3	Can complete task within deadline
p_5	Ready for executing task	t_4	Sending task to local scheduler
p_6	Ready for executing remote task	t_5	Assigning task to home scheduler
p_7	Completed tasks	t_6/ t_8	Executing remote/ home task
p_8	Completed remote subtask	t_7	Submitting completed remote subtask
pn_1, pn_3, pn_5	Output units of submitting task, completing subtask and machine information.	t_9	Return completed task
pn_2, pn_4	Input units of assigning remote subtask and completing task	t_{10}	Providing machine information

(c) . $P_3=\{p_{3i}|i=1,2,\ldots, 2n$, where n is the number of LAN} is a finite set of output units for local schedulers.

(d) $P_4=\{p_{4i}|i=1,2,\ldots, m_1, m_1+1,\ldots, m_1+ m_2, \ldots, m_1+ m_2+\ldots+m_n$, where n is the number of LAN, m_j is the number of machines of $LAN_j\}$ is a finite set of input units for home schedulers.

(e) $P_5=\{p_{5i}|i=1,2,\ldots, m_1, m_1+1,\ldots, m_1+ m_2, \ldots, m_1+ m_2+\ldots+m_n$, where n is the number of LAN, m_j is the number of machines of $LAN_j\}$ is a finite set of output units for home schedulers.

(2) $T=\{T_1, T_2, T_3, T_4 \}$, where,

(a) $T_1=\{t_{1i}|i=1,2,\ldots, n$, where n is the number of LAN} is a finite set of transitions, sending information from grid scheduler to local schedulers.

(b) $T_2=\{t_{2i}|i=1,2,\ldots, 2n$, where n is the number of LAN} is a finite set of transitions, sending information from local schedulers to grid scheduler.

(c) $T_3=\{t_{3i}|i=1,2,\ldots, m_1, m_1+1,\ldots, m_1+ m_2, \ldots, m_1+ m_2+\ldots+m_n$, where n is the number of LAN, m_j is the number of machines of $LAN_j \}$ is a finite set of transitions, sending information from local schedulers to home schedulers.

(d) $T_4=\{t_{4i}|i=1,2,\ldots, m_1, m_1+1,\ldots, m_1+ m_2, \ldots, m_1+ m_2+\ldots+m_n$, where n is the number of LAN, m_j is the number of machines of $LAN_j\}$ is a finite set of transitions, sending information from home schedulers to local schedulers.

(3) $S=\{S_1, S_2, S_3\}$, where,

(a) $S_1=\{s_{11}\}$ is a finite set of subnet corresponding to grid scheduler.

(b) $S_2=\{s_{2i}|i=1,2,\ldots, 2$, where n is the number of LAN$\}$ is a finite set of subnets corresponding to local schedulers.

(c) $S_3=\{s_{3i}| i=1,2,\ldots, m_1, m_1+1,\ldots, m_1+ m_2, \ldots, m_1+ m_2+\ldots+m_n$, where n is the number of LAN, m_j is the number of machines of $LAN_j\}$ is a finite set of subnets corresponding to home schedulers.

(4) $F\subseteq(P\times T) \cup (T\times P) \cup (P\times S) \cup (S\times P)$ *is a finite set of arcs.*

(5) C is a set of colors. The details are referred to definition 7.

(6) W is a finite set of weighted functions of arcs.

(7) M_0 is an initial marking, where $M_0(p_{4i})=1$ ($i=1,2,\ldots, m_1, m_1+1,\ldots, m_1+ m_2, \ldots, m_1+ m_2+\ldots+m_n$), Other places have no tokens in initial marking.

The graphical representation of HCPN including 2 local schedulers and 3 home schedulers is shown in figure 3 (the weighted functions of arcs are omitted).

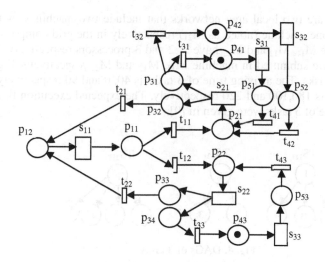

Fig. 3. HCPN model

5   Analysis of System Performance

Proposition 1. The throughput of system can be gotten from following formula:

$$\sum_{k=1}^{n}\sum_{i=1}^{m_k}M_{ki}(p_7)$$

where, $M_{ki}(p_7)$ is the reachable marking of H-ECTDPN model, representing the number of tasks completed in the ith machine of the kth local area network.

Proposition 2. Let μ and σ be mean and standard deviation of $M_{ki}(p_7)$ ($k=1,2,\dots,n;i=1,2,\dots, n_k$). If $\sigma \ll \mu$, then the system load is not balanced. Otherwise, the system load is balanced.

If the system load is not balanced, we should modify the scheduling algorithm to balance the system load.

In order to analyze the time behavior of system, we introduce the concept of reachable task graph of HCPN. The definition and construction algorithm of reachable task graph were given in [9]

Proposition 3. Let RTG(HCPN) be the reachable task graph of HCPN. The sequence composed of "$t[n]/ TS_{kis}$" from M_0 to the end node is the scheduling sequence of task TS_{kis}.

Proposition 4. Let RTG(HCPN) be the reachable task graph of HCPN. $M_j \in$ RTG(HCPN) is the end node. a_j is a tag of M. The makespan of the system (i.e. the complete time of last task) is equal to max $\{ a_j \}$.

6   Example

Suppose that there are two local area networks that include two machines (noted as M_{11} and M_{12}) and one machine (noted as M_{21}) respectively in the grid computing environment. Machine M_{11}, M_{12} and M_{21} have 2, 2 and 3 processors respectively. Three independent tasks are submitted in machine M_{11}, M_{12} and M_{21} respectively. Figure 4 shows DAGs of 3 tasks. The arriving time of 3 tasks is 40, 0 and 90 respectively. The deadline of 3 tasks is 180,100 and 220 respectively. The expected execution time and communication time of 3 tasks were given in [9].

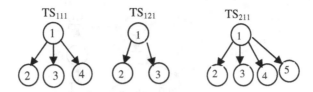

Fig. 4. DAGs of 3 tasks

According to the definitions 7, 8, 9 and 10, we construct hierarchical colored Petri net models for the resource scheduling of the example. The graphical representation of the models is similar to figures 2 and 3 and is omitted here.

Then we construct the RTG(HCPN). The RTG(HCPN) is similar to RTG(HLTDPN) given in [9] and is omitted here.

From the RTG(HCPN), we get the scheduling sequence of tasks. According to proposition 4, we know that M_{115}, M_{24} and M_{323} are dead-end nodes from RTG(HCPN) . The makespan of the schedule is max$\{173,80,303\}$=303.

7   Conclusions

In this paper, a resource scheduling scheme with three-level in grid computing environments is presented. The resource scheduling scheme is modeled and analyzed by hierarchical Petri net. Different Petri net models for resource scheduling of different layers (home scheduler, local scheduler and grid scheduler) are given in this paper. Petri model for different layer has different behavior, which represents heterogeneous and autonomous features of grid computing resources. So, the hierarchical Petri net is an ideal model for resource scheduling scheme with three-level in grid computing environments. Finally, we get some important results such as throughput, load balance and makespan on resource scheduling by analyzing reachability of Petri nets.

References

[1] I. Foster and C. Kesselman, ed., "The Grid: blueprint for new computing infrastructure", Morgan Kaufmann Publishers. San Francisco, CA, 1999.

[2] Vijay Subramani, Rajkumar Kettimuthu, et al, "Distributed task scheduling on computational grids using multiple simultaneous requests", Proceedings of 11th IEEE International Symposium on High Performance Distributed Computing (HPDC'02), July 24 - 26, 2002 Edinburgh, Scotland. pp. 359-366.

[3] Maheswaran M., Ali S., et al, "Dynamic matching and scheduling of a cass of independent tasks onto heterogeneous computing systems", Proceedings of 8th IEEE Heterogeneous Computing Workshop (HCW'99) ,San Juan, Puerto Rico, Apr. 1999, pp. 30-44.

[4] W.M.P. van der Aalst, "Petri net based scheduling", Computing Science Reports. No. 95, Eindhoven University of Technology, 1995.

[5] Yu DA, Zhang Bo, Chen Chen, "An approach to HPN model of the scheduling problem", Computer Research & Development. Vol. 33(5), 1996:321-328.

[6] T. Murata, "Petri nets: properties, analysis and application". Proceedings of IEEE, Vol.77, Apr.1989: 541-584.

[7] Jensen, K. "Coloured Petri nets: basic concepts, analysis methods and practical use", Berlin, Heideberg, New York: Springer-Verlag, Vol. 1, 2. ed. , 1996.

[8] W.M. Zuberek, "Timed Petri nets: definitions, properties and applications". Microelectronics and Reliability, vol.31, no.4, 1991: 627-644.

[9] Yaojun Han, Changjun Jiang, Xuemei Luo, "Resource Scheduling Model for Grid Computing Based on Sharing Synthesis of Petri Net", Proceedings of 9th international conference on Computer Supported Cooperative Work in Design(CSCWD 2005), Coventry, UK, May 24-26, 2005.

The Design and Implementation of Service Adapter in ShanghaiGrid Core*

Hongbo Wan, Qianni Deng, Xinhua Lin,
Xinda Lu, and Minglu Li

The Grid Computing Center, Shanghai Jiaotong University,
200030 Shanghai, China
todaytome@sjtu.edu.cn

Abstract. Up to now, there have been three un-compatible standards in service-oriented grid environment: Standard Web Service (WS), OGSI (Open Grid Service Infrastructure), WSRF (Web Service Resource Framework). In order to make use of these distinct services in a consistent way, we propose the Service Adapter solution. In this p[1]aper, following a brief description of ShanghaiGrid Core (SG-Core), we focus on the design and implementation of Service Adapter that used in the SG-Core. Service Adapter simplifies the invocation procedure of the un-compatible services, and it provides user with a transparent service access interface. It is designed in an extensible way, so new standard adapter or binding extension can be added easily.

1 Introduction

One of the problems with any computing technology is getting the different components to talk to each other. The essence of the Grid is all about distributed computing and resource management. So the standard is very significant in grid computing.

Web Service technology allows applications to be integrated more rapidly, easily and less expensively than ever before. [1] It can be used to provide a backbone for our grid solutions. OGSA represents an evolution towards a Grid system architecture based on Web services concepts and technologies. [2] The Open Grid Services Infrastructure (OGSI, developed by GGF) is the first specification of OGSA. OGSI adds service data through extending standard WSDL (Globus WSDL, GWSDL). [3] The Globus Toolkit (GT) V3 is the major reference implementation of the OGSI. The Web Service Resource Framework (WSRF, developed by OASIS) is the second specification of OGSA. WSRF is to keep grid/web services interfaces stateless, and let them interact with separate stateful resources. [4, 5] The GT V4 is the reference implementation of the WSRF.

During the development of ShanghaiGrid [6], numerous of Web/Grid Services have been deployed in different grid sites. Of course, they have been developed according to different standards (Standard WS, OGSI-compliant, WSRF-compliant), and also

---

* This paper is supported by National Natural Science Foundation of China(60403034) and Shanghai Technology and Science Committee Municipality (03dz15026, 03dz15027).

G. Chen et al. (Eds.): ISPA Workshops 2005, LNCS 3759, pp. 540–548, 2005.

they have been deployed in different service containers, for example, Tomcat+Axis, GT V3 Container, GT V4 Container, etc. Within grid technology concept, grid can be viewed as a virtual powerful computer. So, we want to integrate all these services in a consistent grid environment, and user can make use of these services without consideration of technique details. There are two solutions that we can choose. (1)Transplantation solution: We can transplant all the services according to one standard in ShanghaiGrid, for example, WSRF. This method will involve re-development and re-deployment of existing services. (2) Service Broker solution: No changes on existing services, we add a service broker between service user and service provider. During the interaction with service, the broker will deal with the complex technique details. By all appearances, the latter method is the best choice.

ShanghaiGrid Core (SG-Core) is an innovative service broker solution used in ShanghaiGrid environment. We will give a brief introduction of SG-Core in Section 3. Service Adapter is an integral part of SG-Core, and it is used to adapt ShanghaiGrid for multi-standards service environment. It will be discussed in Section 4. Finally, we present our SG-Core's browser interface based on Service Adapter in Section 5. Our contribution, conclusion, and future work will be discussed in Section 6.

2 Related Works

Both transplantation solution and service broker solution can be adopted according to different conditions.

The Belfast e-Science Centre [7] established in Queen's University Belfast represents an attempt at a systematic approach to the conversion of GT3.x services to GT4 services. This method considers the conversion of Java code to Java WSRF Core. Both OGSI-compliant and WSRF-compliant services are deployed in the form of GAR (Grid Archive) file. In this file we provide the container with the service descriptor, deploy descriptor, implementation files, and associated libraries. There's a direct mapping from OGSI features to WSRF features. In fact, this method is to make transplantation from GT V3 services to GT V4 services.

Systinet Server [8] for IBM WebSphere that enables traditional MOM (Message-Oriented Middleware) infrastructures to take advantage of standardized Web services technology use Web Service Adapter to connect Systinet Server to the Web services environment. It creates Web service endpoints for publishing messages through Systinet Server as well as endpoints where Web service subscribers can listen for messages. When contracts are used, WS Adapter publishes WSDL's describing the endpoints. So WS Adapter is a bridge between MOM and standard Web Service.

But, in Shanghai Grid environment, our Service Adapter will deal with more complex issues. So, we must adopt service broker solution.

3 Brief Introduction of ShanghaiGrid Core (SG-Core)

ShanghaiGrid is a complex service-oriented infrastructure. It has integrated resources from Shanghai Supercomputer Center and four universities: Shanghai Jiao Tong

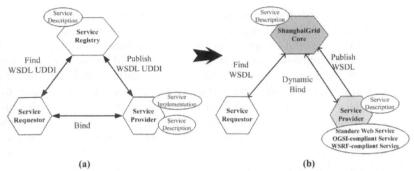

(a)   (b)

Fig. 1. (a) Traditional Web Service Architecture (b) Service Broker Architecture based on ShanghaiGrid Core

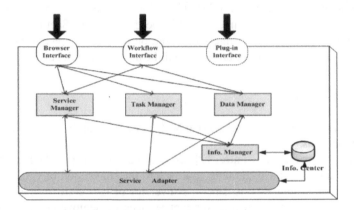

Fig. 2. The Architecture of ShanghaiGrid Core

University, Fudan University, Tongji University, and Shanghai University. Since the WSRF standard was released by OASIS in the early of 2004, we have taken initiative to do research on the problem about how to integrate services based on different standards. Fig. 1 (a) shows that the traditional Web Services architecture is based upon the interactions between three roles: service provider, service registry and service requestor. [1] In this architecture, the service requestor must be familiar with the details of service implementation. But, after the introduction of SG-Core, shown in Fig 1 (b), the service requestor is separated from service provider. With SG-Core, service requestor, including final user, workflow engine, and so on, will not care about the specific implementation of service. The SG-Core can dynamically make match for service requestor according to the different standards.

The architecture of SG-Core is compact and extensible, as illustrated in Fig. 2. On the top layer, there are three interfaces: (1) Browser Interface: Service provider can register their services and user can interact with a service from a conventional web browser. (2) Workflow Interface: This interface allows workflow engine to invoke services transparently. (3) Plug-in Interface: This interface is used for extension, new features can be plugged in through this interface.

There are three kernel function modules in the middle of the SG-Core, as following: (1) Service Manager: It is used to register a new service, index the service and search proper service according to user's requirement. (2) Task Manager: We view service invocation procedure as a task. This module is to manage the input parameter, the output result, etc. (3) Data Manager: It is used to transfer data between user and grid site. Information Manager is used to store all data published by service provider.

All these function modules are based on Service Adapter, so the Service Adapter is an essential part of SG-Core. We will get down to specific in Section 4.

4   Service Adapter in ShanghaiGrid Core

In this section, we will discuss the design architecture of Service Adapter. Then the implementation details will be presented in three parts: Service Data Manager, Service Adaptation and Binding Adaptation.

4.1   The Design Architecture

In service-oriented grid infrastructure, hosting environment and services are basic low level structures, as showed in Fig. 3. The grid environment is made of thousands of services which hosted in different platforms and widespread locations. Also, maybe the services are implemented in distinct standards, and deployed in different service container. Consuming service is the basic method to make use of grid computing technology. Service is the abstraction of resources, including computing capability, application, network bandwidth, etc. Developers use services as fundamental processes. Service composition lets developers create applications on top of service-oriented computing's native description, discovery, and communication capabilities. [10]

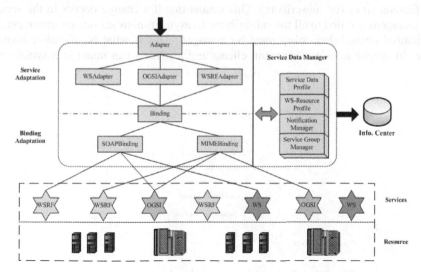

Fig. 3. The Design Architecture of Service Adapter

Service Adapter is the service access module in ShanghaiGrid Core. As showed in Fig. 3, the Service Adapter can be divided into three parts: service data manager, service adaptation, binding adaptation. The top layer is abstract service access interface provided to user and workflow engine. This is a consistent and easy way to invoke service without consideration of services' implementation details.

Service adapter is designed in an adaptive structure. When interacting with services, it will choose proper adapter and binding extensions automatically. All these information comes from information center.

4.2 Service Data Manager

Standard web service is stateless, so there is no need to store any state information between requests. But in grid service (OGSI, WSRF), we must model stateful resources, so service data (extended in OGSI) and WS-Resource Properties (extended in WSRF) are added into standard services.

Service data profile is used to cache some OGSI-compliant service data. Service data is a structured collection of information related to a Grid Service. Based on this information, Grid Services can be classified and indexed according to their characteristics. Efficiency and performance are very important in obtaining these data. We can store static service data as cache in information center. When the service is invoked first time, we can initiate an instance of the service; also we can cache service data in local database. After that, the static service data can be accessed efficiently. When the instance of the service is destroyed, the service data will be removed.

WS-Resource is the set of stateless web service and stateful resources. It is defined in WSRF; WS-Resource profile will be used to manage the WS-Resource. When new WS-Resource is created, we also cache some static resource properties, as done in Service data profile.

A service can be configured to be a notification source, and certain clients to be notification sinks (or subscribers). This means that if a change occurs in the service, that change is notified to all the subscribers. In asynchronous service environment, this publish/subscribe relationship must be managed. This is what Notification Manager done. In synchronous environment, clients and providers can intact in a synchronous

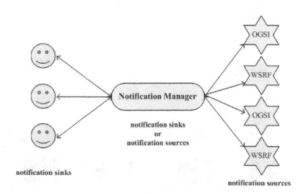

Fig. 4. Notification Manager used in Asynchronous Service

mode. In fact, Notification Manager itself is a service, and some asynchronous clients can subscribe some information to it, as showed in Fig. 4. Notification Manager is source of the clients, and also it is sink (or subscriber) of the service providers. Through Notification Manager we can support asynchronous notification storage mechanism.

4.3 Service Adaptation

This is the integral part of the service adapter. Based on service data manager, it makes choice of the suitable adapter. We have implemented, but not limited, three adapters, including:

- WSAdapter: used for standard web service. We mainly use JAX-RPC and SAAJ API. These are standard API used for web service.
- OGSIAdapter: used for OGSI-compliant service. Before we can invoke the service operations, we must create an instance of the service. This is done automatically, and user does not need to care for this detail. After the creation of service instance, the adapter can interact with this instance. [11] The lifecycle manager of the container will manage this instance. At the end of the session, the adapter will destroy the instance.
- WSRFAdapter: used for WSRF-compliant service. After creation of WS-Resource, we can get an endpoint reference. All methods invocation is done through this reference. [12] The endpoint reference is managed by adapter, and stored in information center.

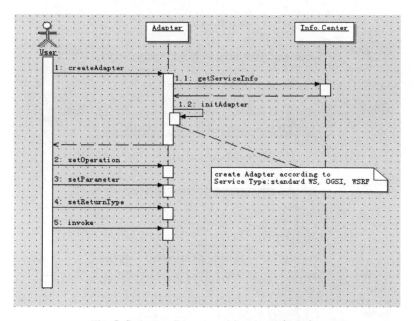

Fig. 5. Sequence Diagram of Service Adaptation

The service adaptation sequence diagram is showed in Fig. 5. The `initAdapter` `(1.2)` method will initialize the service invocation environment according to service type and binding extension. Then proper adapter object will return to user. After setting operation (`setOperation`), parameters (`setParameter`), and return type (`setReturnType`), user can invoke this operation directly without caring for specific issues.

4.4 Binding Adaptation

WSDL defines a common binding mechanism. This is used to attach a specific protocol or data format or structure to an abstract message, operation, or endpoint. WSDL specification defines three binding extensions: SOAP 1.1, HTTP GET / POST and MIME. SOAP binding is used in almost all the service invocation, and MIME binding can be used in an asynchronous way. So binding adaptation in Service Adapter supports these two bindings.

In fact, service adaptation and binding adaptation are done at the same time. A ready-to-run service invocation environment will be constructed after these adaptation procedures.

5 SG-Core's Browser Interface Based on Service Adapter

It is very convenient for user to access grid through a web browser. So, during the development of SG-Core, we do lots of work on browser interface. As Fig. 6 shows,

Fig. 6. SG-Core's Browser Interface based on Service Adapter

user can select a service, and then service's port will be listed. After user's selection of operation, user can fill in parameters of the operation. Finally, user press "invoke" button, and Service Adapter will take manage of all these details of invocation, as described in Section 4.

6 Our Contribution, Conclusion and Future Work

We design and implement a Service Adapter which used in multi-standards service-oriented grid environment. It is very suitable for complex service-oriented grid, for example, ShanghaiGrid. It can help user to finish some complex issues, and give user a transparent service access interface. User properly is not an experienced service-oriented programmer, but service adapter can help them. Workflow is key technology in service composition. Service adapter also is used to simplify workflow engine implementation. Workflow engine can use service adapter to simplify service interaction procedure.

ShanghaiGrid Core now is under development. Service adapter is the fundamental module of the SG-Core. Some more new features, for example, security service access, must be added in adapter level. In addition, service-oriented grid is rapidly evolving in concepts, technologies and implementations. So, the SG-Core and Service Adapter will also change.

References

1. Heather Kreger. Web Services Conceptual Architecture. Technical report, IBM Software Group, 2001
2. Foster, I., Kesselman, K., Nick, J., Tuecke, S., "The Physiology of the Grid. An Open Grid Services Architecture for Distributed Systems Integration", in Grid Computing: Making the Global Infrastructure a Reality, Fox, G. Ed. Wiley, 2003.
3. S.Tucke, K. Czajkowski, J. Frey, et al. Open Grid Services Infrastructure(OGSI) Version 1.0. Technical report, Global Grid Forum, 2003.
4. I.Foster,J.Frey,S.Graham, et al. Modeling Stateful Resources with Web Services. Technical report, Globus alliance, 2004
5. Web Services Resource Framework (WSRF) http://www.oasis-open.org/committees/ tc_ home.php?wg_abbrev=wsrf
6. Xinhua Lin, Qianni Deng, Xinda Lu, Information Grid Toolkit: Infrastructure of Shanghai Information Grid, in Proceedings of the Second International Workshop on Grid and Cooperative Computing (GCC 2003), Vol.3032.
7. The Belfast e-Science Centre http://www.qub.ac.uk/escience/
8. Systinet Server http://www.systinet.com/
9. I. Foster, C. Kesselman, S. Tuecke. The Anatomy of the Grid Enabling Scalable Virtual Organizations. International J. Supercomputer Application,2001,15 (3). Also in: Cluster Computing and the Grid, 2001. Proceedings. First IEEE/ACM International Symposium on, 2001,6-7

10. David Mennie, Bernard Pagurek: An Architecture to Support Dynamic Composition of Service Components. Proceedings of the 5th International Workshop on Component-Oriented Programming (WCOP 2000), Sophia Antipolis, France, June 13, 2000.
11. Borja Sotomayor. The Globus Toolkit 3 Programmer's Tutorial, Technical report, University of Deusto, 2003
12. Borja Sotomayor. The Globus Toolkit 4 Programmer's Tutorial, Technical report, University of Deusto, 2004

MCRM System: CIM-Based Multiple Clusters Manager

Yutong Lu, Zhiyu Shen, Enqiang Zhou, and Min Zhu

School of Computer, National University of Defense Technology,
410073 Changsha, China
ytlu@nudt.edu.cn

Abstract. As the developing of parallel and distributed computing, the needs of large computing resources and cooperative computing increase quickly. Multiple clusters belong to different organizations and locate on different places need to be used by some collective purposes. The corporation of multiple resources is a key problem of such distributed computing. We design and implement a multiple cluster management system MCRM based DPSCIM extension to CIM(Common Information Model), with a cascade CIMOM architecture to satisfy the requirements of large scale parallel and distributed computing.

1 Introduction

As the developing of parallel and distributed computing, the needs of large computing resources and cooperative computing increase quickly. Multiple clusters belong to different organizations and locating on different places need to be used by some collective purposes. The corporation of multiple resources is a key problem of such distributed computing.

The main issue of managing multiple clusters is to settle its heterogeneity in different levels, despite the hardware is different too, such as CPU, memory, disk, the network connecting the nodes, the software scheduling the resources and so on. When users use these clusters they must know how to designate the resources they need, and how to use different commands to run their applications and obtain the results. Therefore, system developers must be exactly familiar with interfaces of each cluster's monitor and scheduler to achieve the functions of the management they need. In fact, the essential question is that the representation of resources is varied in various cluster systems.

We need a uniform criterion for defining resources in the multi-cluster environment. Ideally, information used to manage the computerb systems should be organized or structured to allow disparate groups of people to understand and use. This can be accomplished by establishing a model or representation of the details required by people working within a particular domain. Such an approach can be referred to an information model. An information model requires a set of legal statement types or syntax to capture the representation, and a collection of actual expressions to match common aspects of

G. Chen et al. (Eds.): ISPA Workshops 2005, LNCS 3759, pp. 549–558, 2005.

the complex computer systems. The Common Information Model is nicely satisfied with these requirements.

We propose the DSPCIM model which extend CIM and a multiple level CIMOM cascade architecture to manage the multiple clusters resource efficiently

In this paper, the related work will be discussed in section 2, the implement of CIM model will be discussed in section 3, the architecture of the MCRM will be presented in section 4, and the implementation of the management for a hybrid system with Linux and windows clusters will be introduced in section 5. At last, we will analyze the characters of MCRM, and give a conclusion and future works in section 6.

2 Related Works

The issues of MultiCluster Management mainly stress on the following two aspects, firstly the management model of the MultiCluster, secondly, the management architecture and mechanism of it.

Now there are so many types of managing system for the cluster that almost every cluster has its own cluster manager system provided by its vendor, such as sycly for Beowolf and clusterworkx for Linux Networkx. Furthermore, in many universal job schedulers, such as LSF, NQE, SGE and PBS, the definition of the same resource has different object and different data structure. The multiple clusters management becomes very hard to use, let alone to migrate and integrate.

Some kinds of MultiCluster management software emerge in recent years, most of their purpose is to partly support the grid computing.LSF (Load Sharing Facility) MultiCluster is the enabling software which allows load sharing among disparate LSF clusters. It supports transparent access to remote cluster configuration and load information, distribution of jobs among clusters, importing and exporting of batch queues between clusters, configurable user account mapping at the individual user level and automatic file transfer[5].

PBSpro[6] also could do co-scheduling for one job to allocate the resources in multi pbs clusters.

Condor-G[9] could configure and manage multiple computing resources, provide with a combination of dedicated and opportunistic scheduling policy to meet the needs of vary kinds of jobs including serial jobs and parallel jobs.

Above system mainly emphasis on the resources using, and jobs running, and the each unit in multicluster must use the same job manager system, each management architecture and mechanism are different, so they hard to integrated.

At the same time, some cluster monitoring tools such as ganglia[10], have been used widely. Ganglia is comprised of separate components that can work alone or together, provides a complete real-time monitoring and execution environment. It is not just a way to link nodes in a cluster together in a logical way but also a way to link clusters to other clusters. It could do monitor work well, but lack of management fuctions.

We propose a new way to define the multicluster resources and manage them by using CIM.

3   Information Model

In order to manage the multicluster, we must define the resources model of it. We hope the model can cover all information of the multicluster system, and it should be a standard if we want to use it to manage variable system and fulfill the increasing needs of application.

The common information model(CIM) is the right prototype of our model.

3.1   The Characteristics of CIM

The CIM is defined and maintained by Distributed Management Task Force (DMTF)[1], whose purpose is to define an object-oriented model for information technology managers, system administrators, application developers, and provider/instrumentation developers. It's an extension of information model and object model. It could get the system information by defining a group of object class. It mainly concerns about the manageability and components of the system, so it emphasizes the common characteristics of various systems.

CIM defines many classes for hardware and software, it also has logical and physical models for the defining of abstract and concrete objects. CIM supplies a set of classes with properties and associations that provide a well-understood conceptual framework within which it is possible to organize the available information about the managed environment. It is assumed that CIM will be clearly understood by any programmer who will operate against the object schema, or by any schema designer intending to make new information available within the managed environment.

The CIM also is hierarchy, the core model of which is an information model capturing notions that are applicable to all areas of management. The Common model is an information model that captures notions that are common to particular management areas such as systems, applications, networks and devices, but independent of a particular technology or implementation. The information model is specific enough to provide a basis for the development of management applications. Extension model represent technology-specific extensions of the Common model. These schemas are specific to environments, such as operating systems (for example, UNIX or Microsoft Windows) and the way of implementation. The detail description of CIM can be found in [1] [2].

According to its standardization, easy understanding, scalability, the CIM is already used by many network management system such as SAN and some others. Now many companies such as IBM, SUN, HP, Microsoft, announce to support it in their products. We decide to choose CIM for describing the multiple clusters resources, and implement the management systems.

3.2   The Implementation of CIM

The CIM specification includes four parts: modeling language and syntax, management schema (core, common, extension), protocol to encapsulate syntax and schema (XML/HTTP), and compliance document. But it does not include the implementation. The CIM object managers (CIMOM) are implemented differently by different developers. Now, there are three main CIMOM implementations for users to choose,

SNIA, Pegasus and Openwbem. Among them, SNIA[2] is written by Java, while Pegasus[3] and Openwbem[4] are written by C++.

We use the CIMOM architecture to construct the system. The main purpose is to set up a scalable structure for easily adding managed objects. The architecture of CIMOM looks like the following figure 1.

The CIMOM is a core of Common Information Model Object Manager to hold or host instances of objects. Providers are instruments that obtain vendor data, especially the resource information that change dynamically. The relative static resource information usually store in the repository with consistent format, such as database or text file. The core has an Asset Query Engine to analyze and summarize objects. Http and xml are used for communication with client.

The model is expected to used consistently when the target system is flexible and wide ranging, so the provider writers need to piece together the CIM objects in unique ways. Model richness is both good and evil, the CIM model object classes are fully rich, we usually could use the part of it, so we can slim it down to decline the usage of system memory, increase the efficiency of hole system. In the other hand, CIM model address by definition of standard "profiles" or "structures", it is data centric, we also need to extent and implement more methods to have more ability to "do managing things".

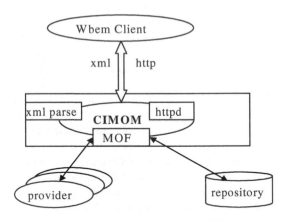

Fig. 1. The architecture of CIMOM

3.3 DPSCIM — Extension and Modification of CIM

To fulfill the needs for the multicluster management, we have done some modification of the CIM, define our own DPSCIM model, which include the core model and common model, we also add the Domain objects, JMS management objects, events management objects, license management objects, and IPMI-based power management objects.

The Domain objects–Domain_CIM can be the deprive class of the system, it has more attributes including cluster type, JMS type, system architecture info,etc.

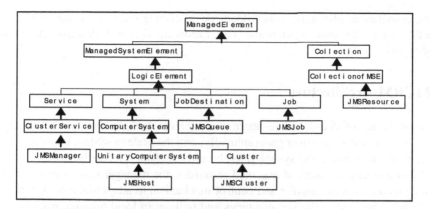

Fig. 2. JMS related objects, JMSManager is one kind of system service, so it is extended from the Sevice class, JMSHost is just a kind of computer system, it could be extended from the UnitaryComputersystem class, and the JMSCluster is the same. JMSResource is the collection of all the system elements, so it could be extended from Collection class.

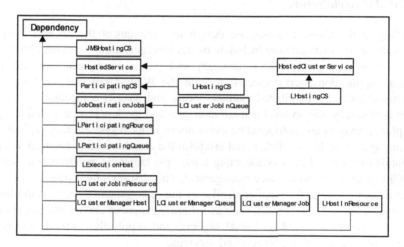

Fig. 3. JMS objects related associations

The JMS management objects include the whole Multicluster jobs management system information. In January 2004, NCSA announced their openpbs cim schema[11] for the cluster scheduling by openpbs. We have defined the common JMS model for supporting multiple job management system, including Openpbs, PBSpro, LSF, SLURM and SGE.

The JMS objects divide in three kinds, JMS services information, JMS queues information, JMS jobs information, and also define the association between the objects, the model we defined named DPSCIM, described in following figure 2.

The associations also need to be added for describing the relationship of the new objects, and to do some operations. The following figure 3 describes the main associations.

4 MCRM Architecture

The main issues of distributed resource management include: Firstly, the managed system may be distributed over geographically, and the scale of system usually change dynamically, so it needs the system must be easy scalable. Secondly, because of the variability and heterogeneity of managed resources, the manager system needs proper resource model, schema handler and control mechanism to adapt to the complexity of that. Thirdly, because of the variable types and policies of local resource management systems, they often have strongly autonomy, the manager system needs to support inter operation over multiple local systems, and support the multi-cluster management independent of platform.

4.1 MCRM Architecture

According to the above requests, we design and implement the MCRM system, it constructs with the manager core(including model manager, storage manager, information service, event manager, provider manager, and global queue manager, global job manager), application interface(according with the WBEM criterion), and supporting environment(including distributed monitor library and parallel computing library). The system is hierarchy, the up level is main manager, and the low level is uplink manager. The uplink managers are distributed on every nodes or local systems, they register to the main manager or up-level uplinker, and establish the communication connection and the association of control, finally constructing a multiple hierarchy architecture to solve the scalability of large system resource management. This describes by Figure 4

The manager core is the main controller of the management system, it implements the management of kernel object, such as schema, instances and events etc, construct the service mechanic based on kernel objects, and supply the methods and control mechanic of accessing those objects and services.

HTTP service and RMI provide the entries of accessing the manager core, the manager core hasn't the direct interface to the upper environment. Instead, it provides APIs to allow the client accessing the server function as client/server model. Those APIs are the images on the client of the core function modules, when applications use this APIs to access kernel, they pack the accessing entries and parameters into a XML packet or a RMI call, transfer it to the corresponding core function module, and then execute the specific method. The security controller responses for identity authentication of users, which could integrate with other security mechanics. Till now we use the unified authentication based on LDAP.

The supporting environment includes two parts: parallel computing library which implements MPI-MD to support the MPI application running under the multi-cluster environment, and the distributed monitor library which contains the GUI library and communication library, providing the basic monitor GUI components and the client components based on HTTP.

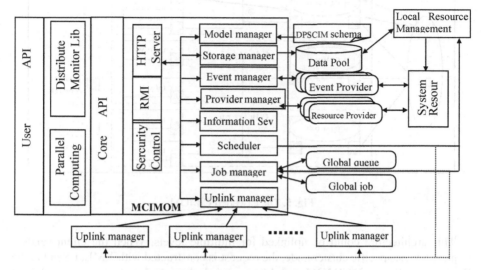

Fig. 4. The architecture of MCRM

Event manager supports the event registration, system administrator or authority user could define the events they care, system support to custom the event classes, event instants and the event methods. When some registered events happen, we would get the warning information from MCRM system, and the system would automatically execute the method appointed by event class.

4.2 Cascade CIMOM

Each domain in the multiple clusters has it own resource management system, with its extinct schedule policy and has different node scale, so we need to know the whole system resource information to set some system arguments, operate and manage the resource. The SNIA CIMOM architecture is for single node, we can use client SRI to access multiple nodes in one graphic interface. However, these nodes have no relationship with each other, they are independent.

Another case is some time the cluster itself is single system image, not all nodes of cluster can be connected from extend, for some reason such as security, only one main node can be access from extent network, and other nodes in the cluster is connected with internal network, so the CIMOM architecture need to be changed for this situation.

We implement the cascade CIMOM to support registration. The main CIMOM (MCIMOM) opens a registration port and maintains a registration nodes list, thus the internal node can set the Registration Server to the main node, and register to main CIMOM, so the client from extent network can see the internal node, and can get the information or operate the system resources. In fact all the connection is transmitted through the main CIMOM, see also the following figure.

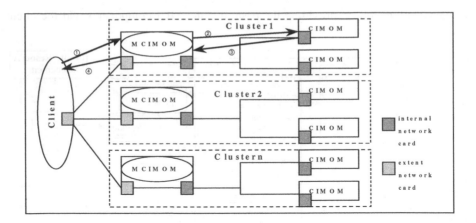

Fig. 5. The cascaded CIMOM

This architecture could be uplinked for multiple levels. When the client sends a request for the specific cluster node, the request is constructed with XML, it send to the Registration Server MCIMOM with http protocol, the actual node name is packed in the http header; When the MCIMOM receives the http pack, it parses it's header. If the node name is other than itself, it will transmit the XML request with new http header to the actual node. After the end node receives the request, it will do the following steps:

- parse the XML request, get the resource information or operates the specific resource
- construct the result XML pack, with the client information in it's http header
- send it to it's Registration Server MCIMOM

When MCIMOM receives the result, it will be transmitted to the client.

During the above course, there aren't many overheads, because the MCIMOM doesn't unpack the XML request, only checking the http header, so it doesn't contain any package reconstruction. So does for the result transmission procession.

5 The Hybrid System Management

In some large scale distributed computing environments, such as cooperating simulator, CAE and CAD application, there are some traditional applications running under the windows systems, and others running on UNIX or Linux systems. They need a uniform management view for system administrator to lighten the complex management burdens, and also a uniform interface for system users to monitor and use the computing resources.

The uniform interface could only be implemented according to the consistent resource model. Our MCRM architecture fits the need properly with easily implementation.

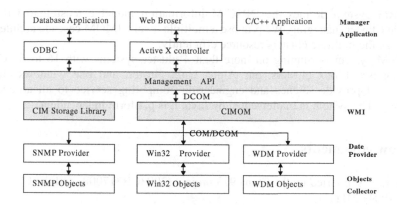

Fig. 6. The WMI architecture

The windows system provides WMI to access system resources, and do management operations. The WMI is the windows management instrumentation, it also compels to CIM. The WMI architecture is described in Figure 6.

The WMI has powerful functions to manage the windows system including many nodes, but it is implemented with DCOM interface which is not platform-independent. So we design a translator mapping the CIM requires to WMI-DCOM requires, described as the following Figure 7.

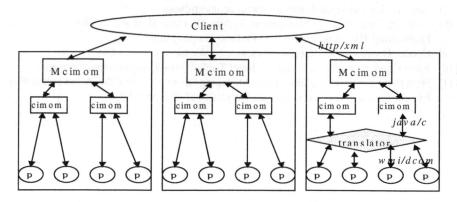

Fig. 7. A translator mapping the CIM requires to WMI-DCOM requires

6   Conclusion and Future Work

MultiCluster manager should have consistent resource definition, consistent managing mechanism and consistent transporting protocol. The first two elements need the consistent information model, the third one dependents by the reasonable implementation.

MCRM system defines the DPSCIM information model extension to CIM for Multiple Cluster managing. We propose a multiple level CIMOM cascade architecture to manage the multiple clusters resource efficiently.

MCRM system is running on more than 4 cluster systems with 16 to 64 CPUs, including two Linux clusters, one Alpha Unix cluster, and one windows cluster, manage and provide science and engineering computing service to all around the university. The system is implemented by Java, it is platform independent.

Acknowledgements

This work is supported by the China 973 project (2003CB317008) and the China NSF project (90412011).

Reference

[1] Open Group Technical Standard, "System Management: Common Information Model(CIM)", ISBN: 1-85912-255-8, 1998
[2] SNIA CIM Object Manager Architecture and Developers Guide□Draft□ DMTF
[3] Openpegasus Document Set, http://www.openpegasus.org
[4] Web-Based Enterprise Management (WBEM) Initiative, DMTF
[5] LSF Document Set, http://www.platform.com
[6] PBSpro Document Set, http://www.pbspro.com
[7] Sun Grid Engine Manual, http://www.sun.com/gridware
[8] Issues in Selecting a Job Management System, By Omar Hassaine - CPRE Engineering-HPC Sun BluePrints™ OnLine - January 2002
[9] Condor Document Set, http://www.cs.wisc.edu/condor
[10] Brent Chun, Matt Massie, Ganglia Cluster Toolkit, http://ganglia.sourceforge.net/
[11] High Performance Computing (HPC) Managing OpenPBS with CIM, A Job Scheduling Environment in Cooperation with the University of Illinois (NCSA)

Introduction to an Agent-Based Grid Workflow Management System*

Lei Cao, Minglu Li, Jian Cao, and Yi Wang

Department of Computer Science and Engineering,
Shanghai Jiao Tong University, Shanghai 20030, China
{lcao, li-ml, cao-jian, wangsuper}@cs.sjtu.edu.cn

Abstract. Grid computing is becoming a mainstream technology for large-scale distributed resource sharing and system integration. One of the most important grid services is workflow management. Grid workflow applications are also emerging as one of the most interesting application classes for the grid. In this paper, we give an introduction to our agent-based grid workflow management system (AGWMS). AGWMS has a four-layer framework. It bases on the adapter middleware and uses a multi-agent platform to make the system more robust, flexible and intelligent. Artificial Intelligence (AI) planning technology is also utilized to generate the agent plan automatically. Our AGWMS is a novel one.

Keywords: Grid Computing, Workflow, Multi-Agent, Planning

1 Introduction

Grid computing[1] facilitates the sharing and aggregation of heterogeneous and distributed resources, such as computing resources, data sources, instruments and application services. With the advent of grid technologies, scientists and engineers are building more and more complex applications to manage and process large data sets, and execute scientific experiments on distributed grid resources. Means of composing and executing distributed applications to form complex workflows are needed. Some efforts in the research of business workflow and web services composition can be reused in grid workflow systems.

Grid workflow[2] is "a workflow intended to solve sophisticated scientific problems that occur in highly heterogeneous, distributed, complex, and dynamic Grid environments that comprise of one or more Virtual Organizations(VOs)[3]." We develop a grid workflow management system to help scientists streamline, manage, and monitor their routinely scientific problem solving processes without knowing any details of the underlying complex structure and dynamic state of VOs. However, there are new challenges needing to be addressed: (1)Computational and networking capabilities can vary significantly over time; (2)There is no

* This paper has been supported by the 973 project (No.2002CB312002) of China, grand project of the Science and Technology Commission of Shanghai Municipality (No.03dz15027).

central ownership and control in grids; (3)The execution of a grid workflow faces many uncertain factors such as unavailability, incomplete information and local policy changes, so a full-ahead plan is not always suitable; (4)The processing of resource discovery and selection could be quite complicated in grids. Workflow and agent technologies are complementary to each other, and there has been a lot of work on integrating the two[4,5]. In our grid workflow management system, we use multi-agent technology to meet those challenges. Our AGWMS has a four-layer framework to make itself more adaptive. Our AGWMS is distributed to improve its execution efficiency. The workflow engine services may scatter in many hosts to balance the system's workload using Jini[6] technology. Our AGWMS applies AI planning technology to make itself more intelligent and robust. Planning is used to generate the agent plan automatically.

The paper is organized as follows. We discuss related work in Section 2. Section 3 presents the framework of AGWMS in detail. Section 4 presents AGWMS' multi-agent platform. We also describe the adapter middleware of AGWMS in Section 5. A case study and the implementation of system are given in Section 6. We conclude in Section 7 with lessons learned and future research plans.

2   Related Work

Many efforts toward grid workflow management have been made. DAGMan[7] was developed to schedule jobs to Condor system in an order represented by a DAG and to process them. With the integration of Chimera[8], Pegasus[9] maps and executes complex workflow based on full-ahead planning. In Pegasus, a workflow can be generated from metadata description of the desired data product using AI-based planning technologies. The Taverna project[10] has developed a tool for the composition and enactment of bioinformatics workflow for the life science community. The tool provides a graphical user interface for the composition of workflows. The workflow management system for grid computing, called GridFlow[11], is presented, including services of both global grid workflow management and local grid sub-workflow scheduling. Simulation, execution and monitoring functionalities are provided at the global grid level. McRunjob[12] is a grid workflow manager used to manage the generation of large numbers of production processing jobs in High Energy Physics. It converts core metadata into jobs submitted in a variety of environments. GALE[13] is an HPC workflow vocabulary that uses key grid services to provide a "run code X anywhere, then post process results, then ..." grid-level scripting language for users and problem solving environments.In addition, many efforts on the composition of Web services[14] can also be complementary to the development of grid workflow management systems.

3   The Framework of AGWMS

From the Fig. 1, you can see that there are four layers in our agent-based grid workflow management system.

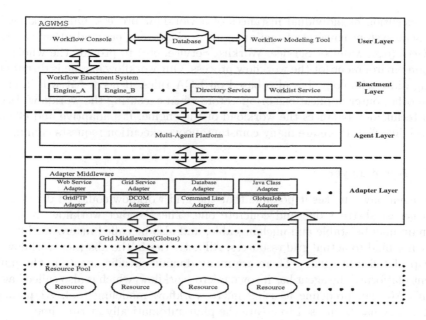

Fig. 1. AGWMS's four-layer framework

3.1 User Layer

The user layer is the interface between user and system. There are mainly two modules in it:

1. Workflow Modeling Tool: It is used to model the complex grid application, which can be seen as a collection of activities (mostly computational tasks) that are processed in some order. It's based on Event-Condition-Action (ECA) rules. By modeling, related data are stored in files or database with multiple formats. In the system, we provide two kinds of modeling tool. One is the macro-workflow modeling tool, which is used to model abstract work-flows of some application domains. The other is the micro-workflow modeling tool, which is used to model the plan of domain-specific agent.
2. Workflow Console: Users can submit the preferred workflow model to the system for execution using Workflow Console. It's also used as the monitoring tool about execution status of the submitted workflow. We have two types of Workflow Console: Web-based and Application-based.

3.2 Enactment Layer

The enactment layer is the core layer to provide the execution environment for the workflow process. The workflow enactment system interprets the process description and controls the instantiation of processes and sequencing of activities, adding work items to the user work lists and invoking application tools as necessary. The workflow engine refers to a specific run-time component which manages the execution of individual instances of a workflow process. Our workflow enactment system consists of one or more workflow engines and other run-time services (e.g., Monitor Service, Worklist Service, etc) to provide the whole execution environment for the workflow process. Our workflow engine is distributed using Jini technology. It's also based on ECA rules. If needed it will interface with other outer applications or operators when executing the workflow. Use of Jini technology balances the workload of the engine. It's adaptive and efficient especially when there are many coinstantaneous execution requests coming.

3.3   Agent Layer

The agent layer makes it possible that the grid workflow could be divided into two types: abstract one and concrete one. The abstract workflow in specific domain may be stable and unchangeable, and also be called macro-workflow. It may not bind to actual grid resources. All activities in the abstract workflow are encapsulated into agents. There are many domain-specific agents in the multi-agent platform. The agent has its own micro-workflow, which is also called "agent plan". We can predefine it using micro-workflow modeling tool. AI planning technology has been used to create the plan automatically at run time.

3.4   Adapter Layer

The adapter layer makes it easily that AGWMS invokes external applications. Adapter is the proxy for the invokable application. Our adapter library contains many adapters corresponding to different application types, such as Web Service, Grid service, Database operation, DCOM, Java Class, Command Line and so on. The adapter encapsulates complex invoking details. Upper functionality modules only need to know the interface parameters of adapter. Doing so makes the system more scalable. More application types only need more adapters plugged in.

4   Multi-agent Platform Used in AGWMS

Currently, there is not much consensus on what an "agent" is, and many definitions abound. We define an agent as "a software component that acts autonomously on behalf of a person or organization, and is also able to interact with its environment and with other agents". A 7-axis characterization of agents can be found in[4], and has the following dimensions: Adaptability, Autonomy, Collaboration, Intelligence, Mobility, Persistence and Sociability. Agents here should be complex including features: autonomous, communication, self-consistent, goal-oriented, and reacting to environment. Other high-level features such as learning, negotiation are also of benefit. All agents in the agent layer are constructed according to Belief-Desire-Intention (BDI) model. There are four kinds of agents in the layer depicted in Fig. 2. They communicate with each other via Agent Communication Language (ACL)[15]channel.

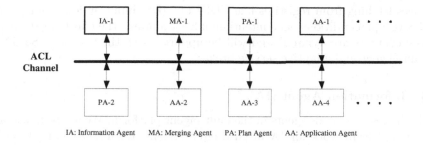

IA: Information Agent   MA: Merging Agent   PA: Plan Agent   AA: Application Agent

Fig. 2. Multi-agent platform structure

4.1 Plan Agent (PA)

PA is the main component of abstract workflow. It is domain specific, and its capability is always stable and predefined. In some sense, PA takes the role of host of sub-workflow denoted in business workflow domain. The plans in PA can be built either manually by agent designer or automatically by the planner.

1. Build manually: The agent designer predefines some plans for the agent according to its capability. The plan can be made with the micro-workflow modeling tool. Each plan behaves externally as three parts: (1)Goal(Post-conditions of the plan); (2)Context(Pre-conditions of the plan); (3)Content(Actions' sequence of the plan). To find a suitable plan only means to search in the plan library to get the plan whose context can be meet by the given conditions and goal can contain the required intention.
2. Build automatically: The AI planning technology is utilized here. If the plan library has no required plan to use, PA will build a new one automatically. Given the designed capability, the present world state and a set of action, PA can generate a plan using POP[16] algorithm. Thus, PA involves the construction of a plan from scratch.

4.2 Application Agent (AA)

Each AA corresponds some application adapters from the same domain. Both preconditions and effects of its capability are the conjunctive ones of its all application adapter instances. According to different application types, AAs have different names: Service agent (SAg), Java Class agent (JCAg), Database agent (DBAg), Command Line agent (CLAg), etc.

Service agent (SAg) is the broker of some grid services or web services. Those services belong to the same type. That means their action effects and preconditions have intersection. When planning, SAg is responsible for binding to the best service, which meets the action requirements of precondition and effect and has the maximum QoS value. Its behavior can invoke only one service. The QoS of a service can be divided into several dimensions[17]. The belief set of SAg includes descriptions of its corresponding services, dynamic states of those services fetching from registries like UDDI or MDS, input action requirements, and SAg's preconditions. The intention of SAg contains the effects of the agent. Those contents are dynamic and will be updated with time passing. So SAg is the intelligent and adaptive service broker.

4.3   Information Agent (IA)

IA is the registry of all agents in the multi-agent platform. We adopt multi-layer distributed framework for IA in Grid environment. Each VO has its local IA. The local IA keeps the information about capabilities of all PAs and AAs in the VO. AAs are chosen preferentially from the same VO when building a plan in order to get better efficiency in time of processing. The general IA has the registration information about all local IAs.

4.4   Merging Agent (MA)

MA is responsible for merging all related plans of PAs in a user-defined abstract workflow to get the final concrete workflow. Both POP and HTN[16] are utilized by MA.

5   Adapter Middleware

Adapter is the proxy for the invokable application. It encapsulates the complex invoking details. Our adapter library allows one to plug in different execution models into workflows. Individual workflow steps are implemented as reusable adapters that can represent data sources, sinks, data transformers, analytical steps, or arbitrary computational steps. An adapter can have multiple input and output ports, through which streams of data tokens flow. Additionally, adapters may have parameters to define specific behavior. Some adapter types are as follows:

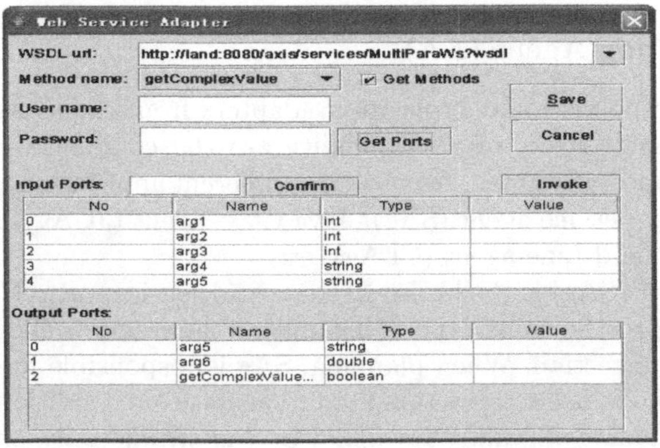

Fig. 3. Web service adapter

1. Distributed Execution (Web and Grid Services): Our web and grid service adapters allow users to utilize computational resources on the grid in a distributed scientific workflow. Generic web service adapter provides the user with an interface to seamlessly plug in and execute any WSDL-defined web service (See Fig. 3). In addition to generic web services, adapter library also includes specialized adapters for executing jobs on the grid, e.g., adapters for certificate-based authentication (ProxyInit), grid job submission (GlobusJob), and Grid-based data access (DataAccessWizard, GridFTP)[18].

2. Database Access and Querying: Adapter library includes Database adapter, which emits a database connection token (after user login) to be used and executes submitted SQL requests (See Fig. 4).

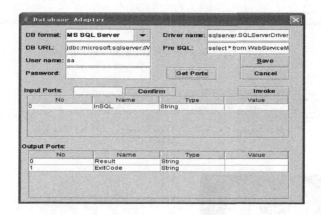

Fig. 4. Database adapter

3. Other Types: Adapter library includes a suite of data transformation adapters (XSLT, XQuery, Perl, etc.) for linking semantically compatible but syntactically incompatible web services together. We also have Java Class adapter, Command Line adapter, COM/DCOM adapter, etc.

6   A Case Study and the Implementation

Our AGWMS is developed with Java language. Fig. 5 gives a screenshot of the macro-workflow modeling tool. Here we give a simple grid application as the example. We design a workflow model of medical image processing. Because the model is simple, we do not use agents to represent domain-specific activities. It is only composed of three activities, two of which are web services. Another is a setting-value activity. The model is based on ECA rules. It will be saved into SQL Server database automatically after modeling. Through the simple

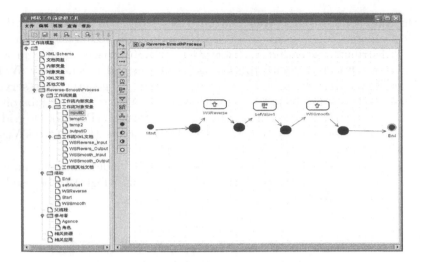

Fig. 5. Grid macro-workflow modeling tool

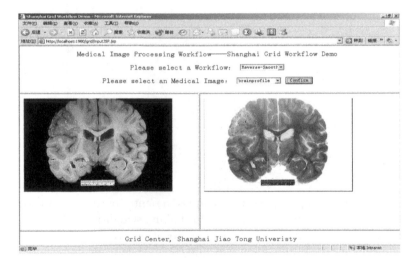

Fig. 6. Medical image processing workflow demo

Web Portal, we may choose the proper workflow model to run. In the back-end, the engine will invoke actual web services deployed in two nodes after the user submits the selected workflow model. The engine does not care about the invoking details because the web service adapter has done the work for it. The execution result is showed in Fig. 6. Our multi-agent platform is developed using JADE[15] technology. JADE has been used by researchers widely. That is why we choose it. We also give the screenshot of Jini-based workflow enactment system in Fig. 7.

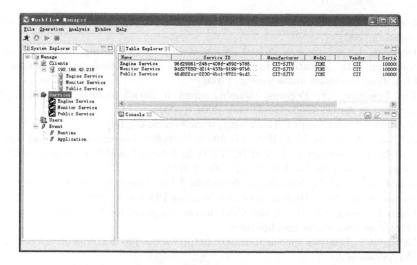

Fig. 7. Jini-based workflow enactment system

7   Conclusion and Future Work

This paper describes an agent-based grid workflow management system (AG-WMS). We give its four-layer framework and describe its components. The adapter middleware layer increases the scalability of AGWMS. Use of agent technology makes AGWMS more intelligent. AI planning technology has been adopted. Our JADE-based multi-agent platform makes the system meet challenges from the grid context. Distributed multi-agent platform architecture, autonomous and other characters of agent, good communication between agents, all those could benefit it. In the near future, we plan to go further using AI planning technology in AGWMS and to do a practical performance evaluation to show that our agent-based workflow management system can be efficiently used in the Grid environment.

References

1. I. Foster, C.K.: The Grid Blueprint for a Future Computing Infrastructure. Morgan Kaufmann, USA (1999)
2. Hwang, S.: Grid workflow-a flexible framework for fault tolerance in the grid. In: PhD Thesis. (2003)
3. I. Foster, C. Kesselman, S.T.: The anatomy of the grid: Enabling scalable virtual organizations. International J. Supercomputer Application **15** (2001) 10
4. Griss, M.: My agent will call your agent. Software Development Magazine **Feb.** (2000) 4
5. Zeus: The zeus agent building toolkit.(In: http://www.labs.bt.com/projects/agents/zeus/index.htm)
6. Jini: Jini community. (In: http://www.jini.org/)

7. Condor: The directed acyclic graph manager.In: http://www.cs.wisc.edu/condor/dagman. (2004)
8. Deelman, E.: Chimera, a virtual data system for representing, querying, and automating data derivation. In: Proceedings of 14th Conference on Scientific and Statistical Database Management. (2002)
9. Ewa Deelman, e.a.: Pegasus: Mapping scientific workflows onto the grid. In: Proceedings of Across Grids Conference 2004. (2004)
10. MyGrid: Mygrid project. (In: http://www.mygrid.org.uk)
11. J. Cao, S. A. Jarvis, S.S.G.R.N.: Gridflow: Workflow management for grid computing. In: Proceedings of the 3rd IEEE/ACM International Symposium on Cluster Computing and the Grid (CCGRID'03). (2003)
12. G.E. Graham, D.E., Bertram, I.: Mcrunjob: A high energy physics workflow planner for grid computing. High Energy and Nuclear Physics **3** (2003)
13. Hugh P. Bivens, J.I.B.: Gale: Grid access language for hpc environment. (In: http://ass3186.sandia.gov/hpbiven)
14. BPEL4WS: Bpel4ws specification.(In: http://www-106.ibm.com/developerworks/library/ws-bpel)
15. JADE: Jade project. (In: http://jade.tilab.com)
16. Stuart Russell, P.N.: Artificial Intelligence: A Modern Approach (Second Edition). Prentice Hall (2002)
17. Jian Cao, e.a.: A dynamically reconfigurable system based on workflow and service agents. Engineering Applications of Artificial Intelligence **17** (2004)
18. S. Tuecke, e.: Open grid services infrastructure (ogsi) version 1.0. In: Specification of GGF by OGSI-WG. (2003)

An XML Query Mechanism with Ontology Integration

Heping Chen[1], Jinguang Gu[2], Xiaohui Li[1], and Hongping Fang[1]

[1] College of Information Science and Engineering,
Wuhan University of Science and Technology, Wuhan 430081, China
chp@mail.wust.edu.cn
[2] College of Computer Science and Technology,
Wuhan University of Science and Technology, Wuhan 430081, China
simongu@ieee.org
simongu@acm.org

Abstract. Ontology Integration plays a key role in information integration systems, especially in the semi-structured information integration systems. This paper develops an ontology integration mechanism which is based on the complex semantic mapping to avoid the insufficient of simple and direct semantic mapping. It introduces an ontology-based extension to the XML query algebra at first, and discusses the ontology-based query mechanism, which includes ontology integration procedures and XML query rewriting mechanism secondly.

1 Introduction

The development of information technologies such as Internet technology, Web based commercial business technology and their applications, demands for complete access to available information, which is often heterogeneous and distributed. The technology of bringing together heterogeneous and distributed computer systems and establish efficient information sharing is known as information integration. In short, information integration not only needs to provide full accessibility to the data, it also requires that the accessed data may be processed and interpreted by the remote system. Problems that might arise due to heterogeneity of the data are already well known within the distributed database systems community: *structural heterogeneity* and *semantic heterogeneity*. Structural heterogeneity means that different information systems store their data in different structures. Semantic heterogeneity considers the content of an information item and its intended meaning[1].

The use of ontologies for the explication of implicit and hidden knowledge is a possible approach to overcome the problem of semantic heterogeneity. Ontologies can be used in an integration task to describe the semantics of the information sources and to make the content explicit. With respect to the integration of data sources, they can be used for the identification and association of semantically corresponding information concepts. A possible approach to remove the semantic heterogeneity is to integration the distributed local ontologies to a global ontology with semantic mapping technology.

G. Chen et al. (Eds.): ISPA Workshops 2005, LNCS 3759, pp. 569–578, 2005.

Two topics should be discussed in semi-structured information integration system. The first one is the representation of semi-structured information. Because XML has been the standard language to represent Web information and semantic web resources, using XML to represent integrated information is a better choice, and users can query information with XML languages. XPath based languages such as XQuery, XUpdate are suitable for retrieving information in distributed integration systems. The other problem is the topic we will discuss in this paper, how to accessing distributed information with a consistent semantic environment and how to make the XML query mechanism with semantic enabled, TOSS[2] is a research on this topic. However, previous integration technologies of ontology is based on the one to one semantic mapping(or directly mapping), with which users can map one local concept or ontology to a global concept or ontology. however, it can not convert the local concept to the global concept exactly with the simple one to one mapping at most time, for example, the mapping: $payment = total(commodity\_amount * (unit\_price + tax))$, can not express the concept *payment* using the concept *total* with the directly mapping.

We developed an ontology enabled information retrieval mechanism on integration information system, which is based on the complex semantic mapping mechanism. Our contribution can be described as:

1. Discussed the ontology integration mechanism based on the complex ontology mapping;
2. Discussed the ontology enabled query mechanism on semi-structured information integration system, including ontology enhanced XML query algebra and XML query rewriting technologies with complex semantic mapping.
3. An implementation of query mechanism in OBSA[3] information integration system, especially the semantic adapter architecture of OBSA.

The remainder of this paper is structured as follows. Section 2 gives the general discussion about ontology based information integration. Section 3 discusses the ontology integration mechanism including ontology fusion and canonical fusion. Section 4 discuss the ontology enabled query mechanism on XML based semi-structured integration systems, such as ontology enhanced XML algebra and XML query rewriting. Section 5 summarizes the whole paper.

2 Ontology Based Information Integration System

The Information Integration system can be express as a mapping process, in which the distributed local information sites can be mapped to a global information site. It can be expressed as $I : (S_1, S_2, \ldots, S_n) \rightarrow S_0$ while S_i $(1 \leq i \leq n)$ denotes the local information sites, S_0 denotes the global information site, I denotes the Integration procedure. Every local site contains the local ontology based structured or semi-structured information source, the information source maybe the relational database, native XML database, web sites, XML based applications or other autonomous systems, from the opinion of information integration, all the local information sites can be expressed as the collections of XML instances, the XML instances can be described as:

Definition 1. *A **XML instance** can be described as a structure $I_d :=$ $(V_d, E_d, \delta_d,$ $\mathcal{T}_d, \mathcal{O}_d, t_d, oid_d, root_d)$, consisting of:*

i. *I_d is a rooted and directed tree, and V_d is the node set of the tree, E_d is the edge set of the tree and $E_d \subseteq V_d \times V_d$, δ_d is the mapping function between nodes which identify the direction of the edges, $root_d$ is the root of the tree;*

ii. *Every node has a unique identifier which belongs to $\mathcal{O}_d$, which means for every node e exists $\forall(e)\{e \in V_d \rightarrow \exists(o)\{o = oid_d(e) \wedge o \in \mathcal{O}_d\}\}$;*

iii. *There exist a mapping function $t_d(e, string)$ which maps the attribute of the node a type $\tau \in \mathcal{T}_d$, and the function has the following rules:*

   - *if **string** = tag, then maps it to the type of tag;*
   - *if **string** = content, then maps it to the type of content.*

iv. *Every type $\tau \in \mathcal{T}_d$ has a domain denoted as $dom(\tau)$;*

v. *δ_d is the identifier of edge, with which the parent nodes can access the child nodes. On the other hand, the child nodes can access parent nodes by the identifier δ_d^{-1}.*

Ontologies are used for the explicit description of the information source semantics, the ontology can be express as[4]:

Definition 2. *A core **ontology** is a structure $O := (C, \leq_C, R, \leq_R, \sigma)$ consisting of:*

i. *Two disjoint sets C and R whose elements are called concept identifiers and relation identifiers, We will call concept identifiers and relation identifiers just **concepts** and **relations**;*

ii. *A partial order $\leq_C$ on C, called **concept hierarchy** or **taxonomy**;*

iii. *A function $\sigma : R \rightarrow C^+$ called **signature**;*

iv. *A partial order $\leq_R$ on R, called **relation hierarchy**, where $r_1 \leq_R r_2$ implies $|\sigma(r_1)| = |\sigma(r_2)|$ and $\pi_i(\sigma(r_1)) \leq_C \pi_i(\sigma(r_2))$, for each $1 \leq i \leq |\sigma(r_1)|$.*

This paper employed a mediator based approach to use ontology in information integration system, which can be express as figure 1. In this approach, the semantics of each source is described by its own ontology, a global shared ontology is build to make the local ontologies comparable to each other. The advantage of the mediator-based approach is that new sources can easily be added without modification. It also supports the acquisition and evolution of ontologies. The use of a shared global ontology makes the source ontologies comparable and avoids the disadvantages of multiple ontology or single ontology approaches[1].How to construct local ontology is not the topic we should discuss, several works had been done on this topic, we will focus on the integration of local ontology to the global ontology and the global ontology-based information query mechanism in this paper.

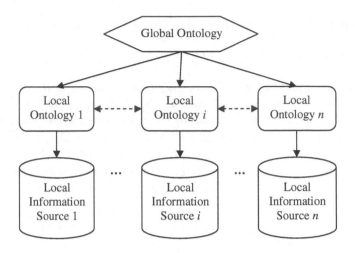

Fig. 1. A hybrid approach for Ontology Integration

3   Ontology Integration with Complex Semantic Mapping

Two different concepts at different local sites may express the same or similar meaning, the task of integration is to combine these local concepts which have acceptable semantic similarity to a single global concept or mapping the different local concepts to a global concept, it uses ontology to express local semantic in this paper, so the semantic mapping changes to ontology mapping.

3.1   The Definition of Semantic Mapping Based on the Semantic Similarity

The mapping patterns can be categorized into four expressions: direct mapping, subsumption mapping, composition mapping and decomposition mapping[5], a mapping can be defined as:

Definition 3. *A **mapping** is a structure $\mathcal{M} = (\mathcal{S}, \mathcal{D}, \mathcal{R}, v)$, where $\mathcal{S}$ denotes the concepts of source ontology, $\mathcal{D}$ denotes the concepts of target ontology, $\mathcal{R}$ denotes the relation of the mapping and v denotes the confidence value of the mapping, $0 \leq v \leq 1$.*

A direct mapping relates the local ontology concept to global ontology concept directly, and the cardinality of direct mapping could be one-to-one. A subsumption mapping is used to denote concept inclusion relation especially in the multiple IS-A inclusion hierarchy. The composition mapping is used to map one concept to combined concepts. For example, the mapping *address=contact(country, state, city, street, postcode)* is a composition mapping, in which the concept *address* is mapped to combined concept "*contact, country, state, street, and postcode*" of local schema elements. The decomposition mapping is used to map a combined concept to one local concept. The example

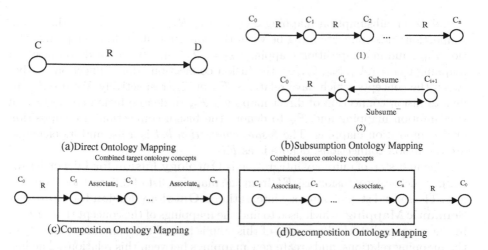

Fig. 2. The Patterns of Semantic Mapping

for the decomposition is the reverse of the composition. These four mapping patterns can be described in the figure 2.

3.2 The Ontology Integration Mechanism with Semantic Similarity Enhanced

We introduce some concepts before we begin to discuss the ontology integration mechanism, the first one is the formal definition of Ontology Integration, it can be expressed as[2]:

Definition 4. *Suppose O_i ($1 \leq i \leq n$)are n different ontologies and suppose* **IC** *is a finite set of interoperation constraints, an ontology O is said to be an* **integration** *of O_i ($1 \leq i \leq n$) iff there are n injective mapping $\mathcal{M}_i$($1 \leq i \leq n$)from O_i ($1 \leq i \leq n$) respectively to O such that:*

   i. $(\forall i \in \{1, 2, \ldots, n\})(O_i : x \preceq O_i : y \to \mathcal{M}_i(O_i : x) \preceq \mathcal{M}_i(O_i : y))$;

   ii. $(\forall x, y)((x \in O_i \wedge y \in O_j) \wedge (x\ op\ y) \in \textbf{IC} \to (\mathcal{M}_i(x)\ op\ \mathcal{M}_j(y)) \in \textbf{IC})$.

Axiom *i*) above says that the integrated ontology must preserve the ordering associated with each of the input ontology; Axiom *ii*) above says that they must preserve the interoperation constraints.

Definition 5. *Fusion Connection is a structure $\mathcal{F}_c(O_1 : C_1, O_2 : C_2, \mathcal{M})$, where C_1 denotes a concept or concept set of ontology O_1, C_2 denotes a concept or concept set of Ontology O_2, $\mathcal{M}$ denotes the direct mapping relationship between C_1 and C_2.*

The function of Ontology fusion is to add connection tag between the concepts which have direction mapping relationship. In direction mapping $\mathcal{M} = (\mathcal{S}, \mathcal{D}, \mathcal{R}, v)$, the fusion connection adds connection tag between the elements of

$\mathcal{S}$ and $\mathcal{D}$; in subsumption mapping $\mathcal{S}_{\mathcal{M}} = (\mathcal{D}_m, \mathcal{R}_m, \mathcal{B}_m, \preceq_m, \mathcal{I}_m, v)$, the fusion connection adds connection tag between the concepts which have mapping relation $\mathcal{D}_m$, and in composition mapping $\mathcal{C}_{\mathcal{M}} = (\mathcal{F}_m, \mathcal{A}_m, \mathcal{B}_m, v)$ or decomposition mapping $\mathcal{C}_{\mathcal{M}} = (\mathcal{A}_m, \mathcal{B}_m, \mathcal{L}_m, v)$, the fusion connection adds connection tag between the concepts which have relations $\mathcal{F}_m$ or $\mathcal{L}_m$ respectively. We use $\mathcal{F}_{cd}$ to denote fusion connection of direct mapping, $\mathcal{F}_{cs}$ to denote fusion connection of subsumption mapping and $\mathcal{F}_{cc}$ to denote the fusion connection of composition or decomposition mapping. The *fusion connection list* is a list and its elements are the fusion connections, denote it as FL.

The first step of ontology integration is **Ontology Fusion for Direct Mapping**, which creates fusion list FL from the mapping list of different local ontologies. The second step of ontology integration is **Ontology Fusion for Complex Semantic Mapping**, which used to find the mappings of the concept that are not in the mapping list, the basic idea of this step is to find the semantic similarity of the mapping relations, and create new mappings between this relations. The last step of ontology integration is **Canonical Fusion**, which merges the concepts of the fusion connection into one concept if the fusion connection type is $\mathcal{F}_{cd}$ or $\mathcal{F}_{cc}$, and add a real relation connection to the concepts if the fusion connection type is $\mathcal{F}_{cs}$. For example the fusion connection $\mathcal{F}_{cd} = (C_1, C_2, M)$, C_1 and C_2 are concepts of different ontologies, merge it to a concept (C_1, C_2) and all the hierarchy of the concepts will be kept. But not all the concepts with the same mapping relation can be merge into one concepts, only the concepts which have strong mapping relation can be merged. For example, if the mappings $\mathcal{M}(C_1, C_2, \mathcal{R}, v_1), \mathcal{M}(C_2, C_3, \mathcal{R}, v_2)$ and $\mathcal{M}(C_1, C_3, \mathcal{R}, v_3)$ satisfy the strong mapping property, we can merge the concept C_1, C_2, C_3 into one concept (C_1, C_2, C_3), otherwise, we have to merge them into two concepts (C_1, C_2) and (C_2, C_3).

4   XML Query Mechanism with Ontology Integration

4.1   The Extension of XML Algebra with Semantic Query Enhanced

We extended XML algebra TAX[6] and OrientXA[7] to enable semantic query on XML instances, TAX uses Pattern Tree to describe query language and Witness Tree to describe the result instances which satisfy the Pattern Tree. However, OrientXA improves TAX by focusing on XQuery based querying, it introduces sequence operator to satisfy the property of XQuery languages, and making the logical planning and physical planning of the query more operable, it also redefines pattern tree, renaming it as *Source Pattern Tree* and *Constructor Pattern Tree* for the purpose of optimizing result construction. The definition of pattern tree with ontology extension can be described as follows:

Definition 6. *A Ontology Enhanced Pattern Tree is a 2-tuple* $SPT := (T, F)$, *where* $T := (V, E)$ *is a tree with node identifier and edge identifier. F is a combination of prediction expressions.*

The prediction expression F supports the following **atomic condition** or **selection condition**[2]. Atomic condition have the form of $XopY$, where:

- $op \in \{=, \neq, <, \leq, >, \geq, \sim, \textbf{instance of, isa, is\_part\_of, before, below,}$
  $\textbf{above}\}$
- X and Y are conditional *terms*, which are attributes ,types,type values $v : \tau$
  and $v \in dom(\tau)$, ontology concepts and so on;
- $\sim$ stands for the estimation of semantic similarity.

The selection condition is:

- Atom conditions are selection conditions;
- If c_1 and c_2 are selection condition, then $c_1 \wedge c2, c_1 \vee c_2$ and $\neg c_1$ are both selection
  conditions;
- No others selection conditions forms.

4.2   XML Query Rewriting

In order to simplify the discussion, this paper just pays attention to the rewriting
mechanism of the selection operation. A selection operation can be expressed as :
$\sigma_{P_i, P_o, PE}(X) = \{x | x \prec X, P_0(X), PE(X)\}$, P_i is input pattern tree, P_o is output
pattern tree, PE is predication list. Briefly, it can be expressed as $\sigma(X, Y)$, $\{X \subseteq P_i \cup P_o, Y \subseteq PE\}$, we define two operator $\cup$ and $\bowtie$ to represent $Union$ and $Join$
operation separately.

Firstly, we discuss how to rewrite pattern tree (which is the X element of expression $\sigma(X, Y)$), there maybe several cases as follows:

1. X is one of the elements of input pattern tree or output pattern tree, and it is
   also a concept in the global ontology hierarchy. $X_i(1 \leq i \leq n)$ are the concepts
   for different local ontologies. X and X_i were combined into one concept in the
   integrated global ontology with strong direct mappings, which means that X
   and X_i can match each other, then rewrite X as $X \cup \bigcup_{1 \leq i \leq n} X_i$;
2. The concept of X is generated by the subsumption mapping or composition
   mapping of $X_i(1 \leq i \leq n)$, then rewrite X as $\bigcup_{1 \leq i \leq n} X_i$.

The responding selection rewriting can be expressed as:

$$\sigma(X_1 \cup X_2, Y) = \sigma(X_1, Y) \cup \sigma(X_2, Y) \tag{1}$$

And then, we discuss how to rewrite the predication expressions (which is the
Y element of the expression $\sigma(X, Y)$), there are also several cases, which can be
described as follows:

1. If there are lots of concept $Y_i(1 \leq i \leq n)$ combined in the concept Y of global
   Ontology, rewrite Y as $Y \cup \bigcup_{1 \leq i \leq n} Y_i$;
2. If the concept Y is generated by the subsumption mapping of $Y_i(1 \leq i \leq n)$,
   rewrite Y as $\bigcup_{1 \leq i \leq n} Y_i$;
3. If the concept Y is generated by the composition mapping of $Y_i(1 \leq i \leq n)$,
   suppose the composition condition is F, rewrite Y as $(Y_1 + Y_2 + \ldots Y_n) \cap F$.

Accordingly, the corresponding selection rewriting can be described as the following expression:

$$\sigma(X, Y_1 \cup Y_2) = \sigma(X, Y_1) \cup \sigma(X, Y_2) \tag{2}$$

$$\sigma(X, (Y_1 + Y_2) \cap F) = \sigma(X, Y_1 \wedge F) \bowtie (X, Y_2 \wedge F) \tag{3}$$

It is worth to point out that rewriting process maybe a recursion for the transitivity property of semantic mapping. The process of rewriting pattern tree and predication expressions can be described as algorithm 1 and 2.

Algorithm 1. SEL_Rewrite_X(X)

Input: X is the pattern tree of selection query $\sigma(X, Y)$.

1 **foreach** $x \in X$ **do**
2   **switch** *Mappings of X node* **do**
3   **case** *funsion_node*
4             $x \leftarrow x \cup \bigcup_{1 \leq i \leq n} x_i$;
5   **foreach** x_i **do**
6   SEL_Rewrite_X(x_i);
7   **end**
8   **case** *subsumption or composition*
9             $x \leftarrow \bigcup_{1 \leq i \leq n} x_i$;
10   **foreach** x_i **do**
11   SEL_Rewrite_X(x_i);
12   **end**
13   **end**
14   **end**
15 **end**

Now we discuss the problem of reducing redundancy in the process of ontology query, A selection is redundancy if it satisfy

$$\forall(i, j)\{X_i \in P_o \wedge X_j \in P_o \wedge X_i \cap X_j \neq \emptyset\} \tag{4}$$

and corresponding rewriting of selection can be described as:

$$\sigma(X_1, X_2, Y) = \sigma(X_1, Y) \cup \sigma(X_2 - (X_1 \cap X_2), Y) \tag{5}$$

The advantage of complex ontology mapping with semantic similarity enhanced can be expressed as follows:

- It can match the semantic similar concepts more exactly, especially for the concepts which is a part of concept hierarchy;

Algorithm 2. SEL_Rewrite_Y(Y)

Input: Y is the predication list of selection query $\sigma(X, Y)$.
Output: E is rewriting expression

1 **foreach** $y \in Y$ **do**
2   **switch** *Mappings of Y concept* **do**
3   **case** *funsion_node*
4              $y \leftarrow y \cup \bigcup_{1 \leq i \leq n} y_i$;
5   **foreach** y_i **do**
6   SEL_Rewrite_Y(y_i);
7   **end**
8   **case** *subsumption*
9              $y \leftarrow \bigcup_{1 \leq i \leq n} y_i$;
10   **foreach** y_i **do**
11   SEL_Rewrite_Y(y_i);
12   **end**
13   **case** *decomposition*
14             $y \leftarrow (y_1 + y_2 + \ldots y_n) \cap F$;
15   **foreach** y_i **do**
16   SEL_Rewrite_Y(y_i);
17   **end**
18   **end**
19 **end**
20 **end**

- It can reduce the semantic inconsistent by solving problem semantic absent. For example, both the concept $O_1 : C_1(a, b, c, d, f)$ and $O_2 : C_2(a, c, d, e, f)$ represent part of the real concept C with a,b,c,d,e and f attributions, the complex mapping mechanism can supply complete view of concept C at the global site;
- It can reduce the redundancy of the global ontology by finding more semantic matching in subsumption and composition (decomposition) mappings;
- The complex mapping mechanism refines the process of query, and it makes the result more precisely.

5   Discussion and Conclusion

The paper mainly discusses complex semantic mapping and integration mechanism, and the semantic based XML query mechanism. It discuss the ontology integration mechanism based on complex mapping, such as support subsumption mapping, composition mapping and so forth, it also discuss the semantic query mechanism based on global and integrated ontology. It primarily extends XML query algebra based on TAX. Because common XML query languages such as XQuery and XUpdate can be transferred into XML query algebra based on TAX, so the extension is feasible. Ontology integration based on complex mapping ensures distributed query can solve the problem of the inconsistency of part semantic and increases the query efficiency by refining on querying and reducing redundancy. A Mediator based Query Rewriting mechanism with ontology integration is implemented in OBSA system[8].

Acknowledgment

This work was partially supported by a grant from the NSF (Natural Science Fundation) of Hubei Prov. of China under grant number 2003ABA049 and by a grant from the NSF of Hubei Education Agency of China under grant number 2003A012.

References

1. Wache, H., Vögele, T., Visser, U., Stuckenschmidt, H., Schüster, G., Neumann, H., Hubner, S.: Ontology-based integration of information - a survey of existing approaches. In: Proceedings of IJCAI-01 Workshop: Ontologies and Information Sharing, Seattle, WA, Springer (2001) 108–117
2. Hung, E., Deng, Y., V.S.Subrahmanian: TOSS: An Extension of TAX with Ontologies and Simarity Queries. In G.Weikum, ed.: Proceedings of the 2004 ACM SIGMOD international conference on Management of data, Paris, France, ACM Press (2004) 719–730
3. Gu, J., Chen, H., Yang, L., Zhang, L.: OBSA:Ontology-based Semantic Information Processing Architecture. In Liu, J., Cercone, N., eds.: Proceedings of IEEE/WIC/ACM International Conference on Web Intelligence 2004, Beijing, IEEE Computer Society Press (2004) 607–610
4. Bozsak, E., Ehrig, M., Handschuh, S., et al.: KAON:Towards a Large Scale SemanticWeb. In: Proceedings of EC-Web 2002, LNCS, Springer-Verlag (2002)
5. KWON, J., JEONG, D., LEE, L.S., BAIK, D.K.: Intelligent semantic concept mapping for semantic query rewriting/optimization in ontology-based information integration system. International Journal of Software Engineering and Knowledge Engineering 14 (2004) 519–542
6. H.V.Jagadish, L.V.S.Lakshmanan, D.Srivastava, et al: TAX: A Tree Algebra for XML. Lecture Notes In Computer Science 2379 (2001) 149–164
7. MENG, X.F., LUO, D.F., JIANG, Y., WANG, Y.: OrientXA: An Effective XQuery Algebra. Journal of Software 15 (2004) 1648–1660
8. Gu, J.: Research on the Mechanisms of the Semantic Based Semi-structured Data Processing. PhD thesis, Wuhan University (2005)

Implementation of Cooperative Cognition Under Web Environment

Wanchun Dou[1,2], Guihai Chen[1,2], Feng Su[1,2], and Shijie Cai[1,2]

[1] State Key Laboratory for Novel Software Technology,
Nanjing University,
douwc@nju.edu.cn
[2] Department of Computer Science and Technology,
Nanjing University, 210093, P. R. China

Abstract. Since cognition could be treated as problem-solving issues based on dynamical knowledge transferring and propagation, the meta-learning and group learning are put forward in conformance with meta-cognition and group cognition through New Product Development (NPD) analysis. To meet the globally distributed tendency of problem solving with cognitive intention based on Internet technology, a P2P-based Problem Solving Environment (PSE) is explored to facilitate Web-based knowledge transferring and propagation. By taking advantage of P2P-based PSE, an infrastructure of knowledge grid oriented toward cooperative cognition is structured to support E-Science.

1 Introduction

Now, knowledge management (KM) is a topic of considerable interest. However, the majority of extant KM research treats knowledge as a static object that can be acquired, stored, and retrieved through information technology [1]. Generally, there stand two fundamental problems in domain of KG from this current viewpoints: (1) many researchers view knowledge as distinct from information, and (2) very little attention is paid to the dynamics of knowledge processing which is often called as "knowledge flow" [1,2,3]. Universally, the concept and the methodology employed in knowledge flow research can be popularized in cognition-based problem-solving process executed in cooperative way. Problem-solving process is often executed in a Problem Solving Environment (PSE) that is a complete, integrated environment for composing, compiling, and running applications in a specific area [4].

As a tendency, the Internet technology enables the cognition-based problem solving to be globally distributed for upgrading the competitiveness and promoting the innovation of teams that collaborate in a virtual organization [3], which underlies an e-Science infrastructure. To facilitate Web-based knowledge transferring and propagation, Knowledge Grid and semantic web attract more and more attentions.

Roughly, Knowledge Grid and semantic web are treated as the high-level application of the Grid that is advocate as the next generation web [5]. PSEs provide some backend computational resources and convenient access to their capabilities, and the integration of different PSEs oriented toward Web environment make up of the

G. Chen et al. (Eds.): ISPA Workshops 2005, LNCS 3759, pp. 579–588, 2005.

backend of Grid computational, especially the Knowledge Grid. [4]. As suggested in [4], knowledge flow features the dynamical environment of Knowledge Grid, typically. Accordingly, the infrastructure of grid middleware plays a critical role in facilitating knowledge flow execution and knowledge discovery when Knowledge Grid is exploited for their application needs [6]. For mental learning for problem solving is always companied by cognition–compliant that are often performed by individual participator or work group based on questions understanding, this paper focuses on the cognition-compliant learning mechanism from the viewpoint of knowledge flow to facilitate teams' collaboration. Furthermore, the P2P technology is exploited to structure the middleware infrastructure and web-based portal supporting Knowledge Grid application oriented toward cooperative cognition.

The remainder of this paper is organized as follows. In section 2, meta-learning and group-learning mechanism supporting meta-cognition and cooperative cognition were explored based on new product development analysis. In section 3, by taking advantage of P2P technology, a P2P-based PSE was structured based on the framework of cooperative cognition. In section 4, the integrated infrastructure of cooperative cognition oriented knowledge grid based on P2P technology was presented. Section 5 presented the conclusions of this paper.

2 Cognition Framework and Learning Mechanisms with Cognitive Intentions

According to the participator's intervention, the cognition process was classified, in this paper, into individual cognition process, i.e. meta-cognition, and cooperative cognition.. Question understanding and individual reflection characterizes the meta-cognition; problem discussion based on knowledge interaction, and cognitive consequence's refinement and formalization based on meta-cognitions make up of the evolution steps of group cognition process [1, 7, 8].

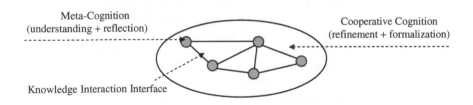

Fig. 1. A Framework of Cooperative Cognition Process

Fig.1 illustrated a framework of cooperative cognition. For learning has been a central aspect of AI from its earliest days and is a vital characteristic of any intelligent system that has to deal with changing environment, certain learning mechanism is indispensable, during cognizing, to pilot and promote cognitive activities, which may be the only way to discover complex problems or systems. And learning algorithms could be classified into supervised learning, unsupervised learning, and reinforcement learning [9]. In conformance with the meta-cognition and group cognition, the learning mechanisms with cognitive intentions are categorized into meta-learning mechanism and group learning mechanism in this paper.

For better understanding the cognitive principle, cognitive pattern in New Product Development (NPD) are exploited to illustrate generic cognition based on meta-learning and group learning. Roughly, NPD is a knowledge-driven action that concentrates on the transformation from tacit knowledge to explicit knowledge. Generally, the conceptualization of existed and expected product is indispensable in reifying the tacit knowledge. By conceptualizing the product, categorizing, correcting and condensing the related data in enterprise's repository becomes effective, which are important in decision discovery, concept design and early decision-making [10]. Here, the hierarchical reification relation from tacit knowledge to explicit knowledge is identified as following 4 stages.

(1) Conceptualize the expected product and existed product;
(2) Frame case structure and gather related decision cases;
(3) Learn from feedback; and
(4) Develop solution through iteration of ideas exchange.

Now, access to a wide range of information is easy, while the increasing size and complexity of database or repository make it more and more difficult to analyze this vast amount of data by hand with the goal of gaining new insights. Conceptualizing and formalizing the existed and expected product could lay a foundation for data mining or knowledge discovery.

For facilitating the following discussion, some hypotheses are presented, firstly. Let Set_of_Product = {Product_1, Product_2, ..., Product_n} be the product set that have been developed related to expected product, i.e. there are n feasible design patterns or cases that have been proved practicability and can be consulted as design guidelines in NPD. These accumulated effective design proposals can be treated as a knowledge base of an enterprise that underlies a NPD. Moreover, let Set_of_CA = {c_a_1, c_a_2, ..., c_a_n} be set of expected product's characteristic attributes in modeling from functional aspect, which is treated as a basic set of attribute piloting decision-making. Let Set_of_CA_Inherited be the subset of Set_of_CA, which stands for the inherited characteristic attributes that could be mapped into some existing products. The image of element c_a_i is presented as c_a_i' in this paper. Obviously, there could be more than one image in relation to c_a_i in practice. Let Set_of_CA_Innovated be the subset of Set_of_CA, which stands for the original characteristic attributes without images in existing products. The number of elements contained in Set_of_CA_Innovated measures the innovation of NPD. The smaller it is, the less innovative NPD is. If Set_of_CA_Innovated = Set_of_CA, the product development could be treated as a totally innovation. Obviously, Set_of_CA_Inherited or Set_of_CA_Innovated is a partition of Set_of_CA and there are some relationships among those sets:

i) Set_of_CA = Set_of_CA_Inherited $\cup$ Set_of_CA_Innovated
ii) Set_of_CA_Inherited $\cap$ Set_of_CA_Innovated = Φ

According to the rough set theory [11], a reified attribute defined above can factor a partition related to expected product and aggregate all the related information from enterprise knowledge base. Here, the reification from tacit knowledge to explicit knowledge can be defined as follows.

Definition 1. Let element_$i \in$ Set_of_CA_Inherited, in the mapping from Set_of_CA_Inherited to enterprise knowledge base, the collection of images of element-i is viewed as the reification of tacit knowledge in related to element-i, which is formalized as Set_of_CA/element_i in the paper.

Definition 2. Let SubSet_of_CA_Inherited $\subseteq$ Set_of_CA_Inherited, in the mapping from Set_of_CA_Inherited to enterprise knowledge base, the image collection of all the elements belong to SubSet_of_CA_Inherited is viewed as a reification of tacit knowledge in related to new product from a dimension, which is formalized as Set_of_CA/ SubSet_of_CA_Inherited in the paper.

If SubSet_of_CA_Inherited = Set_of_CA_Inherited, Set_of_CA/Set_of_CA_Inherited can be viewed as a complete reification of tacit knowledge in related to expected product from enterprise's repository. Accordingly, a cognitive pattern directing NPD can be formalized as follows [11].

Definition 3. The cognitive pattern supporting NPD can be presented as a quadruple form of (Q, A, Θ, f).

In the quadruple, Q is the domain of expected product, i.e. Q = Set_of_CA; A is a set of attributes; $\Theta = \bigcup_{a \in A} \Theta_a$, Θ_a is value collection of attribute of a; and $f: Q \times A \rightarrow \Theta$ is a cognitive function, i.e. $\forall a \in A, x \in Q, f(x, a) \in \Theta_a$.

Essentially, cognizing process is a learning process from some cognitive ground of some related data, information or cases based on personal knowledge or past experience [9]. Decisions in the early design phase of NPD are often based on incomplete, ill structured and poor quality information. So, they are often made in an empirical manner by using only personal knowledge and experience achieved during the past problem solving processes [10]. It is widely cited that most managers/designers refer to previous solutions to related problems as a first step in the design process. So, the solution of a problem or difficulty that was found in an earlier project, and subsequently resolved, could be consulted in a new project. Accordingly, a meta-learning pattern performed by an individual person is defined as follows by what-if analysis method [12].

Definition 4. Let f be the cognitive function, θ_j be a cognitive ground. So, the cognition-intended meta-learning performed by participator i can be formalized as below:

$$f_i: Q \xrightarrow{\theta_j} \Theta_{i\text{-}Q}$$

Where $\Theta_{i\text{-}Q}$ is the cognized output, i.e. collection of cognitive results. The cognitive ground could be instantiated into Set_of_CA/element_i or Set_of_CA/SubSet_of_CA_Inherited, as defined in Def.1 and in Def.2, in NPD. Let SubSet_of_CA_Innovated $\subseteq$ Set_of_CA_Innovated, the cognition-intended meta-learning pattern can be demonstrated in details as shown in Fig.2.

In Fig.2, f_i, f'_i and f''_i are cognitive functions, respectively, but their cognitive ground are different in details. The cognitive ground of f'_i is Set_of_CA/SubSet_ of_CA_Inherited, the cognitive ground of f''_i is personal knowledge or past experience in design related to Set_of_CA_Innovated, while that of f_i is the cognized output of f'_i and f''_i.

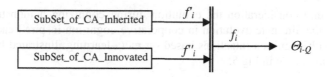

Fig. 2. Meta-learning Mechanism with Cognition Intentions in NPD

When dealing with a product, value analysis shows that the product can be considered either by customers as a set of functions or by designers as a set of components. It is difficult to prescribe the correlations among the components in details based on individual personal knowledge. Iterative detailed design just comes from the impossibility to provide a direct detailed description of the expected product in terms of detailed functions or correlations among the components designed by distributed individual technical personnel, which necessitates the group learning based cognitive cooperation and knowledge sharing in NPD [13].

NPD is typically carried out in a validating manner in terms of generating the initial design and then testing. Other team members' assessment of the acceptability of the decision should be based on decision support data or knowledge. Group learning provides an interdisciplinary fashion that harmonizes contributions from nearly all the functions of team group. The appreciation of upgrade/improvement of an exiting product will greatly benefit the expected product. Figure 3 demonstrates the group learning or team learning mechanism based on meta-learning pattern.

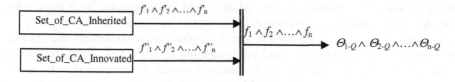

Fig. 3. Group Learning with Cognition Intentions Based on Meta-Learning

The group learning can be treated as a knowledge configuration process that is composed of various functional activities performed in stages from concept development to product delivery. It degrades the disadvantage of mismatch understanding among teams, iterative detailed design or upstream reconsideration thanks to product knowledge gathering and sharing.

As we know, cognition of some problems is usually a recursive process in a progressive way with respect to the grain size of the defined attributes. The cognition's evolution results in the hierarchy of learning process in design analysis and decision-making. According to the learning fashion discussed above, the learning hierarchy can be formalized by Fig.4, where $\Theta'_{i-Q} \subseteq \Theta_{i-Q}$. Fig.4 could be also treated as a reinforcement-learning pattern.

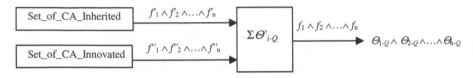

Fig. 4. The Hierarchy in Conformance with Cognition Evolution

Taking into consideration the evolution during cognizing demonstrated by Fig.4, especially the alternate evolution in cooperative cognition inspired each other, group learning with cognition intentions based on meta-learning illustrated by Fig.3 can be improved as shown in Fig.5.

$$\boxed{\text{Set\_of\_CA\_Inherited}} \xrightarrow{f'_1 \wedge f'_2 \wedge ... \wedge f'_n} \Sigma\Theta'_{i\text{-}Q} \xrightarrow{f_1 \wedge f_2 \wedge ... \wedge f_n} \Theta_{1\text{-}Q} \wedge \Theta_{2\text{-}Q} \wedge ... \wedge \Theta_{n\text{-}Q}$$

$$\boxed{\text{Set\_of\_CA\_Innovated}} \xrightarrow{f''_1 \wedge f''_2 \wedge ... \wedge f''_n}$$

Fig. 5. Group Learning with Cognition Intentions Based on Cognition Evolution

According to those two cognitive patterns, a generic cognitive pattern based on inductive learning and case based reasoning can be defined as follows.

Definition 5. The generic cognitive pattern based on inductive learning and case based reasoning can be formalized into a quintuple form of (Q, A, Θ, f, Q'). Where Q' is the case set for case based reasoning, i.e. domain related to NPD, which is, obviously, helpful in reinforcing the cognitive validity.

Accordingly, a generic cognitive cooperation description is presented in this section.

Definition 6. Cognition process is composed of a set of evolutionary cognition behaviors or evolutionary cognition stages, which could be formalized by a triple form Procedure-Of-Cognition-i = <PreviousState-i, $\Rightarrow$, SucceedState-i >.

A cognition behavior would often be unfolded with certain constraints such as timing, tools, explicit knowledge-related understanding or individual's tacit knowledge accumulation. Where, Procedure-Of-Cognition-i stands for a cognition behavior, PreviousState-i stands for the set of problem for settled before the cognition behavior, '$\Rightarrow$' stands for the introspective process against the problem for settled, and Succeed-State-i stands for the set of problem after the cognition behavior. For knowledge innovation are derived from the introspection during cognition process, the cognition process could be characterized by the following features:

1. If reviousState-i = SucceedState-i, we believe that the cognition behavior achieve no evolutional progress, and the cognition behavior stand in a logjam with individual's introspection or team's discussion.

2. If SucceedState-i $\subset$ PreviousState-i, we believe that the cognition behavior achieve some evolutional progress after individual's introspection or team's discussion.

3. Let Q-Element be a problem element, if (Q-Element∈ SucceedState-i) ∩ (Q-Element∉ PreviousState-i), we believe that the cognition behavior achieve some evolutional progress after individual's introspection or team's discussion. Note that the

evolutional progress is different from 2. This evolutional progress lead a new problem that may be helpful for systemic evolutional.

4. If SucceedState-i = Φ, we believe that the cognition process have finished all the cognitive tasks, i.e. the end of cognition process.

For achieving system cognition, there often stand some related cooperative relation among individual cognitive behaviors. We call the group cognitive activities the *Cognitive Cooperation*, which is characterized, here, with some dependency relation in cognition's pre-condition. For example, let Cognizing-Agent-m and Cognizing-Agent-n be two cognition agent, <Cognition-Precondition-i: PreviousState-i, $\Rightarrow$, SucceedState-i> is a cognitive stage of Cognizing-Agent-m based on a pre-condition of Cognition-Precondition-i. <Cognition-Precondition-j: PreviousState-j, $\Rightarrow$, SucceedState-j > is a cognitive stage of Cognizing-Agent-n based on a pre-condition of Cognition-Precondition-j. Let Q-Element' be the cognitive result of problem element of Q-Element, if (Q-Element$\in$ (PreviousState-$i\Box$SucceedState-i)) $\cap$ (Q-Element'$\in$ Cognition-Precondition-j), we treat there stand a direct learning relation between those two cognition behaviors. Cognizing-Agent-n is a learner during their cognitive cooperation.

3   Cooperative Cognition Under P2P-Based PSE

With recent advances in pervasive devices and communication technologies, there are increasing computing behaviors are deployed with networked services. These services extend supports from Web browsers on personal computers to handheld devices and sensor networks. Considering the technology advance, an application paradigm would be discussed supporting cognitive cooperative in distributed fashion on Grid. From the Grid point of view, P2P's main interesting aspects are scalability, self-configuration, autonomic management, dynamic resources discovery, and fault tolerance. The P2P systems focus on promoting peers stay at the edge of a network in which everyone stay creates as well as consumes and P2P's main potential is its ability to exploit idle computing resources, facilitating information exchange [7].

To enhance cognition's validity and efficiency, P2P approach is exploited for supporting cooperative cognition under Knowledge Grid environment. Accordingly, a peer could be cut out for depicting a meta-cognition process, while the P2P approach is exploited to explore the group cognition in cooperative cognition process in the paper. Cooperative Cognition in distributed, decentralized, and self-organizing environment can be viewed as a P2P application in E-Science that is essentially a cooperative cognition composed of a set of meta-cognition. Additionally, service-based architecture and decentralized coordination will take on more importance in Knowledge Grid. As resource-location mechanism playing in generic grid [15], knowledge-location and collaborator-location mechanisms play a key role for facilitating cooperative cognition under knowledge grid environment. P2P-based Problem-Solving Environment supporting distributed cognition process could be illustrated as in Fig.6.

The proposed P2P-based Problem-Solving Environment is characterized by two concepts of Web Knowledge-Flow Peers (WKFP) and Web Knowledge-Flow Peers Directory (WKFPD). WKFPD is defined dynamically by overly prescription component and is an active directory system that maintains a list of all peers that are available to participate in Web cognition process. P2P-Based Problem-Solving Environment allows a WKFP to register with the system and offer their services and resources to other WKFPs through P2P protocols. The services and resource would be the methods and knowledge helpful for certain WKFP in problem solving, i.e., WKFPD assists a WKFP to locate other WKFPs and use their service and resources by providing the live profile information about peer availability during the e-science development. The dynamic knowledge-location and collaborator-location mechanism are based on the WKFPD-location in practice. The infrastructure of location mechanism is based on the overlay networks. Each WKFP encapsulates adequate functionality and knowledge to execute meta-cognition. Through WKFPD, a WKFP could decide which WKFP would be invoked next in the knowledge flow.

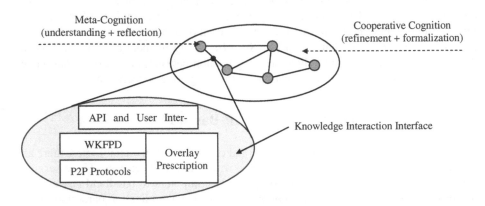

Fig. 6. P2P-based Problem-Solving Environment Supporting Distributed Cognition

4 Infrastructure of Cooperative Cognition Oriented Toward Knowledge Grid

An infrastructure of cooperative cognition oriented knowledge grid based on P2P technology is structured as shown in Fig.7. In Fig.7, the layered Semantic Web consist of a set of Web resources, a set of basic services, and a set of high-level application developed by using basic services; the Web resources is compiled from Generic Grid, and generally, the Web resources are described by metadata in a common and [16]. The basic services include reasoning and querying over metadata, and ontologies and semantic search engines that greatly improved the current Internet services such as Domain Name System and key-based search. By invoking a web service through a method invocation mechanism, a peer can perform complex task that is impossible to deal with if there stood no supporting from other peers.

To improve the static knowledge access service, it is necessary to integrate knowledge discovery and knowledge mining techniques in grid-based problem-solving environment. The P2P approaches reduce the increasing complexity in dealing with the self-management issues for such tasks. The unambiguous representation of the knowledge through metadata and ontologies is a key aspect in knowledge grid's building. Knowledge flow management based on P2P approach facilitates the dynamic knowledge interoperability among grid applications

The component of Grid Application Toolkit (GAT), as shown in Fig.7, plays a major role in providing seamless, pervasive, and secure resource use based on the Open Grid Services Architecture (OGSA) in which grid services conform to a set of conventions for controlled, fault-resilient, and secure management of services and exposes capabilities via standard interfaces. OGSI-compliant services have been reified into the OGSA's Globus Toolkit 3. In practice, GAT concludes a set of functions that support resource management, support for security, support for defining available resources, monitoring and discovery service, and even I/O control (for instance, Globus Resource Allocation Manager (GRAM), Grid Security Infrastructure (GSI), Resource Specification Language (RSL), and GridFtp contained in the Globus Toolkit could perform those functions, respectively) [4].

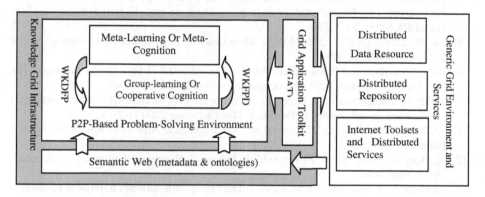

Fig. 7. Cooperative Cognition Oriented Knowledge Grid Infrastructure Based on P2P Technology

5 Conclusions and Future Work

Knowledge Grid Infrastructure provides a Grid-based problem-solving environment for not only data analysis, inference, and discovery, but modeling, simulation, and analysis of scientific experiments. In our prototype system, the cognitive cooperation is originated by knowledge flow that is instantiated by domain ontology, method ontology, and metadata ontology in a certain PSE. Additionally, the P2P technology is exploited to pilot the peer location mechanism as a knowledge flow engine. For our future research, we will apply the P2P approach to more Grid applications or paradigm; especially Knowledge Grid in despite of additional challenges that would cause some new expected issues.

Acknowledgement. This paper is based on Project 60303025 supported by NSFC, Jiangsu Provincial NSF research funds (No. BK2004411 and No. BK2005208).

References

1. Mark E.Nissen and Raymond E.Levitt..Agent-Based Modeling of Knowledge Flows: Illustration from the Domain of Information Systems Design. Proceedings of the 37th Hawaii International Conference on System Sciences, 2004 IEEE.
2. Zhuge, Hai. A Knowledge Flow Model for Peer-to-Peer Team Knowledge Sharing and Management. Expert Systems with Applications, July, 2002, 23(1):23-30.
3. Zhuge, Hai. Knowledge Flow Management for Distributed Team Software Development. Knowledge-Based Systems, 2002, 15(8):465-471.
4. Ian Taylor, Matthew Shields, et al. Triana Application within Grid Computing and Peer to Peer, Journal of Grid Computing, 2003, 1(2):199-217.
5. Zhuge, Hai.China's E-Science Knowledge Grid Environment. IEEE Computer Society, 2004, 37(1):13-17.
6. Kielmann,Thilo. Editorial. Journal of Grid Computing, 2003, 1(2):99-100.
7. F.Schintke et al. A Framework for self-optimizing grids using P2P Components. Proceedings of the 14th International Workshop on Database and Expert Systems Applications(DEXA'03), 2003 IEEE.
8. Nicolas Schweighofer and Kenji Doya. Meta-Learning in Reinforcement Learning. Neural Networks, 2003, 16(1):5-9.
9. Robert A.Wilson and Frank C.Keil.The MIT Encyclopedia of the cognitive sciences. The MIT Press Cambridge, 1999, Massachusetts London, England.p:lxxxiii.
10. 10.Michel Aldanondo, et al. Expert Configurator for Concurrent Engineering: Came´le´on software and model. Journal of Intelligent Manufacturing, 2000 11(2), 127-134.
11. 11.Zhang Wen-Xiu, et al. Theoretical and Methodological Aspects of Rough Set. Science Publish House, 2001.
12. 12.Deng JU-Long. Grey Theory.Publish House of Huazhong University of Scence& Technology, 2002.
13. 13.Bonney, M, Ratchev, S & Moualek, I. The Changing Relationship Between Production and Inventory Examined in a Concurrent Engineering Context. *Production Economics*, 2003. 6(3):243_254.
14. 14.Mario Cannataro and Domenico Talia. Semantics and Knowledge Grids: Building the Next-Generation Grid.IEEE Intelligent Systems, 2004, 19(1):56-63.
15. 15.Daniel A.Menasce, et al. Scalable P2P Search. IEEE Internet Computing(Published by the IEEE Computer Society), 2003, 36(3):83-87.
16. 16.Ian Foster, Carl Kesselman and Steven Tuecke. The Anatomy of the Grid. International Journal of Supercomputer Applications, 2001, 15(3):1-21.

Access Authorization Policy for XML Document Security*

Sun-Moon Jo[1], Ki-Tac Kim[1], Hoon-Joon Kouh[2], and Weon-Hee Yoo[1]

[1] Department of Computer Science and Information Engineering, Inha University,
253 YongHyun Dong, Nam Ku, Incheon, Korea
sunmoon@inhaian.net, Kimkitae@inha.ac.kr, whyoo@inha.ac.kr
[2] School of Computer Information Technology, Kyungin Women's College,
101 GyeSan Dong, GyeYang Ku, Incheon, Korea
hjkouh@kic.ac.kr

Abstract. XML has recently emerged as the most relevant standardization effort in the area of document representation through markup languages. XML-based access control aims at providing an authorization policy that can be consistently applied to various products for access control services on Internet and different kinds of environment for the products. In this paper, we propose an access authorization policy for XML document security. We also suggest a separation of DOM (Document Type Definition) and SAX (Simple API for XML) for parsing of XML documents. Therefore, it becomes easy to manage information on users and access privilege.

1 Introduction

XML (eXtended Markup Language) is the SGML-based, simple, and very flexible text model, which is appearing as a new standard to express and exchange data on Internet [12]. By using its advantage of describing meaningful information directly, XML can provide a standard data model for exchanging information on a lot of data generated during the operation of corporate database or applied program. For this reason, it is so suitable for documentation management system or component specification requiring definition and description of detailed information and its meaning. XML [2] documents were opened to users who accessed them without any restriction all contents to share data as in HTML and SGML.

In case of such specific fields as e-commerce, however, it is necessary to take a measure to protect personal information prevented from being opened to others, thus requiring management of access to documents. In generating documents, it is therefore necessary to privilege users to access their contents and to take a measure to enable only those users who possess the privilege to access specific contents. As for the existing access control, an access control technique becomes complicated for each operation as a operation is added; labeling and DTD verification processes consume

---

* This work was supported by the Korea Research Foundation Grant funded by the Korean Government (MOEHRD)" (R05-2004-000-11694-0).

G. Chen et al. (Eds.): ISPA Workshops 2005, LNCS 3759, pp. 589–598, 2005.

much memory on repetitive DOM tree retrieval and parsing of XML documents, which can reduce the efficiency of the system [5]. The object within DOM enables a developer to read, explore, revise, add, or delete data from documents. It also provides standard functional definition for document navigation and a function to operate contents and structure of HTML and XML documents. However, DOM, which enters the entire document in memory and parses it to document tree, may use very large memory too much and reduce the efficiency of application rapidly. Of course, it can vary with library being used or the internal structures, DOM expression can require memory about ten times as large as the original.

To solve these problems, we propose an access authorization policy for XML document security. We also suggest a separation of DOM and SAX for parsing of XML documents. What is therefore expected is possibility of maintaining more rapid access control policy security with higher efficiency than that of the existing assess control by managing users and access authorization information management more easily and removing unnecessary parsing and DOM tree retrieval.

The remainder of this paper is organized as follows: In Section 2 describe basic concepts of DOM and SAX. We also examine studies and problems about XML access control. Section 3 defines the concept of XACML and an action label type group for access authorization policy rules to describe tree labeling algorithm technique. Section 4 evaluates the access authorization policy and section 5 draws a conclusion and describes the future course of studies.

2 Related Works

As the definition of interface that can be used by operating and accessing objects (tags) and documents, DOM[3] Level 1 can express contents of HTML or XML documents parsed without a loss, support HTML 4.0 and XML 1.0, generate a hierarchical structure of documents, and easily are expanded to use high-level API with ease. Level 2 defines the function of supporting an object model applying style sheet and operating information on the style of documents. DOM higher than Level 2 also includes description of user interface usable in Windows environment. By using this, a user can also define the function and security level of operating DTD of documents. That is, DOM higher than Level 2 serves to design API that enables a user to define, operate, change, and access all the things of documents, including style, events, structure, contents, and security level.

As a standard interface to analyze event-based XML, SAX serves to deal with XML documents using DOM with rapidity and low-level memory. It also analyzes XML documents to extract necessary information and provides API to analyze large-size XML documents more efficiently. The following examines advantages and disadvantages of SAX [10]. Figure 1 compares the styles of dealing with XML documents between DOM and SAX.

- Advantages of SAX
  - □ SAX API is generally simple, compared with DOM.
  - □ SAX doesn't enter the entire documents in memory.

□ It can form a data structure containing key information which needs less memory than DOM.

□ It can conduct operations rapidly because it doesn't read the entire document before beginning the operations.

□ It is proficient in filtering and selecting data.

● Disadvantages of SAX

□ The sequential model provided by SAX doesn't permit random access to XML documents.

□ It cannot make another DTD or revise existing one.

□ Since it doesn't have the entire document within memory, it is necessary to prepare modifications for each structure or content.

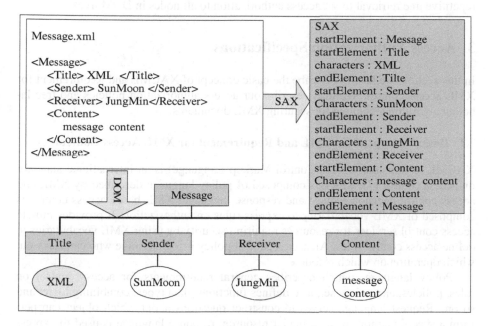

Fig. 1. XML of DOM and SAX a document processing comparison

The existing access control models [4], [5] uses such a DOM tree to set access authorization to elements of DTD and XML documents and control users' access to XML data according to information on access authorization set.

According to the process of changes in documents in [4], [5], [6], there is a request for seeing XML documents. As for all XML documents and DTD concerned, information on access authorization is specified in documents called XAS (XML Access Sheet). XML documents are parsed to obtain DOM trees; then, a value of sign is set which means admission (+) or rejection (-) of access to nodes of DOM trees based on XAS of DTD and XML documents. It is called labeling to set authorization to nodes of DOM trees. The nodes with the value of sign set as - are removed from the labeled DOM trees and only those with the value set as + are restored to the user [1], [3], [4], [5]. Here, although XML documents with nodes removed from DOM trees can fail to be valid (its solution requires the loosening process, with all elements and attributes set as optional in DTD), they can maintain the existing DTD despite the removal of nodes from DOM trees.

To solve the problem that XML documents with nodes removed from DOM trees can fail to be valid for DTD, the loosening technique is suggested to maintain the existing DTD despite the removal of nodes from DOM trees [4]. However, this method causes a semantic conflict due to the loss of information on the structure. The tree labeling technique is used to maintain information on the structure of documents, which has a problem that it can violate secrecy by showing the existence of data and information on the structure with rejection (-) labeling [4], [5].

Above-mentioned studies have a problem of reducing the efficiency of system as the entire DOM trees should be loaded in memory and much memory is used due to repetitive tree retrieval to set access authorization to all nodes in DOM trees.

3   Access Authorization Specifications

In this section, we briefly describe the basic concept of XACML and Requirement for XML access control. We also describe our access authorization policies and tree labeling algorithm technique for securing XML documents.

3.1   Basic Concept of XACML and Requirement for XML Access Control

XACML (eXtensible Access Control Markup Language) is an international standard on access control [7], which is composed of policy language described by XML and access control decision request and response language. XML-based access control is composed of XML vocabularies to express rules on authorization. It provides minute access control services for resources requiring security by using XML vocabularies to define access control rules. An access control policy is to determine who can carry out which operation on which resource.

Policy language, which describes general requirements for access control on rules, policies, and policy set, also defines functions, data types, combining logic, and so on. Request language serves to construct questions about which object can perform a specific action for a particular resource; response language is used to express results of the request, with responses indicated in four results: permit, deny, indeterminate, and not applicable [8], [9], [11].

The existing web-based access control models can describe authorization in a unit or part of files. However, this method fails to make access based on a meaning of information in order to deal with information by the meaning, which characterizes XML documents most remarkably, or access to such small units as elements. Therefore, requirements for access control to XML documents can be summarized as follows [6]:

- Authorization should be provided in many structural levels. It is necessary to designate authorization in various classes because organizational authorization in the same document can vary with properties of the organization.
- It should be possible to expand the existing web server technology. In other words, it should be possible to apply the access control system to XML documents

by expanding the existing web server because XML documents are usually used on the ground of web site.

- It is necessary to support fined-grained access control. The access control model should provide access control in many levels such as document set or one element.
- It is necessary to secure transparency. If it should be transparent to a user to conduct operations of an access control system, it should be impossible to know which part is provided with no privilege in a document a requester looks at.
- The user authorization process should be combined easily with the existing techniques.

3.2 Access Authorization Policy Rules

The authorization rule is used not only to authorize general users and objects to access the documents but also to settle any dispute over the same object between subjects or to resolve the question of overlapped authorities over the same subject between objects. XML document access authorizations are composed of subject, object, action, action label type group, sign, and type:

- Subject: User name, IP address, computer name (A subject who accesses XML documents and provides user group and pattern);
- Object: XPath 1.0 (An element of XML documents, which is expressed in XPath);
- Action: Read, write, create, delete (An operation the subject can implement);
- Action Label Type Group: R(read operator group), DSLG(Document and Structure Label Group; operator group);
- Sign: {+, -} is the sign of the authorization, which can be positive (allow access) or negative (forbid access);
- Type: {L, R, LDH, RDH, LS, RS, LD, RD} is the type of the authorization (Local, Recursive, Local DTD Hard, Recursive DTD Hard, Local Soft, Recursive Soft, Local DTD, and Recursive DTD, respectively).

Privilege subject is described by ID or a position of requesting access. The position can be expressed by an IP address or a symbolic name. Privilege object means a resource to protect access. To express the object, XPath language [13] is used which is norm of W3C for path expression, or the expansion of uniform resource identifiers (URI). Path expression is an array of element names divided by a split (/) on a document tree or predefined functions. Besides, it can include a function. A function can be used according to diverse requirements; a few predefined functions are provided in language. For example, child returns a child node of a certain node; descendent returns all descendent nodes of a certain node; and ancestor returns all ancestor nodes of a certain node. A function and its factors are divided by ::. Action Label Type Group(ALTG) can be classified into operator groups according to the highest level at which operators can change XML documents. Access authorization describes permission or denial of actions that a subject can take on an object stored in a specific site.

□ Read Label Group: A set of operators that read but never change documents in XML (Read).
□ Document Structure Label Group: A set of operators that change XML documents and structures (Insert, Delete, Rename).

Authorization can describe both permission and denial; by using both methods, it is possible to describe authorization with efficiency and convenience through application to subject or object group including exceptions.

3.3 Propagation Policy Rules

A Propagation policy rule is a security policy to use for regulating authorization conflicts to set access authorization. As for authorization interpretation, the final sign (+ or -) is determined by reflecting propagation and overriding in each element. If there are both permission and denial for the same subject, only one access authorization is determined according to the conflict settlement principle. The following steps are rules to determine precedence of authorization in case of authorization conflicts.

Rule 1: Authorization on the most specific subject described according to partial order of subjects takes precedence.
Rule 2: Directly described authorization rather than that occurring by transmission takes precedence.
Rule 3: Authorization directly described on XML documents rather than that described on DTD takes precedence.
Rule 4: Authorization on nodes rather than that of its forefather takes precedence.

3.4 Default Policy

When there is no permission(grant or deny) for an access request or when the confliction resolution policy "nothing takes precedence" is enforced, we need to make a decision according to the specified default policy. This can be specified in the <default> element for each action the default policy is "deny" by default for every action.

3.5 Tree Labeling Algorithm and Technique

Labeling is the process of using information on access authorization defined by a security manager to set access authorization to nodes of DOM trees requested by a user. The information on labeled authorization is used in determining whether to admit or reject the user's request. To label information on authorization to DOM trees based on an operator, it was necessary to repeat the labeling process as many times as the number of kinds of operators included in a question. Suggested is labeling algorithm based on the ALTG to remove such a repetitive labeling process.

■ Tree Labeling Algorithm ■

Input : A requester rq and an XML document URI
Output : The view of the requester rq on the document URI
Method : /* L is local, R is recursive, LDH is Local DTD Hard, RDH is Recursive DTD Hard, LS is Local Soft, RS is Recursive Soft, LD is local DTD-level, RD is recursive DTD-level */
1. A.xml A = {a= <subject, object, action, ALTG, sign, type> | a ∈ authorization, rq ≤ AS subject, uri(object)= =URI OR uri(object) = =dtd(URI)}
2. Let r be the root of the tree T corresponding to the document URI, n is a node other than r, p is the parent node of n

3. AM( ) : returns the ALTG of a node specified in the authorization rule,
4. Type() : returns the type specified in the authorization rule,
5. Propagation_rule() : returns the ALTG determined by propagation rules
6. For each c ∈ children(r) do label(c, r)
7. For each c ∈ children(r) do prune(T, c)
8. L1r = AM(r) in A.dtd , L2r = AM(r) in A.xml
9. initial_label(r)
10. For each c ∈ children(r) do label(n,p)

```
void main() {

                initial_label(n);

                label(n,p);

                prune(); }

void initial_label(n) {

        if  L1r ∪ L2r ={ }, Lr=default(r)

        else  Lr = propagation_rule([L1r, L2r]); }

void label(n,p) {

if type (p) in [L, R, LDH, RDH, LS, RS, LD, RD]

        if  L1n & L2n = { }, Ln = Lp

        else Ln = propagation_rule([Lp, L1n, L2n]);

else if  L1n & L2n = { }, Ln = default(n)

        else  Ln = propagation_rule([L1n, L2n]); }

void prune(T, n) {

    /* Tree representing the document, Determines if n
has to be removed from T */

For each c ∈ children(n)  do prune(T, c);

if children(n) == { } and Ln ≠ '+'   then

    remove the current node from T; }
```

Labeling makes it possible (+) or impossible (-) to access each node n. □, which is the labeling value of each node, has the authorization undescribed and can be interpreted as denial or permission, respectively, according to closed or open policy. To maintain the structure of documents, the part of documents, which is shown to a requester, is a child node of an accessible part; even those parts which are unaccessible or have authorization undescribed include beginning and ending tags. Since the tree of the original document includes even unauthorized parts, a view is generated which shows a requester only permissible parts through tree-pruning according to signs of each node.

Existing XML access control techniques determine whether to allow a query to access or not after labeling the DOM tree. To address this problem, the proposed access control technique divides the access control process into five steps

Step 1: If a user requests a desired resource, preprocessing is implemented.

Step 2: If a user requests XML documents, whether to process it by DOM or by SAX is first determined in the preprocessing process.

Step 3: If the user has only reading privilege, it is processed by SAX.

Step 4: If the user has privilege to change XML documents and structures, it is processed by DOM.

Step 5: At the DOM labeled tree stage, operators with requests opposite to user privilege group are removed (If a user who has no privilege to change XML structure requests to change XML structure, the request is removed in advance).

4   Evaluation

Our processor takes as input a valid XML document requested by the user, together with its XML Access Sheet (XAS) listing the associated access authorizations at the instance level. The processor operation also involves the documents DTD. The processor output is a valid XML document including only the information the user is allowed to access. To provide a uniform representation of XASs and other XML-based information, the syntax of XASs is given by the XML DTD depicted in Figure 2.

The existing access control is the repetitive tree labeling process and DTD verification process consume a lot of memory for XML parsing and DOM tree search, which may degrade system performance.

```
<!ELEMENT set of authorizations (authorization)+>
<!ELEMENT authorizations (subject, object, ALTG, action, sign, type)>
<!ELEMENT subject (#PCDATA)>
<!ELEMENT object (#PCDATA)>
<!ELEMENT ALTG empty>
<!ELEMENT action empty>
<!ELEMENT sign empty>
<!ELEMENT type empty>
<!ATTLIST set of authorizations about CDATA #REQUIRED>
<!ATTLIST ALTG value(R, DSLG) #REQUIRED>
<!ATTLIST action value (read, write, create, delete) #REQUIRED>
<!ATTLIST sign value (+ | − ) #REQUIRED>
<!ATTLIST type value (L|R|LDH|RDH|LS|RS|LD|RD) #REQUIRED>
```

Fig. 2. XML Access Sheet

If the existing access control is used as in the case that a user's authorization changes XML documents and structures, the following procedure is necessary [4], [6].

Step 1: User sends an access request.

Step2: Parsing of XML documents to examine an operator's authorization

Step 3: Labeling of authorization to DOM trees using information on access authorization
Step 4: Determining if structure is changed in the stage of testing DTD
Step 5: Conducting exchange operation if the DTD test identifies that operation leads to no structure change
Step 6: Parsing to obtain new DOM trees as XML contents were changed after the operation
Step 7: Testing authorization of insertion operation
Step 9: Labeling authorization to DOM trees and testing DTD
Step 10: An insertion operator is denied because it was shown to change DTD

As seen above, the existing access control can make the system inefficient with the labeling process to assess authorization after each demand by a user and repetitive visits to DOM trees.

To the contrary, the suggested access control policy model can separate operators' collection into ALTG and thus prevent delay in complicated authorization assessment and responding. To define the action label type group has the following advantages. ① It can remove unnecessary access controls; ② It can reduce repetitive tree retrievals; ③ It can reduce memory; and ④ It provides correct XML documents demanded by a user who has the privilege to access them on the web.

5   Conclusions

Access control policy is important is every enterprise. In this paper, we proposed an access authorization policy for XML document security. We also suggested a separation of DOM and SAX for parsing of XML documents. The definition of an action label type groups made users and access authorization information management easy and provided rapid access control by removing unnecessary parsing and DOM tree retrieval. It is therefore possible to reduce a drop in efficiency of the system that was caused by repetitive visits to DOM trees and labeling to evaluate privilege each time a user makes a request, which is a disadvantage of access control. It is necessary to realize privilege management tool to provide users with convenient interface in the future.

References

1. A. Gabillon and E. Bruno, "Regulating Access to XML Documents", In Proc. IFIP WG11.3 Working Conference on Database Security, 2001
2. C. F. Goldfarb and P. Prescod. The XML Handbook, Prentice Hall, 1998
3. Document Object Model(DOM), Avaiable at http://www.w3.org/DOM/
4. E. Bertino, S. Castano. E. Ferrari, M. Mesiti, "Specifying and Enforcing Access Control Policies for XML Document Sources", WWW Journal, Baltzer Science Publishers, Vol.3, N.3, 2000.
5. E. Damiani, S. De Capitani di Vimercati, S. Paraboschi, P. Samarati, "Securing XML documents," in Proc. Of the 2000 International Conference on Extending Database Technology(EDBT2000), Konstanz, Germany, March 27-31, 2000

6. E. Damiani, S. Vimercati, S. Paraboschi, and P. Samarati, "Design and implementation of an access control processor for xml documents". In proceedings of the 9th International WWW Conference, Amsterdam, May 2000.
7. IBM Tokyo Lab, "XML Access Control Language", 2000, http://www.tr.ibm.com/projects/xml/xacl/xaclpec.html
8. Michiharu Kudo. Satoshi Hada "XML Document Security based on Provisional Authorization" CSS 2000, Athens, Greece
9. OASIS-XACMLTC, "OASIS eXtensible Access Control Markup Language", Working Draft 15, 12 July 2002, http://www.oasisopen.org/ommittess/xacml/repository/draft-xacml- schema-policy-15.doc
10. Simple API for XML http://www.megginso.com/SAX
11. Sun's XACML Implementation. http://sunxacml. soureefore.net/.
12. T. Bray et al. "Extensible Markup Language(XML) 1.0". World Wide Web Consortium(W3C). http://www.w3c.org/TR/REC-xml(October 2000).
13. World Wide Web Consortium(W3C), "XML Path Language(XPath) Version 1.0", http://www.w3.org/TR/PR-XPath 19991008, (October 1999).

OWL2Jess: A Transformational Implementation of the OWL Semantics*

Jing Mei[1,2], Elena Paslaru Bontas[2], and Zuoquan Lin[1]

[1] Department of Information Science,
Peking University, Beijing 100871, China
{mayyam, lz}@is.pku.edu.cn
[2] Freie Universität Berlin, Institut für Informatik,
AG Netzbasierte Informationssysteme,
Takustr.9, D-14195 Berlin, Germany
{mei, paslaru}@inf.fu-berlin.de

Abstract. The wide scale usage of OWL for the formalization of real-world ontologies is currently influenced by important limitations which concern both its expressivity and the efficiency of OWL specific reasoning tools. While the expressivity limitations may be overcame by extending the OWL language (e.g. with rules), the reasoning with such heterogeneous knowledge bases is still an open issue. In this paper we propose OWL2Jess, a prototypical tool which enables the transformation of OWL ontologies to Jess rule bases and thus enables OWL models to be extended by means of rules. Facts are derived from an initial OWL file by one XSLT stylesheet, while the RDF(S) and OWL Semantics are pre-defined as Jess rules. By making hidden knowledge explicit, OWL2Jess achieves the knowledge compilation: the implicit subsumption and membership relations can be subsequently identified using the Jess rule engine.

Keywords: Semantic Web, ontologies, rules, reasoning.

1 Introduction

The increasing use of ontologies in various application domains has led to the development of OWL [14], a Web based ontology representation language, which offers a reasonable trade-off between expressibility and decidability [8]. However representing knowledge in OWL provides two important limitations: on one hand efficient reasoning on real-world ontologies containing a large set of individuals is still a challenging task with current Description Logics-based technologies. On the other hand though OWL is sufficiently rich to be used in many situations, it can not be used efficiently or intuitively by domain experts to model certain application domains (e.g. [1]).

* Supported partially by NSFC (grant numbers 60373002 and 60496322) and by NKBRPC (2004CB318000).

G. Chen et al. (Eds.): ISPA Workshops 2005, LNCS 3759, pp. 599–608, 2005.

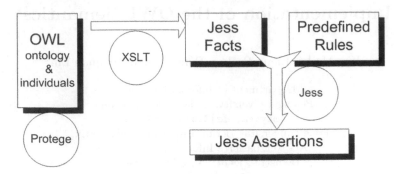

Fig. 1. OWL2Jess Model

The Semantic Web community tries to overcome these drawbacks by proposing two directions for further research: efficient reasoning over individuals could be achieved by identifying fragments of OWL which can be possibly translated to Datalog [4] [2], while the limited expressibility is extended by Semantic Web-enabled rule languages [7] [13].

Generally speaking, both ontology languages, which inherit from frame-based systems or semantic networks, and rule languages are FOL-related formalisms of Knowledge Representation. Some rule-based languages rely on Horn clauses, taking advantage of their well-defined semantics and well-understood and powerful inference mechanisms [9]. Some ontology languages like OWL rely on Description Logics(DL) and can be used for certain modelling tasks in a more intuitive manner [8]. Ideally, each representation paradigm should be used for the particular types of knowledge representation and reasoning tasks it better fits, while transformational implementations could be a solution to the heterogeneous representation.

OWL2Jess(cf. OWLTrans[1]) is proposed as a transformational implementation of the OWL Semantics[2] (Figure-1), which puts these ideas into practice. The tool can be used to fill the gap between OWL and Jess[3], a Java-based rule engine and scripting environment. While domain knowledge is still modelled with OWL, using common ontology editors, we transform OWL ontologies to Jess facts by XSL transformations processing the XML-based syntax of OWL. In addition we use pre-defined Jess rules to encode the OWL Semantics. Finally, the Jess rule engine can be run, so as to implement application-dependent reasoning services.

This approach is related to OWLJessKB[4], ROWL[5], TRIPLE[6] and Euler[7], each of which gives its own implementation corresponding RDF and OWL rules.

---

[1] http://www.inf.fu-berlin.de/inst/ag-nbi/research/owltrans/

[2] In this paper, we term the W3C recommendation document, OWL (RDF-compatible) Model-Theoretic Semantics [14], simply OWL Semantics.

[3] Java Expert System Shell, http://herzberg.ca.sandia.gov/jess/

[4] http://edge.cs.drexel.edu/assemblies/software/owljesskb/

[5] http://mycampus.sadehlab.cs.cmu.edu/public-pages/ROWL/ROWL.html/

[6] http://triple.semanticweb.org/

[7] http://www.agfa.com/w3c/euler/

A theoretical work has been elaborated in [12], with algorithms to reduce a DL syntactic variant of OWL to disjunctive Datalog. The key contribution of OWL2Jess is a translation of the OWL Semantics, providing more additions beyond the previous solutions, to maximize the knowledge compilation.

Note that our pre-defined rules are used to check the consistency, to compute the taxonomic classification, the characteristics of RDF&OWL vocabulary etc. The inferred Jess assertions are helpful for the ontology engineer to evaluate and refine the original OWL ontology.

The remainder of the paper is organized as follows: we describe our approach in Section 2 and give a detailed explanation of the translation of the most important RDF and OWL constructs in Section 3, focusing on the corresponding expressivity restrictions for rule-based languages. Section 4 is dedicated to the evaluation of our tool, which is compared to related approaches in Section 5. Current limitations and planed future work are presented in Section 6.

2   OWL2Jess

This section introduces OWL2Jess, a tool that converts OWL ontologies to Jess knowledge bases. According to different expressivity levels, it actually could be either reduced to pure RDF2Jess, or extended to SWRL2Jess to support SWRL [7], the W3C proposal extending the set of OWL axioms to include Horn-like rules. By syntactically and semantically converting OWL to Jess the tool enables the usage of the Jess reasoning engine over OWL ontologies, which might be more efficient than DL reasoners for particular tasks. In this way OWL2Jess offers a common reasoning engine for the corresponding heterogeneous data sources (OWL plus rules), while preserving the advantages of using OWL and/or rules for particular modelling tasks.

2.1   Transforming OWL to Jess

Converting OWL knowledge bases to Jess is realized in four steps.

1). The first step is the ontology building. An ontology editor like Protege[8] provides an OWL Plug-in to support the development of OWL ontologies. Organizing knowledge in terms of classes, properties, restrictions and individuals has been proven to be well accepted by domain experts and software developers, since this paradigm is very similar to object-oriented modelling or UML. Besides, in the last decades various ontologies for almost every application domain have been formalized in RDF(S) and OWL and can be therefore re-used and extended with rules if required.

2). In the second step we transform the XML syntax of OWL into the Jess syntax by means of XSLT. Starting from the root, recurrent processes of ABox-class and ABox-property are called via a set of named templates. The output file consists of Jess facts. If the semantics of the underlying ontology languages

---

[8] http://protege.stanford.edu/

is already specified as Jess rules, specific keyword matching is unnecessary in the OWL2Jess XSL transformation – as opposed to the ROWL[5] approach.

3). During the third step we combine the Jess file resulting from the XSL transformation with a pre-defined Jess formalization of RDF&OWL entailment rules. Furthermore, external Jess-style queries and rules can also be appended (such as the composition of properties, see example below: "hasUncle(x,z) ← hasFather(x,y), hasBrother(y,z)"). Such rules could also be represented using SWRL in OWL-style and another SWRL2Jess transformation tool.

4). The Jess rule engine is run in step four. Among our pre-defined rules, we mention consistency checking, classification and characteristics. Output results with error messages indicate invalid or illegal issues in the incoming OWL ontology. The engine deals with uncertainty (like $\exists$ or $\vee$) in a random fashion – based on the currently given knowledge base. In this case caution messages are used to signal when discovering that an individual is assigned to a certain class.

2.2   Variants of OWL2Jess

Since the OWL (RDF-compatible) Model-Theoretic Semantics [14] is based on RDF Semantics [6], our Jess rule file "owlmt.clp" includes a separate "rdfmt.clp", resulting that a pure RDF document would also be applied using a simpler RDF2Jess model, which will avoid unnecessary, expensive computations on the more complex OWL semantics.

Another possible alternative to OWL2Jess is its extension to support SWRL-enhanced OWL ontologies [11]. Consequently, by "SWRL2Jess.xsl" stylesheet, the translation from the SWRL syntax to Jess syntax could be easily accomplished. However, unlike the above OWL2Jess XSL transformation, we need additional keyword matching templates to distinguish among different types of SWRL components. The output consists of Jess rules, which will be handled in the same way as other pre-defined rules sharing the common ontology knowledge.

2.3   Discussion

As mentioned above, our proposal suggests to build ontologies in OWL and transform the OWL knowledge base to Jess for particular reasoning purposes. However, the semantics of OWL currently adopts an open world assumption(OWA), while almost all logic programming languages including Jess are based on a close world assumption(CWA).

In OWA, everything which was not specified explicitly is unknown to the reasoning service. For example, an owl:Class is defined as $C = \forall P.D$, but we can not conclude $u \in C$ even if we have currently found out that "for any given $v, P(u,v)$ there is $v \in D$". The reason is that there are more unknown t, maybe $P(u,t)$ but $t \notin D$. This fact can not be derived automatically due to the open world assumption. However, in practice, we indeed need such real-time conclusions, especially when we want to know whether there is something wrong or something missing about an existing ontology.

Consequently, our intention is merely to check the given OWL ontology, drawing attention on the errors or cautions, and to suggest the modifications, rather than attempt to really modify potential modelling errors. According to the error or caution messages, the author can revise the ontology manually. Furthermore, the inferred Jess assertions are helpful for the author to take into account the semantics of the implicit content of the ontology, such as that an individual currently belongs to an OWL restriction or an OWL boolean combination, even if this assertion is missing from the original ontology.

Another important issue is related to the "if-and-only-if"(iff) conditions. In RDF Semantics [6], there are extensional semantic conditions (i.e., iff conditions) for rdfs:domain, rdfs:range, rdfs:subClassOf, and rdfs:subPropertyOf, which are so strong that some consequences inferred are useless in practice. For instance, the domain and range of every property are extended to the largest one, namely rdfs:Resource, resulting in confusions with original definitions. A similar situation appears for the OWL (RDF compatible) Semantics [14]. We ignore these extensions here, however they are easy to be included if they are required.

3   Pre-defined Rules

Since the RDF(S) vocabularies are involved in the OWL Semantics, we first present rules for the RDF Semantics [6], and then the most important OWL-specific ones with a focus on owl:Restrictions and boolean expressions, which are viewed as expressive restrictions [4] for rule-based languages (see [10] for a detailed description of RDF(S) and OWL constructs).

3.1   RDF Semantics

RDF(S) axiomatic triples are transformed to facts, and RDF(S) semantic conditions are transformed to rules. The below Jess fact corresponds to "rdf:type rdf:type rdf:Property", followed by an example rule for rdfs:range.

```
(deffacts RDF_axiomatic_triples
   (triple (predicate "rdf:type")(subject "rdf:type")(object "rdf:Property")))
(defrule RDFS_semantic_conditions_range
   (triple (predicate "rdfs:range") (subject ?x) (object ?y))
   (triple (predicate ?x) (subject ?u) (object ?v))
=>(assert (triple (predicate "rdf:type") (subject ?v) (object ?y))))
```

It is unnecessary to assert triples mentioned as RDFS-valid, such as "rdfs:Class rdf:type rdfs:Class", for these would be inferred by other existing rules.

3.2   OWL Semantics

The implementation of the OWL semantics are more challenging, since OWL is an extension of RDFS to provide restrictions on how properties behave in a local class scope [8]. We define additional facts to represent typical OWL primitives and their relationship to RDFS such as owl:Class is subclass of rdfs:Class. In the remaining of this section we focus on OWL restrictions and boolean expressions, which are in our opinion the most relevant for the OWL to Jess conversion.

Some works-around are helpful to cope with the semantic discrepancy between OWL and rule-based languages: error messages indicating some illegal or invalid issues in the ontology or caution messages pointing out potentially missing ontology statements.

owl:unionOf

In OWL, the subject-value of owl:unionOf is a sequence of rdf:first, rdf:rest constructs. However, via XSLT, we directly catch an owl:Class as the subject-value, hence we skip the verbose syntax of rdf:List. Moreover, in Set Theory, the set equation $A = B$ means $A \subseteq B$ and $A \supseteq B$. Therefore we decompose the set equation of owl:intersectionOf into two rules "subset" and "supset". owl:intersectionOf and owl:oneOf are treated in a similar way.

Suppose $\langle x, y \rangle \in EXT_I(S_I(\text{owl:unionOf}))$ and y is a sequence of $y_1, \cdots, y_n$, we can easily state the supset relation, because $CEXT_I(x) \supseteq CEXT_I(y_1) \cup \cdots \cup CEXT_I(y_n) \supseteq CEXT_I(y_i)$.

However, the subset relation is troublesome due to the uncertainty factor. Given an individual $u \in CEXT_I(x)$, if we check out $\forall y_i, u \notin CEXT_I(y_i)$, then it indicates something missing about the subclasses of the union x in the existing ontology, else $u \in CEXT_I(y_i)$ has been satisfiable. The engine would randomly assign u to certain y_i after generating a caution message, which suggests the ontology author to assert similar statements in the original ontology.

```
(defrule OWL_unionOf_supset
    (triple (predicate "owl:unionOf") (subject ?x) (object ?y))
    (triple (predicate "rdf:type") (subject ?u) (object ?y))
 =>(assert (triple (predicate "rdfs:type") (subject ?u) (object ?x))))
(defrule OWL_unionOf_subset
    (triple (predicate "owl:unionOf") (subject ?x) (object ?y))
    (triple (predicate "rdf:type") (subject ?u) (object ?x))
    (not (and (triple (predicate "owl:unionOf")(subject ?x)(object ?v))
              (triple (predicate "rdf:type")(subject ?u)(object ?v))))
 =>(printout t "Caution!" ?u " now is assigned to " ?y crlf)
    (assert (triple (predicate "rdf:type") (subject ?u) (object ?y))))
```

owl:someValuesFrom

Suppose $\langle x, y \rangle \in EXT_I(S_I(\text{owl:someValuesFrom}))$ and $\langle x, p \rangle \in EXT_I(S_I(\text{owl:onProperty}))$, the supset relation is $CEXT_I(x) \supseteq \{u | \exists \langle u, v \rangle \in EXT_I(p)$ such that $v \in CEXT_I(y)\}$. Once we find out one existence, we can assert it as below:

In order to specify the subset relation, for $\langle u, v \rangle \in EXT_I(p)$, we first find out all possible types s of the individual v, and then check whether y is one possibility of s. If it fails, a possible solution is to randomly assign one belonging to y, else $v \in CEXT_I(y)$ has been satisfiable.

```
(defrule OWL_someValuesFrom_supset
   (triple (predicate "owl:someValuesFrom") (subject ?x) (object ?y))
   (triple (predicate "owl:onProperty") (subject ?x) (object ?p))
   (triple (predicate ?p) (subject ?u) (object ?v))
   (triple (predicate "rdf:type") (subject ?v) (object ?y))
=>(assert (triple (predicate "rdf:type") (subject ?u) (object ?x))))
(defrule OWL_someValuesFrom_subset
   (triple (predicate "owl:someValuesFrom") (subject ?x) (object ?y))
   (triple (predicate "owl:onProperty") (subject ?x) (object ?p))
   (triple (predicate "rdf:type") (subject ?u) (object ?x))
   (triple (predicate ?p) (subject ?u) (object ?v))
   (not (and (triple (predicate ?p) (subject ?u) (object ?o))
             (triple (predicate "rdf:type") (subject ?o) (object ?s))
             (test (eq 0 (str-compare ?s ?y)))))
=>(printout t "Caution!" ?v " now is assigned to " ?y crlf)
   (assert (triple (predicate "rdf:type") (subject ?v) (object ?y))))
```

owl:cardinality

Suppose $\langle x, y \rangle \in EXT_I(S_I(\text{owl:cardinality}))$ and $\langle x, p \rangle \in EXT_I(S_I$ (owl:onProperty)), the subset relation is $CEXT_I(x) \subseteq \{u | card\{\langle u, v \rangle \in EXT_I(p)\} = y\}$. We can compute the number of v using the Jess function "count-query-results", and error messages are thrown in case the result does not equal to y. However, OWL does not use the Unique Name Assumption(UNA), the above matching failure actually indicates some individuals are the same. On the other hand, the supset relation is asserted via the "count-query-results" function, as well.

```
(defquery OWL_cardinality_query
    (declare (variables ?P ?S))
    (triple (predicate ?P) (subject ?S) (object ?O) ))
(defrule OWL_cardinality_subset
   (triple (predicate "owl:cardinality") (subject ?x) (object ?y))
   (triple (predicate "owl:onProperty") (subject ?x) (object ?p))
   (triple (predicate "rdf:type") (subject ?u) (object ?x))
   (test (<> ?y (count-query-results OWL_cardinality_query ?p ?u)))
=>(printout t "Error!" ?x " has no " ?y " relating to " ?p crlf))
(defrule OWL_cardinality_supset
   (triple (predicate "owl:cardinality") (subject ?x) (object ?y))
   (triple (predicate "owl:onProperty") (subject ?x) (object ?p))
   (triple (predicate ?p) (subject ?u) (object ?v))
=>(if (= ?y (count-query-results OWL_cardinality_query ?p ?u)) then
      (assert (triple (predicate "rdf:type") (subject ?u) (object ?x)))))
```

4   Test Cases

A first version of the presented Jess rule base and XSLT stylesheets has been published on OWLTrans[1]. The prototypical implementation was evaluated by means of the following test cases.

In a first step all entailment rules were tested. The output file contained 55 pre-defined assertions (the RDF(S) axiomatic triples) and 108 inferred assertions, including the triples mentioned as RDF(S)-valid, such as (pred sub obj)=(rdf:type rdfs:Class rdfs:Class). In order to support the OWL semantics, this file was extended with 300 assertions, most of which are simple ones resulting from the reflexivity of rdfs:subClassOf and rdfs:subPropertyOf.

In a second step a small OWL ontology representing the family terminology and some individuals asserting their relationships was tested. Besides the obvious conclusions like those related to owl:Thing, more attention was paid to owl:Restriction and boolean expressions. A constraint like $Father \equiv Man \sqcap \exists hasChild.Person, hasChild(mdg, mj), Person(mj), Man(mdg)$ could be formalized in the original OWL ontology. A caution message was thrown after running Jess stating that "mdg is now an individual of the class Father".

In the third step we considered the often cited wine ontology[9]. A set of 1418 facts was obtained after executing the XSLT, and 5840 assertions were inferred by Jess. Running the XSLT took 1 second, while the Jess assertions were generated in 29 seconds. Besides rdf:type and rdfs:subClassOf, user-defined properties like "hasMaker" or "locatedIn" were the source of new Jess assertions, and many caution messages of OWL restrictions or boolean combinations were thrown, indicating implicit facts of the "wine" ontology.

Finally, a larger ontology with approximately 1000 concepts from the medical domain was tested (its source code had 33246 lines). 20700 facts were generated after performing the XSLT. However the inferred 74238 assertions were almost all about rdf:type and rdfs:subClassOf since the ontology mainly consisted of TBox assertions. The XSLT engine needed 1 second for the syntactical transformation, while running the Jess rule engine took approximately 300 seconds.

5   Related Work

Related work towards the integration of rules and ontologies in the Semantic Web can be roughly divided into two categories: (1) extension approaches, which directly extend OWL knowledge bases with rules, such as SWRL [7], a combination of the OWL with the Unary/Binary Datalog Rule Markup Language or the latest SWRL FOL [13] proposed to include an axiom for arbitrary first-order formula; (2) limitation approaches, which focus on some fragment of OWL, such as DLP(Description Logic Programs) [4], an intermediate KR contained within the intersection of DL and LP, or OWL Lite⁻ [2], a strict subset of OWL Lite which can be translated into Datalog.

In the first category we mention SWRLJessTab [3] combining SWRL rules and OWL ontologies within the Protege environment: Protege OWL Plugin, Jess and Racer. Similarly, SweetJess [5] (Semantic WEb Enabling Technlogies for Jess) defines a "DamlRuleML" ontology to deal with the Courteous Logic Programs. ROWL[5] (Rule Language in OWL and Translation Engine for JESS) also uses a specially developed ontology to embody rules. As mentioned among these

---

[9] http://www.w3.org/TR/owl-guide/wine.rdf

approaches, a specified namespace is required, like "swrl:","damlRuleML:" or "rowl:", to declare the elements of a rule such as head, body, variable, atom and so on. We do not use special namespaces in our approach, since all classes, properties and individuals are handed over from the OWL ontology and are expressed directly in rules. Furthermore the combination of properties could also be defined as a new rule to add more expressive power. On the other hand, as to the knowledge of the authors, the mentioned systems do not cover the RDF&OWL semantics to a satisfactory extent, ignoring owl:Restrictions or boolean expressions, which are emphasized in our model.

The second class of approaches concentrates on isolating proper subsets of OWL so as to be translated directly and completely without any loss of semantics to other knowledge representation formalisms. KAON[10] and TRIPLE [15] are reasoning platforms for such OWL subsets: for DLP and OWL Lite⁻ respectively. However, our intension was to allow OWL ontologies to be extended with rules, which means that we focus on scenarios where one needs to represent facts beyond the OWL expressive power.

The Euler proof mechanism[7] provides OWL, RDF, XSD rules described in Notation3; TRIPLE [15] is based on Horn logic and borrows features from F-Logic; and Vampire [16], a FOL prover, also is used to reason with OWL and SWRL. Our work is more similar to OWLJessKB[4] and ROWL[5], where Jess acts as the underlying rule engine as well. However, our implementation provides extended support for the OWL Semantics. The aim of OWL2Jess is to serve for translating the OWL Semantics completely and soundly offering a practical and efficient implementation of OWL reasoning in the same time.

6   Future Work

The transformation process of OWL files with XSLT was implemented in Java. Inferences on OWL ontologies and individuals were performed with the Jess reasoning engine (cf OWLTrans[1]). Expressive restrictions are handled with the help of error or caution messages, and the inferred assertions are helpful for the author to recognize possible extensions of the ontology.

We are aware of the high space complexity required by the Rete algorithm [9] used in Jess, but we note that the time complexity could be linear. To tackle the space problem one can consider using a persistent storage system. In order for Semantic Web to work in real-world scenarios outside the research community, it must offer techniques to reason with scalable collections, for example by using database techniques. We plan to investigate this issue in the future in order to develop a tool taking advantages of the three technologies. Building ontologies including classification and consistency checking can be realized efficiently using Description Logics. Reasoning over large sets of individuals can be performed preferentially using Logic Programming systems, while retrieving and storing information persistently can rely on databases.

---

[10] http://kaon.semanticweb.org/

Acknowledgement. This work was realized during the stay of Jing Mei as a visiting researcher at the Free University Berlin, Institute of Computer Science, Working Group Network Information Systems (NBI). Jing Mei wants to thank her host Prof. Robert Tolksdorf and the NBI working group for the fruitful collaboration during her stay. This work was partially supported by the KnowledgeWeb - EU Network of Excellence and by the Project "A Semantic Web for Pathology" funded by the German Research Foundation (DFG).

References

1. Werner Ceusters, Barry Smith, and Jim Flanagan. Ontology and medical terminology: Why description logics are not enough. In *Proc. Towards An Electronic Patient Record, TEPR2003*, 2003.
2. Jos de Bruijn, Rubén Lara, Axel Polleres, and Dieter Fensel. OWL DL vs. OWL flight: conceptual modeling and reasoning for the semantic Web. In *WWW 2005, Chiba, Japan, May*, pages 623–632. ACM Press, 2005.
3. Christine Golbreich. Combining rule and ontology reasoners for the semantic web. In *RuleML 2004, Hiroshima, Japan, November*, pages 155–169. LNCS 3323, 2004.
4. Benjamin Grosof, Ian Horrocks, Raphael Volz, and Stefan Decker. Description logic programs: Combining logic programs with description logics. In *WWW 2003, Budapest, Hungary, May*, 2003.
5. Benjamin N. Grosof, Mahesh D. Gandhe, and Timothy W. Finin. Sweetjess: Translating damlruleml to jess. In *RuleML 2002, Sardinia, Italy, June*, 2002.
6. Patrick Hayes and Brian McBride.   Rdf semantics.   *Available at http://www.w3.org/TR/rdf-mt/*, 2004.
7. Ian Horrocks, Peter F. Patel-Schneider, Harold Boley, Said Tabet, Benjamin Grosof, and Mike Dean. Swrl: A semantic web rule language combining owl and ruleml. *Available at http://www.w3.org/Submission/SWRL/*, 2004.
8. Ian Horrocks, Peter F. Patel-Schneider, and Frank van Harmelen. From shiq and rdf to owl: The making of a web ontology language. *Journal of Web Semantics*, 1(1):7–26, 2003.
9. John W. Lloyd. *Foundations of logic programming; (2nd extended ed.)*. Springer-Verlag New York, Inc., 1987.
10. Jing Mei and Elena Paslaru Bontas.   Technical reports: Reasoning paradigms for owl ontologies.   *Available at http://www.inf.fu-berlin.de/inst/pubs/tr-b-04-12.abstract.html*, 2004.
11. Jing Mei and Elena Paslaru Bontas. Reasoning paradigms for swrl-enabled ontologies. In *Workshop Protégé with Rules, Madrid, Spain, July*. CEUR: To appear, 2005.
12. Boris Motik, Ulrike Sattler, and Rudi Studer. Query answering for owl-dl with rules. In *ISWC 2004, Hiroshima, Japan, November*, pages 549–563. LNCS 3298, 2004.
13. Peter F. Patel-Schneider. A proposal for a swrl extension to first-order logic. *Available at http://www.daml.org/2004/11/fol/proposal*, 2004.
14. Peter F. Patel-Schneider, Patrick Hayes, and Ian Horrocks. Owl web ontology language semantics and abstract syntax. *Available at http://www.w3.org/TR/owl-absyn/*, 2004.
15. Michael Sintek and Stefan Decker. Triple – a query, inference, and transformation language for the semantic web. In *ISWC 2002, Sardinia, Italy, June*, 2002.
16. Dmitry Tsarkov, Alexandre Riazanov, Sean Bechhofer, and Ian Horrocks. Using Vampire to reason with OWL. In *Proc. of the 2004 International Semantic Web Conference (ISWC 2004)*, pages 471–485. Springer, LNCS 3298, 2004.

Security Frameworks for Open LBS
Based on Web Services Security Mechanism

Kiyoung Moon[1], Namje Park[1], Kyoil Chung[1],
Sungwon Sohn[1], and Jaecheol Ryou[2,*]

[1] Information Security Research Division, ETRI,
161 Gajeong-dong, Yuseong-gu, Daejeon, 305-350, Korea
{kymoon, namjepark, kyoil, swsohn}@etri.re.kr
[2] Division of Electrical and Computer Engineering, Chungnam National University,
220 Gung-dong, Yuseong-gu, Daejeon, 305-764, Korea
jcryou@home.cnu.ac.kr

Abstract. Location-based services or LBS refer to value-added service by processing information utilizing mobile user location. For this kind of LBS, the role of security service is very important in the LBS that store and manage the location information of mobile devices and support various application services using that location information. And in all phases of these functions that include acquisition of location information, storage and management of location information, user management including authentication and information security, and management of the large-capacity location information database, safe security service must be provided. In this paper, attempts are made to present a platform that features LBS and methods of authentication between service systems and of security technology application.

1 Introduction

Recently, with the rapid development of mobile communication technology and wide spread of mobile devices such as cellular phones equipped with a GPS (Global Positioning System) receiver, PDA (Personal Digital Assistant), notebook PCs, LBS technology which uses location information of mobile devices is being more important. LBS platform should provide fundamental functions such as the acquisition of location information, security, user privacy management, authentication, and management of a large volume of location data. To be successful, an LBS technology has to provide an accurate location, as well as suitable information for users required by the corresponding service, with minimal expenditure including establishing infrastructure and overhead.

LBS requests can span multiple security domains. Trust relationships among these domains play an important role in the outcome of such end-to-end traversals. Furthermore, an open LBS infrastructure will extend the use of the LBS technology or

---

* The fifth author of this research was supported by University IT Research Center Project of Korea MIC (Ministry of Information and Communication).

G. Chen et al. (Eds.): ISPA Workshops 2005, LNCS 3759, pp. 609–618, 2005.
© Springer-Verlag Berlin Heidelberg 2005

services to business areas using web service technology. Therefore, differential resource access is a necessary operation for users to enable them to share their resources securely and willingly. In this paper, we suggest security guidelines for open LBS using XKMS (XML Key Management Specification) and SAML (Security Assertion Markup Language), XACML (eXtensible Access Control Markup Language) in Web Services security mechanism. In this paper, attempts are made to present a platform that features LBS and methods of authentication between service systems and of security technology application.

2 Security Considerations of Open Location Services

2.1 Security Problems of Open LBS

For the revitalization of LBS, their negative effect, i.e., ensuring user's privacy and securing authentication through prevention, is as important as their positive effect. One notable adverse effect of LBS is that the location of each user is exposed 24 hours a day in real time. Considering the present situation wherein the issue of network hacking has become a serious social problem, the fact that the location information of an individual is disseminated freely on the Internet is a serious encroachment of the user's privacy. Abuse of location information not only exposes an individual's private life; it can also be used to commit a crime.

Therefore, ensuring the trust relationship for the authentication of the transmission and reception of location information between mobile terminals of the LBS system and Service Providers and for non-repudiation requires the kind of LBS structure and protocol that can protect the personal information and privacy of an individual. Moreover, when LBS are used, location information can be leaked by a third party illegally. To protect location information from such risks, the Location Information Protection Act was established. Still, provisioning of related authentication and security service is urgently required. When using location information services, many problems may arise including the invasion of users' privacy, falsification and confidentiality of location information, user authentication, and illegal access to the LBS platform server. Unless properly controlled, these can lead to the disclosure of personal information and possible involvement in a criminal activity. Thus, authentication and security are very important. Measures that can enhance the confidentiality of location information, authentication for local services, integrity of location information, and access control to the LBS platform server are essential.

When the location information provided by Service Providers are disclosed, falsified, or accessed illegally, the location information service will suffer a decline in quality, and corporate assets (database) may be used illegally. Preventing such occurrences and stabilizing related services also necessitate a reliable mechanism for security and authentication between the LBS platform and the location-based Service Providers. If personal information is leaked through hacking and illegal disclosure, both the corporation and subscribers will suffer considerable damage. Thus, from the business viewpoint as well, security is very important.

2.2 Security Requirement for Open LBS

As a standard providing semantic access and expandability for data, XML performs the role of a linguistic middleware; it also reveals the structure of important information in its expression. As such, various information displayed on XML documents are totally unprotected from outsiders.

Since the security and authentication requirements of the current LBS platform are not clearly presented, attempts are made to establish the concrete security and authentication requirements of the LBS platform and define the security/authentication system. Thus, the LBS platform should be able to process the authentication result; when the authentication result of the LBS platform is different from that of the mobile telecommunications network, the authentication result of the mobile telecommunications network should have precedence.

The following is an analysis of the security service, which is deemed necessary to provide safe location information service for risk factors such as confidentiality, integrity, authentication, and non-repudiation:

Since location information documents operate based on XML, security/authentication requirements for the LBS platform are specified considering the XML Signature and XML Encryption of IETF and W3C as well as SOAP (Simple Object Access Protocol) Sec, SAML, XACML, and SSO (Single Sign On) standards of OASIS (Organization for the Advancement of Structured Information Standards). The LBS security platform should define the confidentiality and integrity of location information and security requirements for user authentication and satisfy the following requirements:

1) Confidentiality of Location Information

Security requirements that can create encrypted sentences or phrases for diverse LBS information including XML in XML format and decrypt them to enable the transmission of information to the final recipient without leakage to a third party. When data protection is necessary in the transmission process of location information, the LBS platform should be able to encrypt the relevant location information or all location information that are transmitted. Any location measurement requested should be provided to the service requester using a reliable and safe method.

2) Integrity of Location Information

XML digital signature requirements for the creation and verification of digital signatures for LBS information including XML in XML format. Data integrity should be ensured in the transmission process of location information. Specifically, falsification or alteration of location information should not be allowed.

3) Authentication of Location Service

Framework requirements for the safe exchange of XML-based authentication and approval information. The LBS platform should prohibit access by unauthorized users. In other words, location information should be safe for authorized users. Authentication information should be included in the transmission process of location information.

4) Access Control to the LBS Platform Server

Requirements for the provisioning of detailed access control service to resources that require security through an access control list and for the establishment and application of the access policy to the LBS information by user. Monitoring and blocking all requests for location information and response thereto should be enabled in accordance with the laws established by the state. To aid in the interpretation of security violations, monitoring records of requests for location information and response thereto should be maintained.

3   Framework Model for Providing Secure Services

3.1   Security Service Framework

Web Services can be used to provide mobile security solutions by standardizing and integrating leading security solutions using XML messaging. XML messaging is considered the leading choice for a wireless communication protocol. In fact, there are security protocols for mobile applications that are based on XML messaging. Some of these include SAML, which is a protocol for transporting authentication and authorization information in an XML message. It can be used to provide single sign-on web services. On the other hand, XML signatures define how to sign part or all of an XML document digitally to guarantee data integrity. The public key distributed with XML signatures can be wrapped in XKMS formats. In addition, XML encryption enables applications to encrypt part or all of an XML document using references to pre-agreed symmetric keys. Endorsed by IBM and Microsoft, WS-Security is a complete solution to providing security to web services. It is based on XML signatures, XML encryption, and same authentication and authorization scheme as SAML.

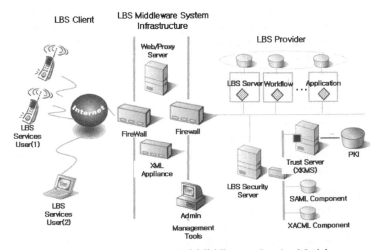

Fig. 1. Proposed Secure LBS Middleware Service Model

When a LBS-mobile device client requests access to a back-end application, it sends authentication information to the issuing authority. Depending on the credentials presented by the LBS-mobile device client, the issuing authority can then send a positive or negative authentication assertion. While the user still has a session with the mobile applications, the issuing authority can use the earlier reference to send an authentication assertion stating that the user was in fact authenticated by a particular method at a specific time. As mentioned earlier, location-based authentication can be done at regular time intervals. This means that the issuing authority gives location-based assertions periodically as long as the user credentials enable positive authentication.

Security technology for LBS is currently based on KLP (Korea Location Protocol). Communication between the LBS platform and Application Service Providers should be examined from the safety viewpoint vis-à-vis Web Services security technology. As shown in the security service model of the LBS platform in figure 1, the platform should have an internal interface module that carries out authentication and security functions to provide the LBS application service safely to the users.

3.2 Structure of Mobile Location Protocol in Korea

The protocol used for data exchange between the LBS server and terminals operates based on the MLP (Mobile Location Protocol) protocol established by LIF (Location Inter-Operability Forum). KLP is Korea location protocol. The application of the authentication and security factors to KLP should be configured considering the following points:

The KLP is an application-level protocol for querying the position of mobile stations independent of underlying network technology. The KLP serves as the interface between a Location Server and a location-based application. The details of the location information security structure between the Location Information Providers and the LBS Providers should be defined in terms of confidentiality, integrity, and authentication and access control element as shown in figure 2.

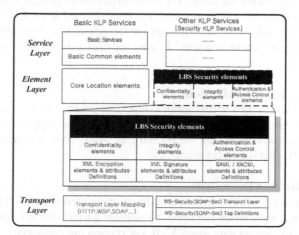

Fig. 2. Security Protocol for Secure Open LBS Services

These elements should be configured into a standard reference system for LBS security and authentication on WS-Security-based transport layers. Based on this structure, the LBS security service transmits location information safely between the LBS platform and the Service Providers in accordance with the XML-based request and response model.

3.3 Standard Element Layer Definition for LBS Security

For LBS provided on the service layers of KLP, KLP service protocols can be divided into five different services, where as message transmission can be defined in three types: request, answer, and report.

- **Request:** Refers to a message that requests information related to location information transmitted from the LBS clients to the location-based server.
- **Answer:** Refers to a message that is transmitted from the location-based server transmitting the result of the requests among LBS clients.
- **Report:** Refers to a message that is transmitted from the location-based server to the LBS clients as requested by the LBS clients or as required by the location-based server. The message format is either regular or unspecified time message.

Security functions that should be provided to LBS service layers should be defined as LBS security elements. For element layers, there are seven main definitions: subscriber identification element, functional element, location element, configuration element, location accuracy element, network element, and context element. For the seven types of element definition DTD (Data Type Definition), the attribute parameters requiring security are displayed in bold font.

1) Subscriber Identification Elements Definitions
Among subscriber identification elements, there are three elements requiring security: 'msid', which represents the identification information of mobile telecommunications subscribers; 'codeword', which is the access code defined in each subscriber terminal, and; 'session', which is the information on the session of the LBS client with the subscriber terminal. There is a need to encrypt data using XML encryption tag elements.

2) Functional Element Definitions
As an element requiring security among functional elements, the 'url' represents the necessary address information to send an answer to the report. 'url' is part of the 'pushaddr' item that can contain the ID and password. Thus, it is necessary to encrypt data using XML encryption tag elements.

3) Location Element Definitions
As the element requiring security among location elements, 'time' represents the time when the service was carried out upon the request for location information. It is therefore necessary to encrypt data using XML encryption tag elements.

4) Shape Elements Definitions

'X', 'Y', and 'Z' are elements requiring security among configuration elements. As coordinate values, 'X', 'Y', and 'Z' are the basic units of location information. Thus, these data have to be encrypted using XML encryption tag elements.

5) Quality of Position Definitions

Since location accuracy elements represent accuracy based on the location information for which security has already been dealt with, there is no need for separate security. Nonetheless, it is necessary to examine security elements that can be applied to the necessary attribute parameters for enhancing the quality of the future LBS service.

6) Network Parameter Element Definitions

CDMA (Code Division Multiple Access), GSM (Group Special Mobile), CDMA-2000, and WCDMA (Wideband CDMA) are defined in network elements. As such, transport layer security should be dealt with on the transport layer of KLP. Likewise, the security function depending on the network infrastructure should be examined separately.

7) Context Element Definitions

As an element requiring security among context elements, an identifier can be used in an element for the provisioning of the privacy structure. This includes ID that allows the use of location information service, 'sessionid' that can substitute for 'pwd', 'pwd' as the password for a registered user implementing the location service, and 'serviceid' as an identifier for distinguishing services and applications that access the network. For 'sessionid' and 'pwd', it is necessary to encrypt data using XML encryption tag elements. In addition, since 'serviceid' requires security to access service, such security should be based on authentication using the PKI (Public Key Infrastructure) interface.

4 Security Services Protocols

Three types of principals are involved in the proposed protocol: LBS application (server/client), SAML processor, and XKMS server (including PKI). The proposed invocation process for the secure LBS security service consists of two parts: initialization protocol and invocation protocol.

The initialization protocol is a prerequisite for invoking LBS web services securely. Through the initialization protocol, all principals in the proposed protocol set the security environments for their web services (Fig. 3). The following is the flow of setting the security environments:

The client first registers information for using web services. It then gets its id/password, which will be used for verifying its identity when it calls web services via a secure channel. The client gets SAML assertions and installs a security module to configure its security environments and to make a secure SOAP message. It then generates a key pair for digital signature and registers its public key to a CA.

The client creates a SOAP message containing authentication information, method information, and XML signature. XML then encrypts and sends to a server such message. The message is in the following form: $Enc_{session}(Envelope\ (Header\ (SecurityParame\text{-}$

ters,Sig$_{client}$(Body))+Body(Method, Parameters)))), where Sig$_x$(y) denotes the result of applying *x'* s private key function (i.e., the signature generation function) to *y*. The protocol shown in Fig. 3 shows the use of end-to-end bulk encryption [4,5]. Security handlers in the server receive, decrypt, and translate the message by referencing security parameters in the SOAP header. To verify the validity of the SOAP message and authenticity of the client, the server first examines the validity of the client's public key using XKMS. If the public key is valid, the server receives it from a CA and verifies the signature. The server invokes web services upon completion of the assessment of the security of the SOAP message. It then creates a SOAP message that contains the result, signature, and other security parameters. The server encrypts the message using a session key and sends it back to the client. Finally, the client evaluates the validity of the SOAP message and server and receives the result.

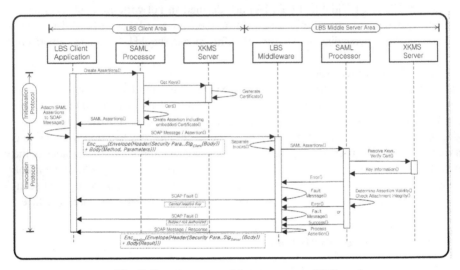

Fig. 3. Security protocol for secure open LBS service

In the existing LBS service, there is no mechanism for differential resource access. To establish such security system, a standardized policy mechanism is required. The XACML specification is employed to establish the resource policy mechanism that assigns a differential policy to each resource (or service)[6,7,9] SAML also has such policy mechanism, whereas XACML provides a very flexible policy mechanism that is applicable to any resource type. For the proposed implementing model, SAML provides a standardized method of exchanging authentication and authorization information securely by creating assertions from the output of XKMS (e.g., assertion validation service in XKMS). XACML replaces the policy part of SAML. Once the three assertions are created and sent to the protected resource, verification of authentication and authorization at the visiting site is no longer necessary. SSO (Single Sign-On) is a main contribution of SAML in distributed security systems[10,11].

5 Conclusion

LBS are so attractive that they can cover all walks of life. However, current LBS are growing slower than expected. Many problems like accuracy, privacy, security, customer requirement have to be addressed. It should be understood that there is no single universal solution to LBS.

We suggest security frameworks for open LBS using web Services security mechanism. And proposed secure LBS middleware service model allows a client to offload certificate handling to the server and to enable the central administration of XKMS polices. To obtain timely certificate status information, the server uses several methods such as CRL (Certificate Revocation List), OCSP (Online Certificate Status Protocol), etc. The proposed approach is expected to be a model for the future security system that offers open LBS security.

References

1. W3C Working Draft: XML Key Management Specification Version 2.0. (2003)
2. E. Faldella and M.Prandini: A Novel Approach to On-Line Status Authentication of Public Key Certificates. in Proc. the 16th Annual Computer Security Applications Conference (2000)
3. Y. Elley, et. Al, Building Certification Paths: Forward vs. Reverse. Proc. the Network and Distributed System Security Symposium Conference (2001)
4. M. Naor and K. Nissim: Certificate Revocation and Certificate Update. IEEE Journal on Selected Areas in Communications, 18 (4) (2000)
5. Euinam Huh, Jihye Kim, Hyeju Kim, Kiyoung Moon: Policy based on grid security infrastructure implementation for dirrerential resource access. ISOC Conference. (2003)
6. Yuichi Nakamur, et. Al.: Toward the Integration of web services security on enterprise environments. IEEE SAINT Conference (2002)
7. Boudewijn R. Haverkort John: Performance of Computer Communication Systems: A Model-Based Approach. Wiley & Sons (1999)
8. Sung-Min Lee et.al.: TY*SecureWS:An Integrated Web Service Security Solution Based on Java. Lecture Notes in Computer Science, Vol. 2738. (2003) 186-195
9. Minsoo Lee, et. Al: A Secure Web Services for Location based Services in Wireless Networks. Networking2004 (2004)
10. Junseok Lee, et. Al.: A DRM Framework for Distributing Digital Contents through the Internet. ETRI Journal, Vol.25, No.6 (2003) 423-436
11. Namje Park, et. Al.: The Security Consideration and Guideline for Open LBS using XML Security Mechanism. ASTAP 04/FR08/EG.IS/06. (2004)
12. Seunghun Jin, et. Al.: Cluster-based Trust Evaluation Scheme in Ad Hoc Network. ETRI Journal, Vol.27, No.4 (2005)
13. Jose L. Munoz et. Al.: Using OCSP to Secure Certificate-Using transactions in M-Commerce. Lecture Notes in Computer Science, Vol. 2846. (2003) 280-292

ANNEX A. Elements and Attributes in DTD

<!--// Subscriber Identification Element Definitions //-->
1) Line <!ELEMENT msid   (#PCDATA)>
5) Line <!ELEMENT codeword (#PCDATA)>
10) Line <!ELEMENT session   (#PCDATA)>
12) Line <!ELEMENT start_msid (msid)>
13) Line <!ELEMENT stop_msid (msid)>

<!-- // Function Element Definitions // -->
11) Line <!ELEMENT pushaddr (url, id?, pwd?)>
17) Line <!ELEMENT url (#PCDATA)>

<!--// Shape Element Definitions //-->
5) Line <!ELEMENT coord   (X, Y?, Z?)>
6) Line <!ELEMENT X (#PCDATA)>
7) Line <!ELEMENT Y (#PCDATA)>
8) Line <!ELEMENT Z (#PCDATA)>

<!--// Location Element Definitions //-->
1) Line <!ELEMENT pos (msid, (pd | poserr), net_param?)>
2) Line <!ELEMENT eme_pos (msid, (pd | poserr), esrd?, esrk?)>
3) Line <!ELEMENT trl_pos (msid, (pd | poserr))>
5) Line <!ELEMENT pd (time, shape, (alt, alt_acc?)?, speed?, direction?, lev_conf?)>
10) Line <!ELEMENT time (#PCDATA)>

<!--// Context Element Definitions //-->
2) Line <!ELEMENT sessionid (#PCDATA)>
4) Line <!ELEMENT requestor (id, serviceid?)>
5) Line <!ELEMENT pwd (#PCDATA)>
6) Line <!ELEMENT serviceid (#PCDATA)>
9) Line <!ELEMENT subclient (id, pwd?, serviceid?)>

<!--// Quality of Position Definitions //-->
None

<!--// Network Parameter Element Definitions //-->
None

Testing and Fault Diagnosis for Web Application Compatibility Based on Combinatorial Method[*]

Lei Xu[1,2,**], Baowen Xu[1,2,3,4], and Changhai Nie[1,2]

[1] Department of Computer Sci. & Eng., Southeast University,
Nanjing 210096, China
[2] Jiangsu Institute of Software Quality, Nanjing 210096, China
[3] State Key Laboratory of Software Eng., Wuhan University,
Wuhan 430072, China
[4] Computer School, National University of Defense Technology,
Changsha 410073, China
xlei@seu.edu.cn

Abstract. The testing and fault diagnosis for Web application compatibility are concerned with multiple kinds of software and hardware facilities, enormous numbers of equipments' trademarks and types, and the combination of all the situations. How to test and find faults efficiently and quickly is a difficult and important task to complete. Combined with the characters of the Web application compatibility testing and the combinatorial method, we obtained acceptable number of test cases for the compatibility testing. After executing the test cases, we analyzed the results so as to find the fault factors by the properties of combinatorial method. Then we retested with some complementary test cases based on the elementary analytic results, and made further analysis and validation with the retesting results. Thus we obtained the factors that cause the errors in a very small range, and provided a very efficient and valuable guidance for the debugging and testing of Web application compatibility.

Keywords: Web Applications, Combinatorial Method, Compatibility Testing, Fault Diagnosis

1 Introduction

Web applications have characters of universality, interchangeability and usability, and they attract more and more users' attentions and develop very quickly [12]. On the one hand, Web applications realize the information sharing in the wide worlds through the broad Internet platform; on the other hand, because of the differences among the compositive components of Web applications, Web topological architectures, access

---

[*] This work was supported in part by the National Natural Science Foundation of China (NSFC) (90412003, 60373066), National Grand Fundamental Research 973 Program of China (2002CB312000), Young Scientist's Foundation of the National Natural Science Foundation of China (NSFC) (60403016), Opening Foundation of State Key Laboratory of Software Engineering in Wuhan University, Innovation Plan for Jiangsu High School Graduate Student, and High Technology Research Project in Jiangsu Province (BG2005032).
[**] Corresponding author.

G. Chen et al. (Eds.): ISPA Workshops 2005, LNCS 3759, pp. 619–626, 2005.
© Springer-Verlag Berlin Heidelberg 2005

methods and physical equipments, problems such as heterogeneousness and autonomy are brought out by these factors.

In order to ensure the normal running of the Web application under various browsers and equipments of the client side, the compatibility testing [5] is needed. And the main work is testing the displays of Web applications under various client side environments, so as to guarantee the displaying functions of Applets, ActiveX Controls, JavaScript, CSS and other HTML elements in all kinds of system configurations. After the testing is completed, further analysis is needed to the testing results so as to diagnose, search and eliminate the faults [6]. These tasks are quite fussy, so we demand a suitable number of test cases to cover the huge combinations and an effective and quick strategy for the fault diagnosis.

At present, researchers pay more and more attentions to web testing, and they have proposed many methods and obtained many important results [3,5,7]. And we also attempted some research in the area of Web testing modeling, performance improvement, and testing methods [11,12,13,14,15]. This paper focuses on how to improve the testing and fault diagnosis for Web application compatibility. So in Section 2, we analyze the specialties of compatibility testing for Web applications and present the model and characters of combinatorial method, so as to explain the necessity and feasibility of adopting the combinatorial method for the testing and fault diagnosis of the Web application compatibility. In Section 3, we present a Web compatibility testing scene as an example, and generate the test cases with the combinatorial method of pair-wise coverage, which is a great reduction in the testing cost; Then in Section 4, we analyze the combinatorial testing results firstly, then retest with some complementary test cases based on the elementary analytic results, and finally make further analysis and validation with the retesting results, so as to obtain the factors that cause the faults in a very small range. Section 5 is concerned with the conclusions and our future work.

2   Related Work

By analyzing the specialties of compatibility testing for Web applications, we can gain the necessity and feasibility of adopting combinatorial method for the testing and fault diagnosis; and combined with the model and characters of combinatorial method, we can test the Web application compatibility and find the fault factors more efficiently.

2.1   Specialties of Compatibility Testing for Web Applications

Web application is consisted of multiple pages, and browsers take charge of parsing and displaying these pages. Browsers are the communicating tools between users and the Web servers, which are running at the client sides. By now, there are many types of browsers, such as Navigator Netscape, Internet Explorer, AOL and Opera. Each type of browser has different versions, and the browsers can be applied on such platforms as Windows, Macintosh, Unix Linux, and etc. As the same content is referred, different browsers may have different parsing results; different version browsers may have different functions; different type of computers may have different font types and sizes; different screen sizes may have influences to the page displaying effect; and different browsers may have different fault-tolerance. So it is urgent to test the displaying of

Web applications in different client environments, so as to ensure the normal running of Web applications on the broad operating platforms.

Therefore, before executing the compatibility testing for Web applications, we must well design the test cases, making the number of test cases acceptable and these test cases can cover the combinations as many as possible. Combinatorial method [1,2,4,6,8,9,10] can realize a scientific and effective testing with fewer test cases, and is specially applied to the systems whose states are influenced by the parameters and their interactions. The client sides of Web applications are usually consisted of equipments such as browser, operating system, video, audio and printer. Each one can be represented as a parameter, and each parameter can have multiple values. Thus, the combinatorial testing method can be adopted to produce high quality test cases. After executing the test cases, if faults are produced, then further analysis is needed to find the factors of the faults, so as to exclude these faults. Then, by analyzing the model and characters of the combinatorial method, we can obtain an effective method for the compatibility testing and fault diagnosis.

2.2 Basic Model and Characters of Combinatorial Method

The precondition of applying the combinatorial method to the system under testing is that the test scenes should be determined by a group of parameters. Now suppose the software under testing (SUT) has n parameters $d_1, d_2, \cdots, d_n$, and $T_1, T_2, \cdots, T_n$ is the value-set of $d_1, d_2, \cdots, d_n$ respectively (supposing $a_1 = |T_1|, \ldots, a_n = |T_n|$).

Let $Num = a_1 * a_2 * \cdots a_n$. If Num is small, we can do the total testing, i.e. considering all the possible combinations. But generally speaking, this value is very large, so it is impossible to run the total testing. Then we should consider how to obtain coverage as high as possible with the acceptable number of test cases. It will at least need $Num = \max a_i (1 \le i \le n)$ test cases to cover all the values of every parameter, $Num = \max a_i * a_j (1 \le i \ne j \le n)$ test cases to cover all the pair-wise combinations of every two parameters ... and so on. With the increase of parameters, the number of test cases increases quickly. Therefore, we need some methods to reduce the number of testing cases, and the orthogonal array and the pair-wise covering table (shown in Definition 1) are very effective.

Definition 1. Suppose $A = (a_{i,j})_{n \times m}$. The j-th column represents the j-th parameter, and the elements of the j-th column are coming from the finite symbol set T_j ($j=1, 2, \ldots, m$), i.e. $a_{ij} \in T_j, i = 1, 2, \ldots, n$. Further more, the number of the j-th parameter is recorded as t_j, i.e. $t_j = |T_j|$. If the arbitrary two columns (the i-th column and the j-th column) of A satisfy these conditions: the total symbol combination of T_i and T_j are occurred in the same probability in the pair-wise which consists of the i-th and j-th column, we call A the orthogonal array; if the occurrence is not in the same probability, we call A the pair-wise covering table.

How to construct the orthogonal array or the pair-wise covering table is not discussed in this paper, and more details are shown in paper [10]. We only use these good properties to generate test cases, and in this way we can have the same covering qualities with as less as possible number of test cases. Now we present two definitions about Test Case and k–value Mode, shown in Definition 2 and 3, which will be used in the next Sections.

Definition 2. Test Case: we define a test case of SUT as n-tuple $(v_1, v_2, \cdots, v_n)$, and $v_1 \in T_1, v_2 \in T_2 \cdots v_n \in T_n$.

Definition 3. k–value Mode: only determining certain k $(1 \le k \le n)$ parameters' values in the SUT, we obtain such n-tuple $mod=(-, \cdots, v_{l1}, -\cdots, v_{l2}, -\cdots, v_{lk}, -\cdots, -)$, and mod is a k–value mode of SUT, "–" indicating that the parameter value of the corresponding location is to be determined.

3   Test Cases Generation Process for Web Application Compatibility

Most browsers consist of several independent parsers, such as HTML Render, Java VM, JavaScript Interpreter and Plug-in Handler. So the Web page elements and the relative parsing software and hardware in the client side are contacted directly, and they generally have little mutual influences. Thus in order to test all the possible instances, only pair-wise coverage is enough.

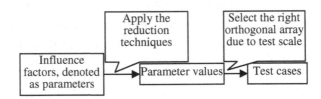

Fig. 1. Test Cases Generation by Combinatorial Method

Now we present a test case generating method for Web application compatibility testing based on the combinatorial method. And the general process is shown in Figure 1: firstly, we select several parameters to denote the different software and hardware in the client side; then apply the reduction techniques to determine the value range of these parameters; thus we obtain the number of each parameter's values, and we can choose the proper orthogonal array or the pair-wise covering table to generate the test cases. So in this way, we realize the minimal number of test cases covering the maximal combinatorial situations. And we also consider these factors such as the test case scale, cover ability, testing cost and time. So we can well improve the testing efficiency finally.

Now we give an example of compatibility testing under the popular client-side configurations. Supposing the software under testing (SUT) is a network game, we only consider five kinds of equipments for simplify, and d_1=video, d_2=audio, d_3=printer, d_4=browser, and d_5=operating system (OS), each one has two kinds of popular types, i.e. $a_1 = a_2 = a_3 = a_4 = a_5 = 2$, as shown in Table 1.

Table 1. Equipments Types for Web Application Compatibility Testing

Video	Audio	Printer	Browser	O S
A1	B1	C1	D1	E1
A2	B2	C2	D2	E2

In Table 1, we find that if we consider all the possible combinations, we need 32 test cases ($2^5 = 32$). And in realities, we should consider more factors, and then the factors' total combinations will increase exponentially. So we apply the generating method to the Web application compatibility, which is based on the pair-wise covering table. And by the table has been constructed in advance, we only need six test cases to achieve the pair-wise combinatorial coverage, and the set of test cases can be described as T, and $T=\{$(A1, B1, C1, D2, E1), (A1, B1, C2, D1, E2), (A1, B2, C1, D1, E1), (A2, B1, C2, D1, E2), (A2, B2, C1, D2, E2), (A2, B2, C2, D2, E1)$\}$.

So by the set T, we can realize the pair-wise combinatorial coverage to fulfill the Web application compatibility testing with only 6 test cases. And this is a great reduction to the testing cost. After executing the test cases in the set T, the fault diagnosis is demanded to search and exclude the faults in Web applications. And this process also can be carried out base on the properties of the combinatorial method, and the details are shown in Section 4.

4 Fault Diagnosis Process for Web Application Compatibility

After executing the test cases in the set T ($|T| = m$), if there is no fault, then no fault diagnosis, indicating that the Web application function is normal in this testing level. Now we suppose that there is a fault occurred in l test cases (denoted as set X), and other $m-l$ test cases all have normal running results (denoted as set Y). Then further analysis is needed to judge that this fault is caused by what valued modes. Our process for the fault diagnosis is carrying out in three steps: first, analyze the testing result; second, generate complementary test cases to assist fault diagnosis; last, analyze and validate the retesting result by the complementary test cases.

4.1 Testing Result Analysis for Web Application Compatibility

Theorem 1. If one fault of a SUT is caused by a k-valued ($1 \leq k \leq n$) mode mod, and $mod=(-,\cdots,v_{l1},-\cdots,v_{l2},-\cdots,v_{lk},-\cdots,-)$, then $\forall x \in X$, mod must exist in x; $\forall y \in Y$, mod must not exist in y.

Proof: If the value-selected combination of k parameters is the reason of the system fault, and this combination also occurs in the other test case that do not cause fault, then there must be a fault in the testing when using this test case. This is inconsistent with the condition.

We can deduce the following characters by theorem 1: (1) If the fault of SUT is caused by a k-valued ($1 \leq k \leq n$) mode, then all the test cases that include the k-valued mode will cause the SUT error; (2) If the fault of SUT is caused by more than a k-valued ($1 \leq k \leq n$) mode, then these modes that cause the SUT error are only occurring in the set X and not occurring in the set Y; (3)If we can find the common modes, namely the certain value-selected (or value-selected combinations) of a certain parameter (or parameters) all occur in the set X, and not occur in the set Y, then these common modes are the most possible reason for the fault.

Based on the above theorem and deduced characters, before determining the fault reason, we must find the common mode in the set X firstly, and then exclude those modes occur in the set Y. Thus we call the results as the common modes, denoted as the set M. This set includes the most possible reasons that cause the fault.

Generally speaking, when we use the test cases in T to test the Web application compatibility, we only consider the instance of one test case cause fault, and others also can be analyze in the same way. Suppose this test case is (A2, B2, C2, D2, E1), i.e. the sixth one in the set T, then by the method described in the above, we obtain the common set M, and M= {(A2, –, –, –, E1), (–, B2, C2, –, –), (–, –, C2, D2, –), (A2, B2, C2, –, –), (A2, B2, –, D2, –), (A2, B2, –, –, E1), (A2, –, C2, –, E1), (A2, –, C2, D2, –), (A2, –, –, D2, E1), (–, B2, C2, D2, –), (–, B2, C2, –, E1), (–, B2, –, D2, E1), (–, –, C2, D2, E1), (A2, B2, C2, D2, –), (A2, B2, C2, –, E1), (A2, B2, –, D2, E1), (A2, –, C2, D2, E1), (–, B2, C2, D2, E1), (A2, B2, C2, D2, E1)}, which includes all the possible factors that cause the system error. In this circumstance, single parameter is not the fault reason, for the value of the single parameter has occurred several times in other test cases, and the modes in set {(A2, B2, –, –, –), (–, B2, –, D2, –), (–, B2, –, –, E1), (A2, –, C2, –, –), (A2, –, –, D2, –), (–, –, –, D2, E1), (–, –, C2, –, E1)} are also not the fault reason, for they can be ensured in the other five test cases.

Now we consider the set M, which have too many possible factors. Thus we must further reduce the range so as to find the fault factors quickly.

4.2 Retest with the Complementary Test Cases

In order to further determine which parameters' value-selected combinations cause the system error, we must add n test cases, denoted as T_{at}, and $T_{at} =\{(\,*, v_{2i_2}, \cdots, v_{ni_n}),$ $(v_{1i_1}, *, \cdots, v_{ni_n}), \ldots, (v_{1i_1}, v_{2i_2}, \cdots, v_{(n-1)i_{n-1}}, *)\}$. The "*" signal presents any value that is different from the selected value in the related position of the original test case $(v_{1i_1}, v_{2i_2}, \cdots, v_{ni_n})$. Thus we need nl test cases and we call them as the complementary test cases. Then based on the retesting results, we can determine the factors that cause faults in a less range. Furthermore, if there are multiple faults in the combinatorial testing, then the above theories are all fit.

So we generate 5 test cases (denoted as the complementary test cases T_{at}) for the test case (A2, B2, C2, D2, E1), which may cause the fault; then retest the system with these new test cases. As shown in Table 2, the "*" signal denotes that the parameter value in the corresponding position is different from the original value, and we choose the value in the bracket.

Table 2. Complementary Test Cases

Video	Audio	Printer	Browser	O S
*(A1)	B2	C2	D2	E1
A2	*(B1)	C2	D2	E1
A2	B2	*(C1)	D2	E1
A2	B2	C2	*(D1)	E1
A2	B2	C2	D2	*(E2)

After we retest the Web application with this suit of test cases, we can determine the fault reason based on the testing result, namely reduce the possible fault reason range, and judge the complementary test cases that do not cause faults, then generate the whole modes from them and get rid of these inconsistent modes from the set M. Then the final modes are the possible fault reasons.

4.3 Further Analysis and Validation for Retest Result

After executing the complementary test cases, we illustrate how to determine the fault reasons based on the detailed fault numbers.

Case 1. No fault occurs. Based on the before method, the set M is reduced to {(A2, B2, C2, D2, E1)}, i.e. only the mode (A2, B2, C2, D2, E1) is the fault factor.

Case 2. Only one test case generates fault. Suppose that the second one in Table 2 arouses a fault in the retest process. Then the set M will reduce to {(A2, –, C2, D2, E1), (A2, B2, C2, D2, E1)}, and the fault factors may be the mode (A2, –, C2, D2, E1) or (A2, B2, C2, D2, E1).

Case 3. Two test cases generate fault, and suppose which are the second and fourth one in Table 2. Then the set M will reduce to {(A2, –, C2, –, E1), (A2, B2, C2, –, E1), (A2, –, C2, D2, E1), (A2, B2, C2, D2, E1)}, and the fault factors may be the sub-mode they both including (A2, –, C2, –, E1), or the mode (A2, –, C2, D2, E1) or (A2, B2, C2, –, E1) or (A2, B2, C2, D2, E1).

Similarly, we can discuss the situation that multiple test cases cause system faults. So based on the original testing result, and add some necessary related test cases, we can find the fault factor effectively and quickly so as to facilitate the system debugging and testing. But if multiple complementary test cases generate system faults, then the analysis process is a little complex and the result is not perfect. Furthermore, if all the complementary test cases cause fault, then it is sure that the complementary test cases add new fault modes themselves.

But in most circumstance, the number of complementary test cases that arouse fault is few (they are high quality test cases for the testing), otherwise the system has serious quality problem and need careful analysis and inspect over again.

5 Conclusions and Future Work

In order to ensure the normal running of Web applications under the different equipments in client sides, the compatibility testing is demanded; and it is urgent to generated acceptable number of test cases to cover the combinations as many as possible; after executing the test cases, further analysis for the testing result is also needed so as to diagnose faults quickly. These tasks must be carried out based on a certain strategy, so as to reduce the testing cost and improve the testing efficiency.

This paper began with the specialties of compatibility testing for Web applications and the model and characters of combinatorial method, so as to explain the necessity and feasibility of adopting combinatorial method for the testing and fault diagnosis. Then this paper presented a Web compatibility testing scene and generated the test cases with the combinatorial method of pair-wise coverage; Next followed with the whole process of the fault diagnosis, i.e. firstly analyzed the combinatorial testing results, then retested with some complementary test cases based on the original analytic results, and further analysis and validation were made with the retesting results so as to obtain the factors that cause the errors in a very small range.

Future work includes the algorithm optimization and generalization for the test case generation and the fault diagnosis of Web application compatibility based on combinatorial testing, and develops the interrelated assistant testing tools. Furthermore, we will pay more attention to the developing trends and the influence to Web applications, so as to guide and encourage the compatibility testing and fault diagnosis more excellent.

References

1. Cohen, D. M. and Fredman, M. L.: New Techniques for Designing Qualitatively Independent Systems. Journal of Combinational Designs, 1998, 6(6): 411-416.
2. Cohen, D. M., Dalal, S.R. and Fredman, M. L.: The AETG System: An Approach to Testing Based on Combinatorial Design. IEEE Trans on Software Engineering, 1997, 23(7): 437-444.
3. Kallepalli, C. and Tian, J.: Measuring and Modeling Usage and Reliability for Statistical Web Testing. IEEE Trans. Software Engineering, 2001, 27(11): 1023-1036.
4. Kobayashi, N., Tsuchiya, T. and Kikuno, T.: A New Method for Constructing Pair-wise Covering Designs for Software Testing. Information Processing Letters, 2002, 81(2): 85-91.
5. Liu, Chien-Hung: A Formal Object-Oriented Test Model for Testing Web Applications. 2002, Doctor Dissertation.
6. Nie, Changhai, Xu, Baowen and Shi, Liang: Software Fault Diagnosis Method Based on Combinatorial Testing. Journal of Southeast University (in Chinese), 2003, 33(6): 681-684.
7. Ricca, F. and Tonella, P.: Web Site Analysis: Structure and Evolution. Proc. of Int. Conference on Software Maintenance (ICSM) (2000): 76-86.
8. Tai, K.C. and Lei, Y.: A Test Generation Strategy for Pairwise Testing. IEEE Trans on Software Engineering, 2002, 28(1): 109-111.
9. Williams, A.W. and Probert, R. L.: A Practical Strategy for Testing Pair-wise Coverage of Network Interfaces. Proc. of 7th Int. Symp. Software Reliability Engineering (1997): 246-254.
10. Xu, Baowen, Nie, Changhai, Shi, Qunfeng and Lu, Hong: An Algorithm for Automatically Generating Black-Box Test Cases, Journal of Electronics, 2003, 20(1): 74-77.
11. Xu, Lei, Xu, Baowen and Chen, Zhenqiang: A Scheme of Web Testing Approach. Journal of Nanjing University (in Chinese), 2002, 38(11): 182-186.
12. Xu, Lei, Xu, Baowen and Chen, Zhenqiang: Survey of Web Testing. Computer Science (in Chinese), 2003, 30(3): 100-104.
13. Xu, Lei, Xu, Baowen, Chen, Zhenqiang and Chen, Huowang: Website Evolution Based on Statistic Data. Proc. of the 9th IEEE Int. Workshop on Future Trends of Distributed Computing Systems (FTDCS 2003), 301-306.
14. Xu, Lei, Xu, Baowen, Chen, Zhenqiang, Jixiang Jiang and Chen, Huowang: Regression Testing for Web Applications Based on Slicing. Proc. of the 27th Annual Int. Computer Software & Applications Conference (COMPSAC 2003), 652-656.
15. Xu, Lei, Xu, Baowen, Nie, Changhai, Chen, Huowang and Yang, Hongji: A Browser Compatibility Testing Method Based on Combinatorial Testing. Proc. of the 3rd Int. Conference on Web Engineering (ICWE 2003), 310-313.

A K-Anonymizing Approach for Preventing Link Attacks in Data Publishing*

Xiaochun Yang, Xiangyu Liu, Bin Wang, and Ge Yu

School of Information Science and Engineering,
Northeastern University, China 110004
{yangxc, binwang, yuge}@mail.neu.edu.cn

Abstract. K-anonymization is an important approach to protect data privacy in data publishing. It is desired to publish k-anomymized data with less information loss. However, the existing algorithms are not feasible enough to satisfy such a requirement. We propose a k-anonymization approach, Classfly for publishing as much data as possible. For any attribute, in stead of generalizing all values, Classfly only generalizes partial values that do not satisfy k-anonymization. As a side-effect, Classfly provides higher efficiency than existing approaches, since not all data need to be generalized. Classfly also considers the case of satisfying multiple anonymity constraints in one published table, which makes it more feasible for real applications. Experimental results show that the proposed Classfly approach can efficiently generate a published table with less information loss.

1   Introduction

Numerous organizations publish data for a variety of different purposes, including demographic and public health research[1,2]. Often values of attributes that can uniquely identify individuals need to be removed from the published table so that adversary cannot build a linkage between an individual and his/her published data. For example, Name and Social Security Number(SSN) are common identifiers. However, this mechanism fails to account for the possibility of combining seemingly innocuous attributes with external data to uniquely identify individuals. According to one study, approximately 87% of the population of the United States can be uniquely identified on the basis of their 5-digit Zipcode, sex, and date of birth[3].

The uniqueness of such attribute combinations leads to a class of attacks where data is "re-identified" by linking multiple (often publicly-available) data sets. For example, Fig. 1 shows this type of attack. Assume that a user, Eve, gets a published table PT (the right table) from her cooperator and she also has a table ET (the left table) from other sources. If she only examines PT,

---

* Supported by Natural Science Foundation for Doctoral Career of Liaoning Province (20041016), National Research Foundation for the Doctoral Program of Higher Education of China (20030145029), and Natural Science Foundation China (60473074).

G. Chen et al. (Eds.): ISPA Workshops 2005, LNCS 3759, pp. 627–636, 2005.

she cannot know who has "chest pain", however, when she link the two tables *PT* and *ET* on Race, Birth, Gender, and Zipcode, she is able to determine Beth's medical information. The combination of these attributes, which often be combined uniquely and can be linked to publicly available information to re-identify individuals is said to be a quasi-identifier of the published table[3].

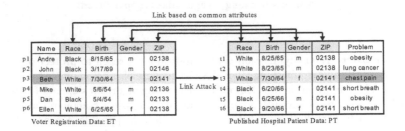

Fig. 1. Tables vulnerable to a linking attack

An approach to avoid such linking attacks is to generalize partial values using generalization hierarchy[5] from the published table so that each record is indistinguishable from at least $k - 1$ other records based on the attributes of the quasi-identifier of the published table. Such a process is called k-anonymization. Fig. 2 show possible value generalization hierarchies for different attributes.

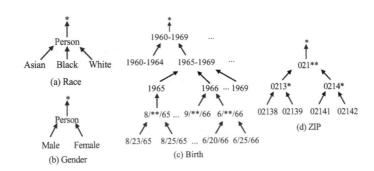

Fig. 2. Value generalization hierarchies for attributes Race, Gender, Birth, and ZIP

For example, GT_1 and GT_2 in Fig. 3 are two 2-anonymized tables of *PT* in Fig. 1. Comparing these two tables, $t_4[race]$ and $t_5[race]$ in GT_1 are **Black**, whereas in GT_2 they are **Person**. Similar, $t_3[gender]$ and $t_6[gender]$ in GT_1 and GT_2 are different. Obviously, the concept of **Person** subsumes **Black**, i.e. GT_2 loses more information than GT_1 although both of them satisfy 2-anonymities.

In real applications, not all quasi-identifiers cause the same probabilities of information leakage. In order to publish as more data as possible, we can set different k for different attribute sets in the published table. If a set of attributes

	Race	Birth	Gender	ZIP	Problem
t1	White	8/**/65	m	02138	chest pain
t2	White	8/**/65	m	02138	lung cancer
t3	Person	**/**/**	f	02141	obesity
t4	Black	6/**/66	Person	02141	short breath
t5	Black	6/**/66	Person	02141	obesity
t6	Person	**/**/**	f	02141	short breath

(a) Table GT1

	Race	Birth	Gender	ZIP	Problem
t1	White	8/**/65	m	02138	chest pain
t2	White	8/**/65	m	02138	lung cancer
t3	Person	**/**/**	Person	02141	obesity
t4	Person	6/**/66	Person	02141	short breath
t5	Person	6/**/66	Person	02141	obesity
t6	Person	**/**/**	Person	02141	short breath

(b) Table GT2

Fig. 3. Comparison of two k-anonymized tables

have more potential to leak information, the corresponding k can be set larger than other attribute sets, vice versa. For example, in Fig. 3, let k of attributes {Race, Birth, Gender} be 3 and k of {Gender, ZIP} be 2, since using the former attribute set is easier to cause linking attack than using the later. Simply adopting the existing k-anonymization approaches cannot solve the problem of multiple quasi-identifiers.

So far, k-anonymization algorithms process all values of an attribute if it doesnot satisfy the anonymity requirement, which result in values of attributes that meet the anonymity requirement have to attend further k-anonymization and lose unnecessary information. In this paper, we propose an approach, Classfly, to process partial values that donot satisfy k-anonymity for single as well as multiple quasi-identifers. It efficiently provides published table with less information loss. Experimental results show that Classfly outperformances the classic k-anonymization approach, Datafly[4].

1.1 Related Work

Samarati and Sweeney first propose the concept of k-anonymity to avoid linking attacks while preserving the integrity of the released data. Literature [7] proposes an algorithm, which starts with a full generalized dataset and systematically specializes the dataset into one that is k-anonymous. The approach of [8] produces a progressive generalization process that the user can step through to determine a desired trade-off of privacy and accuracy.

Some k-anonymization approaches employ incomplete stochastic search[9,10], and the others employ heuristic bottom-up generalization methods[4,11,12] to k-anonymize published data. These algorithms cause a lot of information loss, less utility of published data and the efficiency of performance is not high. Take typical k-anonymization algorithm Datafly[4], for example, Datafly k-anonymize data based on attributes of the published table. So some tuples that have achieved k-anonymity still have to join the subsequent k-anonymization. It results in unnecessary information loss.

Literature [6] proposes an efficient full-domain k-anonymization algorithm to improve the efficiency of full-domain k-anonymization on single quasi-identifier without paying more attention to information loss. Due to the characteristic of full domain, in the case of k-anonymizing with multi quasi identifiers, Datafly only makes simple modification and transplantation of k-anonymization algorithm with single quasi identifier. Literature [8] adopts a top-down specialization approach based on the precision of classification, by which k-anonymizes publishing data and preserves high precision of classification. This method can be adopted for k-anonymization with multi quasi identifiers. However, it only considers preserving the precision of classification but not information loss.

2   Problem Statement

Given a table T, a data owner can define a set of k-anonymity constraints on T. Each constraint has the form of $\langle QI, k \rangle$, where QI is a set of attributes in T and k is a constant. The owner requires the publishing table satisfy the following condition. For each QI, there exist more than k tuples, $t_1, \ldots, t_m (k \leq m)$, such that $t_i[QI] = t_j[QI], i \neq j, 1 \leq i, j \leq m$.

Definition 1. *Given a releasable table T with a quasi-identifier QI, we do a projection $\pi_{QI}(T)$ to get a set of distinct values $\Gamma = \{\tau_1, \ldots, \tau_n\}$. Each τ_i (1 $\leq i \leq n$) is called a representative class to QI and n is the number of Γ. For any representative class τ, there exist a set of tuples $\{t_1, \ldots, t_h\}$ in T, such that $t_i[QI] = \tau$ (1 $\leq i \leq h$). We say t_i belongs to representative class τ, denoted $t_i \lhd \tau$, and h is the size of τ, denoted $|\tau|$. For any two different tuples t_1 and t_2 in T, t_1 and t_2 belong to the same representative class, iff $t_1[QI] = t_2[QI]$, denoted $t_1 \simeq t_1$.*

It is nature that a data owner defines multiple such anonymity constraints. For example, let constraint C_1 be $\langle \{\texttt{Race, Birth, Gender}\}, 3 \rangle$ and C_2 be $\langle \{\texttt{Gender, ZIP}\}, 2 \rangle$.

Definition 2. *Given two anonymity constraints $C_1 = \langle QI_1, k_1 \rangle$ and $C_2 = \langle QI_2, k_2 \rangle$. We call C_1 and C_2 are overlapped, if $QI_1 \cap QI_2 \neq \emptyset$, otherwise, they are independent.*

Problem Statement. Given a publishing table T with multiple anonymity constraints $C = \{\langle QI_1, k_1 \rangle, \ldots, \langle QI_n, k_n \rangle\}$ $(k_i \leq |T|, 1 \leq i \leq n)$ and domain generalization hierarchies DGH_A for each attribute A in T, find a releasable table T' to make the size of each representative class to QI_i larger than or equal to k_i.

3 K-Anonymization with Less Information Loss

In this section, we propose a k-anonymization approach based on representative classes. According to the problem statement, in the process of k-anonymization, if the size of a representative class is not less than k, tuples belong to this representative class need not to attend further generalization, since these tuples have met the requirement of k-anonymity.

We consider the case where all constraints are independent constraints in Section 3.1, and the case of overlapped constraints in Section 3.2.

3.1 *K*-Anonymization for Independent Constraints

If given constraints are independent, we can separately process the table to satisfy individual constraint. Obviously, if two constraints are independent, generalizing values for one constraint doesnot affect the other constraint.

Function `single_cons_proc` shows the algorithm of processing table for one anonymity constraint. The algorithm finds tuples satisfying k-anonymity and moves them to the releasable table T'. For each iteration, values of the attribute having the most number of distinct values are generalized first. If the occurrence of remaining tuples is less than k, suppress them by replacing values with the top value in the corresponding DGH.

```
Function: single_cons_proc
Input:    A table T, QI = (A₁,...,Aₙ), constant k ≤ |T|,
          generalization hierarchies DGH_A₁,...,DGH_Aₙ
Output:   releasable table T' satisfying k-anonymity

   while (|T|≥k)  {
     for (each representative class τ in π_QI(T))
         if (|τ| ≥ k)  {
             insert V(τ) into T';
             T = T - T';
         }
         choose an attribute Aᵢ in QI that has largest |π_Aᵢ(T)|;
         generalize values of Aᵢ using DGH_Aᵢ;
   }
   suppress the remaining tuples in T;
   T' = T' ∪ T;
   return T';
```

3.2 *K*-Anonymization for Overlapped Constraints

If anonymity constraints are overlapped, generalizing values to satisfy one constraint may make another constraint invalid, some of them may not. In this section, we study different cases of constraints, and give solution for those cases.

Definition 3. *Given two overlapped anonymity constraints $C_1 = \langle QI_1, k_1 \rangle$ and $C_2 = \langle QI_2, k_2 \rangle$. If $QI_1 \subseteq QI_2$ and $k_1 \leq k_2$, then C_2 subsumes C_1, denoted $C_1 \preceq C_2$.*

Theorem 1. *Given two anonymity constraints $C_1 \preceq C_2$. If a table T conforms to the anonymity constraint C_2, then T must conform to C_1.*

Proof. Let C_1 be $\langle \{A_1\}, k_1 \rangle$ and C_2 be $\langle \{A_1, A_2\}, k_2 \rangle$, $k_1 < k_2$. If there exists k_2 tuples belong to the same quasi-identifier $\{A_1, A_2\}$, then these tuples have the same project values on $\{A_1, A_2\}$, they also have the same project values on A_1. Since $k_1 < k_2$, these k_2 tuples conform to C_1.

Lemma 1. *Given a table T and a set of anonymity constraints $C = \{\langle QI_1, k_1 \rangle,$
$\ldots, \langle QI_n, k_n \rangle \}$. If T conforms to $\langle \bigcup_{i=1}^{n} QI_i, max\{k_1, \ldots, k_n\} \rangle$, then T conforms
each constraint in C.*

According to Lemma 1, the algorithm first classifies constraints into a set
of independent clusters, each of which is a set of overlapped constraints. For a
cluster with several overlapped constraints, according to Lemma 1, tuples that
satisfy the compound constraint $\langle \bigcup_{i=1}^{n} QI_i, max\{k_1, \ldots, k_n\} \rangle$ must satisfy each
constraint of the cluster. Thus we can use single_cons_proc with the compound
constraint of the cluster to k-anonymize the publishing table.

In a cluster, if there is a constraint that subsumes the other constraints, then
the algorithm invokes function `single_cons_proc` for the dominate constraint.
Thus, constraints in the cluster are validated in the publishing table.

The above strategy is safe but causes more information loss. The reason
is that some tuples satisfying each constraint may not satisfy the compound
constraint $\langle \bigcup_{i=1}^{n} QI_i, max\{k_1, \ldots, k_n\} \rangle$. In order to decrease information loss,
the algorithm uses post-processing to examine each tuple in the anonymized
table T'. For each tuple t in the table T', if degeneralizing $t[QI_i]$ and the table
still satisfy all constraints, it keeps the new degeneralized value. The algorithm
is depicted as follows.

```
Algorithm: Classfly
Input:     A table T, constraints C = { ⟨QI₁, k₁⟩,..., ⟨QIₕ, kₕ⟩},
           generalization hierarchies DGHₐ₁,...,DGHₐₙ
Output:    releasable table T' satisfying C

   C' =∅;   // a set of independent constraint clusters
   C₀ = C;
   for (each constraint c in C'') {
     if (c is an independent constraint) {
        C' = C' ∪ {c};
        C = C - {c};
     }
     else if (c is subsumed by another constraint)
        C = C - {c};
   }
   classify constraints in C into non-overlapped clusters;
   for (each cluster CC) {
        QI =∪꜀∈CC(c.QI);
        k = max{c.k}, c ∈ CC;
        C' = C' ∪ {⟨QI,k⟩};
   }
   for (each independent constraint c in C')
        T' = single_cons_proc(T, c.QI, c.k, c.DGH);
   for (each tuple t in T') {
        degeneralize t to t' using DGHₐ₁,...,DGHₐₙ;
```

```
    TT = (T'∪ t' - t);
    if (TT satisfy C₀)
        T' = TT;
}
return T';
```

4   Experiments

We implement Classfly algorithm in C programming language and compare it with the classic *k*-anonymization algorithm Datafly.

4.1   Experimental Setting

We use a synthetic table to test the proposed Classfly approach. We adopt nine anonymity constraints (shown in Table 1) and vary table sizes from 1,024 to 10,240 (denoted 1K to 10K). Values in the publishing table are generated in normal distribution. Given anonymity constraint set C, we use $C = \{C_1, \ldots, C_m\}$ to process the publishing table, where m is the number of constraints (i.e. $|C|$).

The experiments were run on a single-processor Intel Pentium 4, 2.8GHz machine with 512M physical memory.

Table 1. Anonymity constraints for experimental test

Constraint	Definition
C_0	$\langle\{\text{Race, Gender, Birth, ZIP}\}, k\rangle$
C_1	$\langle\{\text{Race, Birth, Gender}\}, 5\rangle$
C_2	$\langle\{\text{Birth, Gender, ZIP}\}, 3\rangle$
C_3	$\langle\{\text{Gender, ZIP}\}, 5\rangle$
C_4	$\langle\{\text{ZIP, Height}\}, 3\rangle$
C_5	$\langle\{\text{Weight, Work\_Hrs, Salary}\}, 6\rangle$
C_6	$\langle\{\text{Work\_Hrs, Salary, Education}\}, 3\rangle$
C_7	$\langle\{\text{Race, Birth, Education}\}, 4\rangle$
C_8	$\langle\{\text{ZIP, Weight}\}, 8\rangle$

We estimate Classfly and Datafly based on the metrics described below:

Precision. Precision is used for measuring the strength of information loss. Given a table $T(A_1, \ldots, A_n)$ with m tuples and domain generalization hierarchies DGH_{A_i} $(1 \leq i \leq n)$, let T' be the anonymized table of T. The precision of T', denoted $prec(T')$, based on generalization and suppression is:

$$prec(T') = 1 - \frac{1}{n \cdot |T|} \sum_{i=1}^{n} \sum_{j=1}^{m} \frac{level(t_j[A_i])}{hight(DGH_{A_i})}, \qquad (1)$$

where, $level(t_j[A_i])$ represents the level of $t_j[A_i]$ in DGH_{A_i}, $hight(DGH_{A_i})$ represents a total generalization level in DGH_{A_i}.

In case of $T = T'$, no value is generalized, i.e. for any element $t_j[A_i]$ in T', $level(t_j[A_i])=0$, and $prec(T')=1$. Whereas, in case of all elements in T' are suppressed, $level(t_j[A_i])=hight(DGH_{A_i})$ and $prec(T')=0$. The higher the precision is, the less the information loss is. Using the hierarchies in Fig. 2, the precision of tables GT_1 and GT_2 in Fig. 3 are: $prec(GT_1)=0.8$, $prec(GT_2)=0.717$, that is, GT_1 has less information loss than GT_2.

Relative Precision. The relative precision between algorithms A and B is:

$$prec_R = \frac{prec_A(T') - prec_B(T')}{prec_B(T')}, \qquad (2)$$

4.2   Experimental Evaluation and Analysis

We estimate Classfly and Datafly using variable table sizes (number of records) and k values.

Precision Estimation. Now we compare precisions and relative precisions between Datafly and Classfly approaches.

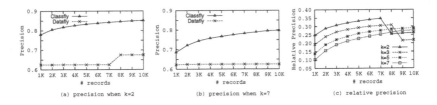

(a) precision when k=2   (b) precision when k=7   (c) relative precision

Fig. 4. Comparison of precisions under independent constraint C_0

Fig. 4(a) and (b) show precisions of anonymized table using Classfly and Datafly under single anonymity constraint C_0. Let k value be 2, 7, resp., and table size varies from 1K to 10K. It can be seen when fixing table size and k value, precisions of Classfly are higher than that of Datafly by 10% to 20%. When k value keeps stable, precisions of Classfly increase with the increment of table sizes. On the contrary, precisions of Datafly do not change much when varying table sizes, since Datafly generalizes all values for a chosen attribute using the same generalization hierarchy, even partial values conform to anonymity constraints before performing generalization. Note that, when $k=2$ and table size is larger than 7K, precision of Datafly increases rapidly. The reason is when k value is small and table size is large enough, lower generalization hierarchies would satisfy the k-anonymity requirement.

Fig. 4(c) shows relative precisions between Classfly and Datafly under constraint C_0 when varying k and table sizes. Since the precision using Classfly becomes more predominant when table size gets larger, the relative precision

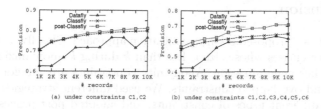

Fig. 5. Comparison of precisions under overlapped constraints

between Classfly and Datafly increases with the increment of table size. It can be observed that, when table size is larger than 8K and k value is 2 or 3, the relative precision drops down a little bit. The reason is that when k value is small and table size is large enough, the precision of Datafly will increase accordingly. Fig. 5(a) and (b) show comparison of precisions using Classfly and Datafly under overlapped constraints $\{C_1, C_2\}$ and $\{C_1, C_2, C_3, C_4, C_5, C_6\}$ when table size varies from 1K to 10K. It can be seen that Classfly with post-processing (named post-Classfly) gets the highest precision. Datafly gets the lowest precision of publishable table. When table sizes get larger, the difference of precisions between post-Classfly and Classfly also gets larger, since more values that need to be degeneralized to decrease the information loss.

Efficiency Estimation. Fig. 6(a) shows the comparison of CPU time using Datafly and Classfly under constraint C_0 when k value is 5 and table size varies from 1K to 10K. Both of the two approaches promote CPU time when increasing table sizes. When fixing table size and k value, Datafly spends more CPU time than Classfly for generating a releasable table. Fig. 6(b) shows comparison of CPU time using two algorithms under overlapped constraints $\{C_1, C_2, C_3, C_4, C_5, C_6\}$. When anonymity constraints are fixed, CPU time of k-anonymization increases with the increment of table size. In general, Datafly spends more CPU time to generate a publishable table than Classfly.

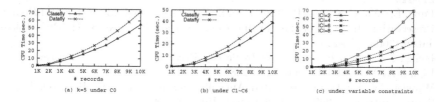

Fig. 6. Comparison of CPU Time

Fig. 6(c) shows more anonymity constraints require Classfly to spend more CPU time on generating a publishable table. In a publishing table, number of tuples that satisfy k-anonymity constraints drops when constraints number increases. Therefore, Classfly needs spend more time on extracting and generalizing tuples donot satisfy constraints.

5 Conclusion

In this paper, we proposed a k-anonymization approach, Classfly, which extracts representative classes whose size is less than k during k-anonymizing published data for further generalization. Anonymity constraints are categorized into independent and overlapped constraints. We used different strategies to solve the problem for different types of constraints, and adopted post-processing for improving precision under overlapped constraints. Experimental results show that Classfly outperforms Datafly, by increasing the precision of k-anonymized data, i.e. causing less information loss, and improving efficiency of k-anonymization.

References

1. Yang, X., Li, C.: Secure XML Publishing without Information Leakage in the Presence of Data Inference. In Proc. of the 30th Int. Conf. on Very Large Database (VLDB). Toronto, Canada. (2004) 96-107
2. Yang, X., Li, C., Yu, G., Shi, L.: XGuard: A System for Publishing XML Documents without Information Leakage in the Presence of Data Inference. In Proc. of the 21st Int. Conf. on Data Engineering (ICDE). Tokyo, Japan (2005) 1124-1125
3. Sweeney, L.: Uniqueness of Simple Demographics in the U.S. Population. In LIDAP-WP4. Carnegie Mellon University, Laboratory for Int. Data Privacy, Pittsburgh, PA (2000).
4. Sweeney, L.: Guaranteeing Anonymity when Sharing Medical Data, the Datafly System. J. of the American Medical Informatics Association, Washington, DC: Hanley & Belfus, Inc (1997)
5. Sweeney, L.: Achieving K-anonymity Privacy Protection using Generalization and Suppression. Int. J. on Uncertainty, Fuzziness and Knowledge-based Systems (2002) 571-588
6. LeFevre, K., DeWitt, D., Ramakrishnan, R.: Incognito: Efficient Full-Domain K-Anonymity. In SIGMOD (2005)
7. Bayardo, R.. J., Agrawal, R..: Data Privacy Through Optimal K-Anonymization. In Proc. of the 21st Int. Conf. on Data Engineering (ICDE). Tokyo, Japan (2005) 217-229
8. Fung, B., Wang, K., Yu, P.: Top-Down Specialization for Information and Privacy Preservation. In Proc. of the 21st Int. Conf. on Data Engineering (ICDE). Tokyo, Japan (2005) 205-216
9. Iyengar, V.: Transforming Data to Satisfy Privacy Constraints. In Proc. of the Eighth ACM SIGKDD (2002) 279-288
10. Winkler, W. E.: Using Simulated Annealing for K-anonymity. Research Report Series (Statistics #2002-7), U.S. Census Bureau (2002)
11. Hundepool, A., Willenborg, L.: μ- and τ-argus: Software for Statistical Disclosure Control. The 3rd Int. Seminar on Statistical Confidentiality, Bled (1996)
12. Sweeney, L.: Towards the Optimal Suppression of Details when Disclosing Medical Data, the Use of Sub-combination Analysis. In Proc. of MEDINFO'98. International Medical Informatics Association. Seoul, Korea. North-Holland (1998)

Transformation-Driven Development of Composite Web Services*

YanPing Yang[1], QingPing Tan[1], and YongXiao[2]

[1] Computer College of National University of Defense Technology, China
yanpingyang@nudt.edu.cn, eric6508@21cn.com
[2] National Lab of Parallel Distributed Process, China
yongxiao@nudt.edu.cn

Abstract. The numerous Web services in existence and complex service requests make it natural to compose simple Web services to get value-added composite ones. In this paper, we present an approach driven by Model Driven Architecture (MDA) to develop composite Web services: using UML Class diagram to model structure PIMs (Platform Independent Models) and UML Activity diagram to model behavior PIMs; then converting the PIMs to specific Web services specification platforms and execution platform to get the corresponding PSMs (Platform Specific Models) by model transformation.

1 Introduction

A number of Web services are now available and it therefore seems natural to reuse existing Web services to create composite Web services. The problem of Web services composition can be reduced to three fundamental problems, which, generally speaking, are discovery of useful partner Web services, calculation of their possible composition, and execution of the new generated Web service.

On one hand, many composition languages specification such as Business Process Modeling Language (BPML), Business Process Execution Language (BPEL) and Web service Choreography Interface (WSCI) provide platforms for the description and execution of the composite Web services; and on the other hand, none of them has been declared so far. This implies that a migration between different environments or a migration to updated composition specifications needs much effort.

Many researchers [1-5] try to describe Web service and Web services composition in more abstract models such as Petri Nets, linear logic, state charts or finite state machines, but none of them has provided the transformation from these abstract models to any execution platforms, which hinders their practical application.

Object Management Group's (OMG's) Model Driven Architecture (MDA) [6] provides an open and vendor-neutral approach to the challenge of business and technology change. MDA is an initiative to automate the generation of Platform Specific Models (PSMs) from Platform Independent Models (PIMs). Web services development driven by MDA has recently attracted considerable attention [7-12].

---

* The paper is supported partially by the National Grand Fundamental Research 863 Program of China under Grant No.2003AA001023.

G. Chen et al. (Eds.): ISPA Workshops 2005, LNCS 3759, pp. 637–646, 2005.

However, most of existing researches enlightened by MDA mainly focus on platform-independent modeling of the static structure of Web service, and have not given the guidance to model the dynamic behavior of Web services, which is especially vital to Web services composition.

This paper studies MDA-driven composite Web services development approach. [12,13] claim that platform-independent UML models are sufficient for Web services structure and behavior modeling. Especially when modeling the complex Web service, a pure conceptual view is helpful to the modeler's comprehension. So we use UML Class diagram [14] to model structure PIMs and Activity diagram [14] to model behavior PIMs. These PIMs can be converted to specific Web services specification platform such as Web services Definition Language (WSDL) [15] and flow execution platform such as BPEL [16] respectively by model transformations.

Thöne et al. in [17] present platform-independent service and workflow modeling, but have not defined the conversion rules to any target platform. Gardner [18] and Grønmo [12] introduce UML profiles of Activity diagram for business process, but the introduced UML profile contains too much information being irrelevant for understanding the semantics of the We services and increases the complexity of modeling.

This paper is organized as follows: Section 2 introduces our development process of composite Web services. Section 3 sketches the Web services composition setup algorithm. Section 4 explains the structure and behavior transformation in details. Section 5 provides an example of how the development works. Finally, conclusions are given in Sections 6.

2   Development Process

Fig.1 shows the flow diagram indicating the steps of development process of composite Web services driven by model transformation.

The goal of step 1 is to create a preliminary interface model of the new Web service, which shall describe the operations signatures of the Web services in the form of a UML Class diagram.

The goal of step 2 is to use relevant discovery and composition algorithm to setup possible service composition. As the solution to this problem, we propose the concept of "invocation layer" based on data dependency between web services invocation. We design three algorithms to jointly get the least invocation layers of candidate web services satisfying the given service request. Firstly, we find the relevant web services from the repository. Secondly, we pick out the contributed web services based on dataflow optimization. At last, we use a search algorithm to find the best composition setup. In this paper, our emphases are put on the model transformations scheme and the details of the algorithms can be referred to [19].

The goal of step 3 is to identify and modify the interface definition of the new generated Web services in UML Class diagram according to the result of step 2. The goal of step 4 is to get the structure PSM of the new generated Web service on specific platform (such as WSDL) from the platform-independent UML model by model transformation. The same model may be used as a basis for conversion to more than one target platform (IDL, Java etc), or to later version of the same platform. This

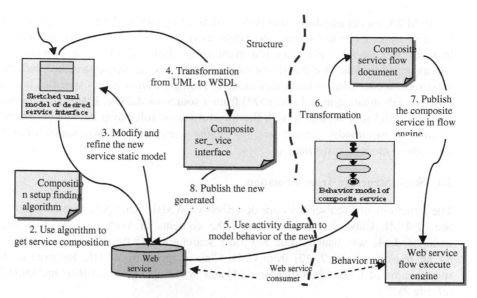

Fig. 1. Model-driven development steps of composite Web service

transformation can be done automatically or semi-automatically by transformation engines. The goal of step 5 is to model the details of the compositions in UML activity models. The composition model is a functional decomposition of the main task identified by the operation. The resulting composition model consists of smaller, manageable Web services that are found as existing Web services The goal of step 6 is to get the flow execution document on specific platform (such as BPEL) of the new Web services from the platform-independent UML behavior model by model transformation. The same model may be used as a basis for conversion to more than one target platform (BPML, WSCI etc), or to later version of the same platform. This transformation can also be done automatically or semi-automatically by transformation engines. The goal of step 7 is to configure the execution engine to run the new Web service. The engine runs according to an executable specification. This specification aligns totally with the activity model resulting from step 5. Therefore, the modeler transforms the activity model to an XML document serving as input to the execution engine. The goal of step 8 is to publish the new generated Web services in an appropriate registry, so it can be discovered and used by Web services consumers.

For the convenience of specification, we draw the flow diagram as a waterfall process, but in practical application, there is much iteration among the steps.

3 Model Transformation

There are various methods for specifying model transformation [20]. Currently, there is no standardized language for definition transformation definitions.

In MDA, model transformation is defined as a mapping to define correspondences between elements in the source and target models. The mainly modeling concepts include: *Metamodel* - plays an important role within MDA, as it provides the language and the rules for describing models. *MOF* - is the well-established and only meta-meta-model used to build metamodels. *Transformation rule* – specifies how to generate a destination model (i.e. PSM) from a source model (i.e. PIM). To transform a given model into another model, the transformation rules map the source into the destination metamodel. *Transformation engine* - executes transformation rules to accomplish model transformation.

3.1 Static Structure Transformation

The structures of Web services are described in WSDL. This paper investigates the use of UML Class diagram to express the contents of Web services in a more understandable way than WSDL. Several researchers have devoted to the automatic model transformation [7, 12] from UML Class diagram to WSDL. Referred to the specification of UML Class diagram [14] and WSDL [15], we get their metamodels (cf. Fig.2).

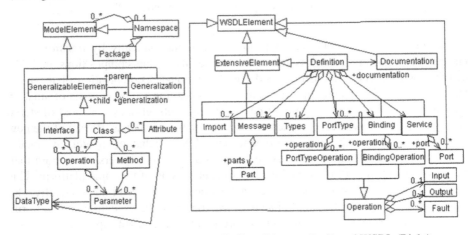

Fig. 2. Metamodel Fragment of UML Class Diagram (Left) and WSDL (Right)

Having analyzed the semantics of each eclement of both metamodels, we give the main transformation rules of structure models of composite Web services in Table 1.

For the limitation of space, we only detail the rule of UMLInterface2WSDLPortType. We express the transformation rules with the Object Constraint Language (OCL) [21].

```
rule UMLInterface2WSDLPortType {
  from itf: UML!Interface
  to pt: WSDL!PortType
  mapsTo itf(
    name<-itf.name,
```

```
operations <-[ UMLInterface2WSDLPortType.wsdlop]
itf.feature->select(e|e.oclIsKindOf(UML!Operation)))
}
```

Table 1. The main mapping rules from UML Class to WSDL

Rule name	Rule description
UMLPackage2WSDLDefinition	Set the value of WSDL element definition according to UML package
UMLDataType2WSDLTypes	Set the corresponding value for every UML DataType in WSDL Types container
UMLClass2WSDLTypes	Set the corresponding definition for every UML class in WSDL Types container
UMLParameter2WSDLPart	Set the value of WSDL part according to UML Parameter
UMLOperation2WSDLOperation Type	Set the value of WSDL Operationtype according to UML Operation
UMLInterface2WSDLPortType	Set the value of WSDL PortType according to UML interface

3.2 Dynamic Behavior Transformation

Modeling collaborations between Web services is a more complex task than modeling individual Web service. There exist several workflow-related specifications in the

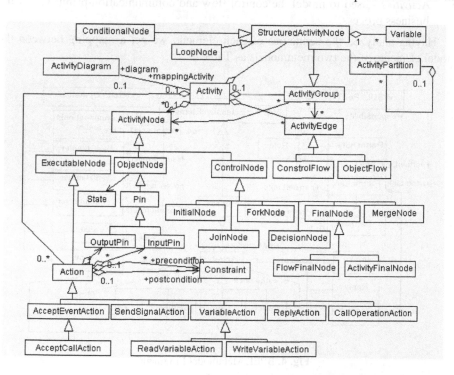

Fig. 3. UML Activity Diagram Metamodel Fragment

world of Web services. Several organizations have proposed their own composition languages specification (BPML, BPMN, BPEL, BPSS, WSCI), and no winner has been declared so far. So it is essential to use a language independent of all these platforms to preserve the business logic of Web services in a more abstract way and to map this model to platform variants and new versions. UML Activity diagram is one best choice [13]. To get the metamodel (cf. Fig.3) of Activity diagram, we have referred to the UML 2.0 Superstructure Specification [22].

As demonstration, we choose BPEL [16] as the target platform and present a mapping of behavior models from UML Activity diagram to BPEL.

BPEL is a promising candidate for the expression of behavior of Web services. It defines the control flow between the services and the information flow by the means of data containers called variables. Fig.4 depicts the fragment of BPEL metamodel, and the main modeling concepts include:

- *Business process* - the central concept of BPEL. It is a stateful process that coordinates a possibly workflow between a set of Web services.
- *Partner links* - refer either to the interfaces that are provided by the invoked services, and possibly to the corresponding call-back interfaces of the business process; or to the provided interfaces of the business process itself, or possibly to the corresponding call-back interfaces of its clients.
- *Partners* - a set of partner links that refer to the same Web service.
- *Variables* - the state-preserving entities of the business process.
- *Activities* - used to model the control flow and communication primitives of the business process.

Having analyzed the semantics of each element, we get a mapping between the model elements of the two metamodels as Table 2.

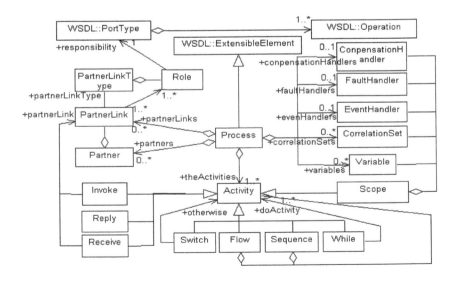

Fig. 4. BPEL Metamodel Fragment

Table 2. The main mapping rules from UML Activity diagram to BPEL

Rule name	Rule description
UMLActivity2BPELProcess	Activity element acts as a container where behavior specification can be defined, and it should be mapped to Process of BPEL.
UMLActivityPartition 2BPELPartitionLink	Activity Partitions element often corresponds to organizational units in a business model and can be used to set the value of PartitionLink element correctly.
UMLExcutableNode2 BPELActivity	Both elements represent the activity units of business process.
UMLConditonalNode 2BPELSwitch	Choice vertices which, when reached, result in the dynamic evaluation of the guards of the triggers of its outgoing transitions. This realizes a dynamic conditional branch.
UMLLoopNode2BPE LWhile	Both elements realize iteration.
UMLVariable2BPEL Variable	Both elements buffer information.
UMLControlFlow2BP ELSequence	Both elements represent the container which contains one or more activities performed in a serial order.
UMLAcceptCallActio n2BPELReceive	AcceptCallAction element represents the receipt of a synchronous call request, and can be used to set the value of Receive element of BPEL.
UMLCallOperationAc tion2BPELInvoke	CallOperationAction element transmits an operation call request to the target object, and can be used to set the value of Invoke element correctly.
UMLReplyAction2BP ELReply	ReplyAction element accepts a set of return values and token containing information produced by a previous acceptcall action, and conforms to the semantics of reply element of BPEL.
UMLVariableAction2 BEPLAssign	VariableAction element support the reading and writing of variables and specifies the variable being accessed, and can be used to implemented the semantics of assign element of BPEL.
UMLOutputPin2BPE LFrom	OutputPin element holds output values and delivers them to other actions, and should be mapped to From element of BPEL.
UMLInputPin2BPEL To	InputPin element holds input values to be consumed by an action and receives values from other actions, and should be mapped to To element of BPEL.

For the limitation of space, we only detail the rule of UMLActivity2BEPLProcess below:

```
rule UMLActivity2BPELProcess{
 from uat: UML!Activity
 to bp: BEPEL!Process
 mapsTo uat{
  name<-uat.name,
  targetNameSpace<-"http://www."+uat.name+".com",
  abstractProcess<-false,
  xmlns<-"http://schemas.xmlsoap.org/"+"...",
  Variable<-[UMLVariable2BPELVariable.bv]
  uat.feature<-select(e|e.oclIsKindof(UML!Variable)),
  PartnerLink<-
[UMLActivityPartition2BPELPartitionLink.bpl]
  uat.feature<-
```

```
select(e|e.oclIsKindof(UML!ActivityPartition)),
  Activity<-[UMLAction2BEPLActivity.ba]
  uat.feature<-select(e|e.oclIsKindof(UML!Action)),
  ...
}
```

4 A Worked Example

This section presents an example of Web service composition development driven by MDA. The scenario is: On receiving the purchase order from a customer, the process initiates GetInvoice and GetSchedule tasks in parallel. While some of the processing can proceed in parallel, there are control and data dependencies between the tasks. In particular, the shipping price is required to finalize the price calculation, and the shipping date is required for the complete fulfillment schedule. When all the tasks are completed, the invoice is sent to the customer.

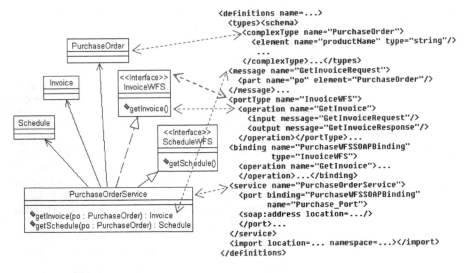

Fig. 5. Structure PIM (Left) / PSM (Right) of New Web service and Their Mappings

First, we use Class diagram to sketch the interface of the new Web service. The diagram representing the purchase order service is shown on the left of Fig.5. The right part shows the transformation result by UML2WSDL mapping, and the mapping relations are notated by the broken lines.

Now we have a local repository that contains information for a set of existing web services, which are used to find a solution to composing. Enlightened by the result of our search algorithm, we describe the way of composition using an UML Activity diagram for the purchase order process, which is shown on the left of Fig. 6. The partners with which the process communicates are represented by the UML partitions. Activities that involve a message send or receive operation to a partner appear in the

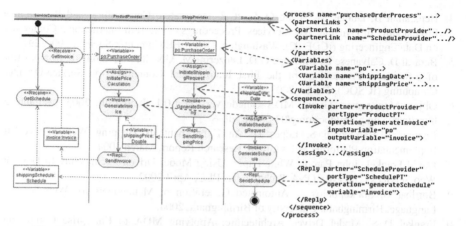

Fig. 6. Behavior PIM (left) / PSM (Right) of new Web service and their Mappings

corresponding partition. The arrows indicate the order in which the process performs the activities. The right part of Fig.6 shows the transformation result by UML2BPEL mapping, and the mapping relations are notated by the broken lines.

5 Conclusions

In this paper, a MDA-driven development approach to web services composition is proposed. Even though Web services have been hyped for some time, it is a relatively new and evolving technology. As a consequence the dependencies between Web services solutions and their development and runtime environments are very strong. This implies that a migration between different environments or a migration to updated Web services specifications needs much effort. Using an MDA approach helps to preserve the business logic of Web services in a more abstract model and to map this model to platform variants and new versions.

We have demonstrated that the MDA idea of model transformation applying in Web service composition is feasible. It is especially important that we not only demonstrated this for structural models, but also for behavior models, because modeling collaborations between Web services is a more complex task than modeling individual Web service. In the future we will concentrate on transformation to more other platforms such as WSCI.

References

1. Hamadi R, Benatallah B. A petri net-based model for web service composition. Proceeding of the Australasian Database Conference (ADC), Australasian Computer Society, 2003. 191-200.
2. Narayanan S, McIlraith S A. Simulation, Verification and Automated Composition of Web Services. Eleventh International World Wide Web Conference (WWW), Hawaii, 2002.77-88.
3. Rao J H, Kuungas P, Matskin M. Application of Linear Logic to Web Services Composition. Proceedings of the First International Conference on Web Services (ICWS'2003), Las Vegas: IEEE Computer Society, 2003. 3-9.

4. Benatallah B, Dumas M, Sheng Q Z., et al. Declarative Composition and Peer-to-Peer Provisioning of Dynamic Web Services. Proceedings of the 18th International Conference on Data Engineering (ICDE'02). Washington, DC: IEEE Computer Society, 2002. 297.

5. Berardi D, Calvanese D, Giuseppe G D, Lenzerini M, Mecella M. Automatic Composition of e-Services. Proceedings of the First International Conference on Service-Oriented Computing (ICSOC), Trento, 2003. 43-58.

6. Object Management Group, MDA Guiede version 1.0.1, June 12th, 2003, available at http://www.omg.org/docs/omg/03-06-01.pdf.

7. Bezivin J, Hammoudi S, Lopes D, An Experiment in Mapping Web Services to Implementation Platforms, Atlas Group, Research Report, March 2004

8. David Frankel, John Parodi, White Paper: Using Model Driven Architecture to Develop Web Services (2nd Ed), IONA Technologies PLC, April 2002.

9. Bordbar B, Staikopoulos A. Automated Generation of Metamodels for Web Services Language. Birmingham: University of Birmingham, 2004.

10. Frankel D S. Model Driven Architecture: Applying MDA to Enterprise Computing, U.S.A., OMG Press, 2003.

11. Anneke Kleppe, Jos Warmer, Wim Bast. MDA Explained: The Model Driven Architecture: Practice and Promise. U.S.A., Addison-Wesley, April 2003.

12. Grønmo R, Skogan D, Solheim I, et al. Model-driven Web Services Development. Proceedings of the International Conference on e-Technology, e-Commerce and e-Service (EEE-04), Taipei: IEEE Computer Society, 2004.

13. Marlon Dumas, Arthur H.M. ter Hofstede. UML Activity Diagrams as a Workflow Specification Language. Proceedings of the International Conference on the Unified Modeling Language (UML2001). Toronto, Canada, Springer Verlag., October 2001.

14. J. Rumbaugh, I. Jacobson, and G. Booch *The Unified Modeling Language Reference Manua* Addison-Wesley, 1999.

15. Christensen E, Curbera F, Meredith G. Sanjiva Weerawarana, Web Services Description Language (WSDL), available at http:// www.w3.org/TR/wsdl, March 2001,

16. Andrews T, Curbera F, Dholakia H, et al. Business Process Execution Language for Web Services (BPEL4WS) version, ftp://www6.software.ibm.com/software/developer/library /ws-bpel.pdf , May 2003.

17. Thöne S, Depke R, Engels G. Process-Oriented, Flexible Composition of Web Services with UML. Proceedings of the International Workshop on Conceptual Modeling Approaches for e-Business: A Web Services Perspective (eCOMO 2002), Tampere, 2002.

18. Gardner T. UML Modelling of Automated Business Processes with a Mapping to BPEL4WS. Proceedings of the Seventeenth European Conference on Object-Oriented Programming (ECOOP2003), Darmstadt, 2003.

19. YanPing Yang, QingPing Tan etc., Setup Algorithm of Web Services Composition, Proceedings of the International Conference on Algorithms and Architectures (ICA3PP-2005), 2005, Melbourne, Australia., Springer-Verlag LNCS.

20. 20. Krzysztof Czarnecki, Simon Helsen, Classification of Model Transformation Approaches, OOPSLA'03 Workshop on Generative Techniques in the Context of Model-Driven Architecture, University of Waterloo, Canada,2003,33-50

21. Object Management Group. UML 2.0 OCL 2nd revised submission, version 1.6, January 6, 2003, 2003. http://www. omg.org/cgi-bin/doc?ad/2003-01-07.

22. Unified Modeling Language: Superstructure (version 2.0), http://www.omg.org/docs/ptc / 03-08-02.pdf

Badness Information Audit Based on Image Character Filtering*

Fei Yu[1,2], Hunag Huang[1], Cheng Xu[3], Xiao-peng Dai[1], and Miao-liang Zhu[2]

[1] Institute of Computer & Information Engineering, Hunan Agricultural University,
Changsha 410128, Hunan, China
{yufei,huangh,dxp}@hunau.net
[2] Institute of Artificial Intelligence, Zhejiang University,
Hangzhou 310027, Zhejiang, China
zhum@zju.edu.cn
[3] College of Computer & Communication, Hunan University,
Changsha 410082, Hunan, China
cheng_xu@yeah.net

Abstract. Along with high development of multimedia information technique, the provider of badness information embeds some badness information to image or directly saves as a image file, avoiding the filter of image, which brings extreme effect of security hidden trouble in society. An information audit system based on image content filtering is provided in this paper. At first, we discuss some basic method filtering physical badness image content, analyze some key technology of filtering image content, and mark as texture character by four eigenvectors: contrast, energy, entropy and correlation. Afterwards, we utilize dynamic programming method to segment image objects, and utilize similarity measurement to denote similarity degree of two character measures. At last, we give an example of identify yellow content, which distill the texture character of image and match it with defined character database. Our system can supervise and control badness information of physical badness image content, and realize automation audit of multimedia information.

1 Introduction

At present, network information audit system realizes information filtering function mostly through capturing and analyzing text information[1]. Comparing with network filtering technique that depends purely on IP address and URL access control list, based text information filtering technique may filter real-time badness in the network, such as network information in some e-mail, chat-room etc[2]. But then, this technique exists itself in obvious limitation: some badness information providers transfer their badness information which are embedded to another image file or formed directly as image file, in order to avoid audit of network information audit system. Along with the development of multimedia technology and obviously advance of network band-

* Foundation item:Supported by Hunan Provincial Natural Science Foundation of China(03JJY3103).

G. Chen et al. (Eds.): ISPA Workshops 2005, LNCS 3759, pp. 647–656, 2005.

width, image and video information increase more and more in the Internet. Pictures added newly to the Internet each year have exceeded 80 billion pages in which there have respectable harmful information[3]. A research in Carnegie Mellon University shows that there has 83.5% picture information contain pornographic content stored in USENET newsgroup. It is a non-disputed fact that there has a great deal of badness information spread in the Internet. Thereby, it is very necessary to audit image content in the network.

2 Key Technology

The content of image is the semantic information contained in the image. From the point of view of image processing, the image character can be divided into the basic empty area character and transformation character. Basic character by which image content filtering is used include as follows: Color texture character, order and edge shape and contour etc. The transformation character is a new characteristic obtained from every kind of transformation through basic character. Commonly used transformations contain the Fourior transformation, the K- L transformation, the Hough transformation and the Wavelet transformation[4].

Relative to another character, color character is consistently dependable, which is not sensitive to circumrotate image、 transfer image flatly、 change measure of image, indeed every kind of form transformation, and has quite robustness property. And that it's computation is simple, thus the character is applied by widely. Typical methods of classification based on image color character have histogram cross method and histogram distance method, which makes use of the relationship between color and its probability appeared in the image to show whole color information of image.

2.1 Basic Method Filtering Physical Badness Image Content

Making use of this characteristic which is the tightness degree of aggregation region of complexion in color space, we establish a model for complexion, which can implement the detection of skin. There have three types of skin detection method:

1)   experimental threshold method

This method mainly utilizes the aggregation character of skin color, after removing brightness interference from skin, adopts adaptive color space as possible as to compress the distribution of skin, and sets a threshold value to lay off definite range, moreover according to this means, it can judge that there is a skin image content when the character value locates in this threshold range, otherwise there is a background image content.

Though this method is a simple and advantageous computation method, it depends on sample database excessively. It is very difficult to identify skin image content exactly, because that this method have not mathematical model of skin, and entirely via by test to stat distribution region, and then it has bigger chanciness.

2)   Bayes decision method

Jones stats directly vertical square in RGB color space, and thus can obtain conditional probability distributions as p(rgb|skin)、p(rgb|non-skin)、p(skin)、p(non-skin). And then we can compute out p(skin|rgb) by Bayes formula, which can set threshold value (commonly there is [0,1]) to identify skin image content. In a word, Jones utilizes Bayes method to make a decision, which increases its expansibility and adaptability to some extent.

3)   Gaussian model method

It has a obvious wave crest in the distribution of skin color in the chroma space. And the distribution of skin color in the chroma space can be marked as Gaussian distribution, which is one of familiar complexion model.

Gaussian model parameters are not complex because of its mathematical denotation. And then we only need those parameters from stat. sample in its realization process. And that model parameters can be readjusted along with the update of sample.

2.2 Denotation of Image Character

Texture character is widely adopted by filtering badness image information. Character measures distilled usually include the degree of uniformity、contrast and direction etc[5]. The degree of uniformity reflects the size of texture, contrast reflects definition of texture, direction reflects whether the entity have regular orientation or not. The method of distilling image texture character contain commonly Symbiosis Matrix Method、K-L Transformation、Texture Spectral Analysis and so on which are based on classic mathematics model, and which bring forward presently Multi-Resolution Analysis、Gabor Filter、Wavelet Analysis and so on which are based on vision model.

We use four character measures to denote texture character which are shown as follows:

1) Contrast (also called principal diagonal moment of inertia):

$$CON = \sum_h \sum_k (h-k)^2 m_{hk} \tag{1}$$

For thick texture, because m_{hk} value near in main diagonal, and $(h-k)$ is small, the relative CON is also small. On the contrary, relative CON is big for thin texture.

2) Energy (also called moment of angle second order):

$$ASM = \sum_h \sum_k (m_{hk})^2 \tag{2}$$

This is a measurement about distributing uniformity of image intensity. When m_{hk} value near in main diagonal, the relative ASM is big; On the contrary, ASM value is small.

3) Entropy:

$$ENT = -\sum_h \sum_k m_{hk} \log m_{kh} \tag{3}$$

In symbiosis matrix of intensity, when m_{hk} value distribute loosely, the relative *ENT* is big; On the contrary, m_{hk} value distribute centralized and tightly, and *ENT* value is small.

4) Correlation:

$$COR = \left[\sum_h \sum_k hk m_{hk} - \mu_x \mu_y \right] / \sigma_x \sigma_y \qquad (4)$$

Where $u_x, u_y, \sigma_x, \sigma_y$ is respectively mean and standard variance of m_x, m_y , $m_x = \sum_h hk$ is the sum of value of all column element, $m_y = \sum_h hk$ is the sum of value of all row element. Correlation is described as the degree of similarity between row element and column element, which is a measure of the degree of linear relationship of intensity.

2.3 Stablishment of Character Library

Character data in character library describe property of image object filtered, which is also warranty of classification for those images that the information audit system have captured, thus the design and implement of character library will directly impact system performance. By way of getting character data of such kind of image, we collect commonly certain relative kind of image as the sample images, and the amount of sample images must be wealthy and representative. And then we can get sample data through distilling the character of sample image, and use these sample data, apply to certain sample training algorithm, at last, can obtain basic character data of relative kind of image object. At practice, character data in character library would be updated at a period of time or be supplied continuously and dynamically through learning and training these sample images.

Character data are commonly vector in high-dimension character space, in which the dimension of vector is decided by the select and distill process of image character. Moreover, the number of vectors in character library is decided together by the varieties of image filtering, filtering precision and processing speed. In order to improve efficiency of retrieval, there would decrease the number of character vectors as possible as under the condition of keeping the same filtering precision. At the same purpose, character data of different kind of image store in different character library, so that there can realize filtering function of different kind of image object through selecting different character library[6].

2.4 Segmentation of Image Object

From the segmentation process of image object, it mostly identifies and locates image object, and distills the contour of image object[7]. The identification and location of image object confirms of the probable position of image object and knows from another object. Moreover, the distilling of object contour makes certain accurately the edges of image object, and draws the outline of image object. The process is shown in Fig 1.

The segmentation method of image object include mostly Flood Fill, Active Contour based on Snake and alternating Dynamic Programming.

Dynamic Programming Method consider that pels array of image constitutes a directed graph, in which each pels in the image correspond to a point in the directed graph, and two neighboring pels compose of a side in the directed graph. Each side is set a value of character measure according as the edge character of image that is called weight in the side. In the segmentation process of image object, the edge detection of image object is namely how to look for a shortest route from this weight directed graph, and uses Dynamic Programming Method to compute this route.

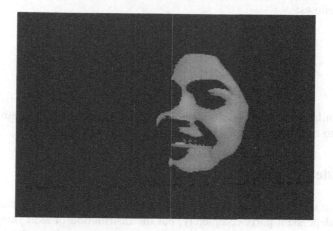

Fig. 1. Distilling of object contour

We use alternating Dynamic Programming Method to realize the segmentation of image object, and the procedure describes as follows:
1. Define the directed graph of image;
2. Define the weight in each side;
3. Select the edge character of image and translate into weight in each side.

Compute the shortest route between start point and end point confirmed in directed graph.

2.5 Network Data Collection

The network processor is a special CPU to process network data[8], and be designed for optimizing the process of data packet, which transmits the packets to the next node at the arrived speed. The network processor is composed of network processor unit and appropriative coprocessor unit. The network processor unit is the kernel of network processor. It can intelligently process large capacity data at a high speed, such as data analysis, classification and forwarding etc. So network processor unit is also called data packet process engine. Different coprocessors have the functions of frame subsection/recombination, accelerate sort, queue/ buffer management, sequence management, memory control and so on. IXP 1200 is composed of 7 RISC processors, secondary storage interface. IX bus interface and PCI bus interface. In the 7 RISC processor, 6 are the packet processing engines and the rest one, called "StrongARM", is used to manage/control the pack processing engine. IXF1002 has 2 full duplex Gbytes MAC interfaces. The speed of data collection can reach 5.12Gbps. IXF440 has 8 full duplex 10/100M MAC interface. IXF1002 and IXF440 are connected with IXP1200 by a IX bus. They transmit the collected data packets to network processor through the IX bus.

2.6 Similarity Calculation

In this paper, the formula that is used to calculate similarity of image character describes as follows:

$$S(X,Y) = \frac{\sum\limits_{i=1}^{n}(x_i \times y_i)}{\sqrt{\sum\limits_{i=1}^{n}x_i^2 \times \sum\limits_{i=1}^{n}y_i^2}} \tag{5}$$

When similarity denotes similar degree of two character measures, similarity value is very big to mean that two character measures are more similar.

3 Skin Identification

Sample point of skin and non-skin overlap in Character space, and it can't be divided into two independent parts completely, but the distribution of skin sample point accord with basically Gaussian distribution from the point of view of each dimensionality[9].

3.1 Modeling of Skin Identification

Therefore, we adopt Bayes Statistics Model to classify skin and non-skin in the image. These formulae describes as follows:

$$P(O|S) = \frac{P(S|O)P(O)}{P(S|O)P(O) + P(S|B)P(B)} \tag{6}$$

$$P(S|O) = P(s_1|O)P(s_2|O)P(s_3|O)P(s_4|O)P(s_5|O)P(s_6|O) \tag{7}$$

$$P(S|B) = P(s_1|B)P(s_2|B)P(s_3|B)P(s_4|B)P(s_5|B)P(s_6|B) \tag{8}$$

Where, O is skin, B is non-skin, S is six dimension character vector. We suppose that $P(s_i|O)$ is Gaussian distribution, and the six character vectors are independent random variables one another. So, Gaussian distribution of skin and non-skin at each dimension can describe as follows:

$$P(s_i|O) = \frac{1}{\sqrt{2\pi}\sigma_o} e^{-\frac{(s_i-\mu_o)^2}{2\sigma_o^2}} \tag{9}$$

$$P(s_i \mid B) = \frac{1}{\sqrt{2\pi}\sigma_B} e^{-\frac{(s_i - \mu_B)^2}{2\sigma_B^2}} \tag{9}$$

Where μ_0 and σ_0 is mean and variance of sample of skin respectively at each dimension, μ_B and σ_B is mean and variance of sample of non-skin respectively at each dimension, i is the number of dimensionality.

3.2 Experimentation of Skin Identification

In this research, four datasets are used to build Pornocide. The color histograms are established by 339 images with skin pixels and 16376 images without skin pixels. Pornocide is trained with the second dataset, which includes 999 pornographic images and 1203 non-pornographic images. The third and the fourth dataset are used to prove the generalization of Pornocide. The third dataset is consisted of 559 benign images and 559 pornographic images. There are 109 benign images and 49 pornographic images in the last dataset. The images in the first three dataset are extracted from images downloaded during a random crawl of the Internet or obtained from "Corel Gallery". The last dataset is obtained from Baltimore Technologies.

In paper[10], the counter of each bin stores the number of times that color value occurred in the entire database of images. In Pornocide, we make the contribution made by each images the same. It means that the contribution of one pixel in "a" image is different from one in "b" image. It depends on the number of pixels extracted from an image. More pixels one image has less weight its pixel represents. We constructed skin and non-skin histogram models using our 339 and 16376 image dataset. The skin pixels in the 339 images containing skin pixels were extracted manually and placed into the skin histogram. The 16376 images that did not contain skin pixels were placed into the non-skin histogram. After collecting pixels into the histograms, we employ the distribution of the histogram in people detection.

Instead of conventional methods such as paper [10], we propose a novel approach to make use of the distribution. The approach is depicted as follows:

First, we define some terms used in the following section.

$Ps(i)$: the probability of the ith bin in the skin histogram.

$Pns(i)$: the probability of the ith bin in the non-skin histogram.

$\beta(i)$: skin-to-nonskin factor, equals to $Ps(i)/Pns(i)$.

$w(\beta)$: weighting function depends on β, the skin-to-nonskin factor.

Second, we construct the new histogram derived from the weighting functions.

Third, we apply the histogram to determine if there is skin in the images of the dataset. After numerous trials on the dataset, we find the optimal θ when the product of sensitivity and specificity is maximized.

Finally, we exploit the histogram and θ to make the skin tone filter.

Skin in the image is a very essential indication that the image is pornographic. It means that if the image is pornographic or objectionable, the image must be composed of skin color. As a result, in Pornocide, skin tone filter is the first mechanism used to detect pornographic image. We believe that a good skin tone filter could be a reliable and preliminary tool for filtering the pornographic images. In other words, it can get rid of most benign images, like scene or landscape, in this stage without difficulty. In this section, we are going to show how effective skin tone filter alone can be in this task.

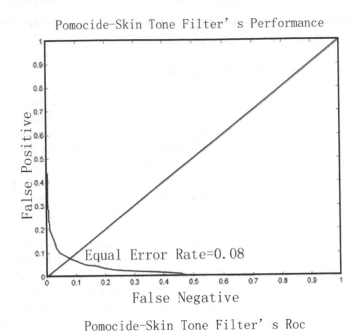

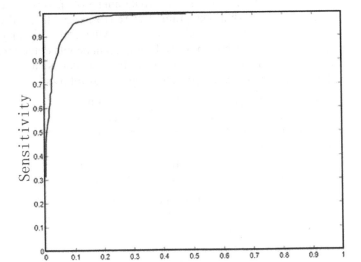

Fig. 2. Skin Tone Filter's Performance

3.3   Analysis of Experiment Result

From above figure, we can find out that statistical probability value of the mass skin sample point nears to in 1, rather than statistical probability value of the mass non-skin sample point nears to in 0,and distributes loose relatively.

Bayes probability skin color model can identify the skin part of image effectively, even as shown as fig 2, provides the relative basis for filtering the pornographic picture.

The results show that simply probing color values allows reasonably good classification of images into those being pornographic and those not. According to the experimental results, ρ is chosen to maximize the product of sensitivity and specificity (the product of sensitivity (95.5%) and specificity (90.1%) is 86.0%) to be the criterion to evaluate whether the image is pornographic or not. If there are more than 8.1% skin region in the image, the image will be passed to the next stage for advanced exam. Otherwise, the image will be thought as a benign image and leave the system.

4   System Architecture

Image monitoring based on image content may divide into two steps: one is offline establishing image character library, the other is online information retrieval of image[11]. Information retrieval consists of server and client part. Server part consists of library subsystem and query engine module, client part finishes how to capture image file in the network and submit this file to server for matching image, and audits manually those shadiness image files that can not be ensured by the system.

1)   Pretreatment

After establishing image character library, it needs to make stated process for image content: filtering noise、adjusting contrast of image、diversification of image、transform of compressed format of image、transform of color space etc. The function of pretreatment is called by existing image process software via interior process.

2)   Object segmentation

Because existing image process software cannot reserve some character information after distilling image object (such as contour line of image object), our system has the function that it marks image object.

3)   Image Character Library

Image character library have mostly image information□character indexing information and some assistant information.

4)   Query and Process

Audit artificially those shadiness image files that cannot be ensured by the system

5)   Retrieval engine

Use image character library to match with checked image.

5 Conclusion

The meaning of image and video information is more abundant rather than text information, thus it is more complex and difficult to analyze and understand them. Existing technique based on image content makes use of almost low-grade character of image, and there is great difference with human's understand about a whole image on the basis of knowledge. The technique about high-level semantic understand should dip into study in the area of image processing and pattern identification all the same, which is also most key technique to improve the performance of network information audit system based on image content. There need us to take into the research hard.

References

1. Dong Kai-Kun, Hu Ming-Zeng, Fang Bin-Xing. A Survey of Firewall Technology Based on Image Content Filtering[J]. *Journal of China Institute of Communications*, 2003,24(1):83-90.
2. Xu Qiang, Jiang Zao, Zhao Hong. Research and Implementation of an Intelligent Firewall System Based on Image Content Filtering[J]. *Journal of Computer Research and Development*, 2000, 37(4):458-464.
3. National Research Council White Paper. Tools and Strategies for Protecting Kids from Pornography and Their Applicability to Other Inappropriate Internet [EB/OL]. http://www7.nationalacademies.org/itas. March,2004
4. Guo F, Jin J S, Feng D. Measuring Image Similarity Using the Geometrical Distribution of Image Contents[A]. Fourth International Conference on Signal Processing, Proceeding[C]. Washington:SPIE Press, 1998. 2: 1108-1112.
5. Forsyth D A, Fleck M M. Identifying Nude Pictures[A]. IEEE Workshop on Applications of Computer Vision, Proceeding[C]. New York: IEEE computer Society Press, 1996. 103-108.
6. Gao Yong-Ying, Zhang Ming-Jin. Progressive Image Content Understanding Based on Multi-Level Image Description Model[J]. Acta Electronica Sinica, 2001, 29(10):1376-1380.
7. Wang J Z, Li J, Wiederhold G, et al. System for Screening Objectionable Images[J]. Computer Communications, 1998, 21(15): 1355-1360.
8. Yu Fei, Zhu Miaoliang, Chen Yufeng, et al. An Intrusion Alarming System Based on Self-Similarity of Network Traffic[J]. Wuhan University Journal of Natural Sciences, 2005,10(1): 169-173.
9. Drimbarean A F, Corcoran P M, Cuic M, et al. Image Processing Techniques to Detect and Filter Objectionable Images Based on Skin Tone and Shape Recognition[A]. International Conference on Consumer Electronics, Proceeding[C]. Boston: USENIX Press,2001. 278-279.
10. Su Kuan-Lun. Pornocide–Design and Implementation of a Content-based Objectionable Image Filtering System[D]. Taiwan :National Taiwan University,2002.
11. Li Xiang-Yang. Research on Image Database Retrieval Technology and it's Model Based on Image Content[D]. Computer Department of ZheJiang University, 1999.

User's Rough Set Based Fuzzy Interest Model in Mining WWW Cache*

Weifeng Zhang[1,3,**], Baowen Xu[2,3], and Guoqiang Zhou[1]

[1]Department of Computer Science and Engineering,
Nanjing University of Posts and Telecommunications, Nanjing 210003, China
wfzhang@yahoo.com
[2]Department of Computer Sci. & Eng., Southeast University, Nanjing 210096, China
[3]Jiangsu Institute of Software Quality, Nanjing 210096, China

Abstract. The WWW Cache technology can store the popular WWW pages in the user's places through which the browsers can speed up fetching these pages. The information in the WWW Cache shows the users' recent interest. The users' interest can be widely used: for example, to customize the WWW pages, to filter the information, to pre-fetch the information and so on. How to use the information in the WWW Cache effectively lies in how to build an adaptive user interest model and how to construct an adaptive algorithm for interest mining. The interest is really a fuzzy concept, but the granularity in simple interest model is too small to describe users' interest appropriately. Based on the analysis of the WWW Cache model, we bring forward a rough-set-based describing method for users' fuzzy interest. With this method, the web page and the set of web pages in the WWW cache can be modeled conformably, and the historical interest and the interest matching can be easily used.

Keywords: WWW, Internet, Interest Model, Fuzzy Set, Rough Set.

1 Introduction

With the rapid development of WWW application, there is more and more information in the Internet. The authorized data show that the static web pages are developing at about an increase of 15 percent each month. At the same time, the current WWW users are often puzzled by the congestion of network and overload of servers. Though the speed of main network increases annually by 60% in average, with the translation from other application systems to WWW applications and continuous increase of WWW users, the users' demand of network width is far from the increasing speed of network width[1]. If no corresponding measures are taken, there will be a lot of congestion in

* This work was supported in part by the outstanding Young Scientist's Fund of NSFC(60303024), the National Natural Science Foundation of China (NSFC) (90412003), National Grand Fundamental Research 973 Program of China (2002CB312000), Doctor Foundation of ministry of education(20020286004), Opening Foundation of Jiangsu Key Laboratory of Computer Information Processing Technology in Soochow University, Natural Science Research Plan for Jiang Su High School(04kjb520096), Doctor Foundatoin of Nanjing University of Posts and Telecommunications(2003-02).
** Corresponding author.

G. Chen et al. (Eds.): ISPA Workshops 2005, LNCS 3759, pp. 657–665, 2005.
© Springer-Verlag Berlin Heidelberg 2005

WWW and a lot of users' requests will be lost. Therefore, since the early 1990s, a lot of scholars have applied themselves to the researches of WWW performance, among which the WWW caching technology is one important measure to improve the WWW performance in some limit of network width. It improves the users' accessing speed of these objects by putting the popular web pages at the side near the users. At present, this technology is used in web browsers and WWW agents. What the WWW cache stores is the historical information which users have ever visited, and the traditional scheduling method of WWW caching(for example, LRU, LFU, and so on[15]) usually puts the web pages which the users have recently visited and has higher visiting frequency to the WWW caches[5]. These historical information shows the users' recent interest states, and the users' interest information can be widely used in customizing web pages, filtering information, pre-fetching information, and so on[2,3,6,7]. There have been a lot of researches on the field of how to mine the feature information of web pages and to produce the users' interest. These interest models are mainly defined by (item, weight)[8] and we call them the simple interest models. The users' interest is really a fuzzy concept and there may be some relations of approximate items, but the description of simple interest model is too precise to describe the approximate relations between the items. It holds up the approximate relations between the items and it can not do the approximate match of users' interest. For example, the items "calculating machine" and "computer" have approximate relations. If the user is interested in "computer", he will also be interested in "calculating machine".

To solve the problem of simple interest model expressing users' interest, the users' fuzzy describing model based on rough set is brought forward in this paper.

Firstly, the simple interest model and its mining method are introduced. Secondly, the users' rough set based fuzzy interest model is shown. Finally, based on the model, we give the method of mining the users' interest in WWW cache.

2 Simple Interest Model and Its Data Mining

Simple interest model is one type of simple method describing the users' interest. In this model, the interest can be specialized by a tuple (term, weight). The interest set is comprised of several interests, and the complete interest set (interest dictionary) is comprised of all interests. The complete interest set T is expressed as $\{ t_1, t_2 \ldots t_m \}$, in which $t_1, t_2 \ldots t_m$ denotes each interest separately and m denotes the size of the interest dictionary. Based on the interest set, we continue to give more basal concepts for further discussion.

Definition 1: Simple interest node is a tuple (t, weight), denoted as Node(t), where $t \in T$ and 'weight' is the weightiness of the interest term t.

The pages in WWW Cache show the recent states of the user's interests. These interests can be transformed to the simple interest nodes in a given way. Before introducing how to perform this transition, it is necessary to describe the web pages in the WWW Cache in some way. The document set in the WWW Cache is expressed as $\{ d_1, d_2 \ldots d_n \}$, denoted as D. For each term t_i in the dictionary T, its frequency appearing in the document d_j is denoted as tf_{ij} (term frequency); and its frequency appearing in the whole document set D (no matter how many times it appears in a document, the count is always recoded as 1) is denoted as df_i (text frequency), the reciprocal of df_i is named as reversal document frequency, denoted as idf_i .

As for simple interest model, the important step in constructing the model is how to calculate the weights of the simple interest nodes. The data mining in this model is mainly text based mining[6,9], which takes all the documents in the D as hypertexts, and regards the frequency of term in the hypertext as its weight [6,7,9,10,11]. This method is so simple that unavoidably it has some weaknesses. For example, if the frequency of an interest term is very high, the term is hard to differentiate user's interests definitely. So in our consideration, for simple interest model, the term frequency and document frequency should be taken into account all together in calculating the interest weights. That is to say, for simple interest node Node (t_i), we use the following formula to calculate its weight:

$$\text{Node}(t_i).\text{weight} = idf_i \sum_{j=1}^{n} tf_{ij} \qquad (1)$$

Where idf_i denotes t_i 's reversal document frequency in D, tf_{ij} denotes t_i 's term frequency in document d_j , and n is the number of documents in D.

An improvement on this mining method of the simple interest model is to take the pages in the caches as structured text, i.e., the terms in different positions or marked by different tags in the page have different weights. The weight of term t_i in position 'place' and in tag 'tag' in document d_j can be represented as $ptw(t_i, d_j.place, d_j.tag)$, and its weight in document d_j is denoted as $stf_{ij} = \sum_{t_i \in d_j} ptw(t_i.place, t_i.tag)$. Thus the interest weight of the interest node Node(t_i) can be computed as following formula.

$$\text{Node}(t_i).\text{weight} = idf_i \sum_{j=1}^{n} stf_{ij} \qquad (2)$$

Where idf_i is t_i 's reversal text frequency in D and n is number of documents in D.

By analyzing and comparing the simple interest model and its interest weight calculating method, it is shown that the simple interest model has the advantages of simplicity, small store space and high executing performance. This model can be widely used in such fields as personal information customizing, information pre-fetching and filtering, etc.

In addition, the users' interest is a relatively fuzzy concept. The simple interest model uses a definite method (term, weight) to describe the interest, which granularity is too small to relevantly describe the users' interest. Thus, after making research on WWW cache structure, we give another user interest model based on rough set and fuzzy theory, which describes the user's interest as rough set based fuzzy concepts. Based on this model, the user's interest can be constructed by mining web contents and web structures, and the web pages currently visited by the users are regarded as users' current interest which is also described by the fuzzy concepts of interest. This method can preferably resolve the problems of the presentation, matching of users' historical interest and current interest.

3 Description of Fuzzy Concepts of Rough Set Based Documents

The users' interest is essentially fuzzy, so the originally fuzzy concepts can not be described well by the simple interest model[24]. Meanwhile, the users' interest is usually represented by different items. For example, "computer" and "calculating machine" in fact state the same concept. Therefore, the theory of rough set is brought forward. By building the classification of approximate items, the items with approximate meaning are put to the same equivalent class.

The theory of rough set, brought forward by Poland mathematician Pawlak in 1982, is the extension of the standard theory of aggregate. It can support the approximate decision-making in procedure of decision-making. It can efficiently analyze and process the. imperfect information such as imprecise information, inconsistent information, half-baked information and etc, discover the hidden knowledge, and reveal the potential rules. Its basic idea is as follows: based on the equivalent relations in the considering field, the sets in the field are described by a pair of approximate operators(the inferior approximation and the superior approximation). These operators can be used in many application systems which need the approximate computing. Based on the approximate relations, we will construct the rough operators. The size of document representing can be reduced by representing the documents according to the equivalent relations, so the documents of different sizes can be mapped to the relatively small space, through which the imprecision caused by the problem of understanding the approximate relations in the procedure of document classification can be decreased.

Let R be the approximate relations on the dictionary T. An approximate space apr=(T,R) is constructed by the non-empty field of objects. The division based on the approximate items can be denoted as $T/R=\{ C_1, C_2, ..., C_m \}$, where C_i is an equivalent class of R, i.e. a group of approximate items. For the arbitrary subset S of T,

The inferior approximation of S is: lower_apr (S)=$\{x \in C_i \mid C_i \subseteq S\}$,

The superior approximation of S is: upper_apr(S)=$\{ x \in C_i \mid C_i \cap S \neq \Phi \}$.

The two kinds of approximation are actually the approximate description of S on the approximate space (T, R).

We can directly map a document to its rough set based representation now. To measure the importance of document on each equivalent class, we further describe the document by constructing the fuzzy set for each equivalent class.

To build up the relation between the rough set and the fuzzy theory, we give a rough set based subjecting function, through which the rough set and the fuzzy set can be associated.

Definition 2: The fuzzy set on the discussion field T: If the discussion filed T is given, x is the arbitrary subset of T, R is the relations of approximate items, and $[x]_R$ is the x existing equivalent class of R, the fuzzy set $\widetilde{X}$ on T is decided by X and R as formula(3).

$$\widetilde{X}_R(x) = \frac{\mid X \cap [x]_R \mid}{\mid [x]_R \mid} \tag{3}$$

Definition 3: The fuzzy set on the discussion filed T/R: Based on the fuzzy set on the discussion field T, the fuzzy set on the discussion field **T/R** can be defined as formula(4).

$$\tilde{X}_{T/R}(C_i) = \underset{x \in C_i}{Max}(\tilde{X}_R(x)) \tag{4}$$

In the fuzzy set on the T/R in definition 2, the frequency of items occurring in the document is not considered, and the importance relative to the set of all documents of items is also not considered. But these two aspects are very important to consider the subjecting degree of item existing in some equivalent class. Therefore, for the item t ($t \in T$), the place in the document d_j ($d_j \in D$) and the weight of tag $ptw(t, d_j.place, d_j.tag)$, the weight of item t in document d_j is denoted as $stf_j(t) = \sum_{t \in d_j} ptw(t.place, t.tag)$, through which the importance of some document in its equivalent class can be calculated by formula(5)(the normalized importance can be calculated by formula(6))..

$$D_j(C_i) = \sum_{t \in C_i}(stf_j(t) \times idf(t)) \tag{5}$$

$$\tilde{D}_j(C_i) = \frac{D_j(C_i)}{\sum_{k=1}^{m} D_j(C_k)} \tag{6}$$

If the importance of the documents relative to every equivalent class can be computed, the fuzzy concept of the document D relative to the equivalent class of approximate items can be easily defined.

Definition 4: Let the fuzzy set of document D relative to the equivalent class of approximate items be $\{w_1(C_1), w_2(C_2)...w_m(C_m)\}$, denoted as $\tilde{D}$, where $C_1, C_2,..., C_m \in$ T/R and $w_1, w_2,..., w_m$ are the subjecting degree of the corresponding equivalent class belonging to document D, which are calculated by formula(8) and there is apparently $0 \le w_1, w_2,..., w_m \le 1$.

To make the comparison and operations of fuzzy concept based documents easy, we define the equivalence, inclusion and complement of fuzzy concepts of documents.

Definition 5: Assume there are a document F and a document G. For arbitrary $C_i \in$ T/R, i=1,...,m, there are:

$$w_F(C_i) = w_G(C_i)$$

We say document F is fuzzily equivalent to document G, denoted as F=G.

Definition 6: Assume there are a document F and a document G. For arbitrary $C_i \in$ T/R, i=1,...,m, there are:

$$w_F(C_i) \leq w_F(C_i)$$

We say document F is fuzzily included to document G.

Definition 7: Assume there is a document F. We name $\neg$F the complement of F and its subjecting function is:

$$\neg F: w_{\neg F}(C_i) = w_F(C_i)$$

Having the above definitions, we can describe the documents in users' browsing procedure(including the documents in WWW cache and users' browsing documents) as the fuzzy concepts of approximate items based equivalent classes. By the representation of fuzzy concepts of documents, we can use the distance to measure the difference between the documents. Here we use the Haiming distance to measure the meaning distance of documents.

Definition 8: Assume there are a document F and a document G. Their Haiming distance can be defined by:

$$d(F,G) = \frac{1}{m} \times \sum_{i=1}^{m} |w_F(C_i) - w_G(C_i)| \tag{7}$$

Therefore, for the documents described by fuzzy concepts, 1-d(F,G) can be used to represent the matching degree of these two documents. When the matching degree is greater than some given threshold, these two documents are regarded as match.

When having the description of fuzzy concepts of a single document, every document in WWW cache can be described as the corresponding fuzzy concept. The linkages between the web pages include important meaning information. They build the associations between the web pages, which show the associations between the users' interest. Therefore, when describing the users' interest in WWW cache, these relations should be considered.

4   Mining the Users' Interest in WWW Cache

The popular WWW mining algorithms are as follows: WWW content mining, WWW structure mining and WWW access logs mining. The mining method in the simple interest model mentioned above only takes into account the inside structure of the pages but ignores the relations between the web pages. In fact, the hyperlink relations of the pages include a lot of potential semantics, which is helpful for analyzing the users' interest automatically. If the author of the WWW pages builds up a hyperlink from his page to other page, the text in the hyperlink can be regarded as the comment of this page [9]. By analyzing these different texts pointing to the same page and built up by the different authors, we can evaluate the importance of this page synthetically. At present, the process of obtaining the user's interest regards each page equally, which cannot reflect the user's interest efficiently while users are browsing the web pages. Actually, while a user is browsing the web pages, he trends to visit the more authoritative web pages. As a result, in order to reflect the user's interest efficiently, we should deal with the different pages separately while mining the interest in the WWW cache.

While mining the interest in the WWW cache, we should obtain the weight of each interest and the transform weight between the interests. The pages in the WWW cache can be represented by a graph, G=(V, E), in which the node in G denotes the page, V is the set of the nodes in the cache, the directional edge in G denotes the hyperlink between the pages and E is the set of the directional edges. The input edge s of the node in G represents the references from other pages, and the output edges represent the references to other pages. Obviously, the hyperlink between the pages in the WWW cache reveal the structures of the pages in the WWW cache. The basic idea of Pagerank[8] is that: one page may be important if it is referenced many times or the important pages reference it; the importance of one page is divided equally and is transformed to its referring pages. In Pagerank's algorithm, the importance of one page can be calculated according to the formula (8).

Assuming in the digraph G, the page node A is referenced by nodes $T_0, T_1, ..., T_n$ ($A, T_0, T_1, ..., T_n \in V$), and the number of the nodes that A refers to is $C(A)$, then the reference relation(RR) of A is :

$$RR(A)=(1-d)+d(RR(T_0)/C(T_0)+...+RR(T_n)/C(T_n)) \qquad (8)$$

Where d is the damping factor, $0<d<1$, and d is set by system (generally is 0.85). $RR(A)$ is the weight produced by the referring relations of the pages. The reference analysis has been researched for a long time in the area of information retrieving. There is also Hub/authority method [9] about the analysis of referring relations, whose main idea is that not all the references have the same influence. The detail about this method will not be discussed here. The chief problem in this part is how to indicate the relative importance of the pages in the samples' training.

It has been a long time to make research on reference analysis in the field of information retrieval. There is also a method of computing reference relativity, Hub/authority, which mainly regards that not all references have the same influence. Its detailed thought will not be discussed here. The main problem in this section is how to distribute the relative importance of web pages into the representation of users' fuzzy interest.

Based on the relative importance of web pages, it can be computed by formula(9) the importance of every classification of rough set in WWW cache G. Then it can be normalized by formula(10) and the relative importance of every classification of rough set can be got.

$$G(C_i)= \sum_{d_j \in V} \left(RR(d_j) \times \sum_{t \in C_i}(stf_j(t) \times idf(t)) \right) \qquad (9)$$

$$\tilde{G}(C_i) = \frac{G(C_i)}{\sum_{j=1}^{m} G(C_j)} \qquad (10)$$

The relative importance reflecting users' historical interest in formula(10) can be got by WWW cache mining. When users are browsing web pages, their currently visiting web pages are regarded as users' current interest which are described by the rough set based fuzzy concepts of documents. Based on users' historical information and users' currently visiting web pages, information pre-fetching, query extending, and so on are realized.

5 Conclusion

There has been a lot of research on the representation of users' interest. Some description methods have been put forward to represent the users' interest such as one member tuple, two-member tuple and three member tuple. The users' interest can also be divided into long-term interest and short-term interest. The model of rough set based fuzzy concepts of documents is brought forward to mine the interest in WWW cache. This model can represent the users' interest information in WWW cache properly. The fuzzy concept of users' rough set based historical interest is got by analyzing the linkage relations between the web pages in WWW cache. This consistent representation provides the advantage of matching the users' interest. In this paper, we don't consider that some customers may share one computer. If some customers are related to a same WWW cache, the information in the WWW cache will not only reflect a user's interest. Some existing operating systems, such as Windows NT and Windows 2000, manage the WWW cache respectively according to the accounts, which can solve this problem. We will make a further research on the interest model of WWW cache and the data mining method, such as , how to realize the mining of users' common interest, and how to manage the storage space reasonably for the multi-users system (for instance, we can put some pictures and voice resource into the WWW cache that can be shared by multi-users).

References

1. Jia Wang.: A survey of WWW caching schemes for the internet. ACM Computer Communication Review, October 1999, 29(5):36-46.
2. Carlos, C. and Carlos, F. B. J.: Determining www user's next access and its application to pre-fetching. In Proceedings of ISCC'97: The Second IEEE Symposium on Computers and Communications, Alexandria, Egypt, July 1-3, 1997,6-11.
3. Bestavros, A.and Cunha, C.: A prefetching protocol using client speculation for the WWW. Boston University, Department of Computer Science, Boston, MA 02215, Tech.Rep:TR-95-011, Apr. 1995.
4. Kroeger, T. M., Long, D. D., and Mogul J. C.: Exploring the bounds of WWW latency reduction from caching and prefetching. In Proceedings of the USENIX Symposium on Internet Technologies and Systems (USITS), Monterey, CA, Dec. 1997,13-22.
5. Greg Barish and Katia Obraczka: World wide WWW caching: trends and techniques. IEEE Communications Magazine Internet Technology Series, May 2000, 38(5):178-184.
6. Baowen Xu, Weifeng Zhang, William C.Chu and Hongji Yang: Application of data mining in WWW pre-fetching. In Proceedings of IEEE MSE2000, TaiWan, 2000, 372-377
7. Baowen Xu and Weifeng Zhang: Research on WWW pre-fetching by data mining. Journal of Computer, 2001, 24(4):430-436.
8. Brin S. and Page L.: The anatomy of a large-scale hypertextual WWW search engine. In: proc of 7th world wide WWW conf(www'98). Brisbane, Australia, 1998, 30: 107-117

9. Jiahui Han, Xiaofeng Men, et al.: Research on WWW mining. Journal of Computer Research and Development, 2001, 38(4):405-414.
10. Weifeng Zhang, Baowen Xu, William C. Chu and Hongji Yang: Data mining algorithms for WWW pre-fetching, Proceedings of the 1st International Conference on WWW Information Systems Engineering(WISE'2000), Hong Kong, China, 2000:34-38.
11. Weifeng Zhang, Baowen Xu, William Song and Hongji Yang: Pre-fetching WWW pages through data mining based prediction. Journal of Applied System Studies, Cambridge International Science Publishing, England. 2002, 3(2): 384–398.
12. Leggett J. et al.: Special issues on hypertext. Communication of ACM, 1994,37(2):26-108
13. S. Chakrabarti, B. Dom, P. Raghavan, S. Rajagopalan, D. Gibson and Kleinberg J.: Automatic resource compilation by analyzing hyperlinkage structure and associated text. In Proceedings of the Seventh International World Wide Web Conference, 1998, 65-74.
14. Weifeng Zhang, Baowen Xu, Hongji Yang and William C.Chu: A genetic algorithm based general search engine. In Proceedings of IEEE Multimedia Software Engineering'2000 (MSE2000), TaiWan, 2000, 366-371.
15. Weifeng Zhang, Baowen Xu, Lei Xu, et al.: Personalizing search result using agent. Mini-Micro Systems, 2001, 22(6):724-727.
16. Weifeng Zhang and Baowen Xu.: Research on framework supporting web search engine. Journal of Computer Research & Development 2000, 37(3):376-378.
17. Weifeng Zhang, Baowen Xu and Xiaoyu Zhou: Counting techniques in web pages. Mini-Micro Systems, 2000, 21(10):1096-1099.
18. Weifeng Zhang, Baowen Xu and Xiaoyu Zhou: Web page techniques for interacting between elements. Computer Engineering, 2000, 26(8):62-64.
19. Tao Zhou, et al.: Information mining technologies and realization on WWW. Journal of Computer Research and Development, 1999, 36(8):1021-1024.
20. Weifeng Zhang, Baowen Xu and Xiaoyu Zhou: An improved relativity technology in reference search. Journal of Software, 2001,12, 317-322.
21. Baowen Xu and Weifeng Zhang: Research on the improved reference search model. Journal of Computer Research and Development, 2002, 39(5): 599-606.
22. Pawlak, Z.: Rough Sets. International Journal of Computer and Information Sciences, 1982, 11(5):341-356.
23. Dell Zhang and Yisheng Dong: An efficient algorithm to rank Web resources. In Proceedings of the 9th International World Wide Web Conference, Amsterdam, Netherlands, May 2000, 449 – 455.
24. Shitong Wang: Theory of fuzzy inference and fuzzy expert system. Shanghai Scientific Literature Press, 1995.

Author Index

Lecture Notes in Computer Science

For information about Vols. 1–3672

please contact your bookseller or Springer

Vol. 3717: B. Gramlich (Ed.), Frontiers of Combining Systems. X, 321 pages. 2005. (Subseries LNAI).

Vol. 3716: L. Delcambre, C. Kop, H.C. Mayr, J. Mylopoulos, O. Pastor (Eds.), Conceptual Modeling – ER 2005. XVI, 498 pages. 2005.

Vol. 3715: E. Dawson, S. Vaudenay (Eds.), Progress in Cryptology – Mycrypt 2005. XI, 329 pages. 2005.

Vol. 3714: H. Obbink, K. Pohl (Eds.), Software Product Lines. XIII, 235 pages. 2005.

Vol. 3713: L. Briand, C. Williams (Eds.), Model Driven Engineering Languages and Systems. XV, 722 pages. 2005.

Vol. 3712: R. Reussner, J. Mayer, J.A. Stafford, S. Overhage, S. Becker, P.J. Schroeder (Eds.), Quality of Software Architectures and Software Quality. XIII, 289 pages. 2005.

Vol. 3711: F. Kishino, Y. Kitamura, H. Kato, N. Nagata (Eds.), Entertainment Computing - ICEC 2005. XXIV, 540 pages. 2005.

Vol. 3710: M. Barni, I. Cox, T. Kalker, H.J. Kim (Eds.), Digital Watermarking. XII, 485 pages. 2005.

Vol. 3709: P. van Beek (Ed.), Principles and Practice of Constraint Programming - CP 2005. XX, 887 pages. 2005.

Vol. 3708: J. Blanc-Talon, W. Philips, D. Popescu, P. Scheunders (Eds.), Advanced Concepts for Intelligent Vision Systems. XXII, 725 pages. 2005.

Vol. 3707: D.A. Peled, Y.-K. Tsay (Eds.), Automated Technology for Verification and Analysis. XII, 506 pages. 2005.

Vol. 3706: H. Fuks, S. Lukosch, A.C. Salgado (Eds.), Groupware: Design, Implementation, and Use. XII, 378 pages. 2005.

Vol. 3704: M. De Gregorio, V. Di Maio, M. Frucci, C. Musio (Eds.), Brain, Vision, and Artificial Intelligence. XV, 556 pages. 2005.

Vol. 3703: F. Fages, S. Soliman (Eds.), Principles and Practice of Semantic Web Reasoning. VIII, 163 pages. 2005.

Vol. 3702: B. Beckert (Ed.), Automated Reasoning with Analytic Tableaux and Related Methods. XIII, 343 pages. 2005. (Subseries LNAI).

Vol. 3701: M. Coppo, E. Lodi, G. M. Pinna (Eds.), Theoretical Computer Science. XI, 411 pages. 2005.

Vol. 3699: C.S. Calude, M.J. Dinneen, G. Păun, M. J. Pérez-Jiménez, G. Rozenberg (Eds.), Unconventional Computation. XI, 267 pages. 2005.

Vol. 3698: U. Furbach (Ed.), KI 2005: Advances in Artificial Intelligence. XIII, 409 pages. 2005. (Subseries LNAI).

Vol. 3697: W. Duch, J. Kacprzyk, E. Oja, S. Zadrożny (Eds.), Artificial Neural Networks: Formal Models and Their Applications – ICANN 2005, Part II. XXXII, 1045 pages. 2005.

Vol. 3696: W. Duch, J. Kacprzyk, E. Oja, S. Zadrożny (Eds.), Artificial Neural Networks: Biological Inspirations – ICANN 2005, Part I. XXXI, 703 pages. 2005.

Vol. 3695: M.R. Berthold, R. Glen, K. Diederichs, O. Kohlbacher, I. Fischer (Eds.), Computational Life Sciences. XI, 277 pages. 2005. (Subseries LNBI).

Vol. 3694: M. Malek, E. Nett, N. Suri (Eds.), Service Availability. VIII, 213 pages. 2005.

Vol. 3693: A.G. Cohn, D.M. Mark (Eds.), Spatial Information Theory. XII, 493 pages. 2005.

Vol. 3692: R. Casadio, G. Myers (Eds.), Algorithms in Bioinformatics. X, 436 pages. 2005. (Subseries LNBI).

Vol. 3691: A. Gagalowicz, W. Philips (Eds.), Computer Analysis of Images and Patterns. XIX, 865 pages. 2005.

Vol. 3690: M. Pěchouček, P. Petta, L.Z. Varga (Eds.), Multi-Agent Systems and Applications IV. XVII, 667 pages. 2005. (Subseries LNAI).

Vol. 3689: G.G. Lee, A. Yamada, H. Meng, S.H. Myaeng (Eds.), Information Retrieval Technology. XVII, 735 pages. 2005.

Vol. 3688: R. Winther, B.A. Gran, G. Dahll (Eds.), Computer Safety, Reliability, and Security. XI, 405 pages. 2005.

Vol. 3687: S. Singh, M. Singh, C. Apte, P. Perner (Eds.), Pattern Recognition and Image Analysis, Part II. XXV, 809 pages. 2005.

Vol. 3686: S. Singh, M. Singh, C. Apte, P. Perner (Eds.), Pattern Recognition and Data Mining, Part I. XXVI, 689 pages. 2005.

Vol. 3685: V. Gorodetsky, I. Kotenko, V. Skormin (Eds.), Computer Network Security. XIV, 480 pages. 2005.

Vol. 3684: R. Khosla, R.J. Howlett, L.C. Jain (Eds.), Knowledge-Based Intelligent Information and Engineering Systems, Part IV. LXXIX, 933 pages. 2005. (Subseries LNAI).

Vol. 3683: R. Khosla, R.J. Howlett, L.C. Jain (Eds.), Knowledge-Based Intelligent Information and Engineering Systems, Part III. LXXX, 1397 pages. 2005. (Subseries LNAI).

Vol. 3682: R. Khosla, R.J. Howlett, L.C. Jain (Eds.), Knowledge-Based Intelligent Information and Engineering Systems, Part II. LXXIX, 1371 pages. 2005. (Subseries LNAI).

Vol. 3681: R. Khosla, R.J. Howlett, L.C. Jain (Eds.), Knowledge-Based Intelligent Information and Engineering Systems, Part I. LXXX, 1319 pages. 2005. (Subseries LNAI).

Vol. 3680: C. Priami, A. Zelikovsky (Eds.), Transactions on Computational Systems Biology II. IX, 153 pages. 2005. (Subseries LNBI).

Vol. 3679: S.d.C. di Vimercati, P. Syverson, D. Gollmann (Eds.), Computer Security – ESORICS 2005. XI, 509 pages. 2005.

Vol. 3678: A. McLysaght, D.H. Huson (Eds.), Comparative Genomics. VIII, 167 pages. 2005. (Subseries LNBI).

Vol. 3677: J. Dittmann, S. Katzenbeisser, A. Uhl (Eds.), Communications and Multimedia Security. XIII, 360 pages. 2005.

Vol. 3676: R. Glück, M. Lowry (Eds.), Generative Programming and Component Engineering. XI, 448 pages. 2005.

Vol. 3675: Y. Luo (Ed.), Cooperative Design, Visualization, and Engineering. XI, 264 pages. 2005.

Vol. 3674: W. Jonker, M. Petković (Eds.), Secure Data Management. X, 241 pages. 2005.

Vol. 3673: S. Bandini, S. Manzoni (Eds.), AI*IA 2005: Advances in Artificial Intelligence. XIV, 614 pages. 2005. (Subseries LNAI).